The foundations of
POLICY ANALYSIS

The Dorsey Series in Political Science
Consulting Editor   Samuel C. Patterson   *The University of Iowa*

The foundations of
POLICY ANALYSIS

Garry D. Brewer
Yale University

Peter deLeon
The Rand Corporation

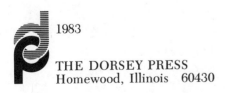

1983

THE DORSEY PRESS
Homewood, Illinois 60430

H
97
.B732
1983

ISBN 0-256-02323-9

Library of Congress Catalog Card No. 82–72369

Printed in the United States of America

1 2 3 4 5 6 7 8 9 0   K   0 9 8 7 6 5 4 3

In gratitude for the inspiration of
Harold D. Lasswell
scholar, spirit, and colleague

Preface

Facing a class of crusty and very skeptical California city managers one day in 1972, the senior author failed miserably with his explanation of the mysteries and beauties of methods to do evaluation research—the nominal subject of a semester's course work.[1] The failure was due less to his lack of technical or substantive knowledge than simply not knowing how things really worked and not being able to locate evaluation methodologies within the richer frames of reference or experience represented by the students. Because they knew better, just learning evaluation methods and procedures was not enough. They knew better partly because their experiences with other techniques—such as planning, programming, and budgeting and management information systems (both quite fashionable at the time)—had been far from successful. And they knew better because technical words such as *effectiveness, efficiency,* and *equity,* all mainstays of evaluation research, had meant so many different practical things to them over the years. As one class member said, an efficient program was one that "kept being funded year after year without having to knock heads with city council or the taxpayers" Or in the words of another city manager, "an effective program is one that keeps council members happy and helps me keep my job." Or, "an equitable policy is one that spreads the resources around to the departments so that no one screams about getting a raw deal." From a practitioner's perspective, it was hard to argue otherwise.

The semester was a long one. But out of the mutual struggle between the technical/theoretical and practical bodies of knowledge we each brought to it, the course gradually became a dissection and exploration of the entire policy process, in which knowledge of (what the instructor knew best) and knowledge in (what the class had in abundance) played off one another for the benefit of all. Ideas from the policy sciences helped, but the precise terminology that policy scientists like Lasswell employed sometimes did not communicate very well.[2] Nevertheless, together we learned that evaluation research offered something to the practitioners, but the realistic details of their complex worlds offered at least as much. And so the course evolved.

Its next iteration occurred in 1973 at the newly founded Rand Graduate Institute, where the modified course was presented under the title "The Scope of the Policy Sciences."[3] It was intended to provide a contextual frame of reference for technically oriented, disciplinary-based young analysts. The course elaborated upon the considerable political and institutional difficulties one encounters in doing analytic work for actual clients in a variety of complex settings. Considerable effort was devoted to the exploration of normative, ideological, political, and institutional opportunities and constraints. The course was at least as challenging to teach as it had been in its first incarnation, but the challenges were quite different. A lack of suitable published materials was one of the main difficulties; finding appropriate examples to illustrate the policy process framework was another. Responses from the students and RGI's advisory board were encouraging and resulted in the decision to write this book.[4]

The Scope course, and several derivatives of it, have been taught by one or the other of us since 1974. For example, at Yale University, where Brewer assumed residence in 1975, increasingly sophisticated versions have been taught to undergraduates majoring in administrative and political science, psychology, economics, and other policy-related disciplines; to Master of Public and Private Management (MPPM—a combined public and business administration curriculum) graduate-professional students in the School of Organization and Management; and to doctoral students in operations research, organizational behavior, and political science. Research seminars on "Policy Evaluation" and "Policy Termination" were conducted for graduate students in administrative science and public health and for law students, respectively. Materials covered in the selection chapters of the book were developed and used in a course entitled, "Political Analysis for Managers," a required introductory offering for MPPM students. At the same time, Brewer was an active policy analyst in such diverse areas as social welfare programs and national security. For his part during this period, deLeon continued working as a professional policy analyst at The Rand Corporation, the Solar Energy Research Institute, and Science Applications, Inc.; he has also adopted this framework for teaching graduate seminars in policy analysis at the University of Southern California. Both authors have served as editors of the journal *Policy Sciences*. This book is a joint product of these diverse but overlapping experiences.

We are reasonably confident that the approach has wide applicability. It has helped many different kinds of students and practitioners at varying levels of intellectual and professional development and sophistication to understand extremely intricate policy problems. It has provided them with a reliable framework to orient their efforts and with operational principles to proceed with their work. It has opened vistas of research and inquiry and stimulated many new perspectives. Because we have used it in our own professional work as scholars and analysts, we are equally confident that the approach is not simple, nor is it always as easy to follow as we would like. Nevertheless, on those occasions where we have been relatively more successful, the results have been well worth the additional effort. The approach and the book are not easy how-to-do-its, nor are they primers or methods for pat or simple solutions. The workaday policy world does not allow that.

This book is intended to document and elaborate the policy sciences approach as we perceive and practice it. It reflects our mutual and evolving experiences, both as teachers and practitioners. The presentation and subject matter are directed towards the graduate student level, but there are ample opportunities for the advanced undergraduate, professional policy analyst, and policymaker to benefit as well.

At this stage of its development, no one can or should claim a monopoly on the policy sciences and how they are practiced. There are no sweepstakes or golden rings, just hard work, new challenges, and, on rare occasions, a glow of gratification. This book, then, should not be seen as an end-all or even a consensual milestone. We view it more as merely marking another phase in the development of the policy sciences as both a discipline and profession, a development in which we urge the readers to participate.

Garry D. Brewer
Peter deLeon

NOTES

1. The School of Public Administration at the University of Southern California was experimenting with a Doctorate of Public Administration program for practicing administrators. Brewer, then a full-time staff member of The Rand Corporation, was hired as a lecturer to teach a seminar on "Policy Evaluation" to a group of twelve city managers and several other California civil servants. At 30, the instructor was the youngest and least practically experienced member of the class.

2. Harold D. Lasswell, *The Decision Process* (College Park: University of Maryland Press, 1956), is one example. Terms like "prescription," "innovation," and "appraisal" for

several of the phases meant much less to the practitioners than more familiar—although possibly less precise—ones such as "implementation" or "evaluation," so they were adopted.

3. The Rand Graduate Institute (RGI) is an accredited, Ph.D.-granting, educational institution within The Rand Corporation. It trains "policy analysts" who work as junior staff members on Rand projects while completing RGI degree requirements. Harold Lasswell was influential in this educational venture from its inception and served as the first chair of the RGI's educational advisory board. Other pioneering policy scientists took active roles as teachers and advisors, such as Abraham Kaplan, Nathan Leites, and Herbert Goldhamer.

4. A considerable debt of gratitude is owed The Rand Corporation and the Rand Graduate Institute for the initial encouragement and support of this project, particularly to Charles Wolf, Jr., Dean of the RGI. The Rand Corporation, the RGI, and Dr. Wolf, of course, bear no direct responsibility for the book and its contents, nor should it be assumed that it reflects the views of The Rand Corporation, the RGI, or any of their respective sponsors.

Institutional/structural issues. Political aspects. Economic concerns. Psychological impediments. Ethical and moral issues. Ideological/mythical issues. Legal aspects.

Some experiences: *Successful partial termination: The Village Nursing Home. Termination on a grand scale: The War on Poverty.* Design issues in termination policy: *Basic principles. Strategic design. Tactical designs. Outcomes and effects.* Bureaucracies and wars: *Runaway bureaucracy. Termination of nuclear wars.* New challenges in termination policy. Termination in the policy process.

1

Introduction

> Reality is not a function of the event as event but of the relationship of that event to past, and future events. We seem to have here a paradox: that the reality of an event, which is not real in itself, arises from other events, which likewise, in themselves are not real. But this only affirms what we must affirm: that direction is all. But only as we realize this do we live, for our own identity is dependent upon this principle.
>
> Robert Penn Warren
> *All the King's Men*[1]

DOES ANYONE KNOW WHAT'S GOING ON?

Much of life appears to be if not actually unreal, then beyond comprehension. A handful of strangers, whose names one hardly knows, shuts down the valves on oil wells in a desolate part of the globe, and in short order lines form at service stations, and gasoline prices skyrocket for something Americans thought was rightfully theirs. Rosa Parks, a working black woman tired from her day's labor, refuses to stand at the back of a Birmingham bus and releases a flood of emotion, energy, and justice whose direction and eventual course no one could (and perhaps still cannot) foretell. A medieval apparition, drawing on a spiritual code from times long forgotten, vanquishes a materially superior opponent armed with the most modern weapons money and management can provide and thus plunges Iran, and much of the industrial world, into confusion and chaos. In school and church, one is told that Communism represents a mortal threat to society and the capitalistic way of life and that nations under its sway deserve fear and reproach. But then one discovers that American banks—capitalism's quintessential institutions—seek business with Communist nations; indeed, so much so that some might fail on account of defaults from such loans. What is one to believe when the government offers aid, comfort, and even interest payments to a faltering Polish economy? Atop this seem-

1

ing confusion and discord rests the virtually unspeakable specter of a nuclear holocaust, a monster entirely of man's own making whose incarnation
threatens all of humanity's artifacts and life's very existence.[2]

If one's perception of events in the public arena is unreal, reference to
private experiences seems even more so, often to the point of dulling
sensibilities. A teenaged boy is arrested for murdering his second or third
victim and then released to terrorize the streets again. A wilderness lake,
supporting abundant life since before recorded time, suddenly grows bar-
ren and sterile as acid literally rains from the skies. A wrong switch is
mistakenly thrown in a power plant, and millions are plunged into darkness.
Even when reason is claimed, the counterclaims ring about as true. Who is
to be believed? Who *really* knows what's going on or what's to be done?
Perhaps Yeats' poetic vision was right:[3]

> Turning and turning in the widening gyre
> The falcon cannot hear the falconer;
> Things fall apart; the center cannot hold;
> Mere anarchy is loosed upon the world,
> The blood-dimmed tide is loosed, and everywhere
> The ceremony of innocence is drowned;
> The best lack all conviction, while the worst
> Are full of passionate intensity.

Yet these signals of societal demise are unduly pessimistic. An indication
of hope is humanity's irrepressible will to confront and master problems
because "he has . . . a spirit capable of compassion and sacrifice and endur-
ance."[4] The paradox Robert Penn Warren addressed above is both a key and
a barrier to such mastery. The way a person perceives reality is itself unreal,
being shaped as it is by the limits of intellect and distorted by the peculiarities of identity and experience. No two individuals will see, comprehend, or value identical events in identical ways. So, for instance, when a
physician bearing fatal news to a dying patient describes the problem, this
description only partly captures the reality felt by this patient or the patient's family or friends, everyone of whom will grasp the matter differently.
Whose perception or grasp is correct or even "better"? No one's and everyone's. The key is to be sensitive to the differences by including them in a
composite, evolving portrait of the problem and what needs to be done to
cope with and overcome it.

The concept of "evolving" is essential. As there are multiple ways to
perceive problems, so there are various means to overcome them, many of
which are not immediately clear; many will depend on special imagination
for their formulation and innovation for their implementation. Events,
furthermore, are neither static nor isolated. Simply being aware of a problem and trying to understand it can affect the field of view and alter the
substance of the problem itself. Knowing that a sulfuric acid rains on a
favorite vacation lake heightens one's awareness of personal shortcomings

at the same time that it changes customary behavior, including a search for solutions to the problem.

Conventional ideas and approaches regarding solutions may actually inhibit their attainment. Much of Western civilization's success is built on rational, disciplined, scientific inquiry. Procedural matters have been devised through the years and refined to a point where science's underlying rational bias is accepted without much reflection.[5] Science's success in framing and answering questions within the scientific realm is indisputable; but for many other problems that fall outside the bounds scientists delineate the rational bias, tight discipline, and quantitative procedures erected to support the scientific edifice provide little help. It is a complex issue, but it usually can be reduced to differences between theory and practice and, hence, the general aims sought by doing intellectual work.

All sciences seek the development of theory by the generation and testing of hypotheses that confirm, refine, and enlarge common understandings of events.[6] Truth, as a concept and objective of science, is contained in such theories. With them, small infusions of evidence from specific settings can be organized and manipulated to yield predictions about the future. A well-developed scientific discipline permits small bits of fresh information, in combination with its laws and theories, to generate valid predictions of wide scope. But science's success is owed in part to the care its practitioners take in selecting their problems. It also results from the consistency of the client for the work: the discipline itself, as represented by its adherents.[7]

For practical problems that demand policy responses, the scientific procedures are not as applicable. There is no theory capable of predicting the civil rights movement in its details, and there is no law powerful enough to explain the consequences of the tired black woman's civil disobedience, the assassination of Martin Luther King, or myriad other related events. Nor is the evidence as reliable or accepted as in the physical sciences. In short, the scientific model and the disciplined, rational principles on which it is based are unable to explain these events or to foretell their consequences. But despite these weaknesses, social events command attention and force action. One can thus legitimately ask, what models and approaches are applicable?

The policy sciences and policy analysts try to describe such events in their real- and unreality. They also try to provide suggestions and guidance for courses of action to persons in authority or with power to change circumstances. Policy analysis is therefore severely disadvantaged compared to conventional science by its inability to choose its own problems, by the complexity of the problems it confronts, and by the limited scope and power of the tools at its disposal. Among its many handicaps, problems of social complexity,[8] human perception and value,[9] and profound uncertainties about the future all figure prominently.[10] Through all of this, the pursuit of a single, optimal, or right solution is thwarted at virtually every turn.[11]

Nevertheless, we expend great energies and considerable resources trying to create simple and durable solutions to problems far more complex than analysts and decision makers admit. For instance, in the initial chill of the energy crisis, some loudly claimed that the solution lay in letting economic markets work unfettered by government or other influences.[12] The issue is more difficult and complex than this, as America's persistent failure to devise an energy policy attests.[13] A rapid increase in the price paid for gasoline ripples through the society until waves of disillusionment and resistance mount. Rather than delve through the apparent facts and understand the complex realities, simple slogans are adopted and scapegoats labeled (e.g., Arabs and/or oil companies). If government is perceived as one of the conspirators, then profound social implications can occur as disillusionment with the government, its processes, and its general ability to serve the public good spread.[14]

The point emphasized here is that the pressing social and political problems of the times are remarkably intricate ones which do not yield to simple solutions. New England pensioners do not see the energy problem or its solution in the same way as economic theorists or as the affluent in the Sunbelt do; changes in habit and taste compelled by higher gasoline prices catch Detroit auto makers off guard and unprepared to retool for smaller and more economical cars; substitute or alternative forms of energy for the radically changed setting provide more hope than heat—and a mad rush to fill the void begins. The theoretical solution is blind to these realistic possibilities; its perception of the problem is too simple and confined. The practical consequences of the problem, however, are neither. Price increases force inequities between classes and regions; changes in driving habits produce crushing unemployment in Detroit and ripple out to other places that depend on the production of automobiles (e.g., steel and rubber); the replacement of traditional forms of energy with new and untried ones demands big outlays, for research and development and for hundreds of other risky and uncertain new ways of living. Academic theoreticians are neither interested in nor responsible for the political decisions that must be made to surmount these problems. Any solution must, however, reflect these considerations, and dozens more, in order to attain political feasibility, for without such attainment, it is no solution at all.[15]

But politics is only partly a rational process, at least according to scientific specifications. Decisions and the analyses on which they are based are always imperfect because the events they deal with are unreal by rational standards. Social problems are intricate and changeable, and they often mean very different things to those involved. Neither problem, context, nor possible solutions stand constant—they all evolve naturally and in reaction to efforts to understand and master them. Despite the considerable temptations of the optimal or best solutions the conventional disciplines seem able to provide, the information they treat is selective and treats only the what-has-been, not the what-will-be that most concerns policymaking, and -makers:

> Policymaking and execution are steps into the future, and it is a source of perpetual concern to political thinkers that, since descriptive knowledge does not encompass the future, uncertainty and risk are inseparable from decision.[16]

Should we reject the scientific method and the disciplines that define and work within it? Clearly not, especially as a normative set of aspirations. But we must learn the limitations of the scientific disciplines by understanding where they can help, where they have less to offer, and where they impede or even harm chances of finding workable solutions to complex policy problems. A prime area where science offers few insights concerns individual human values.[17]

Why does one bother caring about or working on social, which is to say human, problems? A simple question but a very difficult one to answer adequately. As a general matter, human problems should be examined to advance broad human ends, not theoretical, disciplinary, technical, or narrowly particular ones. Much as the Renaissance found direction and accelerated when Donatello, Michelangelo, Leonardo da Vinci, and others at a critical time realized humankind's centrality—not its subservience—in life's general scheme,[18] so might contemporary analytic creativity be released by a similar change in focus.[19] Humanity's highest ambition can thus be defined as a desire to analyze problems to improve the human situation. Because no one can fully appreciate a problem in terms of all who are affected by it, analysts must be careful to include relevant human perspectives, desires, and values as much as possible.

For policy scientists, the most important value is human dignity—a summary idea defined in terms of distinctive human needs for respect, well-being, affection, enlightenment, skill, rectitude, wealth, and power.[20] By definition policy analyses and the policy goals they seek to inform and facilitate are thus means to influence the shaping and sharing of these basic needs and values.[21] Policy scientists are consistently challenged to clarify and specify in operational terms society's long-term goals by relating them to decisions made in a policy process. Lacking such guideposts, policymakers and those who work to advise them simply fly blind: "What's going on and where are we going?"

The analyst has values and policy preferences, and these matter. If understanding why one does policy analysis is difficult, figuring out for whom analysis is done is sometimes even more so. For many analysts the client is whoever pays their wage, which is perfectly acceptable as long as serving the client does not clash with their responsibilities to the general society. Obviously tensions can arise. For many problems an analyst confronts, there is convergence between one's own values, those motivating the sponsor, and those held by other affected parties. In extreme situations of divergent values, however, the analyst is obliged to give precedence to the overriding value of human dignity—which may mean resignation from a project, conspiracy against or open opposition to the client, or, most preferably, concerted efforts to redirect the task to more acceptable ends. Few of these choices confront discipline-based specialists, for their "client" is the discipline or, more generally, science itself.[22]

This book's broad outlines, perspective, and approach are thus: human values are the crux of the policy sciences; problems for analysis are generated by the society at large, not by the theoretical inquiries of the scientific disciplines; and analyses must include many individual perspectives and should aim to be practical while striving to improve the policy processes responsible to and benefiting humankind.

THE FOUNDATIONS: A DISTINCTIVE APPROACH

Although the approach to policy problems and the term *policy sciences* are at least 30 years old, academic and professional attention has rarely centered on the approach nor thoroughly appreciated its various implications. Admittedly the evidence at first seems contradictory: Training programs, courses, books, and many other activities have flourished in recent years where a common aspect is concern for, and identification with, policy, policy analysis, or topics such as health, energy, welfare, national security or transportation policy. Close inspection of the evidence usually discloses only slight variations on the standard disciplinary themes. Books whose titles promise a policy analysis of some problem turn out to be case studies that social scientists have been doing for years with, at best, hastily drawn policy recommendations; methodological courses that claim to teach policy analysis appear to be the standard scope and methods courses using slightly more complicated data sets to teach statistics or data analysis; and training programs for policy analysts or managers are hardly distinguishable from applied programs in economics, political science, sociology, or psychology in the first instance or from routine professional programs in public and business administration in the latter. Policy is a word with many interpretations and interpreters. But if a word represents everything, it risks meaning nothing.

Policy sciences is not a simple, incremental modification of any of the standard disciplinary or professional approaches. It is a fundamental change in outlook, orientation, methods, procedures, and attitude. This is not to say that the traditional disciplines are not valuable or have nothing to contribute; we have already pointed out their importance. It is to say that the challenge of doing policy analysis well is not equivalent to doing disciplinary work well. They are different enterprises with distinctive approaches and objectives.

Some background

It is for this reason we selected the title *The Foundations of Policy Analysis* for this book. Its purpose is to start at ground level and to construct this approach bit by bit as a way of demonstrating its distinctiveness and of guiding would-be analysts and practitioners through the many helpful applications it holds.

We do not claim originality. There is too much history, and the approach is obviously the product of many minds. The policy advisor has attended policymakers since the inception of politics.[23] The philosophy underpinning the policy sciences, however, is distinctly American and can be found in the writings of John Dewey and other pragmatists in the early part of this century, and in Abraham Kaplan's, Harold D. Lasswell's, and others' works more recently.[24] Its theory and technique took form in the 1920s and 1930s at the University of Chicago, largely under the tutelage of Charles E. Merriam,[25] and developed in a variety of fields in the following years. While this book is not meant to detail the intellectural history or sociology of knowledge represented by the policy sciences, it does stress its key discriminating features. The ideas of problem-oriented, multimethod, comprehensive, and human-centered inquiry leading to purposeful action draw heavily upon the cumulative work and effort of many individual scholars, analysts, and practitioners.

The publication in 1950 of the collected work *The Policy Sciences* presented a summary report of selected contributions made during the Depression, World War II, and the period of readjustment and uneasy peace right afterwards.[26] For many reasons, some still unclear, the policy sciences were not taken up by others, nor were its early contributions extended, hence, its promise fulfilled.[27] Lasswell, together with his colleague Myres S. McDougal, pursued a prodigious research, writing, and training program within Yale University's Law School. The law, according to Lasswell's explanation for his preference for it as a base of operations, is one intellectual specialty that appreciates and rewards problem solvers who are also willing to assume responsibility for their actions. Law has its general theories and methods to be sure, but the litmus test of feasibility—the trial of theory and method against reality—is never far from hand or out of mind. But despite its hospitality, law was just a temporary host, an intellectual way station where the policy sciences found refuge and sustenance for the next 20 years.[28]

It is perhaps just as well. The social science disciplines were undergoing a major methodological and philosophical upheaval during this period—what some have called the "behavioral revolution." The historical-descriptive and normative-philosophical wings of the respective disciplines came under heavy attack from the empirical-rational revolutionaries: theory was a holy grail with measurement its quest. The more zealous went so far as to stake their claims on a "value-free" and "objective" new social science that would in short order route and displace the old.[29] Although the behavioralists did bequeath some useful legacies (e.g., a greater appreciation of and sophistication in empirical research as it applies to the social sciences), the passion of the debate distracted the disciplines from research devoted to the recognition of human problems and their alleviation.

Elected president of the American Political Science Association in 1956, in the early days of the revolution, Lasswell used the occasion of his presidential address to remind his disciplinary colleagues of a few of these problems and to encourage them to take an active and responsible interest in their analysis and resolution. In an amazingly prescient tour de force, he singled out nuclear weapons (primarily the threat to world order their diffusion implied), the energy crisis (its probability and the need to begin a diligent search for alternatives, including solar energy), the problems and possibilities of a worldwide communications revolution, and the difficulties posed by technological advances meant to prolong or alter human life.[30] Few took the challenge, many were simply bewildered, and most just returned to the barricades and battlements of the ongoing revolution.

Wars and revolutions run their course in time, and by 1970 most of the costs and benefits occasioned by the behavioral revolution had been absorbed by the social sciences. Again the time seemed apropos to reintroduce the policy sciences. In 1971 Lasswell published *A Pre-View of Policy Sciences,* a handbook summary of what he perceived as the essential elements of the approach. At about the same time, the journal *Policy Sciences* emerged under the sponsorship of The Rand Corporation and the editorial stewardship of Edward S. Quade.[31] Professional training and degree-granting programs oriented to the approach were established at The Rand Corporation (Rand Graduate Institute), Duke University (Institute of Policy Sciences), the University of Michigan (Institute for Public Policy Studies), and Harvard (the John F. Kennedy School of Government), among others. The overall enterprise was publicized by some of its most ardent supporters[32] and received generous foundation support (e.g., the Ford and Alfred P. Sloan Foundations).

The decade of the 1970s was, with minor exceptions, a time of exuberant oversell, burgeoning activity, and limited performance. This is a harsh assessment, but the results of the collective experience are hard to interpret otherwise. While this is not the place or time for an extensive postmortem, it is worth generalizing on some of the limitations common to hundreds— perhaps thousands—of policy analyses performed during the period that claimed to be inspired and directed by the policy sciences. Most show little appreciation for or understanding of the basic elements of the approach. Most are no more than rehashed projects serving disciplinary needs and ends with little appreciation of the fundamental characteristics of the policy sciences; this failure was most apparent in their neglect of the humanistic aspects of the approach. Policy research, analysis, and training were professional fads, and everybody wanted to get with it. The results are now in, and their sober appraisal directs us back to the intellectual drawing board if we are to prepare policy analysts and practitioners for their exceptionally difficult trade.

Back to basics

Lasswell and Daniel Lerner were careful to point out the most general distinctions between the policy sciences and other approaches:

> The term is not to be taken as a synonym for any expression now in current use among scholars. It is not another way of talking about the "social sciences" as a whole, or of the "social and psychological sciences." Nor are the "policy sciences" identical with "applied social science" or "applied social and psychological science." . . . Nor are the "policy sciences" to be thought of as largely identical with what is studied by the "political scientists."[33]

Then and now the term defined an approach concerned with knowledge of the decision or policy process and knowledge in that process. The policy sciences join and integrate theory (knowledge of) and practice (knowledge in) to improve them both for human benefit:

> A policy orientation has been developing that cuts across the existing specializations. The orientation is two-fold. In part it is directed toward the policy process, and in part toward the intelligence needs of policy. The first task, which is the development of a science of policy forming and execution, uses the methods of social and psychological inquiry. The second task, which is the improving of the concrete contents of the information and the interpretation available to policymakers, typically goes outside the boundaries of social science and psychology.[34]

None of the policy-relevant disciplines—including philosophy, history, economics, political science, law, sociology, psychology, and the biological and physical sciences—has precisely this frame of reference, although each has something positive to contribute.

The label, *policy sciences*, was chosen carefully. *Policy* includes society's most important decisions, actions backed by widespread approval and/or threat of sanctions. *Science*, most generally, suggests means to acquire verifiable knowledge. Using sciences, in the plural, invites all scientific disciplines to participate while giving preference to none. Indeed, the entire label, policy sciences, was and still is an invitation to anyone concerned with both policy and science to share the distinctive frame of reference.

Minimum essentials: Getting oriented

"Direction is all," Robert Penn Warren advises. But direction is meaningless without a map; in this case the map is a way to get oriented to the policy process. The map must portray all significant parts of the process, even if some appear only vaguely; otherwise, one might miss opportunities or collide with unexpected problems, either eventuality leading to mis-spent resources.[35] The map must display specific routes and roadsigns. Much like driving across country, policy analysis requires large quantities of very specific factual information, which general, discipline-based the-ories are usually not able to supply. Events are unreal and ever changing, as are the rules (which some call theories) governing those events.[36] The map must post warning signs about this and make allowances for the ana-lyst's intellectual shortcomings (e.g., inadequate theory, inappropriate data), the perceptual and value biases of everyone involved, and the gaps in information that always occur to make the policy process especially resistant to problem solving.[37]

Social science theory and practical experience contribute to the map, but neither alone is reliable. Theory is both incomplete and general, meaning that heavy reliance on it may divert attention away from important aspects of the particular case it does not cover.[38] The solution to the energy crisis dictated by economic theory says nothing about many of its most critical features. Basing decisions on theory alone means believing that general answers exist and that particular details do not count, but for a policy-oriented approach they always do. A case in point regards a simple, but common, assumption underlying many specific decisions made in the Viet-nam War. Maxwell Taylor, who was deeply involved, writes in his memoirs:

> We were inclined to assume . . . they [the North Vietnamese] would seek an accommodation with us when the cost of pursuing a losing course became excessive. Instead, [they] proved to be incredibly tough in accepting losses which, by Western calculation, greatly exceeded the value of the stakes involved.[39]

Taylor adds that the assumption was also based on a feeling that the North Vietnamese would act like the North Koreans had during the Korean War, which is only a way of reminding one that neither theory, Western calcu-lation, nor practical experience, either alone or conveniently reinforced by theory, is sufficient. To address the complexities of the policy arena, we must devise ways to connect theory and practice appropriately, in light of the realistic details (both substantive and normative) of problems that re-quire attention and decision. Improved ways of thinking are required, which provide the fundamental justification for the policy sciences as a distinctive discipline and approach.

One way to proceed is to locate problems with respect to their status or maturity somewhere within the policy process.[40] A problem initially con-ceived is not equivalent to one of long standing, where experience and efforts to contend with it have amassed. So, for instance, when an intel-ligence agency first reports that an adversary has produced a threatening new weapon that may endanger another's national security, an initial and tentative recognition of a problem occurs. Besides trying to learn more (for example, information to verify the threat), the policy analyst will be needed to help decision makers interpret what the threat portends. Information will be sought to estimate the weapon's implications and what might be done to counteract or neutralize it. Once verified and estimated, providing the threat is real and the attention of decision makers can be captured and held, a decision may be made about an appropriate response. Once made, the decision has to be implemented. Time passes and the problem changes; we learn more about it and are actively engaged with it, but so is the adversary. Figuring out the consequences calls for evaluation or appraisal. Did the policy and subsequent decision solve the problem? Make matters worse? Possibly create new problems? Or what? Perhaps the threat was, in retrospect a false assessment, or even à deliberate subterfuge to achieve some other policy goals.[41] Sometime later still, it may be necessary to bring matters to a halt, for example, the decisions and actions taken in its behalf are no longer effective or the problem has evolved to where the issue no longer matters as much or at all. Knowing where a problem is in the policy or decision process is an important procedural matter.

Another way to proceed is to learn how to organize, compare, and cumulate knowledge about the policy process itself. For instance, in creating options and making estimates to counter the hypothetical enemy threat, the analyst utilizes existing tools and methods previously used for these purposes to get organized and oriented; there is no need to start from square zero each time a problem presents itself. Or the problem may be different enough that the analyst has to modify old or create new means to do the estimates. The new means thus add to the general collection of methods and concepts for future use.

The tools are not magical, nor are they chiseled in granite. Indeed their effectiveness is limited by the skill, experience, and judgment of the analyst, by the time and resources available every step along the way, and by the characteristics and contextuality of the problem itself. Rarely, if ever, will an analysis be final or definitive. Not the least reason for this is that the context itself is constantly changing, naturally and in response to the actions taken to master and control it.

Knowledge about the policy process is not just analytic, nor will any one disciplinary perspective provide sufficient coverage. As decisions are reached, different knowledge and requirements than those found earlier in the process enter into play. Weighing various alternatives, sensing their possible implications, and finding bases of acceptance and agreement within parts of the body politic all require knowledge (skill, experience, and judgment) at least as demanding as that needed to do analysis (compare Parts II and III). Likewise, knowing how the various systems work and how to work the systems are essential if one is to transmit decisions into practice (Part IV). But these distinctions in the early rush to embrace policy analysis were not ordinarily appreciated or honored.

It is equally important to understand that no person or institution will be responsible for the entire decision process, nor with the whole analytic endeavor (i.e., the multidiscipline facet). A division of labor is the usual means of coping with both.[42] But this confounds the process. Intelligence agencies, to continue the example, are specialized agencies with particular competence to recognize problems. They are not chartered to make policy or to carry out substantial decisions, although in practice they often do.[43] Distinctive organizations usually practice estimation; its special requirements imply a different mix of skills and talents. So the logic moves through each phase of the policy process. But the different perspectives held by each participant obstruct and impede smooth operations as they enrich the knowledge base of decision. Each literally sees the problem differently; each comprehends its own reality distinctively with its own means and goals; and each values its potential according to separate needs. Further complications arise when each phase of the process is not given adequate weight or, equivalently, when some phases are stressed excessively at the expense of others. Say, for example, a policy counteracting the enemy threat does not include adequate means to evaluate as an ongoing exercise and to adjust the policy as conditions change; in such a case, one would expect that excessive resources would continue building the countermeasures long after their need had passed.[44] When someone finally discovers this, halting production lines and reallocating resources would be very difficult. Or to control the process by ensuring common outlook and values, one finds institutions expanding beyond their particular or authorized competence.

Understandably, competing organizations seldom see events or order their preferences identically, a point of great consequence.[45] The U.S. Congress not only deliberates and makes decisions, it has its own intelligence, research, and evaluation appendages.[46] Thus, information becomes the life blood of policy analysis and policymaking; it is hardly surprising that few agencies treat other agencies' analyses with little more than bare credibility.

Operational principles

Besides a map, one needs operational principles. At a general level, the policy sciences supply guidelines in terms of interdisciplinary, comprehensive, and integrated treatment of the subject matter. Again, these principles specifically emphasize a problem orientation, contextuality, multiple methods, and an overriding concern for human values.

Problem-oriented inquiry consistently and explicitly considers the following questions at every step in the policy process:[47]

What goal values are sought and by whom?

What trends affect the realization of these values? Or, where did the problem originate?

What factors are responsible for the trends? Or, what are the causing, driving, or influencing factors?

What is the probable course of future events and development—especially if interventions are not made?

What can be done to change that course to realize or achieve more of the desired goals, and for whom?

Such questions provide the context of analysis at the same time as they suggest procedures for doing it. Problems designate theory and methods, not the reverse, in sharp contrast to discipline-based inquiry. They also remind one of missing parts of an analysis and thus stimulate imagination to create unexpected policy alternatives for consideration. These questions are pertinent at all stages of the policy process.

Contextuality means understanding the relationship between the parts and whole of a problem. It also means having a clear sense and appreciation of the past, present, and future of events as they interact and change through time. If a choice must be made, we urge comprehensiveness by giving preference to the whole. With this strategy, a problem's tentative appreciation and resolution are always relatively correct but imprecise in detail—a useful situation where time to do analysis is limited or hard to control.[48] In other words, it is better to be approximately right than precisely wrong, to think about a complicated process in the large than to get bogged down in measuring only a few of its minutiae. In short, for important policy issues, it is far preferable and productive to be thinking about many unlikely things than just answering the obvious questions.[49] Being contextual requires a comprehensive conceptual framework to direct one's attention to possibly significant phenomena in a setting and to maintain a tentative, evolving appreciation of the whole.

The following rough sketch illustrates contextuality. Although it is completely imaginary and didactic in purpose, it offers a graphic example of how partial information can be woven into a contextually elaborate and meaningful tapestry. In 1965, an insurance actuary might have estimated that the average 55-year-old Russian male had an expected life of 14.6 years. There may have been a dispute about this, and another equally competent expert could have pointed out that class and race differences and whether or not individuals had suffered undue hardship (e.g., imprisonment, malnutrition, or war traumas), would affect the estimate; maybe it should be as low as 13.3 and maybe it was as high as 16.9 years. Neither actuary would be so bold as to predict the death of a specific 55-year old Russian male, nor would they have the vaguest idea what the numbers meant in other circumstances. But to the contextually-minded analyst of the time, these data might have stimulated some rather unlikely thoughts about the future, even though disputes about the estimates' precision would not matter much at all. The Soviet Union was going to face a political succession crisis, involving most of its top leadership, sometime in the early 1980s. Several other contextual data contributed to this tentative forecast even though deciding whose problem or opportunity it would eventually be was still an open question.

The Soviet Union had already experienced rather bloody and fitful transfers of power from one ruling cadre to the next after long years of Stalin's domination. Experience, unwritten rules, and byzantine procedures existed to cue the next succession.

Experience also suggested that succession could result in a loss of control over the Soviet society or empire. Fearful of such contingencies, decisions by Soviet leaders had to be carefully guarded, tightly limited, and swiftly executed.

Bulganin and Khrushchev, transitional politicans firmly rooted in the Stalinist era, had consolidated power, with Khrushchev finally emerging on top.

Khrushchev's adventurism, notably in the Cuban missile crisis in 1962, had frightened everyone—Russians, Americans, and most of the world—and his time and methods had clearly passed. Less dangerous types were needed to continue the slow and steady progress in military build-up and economic development begun after the devastation of World War II. Advances were precious and had to be protected. Such expectations and hopes, based on vividly shared experiences, were common.

Despite the crude arrangements to transfer power, the unwritten rules did not specify when to do so. It was safe to assume that the cautious *aktiv* succeeding Khrushchev would hang on as long as possible.

But to hang on, an elaborate system of personal political alliances with like-minded and trustworthy comrades would be essential. Thus, members of the new leadership would need to be tightly interdependent and would probably appear, to an outsider, virtually indistinguishable one from the other.

Once established and proven to be effective, the alliances would be extremely stable, mainly out of fear of their disruption and another risky crisis in leadership. Barriers to entry and the infusion of new blood would be, respectively, high and unlikely; more probably, internal coalitions would rearrange the actors until, as in the cases of Lenin, Stalin, Khrushchev, and Brezhnev, a single leader emerged.[50]

For our imaginary analyst, these and many other features together contributed to a provisional map of the whole of the Russian Succession Crisis. As time passed, from 1965 on, more information would be revealed that enriched the initial formulation and enhanced analytic understanding. Accuracy of important details could be improved as available and necessary. Much of the information was qualitative and subject to different interpretations. Some, with the passage of time, would turn out to be less important than initially hypothesized; and some could turn out to be plain wrong. Throughout the period, as the 1980 target date approached, various contingencies and options could be imagined and assessed. Policy questions and thoughts of the following sort would keep occurring:

Is it in America's interest to do anything at all to influence the succession? What groups contribute what kinds of opinions and preferences to the succession crisis?

If the Soviet Union has serious domestic economic or political difficulties at about the same time as the leadership crises, what are the risks that succession will be used as an excuse for an external adventure to divert attention away from them.[51]

Would it be in American interests to work on reducing such pressures, thus to lessen the chance of conflict elsewhere in the world? (The Polish bail-out of 1982 suggests as much.) Or, are the internal contradictions so threatening to the Soviet polity that it would be to the U.S.'s advantage to try to destabilize or excite dissenting passions so as to moderate or maybe even collapse the system? (U.S. reactions to Castro's Cuba during the 1960s and El Salvador in the early 1980s hint at this tactic.)

How far can the Soviet leadership be pushed before it becomes desperate and perhaps dangerous?

Of groups and individuals likely to participate in the Soviet succession struggle, are some preferable to others from the American perspective, and if so, what could be done to assist them or to undercut the less preferred ones? Or should anything be done at all?

Under different, but still plausible, circumstances, how is the succession crisis likely to play out?

This is hardly a definitive analysis; it was not meant to be. However, to quell doubts about its general shape and intent, one could consult one policy scientist's rendition, Leites' *The Operational Code of the Politburo.*[52] This sketch illustrates several aspects of contextuality and portrays the style of thought a policy sciences approach stimulates and demands.

Obviously many disciplines and methods can contribute to the ongoing analysis of a problem. The problem itself, embodied in one's evolving appreciation of it, points out, perhaps demands, which disciplines and what methods might best be brought to bear. Calling attention to multiple methods suggests lessening a prevalent tendency in disciplinary analysis to celebrate methodology at the expense of substance. Any method has blind spots that focus attention on highly selected aspects of a problem while blocking it out for others. A policy analyst must understand this and counteract it by viewing problems with a variety of different methods or approaches and then working to assemble their partial insights into something approximating a composite whole. Furthermore, picking a problem that fits a method, a commonplace activity, is no guarantee that the problem is worth considering at all. Once the actuaries provided estimates of expected life spans, very little else was needed from them. Other methods and perspectives enabled the analyst to abscribe meaning to these numbers. Nonetheless, the actuaries probably continued observing and diligently measuring, even though it no longer mattered much for the problem at hand.

The human-centered operational principle forces analysts to raise questions continually about who the relevant participants are at each phase in the process and further, to try to understand the value demands, expectations, and identifications of each of them. What resources are available to each participant, and how are they using them to affect outcomes? In simpler terms: Who are the players, what do they want, how might they be affected, and what resources do they have at their disposal?

"What do they want?" and "What have they got going for them?" have to be assessed in terms of many different human needs:[53]

Power: Participation in decision making.

Enlightenment: Insight, knowledge, information.

Wealth: Income and property.

Well-being: Health, safety, comfort, security.

Skill: Proficiency in performing tasks.

Affection: Love, friendship, loyalty, solidarity.

Respect: Honor, status, reputation, nondiscrimination.

Rectitude: Conformance with ethical or religious standards.

Rosa Parks' refusal to move to the back of the Birmingham bus released the flood gates of the civil rights movement, not because she was powerful, but because her act symbolized and tapped the deprivation of respect felt by millions of others like her. Many other sympathetic values were certainly involved, and later decisions sought to allocate them more equitably than before. Power and wealth were not sought as ends nearly so much as they were used as means to acquire access to other values: respect (nondiscrimination in jobs and housing), skill (job training and educational opportunities), well-being (nutrition and health programs), and rectitude (realization of long-denied constitutional guarantees and simple recognition as fellow human beings).

The religious values the Ayatollah Khomeini drew upon turned out to be more effective as organizing and mobilizing forces than the wealth and naked power resources available to the Shah of Iran. Indeed, the Iranian revolution is somewhat more understandable as a reaction to the Shah's pursuit of power at the expense of religious and ethical values deemed more important by most of his subjects.

The illustrative wilderness lake, ruined by the acid rain of industrial pollution, stands for an increase in wealth for some at the expense of wealth (lost property value) and well-being (threats to health) for others. Or at the personal level, the dying patient represents a loss of comfort and health (and other values for the family and friends) because of inadequacies in enlightenment (knowledge about the disease) and skill (the physician's inability to do anything).

Lastly, because policy is future-oriented, determining who the relevant participants are in any policy process may involve many who do not yet exist. The responsibility to future generations is key to understanding such disparate movements as ecology and nuclear disarmament. Policy disputes about abortion are notable here, as are decisions about using or conserving energy, or enhancing or holding back certain technologies. Take genetics for example: What would be the legal rights of human clones, identical human replicates? What are the rights and obligations toward a genetic duplicate created primarily as a ready reserve of spare parts for organ transplantation? Should government assume a more active role in controlling genetic engineering with human applications? These admittedly are far-reaching questions but that reason alone should not obscure the point that current policy decisions have significant consequences for future generations which must be taken into account today.

Our discussion could be construed as discouraging, or at least frustrating to many. Some may dismiss it out of hand. Others may see no role for themselves, considering their limited interest or supposedly meager talents. To these views, we simply propose the following: significant decisions are and will continue being made which intimately affect personal values and lives. Is it preferable that others make them without the knowledge, advice, and consent of an informed and participating citizenry?

At base, the policy sciences offer guidance to anyone wishing to understand complex human problems, although one's skill and success with the approach will naturally vary widely. The approach is neither foolproof nor a panacea. It is often frustratingly hard work for reasons we will document at length throughout the book. But the policy sciences do offer an opportunity to help one think through and understand the basic problems confronting the human condition.

More must be said about our proposed map, particularly the phases of the policy process it represents. It, and this book, attempt to move beyond bare essentials and provide guidance for those who wish to pursue this intellectual and professional course.

THE POLICY PROCESS

The policy process can be visualized in several ways, but one simple scheme features six basic phases through which policies and programs pass over time.[54] It is recognizable from the previous illustration of actions following the discovery of a new enemy threat.[55]

Initiation.

Estimation.

Selection.

Implementation.

Evaluation.

Termination.

Initiation begins when a potential problem (which could just as well be an opportunity) is first sensed, i.e., problem recognition or identification. Once a problem is recognized, many possible means to alleviate, mitigate, or resolve it may be explored quickly and tentatively. In this early and most creative phase, one comes to expect numerous, ill-defined, and inappropriate formulations. Indeed, as much as casting about for answers, this phase emphasizes efforts to define (or redefine) the problem, to get a sense of it in terms of its possible importance and whether it merits further time, attention, and resources. Many problems will not or will languish in the initiation state awaiting additional and clarifying information. Initiation also refers to the innovative tasks of conceptualizing and sketching out the rough outlines of a problem, collecting the information necessary to lay out a range of possible responses, and then beginning to specify potential policy choices within that range. Here, as in all subsequent phases, the various operational principles previously discussed apply.

Estimation concerns predetermining risks, costs, and benefits associated with each possible option that emerges from initiation and with new ones analysts discover as they continue their work. This stage emphasizes empirical, scientific, and projective issues to help determine the likelihoods and consequences of the candidate options. It also stresses the assessments of the desirability of such outcomes, a normative concern usually given short shrift by policy analysts. Many technical approaches exist to aid calculations of the first type, such as cost-benefit analysis, various statistical techniques, and computer modeling of great scope and complication. But far fewer aids address the normative aspects of estimation. Pertinent knowledge certainly exists; however, it is rarely integrated within ordinary policy analyses.[56] Estimators should generally try to narrow the range of plausible solutions (e.g., by excluding the infeasible or exploitive) and to order the remaining ones according to scientific and normative criteria. Pursuit of both objectives helps decision makers in the next phase.

Selection refers to the fact that someone may eventually make a decision; the prior analytic work to imagine and define the problem and assess the alternatives usually plays a role in this. A decision or policymaker is anyone authorized or able to alter the flow of pertinent events. Thus, within a properly defined and limited frame of reference, ordinary people act as decision makers all the time. This is the most political of the enumerated steps. Decisions are seldom made only on the basis of prior technical calculations and estimates. Many other aspects need to be considered, not the least of these being the multiple, changing, and sometimes conflicting goals held by those interested in the problem and its resolution. To the extent that the analytic efforts exercised during estimation neglect non-rational or ideological information, decision makers may find themselves forced to rely heavily on their own experience and intuition to integrate these essential ingredients of workable decisions. A nondecision is always possible, especially where previous analyses were inconclusive or contradictory, or where those responsible decide that the risks and uncertainties of doing something exceed those of doing nothing. For large-scale and consequential problems, finding an acceptable and feasible solution may take inordinate amounts of time, attention, and resources as compromises are hammered out, deals are struck, and modifications are made to account for specific contextual details of the setting.

Implementation is the execution of the selected option—an option that may bear only faint resemblance to estimation's orderly recommendations, often to the analyst's wonderment, frustration, or chagrin. Implementation has only lately been accepted as a distinctive phase of the policy process, having its own participants, rules, methods, and procedures. Prior to the mid-1970s, most scholars (and many practitioners) labored under the impression that decision making and implementation were nearly one and the same. The postmortems of numerous policy failures soon gave evidence that they are not.[57] To understand how decisions are carried out and to anticipate institutional effects even beforehand, one must master the details of what has been called implementation analysis. In brief, particulars matter. For example, individuals' and organizations' incentive systems are essential objects of study and later manipulation. Lacking an appreciation of them, one could easily be dismayed to discover that what was intended at the moment of decision and what eventually happened are quite different. Those making the decision and those tasked to execute it are generally not the same individuals, with all that implies concerning perceptions of events, values, and other identified complications of the human condition.[58] Certainly one must thoroughly understand the general mechanisms (knowledge *of*) and their specific operation (knowledge *in*) before performance may be evaluated and improved, the next step in the policy process.

Compared with previous phases, *evaluation* is more retrospective in practice. Initiation and estimation are anticipatory, and selection stresses the present. All three deal with possible, but not yet experienced, events. Implementation is an occasion to transform potential into reality, and the differences between the two need to be assessed. Evaluation asks questions of the following sort: What individuals and what policies and programs were successful or unsuccessful? How can that performance be measured and evaluated? Were any criteria established to make those measurements? By whom? Were the criteria appropriate; did they incorporate pertinent perspectives and values and emphasize important outcomes and effects? Who sponsored and who did the assessment, and why? To what ends was the evaluation directed, and were they accomplished? Good evaluation is a scarce commodity, despite numerous evaluation research studies and related scientific methods. It is also an essential commodity to the next and final phase of the process.

Termination concerns the adjustment of policies, programs, and organizations that have become dysfunctional, redundant, outmoded, or unnecessary. From the conceptual and intellectual point of view, it is a poorly

TABLE 1–1   Phases and characteristics of the policy process

Phase	Characteristics/uses
Initiation	Creative thinking about a problem. Definition of objectives. Innovative option design. Tentative and preliminary exploration of concepts, claims, and possibilities.
Estimation	Thorough investigation of concepts and claims. Scientific examination of impacts; e.g., of continuing to do nothing and for each considered intervention option. Normative examination of likely consequences. Development of program outlines. Establishment of expected performance criteria and indicators.
Selection	Debate of possible options. Compromises, bargains, and accommodations. Reduction of uncertainty about options. Integration of ideological and other nonrational elements of decision. Decisions among options. Assignment of executive responsibility.
Implementation	Development of rules, regulations, and guidelines to carry out decision. Modification of decision to reflect operational constraints, including incentives and resources. Translation of decision into operational terms. Setting up program goals and standards, including schedule of operations.
Evaluation	Comparison of expected and actual performance levels according to established criteria. Assignment of responsibility for discovered discrepancies in performance.
Termination	Determination of costs, consequences, and benefits for reductions or closures. Amelioration as necessary and required. Specification of new problems created during termination.

developed phase. From the practical and operational point of view, it is at least as impoverished. These conditions belie termination's importance and signal areas requiring considerable thought and attention. Interest groups may demand that production lines for the weapons created to counter the enemy threat be ceased, but can one be sure about whether, when, or even how to do so? Others may call for cuts in government spending as a way to reduce its influence on personal lives, but what happens to those put out of work or those who rely on services excised by the economizer's zeal? What will termination cost when measured against the relevant values at stake for all those involved? Who pays? Simply ending something often only creates many new and unexpected problems for attention and resolution, perhaps greater than those they replace.

The policy model as represented so far is greatly oversimplified, as we acknowledge. But it has the distinct advantage of being readily understood and remembered, both important features to help one appreciate the policy orientation and to direct one's intellectual energies. A biological analogy clarifies the point. The human circulatory system does not exist outside the entire body; nonetheless, one can learn something by separating it conceptually. Still, the whole body must be kept in mind when ministering to the heart, an artery, or a vein. So it is with the policy process, although many think and act as if decision making or analysis were each totally self-sufficient, which we argue is surely not the case.

The six-phase model becomes more plausible and useful as its various interactive possibilities are explored, conceptually and in practice. This is the explicit conceptual framework posed here and the organizing theme of this book. General conceptual linkages among the phases are detailed at the end of each chapter, and practical relationships are illustrated by numerous examples throughout.

To summarize the discussion, the phases or steps in the policy process are listed again alongside characteristic activities and reasons for each in Table 1–1.

THE RATIONALE AND POSSIBLE USES OF THE BOOK

The approach, ideas, examples, and experiences presented in the book evolved (rather in keeping with the policy process itself) over more than 10 years. A few words about this may be helpful. We also try to anticipate, based on our experiences in using and teaching the approach, some general questions that nearly always occur. Answers to them comprise a rationale of sorts for the considerable time and effort we have expended over the years. The book has been an eight-year, on-again, off-again thinking and writing process for the two of us. Initial drafts of several of the chapters existed as long ago as 1973. They, and everything done subsequently, have been continually rethought, updated, and revised in light of events—including our own intellectual and professional development as policy scientists. We conclude this section with some speculations and suggestions about how this book can be used.

As graduate students, we were both schooled as political scientists but with substantial training in other disciplines, such as economics, mathematics, history, and engineering. Furthermore, we both had the great good fortune to know and work with Harold D. Lasswell, who encouraged our intellectual imaginations well beyond the strict confines of the traditional academic disciplines. Finally, as instructors and practitioners, we have been forced to define and explain our particular views of policy analysis to any number of curious students and skeptical research sponsors. (It is arguable which audience is more demanding.) Thus, over the years, we have formulated and evolved a contextually rich and practically viable conceptual framework for appreciating and practicing the policy sciences. What it may lack in theoretic elegance is compensated for by its real-world applications.

The thrust of the framework reflects, as it must, our backgrounds and experiences. It is decidedly political in nature. How are policies and programs defined, selected, evaluated, and ended? Again, the motivating purpose is to gain knowledge of and in the policy process, so as to help policy analysis better meet its objectives within the more general goals of the policy sciences. Although there are numerous examples of applied technical methodologies (e.g., statistical analysis, cost-benefit ratios), this is deliberately not a scope and methods text.[59] Rather, the policy process presented here gives the reader a recognition of how the policy process works, how it might work better, and suggests ways and places that the more technical skills of the analyst can be best employed.

Common questions/a rationale

Several questions about the policy sciences show up without fail every time we teach or use the approach. Some are worth pursuing briefly to provide additional background and a rationale for the book. We start with a common question and end with one more complex.

"Isn't the policy sciences just another way of saying the obvious?"

No. It is a potentially powerful scheme that allows or even forces the observer of complex human problems to become oriented to a complicated stream of events; to appreciate the consequences of legitimate but often different perceptions of events; and to become sensitive to the many individuals and institutions affected by and/or trying to cope with real problems. Other approaches may appear to offer simpler or easier solutions, but each usually turns up lacking in important ways—not the least of these being their relative inability to help one think and understand, and hence to become a more humane, creative, and effective problem solver.

"All the terms and concepts confuse me. Aren't there some easier ones that do the same job? Or are we just learning lots more social science jargon?"

The terms used here are the most uncomplicated we have found while still being descriptively powerful enough to meet our purposes. We are not promoting jargon for its own sake, but for the purpose of helping others understand. Certainly other terms or essential equivalents for the ideas exist or could be devised. Whatever is convenient and expedient is certainly appropriate, but only if the fundamental ideas the language conveys are not obscured or lost. If calling selection something like decision making makes its consideration any easier without omitting the essential elements that make selection the richly complex phase that it is, then the change should be made. We are not personally enamoured by inelegant phrases like termination and implementation. They are rather ungainly linguistic concoctions. But we still use them because they are common and convey some meaning when starting to discuss the intricacies they represent.

"Isn't the approach equally guilty of the excessive rationality you fault in others?"

Yes and no, depending on the meaning of rationality. The approach to understanding the policy sciences manifests is itself fundamentally rational as it tries to be systematic, comprehensive, problem-oriented, multi-method, and concerned with human values. However, this in no way compromises the facts that the objects of study and understanding are themselves often irrational, or apparently so, or that various forms of irrationality often figure prominently in the policy process. There is nothing quite so irrational—and misguided—as approaches that claim to be rational and then operate as if the world ought to be the same—neat, simple, and orderly.[60] As distinct from the disciplinary specialists discussed earlier, policy scientists try not to place a rational straitjacket on the decision processes they observe. The world is often crazy, and pretending otherwise does not make it any less so.

"Isn't politics simply a redistributional issue, where power is used to reallocate wealth?"

Yes, but other values are equally at stake and have to be accounted for before decisions are made, so that individuals can think about what the trade-offs are to inform and clarify their preferences; as decisions are made, so that politics' symbolic, ideological, and mythical aspects receive their due; and after decisions are made, so that meaningful assessments and adjustments to outcomes can take place. In such forums, other values besides power enter into analysis. This is one of the strengths of the policy sciences approach.

> "Isn't the incremental approach (or bureaucratic-politics or case study) really a better way to think about the policy process?"

Although each has something to offer, none is sufficient to do the job well. Three very general issues must be considered by any approach to matters of human decision: (1) The problem orientation of decision makers; (2) the context which gives rise to and is affected by decisions; and (3) the mechanisms and processes by which orientation and context are related to decision making and decision experience. Consideration of several well-known approaches according to these issues shows what they emphasize and, more importantly, what they lack.

Incremental theories of decision making have gained acceptance and a large following in the policy analysis community. This is partly justified when one realizes how many decisions are basically only slight modifications of previous practice. But many are not. How, for example, does one increment to or from ground-zero, where there is no previous experience or where past practice has been decisively unsuccessful, e.g., in cases of sharp discontinuity in the social process (war, depression, or revolution) or of a fundamentally new problem demanding action (government regulation of genetics research)?

Incremental approaches focus on just one kind of decision-making process (issue 3, above)[61] while ignoring the problem orientation of decision makers and the contexts in which they operate (issues 1 and 2). On problem orientation: What happens when numerous incremental decisions are made whose consequences are not felt for long periods of time, as could happen in selecting and building a large-scale and untried new technology, like nuclear power plants? Because the built-in self-correction (or evaluation) on which incrementalism is predicated is so long in coming, decision makers wedded to this process must fly blind, destination unknown, until they reach their destination—or crash.

Context does not matter to the incrementalist. Goals are dismissed by assuming that decisions taken are right because, lacking sufficient support, they would not have been made in the first place. The assumption is grievously faulty. No one has any real experience with decisions until they have been enacted. But implementation typically distorts the diverse intentions underlying decisions by making concrete just one of them. One could support a decision and still be displeased with its eventual outcomes. These contextual and process matters are naively slighted by incrementalists, as are unique and chance events, distinctive personalities, human passions and foibles, the clash of conflicting ideologies and beliefs, and numerous other factors given prominence in other approaches to the subject.

What matters most in the incremental approach is one very specific process that matches the demand for political solutions against the available supply. Bared to its essentials, one discovers a discipline-based, micro-economic, market-oriented, and rational perspective of the world. However, the policy process has more than micro frames of reference and is far more complex and interesting than the marketplace.

Bureaucratic politics is a popular approach with a different slant, but it has blind spots as well. Here the context is primarily defined in terms of organizational structures and their particular interests, procedures, and sensitivities to issues and information as decision constraints. Other levels of analysis and perspectives on the matter do not count as much and are hence disregarded. So are the distinctive orientations of specific decision makers; they are less interesting than are the institutions where they sit.[62]

The case study or historical approach is strong on contextual details the other two examples discount, but it is weak on explanations, forecasts, and alternatives beyond the single one described. Cases typically do not generalize and they are hard to use for policy purposes. Casebook solutions tend to mislead one into believing that general answers exist and specific details do not matter. In other words, they overemphasize issue 2 and overlook or ignore issues 1 and 3.

These short examples are not meant to denigrate any one approach. They and the section's other questions rather suggest a rationale for this book. Any approach to the policy process must incorporate and balance its appreciation of the three general issues just defined. It gains advantage if it offers procedural guidance to reduce unwarranted or excessive concentration on any one or two of the three. The policy sciences approach satisfies these requirements.

How to use this book

One should begin by reading the book as a whole, to gain as comprehensive and continuous a sense of matters as possible. For some, this may be enough. It works out to about a semester's effort for the average student or to several days of careful reading for others. Some may wish to delve more deeply into a particular phase to learn more about its special characteristics and details. Take evaluation, from the point of view of an analyst trying to improve the effectiveness of his or her work, or from the perspective of a practitioner sponsoring and using the evaluation product. Both would find something of interest, although there would be different attractions to each. Besides the extensive documentation provided in each chapter, we have assembled pertinent, selected references at the end of each major party to assist in-depth exploration and development.

Individuals interested in classes of problems (e.g., urban renewal or social welfare programs) might use the book differently, providing they have first tried to master its conceptual approach. As soon becomes obvious, our own interests and experiences as policy scientists stand out in the substantive illustrations and materials used. Health, education, national security, housing, energy, civil rights, natural resources, technology, and numerous applications of different research methods recur regularly as examples and could be read selectively by those wishing to develop more familiarity with these topics. With only a little extra effort, the selected references at parts' ends, plus appropriate references within, could also be organized for this purpose.

A third possible, general use might be explored by the more adventuresome. Many parts of the general map are poorly understood, and some have hardly been charted at all. We signal these where they occur. Similarly, many emerging policy areas demand immediate and thoughtful attention, both in terms of developing methodology and, more basically, the human condition.[63] Each warrants ample additional concern and even more hard work. The policy process works poorly enough and might be improved were these weaknesses and gaps attended to with care. Were readers to make this choice, chances are good that they would run into one or the other of us somewhere along the way, an opportunity we would surely welcome.

Each chapter aims to cover particular theories, practices, methods, procedures, and approaches relevant to a distinctive phase of the policy process. The book as a whole encourages their integration. We are well aware of the difficulties here and of our limitations in achieving these goals. We take some comfort, though, in realizing that there are seldom, if ever, definitive, best, or correct answers in the world of political (i.e., human) decisions. Rather here are only limitless possibilities for the imagining, whose ultimate significance shall only be grasped through experience and with time. This represents both the millstone and medallion of the policy sciences, or, perhaps more aptly, reality as best we understand it.

NOTES

1. (New York: Harcourt Brace Jovanovich, 1946), p. 231 in Bantam edition.

2. Jonathan Schell, *The Fate of the Earth* (New York: Alfred A. Knopf, 1982), vividly describes the consequences of a nuclear exchange and wonders why mankind has avoided the moral responsibilities of confronting this ultimate threat to humanity. His fears are not unique; see Mary Thorton, "46% in Poll Say Chance of Nuclear War on Rise," *Washington Post*, March 24, 1982, p. 8; or James Kelly, "Thinking About the Unthinkable," the cover story in *Time*, March 29, 1982, pp. 10–14.

3. Reprinted with permission of Macmillan Publishing Co., Inc. from "The Second Coming," © 1924 by Macmillan Publishing Co., Inc., renewed 1952 by Bertha Georgie Yeats. *Collected Poems* by William Butler Yeats.

4. From his acceptance speech for the 1949 Nobel Prize for Literature by William Faulkner. Even then (1950), Faulkner identified the key issue of our time when he stated: "There is only one question: When will I be blown up?"

5. Some go further and implicate them as troublesome. Richard R. Nelson, "Intellectualizing about the Moon-Ghetto Metaphor: A Study of the Current Malaise of Rational Analysis of Social Problems," *Policy Sciences*, December 1974, pp. 375–414, explores the analytic and practical dimensions; and William Barrett, *Irrational Man* (Garden City, N.Y.: Doubleday/Anchor, 1958), approaches it with a philosopher's mind.

6. James S. Coleman, *Policy Research in the Social Sciences* (Morristown, N.J.: General Learning Press, 1972), guides one through these distinctions.

7. Thomas S. Kuhn, *The Structure of Scientific Revolutions* (Chicago: University of Chicago Press, 1970), is central to the understanding of the progress of science and its short-comings.

8. Ronald D. Brunner and Garry D. Brewer, *Organized Complexity* (New York: Free Press, 1971); and Todd R. LaPorte, ed, *Organized Social Complexity: Challenge to Politics and Policy* (Princeton, N.J.: Princeton University Press, 1975), take up the general topic in various ways.

9. George A. Miller, *The Psychology of Communication* (New York: Basic Books, 1967); Geoffrey Vickers, *Value Systems and Social Process* (New York: Basic Books, 1968); and Abraham Kaplan, *American Ethics and Public Policy* (New York: Oxford University Press, 1963), are essential and fundamental readings here.

10. William Ascher, *Forecasting: An Appraisal for Policy-Makers and Planners* (Baltimore, Md.: Johns Hopkins University Press, 1978), catalogs the results of empirical modeling efforts to predict policy problems in a variety of settings and generally concludes that there has not been much success.

11. Herbert A. Simon, *The Sciences of the Artificial* (Cambridge, Mass.: MIT Press, 1969), offers one compelling interpretation here.

12. Perhaps the purest statement of such advice in the popular press is by Milton and Rose Friedman, *Free to Choose* (New York: Harcourt Brace Jovanovich, 1978).

13. Actual recommendations are not usually so starkly put, and precise details for arriving at this optimal state are considerably more involved, although neither qualification blunts the underlying theoretical rationale and impetus. Hans H. Landsberg et al., *Energy: The Next Twenty Years* (Cambridge, Mass.: Ballinger, 1979); and Sam H. Schurr et al., *Energy in America's Future* (Baltimore, Md.: Johns Hopkins University Press for Resources for the Future, 1979), present several perspectives of energy events while emphasizing an economic-theoretical and technical-economic standpoint, respectively.

14. Ronald D. Brunner and Weston E. Vivian, "Citizen Viewpoints on Energy Policy," *Policy Sciences,* August 1980, pp. 147–74.

15. Garry D. Brewer, "Where the Twain Meet: Reconciling Science and Politics in Analysis," *Policy Sciences,* June 1981, pp. 269–79.

16. Harold D. Lasswell, "Some Perplexities of Policy Theory," *Social Research*, Spring 1974, p. 177. Lasswell goes on to identify several "novel elements" that affect eventual results: human imagination, judgment, and purpose, and "in part their combined impact 'invents' the future."

17. This, of course, is not meant to suggest that scientists as individuals are not deeply concerned with human values.

18. The germination of the Renaissance is literately depicted by Johan Huizinga, *The Waning of the Middle Ages* (Garden City, N.Y.: Doubleday/Anchor, 1949). The standard treatise on its flowering is Jacob Burckhardt, *The Civilization of the Renaissance in Italy* (New York: New American Library, 1960, first published in 1860). The period's glorious art and its relation to man are described by Bernard Berenson, *The Italian Painters of the Renaissance* (New York: Meridan, 1976), pp. 118–27, 170–78.

19. Explicit in their endorsement and explanation of this necessary change are Harold D. Lasswell, "The Policy Orientation," in Daniel Lerner and Harold D. Lasswell, eds., *The Policy Sciences* (Stanford, Calif.: Stanford University Press, 1950), pp. 9–15; and Harold D. Lasswell and Abraham Kaplan, *Power and Society* (New Haven: Yale University Press, 1950).

20. Lasswell and others emphasize the difference between discipline-oriented and human-centered analyses by labeling the latter the policy sciences, a distinction we endorse and

promote throughout this book. Thus we use the more common terms *policy analysis* and *policy analyst,* but in keeping with the policy sciences approach.

21. Harold D. Lasswell, "Policy Sciences,"*International Encyclopedia of the Social Sciences,* vol. 12 (New York: Macmillan and Free Press, 1968), pp. 181–89.

22. Jacob Brownowski, *Science and Human Values* (New York: Harper & Row, 1965), is a clear and sensitive exploration of the general topic; also see Albert O. Hirschman, *Exit, Voice and Loyalty* (Cambridge, Mass.: Harvard University Press, 1970).

23. Herbert Goldhamer, *The Adviser* (New York: Elsevier, 1978), chronicles much of the advisor's history in a variety of historical and cultural milieus.

24. John Dewey, *Reconstruction in Philosophy* (Boston: Beacon Press, 1948); Abraham Kaplan, *The Conduct of Inquiry* (San Francisco: Chandler, 1974); and Lasswell and Kaplan, *Power and Society,* collectively cover the philosophical ground.

25. A comprehensive narrative of the development of American intellectual life is still untold. However, when the job is finally complete, the prominence of the University of Chicago during this time in the human and social sciences will undoubtedly stand out.

26. Lerner and Lasswell, *Policy Sciences.* This is one of the earliest published uses of the identifying label.

27. Policy scientists were located in many governmental agencies and contributed much of practical, policy utility during this period. The Office of War Information, focal point of all propaganda efforts, and analytical divisions of the Office of Strategic Services are two notable illustrations. Many individuals contributed directly to the policy process as analysts and activists, e.g., Beardsley Ruml, Paul Hoffman, and William Benton. One continuing legacy of the era is the Committee for Economic Development, a business research and analysis group in New York City and Washington, D.C., originally established at war's end to explore the possibility of a resumption of the Depression, and policy options to counteract it.

28. Many believe that some of the distinctive character of legal education at Yale, e.g., its acceptance of the social sciences and its orientation toward public service, can be traced to the combined efforts of Lasswell and McDougal during this era.

29. Knowing what counts is as important as knowing how to count, a point sometimes lost on the early behavioralists. Presuming that observation and measurement could be neutral or value free collides with the fact that selecting something to measure is a choice itself based on the observer's values and preferences. The contradiction has since become accepted wisdom.

30. Harold D. Lasswell, "The Political Science of Science," *American Political Science Review,* December 1956, pp. 961–79. Little has been lost in the passage of more than two decades.

31. Harold D. Lasswell, *A Pre-View of Policy Sciences* (New York: American Elsevier, 1971). The book is difficult, but essential, reading. Quade, then head of the mathematics department at The Rand Corporation, is not so much a policy scientist as he is a systems analyst (Chapter 6, tables 6–1, 6–2 for the basic differences). He nonetheless provided meritorious service to the journal in its first years.

32. Representative is Yehezkel Dror, "Approaches to Policy Sciences," *Science,* 10 October 1969, pp. 272–73. The press took notice, too: John Noble Wilford, "New Study Field: Policy Sciences," *New York Times,* August 9, 1970, p. B-16.

33. Lasswell, "The Policy Orientation," p. 4.

34. Ibid., p. 3.

35. Lasswell, *Pre-View of Policy Sciences,* chap. 2.

36. Coleman states this as a general principle of policy research: "For policy research, the criteria of parsimony and elegance that apply in discipline research are not important;

the correctness of the predictions or results is important, and redundancy is valuable."
Similarly, he supports the need for contextual, if not altogether perfect, information
about problems: "For policy research, partial information available at the time an action
must be taken is better than complete information after that time." Coleman, *Policy
Research in the Social Sciences*, p. 4.

37. We are obviously not talking about a real map, in the ordinary sense of the word, but of
a conceptual and intellectual one. Herbert A. Simon, for one, has carefully described the
intellectual, perceptual, and value components of such a map in his various treatments
of a problem he labels "bounded rationality." Simon, *Sciences of the Artificial*; and
Robert M. Axelrod, ed., *The Structure of Decision* (Princeton, N.J.: Princeton University
Press, 1976), are representative. Gaps in information stem not only from intellectual
limitations; they can be intentional, as in the cases of censorship, propaganda, and myth.
See Part III.

38. Valuable lessons on the point are related by Albert O. Hirschman, "The Search for
Paradigms as a Hindrance to Understanding," *World Politics*, April 1970, pp. 329–43;
and Kaplan, *Conduct of Inquiry*.

39. Maxwell Taylor, *Swords and Plowshares* (New York: W. W. Norton, 1972), pp. 400–1.

40. Note in this illustration the need for knowledge both *in* and *of* the policy process.

41. Desmond Ball, *Politics and Force Levels* (Berkeley: University of California Press, 1980),
suggests that the U.S. intelligence community misrepresented the Soviet missile threat
in the late 1960s and that the Kennedy administration seized upon the "missile gap" to
launch a massive strategic buildup even though Secretary of Defense McNamara and
others realized the shortcomings of the intelligence estimates. Much of this is substan-
tiated by McNamara in an interview with Robert Scheer, "Fear of First Strike Seen as
a Cause of Arms Race," *Los Angeles Times*, April 8, 1982, pp. I-1, 13, 14.

42. Of course the frame of reference or level of analysis may mitigate, e.g., in instances of
finely detailed or personal decisions, where the problem's scope and the resources
required are within a single person's reach. Even here though, outside consultation,
advice, and other assistance may enrich the process and improve eventual outcomes.

43. In recent years, the Central Intelligence Agency has been criticized for exceeding the
limits of its competence and authority. Reaction concentrated on redefining its role and
scope of activity.

44. See Ball, *Politics and Force Levels*.

45. Think for a moment why it is that the estimates and assessments of the current state and
future course of the U.S. economy prepared by the Congressional Budget Office and the
Executive Office of Management and Budget routinely disagree and often by wide
margins.

46. Respectively, the Congressional Research Service of the Library of Congress, the Congressional Budget Office, and the General Accounting Office.

47. This organizing principle is used explicitly to focus on political development by Garry
D. Brewer and Ronald D. Brunner, eds., *Political Development and Change: A Policy
Approach* (New York: Free Press, 1975).

48. Such is the norm in policy analysis, as contrasted with discipline research, where time
matters relatively less.

49. Scientific disciplines nearly always choose a partial or reductionist strategy in which
details are pursued and measured precisely. Often lost in the strategy is an appreciation
of what the details mean and how they fit within an evolving conception of the whole in
which they are but a part. William Barrett, *The Illusion of Technique* (Garden City, N.Y.:
Doubleday/Anchor, 1978), is a clear and devastating exposition of this necessity; again
Kaplan, *Conduct of Inquiry*, cannot be neglected.

50. The historical details of this contextual illustration can be found in Jerry F. Hough and Merle Fainsold, *How the Soviet Union Is Ruled* (Cambridge, Mass.: Harvard University Press, 1979); and Alfred G. Meyer, *The Soviet Political System* (New York: Random House, 1965).

51. "During times of crisis—notably during a relatively popular war—the whole body politic acts in support of measures regarded as essential to national identity and interest." Lasswell, "Some Perplexities," p. 188.

52. Nathan Leites, *The Operational Code of the Politburo* (New York: McGraw-Hill, 1951).

53. The specific terms used are less important than the messages they contain: Human beings require a variety of values; trade-offs will exist among and between them; no two individuals, or even the same individual at different times or in different circumstances, will either want or command the same array of values. Any comparable list will do as long as these conditions are recognized and met. This set is posed by Lasswell, *Pre-View of Policy Sciences.*

54. Understanding of the terms "policy" and "program" will come with their continued use throughout the book. Provisionally, a "policy" is a broad or strategic statement of intent to accomplish specified aims; "program" is any one of several possible means, more tactical in nature, to attain a policy objective. A policy, thus, is usually thought of in terms of its constituent program elements. These definitions are sufficient for initial comprehension, but will be elaborated throughout the book.

55. A slightly different model is found in Harold D. Lasswell, *The Decision Process* (College Park: University of Maryland Press, 1956); some additional explanation occurs in idem, *Pre-View of Policy Sciences*, especially chap. 5. We have simplified and relabeled the model for ease of presentation and understanding. The present version first appeared in Garry D. Brewer, "The Policy Sciences Emerge: To Nurture and Structure a Discipline," *Policy Sciences*, September 1974, pp. 239–44.

56. Chap. 4, "The Human 'Ought' and the Rational 'Is'," explores this at length.

57. Jeffrey Pressman and Aaron Wildavsky, *Implementation* (Berkeley: University of California Press, 1973).

58. Thomas B. Smith, "Policy Roles: An Analysis of Policy Formulators and Policy Implementators," *Policy Sciences*, September 1973, pp. 297–307.

59. Ample references to such methodologies and approaches will be found throughout the text and chapter bibliographies.

60. Others share this view as well. See David Berlinski, *On Systems Analysis* (Cambridge, Mass.: MIT Press, 1976); Gunnar Myrdal, *Objectivity in Social Research* (New York: Pantheon, 1969); Richard R. Nelson, *The Moon and the Ghetto* (New York: W. W. Norton, 1977); and Barrett, *Illusion of Technique*, all use this theme in different ways.

61. In extreme cases, claims are made that it is not only how decisions are made, but it is the best way to do so. A discussion critical of these claims is contained in La Porte, *Organized Social Complexity*, "Introduction."

62. This is not as much as can and needs to be said about incrementalism and bureaucratic politics; these discussions are continued in various places throughout the book, especially Parts III and IV.

63. Many of these issues are proposed by Brewer, "Policy Sciences Emerge"; and Peter deLeon, "Policy Sciences: The Discipline and the Profession," *Policy Sciences*, February 1981, pp. 1–7.

PART I

Initiation

The genesis of what we call the policy process occurs in the first stage, initiation: The analyst's perceptions signal the existence of a policy problem or opportunity; the problem is formulated in general terms; the problem context is identified; policy goals are determined; and policy alternatives are generated.

The existence of initiation as a phase is not disputed by most observers. Obviously one cannot have a policy unless a problem is recognized, the policymaking mechanisms are alerted, and policy alternatives are generated. At the same time, the initiation period is one of the most complex and difficult to conceptualize and therefore one of the least studied. It involves such nebulous matters as individual and group perception, pattern recognition, communication networks, creativity, and innovation. The analyst must engage in such disparate activities as the normative definition of goals and the selling of one's view of the problem to the political decision maker.

Work done during initiation pivotally affects the formulation and execution of good policy. Three potential hazards during the initiation stage illustrate why. First, if the problem is misdefined during initiation, the condition might not be discovered and corrected until later in the policy process (perhaps during the estimation stage), at the cost of valuable time and resources. In the meantime, the problem may have changed so much that the policy process must begin anew. If the mistake is never discovered, the eventual policy might—probably would—intensify rather than ease the original problem. One example of faulty problem definition occurred in the early 1960s when there was nationwide concern over decaying urban centers and their residents' flight to the suburbs. Hoping to rehabilitate the areas and stem the centrifugal migration, urban renewal planners redesigned and rebuilt the downtown areas of their cities. Billions of construction dollars and several riots later, federal and local planners recognized that ramshackle buildings were only symptoms of the underlying and more serious problem of urban poverty, that urban renewal had only made the problem worse, and that markedly different strategies were necessary to cope with the root cause.[1]

Second, in the initiation phase, normative goals must be defined and values and policy objectives made explicit.[2] Few policymakers ever completely ignore these things, but most never consider them explicitly.[3] To ensure consistency in the policy process and to make the resulting policies more attentive, it is necessary to specify the goals, values, and objectives being pursued throughout the policy process but especially in the initiation phase. Otherwise, an organization may find itself gradually, unwittingly, and perhaps unwillingly pulled into situations that are antithetical to its consensual goals and forced to adopt policies contrary to its values. The American involvement in Vietnam is regrettable testimony to the consequences of failure to spell out national goals, values, and objectives.[4]

Third, a short circuit in the initiation stage could blind one to the existence of a problem until it had grown too big for treatment with the available policy tools. The collapse of the stock market in 1929 was predictable, but no government agency recognized and acted upon the warning signs. Indeed, even after Black Tuesday the government failed to recognize the severity of the problem and acted as if the market would correct itself.[5] Similarly, the government neglected the civil rights of over 10 percent of its population until the civil rights demonstrations and riots of the early and mid-1960s vividly demonstrated the immediacy and enormity of the problem as well as the inequity of the system, problems continuing to defy resolution, if the Miami riots of 1980 are indicative.[6] The energy crisis was foreseeable prior to the jolt caused by the Arab oil embargo of 1973–74, but for various complex reasons—many of which relate to deficient initiation efforts—America was caught unprepared and has since 1974 suffered incredible difficulties in coming to terms with energy insecurity and other changes in habitual consumption practices.[7]

In short, a dereliction of responsibilities during the initiation phase can postpone, impair, or even negate the rest of the policy process. Therefore, initiation warrants our careful attention.

We can define the origin of the initiation phase as the perceptions and actions that set the policy process in motion. Perceiving a problem does not mean that new and innovative policy alternatives will be generated or chosen; a policymaker might instead decide to modify a current policy or even make no change at all. Still, simply reviewing current policy in light of a recognized problem constitutes an exercise in initiation.

We discern four separate components in the initiation stage. The first is *recognition of the problem.* Without the perception of a problem, threat, or opportunity there is no incentive for the organization to disturb its status quo, or, in our terms, to expend organizational energy initiating the policy process. Recognition is a function of both the information received and one's ability to interpret it. The linkage between the individual and organizational recognition is crucial. Thus, we examine recognition of the problem as both an individual and an organizational phenomenon.

The second component is *identification of the problem context.* Once a problem, threat, or opportunity is identified, it must be defined and bounded analytically. It must also be assigned a priority in an organization's hierarchy of objectives.

Third is *determination of goals and objectives.* Given that a problem exists, the analyst must specify what objectives are desired by its selection, what values should be pursued, and with what means. These issues involve a number of normative and political considerations. Indeed, the acts of problem recognition and analysis imply a certain set of values.

The last component of the initiation phase is the *generation of alternatives.* Often one of the alternatives will be continuation of current policies. But as present and anticipated problems seem increasingly resistant to existing policies (economic theory offers little policy guidance for treating a simultaneous recession and inflation, for instance), analysis often focuses on creative and innovative alternatives.

Although we treat them separately, the components of the initiation stage are highly interactive. The generation of alternatives will almost certainly provide feedback to the identification of the problem context and specification of objectives. Similarly, one should bear in mind the interaction of initiation and the other stages of the policy process. The objectives defined in initiation will surely influence the evaluation' and selection stages, and the care taken during the generation of alternatives will have a bearing on the implementation stage. We will return to consider the effect of the initiation stage on the rest of the policy process at the end of this part.

NOTES

1. For a general overview and several specific case studies, see James Q. Wilson, ed., *Urban Renewal: The Record and the Controversy* (Cambridge, Mass.: MIT Press, 1967). For an analysis of the urban renewal and other city problems, see Douglas Yates, *The Ungovernable City* (Cambridge, Mass.: MIT Press, 1977).

2. Harold D. Lasswell and Abraham Kaplan, *Power and Society* (New Haven: Yale University Press, 1950), suggest a set of general policy values. Also see the discussion of goals and values in Harold D. Lasswell, *A Pre-View of Policy Sciences* (New York: American Elsevier, 1971), chap. 2, "Contextuality: Mapping the Social and Decision Processes."

3. Although the writings of the incrementalist or partial-adjustment school of policymaking imply that decision makers can disregard broader issues of goals, objectives, and values. See Charles E. Lindblom, *The Intelligence of Democracy* (New York: Free Press, 1965).

4. This failing of U.S. policy in Vietnam is thoroughly documented by David Halberstam, *The Best and the Brightest* (New York: Random House, 1972). Frances FitzGerald, *The Fire in the Lake* (New York: Random House, 1971), describes how American policymakers never stopped to consider the horrific impact U.S. involvement would have on the Vietnamese social order.

5. The most readable account of the government's failure to act upon the fiscal warning signs is John Kenneth Galbraith, *The Great Crash, 1929* (Boston: Houghton Mifflin, 1954).

6. The dawning of the import of the civil rights movement upon the government is documented in the memoirs of Presidents Kennedy and Johnson. See Arthur M. Schlesinger, Jr., "The Travail of Equal Rights," and "The Negro Revolution," *A Thousand Days: John F. Kennedy in the White House* (Boston: Houghton Mifflin, 1965), chaps. 35 and 36; and Lyndon B. Johnson, "The Struggle for Justice," *The Vantage Point: Perspectives of the Presidency* (New York: Holt, Rinehart & Winston, 1971), chap. 7.

7. William Ophuls, *Ecology and the Politics of Scarcity* (San Francisco: W. H. Freeman, 1977), is a sobering assessment of what many are coming to realize may be a fundamental change in the world context.

2

Problem recognition and context

RECOGNITION OF THE PROBLEM

The perception and recognition of a policy problem can be treated as both individual and institutional phenomena. Obviously, an institution is not a biological entity endowed with cognitive or sensory powers; it perceives action and problems in its environment only through its human members. Therefore, we first discuss individual perceptions and then the mechanisms necessary to transform an individual recognition of a problem into a group or institutional recognition of the need for action. Thus, the individual analyst needs "guidance on *what* to think about or look for, and on *how* to proceed. The first requirement calls for principles of *content* (or manifest meaning); the second, for principles of *procedure*."[1] Although many individual and organizational characteristics are analogous, one must remember that they are not identical; to equate the two, especially to conceptualize the organization as a unitary decision-making entity, produces a misunderstanding of the policy process.[2]

The very recognition of a problem implies a certain set of values and goals on the part of the individual. For the moment, let us assume that the analyst shares a common set of values with the relevant policymaker and the segment of society being served, an assumption discarded later in the chapter.

Individual problem recognition

Generally speaking, a person will recognize or perceive a problem when two conditions are met.[3] First, conflict or tension must exist between familiar patterns of behavior and expectation and one's environment. Second, information about this conflict must come to attention. "Generally, *information* can be defined as a patterned distribution or a *patterned relationship between events.*"[4] Without some form of reliable information, the individual has no way of perceiving even the most significant alteration of the environment; for nearly 30 years after hostilities had ceased, Japanese soldiers were still being found on Pacific Islands prepared to fight the Second World War. Both existing conflict and attention are necessary, and neither one is sufficient, for the analyst to recognize a potential or actual problem.

The amount of dissonance the individual sees between the situation and unique patterns of expectation and action determines the priority placed on solving the problem.[5] Individual patterns of expectation are laden with complexities that need not concern us here; let us just note that they are conditioned by the individual's personal (e.g., psychological, cultural, educational) and institutional/professional backgrounds, with some overlap between the two.[6] Thus, the threat of famine might appear more dire to an African than to an American and a decline in the London gold market will evoke a different response in an analyst in the Department of the Treasury than in a counterpart in the Department of Commerce. Although the individual may appear to be treating information about a problem rationally or objectively, it is very likely that strong emotions and values—perhaps conscious but probably unconscious—are affecting actual perception.

Finally, even though the individual may perceive a conflict situation, one's thought processes may reject, repress, or downgrade the information to the point that the conflict no longer exists.[7] One reason for this is what psychologists have called *cognitive dissonance,*[8] which acts to suppress information that could be painful to the individual if perceived. Its presence can explain how a person might ignore a personal condition, such as excessive drinking, that other observers would perceive as a problem.

A second reason why a person might ignore a warning signal is that there are limits to the amount of information one can cognitively process; in cybernetics terminology, the existence of an overload condition would short-circuit the system.[9] Toffler argues that one reason people and institutions today are not preparing to deal with the possible dangers of a vastly altered future world is that they have been numbed into inaction by the great number of changes already manifest and the rapidity with which they have occurred.[10]

A final reason why people might not recognize a dissonant stimulus is that they prefer to remain in set cognitive and emotional patterns. Stimuli that counter these patterns operate against internal defenses or inertia—

mental sunk costs—which must be overcome before a problem is recognized and action undertaken. People seek to avoid the distinct costs attached to the rejection of existing patterns and the formation of new ones. By the same token, people fairly quickly accept information that agrees with their thought patterns or buttresses their mental constructs; the cost is negligible and the value, reinforcing their position, is positive. Thus, more information is necessary to convince one to change thinking or perceptions than is necessary to maintain the cognitive status quo. This point is underscored by psychiatrist David Viscott, who writes, "The world which people perceive is in some way distorted because only part of it, the part which can be tolerated, is allowed to filter in. One views the world subjectively and tends to see only the evidence that supports one's way of thinking. Everybody [has] his own psychological blind spots."[11]

Once a problem is perceived to exist and fall within an individual's purview, a number of personal thought processes may be initiated to reduce persistent ambiguities or uncertainties. The analyst duplicates these processes by following conventional professional procedures. Information is compared with existing intelligence to see whether it fits current specifications or whether new models, scenarios, or intellectual constructs are necessary. To the extent that the new information diverges from current estimates of the situation (intelligence), questions about discarding the new information (bad data), searching for new information, or deciding what aspects of the new information should be incorporated into the current estimate all occur.[12] The analyst uses various criteria to help make such determinations. As in initial problem recognition, these criteria are value-laden. McDougal, Lasswell, and Reisman have proposed as an appropriate set of criteria for information in a democratic society "dependability, comprehensiveness (within which we include systematic contextuality), selectivity (relevance), creativity, openness, availability and economy."[13]

Organizational problem recognition

Once the analyst is satisfied that the problem exists (i.e., the information set is reliable and valid), poses a threat, and is appropriate for the analyst's organization to deal with, then the analyst must bring the problem to the organization's attention.[14] How this is done depends upon the analyst's personality, position in the organization, and the character of the organization itself. The analyst's own personality is an important link in the transition of a problem from individual to organizational recognition, but it is the most subject to unique idiosyncrasies and too complex for us to address here. We will focus on the other two factors.

Society contains a number of positions whose charters specifically include the identification and alleviation of problems: ministers plenipotentiary and ombudsmen perform such functions in many governments.[15] The responsibility may be limited to the immediate time frame, as with an emergency vehicle dispatcher,[16] or extend over the long term, as with policy planners in the Department of State.[17] Regardless, the roles are similar and their occupants are furnished special tools and discretion to recognize and act upon problems quickly. They also have immediate access to the agency or persons who hold the authority to implement corrective action.

An organization can impede or facilitate the flow of information and recognition of problems by such qualities as its distribution of authority (pyramidal or horizontal structure); lines of communication; what Thompson refers to as the organizational task environment and domains;[18] size and age; the demands already being made on it; and even the composition and attitude of the work force. For example, a hierarchically structured organization with established channels of communication would probably recognize and act upon a well-defined problem faster than would a horizontally configured organization with diffuse, informal lines of communication. There is some evidence, though not conclusive, that small organizations can react more quickly than larger ones in developing and installing technical innovations.[19] An organization already beset with problems will be more reluctant to tackle additional ones. Deutsch suggests that "communications *overload* and *decision overload* may be a major factor in the breakdown of states and government."[20] Rogers and Shoemaker assert that communications are more likely to occur among people with similar, or homophilous, values: "In a free-choice situation, when a source can interact with any one of a number of receivers, there is a strong tendency for him to select a receiver who is most likely like himself."[21]

Failing to gain the organization's attention, an individual's recognition of the problem will not be shared by the organization nor will it be acted upon.[22] Obviously that consequence can be either good or bad depending upon the situation. The president would not order the U.S. strategic missile force launched solely on the warning of a single radar operator in Alaska. On the other hand, largely because of Ambassador Patrick Hurley's refusal to offend Chiang Kai-shek in the waning days of World War II, middle-level American diplomats serving in China were unable to convince the Department of State or the White House of the emerging dominance of the Chinese Communists. Hurley's intransigence even prevented the personal offer by Mao Tse-tung and Chou En-lai to come to Washington and talk with President Roosevelt from ever reaching the State Department.[23]

If the organization will not accept and act upon the individual's recognition of a threat, then that person must decide whether to abide by that decision or bypass the organization's standard channels of communication (or chain of command) and appeal to a higher authority, either within the organization or outside it, such as the Congress or public opinion. "The segments of the public world—Congress, the news media, the citizenry, even international opinion—are regarded from within the world of the government insider as elements to be influenced."[24] If the individual chooses to circumvent immediate supervisors, a resort to a leak or background briefings not for attribution may follow to bring information to the attention of higher-placed, hopefully more sympathetic, decision makers. Both techniques are common in governmental circles; indeed, leaks by federal bureaucrats are almost a standard operating procedure in Washington.[25] A second alternative might be to recruit an ally in another part of the organization or even in a different agency in hopes of attaining success in raising interest in the problem. For example, when proponents of research on medical insurance and performance contracting for education were unable to persuade the authorities in the old Department of Health, Education, and Welfare of the merit of their studies, they transferred their attentions to the Office of Economic Opportunity and received funding from that agency.

Individuals who do not have organizational ties need not contend with the reluctance or refusal of an organization to act. On the other hand, such individuals have little base of support upon which to build and usually lack resources. Even though a tradition of successful muckraking exists in America—one need only consider the impact of Rachel Carson (pesticides),[26] Michael Harrington (poverty),[27] and Ralph Nader (General Motors)[28]—the isolated individual who can readily transfer problem recognition to a large government bureaucracy is an exception. Virtually all problems an organization chooses to act upon have been formulated by one of its members.

Like the individual, an organization may confront internal obstacles to the recognition that policy changes are needed. Even after the organization's decision makers are convinced that a problem exists, they might with good reason resist searching for a policy alternative. The costs of replacing or revising an existing applicable policy might be greater than the cost of continuing the current policy in face of the problem. An organization has already devoted much time, energy, and other scarce resources to formulating and implementing existing policies.[29] March and Simon have pointed out that institutions invest a substantial sunk cost into a set of programs, which makes the organization reluctant to abandon them. Furthermore, information regarding current policies is fairly reliable because it is experience-based, while knowledge regarding new, untried policies is relatively uncertain. The benefits gained might only be marginal and could be lower (even significantly lower) than those of the current policy. The most economical choice, then, might be to remain with the current policy. For that reason, "individuals and organizations give preferred treatment to alternatives that represent continuation of the present programs over those that represent change."[30] This preference for the institutional status quo (the maintenance of certain states or functions) is what Schon refers to as *dynamic conservatism*: "the corporate society . . . is in a state of dynamic conservatism. It strives for survival, stability, and continuity."[31]

Organizations and individuals share certain inherent limits on their ability to perceive problems. The analogous characteristics include various attention focusing mechanisms that alert the organization to threatening discrepancies between its environment and its pattern of expectation; limited search capabilities that restrict its capability to observe its environment; the obvious reliance upon uncertain information about the problem, the environment, and the effect of different policy alternatives;[32] bounded rationality; and the tendency to avoid or at least reduce uncertainty or ambiguity.[33] The analogy does not hold in some ways (e.g., the organization is not a biological entity with a physiological sensory apparatus), but it is close enough to be illustrative. The two important differences are the organization's quasi resolution of conflict as a form of decision making and the organization's reliance upon communication networks.

Beginning with the work of James March and Richard Cyert, researchers have viewed the process of decision making by an organization as being different from that by an individual.[34] An organization, they asserted, acts on a problem in response to the demands or preferences of a number of its subunits; organizational agreement or decision making involves political coalition building, whereas individual decision making involves merely making up one's mind. The tugging and pulling inherent in organizational decision making result in a series of problem formulations and decisions that are usually not optimal for any member of the organization and may even be irrational in terms of organizational consistency.[35] Rather than sophisticated optimization, organizational decision making reflects such simple decision-making rules as local rationality ("an organization factors its decision problems into subproblems and assigns the subproblems to subunits . . . ") and sequential attention to mutable goals ("Organizations resolve conflict among goals, in part, by attending to different goals at different times"). This is what Cyert and March have termed the "quasi-resolution of conflict."[36]

Organizations, like individuals, rely on information or intelligence regarding their environment.[37] Bardach proposes four criteria for what he terms good political alarm systems: rapidity; selectivity (the ability to discriminate good data from bad); validity; and comprehensiveness (the facility to reach all concerned parties).[38] However, in addition to valid information, the organization must have viable channels of communication appropriate to its task.

Communication networks are so fundamental that they have been used to define a country's development.[39] Executives go to great lengths to establish formal communication channels throughout their organization and then expend as much effort in securing informal, or what Downs calls *subformal*, communication links to others in the organization.[40] The second, not necessarily secondary, network is used to validate the formal information flow as well as provide a trusted early warning system. "The viewpoint of cybernetics suggests that all organizations are alike in certain fundamental characteristics and that every organization is held together by communication."[41] A subunit can perceive and recognize a threat, but if that perception cannot be transmitted to the decision-making center, then appropriate action cannot be taken.[42] The consequences of blocked communication networks to an organization are like the consequences of a severed optic nerve to an individual: the eye can see, but the brain cannot receive or act upon the image.

Difficulties with transmitting information to the relevant decision makers parallel the difficulties discussed earlier in the transition from the individual to institutional perception of a problem. Frequently a subunit of an organization is unable to convince the wider organization of an impending threat or problem because of inadequate communication channels. Or, somewhat digested or preprocessed data may not be transmitted because so much raw data are being collected that essential data reduction and management tasks become overwhelmed. For example, repeated Congressional testimony emphasizes our inability to process the mountains of satellite-collected data concerning the number and disposition of Soviet strategic weapons. One Defense Department official went so far as to state that the United States is rapidly "reaching the point where it simply cannot screen all of the imagery that is available."[43] An organization will go to great lengths to preserve its information and communication channels, especially to the subunits that operate on the organization's periphery and might therefore be the first to identify an external threat.[44] It may also expend considerable resources to improve data management measures: multiple millions of dollars in the strategic satellite case.[45]

In spite of such precautions, and even excluding mechanical failure, communications still may not function properly. Besides being overloaded with raw or unprocessed data, a decision maker may not be able to assimilate and comprehend what actually is transmitted. Data only become information as a result of their being interpreted and compared with realistic situations; often decision makers are simply unable to accomplish these tasks in a timely and discerning way. Wohlstetter demonstrates how U.S. intelligence had ample evidence of the Japanese surprise attack on Pearl Harbor but was not able to winnow the proper intelligence from the masses of data that were being collected every day.[46] In this particular case, the inability to discern the proper information was especially striking because U.S. Naval Intelligence had broken the most secret Japanese code and both President Franklin Roosevelt and Secretary of State Cordell Hull were aware that the Japanese were planning to sever diplomatic relations with the United States.[47]

Finally, even good or reliable information does not necessarily guarantee that an organization will be able to recognize readily and act upon a problem. The various subunits of the organization may not agree on the perception of the problem or that a problem even exists. The conflict between the three branches of the armed forces over the annual defense budget displays three very different views of the threat even when all perceive the same enemy.[48] Even if a consensus is reached, there is the possibility that the organization's communications will not function properly and no directed actions can be taken. To prevent this contingency, the United States has spent vast amounts of money to protect the communication channels to its strategic armed forces, with hot lines, redundancy, and other protective devices in case of a nuclear attack.[49]

To summarize briefly, problem recognition will launch the policy process if an individual recognizes that a problem exists and can then demonstrate to a responsible organization that this perception is valid with respect to the organization's perspective and role.

IDENTIFICATION OF THE PROBLEM CONTEXT

Harold D. Lasswell long urged policy analysts to realize and act upon the fact that they are working in an interactive world and that there is an intimate connection between participants in the policy process, their values, and the resource environment.[50] Having considered above the role of participants, we take a closer look at the resource environment. The next subsection addresses the issues of values and objectives.

The identification of the problem context in terms of threats and resources involves having three general components: (1) criteria used to define the problem, (2) relevant contextual or environmental parameters, and (3) proper time constraints. The identification of these three components permits the analyst to determine the seriousness and extent of the problem, its imminence, its possible effects if left unattended, and, in sum, the priority with which it should be addressed. Although the three components are highly interactive, we treat them separately here.

Selection of criteria

Selection of the proper criteria is fundamental to the work of the policy analyst. Unless the proper questions are asked, one has only a hope of obtaining, or even recognizing, the right answers. Furthermore, lack of proper criteria will introduce error in the selection of the proper policy alternative. How can alternative solutions be generated without a firm idea of the dimensions of the problem?

The definition of criteria is not an easy task. Systems analysts have grappled with the problem for some time, and their comments apply more generally to policy analysis; for example: "Criteria are needed to select preferred alternatives within fixed contingencies,"[51] and "An analysis must begin with problem formulation. A major pitfall is the failure to allocate the total time intelligently, so that a sufficient share of it will be spent in deciding what the problem really is."[52] However, systems analysts (and economists) too often try to reduce criteria to monetary costs or numerical metrics, a convenience that the policy analyst cannot always enjoy.[53]

Virtually every research effort, be it academic or policy-directed, requires the definition of criteria. Although the academic reseacher's efforts to formulate criteria are analogous to those of the analyst, the differences in their respective audiences and purposes are significant.[54] The most important difference is that the analyst is professionally motivated to arrive at an answer or policy alternative, while his academic counterpart can legitimately reach the conclusion that "further research needs to be done in this field." Second, the analyst's criteria could have consequences that are injurious to society, whereas the academician might, at worst, receive caustic comments from colleagues. Finally, the policy analyst is firmly grounded in the empirical world and, hence, cannot conveniently assume away or hold constant elements that might confuse the issue in order to present a lucid, theoretically rigorous—and irrelevant—model.[55] For example, Department of Justice lawyers examining pricing mechanisms in a restricted industry cannot avail themselves of the marginalist theory of price setting despite its theoretical value in explaining the fluctuations in price and the convenience of setting marginal costs equal to marginal revenue.[56] Academicians can "choose to ignore the simple fact that any proposed change impinges on existing social structures," a choice that the policy analyst can afford only if unconcerned about alleviating the problem.[57] In short, the realization that the ultimate product of analysis are programs that will be implemented in the real world should force the policy analyst to consider criteria much more carefully than might an academician.

The prescriptive normative content of the above sentence should be noted, for the mere assertion that problem criteria should be carefully and thoroughly considered does not necessarily mean that they are. In the early 1950s, the Ford Motor Company commissioned a study to determine the car-buying habits of American consumers and discovered that they preferred large, medium-priced cars. To capture this market, Ford brought out the Edsel in 1957. In 1959, the Edsel was discontinued, with losses of over a third of a billion dollars. Had Ford asked about car-buying trends rather than the more static current conditions, it might have noted the accelerating sales of small foreign cars and have avoided introducing the Edsel in the year that the automobile industry came to call "the year of the compact."[58] Present-day distress in the automobile industry, in which the Chrysler Corporation is nearly bankrupt and economic ails pervade all large-car manufacturers, points out the cyclical nature of this trend, including the conditions under which it is more liable to come to prominence.

A common error in determining criteria is to define the problem based upon inadequate information, or solely upon existing conditions without taking future conditions into account. Another danger is to base criteria upon symptoms rather than on underlying or root causes. The earlier example of policies addressing urban renewal instead of urban poverty is relevant here. The analyst should always examine the bath water for the possible baby before dumping it out.

Given that the selection of criteria is very difficult, what might be some good rules or questions to use as guidelines? One is that the set of appropriate criteria should accord with the scope of problem. The larger the scope, the more general the criteria will be. For example, faced with the possibility of the obsolescence of the American nuclear deterrent force or strategies, the analyst would not want to be diverted by second-order questions, such as those relating to the manning of the B–52 bomber force. Broadgauge questions are needed, such as: Is the obsolescence a fact? How does it affect the strategic balance? How will the Soviets react to it? Do we need a B–52 force? If the answers to these questions are contrary to defined national interests, what general strategies might the U.S. undertake to correct the situation?[59] For problems at this level, the analyst might well decide by using criteria on general concepts such as those that Lasswell has termed the five intellectual tasks of problem solving: goal clarification; trend description; analysis of conditions; projection of developments; and the invention, evaluation, and selection of alternatives.[60] These are similar to the types of questions that Allison poses for his Model III analyst.[61]

If the problem is one of narrower scope with discrete parts, one would ask more specific questions directed toward defining a more restricted policy or program. The decision to provide certain community services in model housing communities,[62] interservice conflicts over the command of the primary weapon systems,[63] and even the choice of symphonic works an orchestra plays,[64] are examples of this level of criteria selection. Typical questions might include: What specific organizations and actors are affected? To what extent and in what way? These are the questions that the bureaucratic politics analyst might pose.[65] Criteria selection at this level is mainly attuned to what is possible; there usually is not enough time to strive for the optimal communication channels or obtain complete information. The answers to such questions tell the analyst who the problem might affect, how it will affect them, and when the effects will be felt.

The third and lowest level of attention deals with criteria for specific, fairly concrete policy problems. This does not mean that they are trivial; if they were, they would probably have been solved by routinized procedures. Without careful selection of criteria, even a minor problem can become confused, misspecified, and larger than need be. Brewer provides a general set of criteria for computer simulation models,[66] but a survey of simulation models used within the Department of Defense clearly implies that no such set was applied to the vast majority of formal military analyses which rely on computer models.[67] The guideline questions for this class of problems can be technical (e.g., Are the data available and in usable form?), policy-oriented (e.g., Is the model static and will its results be applicable to policymaking?), or even normative (e.g., Are the underlying ethical, moral, and professional assumptions and standards in harmony with those of the decision maker?).[68] The important point is that although the perceived problem may not have a major impact upon the organization or the society, the analyst must still treat the question of criteria carefully.

Identification of contextual or environmental parameters

After determining the problem criteria, thus becoming able to define the problem so as to describe it with some precision to others, the analyst can begin to identify the relevant contextual or environmental parameters, or, in other words, determine how the problem fits into the general organizational environment. Specifically, this means delineating the people affected (it may be equally important to define who is not affected),[69] how they are likely to interact, and how the problem can be bounded and analyzed.

An examination of the first question—who is affected?—includes the individuals and organizations that are both touched by the problem and likely to be involved in planning its solution, and how they relate to each other and to the perceived problem. The assessment of people affected, both those who benefit and lose, continues throughout the policy process. However, the analyst should make an initial identification at this early stage. A roster of who is hurt or benefited by the problem will suggest how much leeway and discretion the analyst will have. It will also help in making estimates about the general importance of the problem. A threat to a large number of people should receive greater attention than one likely to affect a smaller number. This calculus can change, of course, as the relative numbers affected change or as the problem's significance is reassessed. For instance, in fall 1962 a small number of intelligence analysts were monitoring the Soviet buildup in Cuba. When clear evidence was discovered of a Soviet offensive missile buildup, the threat to the United States suddenly magnified, and the government's human resources assigned to assess it were increased by an exponential factor.[70]

A second purpose for determining the relevant actors is to learn which agencies or organizations are best suited to act upon the problem. This consideration is often overlooked, and unless it is made later, neglect can lead to faulty policy implementation. For example, when President Richard Nixon announced the imposition of a 90-day wage and price freeze in August 1971, he designated the Office of Emergency Preparedness (OEP) to implement the policy.[71] In his rush to embrace Keynesian economics, the President neglected the limited size and preparedness of the OEP. The Internal Revenue Service, with offices and personnel located throughout the nation, would have been a far better choice and was, in fact, later designated the responsible agency.

Once an analyst has determined the people and organizations affected, one should determine how they interact with the problem and with each other. As Lasswell has written, "the world is not only interdependent, but . . . realistic and selective awareness of that interdependence is indispensable to enlightened public policy."[72] Virtually any reallocation of goods—a fundamental political task—will have supporters (those who gain) and detractors (those who lose). These players have been identified earlier in the initiation stage; here the task is to understand what forces motivate the differing coalitions. For example, Senator Robert Kennedy was the principal architect of the evaluation requirements of the 1965 Elementary and Secondary Education Act (ESEA) Title I. His concern, as he stated it during ESEA hearings, was to provide information for parents on the progress of their childrens' education.[73] At the same time, personnel in the Office of Education in the Department of Health, Education, and Welfare (HEW) were advocating evaluation statistics to provide data for their newly designed Program-Planning-Budgeting System. Thus, Senator Kennedy and HEW personnel formed an effective coalition in support of strict evaluation requirements for Title I projects, but for markedly different reasons. Obviously political coalitions are temporary, highly situation-dependent,[74] and influenced by such legislative and bureaucratic tactics as logrolling,[75] pork barreling, and vote trading.[76]

While examining the environment for aspects that are changing or changeable,[77] the analyst also looks for stable elements. For example, one can generally rely on a bloc of Southern senators to vote against the cloture of a filibuster. If too many elements are simultaneously changing, the analyst will have difficulty determining which to base the analysis on; without a suitable reference point, the analysis may become nearly impossible.[78] Imagine Alice's perplexity had she been a card-carrying analyst during her adventures in Wonderland. The Queen of Heart's croquet game featured soldiers as wickets and hedgehogs as balls, both of which moved only when they chose; the mallets were uncooperative flamingoes; and the Queen kept "shouting 'Off with his head!' or 'Off with her head!' about once a minute."[79] In such a melee of madness, Alice could have found no reference point upon which to base an analysis, let alone a policy change. At best, she could only go along with the status quo and hope for a resolution. That was, in fact, what she did:

> Alice . . . had already heard [the Queen] sentence three of the players to be executed for having missed their turns, and she did not like the look of things at all, as the game was in such confusion that she never knew whether it was her turn or not. So she went off in search of her hedgehog.
>
> The hedgehog was engaged in a fight with another hedgehog, which seemed to Alice an excellent opportunity for croqueting one of them with the other; the only difficulty was, that her flamingo was gone across to the other side of the garden, where Alice could see it trying in a helpless sort of way to fly into a tree.
>
> By the time she had caught the flamingo and brought it back, the fight was over, and both hedgehogs were out of sight: "but it doesn't matter much," thought Alice, "as all the arches are gone from this side of the ground." So she tucked it away under her arm, that it might not escape again, and went back to have a little more conversation with her friend [the Cheshire Cat].[80]

The final task in identifying the problem parameters is to bound the problem, that is, delineate the boundaries that distinguish it from the surrounding environment. The analyst or the organization can only process a limited amount of information. Therefore, the size of the problem must be narrowed until it is manageable.

"In . . . analysis, the complexity of the full problem frequently far outruns analytic competence."[81] There are two main ways to confront this. One is to define the problem so tightly that it can be analyzed whole. With significant problems, however, this is rarely possible. The other is to disaggregate the problem into a number of smaller, discrete, or manageable subproblems. The exercise then is to solve each subproblem—what system analysts and operations researchers call suboptimization—in the hope that the summed solutions or alternatives will present a solution to the large problem.

Although disaggregation/suboptimization often appears to be the best way to analyze a problem, the difficulties can be formidable. The design of a large social experiment, for example, requires the skills of many disciplines, such as economics, demography, statistics, each contributing to specific subtasks.[82] In theory, if each subproblem is well defined and each person competently carries out the assignment, the sum of their efforts will produce a successfully designed and implemented social experiment. But, in reality, problems of coordination and differing objectives often arise among the suboptimizing units; what the statistician might design, the interviewer might not be able to implement. "The criteria and objectives for the suboptimization [must] be consistent with those that would apply to the full problem."[83]

Another boundary consideration is the agreement on the initial observations, values, and starting point for the analysis, because "different starting points yield different estimates, which are biased toward the initial values."[84] The determination of these initial observations and values, a phenomenon psychologists call *anchoring*, has an important effect on the formulation of the problem and the alternatives posed to alleviate it.

Identification of time constraints

How much time is available to study the problem before it begins to have adverse effects? Given two problems of equal magnitude in other respects, the one whose adverse impact is the more imminent will receive the highest priority and attention; the other problem would not necessarily be taken in order but would have to wait until it became pressing. An urgent problem implies very tight time constraints. Working against deadlines, the analyst is more prone to make mistakes than one would otherwise make.[85]

The importance of time in activating the policy process is illustrated in the earlier example of President Nixon's 1971 wage and price freeze. The problem was forcefully brought to Nixon's attention by the convergence of an unacceptable level of unemployment, an unacceptable rate of inflation, demands for an expanding economy, a deteriorating balance of trade, and continuing uncertainty and instability in the international monetary markets.[86] In addition, "Politically, the freeze was probably unavoidable, for the pressures for a basic change in policy were terrific, coming not only from the political opposition but also from businessmen, bankers, economists, journalists, and international agencies."[87] Faced with this array of pressures, the president perceived that he had little alternative but to act quickly. Many economists argued at the time that the economy was beginning to correct itself and Nixon's precipitate moves would only worsen the economic situation. But the president decided he must act quickly or the situation would worsen.

The case of the Iranian hostages in 1980 presents a quite different resolution, although the contributing elements are reasonably clear. Precipitate action on the part of President Carter—forceful action designed to free the hostages soon after their seizure—was ruled out for a long period in favor of exploring a full range of alternative responses, e.g., diplomatic, economic, formal, and informal. Among other lessons this experience may offer, the frustrating intractability of many problems to analysis and solution stands out prominently.

In conclusion, the identification of the problem context by delineating the relevant criteria, the environmental parameters and variables, and the time constraints sets the tone for the rest of the policy process. There are no tidy checklists that can be filled out and filed away. Nor is this a one-time activity. As will become apparent, these questions must be reexamined throughout the entire policy process and may receive different answers as different elements, individuals, and constraints enter the analysis.

DETERMINATION OF GOALS AND OBJECTIVES

The initiation stage provides an important opportunity to address and define policy objectives or goals directly. The objectives will determine what priorities are assigned and what policies are selected, provide guidelines for the implementation of the chosen programs, and determine the criteria for program evaluation. Thus, the determination of policy objectives is fundamental to the policy task. That objectives are too often left vague or ambiguous—or even not considered at all—may explain why so many programs flounder, as if they had no clear direction or purpose. Without clear objectives, they do not.

Setting goals or objectives is not easy. The inherent difficulty of defining policy objectives prompted Lindblom to expound upon the virtues of muddling through:

> As to whether the attempt to clarify objectives in advance of policy selection is more or less rational than the close intertwining of marginal evaluation

and empirical analysis, the principal difference established is that for complex problems the first is impossible and irrelevant, and the second is both possible and relevant.[88]

Lindblom's statement is more descriptive than prescriptive, although he presents a good argument for the marginalist approach. We shall later point out its shortcomings with respect to policy estimation and evaluation; here it is sufficient to note that he overstates and biases his contention: the definition of policy objectives is admittedly difficult but not impossible and never irrelevant.

We must first ask if organizations have unitary goals. Early research in sociology assumed that organizations have identifiable goals.[89] However, the works of Simon, Cyert, and March argue strongly that unitary goals do not exist, that organizational goals are a complex amalgamation of sub-organization goals that achieve consensus through a basically political process.[90] "Instead of a goal, then, a set of constraints is offered; which of these, if any, might be considered principal or major depends upon one's vantage point from within the organizational coalition."[91] The bureaucratic politics approach substantiates and expands their postulates.[92] Other research has held that there are two distinct types of organizational goals: Perrow suggests that goals should be classified according to whether their referenced outcomes are internal or external to their organization;[93] Mohr takes this further by classifying goals as either transitive (external) or reflexive (internal).[94] Many managers illustrate this difference by pointing to the different objectives held by production and marketing departments in the same organizations.[95]

These points apply also to a policy objective. To define a policy's goal or objective as simply as Etzioni defines an organizational goal (". . . a desired state of affairs which the organization attempts to realize")[96] masks the complexity of goal definition. Here we will assume that a policy objective can be determined even though it may be vague and the product of many, perhaps conflicting, subunit objectives. Regrettably, in too many cases, policy objectives are determined after the fact rather than before. It is the responsibility of the cognizant organization to assure a unity of objective among the participating organizations or subunits, if not to coordinate the means to that objective.[97]

An analogy from physics is helpful. A vector is defined as a force with two dimensions: magnitude and direction. For any number of vectors, a resultant vector can be calculated that represents the aggregated sum of the directions and magnitudes of all the individual vectors (Figure 2–1). Likewise, the goal or objective of an organization in respect to a specific perceived problem can be seen as the sum of the objectives of the participating subunits.

A policy objective has two primary components, the normative and the political. The first refers to both the manifest and underlying values that the policy symbolizes. The second refers to the different objectives among

FIGURE 2-1

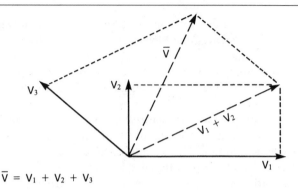

$$\overline{V} = V_1 + V_2 + V_3$$

the people and organizations affected. That is, how would each wish to see the problem resolved and for what reason? Obviously the two are not mutually exclusive.

Normative definition of objectives

No other place in the policy process provides as clear an opportunity to explore normative matters. During initiation, the normative component can be assessed on two levels: the value system of the immediate individuals and organizations and the value system of the larger society. Although logically these can be identical, realistically they more often than not overlap only in certain areas. On the first level, the individual analyst must recognize the internal set of values or ethics that influences the policy perspective taken and then determine if they are congruent with the values of the organization's decision makers. That is, will the values defining or underlying the analyst's own preferences be accepted by the organization? On the second level, the analyst should ensure that the values implied by the policy are in harmony with general societal values.[98] They need not be identical; the difficulty of reconciling differing perspectives, information sets, and demands makes that attainment quite unlikely. But they must be harmonious enough for the society to accept the policy as legitimate and proper, or people will not abide by it unless deceived or coerced. Even then, limits exist; revolutions give violent testimony to such limitations.

Those responsible for the original analysis should engage in an explicit mental calculus to understand the values being expressed or inculcated in the emerging analytic efforts. As with most analytic tasks, difficult trade-offs are to be expected. For example, does the moral value of equality in education outweigh the prospect of serious community strife, such as resulted from the numerous, continuing confrontations over busing school children? How does one compare the value of being able to choose one's neighbors with that of open housing? Obviously, morals and values do not lend themselves to quantification and numeric trade-offs. Still, important value statements underlie most important policy issues, and even though they cannot be measured or weighed precisely, they should be made as explicit as possible in any analysis.[99]

Once an analyst presents a problem formulation to a decision maker, the identification of the policy objectives becomes exceedingly complex for two primary reasons. First, additional individuals and organizations, each with their own viewpoints, expectations, and demands, enter the policy process. Second, the decision maker has to consider the values and preferences of the external environment as well as those of the individual and the organization. If, as happens fairly often, the values presented in the policy formulation are not congruent with those held by decision maker, a policy conflict can occur. Rationality does not necessarily dominate. "The question of what values, and whose values, ultimately are to count is inherently a question that must be answered through political process, not rational analysis . . . . The machinery of legitimate political power may legitimately reject the analysis on the grounds that the analysts's implicit or explicit value judgments are unacceptable, or, more generally, may even deny that there is a problem that needs any solution."[100] President Nixon strongly objected to the philosophic basis of the War on Poverty and moved to terminate the activities of the Office of Economic Opportunity (OEO), which symbolized the War on Poverty in the Washington bureaucracy, by impounding funds that Congress had allocated to OEO.[101]

If analyst and decision maker disagree on value premises, the analyst can hope that either events or their presentation will be persuasive and reduce the divergence. Among remarkable transformations in American politics was Senator Robert Kennedy's conversion to the belief that the American commitment in the Vietnam War was immoral, especially after his intimate involvement in Vietnam decisions in his brother's administration. Representative John Anderson's much publicized effort to impose his strong religious preferences in federal legislation and his subsequent retreat from this objective can be viewed in much the same light. In the long run, though, the analyst and the organization will have a congruent set of values; indeed, were this not the case, the two would part company rather than engage in continual conflict.

There is no phenomenon identifiable as an organizational ethic; individuals have moral tenets, and organizations can only reflect them. A change of key administrators can thus have a definite impact on the tone and direction of an organization, even without other changes of personnel. The Department of Justice under Attorney General Elliot Richardson had a markedly different character and represented different values and priorities than did the department under John Mitchell, though they both served the same president. Therefore, an organization per se does not possess a coherent and consistent set of values. Nevertheless, because of the influence of values on choices later in the policy process it is important to try to clarify an organization's underlying value structure.

Even after reaching agreement between themselves on normative objectives, analysts and clients in the organization cannot rest content. They must ensure accord between their values and the society being served.[102] In many cases, given instantaneous international communications, that society is the world. Witness the worldwide concern over famine in under-developed countries and the obvious posturing among nations to gain (or avoid) international respectability (opprobrium). Domestically, policies whose objectives are out of step with a constituency's values may well be impossible to legislate or enforce except at an unacceptable cost, even if there are pockets of strong support. For example, Washington officials and federal judges have repeatedly ordered open housing and the cessation of prayers in schools, but in communities where those orders are in violent contradiction to local values, they are unenforced.[103] The Volstead Act that introduced Prohibition is another case in point.[104] Declaring the energy crisis to be the "moral equivalent of war," as President Carter did early in his administration, proved to be far less effective in garnering support for various proposals than working to create specific policies and programs in accord with the society's prevailing normative disposition. Although a government can slowly educate its society and marginally alter its values, the old cliché about legislating morality generally holds true.[105]

Finally, a number of vague but nevertheless important values pertaining to human dignity must be upheld. A government can subvert them for a time, but repression, force, and deceit in the long run either undermine the society or provoke political reaction intolerable to the government.[106]

In sum, the policy goals and objectives of the organization cannot be carried out unless policymakers understand the ethical framework upon which the goals and objectives are based.[107]

Political definition of objectives

In defining the problem context, the analyst identified the people and organizations affected by the problem and assessed its effects upon them. Now the analyst begins to consider the particular objectives of the relevant participants. Recalling our vector illustration, each concerned individual or organization acts with respect to two dimensions. Direction: Is it helped or hurt by the problem and the various policies suggested to correct it? And magnitude: How concerned is it and what resources can it mobilize? Much past this illustrative use, vector physics cannot be used to represent the complexity of the organizational determination of policy goals and objectives in either the normative or political sense. Still, as an illustration, the metaphor usefully indicates the tugging and pulling that are inherent in the determination of the policy objectives within and between organizations.

A concrete example is helpful at this point. During the debate on Medicare and Medicaid, members of Congress were subjected to intensive lobbying. Those opposed were represented by the American Medical Association (AMA) and those in favor by groups of the poor and senior citizens. The AMA presented strong political and moral arguments against alleged elements of socialized medicine in the legislation. AMA lobbyists argued that socialized medicine would undermine the tradition of American health care and would undercut the free-enterprise foundation of the nation. The elderly and poor had an attentive audience in Congress, since they represented an increasingly large, visible, and coherent bloc of votes. They argued, also persuasively, that the society should not exclude its less fortunate members from the benefits of first-rate medical service.[108]

From these seemingly contradictory vectors, Congress was able to fashion legislation that, for a time, satisfied each group of clients. The poor and elderly were provided with government health insurance and service through the traditional medical delivery system. However, as events since the passage of Medicare have demonstrated, the resultant policy objectives were satisfactory only in the near term. The price of medical services, escalated by Medicare and other forms of health insurance, has grown at a much higher rate than the economy as a whole until adequate medical care is now beyond the financial reach of people who are uninsured.[109] As a result, the issue of governmental intervention into the health delivery system is again pressing. If greater attention had been given in the original definition of objectives to the long-term stabilization of medical costs, then demands for a nationalized health service would not have occurred less than 10 years after the landmark medical legislation.[110]

CONCLUSION

The political definition of objectives and goals consists of listing and ranking the objectives and goals of the relevant actors.[111] Although this information will not be used explicitly until later in the policy process, it allows the analyst to present to the decision maker as complete an analysis as possible. The decision maker, in turn, will be able to weigh as many factors as possible when choosing among alternative strategies and methods of implementation.

NOTES

1. Harold D. Lasswell, *A Pre-View of Policy Sciences* (New York: American Elsevier, 1971), p. 15; Lasswell's emphasis.
2. The disaggregation of the unitary, decision-making organization is a major contribution of Richard M. Cyert and James G. March, *A Behavioral Theory of the Firm* (Englewood Cliffs, N.J.: Prentice-Hall, 1963).

3. Hans Wallach, *On Perception* (New York: Quadrangle Books, 1976), chap. 10, presents a technical discussion.

4. Karl W. Deutsch, *The Nerves of Government: Models of Political Communication and Control* (New York: Free Press, 1966), p. 147; Deutsch's emphasis.

5. Robert M. Axelrod, "Schema Theory: An Information Processing Model of Perception and Cognition," *American Political Science Review*, December 1973, pp. 1248–66, treats the subject of individual perceptions in depth. See also Robert M. Axelrod, ed., *Structure of Decision* (Princeton, N.J.: Princeton University Press, 1976).

6. The interested reader should consult works in social psychology; a standard reference is Gardner Lindzey and Elliot Aronson, eds., *The Handbook of Social Psychology*, 5 vols. (Reading, Mass.: Addison-Wesley, 1968), especially vol. 1.

7. John D. Steinbruner, *The Cybernetic Theory of Decision* (Princeton, N.J.: Princeton University Press, 1974), points out some of the lengths an individual will go to avoid confronting new realities.

8. The phrase is associated with Leon Festinger, *A Theory of Cognitive Dissonance* (Stanford, Calif.: Stanford University Press, 1957).

9. See George A. Miller, "The Magical Number Seven, Plus or Minus Two," in his *The Psychology of Communication: Seven Essays* (New York: Basic Books, 1967).

10. Alvin Toffler, *Future Shock* (New York: Random House, 1970).

11. David S. Viscott, *The Making of a Psychiatrist* (New York: Fawcett, 1972), p. 112.

12. Axelrod, "Schema Theory," explains this process.

13. Myres S. McDougal, Harold D. Lasswell, and W. Michael Reisman, "The Intelligence Function and World Public Order," *Temple Law Quarterly*, Spring 1973, p. 371.

14. There are, of course, problems that do not require the organization's attention. They may be too trivial for its particular level of attention; e.g., the Washington D.C. police dispatcher need not alert the White House if a municipal bus is robbed.

15. Stanley V. Anderson, "Ombudsman," *Encyclopaedia Britannica* (1972), vol. 16, p. 960, defines ombudsman as "a legislative commission for the investigation of citizens' complaints of bureaucratic abuse." See Stanley V. Anderson, ed., *Ombudsmen for American Government?* (Englewood Cliffs, N.J.: Prentice-Hall, 1968); Donald C. Rowat, *The Ombudsman: Citizen's Defender* (Toronto: University of Toronto Press, 1965); and Larry B. Hill, "Institutionalization, the Ombudsman, and Bureaucracy," *American Political Science Review*, September 1974, pp. 1075–85.

16. Operations researchers have been very active in studying this function. Jan M. Chaiken and Richard C. Larson, "Methods for Allocating Urban Emergency Units: A Survey," in William W. Cooper, ed., "Urban Issues II," *Management Science*, December 1972, pp. P:110–30, provide an excellent and concise review of much of this literature; also see Richard C. Larson, *Urban Police Patrol Analysis* (Cambridge, Mass.: MIT Press, 1972).

17. The policy planning process in the Department of State is addressed by Robert L. Rothstein, *Planning, Prediction, and Policymaking in Foreign Affairs* (Boston: Little, Brown, 1972); for an abbreviated version, see Robert L. Rothstein, "Planning in Foreign Affairs," *Policy Sciences*, December 1973, pp. 453–65.

18. James D. Thompson, *Organizations in Action* (New York: McGraw-Hill, 1967).

19. The empirical evidence has been gathered mostly by economists; it is reviewed without conclusion by James M. Utterback, "Innovation in Industry and the Diffusion of Technology," *Science*, 15 February 1974, pp. 620–26; and F. M. Scherer, "Market Structure and Technological Innovation," *Industrial Market Structure and Economic Performance* (Skokie, Ill.: Rand McNally, 1970), chap. 15.

20. Deutsch, *Nerves of Government*, p. 162; Deutsch's emphasis.

21. Everett M. Rogers and F. Floyd Shoemaker, *Communication of Innovations* (New York: Free Press, 1971), p. 14.

22. George W. Downs, Jr., *Bureaucracy, Innovation and Public Policy* (Lexington, Mass.: D. C. Heath, 1976).

23. For a brief account of the travails of the Foreign Service officers in China, see David Halberstam, *The Best and the Brightest* (New York: Random House, 1972), chap. 7; they are counted among Halberstam's best. A lucid account of their inability to move the American government to support Mao—or appraise him fairly—is Barbara W. Tuchman, "If Mao Had Come to Washington: An Essay in Alternatives," *Foreign Affairs*, October 1972, pp. 44–64. John W. Service, *Lost Chance in China* (New York: Random House, 1974), was one of those officers.

24. Neil Sheehan, "Introduction," to Sheehan et al., *The Pentagon Papers* (New York: Bantam Books, 1971), p. xiii. The context of the quote is that the Executive Office sought to gain support for its Vietnam policies by manipulating the information released to the outside world. However, Daniel Ellsberg was similarly trying to gain public support for his views by supplying the Pentagon study to *The New York Times*.

25. Even though leaks might be standard practice between federal officials and the Washington press corps, the virulent reaction by the Nixon Administration to William Beecher's description of the U.S. negotiating position during the strategic arms limitation talks (*New York Times*, July 23, 1971) and to Jack Anderson's accounting of National Security Council discussions during the India-Pakistan War (late 1971) implies that standard practices are not always acceptable if they do not fit one's purpose. To identify the source of the leaks, President Nixon ordered the formation of the White House "plumbers" that were later to cause him so much distress. See Leon V. Sigal, *Reporters and Officials: The Organization and Politics of Newsmaking* (Lexington, Mass.: D. C. Heath, 1973), especially chap. 3.

26. Rachel L. Carson, *The Silent Spring* (Boston: Houghton Mifflin, 1973), was one of the first to point out (in 1962) the dangers of pesticides to the fragile ecological balance.

27. Michael Harrington, *The Other America: Poverty in the United States* (New York: Macmillan, 1962), is often given credit for having brought the problems of poverty in America to the attention of President John Kennedy and thus having provided some early ammunition for the War on Poverty.

28. Ralph Nader, *Unsafe at Any Speed* (New York: Grossman, 1972), received his initial fame for identifying the mechanical dangers in the Chevrolet Corvair. His findings received wide coverage partially because of the heavy-handed manner in which General Motors responded to his charges (e.g., hiring private detectives to investigate his personal life).

29. The multiple interconnections of the policy process are noteworthy here. One person's initiative nearly always presents a threat of termination to someone else. The idea of creation-as-destruction is considered at length in the final chapter; see Garry D. Brewer, "Termination: Hard Choices—Harder Questions," *Public Administration Review*, July/August 1978, pp. 338–44.

30. James G. March and Herbert A. Simon. *Organizations* (New York: John Wiley & Sons, 1958), p. 173.

31. Donald A. Schon, *Technology and Change* (New York: Dell, 1967), p. 63.

32. Harold L. Wilensky, *Organizational Intelligence* (New York: Basic Books, 1967), is a durable overview of many of these matters. The formal state of intelligence organizations within the United States is surveyed in Tyrus G. Fain, comp., *The Intelligence Community: History, Organization, and Issues* (New York: R. R. Bowker, 1977).

33. These are elaborated upon in Cyert and March, *A Behavioral Theory*, chap. 4. See also Irving L. Janis and Leon Mann, *Decision Making: A Psychological Analysis of Conflict, Choice and Commitment* (New York: Free Press, 1977).

34. For example, see ibid.; and James G. March, "The Business Firm As a Political Coalition," *Journal of Politics*, November 1962, pp. 662–78.

35. See Charles E. Lindblom, "The Handling of Norms in Policy Analysis," in Moses

Abramovitz et al., *The Allocation of Economic Resources* (Stanford, Calif.: Stanford University Press, 1959), p. 179.

36. The two quotations are from Cyert and March, *A Behavioral Theory*, pp. 117–18. This mode of organizational decision making is described and illustrated in Graham T. Allison, *Essence of Decision: Explaining the Cuban Missile Crisis* (Boston: Little, Brown, 1971), Model II.

37. Paul S. Goodman and Johannes M. Pennings, *New Perspectives on Organizational Effectiveness* (San Francisco: Jossey-Bass, 1977).

38. Eugene Bardach, "Subformal Warning Systems in the Species *Homo Politicus,*" *Policy Sciences*, December 1974, p. 417.

39. See Daniel Lerner, "Towards a Communication Theory of Modernization," in Lucian W. Pye, ed., *Communications and Political Development* (Princeton, N.J.: Princeton University Press, 1963), chap. 18.

40. Anthony Downs, *Inside Bureaucracy* (Boston: Little, Brown, 1967), particularly p. 113, where business lunches are described as part of the subformal system.

41. Deutsch, *Nerves of Government,* p. 77; the title is indicative of Deutsch's perspective.

42. John Kimberly, "Managerial Innovation," in P. C. Nystrom and W. H. Starbuck, eds., *Handbook of Organizational Design*, vol. 1 (New York: Oxford University Press, 1980), relates communication and structural issues to the overriding matter of an institution's ability to respond to a changing environment.

43. U.S. Congress, Senate, Committee on Armed Services, *FY 1977 Authorization for Military Procurement* (Washington, D.C.: Government Printing Office, 1976), part 11, p. 5858. See also, Bruce G. Blair and Garry D. Brewer, "Verifying SALT Agreements," in William Potter, ed., *Verification and SALT* (Boulder, Colo.: Westview Press, 1980), for additional discussion of this and related matters.

44. Thompson, *Organizations in Action*, chap. 4, points out how subunits on the frontier of the organization's domain display these characteristics. The high technology analog is suggested in the numerous, often redundant, strategic satellites currently operating and planned for positioning around the globe.

45. William J. Broad, "Computers and the U.S. Military Don't Mix," *Science*, 14 March 1980, pp. 1183–84, 1186–87.

46. See Roberta Wohlstetter, *Pearl Harbor: Warning and Decision* (Stanford, Calif.: Stanford University Press, 1962), for an exemplary study of the paralyzing effects of communication overload on an organization.

47. U.S. cryptologists were so swift that Hull read Tokyo's order to break off diplomatic relations even before it had been decoded for the Japanese Ambassador in Washington; see David Kahn, *The Code Breakers* (New York: Macmillan, 1967).

48. Perhaps in this example the proper question is whether the enemy is the Soviet Union or the Congress; in any event, see W. R. Schilling, P. Y. Hammond, and G. H. Snyder, *Strategy, Politics, and Defense Budgets* (New York: Columbia University Press, 1962), for a general overview; and P. Y. Hammond, "Super Carriers and the B–36 Bombers," in Harold Stein, ed., *American Civil-Military Decisions* (University: The University of Alabama Press, 1963), for a more specific example.

49. It is interesting to note that for such an important subject, interest in the professional, scholarly literature has been scant. As recently as 1978, the importance of what is known in the military jargon as "C^3"—communication, command and control—was only being discovered. See John D. Steinbruner, "National Security and the Concept of Strategic Stability," *Journal of Conflict Resolution*, September 1978, pp. 411–28.

50. For example, see Lasswell, "Contextuality: Mapping the Social and Decision Processes," *Pre-View of Policy Sciences*, chap. 2. This is what Eugene Bardach, *The Skill Factor in Politics* (Berkeley: University of California Press, 1972), refers to as "the attentive public."

51. L. D. Attaway, "Criteria and the Measurement of Effectiveness," in E. S. Quade and W. I. Boucher, eds., *Systems Analysis and Policy Planning: Applications in Defense* (New York: American Elsevier, 1968), p. 75.

52. E. S. Quade, "Pitfalls and Limitations," in ibid., p. 348. See also E. S. Quade and G. Majone, eds., *Pitfalls of Analysis* (New York: John Wiley & Sons, 1980), chap. 1.

53. Charles J. Hitch and Roland N. McKean, *The Economics of Defense in the Nuclear Age* (New York: Atheneum, 1965), chap. 9, "The Criterion Problem."

54. See James S. Coleman, *Policy Research in the Social Sciences* (Morristown, N.J.: General Learning Press, 1972); and Gunnar Myrdal, *Objectivity in Social Research* (New York: Pantheon, 1969), chap. 10.

55. Garry D. Brewer and Ronald D. Brunner, eds., "Introduction," *Political Development and Change: A Policy Approach* (New York: Free Press, 1975).

56. The marginalist argument has long been a point of contention among economists. The pros are presented by Fritz Machlup, "Theories of the Firm: Marginalist, Behavioral, Managerial," *American Economic Review,* March 1967, pp. 1–33. A thorough discussion of the cons is in Scherer, *Industrial Market Structure,* chap. 2, "The Welfare Economics of Competition and Monopoly."

57. Garry D. Brewer, "On Innovation, Social Change, and Reality," *Technological Forecasting and Social Change,* February 1973, p. 19.

58. John Brooks, *The Fate of the Edsel and Other Business Ventures* (New York: Harper & Row, 1959).

59. This exact problem was brilliantly set forth by Albert Wohlstetter in "The Delicate Balance of Terror," *Foreign Affairs,* January 1959, pp. 211–34, an article that had a profound effect on U.S. strategic thinking throughout the 1960s.

60. These were first defined by Harold D. Lasswell, *Politics: Who Gets What, When, and How* (New York: Meridian, 1958), p. 187. They are updated in Lasswell, *Pre-View of Policy Sciences,* chap. 3, "Problem Orientation: The Intellectual Tasks."

61. Allison, *Essence of Decision,* p. 257.

62. Martha Derthick, "Defeat at Fort Lincoln," *The Public Interest,* Summer 1970, pp. 3–39, explains the decision criteria that underlay the policy choice for the Washington, D.C., model community project.

63. Michael Armacost, *The Politics of Weapons Innovation: The Thor-Jupiter Controversy* (New York: Columbia University Press, 1969), documents the debate between the Army and Air Force over which would have the primary command of the U.S. missile arsenal. Frederic A. Bergerson, *The Army Gets an Air Force* (Baltimore, Md.: Johns Hopkins University Press, 1980), examines the disposition of helicopters and other small aircraft in favor of the U.S. Army.

64. Edward Anian, *Bach, Beethoven, and Bureaucracy* (University: The University of Alabama Press, 1971), describes how a coalition between the musician's union, patrons and benefactors, contracting record companies, and management decides what musical selections will be on a given evening's program or record of the Philadelphia Symphony Orchestra.

65. See Allison, *Essence of Decision,* Model II, p. 257.

66. Garry D. Brewer, *Politicians, Bureaucrats, and the Consultant: A Critique of Urban Problem Solving* (New York: Basic Books, 1973), pp. 60–61.

67. Garry D. Brewer and Martin Shubik, *The War Game: A Critique of Military Problem Solving* (Cambridge, Mass.: Harvard University Press, 1979), part 4.

68. Even if they are, and analysis proceeds, there is cause to doubt that the goals will be widely shared or the policies they engender will be feasible. See Dick Kirschten and Robert J. Samuelson, "Carter's Newest Energy Goals: Can We Get There from Here?" *National Journal,* July 21, 1979, pp. 1192–1201.

69. The exclusion of representatives from Czechoslovakia during the Munich Conference in September 1938 was suggestive of the participants' decision regarding German claims on the Sudetenland. See John W. Wheeler-Bennett, *Munich, Prologue to Tragedy* (New York: Duell, Sloan, and Pearce, 1948); the significance of the Munich Conference is debated in Dwight E. Lee, ed., *Munich: Blunder, Plot or Tragic Necessity?* (Lexington, Mass.: D. C. Heath, 1970).

70. The transition of attention from a few intelligence analysts to virtually the entire American defense establishment is detailed by Elie Abel, *The Missile Crisis* (Philadelphia: J. B. Lippincott, 1966).

71. See Roger LeRoy Miller and Raburn M. Williams, *The New Economics of Richard Nixon: Freezes, Floats, and Fiscal Policy* (San Francisco: Canfield Press, 1972); and Arnold R. Weber, "A Wage-Price Freeze As an Instrument of Income Policy: Or the Blizzard of '71," *American Economic Review*, May 1972, pp. 251–58. Weber was a Nixon economic planner at the time of the freeze.

72. Lasswell, *Pre-View of Policy Sciences*, p. 14.

73. Milbrey Wallin McLaughlin, *Evaluation and Reform: The Elementary and Secondary Education Act of 1965, Title I* (Cambridge, Mass.: Ballinger, 1975). For a more general treatment of the politics behind the passage of the ESEA, see Philip Meranto, *The Politics of Federal Aid to Education in 1965: A Study in Political Innovation* (Syracuse, N.Y.: Syracuse University Press, 1967).

74. See Sven Groennings, E. W. Kelley, and M. A. Leiserson, eds., *The Study of Coalition Behavior: Theoretical Perspectives and Cases from Four Continents* (New York: Holt, Rinehart & Winston, 1970); also see Clifford S. Russell, ed., *Collective Decision Making* (Baltimore, Md.: Johns Hopkins University Press, 1979), for a sampling of both theoretical and practical treatments of the issue. The best description of this flux is Robert A. Dahl, *Who Governs?* (New Haven: Yale University Press, 1962).

75. Logrolling is described in any introductory civics text; more rigorous treatments of logrolling and its effects are provided by economists Robert Wilson, "An Axiomatic Model of Logrolling," *American Economic Review*, June 1959, pp. 331–41; and Gordon Tullock, "A Simple Algebraic Logrolling Model," *American Economic Review*, June 1970, pp. 419–26.

76. For formal theoretic approaches to this, see Oran Young, ed., *Bargaining: Formal Theories of Negotiations* (Urbana: University of Illinois Press, 1975). A specific model is presented in William H. Riker and Steven J. Brams, "The Paradox of Vote Trading," *American Political Science Reveiw*, December 1973, pp. 1235–47.

77. Roger Benjamin, *The Limits of Politics* (Chicago: University of Chicago Press, 1980), is especially thoughtful and provocative on the matter of situations that change so rapidly as to outstrip conventional intellectual paradigms for coping.

78. The point is nicely made in R. G. H. Siu, "Management and the Art of Chinese Baseball," *Sloan Management Review* 19, no. 3 (1978), pp. 83–89. Siu's game is just like real baseball, except that anyone can move a base as soon as the pitcher delivers the ball.

79. Lewis Carroll, *Alice's Adventures in Wonderland* and *Through the Looking Glass*, notes by Martin Gardner (New York: Clarkson N. Potter, 1960), p. 112. Alice's marvelous adventures and observations contain many lessons for the policy analyst. This particular version, also known as *The Annotated Alice*, is especially enjoyable since, in addition to the original illustrations by John Tenniel, Gardner provides full notes explaining most of Carroll's allusions, word and number games, and political parodies.

80. Ibid., p. 115.

81. E. S. Quade, "Principles and Procedures of Systems Analysis," in Quade and Boucher, *Systems Analysis and Policy Planning*, p. 38.

82. Garry D. Brewer, "Experimentation and the Policy Process," in *Twenty-Fifth Annual*

Report of The Rand Corporation (Santa Monica, Calif.: The Rand Corporation, 1973), pp. 151–65.

83. Hitch and McKean, *Economics of Defense,* chap. 9, "The Criterion Problem."

84. See Amos Tversky and Daniel Kahneman, "Judgment Under Uncertainty: Heuristics and Biases," *Science,* 27 September 1974, pp. 1124–31, at p. 1128.

85. Failure to match temporal and analytic realities has limited otherwise commendable efforts to do long-range planning. See U.S. Congress, Congressional Research Service, *Long-Range Planning* (Washington, D.C.: Government Printing Office, 1976).

86. This assessment was made by then Secretary of the Treasury John Connally, in a press briefing that immediately preceded the President's address of August 16, 1971. Quoted in Miller and Williams, *New Economics of Richard Nixon,* p. 1. For an account of the pressures leading up to Nixon's decision, see Juan Cameron, "How the U.S. Got on the Road to a Controlled Economy," *Fortune,* January 1972, pp. 74–77 and 156–65.

87. Gottfried Haberler, "Incomes Policy and Inflation: Some Further Reflection," *American Economic Review,* May 1972, p. 235.

88. Charles E. Lindblom, "The Science of 'Muddling Through'," *Public Administration Review,* Spring 1959, pp. 79–88; quoted in Amitai Etzioni, ed., *Readings in Modern Organizations* (Englewood Cliffs, N.J.: Prentice-Hall, 1969), p. 159. For additional statements to this effect, see Lindblom, "Norms in Policy Analysis."

89. For example, see Max Weber, *The Theory of Social and Economic Organizations,* A. M. Henderson and Talcott Parsons, eds. and trans. (New York: Oxford University Press, 1947), pp. 337–41.

90. See Cyert and March, *A Behavioral Theory;* March and Simon, *Organizations;* and March, "The Business Firm."

91. Lawrence B. Mohr, "The Concept of Organizational Goal," *American Political Science Review,* June 1973, p. 472.

92. See Allison, *Essence of Decision;* Richard E. Neustadt, *Alliance Politics* (New York: Columbia University Press, 1970); and Samuel Williamson, *The Politics of Grand Strategy: Britain and France Prepare for War, 1904–1914* (Cambridge, Mass.: Harvard University Press, 1969).

93. Charles Perrow, *Organizational Analysis* (Belmont, Calif.: Wadsworth, 1970), pp. 133–74; the issue is treated somewhat differently, but complementarily, in Herbert A. Simon, *The Sciences of the Artificial* (Cambridge, Mass.: MIT Press, 1969), pp. 8–9.

94. Mohr, "Concept of Organizational Goal," pp. 475–76.

95. A similar distinction has been noted in the Strategic Air Command, which divides its operations into two main components, flying and maintenance. Conflict between the two frequently appears in the scheduling of missions. See Morton B. Berman, "Organizational Behavior and Public Sector Efficiency: An Analysis of the Strategic Air Command" (Santa Monica, Calif.: The Rand Graduate Institute for Policy Studies, unpublished Ph.D. dissertation, October 1974).

96. Amitai Etzioni, *Modern Organizations* (Englewood Cliffs, N.J.: Prentice-Hall, 1964), p. 6.

97. Allison's Models II and III explanations of the Cuban missile crisis offer an instructive example of differing subunit objectives and procedures and how they affected U.S. and Soviet plans; see Allison, *Essence of Decision,* chaps. 4 and 6, "Cuba II: A Second Cut" and "Cuba II: A Third Cut."

98. This determination cannot be made in the abstract, but must be rendered with respect to the concrete setting of choice. Nicholas M. Smith, "A Calculus of Ethics: A Theory of the Structure of Value," *Behavioral Science,* April 1956, p. 112.

99. Hitch and McKean, *Economics of Defense,* warn the analyst about the difficulties of dealing with "incommensurables" in chap. 10. "Incommensurables, Uncertainty, and

the Enemy," especially pp. 182–88. But incommensurables should not be ignored, though they often are because of the difficulties. We return to this topic in later chapters.

100. Richard R. Nelson, "Intellectualizing About the Moon-Ghetto Metaphor: A Study of the Current Malaise of Rational Analysis of Social Problems," *Policy Sciences*, December 1974, pp. 375–414, at p. 376.

101. This experience, and several others, contributed to the pressure for The Congressional Budget and Impoundment Act of 1974, which is summarized in Grover Starling, *Managing the Public Sector* (Homewood, Ill.: Dorsey Press, 1977), pp. 293–303.

102. An important, if convoluted, exposition on morals and the contemporary American political society is Richard N. Goodwin, *The American Condition* (Garden City, N.Y.: Doubleday, 1974). See Abraham Kaplan, *American Ethics and Public Policy* (New York: Oxford University Press, 1963), for a brilliant discussion of these issues.

103. The lack of enforcement of federal open housing and school prayer decisions are the subjects of, respectively, Frederick Aaron Lazin, "The Failure of Federal Enforcement of Civil Rights Regulations in Public Housing, 1963–1971: The Co-optation of a Federal Agency by Its Local Constituency," *Policy Sciences*, September 1973, pp. 263–73; and Kenneth M. Dolbeare and Phillip E. Hammond, *The School Prayer Decisions: From Court Policy to Local Practice* (Chicago: University of Chicago Press, 1971).

104. The history of Prohibition and the Volstead Act is recounted in Herbert Asbury, *The Great Illusion: An Informal History of Prohibition* (Garden City, N.Y.: Doubleday, 1950).

105. The point, with respect to the energy problem, is brought home forcefully in Lewis H. Lapham, "The Energy Debacle," *Harper's*, August 1977, pp. 58–74.

106. The writings of Aleksander Solzhenitsyn, especially *The Gulag Archipelago*, Thomas P. Whitney, trans. (New York: Harper & Row, 1974), had such an impact on the closed Soviet society that its leaders were forced to spare his life and ultimately to exile him.

107. Attaining an understanding is an extraordinarily difficult thing to do, as Steven R. Brown, *Political Subjectivity* (New Haven: Yale University Press, 1980), points out so well. Various practical illustrations are provided in Yerachmiel Kugel and Gladys W. Gruenberg, eds., *Ethical Perspectives on Business and Society* (Lexington, Mass.: D. C. Heath, 1977), especially part I.

108. See Theodore R. Marmor, *The Politics of Medicare* (Chicago: Aldine, 1973), for a comprehensive account of the design and passage of this legislation.

109. The alarming rates of increase of all medical costs are documented in Robert M. Gibson and Charles R. Fisher, "National Health Expenditures, Fiscal Year 1977," *Social Security Bulletin*, July 1978, p. 16.

110. A most welcome and thorough coverage of this subject is provided in Judith Feder, John Holahan, and Theodore R. Marmor, eds., *National Health Insurance: Conflicting Goals and Policy Choices* (Washington, D.C.: The Urban Institute, 1980). Goals are treated directly in the introduction, chaps. 1, 8, 9, and in the summary.

111. As is suggested in Lasswell's title, *Politics;* also see Bardach, *The Skill Factor*.

3

Alternatives and initiation in the
policy process

GENERATION OF ALTERNATIVES

Traditionally, the primary focus of the policy analyst's work has been the generation of policy alternatives and options. The initiation of the policy process has been left to happenstance, the selection of the proper alternative to the decision maker, and the implementation of policy to the bureaucracy. While this division of labor is understandable, isolation borne of poor communication between the primary functional elements in the decision process leads to inadequate performance in case after case. Division and separation extend to the analyst, whose main claim to fame has centered on the examination of the problem and the generation of policy options to ameliorate it. One of our main purposes is to demonstrate that the analyst must, in fact, do far more—and do it consciously—than merely generate alternatives. However, in this section we will examine that task and view it in the context of the initiation stage and then with the entire policy task.

This prologue is not intended to deprecate the generation of alternatives. It is a vital step in the overall policy process. Without a carefully prepared set of policy choices, the decision maker has to rely on a limited set of personal resources or blind luck. However, a brilliantly presented set of policy options will be ineffectual unless the other policy stages are well executed. Rather than downgrade the generation of alternatives, we mean to elevate the other stages and demonstrate the interrelation of them all.

The generation of alternatives is usually performed simultaneously with the estimation of the effect and merit of each alternative. Because of this, many features of the estimation process have been overlooked or obscured. To remedy this neglect, we have rather arbitrarily separated the generation of alternatives from the estimation function. The latter is discussed in the next part. Here we will take a closer look at the formulation of policy alternatives, particularly to encourage creativity and innovation in one's approach to the task. Then we consider the actual process of defining a range of policy alternatives.

Creativity and innovation

Creativity, an illusive quality, is often confused with innovation. We accept Mohr's distinction that creativity "implies bringing something new into being; innovation implies bringing something new into use."[1] Obviously this distinction is much easier to make for technological advances; microcircuitries, or chips, were a product of creativity while hand-size electronic calculators were innovations. Still, the distinction is possible in policy research, for creativity can bring entirely new techniques and concepts to bear on a different problem and is important in what Morton Deutsch calls the "creative resolution of conflict."[2]

What, then, is creativity in the policy context? Lasswell defines it as "the disposition to make and to recognize valuable innovations" and cites the American court system as a creative act of governance that has since been replicated throughout the world.[3] More in keeping with policy terminology, let us define creativity as the capability to view a problem and propose alternatives in perspectives and methods that are unique and unlike any prior attempts to solve similar problems; in the words of psychologist Frank Barron, "The emphasis is upon whatever is fresh, novel, unusual, ingenious, divergent, clever, and apt."[4]

An example of creative policy analysis is The Rand Corporation's so-called Rand basing study.[5] In the early 1950s, the Air Force requested Rand's advice on the most efficient ways to select and construct overseas bases for the Strategic Air Command. Albert Wohlstetter, among others, recognized that the subject had much broader and more important implications than the Air Force had imagined. "Reformulating what appeared to be a routine, logistical study, Wohlstetter came up with a broader range of questions about the vulnerability of the Strategic Air Force to surprise attack and about system-wide costs—both more important than the question of minimum cost for given facilities, the main criterion prevailing among Air Force planners."[6] The Rand basing study was a creative endeavor in that it asked new questions and perceived unrecognized significance. In contrast, innovation would be the application of methodologies proven elsewhere to new situations. Brewer refers to the introduction of the Planning, Programming and Budgeting System (PPBS) into the Department of Defense as a "model of innovation."[7]

A main purpose of introducing creativity and innovation in the policy process, and especially in the generation of alternatives, is to press the analyst to think beyond the company line.[8] Quade agrees with Kahn and Mann when they describe the party line as "the most important single reason for the tremendous miscalculations that are made in foreseeing and preparing for technical advances or changes in the strategic situation."[9] Creativity is usually absent in policy debates because officials generally opt for the safe and quick solution rather than spend the resources necessary to develop creative alternatives. It is regrettable but true that creativity in government bureaucracies is most likely to be found in an organization that is losing its reason for existing and is desperately trying to discover a viable rationale.[10] The arguments presented by the U.S. Army horse cavalry until about 1950 to secure its survival are excellent examples of creativity, albeit creativity misspent.[11]

Given that creativity should be encouraged in principle, how does an organization provide the proper stimuli, motivations, and climate to foster it in the real world? This is a difficult question because creativity is very much an individual attribute, and it seems impossible to define the concept in terms other than tautological.[12] A conference was held in Germany to discuss the nature and nurturing of creativity, which was described as "that ill-defined state of mind which allows the investigator to forge anomalous or apparently unrelated facts into bold chains of theory."[13] The proceedings were unable to offer little in the teaching of creativity besides exposing bright junior scholars to brilliant senior scholars. Deutsch and Barnett each suggest that a number of individual factors (e.g., intelligence, exposure to diverse experiences, the capacity to make remote associations, competition) facilitate creativity, but there seem to be few replicable guidelines on what organizational features would stimulate it.[14] One possibility is the use of the decision seminar, a variation of what business schools call brainstorming sessions, that is focused on relatively specific policy issues.[15] On the other hand, a number of organizational characteristics often attributed to large bureaucracies combine to repress creative problem solving; organizations' strong preference for standard operating procedures and the lack of both time and adequate incentives operate against creativity as alternatives are being generated.[16]

Evidence about what fosters personal innovation is only slightly less amorphous, even as regards technical innovation.[17] It is probably accurate to assume that such factors as higher education, interdisciplinary approaches, and organizational flexibility or receptivity to change all promote innovation in policy analysis and, here, in the design of policy alternatives.[18]

Policy alternatives

The generation of policy alternatives builds directly from the preceding steps of the initiation stage. The individual alternatives are a function of all that has gone before. Specifically, the recognition of the problem, the organizational acceptance of that recognition, the identification of the context (with the relevant criteria and the pertinent actors), and the identification of the normative and political goals and objectives all act as guidelines or constraints upon policy options. The range of alternatives can extend from simply doing nothing to doing something radical with countless policy options in between.

Doing nothing should not be excluded from the list of alternative policies. There are times when inaction is the proper course, permitting exogenous forces to produce the desired effect; not only is this a low cost policy but it also shields the organization from any adverse publicity that might follow.[19] The United States was opposed to many U.N. Security Council resolutions on colonialism, but it let a French or British veto kill the measures rather than use its veto power and suffer criticism from the other Council members. Inaction can be either a negative or a positive decision. It can be negative if a certain policy requires active support to survive. This happened in the presidential elections of 1972, when the American Federation of Labor and the Congress of Industrial Organizations (AFL–CIO), the Democratic Party's traditional allies, chose not to support the Democratic ticket; the Executive Council voted that the AFL–CIO, with its valuable political treasury and volunteers, would remain neutral.[20] "Doing nothing" can also be a positive action. In the example above, the neutrality of organized labor benefited the Republican Party, which did not have to campaign against labor's manpower and funds. Similarly, a nation might assist a rebellion in a neighboring country by doing nothing in regard to rebel sanctuaries. Yugoslavia aided Greek insurgents in the late 1940s by ignoring insurgent camps located in Yugoslavia.[21] Thus, inaction should not always be regarded as doing nothing nor equated with a lack of policy or preference.

At the other extreme, there are times when a threat appears so immediate and so pressing that radical proposals are in order. The Truman Doctrine and the Marshall Plan represented a virtual revolution in U.S. foreign policy, but conditions in Europe seemed to warrant drastic action.[22] Few dispute that the trauma of the Great Depression pushed President Franklin Roosevelt to initiate major social legislation.[23] The inability of an organization to produce radical solutions or alternatives and the decision makers to countenance such policies may gravely handicap its policy process. The inability to recognize and use radical new technologies, such as computers, has seriously hurt some corporations and even some public agencies,[24] just as the French inability to appreciate new military capabilities led to the defeat of France after only six weeks of fighting in the summer of 1940.[25] Abraham Lincoln might well have been speaking to policy analysts when, in his second inaugural address, he cautioned that "The dogmas of the quiet past are inadequate to the stormy present."

The vast majority of the time, the policy alternatives that are formulated will fall between these two extremes. Depending on the requirements discovered previously when the problem was defined, the analyst must work to generate alternatives that meet such requirements. Alternative generation is an iterative process, or, as doctrine from systems analysis holds, "As the study progresses, . . . original ideas are enriched and elaborated upon—or discarded—and new ideas are found."[26] Although alternatives will later be weighed and estimated before a policy is finally selected, the analyst should take pains to outline policy implementation strategies and provide complete documentation for the work so that it can be understood—and, if necessary, reconstructed—later in the exercise.[27] Considerations of implementation and documentation are often ignored. The analyst should avoid proposing plans that apply to a different set of requirements, or suggesting infeasible alternatives, for example, those falling outside the relevant time frame, unattainable with available resources, or beyond the reach of a specified level of technology. Policy selection is a continually winnowing process and the analyst should contribute by sifting alternatives to aid the process.

In summary, the analyst should prepare a menu of policy alternatives that cover the range of appropriate, possible, and feasible solutions to the problem. The range might well include inaction or radical action. It should be varied enough to permit the decision maker to choose between different capabilities, technologies, resources, and policy levers. The policymaker is the proper agent to decide resource trade-offs. The analyst's role at this stage is to provide a list that permits authoritative consideration of the alternatives so that necessary trade-offs may be weighed in selecting a policy option.

INITIATION IN THE POLICY PROCESS

Finally, we widen our view to encompass the impact of initiation on the rest of the policy process.

The estimation stage is the most directly affected, being the next step in the process. The definitions of criteria and objectives are of immediate operational use there because they provide the measures against which the proposed alternatives are assessed. The determination of time priorities made during initiation helps those working in the estimation stage determine the time available to work before presenting their results to the decision maker. Estimation analysts will also rely on the initial priorities set during problem recognition and identification of the problem context.

The selection stage is likewise dependent on the problem definition and identification of criteria and objectives carried out during initiation; however, these will have been filtered through the intervening analytic stage and perhaps altered by the passage of time. New data or evidence may have had a major impact on the previously identified alternatives; their aptness will either have been validated or discredited. If the latter, then initiation processes must be restarted. In most cases, however, the decision maker will choose among the alternatives that were generated in the initiation stage and will base a decision at least partially on the defined objectives. For example, in the Cuban missile crisis, the final options considered before the quarantine decision were a subset of those originally proposed; no new alternatives were developed in the interim even though the conditions had been altered. The objectives were also basically the same. For instance, President Kennedy argued that he had to act forcefully or face impeachment, while Robert Kennedy argued that the United States should not launch a surprise air attack because it would be contrary to the American sense of values.[28]

The implementation and evaluation stages will use the initial statements of objectives and criteria, respectively, although they will probably be altered by this time. Faithful implementation depends partly on the implementor's understanding of the problem (problem definition) and the policy (alternative definition). The clearer and more precise the analytic work done during initiation, the better are chances that actual programs will be consistent with the policy intent. Program evaluation uses the original criteria as amended during the intervening stages. Using these criteria, the evaluators can ask: Has the policy worked? Has the policy solved, alleviated, or ignored the original problem? If the answer is unfavorable, it may be necessary to return to the selection stage and choose another option, to return to estimation for analytic reworking, or even return to the initiation stage to reconsider fundamentals, such as basic definitions and understandings.

Finally, considerations of termination hark back to the recognition of the problem. If the problem no longer exists or, more probably, is no longer threatening (i.e., the stated objectives have been met), the policy will have outlived its usefulness and becomes a candidate for termination. The criteria by which this determination is made may very well have been conceived in the initiation phase. Somewhat differently, one is well advised to think about initiatives in terms of what ongoing practices they will threaten—or even cause to be terminated. This, a creation-as-destruction view, presumes that innovations are not introduced de novo, but rather disrupt or supersede existing practices and arrangements; it also allows one to appreciate many difficulties encountered by innovators, particularly when the innovation has wholesale or readily apparent implications.

Implicit in this discussion of the rest of the policy process is the interactive nature of the phases. We have seen how initiation significantly affects the subsequent policy steps. It is equally important to appreciate that events and constraints can arise in the latter five stages that necessitate a return to some of the activities of the initiation stage. For example, the successful testing of the atomic bomb presented a new alternative for ending the Second World War against Japan. The power and revolutionary nature of the weapon forced American decision makers to reconsider their goals and the means to those goals in light of the new development. Only then were they, and particularly President Truman, able to decide which option to use to force the Japanese surrender.[29] Likewise, policy evaluators might easily realize the criteria are not adequate and return to initiation for further definition or clarification.

An important, but different, form of interaction normally occurs in the realistic setting of decision. The policy process seldom moves in lockstep from stage to stage, nor does it demonstrate equivalent care or attention to each stage. Simply given the sheer number of participants involved in many consequential decisions, such stylized expectations about the process could be shown to err, and often substantially. The real complexity of the context and processes found in the social setting motivates much of this book; however, the book also avers that the failure to understand the roughest outlines of the policy and decision process, evident in many less-than-satisfactory experiences with it, is a correctable shortcoming.

CONCLUSION

The initiation phase constitutes the actual beginning of the policy process and includes the original formulation of the problem and the various policy alternatives. These first steps are critically important; errors introduced here may be corrected later, perhaps during the selection stage, but at a possibly unacceptable and, in any event, needless cost. Much will happen to the products of the initiation analysts' work as new information and requirements are added and choices are made during later phases. With profound enough changes in the environment, their work may even have to be scrapped and the process begun anew. But the foundation laid by sound analysis during initiation strengthens and supports the policy process, whatever contingencies arise.

We noted earlier that we are separating the recognition of the threat and the creation of policy options from the processes involved in analyzing those options.[30] In our scheme, then the analysis of alternatives begins in earnest during the estimation phase.

NOTES

1. Lawrence B. Mohr, "Determinants of Innovation in Organizations," *American Political Science Review*, March 1969, p. 112.

2. Morton Deutsch, *The Resolution of Conflict* (New Haven: Yale University Press, 1973), p. 362.

3. Harold D. Lasswell, "The Social Setting of Creativity," in Harold H. Anderson, ed., *Creativity and Its Cultivation* (New York: Harper & Row, 1959), p. 203.

4. Frank Barron, "The Psychology of Creativity," *New Dimensions in Psychology II* (New York: Holt, Rinehart & Winston, 1965), p. 7.

5. A. J. Wohlstetter, F. S. Hoffman, R. J. Lutz, and H. S. Rowen, *Selection and Use of Strategic Air Bases* (Santa Monica, Calif.: The Rand Corporation, R–266, April 1964). The genesis and history of the study may be found in Bruce L. R. Smith, *The RAND Corporation: Case Study of a Nonprofit Advisory Corporation* (Cambridge, Mass.: Harvard University Press, 1966), chap. 6.

6. Harold L. Wilensky, *Organizational Intelligence: Knowledge and Power in Government and Industry* (New York: Basic Books, 1967), p. 36.

7. Garry D. Brewer, "On Innovation, Social Change, and Reality," *Technological Forecasting and Social Change*, February 1973, p. 22.

8. A fuller treatment and consideration of other purposes are presented in Garry D. Brewer, "On the Theory and Practice of Innovation," *Technology In Society*, Fall 1980, pp. 337–63.

9. H. Kahn and I. Mann, *Ten Common Pitfalls* (Santa Monica, Calif.: The Rand Corporation, RM–1937, July 1957), p. 42; cited in Quade, "Pitfalls and Limitations," in E. S. Quade and W. I. Boucher, eds., *Systems Analysis and Policy Planning: Applications in Defense* (New York: American Elsevier, 1968), p. 351.

10. Herbert Kaufman, *Are Government Organizations Immortal?* (Washington, D.C.: The Brookings Institution, 1976), is full of examples here.

11. See Edward B. Katzenbach, Jr., "The Horse Cavalry in the Twentieth Century: A Study in Policy Response," *Public Policy* 8 (1958), pp. 120–149.

12. This, and many other difficulties, are cogently treated in Richard R. Nelson and Sidney G. Winter, "In Search of a Useful Theory of Innovation," *Research Policy* 6, no. 1 (1977), pp. 36–76.

13. The conference is reported in Thomas H. Maugh II, "Creativity: Can It Be Dissected? Can It Be Taught?" *Science*, 21 June 1974, p. 1273. Maugh's pessimism regarding these questions is disputed in several letters to the editor; see *Science*, 27 September 1974, p. 1110.

14. M. Deutsch, *Resolution of Conflict*, p. 362; and Homer G. Barnett, *Innovation: The Basis of Cultural Change* (New York: McGraw-Hill, 1953), chaps. 2 and 3.

15. The "decision seminar" was first proposed by Harold D. Lasswell, "Technique of Decision Seminars," *Midwest Journal of Political Science*, August 1960, pp. 213–36. See Garry D. Brewer, "Dealing with Complex Social Problems: The Potential of the 'Decision Seminar'," in Garry D. Brewer and Ronald D. Brunner, eds., *Political Development and Change: A Policy Approach* (New York: Free Press, 1975), chap. 12, for a discussion of the implementation of a decision seminar. Also see Sidney J. Parnes, "Do You Really Understand Brainstorming?" in S. J. Parnes and H. F. Harding, eds., *A Source Book for Creative Thinking* (New York: Charles Scribner's Sons, 1962).

16. Robert K. Yin, "Production Efficiency Versus Bureaucratic Self-Interest: Two Innovative Processes?" *Policy Sciences*, December 1977, pp. 381–99.

17. Most economists, for instance, are more concerned with innovation by the firm than by the individual. Edwin Mansfield et al., *Research and Innovation in the Modern Corporation* (New York: W. W. Norton, 1971); and James M. Utterback, "Innovation in Industry and the Diffusion of Technology," *Science*, 15 February 1974 are representative.

18. Everett M. Rogers and F. Floyd Shoemaker, *Communication of Innovations* (New York: Free Press, 1971), offer over 100 different hypotheses on innovations and list both supporting and contradicting references.

19. Often doing nothing allows passions to cool, other issues to displace the topic or fad of the moment, or additional information to be gathered to assist in problem resolution. All of these points are well treated in Anthony Downs, "Up and Down with Ecology: The Issue-Attention Cycle," *Public Interest* 28, no. 1 (1972), pp. 38–50.

20. See Theodore H. White, *The Making of the President, 1972* (New York: Atheneum, 1973), chap. 8, for an explanation.

21. See Thomas G. Patterson, *Soviet-American Confrontation: Postwar Reconstruction and the Origins of the Cold War* (Baltimore, Md.: Johns Hopkins University Press, 1973).

22. This period is lucidly analyzed by Joseph Jones, *The Fifteen Weeks* (New York: Viking Press, 1955).

23. FDR's epochal "First 100 Days" are emphasized in Arthur M. Schlesinger, Jr., *The Coming of the New Deal* (Boston: Houghton Mifflin, 1952).

24. Edward E. David, "Science Futures: The Industrial Connection," *Science*, 2 March 1979, pp. 837–40, argues convincingly on this and related matters. James L. Perry and Kenneth L. Kraemer, "Innovation Attributes, Policy Intervention, and the Diffusion of Computer Applications Among Local Governments," *Policy Sciences*, April 1978, pp. 179–205, present a detailed, empirically-based analysis of several public practices.

25. The French defeat to the German *Blitzkrieg* is described by Jacques Benoist-Méchin, *Sixty Days That Shook the World*, Peter Wiles, trans. (New York: G. P. Putnam, 1963); and Alistair Horne, *To Lose a Battle: France 1940* (Boston: Little, Brown, 1969). Some measure of the blame has been traced to poor problem recognition and even poorer analysis; see Paul Bracken, "Unintended Consequences of Strategic Gaming," *Simulation & Games*, September 1977, pp. 283–318, especially pp. 287–93, wherein "unintended diversion" resulted from a single-minded preoccupation with the imagined invulnerability of the Maginot Line.

26. E. S. Quade, "Principles and Procedures of Systems Analysis," in Quade and Boucher, *Systems Analysis and Policy Planning*, p. 37.

27. The general argument is stressed in Garry D. Brewer, "Operational Social Systems Modeling: Pitfalls and Prospectives," *Policy Sciences*, December 1978, pp. 157–69. Specific instances are presented in Garry D. Brewer and Martin Shubik, *The War Game: A Critique of Military Problem Solving* (Cambridge, Mass.: Harvard University Press, 1979), chap. 14.

28. The transition from option generation to policy decision in that incident is discussed in Elie Abel, *The Missile Crisis* (Philadelphia: J. B. Lippincott, 1966); and in Robert Kennedy, *Thirteen Days: A Memoir of the Cuban Missile Crisis* (New York: W. W. Norton, 1969).

29. The interactions between the political, military, and scientific communities that led to this decision are examined in Herbert Feis, *Japan Subdued* (Princeton, N.J.: Princeton University Press, 1961). The decision stimulated much debate; see Gar Alperovitz, *Atomic Diplomacy: Hiroshima and Potsdam* (New York: Random House, 1967).

30. This distinction is supported by Martin A. Levin and Horst D. Dornbusch, "Pure and Policy Social Science," *Public Policy*, Summer 1973, pp. 383–423.

Discussion questions

1.   Factors exist mainly in the eye of the beholder. With respect to the earliest identification of a problem, discuss the following issues:

    a.   Factors enhancing and impeding recognition.

    b.   Factors required to specify the context or situation in which the problem is embedded.

    c.   Impediments to the creative generation of plausible and feasible solution options.

2.   A problem context can be specified, conceived, or identified in a variety of ways. Specify several of these and discuss them in terms of (*a*) specialization, both individual and institutional; (*b*) professionalization, including an appreciation for the many disciplines and techniques that exist to facilitate initiation; (*c*) problem recognition and definition, with concern for the many different perspectives that can be adopted; (*d*) value preferences exemplified; and (*e*) research resources, capabilities, and constraints.

3.   Recognizing the existence of emerging social problems has been treated as a key component of the initiation phase of the overall policy or decision process. However, there are many partial explanations that one may develop to account for the fact that such problems are frequently overlooked until they have reached crisis proportions. What are some of these expla-

nations? What are their likely, common, and usually undesirable consequences for improved operation of the decision process?

4.   The general conception of perceptions has lately become faddish, at least in the policymaking community. What does it mean? What different kinds of intellectual and technical skills and insights would be necessary to explore the perceptions problem adequately and thoroughly? (Try thinking directly about what is meant by the perceptions problem.) Why should it be that different individuals, groups, and institutions have different, even radically different, perceptions of the identical contextual situation? What might be done to lessen the impact of differential perceptions for the purposes of improving policymaking and analysis?

5.   What kinds of institutions can you identify whose basic purpose and function are initiative or inventive? Identify three or four of them—both public and private in nature. What are the strengths and weaknesses of each with respect to their general contribution to the overall decision process? In your opinion, what improvements are needed in this phase of the process, specifically with respect to institutional design or creation?

6.   What thoughts are stimulated as you reflect on the following judgment about planning and the actual conduct of war:

> Man's attempts at preordination are always risky and require as a minimum precondition for success the cooperation of all concerned. . . . [T]he compilation of a plan which would depend for its success on the smooth interaction of a very large number of mutually dependent elements invites its frustration. [John Keegan, *The Face of Battle* (New York: Viking Press, 1976), pp. 261–62.]

7.   What might account for the often observed fact that good ideas seldom emerge unscathed from public exposure and experience? Could anything be done that would result in (a) the generation of more creative alternatives for problem resolution and (b) realization of some of these alternatives?

Supplementary readings

The following readings are provided to allow the student to explore many questions and issues treated in the chapters in greater detail and at leisure. The listing follows, to a certain extent, the architecture of the part itself.

RECOGNITION OF THE PROBLEM

Individual level

Axelrod, Robert M., ed. *Structure of Decision.* Princeton, N.J.: Princeton University Press, 1976.

Hammond, Kenneth, and Leonard Adelman. "Science, Values, and Human Judgment." *Science,* 12 October 1976, pp. 389–96.

Lindzey, Gardner, and Elliot Aronson, eds. *The Handbook of Social Psychology* vols. 1–5. Reading, Mass.: Addison-Wesley, 1968. [Generally, but especially note, Seymour M. Berger and William W. Lambert, "Stimulus-Response Theory in Contemporary Social Psychology," vol. 1, pp. 81–178.]

Raiffa, Howard. *Decision Analysis.* Reading, Mass.: Addison-Wesley, 1968.

Tversky, Amos, and Daniel Kahneman. "Judgment Under Uncertainty: Heuristics and Biases." *Science*, 27 September 1974, pp. 1124–31.

Social, psychological, cultural, and educational factors

Dawson, Richard E., and Kenneth Prewitt. *Political Socialization.* Boston: Little, Brown, 1969.

Ethredge, Lloyd S. *A World of Men: The Private Sources of American Foreign Policy.* Cambridge, Mass.: MIT Press, 1978.

Geertz, Clifford. *Agricultural Involution.* Berkeley: University of California Press, 1963.

Greenstein, Fred I., and Michael Lerner, eds. *A Source Book for the Analysis of Personality and Politics.* Chicago: Markham, 1971.

Hermann, Margaret. "Effect of Personal Characteristics of Leaders on Foreign Policy." In M. A. East, Stephen A. Salmore, and C. F. Hermann, eds. *Why Nations Act.* Beverly Hills, Calif.: Sage Publications, 1977.

LeVine, Robert A., and Donald T. Campbell. *Ethnocentrism.* New York: John Wiley & Sons, 1972.

Ranney, Austin, ed. *Political Science and Public Policy.* Chicago: Markham, 1968. [See especially Ranney's introductory essay, pp. 3–22.]

Sniderman, Paul, and Jack Citrin. "Psychological Sources of Political Belief." *American Political Science Review*, June 1971, pp. 401–17.

Tajfel, Henri. "Social and Cultural Factors in Perceptions." In Lindzey and Aronson, eds. *Handbook of Social Psychology*, vol. 3. pp. 315–94.

Triadis, Harry C. "Cultural Influences upon Cognitive Processes." In Leonard Berkowitz, ed. *Advances in Experimental Social Psychology.* New York: Academic Press, 1964.

Vickers, Geoffrey. *Value Systems and Social Process.* New York: Basic Books, 1968.

Walton, John. "Discipline, Method, and Community Power: A Note on Sociology of Knowledge." *American Sociological Review*, October 1966, pp. 684–89.

Impediments and defense mechanisms

Abelson, Robert P.; E. Aronson; W. J. McGuire; T. N. Newcomb; M. J. Rosenberg; and P. H. Tannenbaum, eds. *Theories of Cognitive Consistency.* Skokie, Ill.: Rand McNally, 1968.

Aronson, Elliot. "The Theory of Cognitive Dissonance: A Current Perspective." In Berkowitz, ed. *Advances in Experimental Social Psychology*, vol. 3, pp. 2–35.

Festinger, Leon. *A Theory of Cognitive Dissonance.* Stanford, Calif.: Stanford University Press, 1964.

Holsti, Ole R., and Alexander L. George. "The Effects of Stress on the Performance of Foreign Policy-Makers." In C. P. Cotter, ed. *Political Science Annual: Individual Decision-Making.* Indianapolis, Ind.: Bobbs-Merrill, 1975.

Janis, Irving L., and Leon Mann. *Decision Making: A Psychological Analysis of Conflict, Choice, and Commitment.* New York: Free Press, 1977.

Jervis, Robert. *Perception and Misperception in International Relations.* Princeton, N.J.: Princeton University Press, 1976.

Luria, A. R. *The Man With a Shattered World.* New York: Basic Books, 1972.

Miller, George A. *The Psychology of Communication: Seven Essays.* New York: Basic Books, 1967.

Miller, James G. "Adjusting to Overloads of Information." In David Rioch, and Edwin A. Weinstein, eds. *Disorders of Communication.* Baltimore, Md.: Williams and Wilkins Co., 1964, pp. 87–100.

Mednick, Martha, and Sarnoff A. Mednick, eds. *Research in Personality.* New York: Holt, Rinehart & Winston, 1965. [See readings collected under "The Resolution of Conflict: Defense Mechanisms," chap. 3.]

Newell, Allen, and Herbert A. Simon. *Human Problem Solving.* Englewood Cliffs, N.J.: Prentice-Hall, 1972.

Reitman, W. R. *Cognition and Thought: An Information Processing Approach.* New York: John Wiley & Sons, 1966.

Sanford, R. Nevitt. "Individual and Social Change in a Community Under Pressure." In Charles F. Reed, Irving E. Alexander, and Silvan S. Tomkins, eds. *Psychopathology: A Source Book.* Cambridge, Mass.: Harvard University Press, 1963, pp. 763–82.

Schroeder, Harold M.; Michael J. Driver; and Siegfried Streufert. *Human Information Processing.* New York: Holt, Rinehart & Winston, 1967.

von Hippel, Eric. "Users and Innovators." *Technology Review,* January 1978, pp. 31–39.

Organizations, general

Cyert, Richard M., and James G. March. *A Behavioral Theory of the Firm.* Englewood Cliffs, N.J.: Prentice-Hall, 1963.

Goodman, Paul S., and Johannes M. Pennings. *New Perspectives on Organizational Effectiveness.* San Francisco: Jossey-Bass, 1977.

Lawrence, Paul R., and Jay W. Lorsch. *Organization and Environment.* Cambridge, Mass.: Harvard Business School, 1967.

March, James G., and Johan P. Olsen et al., eds. *Ambiguity and Choice in Organizations.* Bergen, Norway: Universitetsforlaget, 1976.

March, James G., and Herbert A. Simon. *Organizations* New York: John Wiley & Sons, 1958.

Nystrom, P. C., and W. H. Starbuck, eds. *Handbook of Organizational Design.* New York: Oxford University Press, 1980.

Schon, Donald. *Technology and Change.* New York: Dell, 1967.

Simon, Herbert A. "On the Concept of Organizational Goal." *Administrative Science Quarterly,* June 1964, pp. 1–22.

Thompson, James D. *Organizations in Action.* New York: McGraw-Hill, 1967.

Intelligence agencies and practices

Deacon, Richard. *The Chinese Secret Service.* New York: Ballantine, 1974.

Fain, Tyrus G., comp. *The Intelligence Community: History, Organization, and Issues.* New York: R. R. Bowker, 1977.

Hilsman, Roger. *Strategic Intelligence and National Decision.* New York: Free Press, 1956.

Kahn, David. *The Codebreakers.* New York: Macmillan, 1967.

Ransom, Harry Howe. *The Intelligence Community.* Cambridge, Mass.: Harvard University Press, 1970.

Smith, R. Harris. *OSS: The Secret History of America's First Central Intelligence Agency.* Berkeley: University of California Press, 1972.

Whaley, Barton. *Codeword BARBAROSSA.* Cambridge, Mass.: MIT Press, 1973.

Winterbotham, Frederick W. *The Ultra Secret.* New York: Harper & Row, 1974.

Wohlstetter, Roberta. *Pearl Harbor: Warning and Decision.* Stanford, Calif.: Stanford University Press, 1962.

Communication

Cherry, Colin. *On Human Communication.* Cambridge, Mass.: MIT Press, 1966.

Deutsch, Karl W. *The Nerves of Government: Models of Political Communication and Control.* New York: Free Press, 1966.

Hermann, Margaret. "How Leaders Process Information and the Effect on Foreign Policy." In James N. Rosenau, ed. *Comparing Foreign Policies.* Beverly Hills, Calif.: Sage Publications, 1974.

Lasswell, Harold D., Nathan Leites et al. *Language of Politics.* Cambridge, Mass.: MIT Press, 1965.

Steinbruner, John D. *The Cybernetic Theory of Decision: New Dimensions in Political Analysis.* Princeton, N.J.: Princeton University Press, 1974.

Weiner, Norbert. *Cybernetics.* Cambridge, Mass.: MIT Press, 1961.

Wilensky, Harold L. *Organizational Intelligence: Knowledge and Policy in Government and Industry.* New York: Basic Books, 1967.

IDENTIFICATION OF THE PROBLEM CONTEXT

General

Churchman, C. West. *The Systems Approach.* New York: Delacorte Press, 1968, chap. 3.

Lasswell, Harold D. *A Pre-View of Policy Sciences.* New York: American Elsevier, 1971.

Quade, E. S. *Analysis for Public Decisions.* (New York: American Elsevier, 1975, chap. 5.

Quade, E. S., and W. I. Boucher, eds. *Systems Analysis and Policy Planning.* New York: American Elsevier, 1968, chap. 3.

Criteria

Attaway, L. D. "Criteria and the Measurement of Effectiveness." In Quade and Boucher, eds. *Systems Analysis and Policy Planning,* chap. 4.

Hitch, Charles J., and Roland McKean. *The Economics of Defense in the Nuclear Age.* New York: Atheneum, 1965, chap. 9.

Kaplan, Abraham. *The Conduct of Inquiry.* San Francisco: Chandler, 1964.

Meehan, Eugene J. *The Theory and Method of Political Analysis.* Homewood, Ill.: Dorsey Press, 1965.

Nagel, Ernest. *The Structure of Science.* New York: Harcourt Brace Jovanovich, 1961, chap. 13.

Participants, individual

Arrow, Kenneth J. *Social Choice and Individual Values.* New York: John Wiley & Sons, 1963.

Buchanan, James, and Gordon Tullock. *The Calculus of Consent.* Ann Arbor: University of Michigan Press, 1962.

Curry, Robert L., and L. L. Wade. *A Theory of Political Exchange.* Englewood Cliffs, N.J.: Prentice-Hall, 1968.

Dahl, Robert A. *Who Governs?* New Haven: Yale University Press, 1961.

Heath, Anthony. *Rational Choice and Social Exchange: A Critique of Exchange Theory.* Cambridge: Cambridge University Press, 1976.

Inglehardt, Ronald. "Values, Objective Needs, and Subjective Satisfaction among Western Publics." *Comparative Political Studies,* January 1977, pp. 429–58.

Lasswell, Harold D. *Politics: Who Gets What, When and How.* New York: Meridian, 1958.

Milbrath, Lester. *Political Participation.* Skokie, Ill.: Rand McNally, 1965.

Olson, Mancur. *The Logic of Collective Action.* Cambridge, Mass.: Harvard University Press, 1965.

Participants, institutional

Katz, Daniel, and Robert I. Kahn, eds. *The Social Psychology of Organizations.* New York: John Wiley & Sons, 1967.

Simon, Herbert A. *Administrative Behavior.* New York: Free Press, 1957.

[And all items listed above under "Organizations, general".]

Boundary conditions

Howard, Ronald N. "Classifying a Population into Homogeneous Groups." In J. R. Lawrence, ed. *Operational Research and the Social Sciences.* London: Tavistock, 1966, chap. 43.

Nelson, Richard R. "Intellectualizing About the Moon-Ghetto Metaphor: A Study of the Current Malaise of Rational Analysis of Social Problems." *Policy Sciences,* December 1974, pp. 375–414.

Quade, E. S., and G. Majone, eds. *Pitfalls of Analysis.* New York: John Wiley & Sons, 1980.

Simon, Herbert A. "The Architecture of Complexity." *General Systems* 10 (1965), pp. 63–75.

Strauch, Ralph. " 'Squishy' Problems and Quantitative Methods." *Policy Sciences,* June 1975, pp. 175–84.

Weaver, Warren. "Science and Complexity." *American Scientist* 36 (1948), pp. 536–44.

Temporal constraints

Ascher, William. *Forecasting.* Baltimore, Md.: Johns Hopkins University Press, 1978, especially pp. 190–214.

Duncan, Otis Dudley. "Social Forecasting: The State of the Art." *Public Interest,* Fall 1969, pp. 88–118.

Shubik, Martin. "Symposium: The Nature and Limitations of Forecasting." *Daedalus,* Summer 1967, pp. 938–46.

Wolf, Charles, Jr., "Heresies About Time: Wasted Time, Double-Duty Time, and Past Time." *Quarterly Journal of Economics,* November 1973, pp. 661–67.

DETERMINATION OF GOALS AND OBJECTIVES

General

Kaplan, Abraham. *American Ethics and Public Policy.* New York: Oxford University Press, 1963.

Lasswell, Harold D. *Pre-View of Policy Sciences,* chap. 2.

Lasswell, Harold D., and Abraham Kaplan. *Power and Society.* New Haven: Yale University Press, 1950.

Vickers, Geoffrey. "Commonly Ignored Elements in Policymaking." *Policy Sciences,* July 1972, pp. 265–66.

————. *Freedom in a Rocking Boat: Changing Values in an Unstable Society.* New York: Basic Books, 1971.

Winter, Gibson. *Elements for a Social Ethic: The Role of Social Science in Public Policy.* New York: Macmillan, 1966, chaps. 6–8.

Organizational goals

Etzioni, Amitai. *Modern Organizations.* Englewood Cliffs, N.J.: Prentice-Hall, 1964.

Gross, Edward. "The Definition of Organizational Goals." *British Journal of Sociology*, September 1969, pp. 277–94.

Mohr, Lawrence B. "The Concept of Organizational Goal." *American Political Science Review*, June 1973, pp. 470–81.

Perrow, Charles. "Organizational Goals." In David Sills, ed. *International Encyclopedia of the Social Sciences*. New York: Macmillan, 1968, vol. 11, pp. 306–09.

Simon, Herbert A. "On the Concept of Organizational Goals." *Administrative Science Quarterly*, June 1964, pp. 1–22.

Political systems

Brecht, Arnold. *Political Theory*. Princeton, N.J.: Princeton University Press, 1959.

Dahl, Robert A. *Modern Political Analysis*. Englewood Cliffs, N.J.: Prentice-Hall, 1963, chaps. 3, 4, and 8.

Meehan, Eugene J. *Theory and Method of Political Analysis*, chap. 8.

Contextual matters

Carritt, E. F. *Morals and Politics*. New York: Oxford University Press, 1935.

Girvetz, Harry K., ed. *Contemporary Moral Issues*. Belmont, Calif.: Wadsworth, 1968.

Kaplan, Abraham. *American Ethics and Public Policy*. On "situational ethics."

Laslett, Peter, and W. G. Runciman, eds. *Philosophy, Politics and Society*. New York: Oxford University Press, 1967.

Rawls, John. *A Theory of Justice*. Cambridge, Mass.: Harvard University Press, 1971.

GENERATION OF ALTERNATIVES

Creativity

Anderson, Harold H., ed. *Creativity and Its Cultivation*. New York: Harper & Row, 1959.

Barron, Frank. "The Psychology of Creativity." In *New Dimensions in Psychology II*. New York: Holt, Rinehart & Winston, 1965, pp. 1–35.

Cox, Catherine M. et al. *Genetic Studies of Genius*. Stanford, Calif.: Stanford University Press, 1926.

Goertzel, V., and M. G. Goertzel. *Cradles of Eminence*. Boston: Little, Brown, 1962.

Gruber, H. E.; Glenn Terrell; and Michael Wertheimer, eds. *Contemporary Approaches to Creative Thinking*. New York: Atherton, 1962.

Guilford, J. P. *The Nature of Human Intelligence*. New York: McGraw-Hill, 1967.

Haefell, John W. *Creativity and Innovation*. New York: Holt, Rinehart & Winston, 1962.

Innovation

Barnett, Homer G. *Innovation: The Basis of Cultural Change.* New York: McGraw-Hill, 1953.

Brown, Lawrence. "Dynamics of Innovation." *Economic Development and Cultural Change,* January 1969, pp. 189–211.

Downs, George W., Jr., *Bureaucracy, Innovation and Public Policy.* Lexington, Mass.: D. C. Heath, 1976.

Kimberly, John. "Managerial Innovation." In P. C. Nystrom and W. H. Starbuck, eds. *Handbook of Organizational Design.* New York: Oxford University Press, 1980.

Mohr, Lawrence B. "Determinants of Innovation in Organizations." *American Political Science Review,* March 1969, pp. 111–26.

Nelson, Richard R., and Sidney G. Winter. "In Search of a Useful Theory of Innovation." *Research Policy* 6, no. 1 (1977), pp. 36–76.

Rogers, Everett M., and F. Floyd Shoemaker. *Communication of Innovations: A Cross-Cultural Approach.* New York: Free Press, 1971.

Zaltman, Gerald; Robert Duncan; and Jonny Holbek. *Innovations and Organizations.* New York: John Wiley & Sons, 1973.

Diffusion of innovations

Aiken, Michael, and Robert R. Alford. "Community Structure and Innovation: The Case of Urban Renewal." *American Sociological Review,* August 1970, pp. 650–64.

Brewer, Garry D. "On the Theory and Practice of Innovation." *Technology In Society,* Fall 1980, pp. 337–63.

Coleman, James S.; Elihu Katz; and Herbert Menzel. *Medical Innovation: A Diffusion Study.* Indianapolis, Ind.: Bobbs-Merrill, 1966.

deLeon, Peter, ed. "Special Issue: Technology and Public Policy." *Policy Sciences,* February 1980.

Gray, Virginia. "Innovation in the States." *American Political Science Review,* December 1973, pp. 1174–85.

Haeffer, Erik A. "The Innovative Process." *Technology Review,* March/April 1973, pp. 18–25.

Hägerstrand, Torsten. *Innovation Diffusion as a Spatial Process.* Chicago: University of Chicago Press, 1967.

————. *The Propagation of Innovation Waves.* Lund, Sweden: Royal University of Lund, 1952.

Lambright, W. Henry et al. *Technology Transfer to Cities: Processes of Choice at the Local Level.* Boulder, Colo.: Westview Press, 1979.

Michaelis, Michael. "Obstacles to Innovation." *International Science and Technology,* November 1964, pp. 40–46.

Rowe, Lloyd A., and William B. Boise. "Organizational Innovation: Current Research and Evolving Concepts." *Public Administration Review,* May/June 1974, pp. 284–93.

Thompson, Victor A. *Bureaucracy and Innovation.* University: The University of Alabama Press, 1969.

Walker, Jack L. "The Diffusion of Innovations in the American States." *American Political Science Review,* September 1969, pp. 880–99.

Wilson, James Q. "Innovation in Organizations: Notes towards a Theory." In James D. Thompson, ed. *Approaches to Organizational Design.* Pittsburgh: University of Pittsburgh Press, 1966, pp. 193–218.

Yin, Robert K. "Production Efficiency Versus Bureaucratic Self-Interest: Two Innovative Processes?" *Policy Sciences,* December 1977, pp. 381–99.

PART II

Estimation

Estimation continues work begun during initiation: systematic investigation of a problem and thoughtful assessment of options and alternatives are its characteristic tasks. Specifically, estimation concerns the accurate determination of all likely costs and benefits that are expected to flow from decisions taken during the subsequent, or selection, stage of the overall process. Consideration is given both to the probable consequences of positive action and to those expected to result from inaction, whether intentional or not. Estimation efforts aim to reduce uncertainties about possible choices to the greatest extent possible, given time, intellectual, and other constraints.

At some point a problem and its tentative solutions pass from an early recognition and inventive phase into one characterized by efforts to explore its full dimensions, to generate refined options for management and resolution, and to calculate the costs and benefits associated with possible action and intervention strategies. For some problems, the move is clearcut: formal ties are instituted with specialized individuals and institutions having experience with the problems. Sometimes the move is made only slowly or hardly at all: many problems fail to capture public attention, fail to displace other, more salient ones, or remain unattended until some precipitate event forces the matter into the full glare of attention. The gasoline lines, created by the Arab oil embargo of 1973–74, and the late 1960s and early 1980 urban race riots, prompted by years of neglect, are clear examples of public policy issues which were predictable but still ignored or unresolved.

In any case, estimation is usefully imagined as a separate phase of the decision process—a phase having many important aspects and functions, distinct participants, and understandable implications for all other phases, the nature and quality of decisions made, and the specific outcomes eventually realized.

Estimation is decisively founded on questions of value. Beginning even with elementary definitions of the problem, one is continually confronted with ethical aspects and judgmental difficulties—the neglect of which does little to reduce their impact or improve the quality of policy analyses. For instance, for many estimation acts taken in support of the MX (missile/experimental) intercontinental ballistic missile system, it is apparent that preliminary definitions of the problem heavily emphasized technological features of exotic weaponry and devalued many social, economic, environmental, and political elements.[1] This case illustrates many inherent dangers of a less-than-comprehensive approach to estimation and decision making. Officials in the Department of Defense simply value differently, or less, many features of the MX problem than do other concerned participants, such as citizens in Utah and Nevada whose patriotism may not extend so far as to risk their lives by placing them in the center of a nuclear bull's-eye.[2]

In technical terms, this problem appears to have been misspecified by those responsible for its estimation; that is, they have selected rather narrowly and incompletely from the whole array of relevant factors and have valued issues of national security over local quality-of-life considerations. This common occurrence stresses the importance of a full and humane development of multiple interpretations of a problem, with a variety of methods, theories, and data, and from a large number of distinct observational and value-based perspectives. At a minimum, the imagined alterations of life and circumstances estimated by many citizens, the governors and U.S. senators from Utah and Nevada probably exceeded the weight given them by national leaders in Washington.[3]

The nation's cities underwent renewal with a virtual vengeance. However, scant attention was given to the preferences of those whose lives were irreparably affected by this policy and the many specific programs undertaken in its behalf.[4] Care for native American Indians, but the continuing shame and failure of the Bureau of Indian Affairs and many other "helpful" programs, must signal a fundamental misunderstanding of the problem: a misunderstanding that, at the very least, has failed to value and take into account the Indian culture, the expressed desires of Indians, and their perspectives of themselves and their relation to the world.[5] In these, and myriad other examples, it is both easy and probably unfair to lay full blame at the feet of those entrusted with the estimation acts that predate policy and programmatic choices; nevertheless, a thoughtful reassessment of such stories would probably tell one much about the limitations and weaknesses of estimation and other phases of the decision process.

In the following chapters we present an interpretation of the complexity of problem and decision settings in which estimation acts are undertaken; we discuss a prevalent orientation in our culture favoring rational analyses: a preference for systematic, formalized, and often quantitative methods and theories for assessing alternatives, which often neglect the root causes of a problem. Many important human and valuational aspects of estimation are identified and discussed to raise the reader's sensitivities to them. Because estimation nearly always results in a simplified and selective treatment of problems and contexts, common simplification strategies are described and samples of prevalent estimation methods and mistakes are discussed. The role of experts and specialized knowledge is featured because much of the practical business of estimation is delegated to those with privileged insights, access, and training. Finally, we emphasize some fundamental differences of purpose, intent, and use for those mainly concerned with both estimation and the linked stage of selection or decision making— differences having implications for all phases of the policy process.

NOTES

1. Eliot Marshall, "MX Faces Stiff Political Test in Nevada," *Science*, 29 February 1980, pp. 961–65.

2. Reagan's decision in 1981 to proceed with a *limited* version of MX, not requiring the use of Nevada or Utah, reflects these concerns: See Richard Halloran, "Reagan Drops Mobile MX Plan, Urges Basing Missiles in Silos: Proposes Building B–1 Bomber," *New York Times*, October 13, 1981, pp. 1, 13.

3. The magnitude of the MX system is hard to comprehend; the twists and turns it took during estimation are even more so. The size, complexity, and rationale for the system— and a sense of the fluid aspects of its life during estimation—are gleaned by reading the following, in order: U.S. General Accounting Office, *The MX Weapon System —A Program with Cost and Schedule Uncertainties* (Washington, D.C.: Government Printing Office, PSAD–80–29, February 29, 1980); Eliot Marshall, "Congress Challenges MX Basing Plan," *Science*, 30 May 1980, pp. 1007–9; R. Jeffrey Smith, "Reagan Proposes Huge Nuclear Buildup," *Science*, 16 October 1981, pp. 309, 312; and James Fallows, "Reagan's MX Surprise," *Atlantic*, December 1981, pp. 8, 10, 14.

4. Jane Jacobs, *The Death and Life of Great American Cities* (New York: Random House, 1961); and Martin Anderson, *The Federal Bulldozer* (New York: McGraw-Hill, 1967), both attest to this.

5. William J. Broad, "The Osage Oil Cover-up," *Science*, 4 April 1980, pp. 32–35, is one more illustration of a long and checkered story.

4

A conception of complexity

COMPLEXITY AND ITS CONSEQUENCES

There should be no doubt that modern social systems are complex. The general problem was long ago recognized by Charles E. Merriam in terms of the trouble one has "in determining specific units, and with many variable factors which may make the accurate interpretation of a result very difficult to isolate successfully. The relations of the variables are not always disentangled, and their confusion may be the source of most serious error."[1]

A complex social system is one made up of "a large number of parts that interact in a nonsimple way. In such systems, the whole is more than the sum of its parts, not in an ultimate metaphysical sense, but in the important pragmatic sense that, given the properties of the parts and the laws of interaction, it is a nontrivial matter to infer the properties of the whole."[2] Confronted with this complexity, the social analyst reacts by simplifying phenomena, ignoring some and emphasizing others, in order to achieve comprehension.[3] Richard Bellman and Robert Kalaba have noted the irony that to understand, we must "throw-away information. . . . We cannot, at least at this level of our intellectual development, grapple with a high order of complexity. Consequently, we must simplify."[4] But while it is difficult to understand the entirety of any social system in terms of its parts, the operation of no one part can be understood without comprehending the whole. Lamentably, human beings have only a limited capacity to deal with complex systems as wholes. George Miller, a social psychologist, puts it this way:

> It seems to me that the very fact of our limited capacity for processing information has made it necessary for us to discover clever ways to abstract the essential features of our universe and to express these features in simple laws that we are capable of comprehending in a single act or thought. We are constantly taking information given in one form and translating it into alternative forms, searching for ways to map a strange, new phenomenon into simpler and more familiar ways.[5]

In short, the complexity of the subject matter, on the one hand, and our limited intellectual and operational capacities for analysis, on the other, require us to simplify; yet the implications of doing so are seldom considered by analysts or decision makers.[6]

A system becomes more complex as the number of interconnected elements (variables and parameters) increases; most social problems and the systems in which they are embedded are both large and highly interconnected.[7] The price increase in Organization of Petroleum Exporting Countries (OPEC) oil, announced in June 1980 at the conclusion of the Algiers meeting, demonstrates the concept of connectedness. As reported in the *Christian Science Monitor*, "This is the story of the sheikh, the banker, and the poor farmer, and it illustrates how a $30 billion oil price increase travels around the world."[8] The sheikh, representing those who stand to gain most directly from the price increase, must do something with the extra resources created by the $1 to $3 per barrel price hike; thus some portion of it will find its way to the banker. The banker's lot is not all that simple, however, not in a world fraught with inflation and plagued by recession—both of which are related partly to previous oil price increases. Places where the demands for the loan resources are greatest, developing countries, present many, often insurmountable problems—not the least of which is the already high level of debt they carry.[9] The poor farmer figures in this seamless web in terms of the increased price he must pay for fuel to run his irrigation pumps and fertilizer to feed his crops, both of which derive from ever more expensive oil; for many of the commodities the farmer produces, however, domestic and world prices have not increased enough to compensate for the rising costs. The double specter of inflation and recession figures prominently here again. Truly, "the sheikh, the farmer and the . . . banker are tied together in the increasingly interconnected world."[10]

Overlapping interactions among numerous elements, positive and negative feedback control loops, nonlinear relationships, and continuous structural changes inhere in social systems. These characteristics largely account for the astonishing diversity of social systems and behavior. Our limited intellectual apparatus, however, prompts us to seek simply-ordered regularity.[11] Our images are poor proxies for reality. Analyses frequently reflect these defective images, and so, too, do our policies. If our intellect persistently "supposes a greater degree of order and equality in things than it really finds," should one expect otherwise?[12]

Multiple interpretations of reality

With increased complexity come increases in the number and diversity of system interpretations, in part because of the biased and distorted views affected individuals bring with them to the problem context.[13] Depending on the general issues at stake, various perceptions of them, and the meanings concerned participants ascribe to each, these diverse interpretations may seriously affect the decision process and overall system operations. For instance, in the early 1960s, President John F. Kennedy dispatched two senior officials, a Foreign Service officer and an Army general, to Vietnam to provide him with fresh and realistic estimates of the situation there. The general's glowing assessment, when matched against the civilian's gloomy pessimism, prompted Kennedy to remark: "Were you two gentlemen in the same country?"[14] Up to some limit (clearly surpassed in the example), diversity of viewpoint may be a positive thing: responsible decision making requires consideration of numerous plausible courses of action before selecting only those having most promise. In highly complex situations, exceeding the limit can lead to trouble.[15]

At one level, decision makers depend on a limited repertoire of responses. Their reversion to tried and true or standard operating procedures, particularly in a novel or crisis setting, is a commonplace. Allison, in his well-known account of the Cuban missile crisis, discusses this issue in terms of "procedures . . . that do not change quickly or easily," but which are "quite limited . . . and cannot be substantially changed in a particular situation. The more complex the action and the greater the number of individuals involved, the more important are programs and repertoires as determinants of organizational behavior."[16] However, presuming that a present situation can be treated just like last time may lead to failure if the problem context differs significantly from one's familiar perception of it.[17]

Incremental decision making will be explored at length in Part III because it describes many realistic choices. Decisions have to be made, and all that a decision maker needs to understand—indeed, can understand in the face of complexity—is the specific detail of the single choice requiring action, or, in the words of two principal exponents of this view, "only those policies are considered whose known or expected consequences differ incrementally from the status quo."[18]

The incrementalist's view of decision making differs fundamentally from that advanced by Simon and other comprehensive rationalists. While not disputing the prevalence of incremental decisions nor the adequacy of many specific outcomes realized in this manner, for many decisions, especially those prompted by distinctive structural changes or cumulative effects, incrementalism becomes increasingly ineffective. With respect to highly complex technological systems, for instance those responsible for nuclear waste disposal, errors in design and performance may not become evident until many years after the system has been operational. Learning, a fundamental tenet of incrementalism, cannot occur until well beyond the point at which effective or efficient intervention can be undertaken. This situation presents the realistic challenge of having to design error-free institutions—a challenge incrementalism cannot meet.[19]

Another prevalent response to heightened complexity is doing nothing. Vacillation and indecision may become routine responses in situations where competing and contradictory interpretations dominate. Failure to formulate a national energy policy,[20] reluctance to agree to a continuation of limitations on strategic armaments,[21] and wavering with respect to ratification of women's equal rights all can be understood to a certain extent in these terms.

Imputing sinister motives in situations of threat or opposition or, the reverse, convincing oneself of dominance or invincibility in possible conflict settings, demonstrates yet another class of response to complex and uncertain problems. The first, or sinister, case has given rise to what is known as the worst-case mentality among strategic warfare analysts. One assumes the most hostile intent of a potential adversary (including a certainty that the enemy's weapon capabilities will be maximized in the future), and then deduces sets of decisions that will respond to these threats by maximizing one's own production and deployment of arms.[22] Invincibility follows from the selected discernment and biased weighting of facts about a likely opponent as compared with one's own capabilities. Stalin's failure to appreciate Hitler's impending invasion of the Soviet Union and America's similar error with respect to Pearl Harbor are most stunning examples of this problem.[23]

Much of the foregoing can be imagined in terms of the diagram shown in Figure 4–1. If one assumes that over some time period an organization will be making decisions that range in their originality all the way from "None," signifying that no decision was taken, to "Radical," signifying a highly innovative, risky decision, then it might be the case that all decisions could be described and found to exhibit a distributional property, such as that indicated by the figure's solid line. This is not to say that organizations either do or should have this characteristic. Possible interpretations of this figure emphasize that most decisions are incremental and differ only slightly from similar, previous choices; that doing nothing and deciding not to decide sometimes happen;[24] and that radically creative acts are relatively rare.

Our previous arguments about the effects of trying to cope with heightened social complexity can be visualized in terms of the dotted-line distribution in the figure. Inaction has become a dominant mode, and creativity becomes less frequent. Such a pattern may suffice in the short term or in

FIGURE 4–1   Hypothetical distribution of decisions according to originality

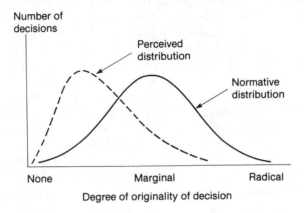

relatively static, benign situations; however, for the longer term and in situations marked by sharp change, such a pattern of behavior cannot long continue until an organization is supplanted by more responsive or adaptive ones.[25]

Inferred from this diagram is that at precisely the time when adaptive and innovative choices need to be considered and explored through estimation procedures, a tendency exists to retreat to safe decision strategies, to take no action at all, or to harbor either overly pessimistic or optimistic views of the world. Robert Jervis, in considering a complementary interpretation of this matter, advances several hypotheses about how estimation might contribute toward improvement. Among other suggestions to aid estimators, Jervis urges one to be as self-conscious as possible about the inherent biases found in policy estimates and to make these available for all to see and consider; to treat all assumptions, beliefs, and perceptions as transparently as possible; and to view the problem at hand from as many different perspectives as time and talent allow.[26] These general estimation prescriptions are treated in some detail in subsequent chapters, on the ground that their thoughtful and consistent elaboration in specific settings do much to enrich decision-making choices in situations of increased complexity.

Increasing chaos

Increasing a system's size may lead to chaos within an affected organization, where no one view or recommendation prevails amid the clamor and no choices are made, or to authoritarianism, where only one or a select few recommendations are heard and acted upon.[27] One needs only reflect momentarily on the aggressive politicization of virtually all of our traditional social institutions in recent years to appreciate organizational chaos: Welfare mothers, those favoring and abhoring abortion, homosexuals, draft resisters, environmentalists, public employees, and many other politically aware groups have become actively involved in complex political and social systems. The interconnectedness of individual and system has always existed; however, in the face of what some believe to be loss of faith in institutions or a decline in their legitimacy, many of these connections are now being energized as citizens take things into their own hands and hence make governance a sometime thing.[28] Appeals to an authoritarian solution, for instance proposals to exempt decisions about nuclear power from broad-scale participation,[29] are one natural and disturbing result: natural when the frustration of inactivity is considered and disturbing when democratic needs for participation are seen to be threatened.

A less extreme variant of the chaos-authority model is the intuitive-analytic one. Confronted with a difficult and pressing problem, the intuitive decision maker often elects to fly by the seat of the pants, taking consequences serially with slight regard for interrelationships, priorities, or other potentially important subtleties. To the extent that one's intuition substitutes for a hearing of others' perceptions of reality, the situation also tends to become authoritarian, and potentially dangerous. Alouph Hareven claims that the strong personalities of Moshe Dayan and other Israeli military commanders contributed to their preference to obtain selective raw intelligence about Egyptian intentions prior to the 1973 Yom Kippur War. Intuition in this case resulted in the suppression of information and substituted for a full portrayal of the actual and threatening situation just before hostilities began; the costly results are well known.[30]

The analytic decision maker, in contrast, strives to collect more data, to do more analyses, and to hear out as many points of view as time and conditions permit. An extreme case of working to gain more information, where the final outcome was affected, is exemplified in the risky decision to send U–2 surveillance overflights of Cuba before and during the peak of the missile crisis. Had the existence of Soviet missile sites not been positively established while still under construction, as they were, the character of the following showdown, in which operational Soviet missiles were not a fait accompli, could very well have "ruled out the successful blockade strategy and the Kennedy-Khrushchev negotiations that ended the crisis."[31] When carried to an extreme, however, marked by an absence of choice or vacillation, such a style may become disoriented or chaotic. Such an assessment appears warranted in the case of President Carter's decisions first to produce and deploy "enhanced radiation weapons" (the neutron bomb) in Europe and then his abrupt reversal, both apparently without much consultation with the European allies.

Time is important. As the time available to make a choice decreases, both the search for alternatives and the opportunity to do analysis decrease and may force intuitive decision-making behavior to take over. Thought yields to intuition. All the time in the world is probably not sufficient to conduct the definitive analysis that would eliminate all uncertainty about choice; our emphasis here is one of relative degree. All realistic decisions will have some element of subjective intuition attached (a feature considered in Part III); a severe compression of the time available to consider and then formulate a decision, we argue, overburdens the intuitive prowess of many decision makers.[32]

In a crisis setting, where many of the distinctions we discuss are most noticeable, the decision focus is narrowed and intensified on a select few alternatives; the number of advisors consulted decreases; and the amount of information brought to bear on the problem also decreases.[33] As the competitive aspects of the situation intensify, analytic thoroughness and precision may both fall by the wayside. In disclosing how the Central Intelligence Agency failed to anticipate and analyze the surprise 1975 North Vietnamese Army penetration of the Vietnamese Highlands, Frank Snepp offers the following illustrative explanation: "Unfortunately, all of us in the analytic business in Saigon had come to rely excessively on . . . electronically obtained intelligence, in lieu of human-source data, in fast-moving crisis situations."[34] During crises, the time spent in estimation acts is foreshortened, often to the point where uncertainties about decisions taken dominate all other aspects.[35] As human, practical limits are approached, one must be prepared either to deal with contradictory and conflicting recommendations and points of view or with an homogenized best choice of less than ideal proportions.[36] All of these behavioral aspects potentially exist in most policy settings, but their worst features tend to be emphasized in the high-stakes, short-time, crisis setting.[37] As the number and diversity of values in question increase, so, too, do opportunities for select participants to be indulged or deprived. Because this eventuality directly threatens the norm of widespread participation upon which the democratic process is founded, many concerned analysts, such as Alexander George, have advanced proposals to avert the problem.[38] Such proposals generally call for more, and better, analysis, not less.[39]

Unintended consequences

Because of their complexity, social systems are capable of producing problems neither expected nor results intended. Participants may perceive these surprises as occurring outside of their spheres of interest or responsibility; with increased complexity, beneficial and harmful externalities (as these surprises are sometimes called) seem to happen more often. The unanticipated consequences of policies and programs can, to a limited extent, be calculated if the estimator works hard to do so. Herbert Simon's general recommendation to treat problems with equal regard for part and whole, for instance, may help the analyst incorporate important consequences normally overlooked.[40]

Two poignant illustrations help one appreciate this argument. Assume that a group of determined parents were able to call the attention of local authorities to the unmet needs of their autistic children in terms of an educational and medical research program whose results, when applied, would help integrate their children into normal society. (Autism, unfortunately, is seldom easily surmounted.) If the cost for this program was estimated at $1 million and there were very few autistic children in the local district, it is doubtful that district officials would select the program; local benefits would be too small when compared with the cost, particularly the cost-per-child. If the program were expanded nationwide, however, the $1 million cost would likely appear small compared with potential nationwide benefits to all autistic children. Were the federal government to fund the research, the high local costs would be minimal when viewed from the national level, and proper balance would exist for reaching a socially optimum level of investment.[41]

In contrast, consider a different case of estimating the likely effects of a major medical breakthrough. With respect to medical diagnostic procedures for the fetus that allow in utero determinations of many serious disorders, simple calculations of cost and benefit fail to raise and resolve a host of noneconomic questions; indeed, the benefit-to-cost ratio of amniocentesis, as the main procedure is known, is resoundingly positive.[42] However, wholeness of analysis requires the estimator to consider other-than-cost aspects, such as: Who shall be tested—all pregnant women or just those assigned to high-risk categories because of age, past history, or other circumstances? What purposes shall the test serve—screening of serious disorders or creating eugenic (breeding) programs? Who should have the right to decide, in cases where test evidence suggests abnormality, about continuation of the pregnancy?[43] All such questions merit the estimator's (and society's) attention. In technical terms, the part-whole estimation strategy attempts to raise and resolve such questions to a far greater extent than a simple partist or reductionist one does.

Perfect foresight and total reduction of uncertainty will never be attainable through sheer force of reason. In remarking on the decline of hubris and assumption of humility evident in the thoughts and works of many policy analysts in the decade of the 1960s, Richard Nelson makes the following central point:

> One can also question the power of the policy analyst to fulfill his implicit promise to be able to trace with any scientific accuracy the consequences [of policy acts] in terms of the relevant benefits and costs of different alternative courses of action. The problems tend to be of the sort that are "poorly understood" [i.e., complex] by scientists as well as laymen.[44]

One especially poorly understood problem appears to be energy supply and demand, at least with respect to expert estimates of the likely demand for energy in America since 1973. The inaccuracy of such forecasts has led at least one decision maker to exasperation: "We've gone through the age of laying a straight edge on a piece of graph paper, and we've just gone through all the econometric models [for forecasting energy] and shown they're no good. And so we're back to crystal ball gazing," which is hardly a rational way to make large and hard-to-reverse investment decisions.[45]

Sensing and assessing the consequences flowing from complex problems are critical functions of the evaluation phase, as an element of the overall decision sequence (Part V). Accurate information is needed to decide whether effects are positive or negative, for whom, and to what extent. Based on such assessments, other policies may be instituted to reinforce the desirable effects and to suppress the unwanted ones. In the energy example, this may mean devising means of pooling or selling off overcapacity to other areas where demand exceeds local supply, or it may mean creating (at some considerable expense) stopgap measures to meet needs where sharing is not feasible. Policymakers need also to be alert for opportunities to adjust or terminate no longer needed or outworn policies and programs. Rationing schemes, termination of preferential pricing for large energy consumers to encourage conservation, and other ideas are all being discussed in the energy field to these ends. As social complexity increases, more externalities appear and are in time recognized.[46] They represent potential policy issues that may become serious, depending on the number of participants and the size of the stakes involved.

System control

The levels and interplay of loads, lags, leads, and gains have great importance for the efficiency, performance, and character of any social system. All of these concepts stem from theoretical work in the areas of social communication and control.[47] Each is an important, alternate way to think about social complexity. *Load* is the degree of stress, tension, or disequilibrium in a system. *Lag* is the time that a system takes to respond to a stimulus. *Gain* is the amount of corrective action taken by a system, expressed as the ratio of output to input. *Lead* is the time between the present and the point in the future at which the state of the system can still be accurately predicted. Generally, control in a system varies inversely with the degree of load and lag, directly with the amount of lead, and, up to the point of overcontrol or overresponse, directly with the amount of gain. Deutsch has related these concepts in the following terms:

> [O]verall performance . . . will depend upon the interplay of all these factors. Since gain is related to power, governments or organizations with little power may have to try to compensate for their low rates of gain by trying to increase their foresight [through estimation] and the speed of their response, that is to say, to cut down their lag and to increase their lead. Great powers, on the other hand, may often succeed in coping with a situation by the sheer size of

their response, even though their reactions may be slow and their predictions poor.[48]

While moderate rates of change or disequilibrium may be dealt with successfully, many governments and organizations "may find themselves unable to control their behavior effectively in times of rapid change that may put an excessive load upon their decision-making system."[49]

Loading a system's decision-making apparatus with numerous, diverse perceptions and recommendations may reduce the prospects for consensual processes to operate. Samuel Huntington responds to system overload in the following terms: "The tensions likely to prevail in a postindustrial society will probably require a more authoritative and effective pattern of governmental decision-making." However, the factors that contribute to the overload, e.g., changing values and ideologies and sharply increased levels of participation, may "make authoritative allocation of resources by government more rather than less difficult."[50] Failure to reduce the system overload, according to proponents of this view, threatens the legitimacy and very existence of political institutions.[51] Attaining and holding a majority on one issue becomes more difficult the greater the number of competing demands or loads requiring attention. In the situation where no one person or institution really comprehends the whole, however imperfectly, coordination and analysis may dissolve.[52]

As systems become loaded, lag times tend to increase. Priority matters dominate the decision maker's attention, routine issues are delayed or delegated to subordinates who treat them cautiously according to tried and true rules and principles, and many matters are simply ignored, either out of necessity or, more tellingly, convenience. Often when choices are finally made, it is necessary to apply more force (gain) than would have been required were the decision made in a more timely fashion. Brute force, extraordinary resources, and coercion tend to replace reason and analysis as dominant modes of operation. In the face of increasing uncertainty, lead times decrease—the time horizon for accurate prediction contracts—rendering decision making all the more susceptible to nonanalytic solutions. Fire fighting and flights by the seat of the pants replace structured problem solving and decision making.

The introduction, evolution, and widespread use of heroin in this society provide one graphic illustration of many of the main theoretical ideas presented here. In the words of former Boston Mayor John F. Collins:

> The slow early growth of heroin addiction, followed by rapid expansion, is typical of many socio-economic problems highly resistant to change. The public gradually becomes frustrated and fearful. Greater sums of money for police, courts, and prisons produce no discernible improvement in abating violence or street crime. . . . Demands to identify and eliminate the root causes of addiction—an endeavor which has so far been unsuccessful and time-consuming—are matched by equally fruitless clamor for eradication of the heroin flow into this country.

> The legal and health authorities have pursued several well-intentioned programs to conclusions far below the anticipated benefits. . . . Intuition and good intentions persuade us that we shall overcome.[53]

In the early stages of introduction, the problem was not given adequate attention but, rather, was allowed to embed itself in the inner cities and, in time, to flow outward to suburbia and the middle class.[54] Lead time had been squandered through inaction. The lag between problem recognition and response was too long, and when responses finally occurred they tended to be too little, too late and inappropriate to the full complexity of the current problem.[55] Intuition and good intentions have yet to yield resolution, and may even have made matters worse.[56] Whatever the eventual disposition of the heroin problem—if there is one—most agree that it will neither be simple nor will it come cheaply.[57] Deficient initiation and estimation, to a considerable extent, lie at the root of the present, nearly intractable situation.

Coping with complexity and working to reduce uncertainty about possible policy alternatives are both self-evidently desirable goals summarizing much of what policy analysis aims to accomplish. Increasing lead time appears to offer particularly attractive benefits. Time—unexpandable, irreplaceable time—may be the most critical element of all. While prescriptions that generally aim at the development of initiation and estimation as distinct policy phases are pertinent, efforts to link large data processing procedures with analytic models and conceptual frameworks merit specific consideration.[58] More appropriate data, interpreted in ways that produce useful information for analysis and estimation, have to improve a present condition too often marked by short or no lead-time decision making. The challenge is formidable and not made any easier by what one observer finds to be a fundamental human limitation:

> It appears that man is willing to learn about himself only after some disaster; after war, economic crisis, and political upheaval have taught him how flimsy is that human world in which he thought himself so securely grounded. What he learns has always been there, lying concealed beneath the surface of even the best-functioning societies; it is no less true for having come out of a period of chaos and disaster. But so long as man does not have to face up to such truth, he will not do so.[59]

Perceiving what has always been there and coping with this reality so as to emphasize human values while reducing the risks of collective catastrophe are the main purposes of policy analysis.[60] The difficult matters are not easily accomplished. The complexity of many social problems coupled with our limited intellectual and technical capacities for dealing with this complexity often conspire to limit the role and impact of analysis. However, it is our conviction that both room and means for improvement exist and can be instituted.

COPING WITH COMPLEXITY

Rationalizing the irrational?

The perceptual problem Barrett alludes to is itself very complicated and, among those who have pondered it, not well or reliably understood.[61] Nonetheless, there is reason to believe that the problem leads to adaptive failures in the acquiring and processing of, and reacting to, signals from a problem context. Furthermore, it seems to involve many human frailties, including perceptual and cognitive distortions that follow from one's limitations to categorize data, process information, and simply remember.[62] All of these cognitive characteristics reduce the accuracy and pertinence of one's estimates.[63] While as individuals we everyday successfully simplify the world around us to reduce uncertainty, the amount of success achieved in collective efforts is not nearly as great.[64]

Analysts and decision makers have different motivations, different life experiences, divergent purposes, and often different intellectual capabilities and training, all of which suggest reasons why identical factual situations so often produce extremely different alternatives for action.[65] This may be important if individual differences become so great as to hamper decision making or to impede system operations. Different goals may help determine whether a problem gets recognized and brought to the attention of an organization (as we saw in Chapter 2). Institutional structure and the roles individuals perform within organizations set out the conditions under which problems and opportunities will be appraised and acted upon.[66] Communication channels, complexity, uncertainty, the age of an institution, and myriad other factors have all been implicated in studies of why problems are seen and treated so differently by diverse organizations—or even the same organization under altered circumstances.[67]

Despite concern for the collective element of misperception, individuals must appreciate and correct (either as individuals or through their organizations) poor or inappropriate system performance. This has been well characterized, albeit pessimistically, by Richard Betts in terms of "[p]olicy premises [that] constrict perception, and administrative workloads [that] constrain reflection," and "The interaction of analytic uncertainty and decisional prudence is a vicious circle that makes the segregation of empirical intelligence [estimation or analysis] and normative policy a Platonic ideal."[68] Largely in anticipation of the very real restrictions Betts emphasizes, the following specifications of and justifications for the policy sciences as a separate discipline and profession were long ago offered by Lasswell:

> A policy orientation . . . is directed toward the policy process, and in part toward the intelligence needs of policy. The first task, which is the development of a science of policy forming and execution, uses the methods of social and psychological inquiry. The second task, which is the improving of the concrete content of the information and the interpretations available to

policymakers, typically goes outside the boundaries of social science and psychology.[69]

This orientation frees the analyst from Betts' vicious circle of institutional requirements and, at the same time, accesses any and all potentially useful intellectual disciplines and estimation methods to solve problems. Or, as Lasswell puts it: "We can think of the policy sciences as the disciplines concerned with explaining the policy-making and policy-executing process, and with locating data and providing interpretations which are relevant to the policy problems of a given period."[70]

In going outside the boundaries, one faces problems that do not inhibit conventional discipline-based inquiries as much. The identification and selection of information for use by decision makers must necessarily be tied to the analyst's judgment about the likely nature and importance of evolving problems; such judgments will be independent of many institutional constraints but still need to be made while considering the decision maker's willingness and capacity to realize the information's pertinence and utility; such properties are worth exploring to discover areas of possible misperception and resistance.[71] Often important factual information is missing and, within the constraints of time and other resources, identifying and assemblying it may not be possible. As Bardach and others have cautioned, those involved in estimation analyses seldom have an embarrassment of data riches—or at least, data bearing directly on the specific policy problem.[72] Besides the exercise of judgment about what is likely to be important and the development of a realistic sense of what a decision maker needs and can use from the analyst, estimation can be viewed in terms of resolving difficult questions of the following sort: Can the decision maker be supplied with defensible estimates of what is likely to happen if a given policy option is pursued (including the option of doing nothing at all)? Can the analyst assess in timely fashion policy alternatives that the decision maker might not have otherwise considered?[73]

Trying to answer such questions by relying on the rationalistic methods and procedures of the usual academic disciplines does not account very well for the irrational components of decision encapsulated in the notions of the perceptions problem or the institutional vicious circle, nor does it respond well to the task of policy creation—a task beyond the reach of technique and method. "Genuine creation," according to philosopher Barrett, "is precisely that for which we can give no prescribed technique or recipe; and technique reaches its limits precisely at that point beyond which real creativity is called for—in the sciences as well as the arts."[74]

Rationalism versus instrumentalism

Unresolved in much current policy analysis is a deeper tension well known to students of the history and progress of thought. Rationalism, an orientation that places great weight on the power of the mind (reason) to discern orderliness and intelligibility in the world, had its adherents (Descartes and Spinoza)[75] and its detractors (Locke).[76] In more recent times, positivism, with its logical postulate that valid inquiry can only follow faithful adherence to scientific method, and irrationalism, in which a denial of the world's posited underlying orderliness raises doubt about the comprehending power of reason, offer distinctly antithetical views and prospects for the analytic enterprise.[77] While not wishing to press final judgment on any of these powerful modes of thought—ours is a different and more practical task—it does appear that rationalism and positivism have had considerable impact on the theories and methods one encounters in estimation. The results have been mixed.

> The normative structure of traditional policy analysis puts a good deal of faith in the power of the logic of choice drawn from economics, statistical decision theory, and operations research, to aid in decision-making in a way regarded as ethically neutral. But the logic of choice depends on prior specification of objectives, or agreement about the nature of relevant benefits and costs. . . . The power of the logic also depends on the strength of the underlying scientific understanding of a problem that enables one to trace relationships between means and ends and to identify salient alternatives.[78]

Prior specification and agreement, in Nelson's terms, are central objectives sought throughout the policy process, but vigorously so during initiation and estimation. Neither can be presumed; both relate to Lasswell's first, or policy-forming and executing, task. Lacking adequately powerful theories or even much fundamental data, the contribution of the rational-scientific approach to policy analysis has been limited: realistic aspects leading to Lasswell's second—the information and interpretation—task.

Another who early recognized many of these problems, John Dewey, responded constructively in a form which has since been labeled instrumentalism.[79] Dewey offers an optimistic grounding for analysis by recognizing that knowledge is conditional on experience and emphasizing experimentation as a means to approach feasible and desirable solutions to human problems. His hopes are conciliatory:

> [The instrumental approach] would permit the co-operation of those who respect the past and the institutionally established with those who are interested in establishing a freer and happier future. For it would determine the conditions under which the funded experience of the past and the contriving intelligence which looks to the future can effectively interact with each other. It would enable men to glorify the claims of reason without at the same time falling into a paralyzing worship of super-empirical authority or into an offensive "rationalization" of things as they are.[80]

Going outside the boundaries: A broader perspective

Attaining a clearer understanding of the use of knowledge in policy- and decision making helps one come to realistic terms with estimation.[81] The central parties, analysts and decision makers, must learn the current condition of the problem context, understand how it evolved to the present state, decide on what direction it is moving, assess where it ought to go in the future, and imagine how various decision options will likely affect the future.[82] Many intellectual traditions and skills will be needed to appreciate and assault the complexity, uncertainty, and conflict that characterize most decision settings. In addition to intellectual ecumenism (stressed earlier in the Introduction as a call for multimethods), the analyst must be prepared to create new methods and techniques in accord with challenges presented by specific problems. Failing to do so, according to the gifted mathematician John von Neumann, leads to "very grave dangers," including "more purely aesthetizing," and "more purely *l'art pour l'art*." That is, "the [technical] discipline will become a disorganized mass of details and complexities," subject to revitalization only by "reinjection of more or less directly empirical [realistic] ideas."[83]

While no one technique or metric will be appropriate for use under all circumstances, combinations may be encountered in specific situations. Besides learning to recognize when to use, blend, or create techniques and procedures, the analyst must also become proficient in appreciating the limitations of technique generally and the shortcomings of any one technique in particular application.[84]

We do not claim that the choice of estimation techniques can be determined solely by technical means; rather we contend that broad and judicious application of such means may improve the number and quality of alternatives eventually considered by those responsible for decisions, and indeed, the quality of the decisions themselves, assuming effective policy is our benchmark. We sympathize with but cannot accept Barrett's gloomy, existential posture.

> Yet the belief in the decisive role of technique has not vanished; it has passed from the philosophers into the culture at large. It has become a general faith, widespread even when it is unvoiced, that technique and technical organization are the necessary and sufficient conditions for arriving at truth; that they can encompass all truth; and that they will be sufficient, if not at the moment, then shortly, to answer the questions that life thrusts upon us.[85]

It is one thing to despair, it is quite another to realize that decisions, for better or worse, continue to be made and often made with scant information, under constricting time pressures, and with slight regard for more than a handful of their most noxious consequences. Certainly we must do better than this. The underlying assumption of this book, and particularly the chapters in this part, is that we can.

A survey of general procedures

Broad categories of procedures showing promise to this end include contextual mapping, decision seminars, developmental constructs, prototyping, and participant observation.[86] Each represents an instrumental (in

Dewey's sense) contribution to the estimation task; each has been employed successfully in specific settings; but each, as with any method or procedure, has limitations.[87] We illustrate many of these procedures subsequently.

Specific procedures for dealing with complexity are summarized in the following table (Table 4–1). The selection of one or more of these is, naturally, an important analytic judgment made with respect to the specific problem at hand.

The main purpose of displaying these diverse procedures is to stress that numerous management tactics exist to reduce complexity, most of these have been used, and could be taken, modified, or fitted to new or different problem situations. The tool kit is not bare; rather the problem seems to be more one of quite limited imagination or professional reluctance in applying the tools.[88]

Other specific procedures, often overlapping those related to complexity reduction, exist and have been used to reduce uncertainty in the problem setting. It is interesting to note that the reduction of complexity may have the added bonus of also reducing uncertainty, depending on the skill and good fortune of analysts. However, complexity and uncertainty are not equivalent. We have treated the former previously in this chapter and consider the latter to mean entities or situations in which one does not have dependable, reliable, or sure knowledge; or, entities or situations that are indeterminate, problematical, or not clearly defined. Insensitive reduction of complexity may, for instance, produce the paradoxical result of increasing uncertainty by allowing actually important elements of a problem to be set aside or downplayed that, in time, may figure prominently in realized outcomes. For instance, decision theory may be used as a means of aggregating preferences in a situation and hence reducing the inherent complexity; however, failure to treat the numerous elements left out of the formal decision calculus may very easily lead to surprises. The importance of analytic judgment and skill and the need to consult other analytic interpretations of the problem are both emphasized once again.[89]

Many specific procedures exist to reduce uncertainty; a sampling of the general types and classes is summarized in Table 4–2.

Effective decision makers instinctively know that rationality and scientific procedures help answer "only one of three crucial questions overarching key decisions: These are: (a) Does it add up? (b) Does it sound okay? and (c) Does it feel right? Logic and science contribute primarily to the first question, less to the second, and even less to the third."[90] In such circumstances one must apprehend, in Siu's lexicon, the context well enough to mitigate conflict and to improve the chances for successful decision making.[91] Besides apprehension, other procedures to these ends can be imagined (Table 4–3).

Evident in many conflict-reducing procedures is a blending of estimation and selection tasks, and this is appropriate. As estimation moves closer to the moment of decision, greater care and attention are demanded to adjust

TABLE 4–1   Procedures to reduce complexity[*]

Model the complexity:
    Decompose, treat serially, reconfigure: simulation, causal models, mathematical analyses.

    Input/output models: especially macroeconomic models.

    "Go for broke": world, regional, total systems and other large-scale models.

Formulate alternatives:
    Morphological analyses: structural/functional models, graph theory.

    Regulations and comparisons: set theory models, logic, semantics.

    Alternative futures: scenario generation, utopian and anti-utopian "stories."

Problem diagnosis and rediagnosis:
    Concentrate on structural certainties: studies of habit, custom, procedural constraints; legalistic, anthropological, and sociological inquiries.

    Focus on changes: marginal analyses, discrete-event analyses (e.g., constitutional as in elections and non-constitutional as in coups d'etat and revolutions).

    Determine priorities among competing problems: market studies, public opinion surveys, elite interviews, psychiatric profiles and surveys, other intensive methods of inquiry (e.g., in-depth interviews and extended or panel surveys), group opinion techniques.

Aggregate information:
    Create data banks: social accounting schemes, cleaning and fine-tuning of existing operational data (e.g., economic and census), collate data from diverse research and operational sources with respect to a given problem area (e.g., Energy Information Agency).

    Establish and/or improve communication structures and networks: information clearing houses, library and archival activities, study and seminar groups (e.g., decision seminars, social planetaria), commissions with a specific subject matter objective.

    Collect expert opinions: Delphi, cross-impact matrices, surveys, interviews.

    Enlist external participation: public hearings, conferences, interviews.

    Build information processing capacities: computer networks, dedicated computer systems, early warning systems.

Aggregate preferences:
    Model the preferences: utility theory, decision theory, public choice models.

    Estimate payoffs under various strategic conditions: game theory.

    Optimize: linear programming, interactive programming.

    Experiment: prototypes, demonstrations, social experiments.

    Propagandize: media events, "blitzes," "arm twisting," "jaw-boning."

---

[*] We are indebted to a colleague, Bruce G. Blair, for suggesting this list, which we have elaborated upon to suit the current discussion.

the options and alternatives to the decisional realities. Failing to do so, even when convinced of the wisdom and desirability of a specific course, may lead to the most egregious outcomes imaginable. American efforts to achieve a natural gas deregulation bill, during the period extending from mid-1977 through late 1978, can be assessed this way; while the underlying

---

TABLE 4–2   Procedures to reduce uncertainty[*]

Model the uncertainty:
> Forecast: time-series models and extrapolations, critical event analysis, path analysis.
>
> Compute: objective probability distributions, subjective probability distributions.
>
> Strategize: game theory, risk analysis, utility analysis and models, decision theory and models.

Generate and test alternatives:
> Heuristics: brainstorming, free-form and scenario-based games, free-association and other psychiatric techniques, synectics.
>
> Simulate: simulation and sensitivity analyses.
>
> Experiment: small-scale models, prototyping, demonstrations, social experiments.

Acquire information:
> Data collection.
>
> Compute: determine expected value of obtaining additional information (e.g., economics of information).
>
> Investigate: a "peak is worth two finesses" in bridge—and in analysis.

Affect consequences:
> Contract with the environment: control of markets, coopt possible opponents, delegate subordinates.
>
> Diversify: develop different tactics to attain objectives, indifference analysis.
>
> Refine objectives: means-ends analysis, goal clarification techniques.

---

[*] Besides the suggestions of Blair, earlier noted, ideas for table 4–2 have been gleaned from Albert Madansky, "Uncertainty," in E. S. Quade and W. I. Boucher, eds., *Systems Analysis and Policy Planning* (New York: American Elsevier, 1968), chap. 5.

TABLE 4–3   Procedures to reduce conflict (and to enhance decision success)

Apprehension:
> Full immersion in the context.
>
> Wholistic strategies: Begin with big picture and reduce unnecessary and less relevant elements to achieve a relatively correct but imprecise appreciation of the total situation.
>
> Use distinct observational perspectives: View the problem from as many different standpoints as there are relevant and concerned participants.
>
> Create and maintain alternative tactical means to desired ends: Resist arguments that favor only one course of action; reject analyses that purport to have optimized or solved a problem once and for all.

Compromise:
> Devise tactical plans which not only result in strategic accomplishment but do so in ways that allow different conditions of quid pro quo to evolve.

TABLE 4–3 (*concluded*)

Explore, through experimentation, trial balloons, or even formal analyses (e.g., game-theoretic in kind) diverse pay-off possibilities to those affected by proposed alternatives.

Anticipate bargaining situations and opportunities using scenarios, seminar-based gaming, and other exploratory and heuristic procedures.

"Leave a little on the table for the dealer": Generate opportunities for third-parties to participate in one's tactical plans, and then reward such interventions appropriately.

Integration:

Game the decision situation to determine areas of potential conflict, including a determination of who might object and the means by which this will be manifest.

Incorporate into the estimation process those whose objections to the plan are least threatening or mainly symbolic—not substantive: Convene study groups, commissions, or other parallel estimation activities.

Diversion and avoidance:

Segment the problem and treat decision serially: Do what is feasible; do what either costs least or benefits most first before proceeding to more costly and/or less beneficial parts of the problem; develop institutional sunk costs that eventually commit one to a course of action.

Redefine the problem to limit the scope of discourse to relatively insensitive or unimportant aspects: Keep the troops occupied.

Classify the problem to limit consideration or deliberation: Use procedural rules and other formalities.

Delegate problem analysis to research groups under direct operational and/or financial control (e.g., in-house or "tame" analytic groups or firms; blue-ribbon panels or commissions).

Swamp the information environment with tons of facts.

Filibuster or otherwise obstruct normal decision-making channels.

Create a diversion to divert attention away from the problem: Take a trip (and take the press corps with you); make a spectacular announcement.

Bring new and sympathetic participants into the situation, i.e., dilute the possible opposition.

Do nothing until a crisis develops with attendant pressure to act.

Create and/or exploit a crisis:

Alienate known opponents to precipitate a crisis.

Symbolize the problem in the most threatening terms to heighten popular insecurity, e.g., boycott the Olympic Games as a national security action.

Withhold analytic results until the environment appears willing to accept hard choices, or at least those that appear possible, albeit Draconian.

---

economic rationale favoring deregulation was simple and appreciated by most economists, determining political feasibility and means to reduce conflict was neither as simple nor as well appreciated.[92] Good analysis made for very bad politics.[93] It added up, but it didn't feel right—to many decision makers.

We return to the world of politics in its relation to estimation at the conclusion of this part. We also illustrate in greater detail many of the specific technical procedures mentioned here, but this, too, must wait until the process of estimation is itself better understood.

THE HUMAN OUGHT AND THE RATIONAL IS

Abraham Kaplan, eminent philosopher and social scientist, has commented: "Political morality . . . is intrinsic to all policy whose decisions significantly affect the value placed on things human. Public morality is the morality of public policy."[94] Those concerned and responsible for the estimation phase are obligated to understand this point and to call attention to the multiple dimensions of complex social contexts. Regard for the man-centered—or hominocentric—basis of these tasks has been stressed by Kaplan and Lasswell, among others:

> As science, [hominocentric politics] finds its subject matter in interpersonal relations, not abstract institutions or organizations; and it sees the person as whole, in all his aspects, not as the embodiment of this or that limited set of needs or interests. As policy, it prizes not the glory of a depersonalized state or the efficiency of a social mechanism, but human dignity and the realization of human capacities.[95]

Human dignity includes freedom, the sharing of power among the many rather than the few, as well as widespread participation in all other value processes. Even though circumstances change, the humane aims of a democratic society are permanent. The task is to specify and respecify them in concrete circumstances via specific policy measures, so that whatever potential for progress exists can be realized.[96]

The problem with most estimation activities, particularly those founded on scientific or other rational philosophies, is that the methods require the projection of order on the problem; however, this projective act, involving the breaking down into parts and the ordering of these in accordance with the dictates of theory and method, presupposes an answer to the problem. Scientific simplification, in short, embeds ethical presumptions that always bias possible outcomes. For instance, confronting the horror of child abuse or negligence, the twin effects of role and training cause the physician's attention to be directed to immediate health needs to reduce suffering and make the child well. In the same circumstance, a judge or lawyer would care less for the immediate well-being of the child, and focus on matters of legal assistance, custody, and long-term care. A psychiatrist, as distinguished from a general practitioner, would respond to the psychological environment that contributed to the abuse and propose therapeutic recommendations to lessen the deep-seated, stress-provoking conditions that lead to abuse.[97] Each specialized perspective, in this example and for many complex problems, carries with it ethical baggage founded on individual personality traits, past experiences, training, and many other factors. Such baggage, or presumptions, help the specialist get oriented to a new situation by providing cues and guidance to some of its aspects while weighting others less. Outcomes, in the sense of determining what is right, best, or most appropriate, are understandably biased as a result.

Failure to understand this fundamental point has many roots, not the least of which is a common lack of appreciation of the contextual nature of values. Values are not absolute and can be appraised only with respect to a concrete setting: "a description of a value of a commodity refers to that commodity in its environment. Value is not a property of the commodity in abstract, but the commodity *in situ*."[98] For instance, the statement "children should not be abused," while having superficial appeal, is relatively meaningless without an adequate specification of the time, place, and other circumstances in which this value is to be sought. Spanking a child in some cultures is commonly regarded as abuse; it may or may not be in American society, depending on who is doing the spanking, the age of the child, the contributing circumstances, and the force with which the punishment is delivered; in ancient Sparta, to make the point vividly, physical abuse reportedly had positive value.[99]

Emphasizing the contextual nature of problems and circumstances is a positive reminder of a fundamental task of policy estimation:

> Policy has to do with man's problems in coping with his future. . . . Policy brings to statement what is judged to be possible, desirable, and meaningful for the human enterprise. In this sense, policy is the nexus of fact, value, and ultimate meaning in which scientific, ethical, and theological-philosophical reflections meet.[100]

Human beings continually orient themselves to the future, and policy is one concrete manifestation or embodiment of the collective perception of the future. This collective image is itself the product of many individual renditions, each of which has been filtered through a value system uniquely determined based on one's identity, expectations, and experience. The future is filled with numerous unrealized potentialities which the individual may imagine and appraise according to a personal set of values before selecting those believed to be best.[101]

Something approaching rationality appears to exist at the level of the individual's abstracted and much simplified view of the world, or one's image of it, in Kenneth Boulding's terms. The difficulty arises in reconciling and aggregating (i.e., estimating) many different views in anticipation of decision. The importance of ensuring that these individual views are well informed and that as many of them as pertain to the problem at hand are considered are fundamental requisites for democratic decision making. Even working hard to these ends, however, does not remove the essential, human element of choice or judgment: "A human must choose or decide on the system requirements. He may derive them from the needs the system is to satisfy or by computations from more primitive information about what is wanted. [But] he must order the requirements as essential and less important."[102]

It is in the future, in our attempts to manipulate the state of the social system through purposive acts, that the true importance and enormous difficulty of the estimation tasks are most pronounced, for "The problem of policy is ultimately how the future is grasped and appraised. The essential meaning of responsibility is accountability in human fulfillment in the shaping of the society's future."[103]

Troublesome impediments

In the absence of any consensually accepted social accounting scheme[104] or estimation standards,[105] much of what passes for policy analysis necessarily deals with qualitative variables of problematic value. Confronted with this condition, the estimation specialist resorts to one or a few simplifying tactics. Primary reliance may be placed on hard indicators, usually expressed in monetary or demographic metrics, thereby slighting the qualitative imponderables; or, as is the case of decision and preference analyses,[106] the policy analyst may boldly attack qualitative aspects of the problem, such as the political values at issue, so as to quantify such soft indicators.[107] The attack is rarely successful, for among other reasons noted by Dahl, "The language of political values is perhaps most easily translated into the language of qualitative data: but it stubbornly resists accurate and satisfying translation into the language of quantitative data."[108] Practically, these troublesome soft variables are not often treated with the sensitivity they warrant and are maligned by the analyst's coarse tools, as in the instance of heroic assumptions made to devise a clean formulation of the problem.[109]

Despite these pessimistic warnings, experience shows that the qualitative features of problems can be analyzed, and often to advantage. Specialized estimation techniques have been devised and used over the years to study values,[110] propaganda,[111] symbols[112] (even including those embodied in public buildings[113]), and goals.[114] Common limitations, from the point of view of ready and frequent use in policy estimation, of many of these otherwise constructive approaches and techniques are that they have been conducted by a very few individuals in quite disparate disciplines so that the cumulative practical impact of the work has been diminished and they are rarely integrated into predominantly technical, quantitative analyses receiving most decision-making attention in our society.

This seductive influence of technique has been recognized; however, awareness either has not been broadly shared or it has been rejected by many technicians. The longer-term description of the matter is presented by Geoffrey Vickers:

During the past two centuries, men gained knowledge and power, which vastly increased their ability to predict and control; and they used these powers to make a world increasingly unpredictable and uncontrollable. . . . Nonetheless, the belief persisted that increased power to alter the environment brought increased control over it. This belief, still far from dead, is a manifest delusion.

*   *   *   *   *

Powerful new tools always change the processes to which they are introduced. In time the entire activity is modified to suit what the new tools can and cannot do. This has been the history of industrial technology and it will surely be the history of technology applied to the political process.[115]

A more practical, and immediate, illustration revolves around American failures, in the wake of years of highly technical analyses of the strategic balance of power, to recognize the legitimate perceptions, needs, and political realities of our European allies in our calculations. Michael Howard makes the basic case for inclusion of these forgotten issues, and Dönhoff and Makins draw the realistic implications of not considering qualitative aspects of decisions about cruise missile and neutron bomb deployments in Europe.[116] Continuing to forget with regard to planned deployment of Pershing II missiles in the fall and spring of 1981–82 resulted in massive public demonstrations and threats to the European alliance.

As all too often seems to be the case, the limits and failures of policy analysis, a form of technology applied to the political process, do not lead to honest assessment of underlying frailties or deficiencies, rather they appear to stimulate increased demands for the same kind of work, and even in increasing amounts.[117]

Among other confounding impediments, the variety of individual preferences, the conflicts that exist among them, and the difficulty of even comprehending what these preferences are all contribute to many estimation difficulties.[118] Preference scales are not stable; they are not wholly, or reliably, determinate.[119] Indeed, to the extent that the familiar political processes of goal determination and consensus building are not somehow captured in a policy analysis, it may become rather academic and benign (at best) or misleading and harmful (at worst). Quite typically, political officials are unable to articulate their own preferences, except in vague platitudes; neither do they demonstrate great awareness of what other's preferences might be.[120] While these limitations may even have some benefit—stating vague goals, a politician may be able to maintain certain flexibility through time—it makes analysis very difficult.

Analysis: To what ends?

The importance of contextual goals, or the ought of society, is a well established fundamental of estimation.[121] It forces attention on the identification of judgmental criteria for use in assessing the worth and value of any proposed decision alternative. These criteria are malleable; they are subject to manipulation and change in the face of changing circumstances. For instance, representative general criteria encountered include the maximization of freedom, rationality, security, and progress;[122] limitations on conflict and rates of social change;[123] incentives for increased stability of economic and social systems, pluralism and consensus;[124] and pleas to increase human dignity.[125]

So many general criteria, and hence reasons for doing analysis, confound estimation. What should an analyst do? Some define their problems so that attaining a single goal is the same as reaching a solution. However, most social problems are not, in the technical sense, well-defined;[126] declaring and attaining a single goal seldom result in satisfactory problem solution.[127] The analyst is required to consider many legitimate goals and to assess the likely consequences of trade-offs, such as those existing generally between equality and efficiency or specifically among program elements. For instance, many public policies to aid the disadvantaged yield few, if any, economic benefits to society; they are enacted to advance equity goals.[128] Within the program portfolio of a single agency, another kind of trade-off occurs: When the secretary of defense proposes an increase in strategic weapons while holding steady or reducing other forces, trade-offs based on estimates have occurred.[129]

By what means?

Policy analysts often oversimplify and hence overlook these important matters. One illustration would be when operations researchers attempt to maximize or minimize a social objective function.[130] Although many policy estimates stress rational calculation, as we have discovered, the problems of multiple and changing goals are seldom directly confronted in such analyses.

Critical path analysis, including Program Evaluation and Review Technique (PERT) and Critical Path Method (CPM), has been used in information theory, research and development project management, and transportation system design; its applications to other social problem areas is often advocated.[131] The basic idea can be pictured (Figure 4–2). The shortest route through the network of nodes is $S—B—D—Goal$, and yields a value of 13. However, for the successful attainment of the goal, a complicating condition might be to accomplish all tasks (i.e., touch all nodes) and to do so in the shortest distance (or least cost). A possible solution to this would be

$$S—C—B \Big\langle{}^{A}_{E}—D—Goal,$$

with a value of 21. Or the job may be complicated by imposing one more condition: all tasks must be accomplished, but in alphabetical (logical) order, a condition that adds to the difficulty (cost or distance) of attainment. In this case, a new link between C and D had to be created, which would add an unexpected increment to the network total cost or value of 28. (Simply moving from C to D has a value of 11; the cost of creating the link would be determined separately.) Of course a possibility exists to explore the feasibility of linking nodes more efficiently (shortening distances/reducing costs), creating links (done to satisfy the final condition), and/or collapsing two or more components into fewer number. More fundamentally, critical path analysis will be appropriate only if a desired goal or end state is known and accepted by those involved with the task and if alternative paths can be posed, evaluated, and rationally chosen. Establishing the instrumental conditions is also an open question. In all of this, the question of valuation becomes as important as the problem of analysis when the path actually followed in realistic social problem solving is a tentative and shifting result of many conflicting and inconsistent norms and where the uncertainties about the value or costs of transiting through the task network are large.

Developing and articulating the nodes and values are prime functions of the policy estimator; discussing how one ought to choose both goals and alternatives falls within the philosopher's domain; but navigating the path is primarily the responsibility of the politician, who "has to balance the myriad forces as he sees best, and the citizens judge him only to a limited extent by his accordance with their preconceived ideas. Rather, a great political leader is judged like a great composer: one looks to see what he has created."[132] To the extent that these ideas and concerns are not adequately understood and integrated into policy estimation, certain tensions and misapprehensions are bound to occur.

FIGURE 4–2   Illustration of critical path analysis: a network diagram

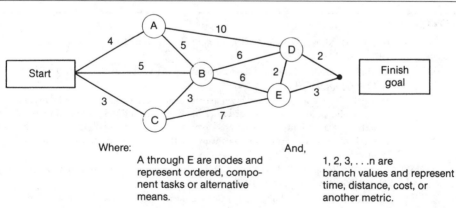

Where:

A through E are nodes and represent ordered, component tasks or alternative means.

And,

1, 2, 3, . . .n are branch values and represent time, distance, cost, or another metric.

There are no "answers"

One must begin to appreciate the extraordinarily difficult tasks represented by estimation. A most striking realization is that there are no answers whose truth can be proved and whose efficacy can be confidently foretold. Rather, one hopes that analysis will enhance understanding of problems and create opportunities to exploit many perspectives of them by using diverse criteria to represent the hopes and expectations of those whose lives will be touched by pending decisions.[133] There are no best or correct answers, only numerous imaginable possibilities whose ultimate significance can only be comprehended in the aftermath of experience.

The decision setting is ever changing and truly knowable only through experience. Estimation precedes this experience; it is synthetic and, hence, nearly always errs.[134] The point is to appreciate the inevitable mistakes by working hard to minimize them—by taking a broader view, working self-consciously with both part and whole of a problem, including the values and perspectives of as many who have a stake and interest in the problem, and using a variety of analytic methods and disciplined perspectives. These essential aspects of estimation suggest attitudes and procedures substantially different from those usually encountered.[135] A strong sense of humility and many explicit measures to anticipate, search out, and correct inevitable errors of prior formulation of alternatives and possible errors in future decision and execution are strongly recommended.

> We must either leave science alone altogether and forgo its tranformation of means, or else integrate it with our moral aspirations and forgo the fixity of traditional ends. A belief is not scientific because it has been "proved" but because it is continuously tested and revised by conformity to experience rather than to axiomatic truths.[136]

We next turn to several means by which science can be used to advantage to help conduct policy estimation.

NOTES

1. Charles E. Merriam, *New Aspects of Politics* (Chicago: University of Chicago Press, 1925), pp. 124–25.

2. Herbert A. Simon, "The Architecture of Complexity," *General Systems Yearbook*, vol. 10 (1965), pp. 63–64.

3. Because of convention, we shall often use the terms "analyst" and "analysis" to stand for, respectively, an individual engaged in estimation work and the product of those labors. Strictly speaking, however, "analysis" is used throughout this book in a much more general sense which allows one to conceive of the whole decision process in "analytic" terms.

4. Richard Bellman and Robert Kalaba, *Dynamic Programming and Modern Control Theory* (New York: Academic Press, 1965), p. 5.

5. George A. Miller, *The Psychology of Communication* (New York: Basic Books, 1967), pp. 49–50.

6. Todd R. La Porte, ed., *Organized Social Complexity: Challenge to Politics and Policy* (Princeton, N.J.: Princeton University Press, 1975), presents a collection of essays that explore this matter in some detail.

7. A theoretical and methodological discussion is contained in Ronald D. Brunner and Garry D. Brewer, *Organized Complexity* (New York: Free Press, 1971).

8. Richard L. Strout, "Poor Nations Bear the Brunt of New Oil Prices," *Christian Science Monitor*, June 12, 1980.

9. Jonathan David Aronson, ed., *Debt and the Less Developed Countries* (Boulder, Colo.: Westview Press, 1979), details the extent and risks inherent in the extraordinarily high levels of debt. One of the more interesting aspects of the fluctuations in world oil prices is that movement up and down in very short periods of time can be as unsettling as the levels finally achieved. The systems are not only connected, but they are not able to absorb rapid changes easily.

10. Strout, "Poor Nations," p. 3. The "sheikh" in this little parable may well come to realize something about complex systems in the event that consumption for oil slacks or buyers find ways to avoid having to pay extremely high prices for it.

11. Robert L. Sinsheimer, "The Brain of Pooh: An Essay on the Limits of Mind," *American Scientist* 59, no. 1 (1971), pp. 20–28, is a delightful exploration of this.

12. Not a new insight, to be sure: Francis Bacon, *Novum Organum* in *Great Books of the Western World*, vol. 35 (Chicago: Encyclopaedia Britannica, 1952), p. 110.

13. Lloyd S. Etheredge, "Personality Effects on American Foreign Policy," *American Political Science Review*, June 1978, pp. 434–51, adopts and elaborates this theme in terms of personal motivations, individual behavioral patterns, and human insecurities.

14. As reported in Morton Halperin, *Bureaucratic Politics and Foreign Policy* (Washington, D.C.: The Brookings Institution, 1974), p. 171.

15. Some have even gone so far as to express their frustration with those in the environmental movement, believing that their efforts have mainly resulted in a slowing and disorientation of necessary energy-related decisions. Attention to the "big picture" gives way to "fragmented and personalized interests and values . . . difficult to reconcile with integrated and rational planning and foresight." Harvey Brooks, "Technology: Hope or Catastrophe?" *Technology In Society*, Spring 1979, p. 15.

16. Graham T. Allison, "Conceptual Models and the Cuban Missile Crisis," *American Political Science Review*, September 1969, p. 700.

17. John Steinbruner refers to this shortcoming as "grooved thinking," in which familiar situations are well handled, at least in the short run and with very little of what we are describing as estimation actions. See his *The Cybernetic Theory of Decision* (Princeton, N.J.: Princeton University Press, 1974), p. 127.

18. David Braybrooke and Charles E. Lindblom, *A Strategy of Decision* (New York: Free Press, 1963), p. 85.

19. The example and the general problem are treated in Todd R. La Porte, "On the Design and Management of Nearly Error-Free Organizational Control Systems," in David L. Sills, C. P. Wolf, and Vivien B. Shelanski, eds., *Accident at Three Mile Island* (Boulder, Colo.: Westview Press, 1981).

20. The problem is acute, and well known by now. For example, see Hans H. Landsberg et al., *Energy: The Next Twenty Years* (Cambridge, Mass.: Ballinger, 1979), chaps. 1, 8, and especially 14.

21. Strobe Talbot, *Endgame* (New York: Harper & Row, 1977), describes this in detail and with lucidity.

22. The "worst-case" mentality is generally treated in Raymond L. Garthoff, "On Estimating and Imputing Intentions," *International Security* 2, no. 3 (1978), pp. 22–32. A specific

example, related to a phantom "missile gap," is documented in Roy E. Licklider, "The Missile Gap Controversy," *Political Science Quarterly* 85, no. 4 (1970), pp. 600–15.

23. The German invasion is described in Barton Whaley, *Codeword BARBAROSSA* (Cambridge, Mass.: MIT Press, 1973); Roberta Wohlstetter, *Pearl Harbor: Warning and Decision* (Stanford, Calif.: Stanford University Press, 1962), is the standard reference for the latter example.

24. These are actually quite different situations, as discussed in Chapter 3.

25. For the classic economic argument, see Joseph A. Schumpeter, *The Theory of Economic Development* (Cambridge, Mass.: Harvard University Press, 1934), "Preface." For a modern interpretation, see Richard R. Nelson and Sidney G. Winter, "Toward an Evolutionary Theory of Economic Capabilities," *American Economic Review*, May 1973, pp. 440–49.

26. Robert Jervis, "Hypotheses on Misperception," *World Politics* 20, no. 4 (1968), pp. 454–79.

27. Empirical work supports this possibility: Thornton B. Roby, Elizabeth H. Nicol, and Francis M. Farrell, "Group Problem Solving under Two Types of Executive Structure," *Journal of Abnormal and Social Psychology* 67, no. 6 (1963), pp. 550–56.

28. Michael N. Danielson, Alan M. Hershey, and John M. Bayne, *One Nation, So Many Governments* (Lexington, Mass.: Lexington Books, 1977), pp. 30–40, provide a tightly argued summary of this main point.

29. Alvin Weinberg, "Social Institutions and Nuclear Energy," *Science,* 7 July 1972, pp. 27–34.

30. Alouph Hareven, "Disturbed Hierarchy: Israeli Intelligence in 1954 and 1973," *Jerusalem Quarterly* 9, no. 1 (1978), pp. 3–19.

31. Frank Stech, a psychologist concerned with national security matters, is not well known outside of a small circle of professional colleagues. His most recent work, *Political and Military Intention Estimation* (Bethesda, Md.: MATHTECH, November 1979), from which this example is drawn [p. 153], suggests he should be.

32. This position differs significantly from that advanced by Charles E. Lindblom and David K. Cohen in *Usable Knowledge: Social Science and Social Problem Solving* (New Haven: Yale University Press, 1979), especially chap. 2. This difference reveals our own bias toward a constructive role for estimation which Lindblom and Cohen do not completely share.

33. C. Smart and I. Vertinsky, "Designs for Crisis Decision Units," *Administrative Sciences Quarterly* 22, no. 4 (1977), pp. 640–57, present an orderly and thorough summary of these and many other limiting factors.

34. Frank Snepp, *Decent Interval* (New York: Random House, 1977), p. 179.

35. Graham T. Allison, *Essence of Decision* (Boston: Little, Brown, 1971), can be read profitably with this point of view in mind.

36. Irving L. Janis, *Victims of Groupthink* (Boston: Houghton Mifflin, 1972), treats the subject with such skill and conviction that the term groupthink has by now passed into the popular culture.

37. Some experimental evidence gives credence to this claim: See Mauk Mulder, "Communication Structure, Decision Structure, and Group Performance," *Sociometry* 23, no. 1 (1960), pp. 1–14.

38. Alexander L. George, "The Case for Multiple Advocacy in Making Foreign Policy," *American Political Science Review*, September 1972, pp. 751–85, is a sophisticated treatment of the problem. His various suggestions warrant consideration and adoption.

39. A consistent theme in many of his writings, the mixed concerns of participation, full

explication, and explicit value analysis all show prominently in Harold D. Lasswell, *A Pre-View of Policy Sciences* (New York: American Elsevier, 1971); for concrete examples, see Harold D. Lasswell, "The Political Science of Science," *American Political Science Review*, December 1956, pp. 961–79.

40. Simon, "Architecture of Complexity," p. 64.

41. Garry D. Brewer and James S. Kakalik, *Handicapped Children: Strategies for Improving Services* (New York: McGraw-Hill, 1979), p. 65, is the source for this and related examples of "Internalization of Externalities."

42. Aubrey Milunsky, *The Prenatal Diagnosis of Hereditary Disorders* (Springfield, Ill.: Charles C. Thomas, 1973), is a thorough treatment of the capability. At the moment, it is estimated that simple custodial care of Mongoloid children (a disorder detected by amniocentesis) in America approaches $1.7 billion per year. The cost of amniocentesis varies across the country, but a planning figure of about $300 is representative.

43. Amitai Etzioni, "Public Policy Issues Raised by a Medical Breakthrough," *Policy Analysis*, Winter 1975, pp. 69–76, is a concise summary of most of these matters.

44. Richard R. Nelson, "Intellectualizing about the Moon-Ghetto Metaphor: A Study of the Current Malaise of Rational Analysis of Social Problems," *Policy Sciences*, December 1974, p. 382.

45. Eliot Marshall, "Energy Forecasts: Sinking to New Lows," *Science*, 20 June 1980, pp. 1353–54, 1356. Marshall, in the cited passage, interviewed Michehl R. Gent, of the National Electric Reliability Council, an industry cooperative formed after the 1964 New York City blackout to ensure that power supply keeps apace with demand. Gent, in this article, also noted that the effect of poor forecasts "is so enormous, on our industry anyway, because of the capital requirements. To be wrong is just catastrophic." All cites at p. 1353.

46. Just as a crisis tends to highlight selected aspects of decision, so, too, for disasters or failures in terms of focusing attention on costly unanticipated consequences. Bo Persson, *Surviving Failures* (Stockholm: Almqvist & Wiksell, 1979), part I, is directed to this theme.

47. Karl W. Deutsch, *The Nerves of Government* (New York: Free Press, 1966); Steinbruner, *Cybernetic Theory of Decision*, chap. 3; and Walter Buckley, *Sociology and Modern Systems Theory* (Englewood Cliffs, N.J.: Prentice-Hall, 1967), present, respectively, the communication, psychological, and sociological interpretations of the cybernetic or control paradigm.

48. Deutsch, *Nerves of Government*, pp. 190–91.

49. Ibid. A precise technical discussion of the control theory paradigm used by Deutsch and other social scientists is contained in G. J. Thaler and R. G. Brown, *Servomechanism Analysis* (New York: McGraw-Hill, 1953), pp. 148–62. As the world price for oil (noted in a previous example) moves up and down the decision-making burdens implicated here will tend to affect both consumers and producers.

50. Samuel P. Huntington, "Postindustrial Politics: How Benign Will it Be?" *Comparative Politics*, January 1974, pp. 163–91.

51. Daniel Bell, "The Revolution of Rising Entitlements," *Fortune*, April 1975, p. 98, is representative.

52. Harold L. Wilensky, *Organizational Intelligence* (New York: Basic Books, 1967), pp. 39–42, supports this point by indicating that estimation failures are more likely to stem from institutional (structural) limitations than individual ones.

53. John F. Collins, "Foreword," to Gilbert Levin, Edward B. Roberts, and Gary B. Hirsch, *The Persistent Poppy: A Computer-Aided Search for Heroin Policy* (Cambridge, Mass.: Ballinger, 1975), p. xiii. While quite late in the game, the analyses presented in this book appear to offer analytic insights to the problem.

54. Lucia Mouat, "Heroin Abuse Reaches Small Towns," *Christian Science Monitor*, October 8, 1974, p. 1. In 1980, heroin abuse had reached epidemic proportions in the European middle class.

55. Levin et al., *Persistent Poppy*, chap. 5, evaluate the standard responses.

56. James M. Markham, "Methadone Found Rising as Killer," *New York Times*, March 14, 1972, p. 48.

57. One symptom, and it is no more than that, reported for New York State, is a decreasing indictment rate for felonies, especially for New York City (i.e., more crimes are being committed, but fewer criminals are standing trial), and a reduction in the average length of stay in state prisons. Both factors appear to be a response to overloading the prison system. Memorandum from State Senator Marino of the New York State Select Committee on Crime, "1980 Crime Control Legislation" (Albany, N.Y.: March 28, 1980). By 1979, violent crimes in New York City, reported in excess of 123,000, were more than four times those in the next most violent city, Los Angeles, on a nominal or simple count basis. Drug related felonies of assault, larceny, and burglary all figure prominently here.

58. Martin Shubik, "Symposium: The Nature and Limitations of Forecasting," *Daedalus*, Summer 1967, pp. 941–46, makes this suggestion.

59. William Barrett, *Irrational Man* (Garden City, N.Y.: Doubleday/Anchor, 1962), p. 35.

60. "Disaster" or "catastrophe" studies are coming to the literature. B. A. Turner, "The Organizational and Interorganizational Development of Disasters," *Administrative Science Quarterly* 21, no. 3 (1976), pp. 378–97; and, Philip M. Boffey, "Investigators Agree N.Y. Blackout of 1977 Could Have Been Avoided," *Science*, 15 September 1978, pp. 994–98, offer general and specific illustrations. The contribution of an explicit consideration of possible disasters is argued well in R. K. Mark and D. E. Stuart-Alexander, "Disasters as a Necessary Part of Benefit-Cost Analysis," *Science*, 16 September 1977, pp. 1160–62. In the aggregate and through time disasters are commonplace; however, individual cases are never anticipated, so the Mark and Stuart-Alexander argument goes.

61. Walter R. Reitman, *Cognition and Thought* (New York: John Wiley & Sons, 1965); and Earl B. Hunt, *Concept Learning: An Information Processing Problem* (New York: John Wiley & Sons, 1962), both provide balanced and well-illustrated summaries of the matter. See Chap. 2, above, "Recognition of the Problem."

62. A standard technical reference is Ulric Neisser, *Cognitive Psychology* (New York: Appleton-Century-Crofts, 1967).

63. Irving L. Janis and Leon Mann, *Decision Making* (New York: Free Press, 1977), variously consider information overload, individual human limitations, group pressures, prejudice, ignorance, organizational and political matters in analyzing the rich interplay of possible contributing factors.

64. Jervis, "Misperception"; Wilensky, *Organizational Intelligence*, p. 39; and, Garthoff, "Estimating and Imputing Intentions," pp. 22–26, move, respectively, from a very theoretical, to an institutional, to a practical consideration of this shortcoming.

65. Robert Axelrod, "Schema Theory: An Information Processing Model of Perception and Cognition," *American Political Science Review*, December 1973, pp. 1248–66, is a serious treatment of this. An in-depth exploration into the foreign policy arena is provided by Lloyd S. Etheredge, *A World of Men: The Private Sources of American Foreign Policy* (Cambridge, Mass.: MIT Press, 1978). Etheredge generously acknowledges his intellectual debt to Harold D. Lasswell, particularly for the many central theoretical insights Lasswell puts forth in his *Psychopathology and Politics* (New York: Viking Press, 1960).

66. Wilensky, *Organizational Intelligence*, passim.

67. James G. March and Johan P. Olsen et al., eds., *Ambiguity and Choice in Organizations* (Bergen, Norway: Universitetsforlaget, 1976); James D. Thompson, *Organizations in Action* (New York: McGraw-Hill, 1967); and James G. March and Herbert A. Simon, *Organizations* (New York: John Wiley & Sons, 1958), all address the topics well.

68. Richard K. Betts, "Analysis, War, and Decisions," *World Politics*, 31, no. 1 (1978), pp. 71, 88.

69. Harold D. Lasswell, "The Policy Orientation," in Daniel Lerner and Harold D. Lasswell, eds., *The Policy Sciences* (Stanford, Calif.: Stanford University Press, 1951), p. 3.

70. Ibid., p. 14.

71. D. A. Summers, "Conflict, Promise, and Belief Change in a Decision-making Task," *Journal of Conflict Resolution*, June 1968, pp. 215–21.

72. Eugene Bardach, "Gathering Data for Policy Research," *Urban Analysis* 2, no. 1 (1974), pp. 117–44.

73. Lasswell, *Pre-View of Policy Sciences*, p. 4.

74. William Barrett, *The Illusion of Technique* (Garden City, N.Y.: Doubleday/Anchor, 1978), p. 19.

75. For basic summaries see: Albert G. A. Balz, *Descartes and the Modern Mind* (New Haven: Yale University Press, 1952); and Lewis S. Feuer, *Spinoza and the Rise of Liberalism* (Boston: Beacon Press, 1958).

76. Isaiah Berlin, *Age of Enlightenment* (New York: Mentor, 1956), chap. 1, is illustrative.

77. The latter is reflected mainly in the works of the existentialists. See Walter Kaufman, *Existentialism from Dostoevsky to Sartre* (Cleveland, Ohio: Meridian, 1956).

78. Nelson, "Moon-Ghetto Metaphor," pp. 380–381.

79. John Dewey, *Reconstruction in Philosophy* (Boston: Beacon Press, 1948).

80. Ibid., pp. 101–2.

81. One sophisticated, concise elaboration of this theme is Max F. Millikan, "Inquiry and Policy: The Relation of Knowledge to Action," in Daniel Lerner, ed., *The Human Meaning of the Social Sciences* (Cleveland, Ohio: Meridian, 1956), pp. 158–80.

82. Such desiderata may be summarily labeled as conditions, trends, projections, goals, and alternatives, respectively. Each emphasizes distinct intellectual traditions and procedures, and none claims superiority in the totality of conceivable estimation acts. Garry D. Brewer and Ronald D. Brunner, eds., *Political Development and Change: A Policy Approach* (New York: Free Press, 1975), explicitly use this scheme for development policy matters.

83. John von Neumann, "The Mathematician," [excerpted] in J. R. Newman, ed., *The World of Mathematics*, vol. 4 (New York: Simon & Schuster, 1956), pp. 2053–63.

84. J. R. Ravetz, *Scientific Knowledge and Its Social Problems* (Oxford, England: Clarendon Press, 1971).

85. Barrett, *Illusion of Technique*, p. 8.

86. Lasswell, "Diversity: Synthesis of Methods," *Pre-View of Policy Sciences*, chap. 4.

87. A summary of the theory and method referred to as the "decision seminar" is contained in Garry D. Brewer, "Dealing with Complex Social Problems: The Potential of the 'Decision Seminar'," in Brewer and Brunner, *Political Development and Change*, pp. 439–61.

88. Abraham Kaplan, *The Conduct of Inquiry* (San Francisco: Chandler, 1964), p. 305, has referred to this as the "methodological hammer," analogous to a circumstance in which a small boy, when presented with a hammer, proceeds to pound everything in sight.

89. In expert hands, decision theory can be a valuable tool: See Duncan Luce and Howard Raiffa, *Games and Decisions* (New York: John Wiley & Sons, 1957).

90. R. G. H. Siu, "Management and the Art of Chinese Baseball," *Sloan Management Review*, Spring 1978, p. 85.

91. *Apprehension* differs from *understanding* in this use in that the former stresses the grasping, recognizing, and valuing of the real meaning of whole circumstances, while the latter connotes more the sense of factual mastery, often incomplete and insufficient

with regard to the whole in which specific facts are lodged. It is more than a semantic difference.

92. Frank A. Camm, Jr., *The Average-Cost Pricing of Natural Gas: A Problem and Three Policy Options* (Santa Monica, Calif.: The Rand Corporation, R–2282–DOE, July 1978), is a sophisticated treatment of the problem.

93. See, for instance, "Carter Says His Aim Is An Eventual End to Gas Price Curbs," *New York Times*, October 29, 1977, p. 1; for the reaction of Congress, U.S. Congress, House, Ad Hoc Committee on Energy, *House Report 534* (Washington, D.C.: Government Printing Office, 1977). Two years later the issue remained as unresolved as ever: Dick Kirschten and Robert J. Samuelson, "Carter's Newest Energy Goals: Can We Get There from Here?" *National Journal*, July 21, 1979, pp. 1192–1201.

94. Abraham Kaplan, *American Ethics and Public Policy* (New York: Oxford University Press, 1963), p. 6.

95. Harold D. Lasswell and Abraham Kaplan, *Power and Society* (New Haven: Yale University Press, 1950), p. xxiv.

96. Lasswell, *Pre-View of Policy Sciences*, pp. 18–26.

97. Joseph Goldstein, Anna Freud, and Albert J. Solnit, *Before the Best Interests of the Child* (New York: Free Press, 1979), is the source inspiring the illustration.

98. Nicholas M. Smith, Jr., "A Calculus of Ethics: A Theory of the Structure of Value," *Behavioral Science*, April 1956, p. 112.

99. Gertrude J. Williams and John Money, eds., *Traumatic Abuse and Neglect of Children at Home* (Baltimore, Md.: Johns Hopkins University Press, 1980), offer an encyclopedic treatment, including programs to reduce the incidence and prevalence of child abuse.

100. Gibson Winter, "Toward a Comprehensive Science of Policy" (Cambridge, Mass.: Harvard University Houghton Lecture, 1969), p. 7.

101. Kenneth Boulding, *The Image* (Ann Arbor, Mich.: Ann Arbor Paperbacks, 1961), pp. 25–26.

102. Ira G. Wilson and Marthann Wilson, *Information, Computers and System Design* (New York: John Wiley & Sons, 1965), p. 236.

103. Gibson Winter, *Elements for a Social Ethic: Scientific Perspectives on Social Process* (New York: Macmillan, 1966), p. 282.

104. Judith Innes de Neufville, *Social Indicators and Public Policy* (New York: Elsevier, 1975), especially chaps. 12 and 13; a rich bibliography is in Leslie D. Wilcox, Ralph M. Brooks, George M. Beal, and Gerald E. Klonglan, *Social Indicators and Societal Monitoring* (San Francisco: Jossey-Bass, 1972).

105. Garry D. Brewer, "Professionalism: The Need for Standards," *Interfaces*, November 1973, pp. 20–27.

106. Howard Raiffa, *Decision Analysis* (Reading, Mass.: Addison-Wesley, 1968), is a primary introduction and sourcebook for the methods noted here.

107. James S. Dyer and Rakesh K. Sarin, "Group Preference Aggregation Rules Based on Strength of Preference," *Management Science*, September 1979, pp. 822–32, is a representative work—technically elegant but practically dubious.

108. Robert A. Dahl, "The Evaluation of Political Systems," in Ithiel de Sola Pool, ed., *Contemporary Political Science* (New York: McGraw-Hill, 1967), p. 174.

109. Ralph Strauch zeroes in on the matter: "It is sometimes argued that such assumptions are made for 'analytical convenience,' and the results must, of course, be interpreted in a larger context. This argument would be valid, if, in fact, the problems of interpretation in a large context were regularly considered and assessed; but they seldom are." *Winners and Losers: A Conceptual Barrier in Our Strategic Thinking* (Santa Monica, Calif.: The Rand Corporation, P–4679, 1972), p. 7.

110. Clyde Kluckhohn, "Toward a Comparison of Value Emphases in Different Cultures," in Leonard D. White, ed., *The State of the Social Sciences* (Chicago: University of Chicago Press, 1956), pp. 116–32; Harold D. Lasswell and Allan R. Holmberg, "Toward a General Theory of Directed Value Accumulation and Institutional Development," in Ralph Braibanti, ed., *Political and Economic Development* (Durham, N.C.: Duke University Press, 1969), pp. 354–99; and, Harold D. Lasswell, Daniel Lerner, and John D. Montgomery, eds., *Values and Development* (Cambridge, Mass.: MIT Press, 1976), chaps. 1, 6, and 10.

111. Alexander L. George, *Propaganda Analysis: A Study of Inferences Made From Nazi Propaganda in World War II* (Evanston, Ill.: Row, Peterson, 1959); Robert Merton, *Mass Persuasion* (New York: Harper & Row, 1949); and J. S. Bruner, "The Dimensions of Propaganda," *Journal of Abnormal and Social Psychology* 41, no. 3 (1941), pp. 311–77.

112. Murray Edelman, *The Symbolic Uses of Politics* (Urbana: University of Illinois Press, 1967); Harold D. Lasswell, Nathan Leites et al., *Language of Politics: Studies in Quantitative Semantics* (New York: George Stewart, 1949); and, Harold D. Lasswell, Daniel Lerner, and Ithiel de Sola Pool, *The Comparative Study of Symbols* (Stanford, Calif.: Stanford University Press, 1962).

113. Harold D. Lasswell, *The Signature of Power: Buildings, Communication and Policy* (New Brunswick, N.J.: Transaction Books, 1979).

114. D. P. Carthwright, "Analysis of Qualitative Material," in Leon Festinger and Daniel Katz, eds., *Research Methods in the Behavioral Sciences* (New York: Dryden Press, 1953), pp. 421–70; Abraham Kaplan, "Content Analysis and the Theory of Signs," *Philosophy of Science* 10, no. 2 (1943), pp. 230–47; and, Philip J. Stone, Dexter C. Dunphy, Marshall S. Smith, Daniel M. Ogilvie, with associates, *The General Inquirer: A Computer Approach to Content Analysis in the Behavioral Sciences* (Cambridge, Mass.: MIT Press, 1966).

115. Geoffrey Vickers, *Value Systems and Social Process* (New York: Basic Books, 1968), pp. 41–42, 103. See also, Barrett, *Illusion of Technique*, chap. 1.

116. Michael Howard, "The Forgotten Dimension of Strategy," *Foreign Affairs*, Summer 1979, pp. 975–86; Marion Dönhoff, "Bonn/Washington: Strained Relations," *Foreign Affairs*, Summer 1979, pp. 1052–64; and Christopher J. Makins, "Bringing in the Allies," *Foreign Policy*, Summer 1979, pp. 91–108.

117. William Ascher, *Forecasting: An Appraisal for Policy-Makers and Planners* (Baltimore, Md.: Johns Hopkins University Press, 1978), documents that most policy forecasts, regardless of substantive field, have slight predictive validity. See also, Wade Greene, "Economists in Recession: After an Inflation of Errors and a Depletion of Theory," *New York Times Magazine*, May 12, 1972, pp. 18–19, 58–65.

118. The environmental impact statement, now required for many policy and program projects, surfaces both the variety and potential for conflict inherent in preferences. H. Paul Friesma and Paul Culhane, "Social Impacts, Politics, and the Environmental Impact Statement Process," *Natural Resources Journal*, April 1976, pp. 339–56, is a fair treatment.

119. Robert A. Dahl and Charles E. Lindblom, *Politics, Economics and Welfare* (Chicago: University of Chicago Press, 1976), pp. 83–90, on unstable goals.

120. Amos Tversky and Daniel Kahneman, "Judgment Under Uncertainty: Heuristics and Biases," *Science*, 27 September 1974, pp. 1124–31; and, Kenneth Hammond and Leonard Adelman, "Science, Values, and Human Judgment," *Science*, 12 October 1976, pp. 389–96, present contrasting, illuminating views.

121. Abraham Edel, *Method in Ethical Inquiry* (Indianapolis: Bobbs-Merrill, 1963).

122. Dahl and Lindblom, *Politics, Economics and Welfare*, pp. 25–54.

123. Stockholm International Peace Research Institute (SIRPI), *Safeguards Against Nuclear Proliferation* (Stockholm: Almqvist & Wiksell, 1975); Barry Commoner, *Science and Survival* (New York: Viking Press, 1966); and, Harold D. Lasswell, "The Continuing Revision of Conceptual and Operational Maps," in Lasswell et al., *Values and Development,* chap. 10.

124. Randall B. Ripley and Grace A. Franklin, *Congress, the Bureaucracy and Public Policy* (Homewood, Ill.: Dorsey Press, 1976), chaps. 1 and 2; and, Karl W. Deutsch, *Politics and Government* (Boston: Houghton Mifflin, 1970).

125. Harold D. Lasswell and Daniel Lerner, eds., *World Revolutionary Elites* (Cambridge, Mass.: MIT Press, 1966), pp. 35–36, provide an explicit statement of this goal.

126. Frederick S. Hillier and Gerald J. Lieberman, *Operations Research* (San Francisco: Holden-Day, 1974), chap. 19, are more forthright than most methodological specialists.

127. Robert A. Dahl, *A Preface to Democratic Theory* (Chicago: University of Chicago Press, 1956), pp. 48–50, supplies the theoretical justification. However, many who advocate efficiency or social optimality—to the near exclusion of other goals—illustrate a contrary and hyperrational approach. Leon S. Lasdon, *Optimization Theory for Large Systems* (New York: Macmillan, 1970), is illustrative.

128. Grover Starling, *The Politics and Economics of Public Policy* (Homewood, Ill.: Dorsey Press, 1979), pp. 269–72, provides a concise discussion of the equality-efficiency trade-off. Specific analytic treatment of many such large-scale trade-offs is elaborated in Congressional Budget Office, *Five-Year Budget Projections and Alternative Budgetary Strategies for Fiscal Years 1980–1984* (Washington, D.C.: Government Printing Office, June 1979).

129. Congressional Budget Office, *The MX Missile and Multiple Protective Structure Basing: Long-Term Budgetary Implications* (Washington, D.C.: Government Printing Office, June 1979), is illustrative of both trade-offs and the estimation procedures used to arrive at such a decision.

130. John Harsanyi, "Nonlinear Social Welfare Functions," *Theory and Decision* 6, no. 3 (1975), pp. 311–32.

131. Hillier and Lieberman, *Operations Research,* chap. 5, is a good introduction to these methods. See Harvey Sapolsky, *The Polaris System Development* (Cambridge, Mass.: Harvard University Press, 1972), for an elaboration of PERT and its application.

132. W. Arthur Lewis, "Planning Public Expenditures," in Max F. Millikan, ed., *National Economic Planning* (New York: National Bureau of Economic Research, 1967), p. 207.

133. Guido Calabresi and Philip Bobbit, *Tragic Choices* (New York: W. W. Norton, 1978); and, Wayne A. R. Leys, *Ethics for Policy Decisions* (Englewood Cliffs, N. J.: Prentice-Hall, 1952), both work on this premise.

134. Three styles of justification for estimation error have been noted by Benno Wasserman: naive realism, which adheres to facts to produce one best answer; inductionism, knowledge produced without benefit of interpretation; and determinism, where the human and intentional aspects of choice are neglected. "The Failure of Intelligence Prediction," *Political Studies* 8, no. 2 (1960), pp. 156–65.

135. Not the least in importance is the man-centered, not thing- or institution-centered basis for estimation, and other treatments of the decision process. A key informant is Harry Stack Sullivan, *The Fusion of Psychiatry and Social Science* (New York: W. W. Norton, 1971).

136. Kaplan, *American Ethics,* p. 103.

5

Estimation as simplification

To analyze a problem, to escape from its complexities, one must simplify. Often this occurs with some appreciation for the possible importance of elements of reality set aside or left out, but more usually simplification occurs and analysis proceeds as if the problem were not embedded within a larger context. Simplification is evident in all social problem analyses, and thus all analyses are erroneous and inadequate in varying degrees. The issue is one of working to limit error, to promote accuracy, and to be ever mindful of the weaknesses attending any given analysis.

MODES OF SIMPLIFICATION

Ralph Strauch has presented three different paradigms of the estimation process.[1] In the first (Figure 5–1), the common means by which mathematics (as a system of symbols including well defined rules of operation and interaction) commonly proceeds is portrayed simply: one constructs a mathematical model, applies the appropriate procedural rules, and thereby generates results. Anyone with requisite familiarity with the kind of mathematics used can, in principle, understand what has been included in the model, can detect errors of formulation and operation, and can appreciate or interpret the derived results. It is all very clean—very rational.

FIGURE 5-1   The mathematics paradigm

A common perception of analysis is derivative of this paradigm. As Figure 5-2 shows, two additional factors have been added: the substantive problem and conclusion. In this paradigm, attention is given the fact that some external reality, out there, exists and serves as the basis for one's formal representation. As Strauch observes, "The directness of [the] two links [A and B] allows the results to be interpreted as conclusions about the substantive problem fairly directly." This paradigm has served well for certain kinds of problems, e.g., "in the physical sciences [and] in statistical experimentation, where the analyst uses a probability sampling procedure in order to make his problem one of analyzing a mathematical model he knows and understands."[2] The paradigm has been far less applicable or successful in situations where the problems treated do not have a well-defined formulation, in short, for "squishy" problems embedded in what we have previously called complex social systems. For this class of problems, a third paradigm is offered (Figure 5-3).

As one moves down the left-hand column, highly selected aspects of a problem are retained and much information is deleted as efforts are made to represent the problem formally or analytically. Moving across the bottom row and back up the right-hand column, presuming those aspects have resulted from stating the problem in a formal, usually verbal, manner and then representing these words in mathematics or some other modes, we see that information is being added back onto the analysis. At points A and A′ key interactions between decision makers and experts occur, with all the attendant perceptual problems mentioned earlier. Subsequent translation steps (noted at points B and B′) are dominated by the analytic expert. The step at point B is often taken for purely technical, rather than substantive

FIGURE 5-2   Common perception of analysis paradigm

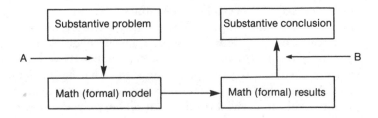

FIGURE 5-3   Estimation of "squishy" or complex problems: A paradigm

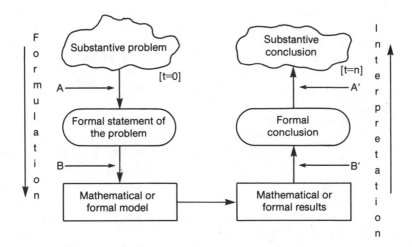

reasons; that the step at point B' is critical for any analysis is poorly appreciated, especially in cases where the formal result is contained on reams of computer printout or numerous, mystifying tables of numbers, the meaning of which can only be deciphered by the technicians responsible for their creation.

Bias enters at every stage and leads to distortions of the analysis and interpretation of the analytic results. To define the substantive problem, for instance, choices must be made about what is important—often by the decision makers on the basis of their own special views of the world, by analysts on the basis of their own perceptions of the problem and the world (modified somewhat if the decision maker's concerns have been enlisted and considered), and then by the technical imperatives of the methods and procedures actually used.[3] Whatever method used, further biases result that are capable of distorting the analytic outcome; many are unaware of the often very strong and constraining assumptions underlying even the most familiar research methods. For instance, although strong statistical assumptions may constrain the measurement and structure of parameters and variables represented in a formal model, we are seldom informed either about them or about their analytic consequences.[4]

As the process moves back up the right-hand column (Figure 5-3), additional information, compensation for that abstracted out in the interest of formalization, must be introduced. As sometimes happens, specialized briefers intervene at point A' to translate and interpret the formal conclusions obtained for the benefit of busy decision makers. These individuals either played no role or only a peripheral one in the preceding analytic steps, which may affect the way analysis is perceived and used. At the very least, the distinctive world views or perceptions held by expert analyst and decision maker will enter at this point to color the outcome.

Were these difficulties not troublesome enough, one must remember that doing analysis takes time—often measured in terms of years for problems of great difficulty or consequence. At the initial step ($t = 0$), the substantive problem possessed certain attributes and aspects; however, the world does not pause for the analyst's benefit. By the time substantive conclusions have been prepared ($t = n$), the initial configuration will have changed simply as a result of its own dynamic and often because of perturbations wrought by the analysts. What was, for the commissioning decision maker, a problem at the onset may no longer be a problem (or at least not a pressing concern) by the time the analysis is completed; other problems may have taken precedence, solutions may have evolved by other means, or the decision maker's initial perception of the problem may have improved to the point where details created in analysis do not provide significant clarification. More than one analyst has been stymied at the conclusion of a long project by a change in client or client perception, which presents dilemmas of an entirely different, but crucial, sort.[5]

At best, any analysis provides a single perspective on a problem, one that is sensitive to and qualified by the steps taken to create it. This truism is seldom appreciated. Once the logic of the problem has been laid out, alternative perspectives (analyses) should be generated and examined for their technical and informational content. Thus, entirely different groups of individuals should ideally be working on complementary analyses to illuminate the problem according to their own distinct capabilities, biases, perspectives, and expectations.[6] At least a second opinion must be developed. As the single-method analyst is impoverished, so too, is the decision maker who relies unduly on one or a small handful of analytic opinions.

Prevalent analytic orientations

One must step back momentarily to acquire a sense of perspective about dominant orientations encountered during estimation. If, because of previous training, personality, past experiences, or for other reasons, one looks at the world as if it were composed simply of a small number of important elements configured in nonlinear, deterministic ways—as an engineer might—certain kinds of analytic methods and procedures would quite naturally follow. Alternatively, one might perceive the world in terms of linear, orderly, and static patterns—as a statistician or actuary might; if so, then different organizing methods for these perceptions could be imagined.

The first orientation has been labeled *simplicity* and the second *disorganized complexity*, where "[though] the number of variables is very large, and . . . each of the many variables has a behavior which is individually erratic, or perhaps totally unknown . . . the system as a whole possesses certain orderly and analyzable average properties."[7] Warren Weaver, who coined these two terms, supplements them with a third, *organized complexity,* characterized by an awareness of problems "which involve dealing simultaneously with a sizable number of factors which are interrelated into an organic whole."[8] Wishing no injustice, it appears as though Weaver's organized complexity, Simon's conception of complex social systems, and Strauch's "squishy" problems are one and the same for all practical purposes. Most social problems, including those of interest in this book, conform more to the third orientation—organized complexity—than to the first two. This is important because the analytic tools developed along with Newtonian mechanics to manage simple problems and those created later to overcome statistical problems of disorganized complexity have not been matched for problems having properties of organized complexity.[9] This crucial distinction has only been partially recognized in the face of repeated and inappropriate efforts to match methods to problems for which they were never intended.[10] Indeed, there may be a complexity threshold beyond which,

> precision and significance (or relevance) become almost mutually exclusive characteristics. It is in this sense that precise quantitative analyses of the behavior of humanistic systems are not likely to have much relevance to the real-world societal, political, economic and other types of problems which involve humans whether as individuals or in groups.[11]

In light of this circumstance, Zadeh concludes with the postulation of a "principle of incompatibility" to account for the mismatch of conventional techniques and social problems.

Concerns for system complexity are encountered, but usually with only the slightest sense of what the concept means. The following is fairly typical:

> The scale and complexity of many urban problems, particularly social problems, are substantially greater than those customarily encountered by defense and space industries . . . [and] the institutions responsible for coping with urban problems are not well suited for the management of change on such a scale.[12]

A close reading of *New Tools for Urban Management,* from which these cautions were drawn, reveals, in case after case, how debilitating urban complexity was for analysis, for constructive alternatives, and even for the prospects of new tools.[13]

Illustrative applications

Depending on the general orientations brought to the analytic setting, different techniques naturally follow and, with them, variations in the quality, pertinence, and utility of the estimation product itself.

Broadly, within the simple orientation, one can discern two analytic subcategories: mechanistic and utopian. Mechanisms are everywhere evident in the work produced by systems and other kinds of engineers. The simple-mechanistic approach is manifest in many studies relying on a so-called multilevel or network conception of the world.[14] Not particularly novel, the approach is directly linked with a classic problem of system decomposition, which implies some powerful assumptions about the real situations in which it is invoked.[15] To the extent that these assumptions are untenable, the view and approach are, too, for the most part. Because of problems of recomposition,[16] data aggregation and information loss,[17] and noncomparability of meaning for elements considered at different levels of analytic detail or resolution,[18] the application of the simple-mechanistic approach has had only modest success, and then mainly when applied to problems having distinct parts.[19] However, the approach regularly continues to be promoted as a means to manage complex soc'al problems,[20] this despite the following, severe limitation:

> In engineering, the use of systems analysis in a given problem is predicated on the knowledge of a family of parameters that describe and define the system in precise terms. There is explicit recognition of a set of values of those parameters in relation to optimal performance of the system. In social planning, no such undisputed parameters or criteria exist.[21]

The simple-utopian view is evident in work spawned by Jay W. Forrester, who was trained as an electrical engineer.[22] The simple solutions produced in this work have been advocated forcefully[23] but at the same time one sees little appreciation given the utopian tradition from which such solutions emanate.[24]

Aggressive marketing of results produced with a single technique (or simply promoting the technique itself) has consequences, not the least of which may be a degraded estimate of analysts and analysis. Philip Handler, President of the National Academy of Sciences in 1980, offered the following editorial view of reasons for "Public Doubts About Science":

> Difficulty arises in the scientific community from confusion of the role of scientist qua scientist with that of scientist as citizen, confusion of the ethical code of the scientist with the obligation of the citizen, blurring the distinction between intrinsically scientific and intrinsically political questions. When scientists fail to recognize these boundaries, their own ideological beliefs, usually unspoken, easily becloud seemingly scientific debate.[25]

Elaborating on the promotional theme, Robert Frosch, a senior national security official and analyst, calls many prevalent techniques into question on the ground that they are "not doing what they are advertised as doing, if they [are] not making things worse. It could be that things would be even worse without these new techniques, but I would like to ask some questions and suggest some reasons for believing that systems engineering, systems analysis, and management, as practiced, are likely to be part of the problem, and indeed causative agents."[26]

Instances of social analyses oriented toward a disorganized-complexity view of the world are too numerous to cite fully. Briefly, two representative subcategories exist: the naive and the regressive. The naive approach is well illustrated in Easton,[27] and in several policy analyses presented by Lineberry and Sharkansky.[28] Extraordinarily complex systems are reduced to simple models having a small number of highly aggregated elements; interactions among elements are usually treated in a reduced and abstracted form as simple tables of correlation coefficients deduced from crosssectional information. While the number of elements explicitly considered is small, their behavior is deduced to be the resultant of average values for more numerous, contributory elements—treated as if the underlying phenomena had regular statistical properties.

The regressive approach has been the special province of economists, and their handiwork is everywhere. For example, the Project Independence Evaluation System (PIES), a large-scale computer model of energy supply and demand,[29] employs statistical estimates based on regression equation techniques to set the values for the coefficients of its many equations. In effect, curves are fitted to plots of data (or to estimates about data) so as to best represent the average properties or central tendencies thought to exist.[30] Among other limitations of the approach, past experiences are emphasized in calculating the likely future course; sharp departures are thereby given less weight. The regressive approach also overemphasizes average and aggregate concepts and behaviors, often at the expense of the underlying contributory factors. In this regard, the naive and regressive approaches are quite similar. For their conservative and aggregational biases, such analyses have limited value in policy deliberations, where the future, creative departures from the norm, and distributional change are all central concerns.

In the face of such limitations, one has reason to wonder at the pervasiveness and attention that regressive analyses have achieved. In those instances where accuracy of forecasts has been sufficient to gain attention, one finds that it was the skill and judgment of the responsible analysts rather than the enabling model, that deserve credit. Bert Hickman, a distinguished economist, puts it this way: "[Accuracy results from] changing the preliminary assumptions on exogeneous variables and constants until the resulting forecast falls within the range thought to be reasonable [by the analyst]."[31] Illustrative of this type of analysis, where the expertness of the analyst dominates, is Martin Feldstein's treatment of the exceedingly complex Medicare health insurance system.[32]

In both general approaches—simplicity and disorganized complexity—certain presumptions about the world (and analysis) seem to hold. Many of these have been well summarized by David Berlinski:[33]

> The world is nonlinear, discontinuous, stochastic, unstable, and inherently complex, but typical models of aspects of the world are none of these things.
>
> Models are used because they are tractable and understandable; the world is seldom either.

Because a model behaves in certain ways, there is a strong tendency for the modeler to believe that the world behaves in similar ways; it usually doesn't.

A social system is not like an engineering system. An engineer is trained to optimize systems that engineers built and understand so as to attain purposes that engineers and others can agree to accept. A policy analyst must understand systems that exist but whose purposes are mysterious and whose components few, if any, understand.

Little wonder then that so few analyses demonstrate a sophistication of understanding associated with the organized complexity approach. Some exhibit parts of such understanding, and these can be grouped according to their utility or realism: utility in the sense that the product of the analysis was taken, considered, and in various ways put to use by decision makers; and realism in the sense that important problem elements were treated directly and with an appreciation of their inherent complexity (as defined earlier).

In the area of criminal justice, the accuracy with which Richard C. Larson was able to portray police behavior and activities in many different urban settings earned for him the Operations Research Society of America's respected Lanchester Prize.[34] The analysis combines a wide variety of complementary methods; it treats messy aspects of the problem directly and still retains an elegance of formulation; the structure of the underlying models is understandable (transparent); and each component model has been explored thoroughly (and improved over time) through repeated application. A utilitarian criminal justice example, which modeled the key processes of court operation, has resulted in several positive policy recommendations and subsequent changes.[35]

Population or demographic analyses are often critical elements in setting the bounds on the who in Lasswell's classic definition of politics as the resolution of *Who Gets What, When, How*.[36] The realistic, explicitly policy scientific, tack taken by John D. Montgomery and his colleagues has much to commend it.[37] A highly useful analysis of evolving structural changes in America's rural population, including consideration of the five intellectual tasks of goal clarification, trend elaboration, condition enumeration, forecasting, and alternative generation (noted earlier in Chapter 4), has been produced by McCarthy and Morrison, two social scientists at The Rand Corporation.[38]

Realistic, comprehensive, value-based, and action-oriented analyses of children's needs and the policies in place and required to meet those needs are found in Nicholas Hobbs' *The Futures of Children*.[39] The book stresses the idea that policy must be directed forward; its recommendations for improvement are already having effects on numerous decision makers, including families themselves.[40] The intense, multidisciplined approach represented in *Before the Best Interests of the Child*, deserves emulation as well.[41] A more utilitarian study, in that it was originally undertaken in response to a request from an influential client—the secretary of health, education, and welfare—*Handicapped Children: Strategies for Improving Services*, attempted to follow the policy science prescription from start to finish.[42] Among other features of this study, it took a policy-analytic, comprehensive view of the system serving handicapped youth to assess the relation of the system's constituent parts to its whole; it looked at this system from the points of view of service providers (public and private, federal, state, and local) and service recipients (including children and families); it collected and analyzed as much available data and information as time and resources allowed to assemble a picture of the system; it created much new data where a need for it existed but where conventional sources proved inadequate to the need; and it was goal-oriented and multimethodological.

Paired examples of mental health studies are Rubenstein and Lasswell, *The Sharing of Power in a Psychiatric Hospital,* and Ronald W. Conley, *The Economics of Mental Retardation,* representing, respectively, realistic and utilitarian points of view.[43] The analytic focus of the former is a single institution (The Yale Psychiatric Institute, YPI), in which the authors were able, over a period of years, to inculcate the broad sharing of decision-making powers for all participants to the greatest extent feasible. The YPI became, as a result, a model therapeutic community. Conley's work treats mental retardation from a broad, analytically-based perspective. In a field where myth, superstition, and simple ignorance about matters of fact (e.g., wide variation existed about a datum as simple as "how many mentally retarded citizens are there in America?") abound, the Conley work has done much to provide essential contextual clarification, to identify areas where policy research is needed, and to inform the bases of debate underlying claims on resources for services and programs for the mentally retarded. As its title suggests, it fails to be as comprehensive in the scope of human values considered as the Rubenstein/Lasswell work, while at the same time being wider in the institutional range and number of participants considered.[44] The point, of course, is that no single study or analysis will satisfy all needs nor will it be able to include all relevant aspects of a problem. What we are strongly suggesting, however, is that adoption of the organized complexity concept increases the chance that more of the essential aspects will be included and that more of the legitimate needs and interests at issue in a given situation will be considered or at least not ignored.

Evidence in support of this contention is contained in Bruce Ackerman (and colleagues), *The Uncertain Search for Environmental Quality,* an exemplary study of pollution problems in the Delaware River Basin.[45] Two other fine analyses, both with what we are calling a utilitarian slant, are Patrick Larkey's *Evaluating Public Programs,*[46] which painstakingly assembles a picture of how municipalities actually spend federal revenue sharing funds and hence provides a much-needed clarification of the important intergovernmental context, and Joel Berke and Michael Kirst's *Federal Aid to Education*.[47] The former work is especially strong in its sensitive and appropriate use of a variety of methodological tools; the latter is noteworthy for the variety of disciplinary perspectives it brings to bear on the subject, including a strong integration of these views.

In summary

Our discussion has emphasized one point above all: Every analysis represents a simplified, abstracted, incomplete, and inadequate view of the world. None will be appropriate or best for all time and circumstances. In this stand, we take comfort in the company kept:

> There is no absolute knowledge. And those who claim it, whether they are scientists or dogmatists, open the door to tragedy. All information is imperfect. We have to treat it with humility. That is the human condition.[48]

DATA, THEORY AND ESTIMATION: CHICKENS AND EGGS

The problem of doing good analysis is nearly as complex as the subject matter it seeks to understand. It even seems as though we have a chicken-and-egg problem: we have very little good analysis because there is so little usable theory; we have little usable theory because there is so little solid information and data; but there are inadequate decent data because there have been so few good analyses to generate theoretical insights that would tell which data to collect. In the following, we attempt to shed light on the circularity in hopes that progress may be made in breaking through the circle in many different places. For the moment we postulate three general statements of the usual situation in policy analysis; each is discussed subsequently in detail.

> Data suitable for analyses are in desperately short supply. Data inputs have obscure, unknown, or unknowable empirical foundations, and the relevance of much data, even if valid, to the effectiveness of social systems is unknown.[49]

> The analytic models and the behavioral assumptions and propositions they contain are often not well verified, and are usually not validated at all.[50]

> Theoretical, technical-institutional, and conceptual deficiencies abound and severely limit efforts to understand and manage social systems.[51]

Data problems[52]

Accurate information on the size, composition, and spatial distribution of a social system's population, i.e., demographic information of the most fundamental sort, is essential to efficient decision making and management and to effective understanding of many social problems. Demographic information is, in many senses, the most basic element of any social analysis, and yet we repeatedly find that such information is inappropriate, outmoded, or simply not available.[53] The 1980 Census of the American people, for example, only became available for analytic purposes slowly, piecemeal, and in forms that did not readily conform to the needs of many specific policy analyses. This delay between enumeration and availability of the data had been foreshadowed by the two- to three-year delay experienced with the 1970 census. It will always be a problem, given the size and complexity of the modern census.

Demographic information is vital. For instance, it is required to set the level of public services, to determine the effectiveness of these services, and to identify future problems that might require action. Decision makers rarely seem to understand which demographic features determine the demand for services or the effects of population on those services.[54] There is only the thinnest of social science knowledge about the relations between demographic processes and social, economic, and political change, nor is there a usable theory of governmental influence on those relations.[55] Given the lack of knowledge about population characteristics and their relationships to resource measures of public program objectives,[56] it is not surprising that sets of demographic information, where they exist at all, are unresponsive to the decision-maker's needs; they are usually not sufficient for the analyst's needs either.[57]

In the absence of basic understanding of elementary social relationships needed to identify, collect, and structure information files, efforts to do analyses that depend on this type of information have not been unqualifiedly successful.[58] Two extreme solutions to the data problem exist: ignoring it by concentrating mainly on theoretical relationships imagined to govern social action,[59] or picking selectively from data whose sources, validity, and interrelationships are not well established, so as to sustain politically-driven preferences.[60] Neither course is recommended. But what alternatives exist?

A simple solution is not to do policy analysis and, hence, to rationalize away the importance, priority, or solvability of the specific problem at hand. Policy analysts find themselves in data-poor environments as compared with basic researchers, who more often have the luxury of following data-rich avenues of research. A basic researcher has more latitude in selecting topics in which adequate data are known to exist; the policy analyst is professionally committed to aid decision makers with problems where data deficiencies are often an integral part of the problem (i.e., had sufficient, adequate, and valid data existed, the problem presented for analysis might have already been treated and resolved). Policy analysis, furthermore, is done under a time constraint; policymakers cannot temporize forever. Evidence or no, decisions get made. The policy analyst has to be responsive to the decision-maker's clock, and thin data are usually better than none at all.

A more satisfactory solution is not to ignore one's professional responsibility. Advice based on poor data may be less than adequate, but it may also be the best available under the circumstances. A decision maker should know—be informed—about data and analytic shortcomings of this and other sorts. The adequacy, expediency, and erroneousness of data collection and use are all relative concepts, to be judged with respect to realistic conditions. Could someone else have done better . . . under the given circumstances? All data and analyses are, as we have noted, more or less erroneous or inadequate, and these qualities apply to both policy and basic research. These properties, too, are not properly considered as absolutes (since all data are erroneous, one should not do analysis), rather one needs to determine the degree of error and the amount of inadequacy tolerable, given time and other circumstances.[61]

Good data should not be expected by the policy analyst. Today's problems were not recognized yesterday, or at least were not given preference. What incentives existed, for example, to record the malaise and plight of the poor until the poor took it upon themselves to make their needs known in the political arena? Therefore, the policy analyst, whose work is rooted in a historical perspective (where only a small fraction of the totality of experience has been recorded) and directed toward the future (where only imaginings and hopes exist), can and should expect data problems. It is the analyst's lot.

In such situations, a basic question that needs to be asked is whether the missing data are needed at all. And, if they are, can they be obtained or adapted from some other source?[62] Time is, always, of the essence, and generating new data is not without time and other costs. To answer the questions the following general issues are often considered:

What is the real purpose of the research? Is it, for instance, merely to supply expert opinion for a specific detail of a policy proposal, or are more fundamental scientific values at stake?

How immediate is the problem? Does the decision maker really need fully validated and reliable data, and need them now?

Are the data indicated unique, or are there close substitutes or even proxies that will "make do?"[63]

The significance of data must be determined by the analyst based on a complex professional judgment about details of the overall context in which the data will be used. Raising these general questions provides other benefits, too. Problem definition and specification are enhanced. Merely collecting data because they exist out there, and doing so in the absence of gaining a workable understanding of the problem can be quite wasteful. Data collection is expensive—not only in the real terms of the time and

effort involved, but in other respects as well. For instance, our ability to
screen for genetic disorders in the unborn has, on first glance, many positive policy attributes; a second, and deeper, consideration of this form of
data gathering indicates that it may have severe costs, too.[64] Finally, omission of superflous data may enhance the communicability of one's analysis,
particularly to a busy decision maker who has time only for the basics or
essential findings of the work.

Often circumstances do not permit the assembly of important, pertinent
data; the situation may be bettered by a forthright admission of the limitation than by trying to make do with dubious proxies for the missing data.
If properly qualified, results from this kind of analysis may make a real
contribution by pointing out what data are needed, providing a justification
for spending resources to do so, and then actually undertaking their collection for future use.

Social indicators

Data problems have not gone unattended; on the contrary, many have
invested heavily in the development of social accounts that include demographic, economic, social, and other kinds of information. Still, an adequate, readily available, and relevant social accounting scheme has yet to
materialize.[65]

Problems with social indicators cause problems for policy analysts. The
treatment of preferences and goals—which is an integral task and responsibility of policy analysis—has not been satisfactorily resolved. Without obtaining precise statements of goals for both individuals and col-
lectivities, attention of those in the social indicators movement has focused
on the development, description, and collection of hard or objective indicators. The basic rationale for collecting and measuring "things" seems to
be that important qualitative elements are too hard to understand and even
harder to measure.[66]

Definitional problems have plagued social accountants, too. For example, there is no rational classification of crimes based on a set of properties
that defines all crimes.[67] Law sometimes helps, but it is incomplete, varies
from locality to locality, and is subject to change and reinterpretation. All
three properties mean that the generation of stable, reliable, time-series
information (a requisite for good policy analysis) is far from being realized.
The definitional issue is general and touches many social problem areas.

Determining a useful level of analysis at which data should be collected
is troublesome. Much social information is aggregated at the national level;
many problems are not. However, our dependence on national-level measures presupposes national-level solutions to problems as, for instance, in
the case of many prevalent energy models.[68] Additionally, very little
evidence—at least the raw data from which evidence could be derived—is
available on individual-level matters related to one's perception, attitude,

expectations, and other concepts indicative of personal satisfaction.[69] A most striking illustration of this lapse is provided by M. Harvey Brenner, in his remarkable penetration of the relationship between economic cycles and mental hospital admissions:

> First, it is clear that instabilities in the national economy have been the single most important source in mental-hospital admissions or admissions rates. Second, this relation is so consistent for certain segments of the society that virtually no other major factor other than economic instability appears to influence variation in their mental hospital rates. Third, the relation has been basically stable for at least 127 years and there is considerable evidence that it has had greater impact in the last two decades.[70]

But can you recall a single reference, especially in times of recession, widespread unemployment, and inflation, of the effects on the mental health of individuals employment or antiinflation (usually creating some unemployment) policies do or will have?

To be truly useful to policy analysts, social indicators need to be standardized so that time series can be generated that bear a close similarity to what is being measured over time. The requirement has not been met because of an incompatibility between the technical/statistical demand for stable definitions and reliability of measures in settings where definitions are changing, where interpretations vary from group to group and time to time (e.g., what is poverty to a Harlem resident in the 1980s could well be affluence to a citizen of Bangledesh; it might even have been tolerable or acceptable to a Depression-era Harlemite), and where differences in both absolute and relative terms from subgroup to subgroup of the same population are not well understood.

Most of these terribly difficult analytic and research problems can be enumerated, if not readily resolved:

Most social phenomena are complex and require multidimensional treatment. A single index (e.g., quality of life) by itself is insufficient to represent most social aspects.

Reinterpretation of data collected for one purpose is seldom completely satisfactory when used for another purpose; significance must be established, not presumed. (E.g., the injudicious use of administrative data for research purposes.)

Data often exist, but not in the public domain—or exist in the public domain but cannot be accessed because of privacy or confidentiality constraints.[71]

Institutional biases contaminate many possible indicators. Social program data more often reflect administrative needs and convenience than they do an individual citizen's view of the situation.[72]

Models and theories: A need for multiple perspectives

Given the long list of formidable data problems one encounters in the policy environment, the importance of the skill and judgment of the individual analyst become all the more apparent. The choice of topics, the organization of the problem, the application of the method, and the formulation of the results all eventually hinge on the judgment, knowledge, and skill of the analyst in carrying out each of these tasks.[73] This has been generally neglected, and the importance of the analyst has been overshadowed by a misplaced emphasis on techniques. The construction and interpretation of formal models and theories about social structures and processes are basically judgmental matters.[74] The approach adopted suggests methods for dealing with the subject matter but it is no guarantee that valid results will naturally follow. Methods applied to problems characterized by their organized complexity have, as suggested earlier, yielded mainly insights and, only occasionally, partial solutions. And such positive, beneficial results usually owe more to the analyst's own capabilities than to the power or rigor of the method used.

For instance, with specific reference to what we describe as the level-of-analysis problem (e.g., relating parts to wholes and making both individual and collective distinctions), if the properties at some higher level of analytic detail cannot be deduced from statements about constituent parts, as seems to be the case for most complex, organized systems, prediction will not always be possible. This aspect of social systems does not absolve the analyst from doing something more than making good guesses, however. Evolving phenomena are always contingent on the total context in which they occur; but because the context may be unique, prediction can be hazardous. Critical configurations defining a context will never reappear in exactly the same fashion, although the likelihood of an event's recurrence is greater if it has happened often in the past. The basic problem is theoretically and practically intractable because there is no sure way to demonstrate that the future will contain configurations analogous (or sufficiently analogous) to those in the past.

A common dilemma faced by an analyst is whether to revise a tentative model or formulation to conform to the realities of data availability or to proceed with poor data. The first strategy is not foolproof. Certain data limitations can be improved by working hard to get supplementary data, but these often must be proxies for the real thing, given time and resource constraints. When proxies are used, the model or theory underlying an analysis may appear improved, while it actually is not: The scope of the analysis could be distorted by adding irrelevant detail; the level of detail may not be appropriate for the problem at hand;[75] accuracy may suffer as slightly wrong factors are allowed to interact in the model to produce very wrong outcomes;[76] and precise identification of what is being modeled may get lost (e.g., results may end up being based on administrative categories, such as a district or political unit, instead of a desired target population of specific people, not all of whom are within the unit). Theories and models developed using these proxies are no more valid or comprehensive than the quality and relevance of the proxies themselves.

Data limitations may be covered by making "guesstimates" to fill in the holes, by adding assumptions, or by extrapolating historical data. Guesstimates sometimes help (particularly if the analyst is truly expert or can enlist the help of those who are); however, guesstimates often end up being used mainly to justify the model and the results it produces and, in any event, they cannot be disproved.[77] Adding assumptions may improve analytic relevance by keeping the model close to essential features of the context; however, each facilitating assumption requires examination and appraisal (e.g., through expert interview, judgment techniques, or direct supplementary measurement) to ensure its appropriateness. Extrapolation can be useful in the near term when social systems tend to be stable, but heavy reliance on extrapolation may blind the analyst to sharp discontinuities or to slowly cumulative effects.[78]

The second, or go-with-poor data, strategy has its own pitfalls: While the analyst may advertise the limitations of the model, and offer the best advice available under the circumstances, it may still not be good advice. A decision maker can accept qualified advice, but will rarely accept blame for poor decisions. Policy analysts are handy scapegoats.[79]

Heavy reliance on just one analysis or model of a problem (the focus of our discussion so far) may also turn out to have unexpected and unwanted outcomes. For instance, in a revealing essay, Paul Bracken exposes the "unintended consequences of strategic gaming," one specific form of model-based analysis, by the British in analyzing threats of German strategic air attack, 1922–39; by the French in constructing defenses between the world wars; and by the Russians in preparing for a German assault on their western border.[80] In the British case, a small group of statistical specialists in the Air Staff prepared assessments of the likely German strategic threat to Great Britain. Only their summary findings, and no documentation or qualifications, were presented to the top decision makers; nor were the findings ever subjected to external evaluation. Highly selective mythical numbers or guesstimates (of the worst-case sort) were used in planning, leading to the construction of day bombers and the virtual exclusion of night bombers, fighters, and other necessary components of a total defense system. Extrapolation from those numbers in fifth- and sixth-order studies generated fear and mistrust in the public: Lloyds of London refused to issue any kind of war insurance; the Home Office determined that civilian losses from German bombing would be greater than the country's capacity to build coffins, so orders were issued for the construction of mass graves; and the Health Ministry judged it necessary to print over 1 million extra death certificates.[81]

Bracken summarizes the following lessons from this experience:

No one questioned the assumptions on which the studies and decisions were based; assumptions must be questioned constantly.

No one reviewed the basic data; such a review would have shown that the numbers had been carefully selected to support the worst possible case, and one that favored airplane development and deployment generally and day bomber production specifically.

The Air Staff models were never scrutinized to determine their structure or to identify what kinds of outputs they were capable of producing. The models were highly classified and closely held.

The simplification technique of selective omission, featured in this illustration, can be used to prove just about anything.

Decision makers in organizations outside the Air Staff were never told what the analyses included, omitted, or could or could not do.

The French case points up another lesson. After the strategic decision to build the Maginot Line was made, most analyses focused on the technical details of that fortification system. Calculations of range, thickness of concrete, firing angle, and the like became a substitute for more comprehensive thought and an anaesthetic for decision makers who refused to confront the real problems posed by a mobile, flexible enemy. The analyses diverted attention away from the real problems facing French military strategists. The lesson is that analyses can be used to keep certain facts and contingencies from scrutiny.

The Soviets learned the same lesson the hard way in preparations for World War II. During the 1930s a series of remarkable strategic games was conducted that might have afforded insight into the coming conflict. However, any deviation from Stalin's doctrine was quickly suppressed. In fact, one brilliant Soviet general was purged partly for his deviation in playing the game.[82] Other Soviet military thinkers saw that it was personally hazardous to dispute the basic strategic assumptions, no matter how fatal they seemed, so dissent ended and the games were increasingly played by the foreordained rules.[83] Bracken terms this "unintended suppression."

Generalizing from historical experience is risky, but failing to learn from the past is even more so.[84] Among other broad prescriptions, the creation and consideration of alternative perspectives of a problem context appear warranted as a partial corrective; besides offering an opportunity to look at the problem differently and hence enrich the informational setting and increase the options considered, relative strengths and weaknesses of a single model or theory tend to become more evident when contrasted with other formulations.[85]

One interpretation of all this begins to come clear: great and continuing need exists to rely on multiple approaches to and perspectives on complex social problems, to use a variety of methodologies (existing and yet to be developed), and to conduct analyses from several distinct but related levels of analytic detail. All such tasks require as rich a contextual or informational setting as possible.

NOTES

1. Ralph Strauch, " 'Squishy' Problems and Quantitative Methods," *Policy Sciences*, June 1975, pp. 175–84.

2. Ibid., p. 176.

3. Numerous technical transgressions of the sort described here are documented in Garry D. Brewer, *Politicians, Bureaucrats and the Consultant: A Critique of Urban Problem Solving* (New York: Basic Books, 1973), pp. 143–52. Among others, it was discovered that a computer programmer was forced, because of the limitations of the computer then being used, to create a totally spurious planning unit ("fract") having no real-world analog and absolutely no substantive or policy relevance.

4. Reading any standard text on statistics will reveal some surprisingly strong assumptions that must be made to employ specific techniques. For instance, in the case of simple regression analysis (a prevalent analytic method), linearity in the relationship between dependent and independent variables is customary. Independent variables may be assumed to have been drawn from a normal or random distribution; if not, somewhat more complicated calculations are required; the variance associated with the dependent variable with respect to each subpopulation of independent variables is assumed to be equal for all subpopulations, e.g., the "residual variance"; and the error term for the regression equation is presumed to be independent and normally distributed. Any or all of these assumptions may or may not be valid; violation of any diminishes the power and utility of the analysis. See Taro Yamane, *Statistics: An Introductory Analysis* (New York: Harper & Row, 1964), p. 429.

5. Garry D. Brewer and James S. Kakalik, *Handicapped Children: Strategies for Improving Services* (New York: McGraw-Hill, 1979), "Epilogue," provide evidence of this.

6. Irving L. Janis and Leon Mann, *Decision Making* (New York: Free Press, 1977), pp. 129–31, make the point as well.

7. Warren Weaver, "Science and Complexity," *American Scientist 36* (1948), pp. 536–44. Emphasis added.

8. Ibid., p. 538.

9. Ronald D. Brunner and Garry D. Brewer, *Organized Complexity* (New York: Free Press, 1971), elaborate this theme.

10. Todd R. La Porte, "Complexity and Uncertainty: Challenge to Action," in Todd R. La Porte, ed., *Organized Social Complexity: Challenge to Politics and Policy* (Princeton, N. J.: Princeton University Press, 1975), chap. 10.

11. L. A. Zadeh, *Outline of a New Approach to the Analysis of Complex Systems and Decision Processes* (Berkeley, Calif.: College of Engineering, Electronics Research Laboratory, Memorandum No. ERL–M342, July 1972), pp. 2–3.

12. R. S. Rosenbloom et al., *New Tools for Urban Management* (Cambridge, Mass.: Harvard University Press, 1971), pp. 19–20.

13. Garry D. Brewer, "Hard Lessons from the Workaday World," *Science*, 12 May 1972, pp. 647–48, reviews the book.

14. David W. Malone, "An Introduction to the Application of Interpretive Structural Modeling," *Proceedings of the IEEE*, March 1975, p. 397f.

15. Albert Ando, Franklin M. Fisher, and Herbert A. Simon, *Essays on the Structure of Social Science Models* (Cambridge, Mass.: MIT Press, 1963), pp. 92–109.

16. James S. Coleman, *Introduction to Mathematical Sociology* (New York: Free Press, 1964), pp. 444–47.

17. Guy H. Orcutt, Harold W. Watts, and John B. Edwards, "Data Aggregation and Information Loss," *American Economic Review,* September 1968, pp. 773–87.

18. Despite considerable effort, "dimensional analysis," one form of social physics, has not penetrated the complexity threshold mainly for the reason stated. H. L. Langhaar, *Dimensional Analysis and Theory of Models* (New York: John Wiley & Sons, 1971); F. J. De Jong, *Dimensional Analysis for Economists* (Amsterdam: North-Holland, 1968); and, R. H. Ewing, "Introducing Dimensional Analysis to Social Sciences," *Socio-Economic Planning Sciences* 7, no. 5 (1972), pp. 533–43.

19. G. K. Chacko, ed., *Systems Approach to Environmental Pollution* (Arlington, Va.: Operations Research Society of America, 1972); M. M. Truitt et al., "Simulation Model of Urban Refuse Collection," *Journal of Sanitary Engineering* 95, no. SA2 (1969); William F. Hamilton, "Systems Analysis of Urban Transportation," *Scientific American* 221, no. 1 (1969); and, D. Drew, "Applications of Multilevel Systems Theory to the Design of a Freeway Control System," in M. D. Mesarovic and A. Reisman, eds., *Systems Approach and the City* (Amsterdam: North-Holland, 1972), pp. 156–175.

20. Maynard M. Baldwin, ed., *Portraits of Complexity: Applications of Systems Methodologies to Societal Problems* (Columbus, Ohio: Battelle Memorial Institute, 1975).

21. Ida Hoos, "Can Systems Analysis Solve Social Problems?" *Datamation,* June 1974, p. 91. Hoos answers her own question in the negative.

22. Jay W. Forrester, *World Dynamics* (Cambridge, Mass.: Wright-Allen, 1971); and, idem, *Urban Dynamics* (Cambridge, Mass.: MIT Press, 1969), are illustrative.

23. An evaluation of 10 professional appraisals of "System Dynamics," as applied to industrial, city, and world problems is provided in Garry D. Brewer, "Professionalism: The Need for Standards," *Interfaces,* November 1973, pp. 20–27; a detailed dissection, in terms consistent with the current discussion, can be found in Garry D. Brewer and Owen P. Hall, Jr., "Policy Analysis by Computer Simulation: The Need for Appraisal," *Public Policy,* Summer 1973, pp. 343–65.

24. Robert Boguslaw, *The New Utopians: A Study in System Design and Social Change* (Englewood Cliffs, N.J.: Prentice-Hall, 1965), provides an historical context; Ida Hoos, *Systems Analysis in Public Policy* (Berkeley: University of California Press, 1972), adds specific case detail.

25. Philip Handler, "Public Doubts About Science," *Science,* 6 June 1980, p. 1093.

26. Robert Frosch, "A New Look at Systems Engineering," *IEEE Spectrum,* September 1969, pp. 24–28.

27. David Easton, *A Systems Analysis of Political Life* (New York: John Wiley & Sons, 1965).

28. Robert Lineberry and Ira Sharkansky, *Urban Politics and Public Policy* (New York: Harper & Row, 1971).

29. Federal Energy Administration, *National Energy Outlook* (Washington, D.C.: Government Printing Office, February 1976); and idem, *Project Independence Evaluation System (PIES) Documentation,* series (Washington, D.C.: Government Printing Office, 1977 et seq.).

30. Lawrence S. Mayer, "The Value of the Econometric Approach to Forecasting our Energy Future" (Princeton, N.J.: Princeton University, Department of Statistics, 1977). (Mimeo.) A more detailed and critical summary is idem, "Econometric Energy Models: A Critical Essay" (Princeton, N.J.: Princeton University, Department of Statistics, 1977). (Mimeo.) Either can be obtained from Mayer, who is currently at the Wharton School of the University of Pennsylvania, Philadelphia, PA.

31. Bert G. Hickman, "Introduction and Summary," in Hickman, ed., *Econometric Models of Cyclical Behavior* (New York: National Bureau of Economic Research, 1972), p. 17.

32. Martin S. Feldstein, "An Econometric Model of the Medicare System," *Quarterly Journal of Economics*, February 1971, pp. 1–20.

33. David Berlinski, *On Systems Analysis* (Cambridge, Mass.: MIT Press, 1976).

34. Richard C. Larson, *Urban Police Patrol Analysis* (Cambridge, Mass.: MIT Press, 1972).

35. J. G. Taylor et al., "Simulation Applied to a Court System," *IEEE Transactions on Systems, Science, and Cybernetics*, vol. SSC–4, no. 4, November 1968. The analysis was done for the District of Columbia. See also, The President's Commission on Law Enforcement and Administration of Justice, *Science and Technology: Task Force Report* (Washington, D.C.: Government Printing Office, 1967), which relates the analysis to decision making.

36. Harold D. Lasswell, *Politics: Who Gets What, When, How* (New York: Meridian, 1958).

37. John D. Montgomery, Harold D. Lasswell, and Joel S. Migdal, eds., *Patterns of Policy: Comparative and Longitudinal Studies of Population Events* (New Brunswick, N.J.: Transaction Books, 1979).

38. Kevin F. McCarthy and Peter A. Morrison, *The Changing Demographic and Economic Structure of Nonmetropolitan Areas in the United States* (Santa Monica, Calif.: The Rand Corporation, R–2399–EDA, 1979).

39. Nicholas Hobbs, *The Futures of Children* (San Francisco: Jossey-Bass, 1975).

40. Hobbs has used the intellectual investment represented in the book and study as a blueprint for subsequent analyses. Also, he has included outside influential participants in a periodic visit and up-dating of ongoing work.

41. Joseph Goldstein, Anna Freud, and Albert J. Solnit, *Before the Best Interests of the Child* (New York: Free Press, 1979).

42. Brewer and Kakalik, *Handicapped Children.*

43. Robert Rubenstein and Harold D. Lasswell, *The Sharing of Power in a Psychiatric Hospital* (New Haven: Yale University Press, 1966); Ronald W. Conley, *The Economics of Mental Retardation* (Baltimore, Md.: Johns Hopkins University Press, 1973).

44. A reapplication of the Brewer and Kakalik, *Handicapped Children*, methodology to a single state for all citizens with respect to both mental illness and mental retardation is J. S. Kakalik, G. D. Brewer, L. L. Prusoff, D. J. Armor, and P. A. Morrison, *Mental Health and Mental Retardation Services in Nevada* (Santa Monica, Calif.: The Rand Corporation, R–1800–FLF, 1976). Seventy-one specific recommendations for change were proposed, and many have been put into effect.

45. Bruce A. Ackerman, and Susan Rose-Ackerman, James W. Sawyer, Jr., Dale W. Henderson, *The Uncertain Search for Environmental Quality* (New York: Free Press, 1974).

46. Patrick D. Larkey, *Evaluating Public Programs: The Impact of General Revenue Sharing on Municipal Government* (Princeton, N.J.: Princeton University Press, 1979). The National Tax Association designated the work as the best book of the year.

47. Joel S. Berke and Michael W. Kirst, eds., *Federal Aid to Education: Who Benefits? Who Governs?* (Lexington, Mass.: D. C. Heath, 1972).

48. Jacob Bronowski, *The Ascent of Man* (Boston: Little, Brown, 1973), p. 353.

49. Judith Innes de Neufville, *Social Indicators and Public Policy* (New York: Elsevier, 1975), is a representative assessment of the situation.

50. William D. Nordhaus, "World Dynamics: Measurement without Data," *Economic Journal*, December 1973, pp. 1156–83, comments on the problem.

51. Several of these are treated in Strauch, " 'Squishy' Problems."

52. Several of the ideas treated here were first presented in Garry D. Brewer, "Operational Social Systems Modeling," *Policy Sciences*, December 1978, pp. 157–69.

53. Peter A. Morrison, *Demographic Information for Cities* (Santa Monica, Calif.: The Rand Corporation, R–618, 1971); and idem, *How Population Movements Shape National Growth* (Santa Monica, Calif.: The Rand Corporation, P–5007, May 1973), are fine illustrations.

54. The relationships of demographic and urban policy aspects are summarized and illustrated (including a guide to many relevant policy analyses where these matters are central) in Peter A. Morrison et al., *Recent Contributions to the Urban Policy Debate* (Santa Monica, Calif.: The Rand Corporation, R–2394–RC, March 1979).

55. James S. Beshers, *Population Processes in Social Systems* (New York: Free Press, 1967), is an exception to the norm. Crude empirical evidence exists that there is a relation of demographic influences on government: In the fall of 1971, the Nixon Administration reorganized the respected Bureau of Labor Statistics, whose unpleasant news about the economy caused political unease. The reorganization led the *New York Times* to editorialize: "President Nixon's decision on Aug. 15 to junk his steady-as-you-go economic policy represented tacit acknowledgement that the B.L.S. economists had been quite precise in their analyses of what was happening to the economy. But the vindication supplied by events has brought no let-up in the Administration's apparent resolve to downgrade the career technicians responsible for these dispassionate appraisals." September 30, 1971, "Editorial." Shortly thereafter, as the action moved onward, Eileen Shanahan, also in the *New York Times,* observed: ". . . the plain fact is that some statisticians of unimpeachable competence and integrity are being shunted into less important work because they have refused to interpret the statistics as their bosses wanted them to." October 10, 1971, "The Reluctant Statisticians: Some Are Reorganized Out of Their Jobs."

56. Carol H. Weiss, ed., *Evaluating Social Action Programs* (Boston: Allyn and Bacon, 1972), emphasizes this.

57. The limitation frequently is not a sufficient deterent, however. See Martin S. Feldstein, *Economic Analysis of Health Service Efficiency* (Chicago: Markham, 1968).

58. In the education area, one needs only remind the reader of the data problems that plagued James S. Coleman, *Equality of Educational Opportunity* (Washington, D.C.: Government Printing Office, 1966).

59. Nordhaus, "World Dynamics"; and Brewer and Hall, "Policy Analysis," both treat this in some detail.

60. J. A. Stockfisch, *Incentives and Information Quality in Defense Management* (Santa Monica, Calif.: The Rand Corporation, R–1827, 1976), is directly on target with respect to national security analyses.

61. These essential insights were provided by Bruce G. Blair in a private communication.

62. Eugene Bardach, "Gathering Data for Policy Research," *Urban Analysis* 2, no. 1 (1974), pp. 117–44, is extremely valuable on this matter.

63. This is a dangerous point in an analysis. Substitute measures are often used, but misinterpreted badly. For instance, the divorce rate is often cited as a measure of satisfaction with the institution of marriage; however, no one really knows whether an increase in the divorce rate indicates a breakdown of the family as an institution as such or the strains and frustrations with other aspects of society.

64. Marc Lappé et al., "Ethical and Social Issues in Screening for Genetic Disease," *New England Journal of Medicine,* May 25, 1972, pp. 1129–32.

65. The promise of the social indicators movement is displayed in Otis Dudley Duncan, *Toward Social Reporting* (New York: Russell Sage Foundation, 1969); the realities are considered in de Neufville, *Social Indicators;* and, for a compendium and bibliography, in Leslie D. Wilcox, Ralph M. Brooks, George M. Beal, and Gerald E. Klonglan, *Social Indicators and Societal Monitoring* (San Francisco: Jossey-Bass, 1972).

66. See James R. Murray, Michael J. Minor, Norman M. Bradburn, Robert F. Cotterman, Martin Frankel, and Alan E. Pisarski, "Evolution of Public Response to the Energy Crisis," *Science*, 19 April 1974, pp. 257–63, for one indication of this.

67. Ramsay Clark, *Crime in America* (New York: Simon & Schuster, 1970), is the basis of this comment.

68. Some hold the view that we have no national energy policy because the problem is predominantly local and regional in scope (not only *is* but *ought* to be): Amory B. Lovins, *Soft Energy Paths* (Cambridge, Mass.: Ballinger, 1977), is a main exponent of this view. For the contrary position, see Federal Energy Administration, *(PIES) Documentation*.

69. Steven R. Brown, *Political Subjectivity* (New Haven: Yale University Press, 1980), is one of the very few treatments of opinions, attitudes, and individual values that appears to have direct relevance to policy analysis in the form presented throughout this book. Angus Campbell, Philip E. Converse, and Williard L. Rogers, *The Quality of American Life* (New York: Russell Sage Foundation, 1976), present the conventional view and approach.

70. M. Harvey Brenner, *Mental Illness and the Economy* (Cambridge, Mass.: Harvard University Press, 1973), p. ix. The argument is not universally accepted, however; see, Frederick C. Redlich and Daniel X. Freedman, *Theory and Practice of Psychiatry* (New York: Basic Books, 1966), p. 539: "Although etiological theories are many, our knowledge of the causative factors [in mental illness] is scanty, and we must view affective behavior disorder as of unknown and exceedingly complex etiology. [Doing otherwise] is a gross oversimplification." Brenner alleges other connections: to death, heart disease, suicides, homocides, and prison admissions. "The Human Tragedy of Unemployment," *U.S. News & World Report*, June 23, 1980, pp. 68–69.

71. Health data represent the first example; and, many examples of the latter are found in: Privacy Protection Study Commission, *Personal Privacy in an Informative Society* (Washington, D.C.: Government Printing Office, 1977).

72. Brown, *Political Subjectivity*; and, Garry D. Brewer, *A Prototype Office of Human Statistics* (Santa Monica, Calif.: The Rand Corporation, P–4439, 1970).

73. David Novick, "Mathematics: Logic, Quantity, and Method," *Review of Economics and Statistics*, November 1954, pp. 357–58, strongly supports this opinion.

74. Strauch, " 'Squishy' Problems"; see also, Edward S. Quade and W. I. Boucher, eds., *Systems Analysis and Policy Planning* (New York: American Elsevier, 1968), pp. 2, 4–5, 11, 17.

75. Orcutt et al., "Data Aggregation," is splendid on this topic.

76. Henri Theil, *Applied Economic Forecasting* (Amsterdam: North-Holland, 1966), pp. 262ff, uses an information-theory approach to consider error propagation problems. William Alonso, "The Quality of Data and the Choice and Design of Predictive Models," in George C. Hemmens, ed., *Urban Development Models* (Washington, D.C.: Highway Research Board, Special Report 97, 1968), pp. 178–92, concludes "[W]e should have research groups in universities and other centers working on complex models, while operational agencies would be working with simpler and safer models." P. 192.

77. Such is very much the case in one very prominent and influential strategic analysis: See Paul Nitze, "Deterring our Deterent," *Foreign Policy*, Winter 1976–77, pp. 195–210; for a detailed assessment, Garry D. Brewer and Bruce G. Blair, "War Games and National Security: With a Grain of SALT," *The Bulletin of the Atomic Scientists*, June 1979, pp. 18–26.

78. William Ascher, *Forecasting: An Appraisal for Policy-Makers and Planners* (Baltimore, Md.: Johns Hopkins University Press, 1978), pp. 63–64, 119–128, documents this.

79. This and other political ("selection") reactions and connections to estimation are discussed in Chapter 6.

80. Paul Bracken, "Unintended Consequences of Strategic Gaming," *Simulation & Games*, September 1977, pp. 283–318.

81. Richard Titmuss, *Problems of Social Policy* (London: HMSO, 1950), pp. 13, 21, is the source for this cited in Bracken.

82. John Erickson, *The Road to Stalingrad* (London: Weidenfeld and Nicholson, 1975), chap. 1.

83. Barton Whaley, *Codeword* BARBAROSSA (Cambridge, Mass.: MIT Press, 1973), corroborates Waller Goerlitz, *Paulus and Stalingrad* (London: Methuen, 1963), pp. 97–120, which Bracken relies on.

84. Brewer and Blair, "War Games," document and argue that many current strategic analyses are at least as flawed. See Garry D. Brewer and Martin Shubik, *The War Game: A Critique of Military Problem Solving* (Cambridge, Mass.: Harvard University Press, 1979), for a more detailed assessment.

85. In effect, this serves as a main justification for the recommendations advanced by Alexander L. George, "The Case for Multiple Advocacy in Making Foreign Policy," *American Political Science Review*, September 1972, pp. 751–85. The recommendations are generalizable to most complex social problems. At least the possibility merits consideration.

6

Methods and estimation
in the policy process

METHODS, TOOLS, AND PROCEDURES

An appropriate tone, at least a chastening one, for a discussion of methods has been set by Barrett:

> All of this would be comic if it weren't also so pathetic—and ultimately dangerous. This worship of technique is in fact more childish than the worship of machines. You have only to find the right method, the definite procedure, and all problems in life must inevitably yield before it.[1]

Different research and scientific approaches rely on somewhat related methodologies—e.g., formal logic, statistics, the calculus—no one of which is either necessary or sufficient to solve social problems. Followers of specialized disciplines, using a familiar tool or method, are occasionally capable of generating specific, narrow insights about a select aspect of a social phenomenon, but this limited success is seldom adequate to comprehend the entirety of the phenomenon or to locate it within the broader decisional context. Limited success may even cause the specialist to overreach; thus, an engineer well grounded in the mysteries of electrical circuitry may be tempted to extend this technical expertise to other areas, such as the urban setting or the entire world,[2] without realizing that this far exceeds the limits of substantive competence.[3] Rather than being cautious or thoughtful about the dangers of inappropriate and limited methodologies, decision makers seem prone to place extraordinary ("comic" in Barrett's terms) reliance on overextended techniques and technicians,[4] the proliferation of which arises from many specific factors too detailed to enumerate here.[5] What the proliferation generally suggests, however, are considerable methodological immaturity and a need to improve our understanding of the relationship of methods to policy knowledge—both in and of the decision process.

Tools

The number and diversity of available tools for policy analysis are staggering and it is not our intent to provide an exhaustive treatment of them. Nor do we claim that the tools illustrated here are the best examples of the class they represent: We are familiar with them and know that they have been used in certain circumstances to advantage.

The uninitiated reader is well advised to consult Claire Selltiz et al., *Research Methods in Social Relations* (New York: Holt, Rinehart & Winston, 1964), for a basic orientation to tools. Though somewhat dated, this resource contains innumerable simple illustrations, suggestions (e.g., how to interview, design a questionnaire, how to sample), and an extensive bibliography; the place of measurement in the social sciences is, commendably, treated from a multidisciplinary perspective.[6]

Statistical tools abound, due in part to our lengthy appreciation for disorganized and complex problems, for which they have particular applicability. A good, basic introductory text is Taro Yamane, *Statistics: An Introductory Analysis* (New York: Harper & Row, 1967); as is A. Mood, F. Graybill, and D. C. Roes, *Introduction to the Theory of Statistics* (New York: McGraw-Hill, 1974). Both texts are relatively uncomplicated technical introductions and neither is encumbered by excessive social science content.[7] Four texts that extend basic understanding to social phenomena are Hubert M. Blalock, *Social Statistics* (New York: McGraw-Hill, 1960); Eric A. Hanushek and John E. Jackson, *Statistical Methods for Social Scientists* (New York: Academic Press, 1977); W. Allen Wallis and Harry V. Roberts, *The Nature of Statistics* (New York: Free Press, 1965); and Carl N. Morris and John E. Rolph, *Introduction to Data Analysis and Statistical Inference* (Englewood Cliffs, N.J.: Prentice-Hall, 1981). The first two are intermediate-level treatments to be considered only if one has already received a grounding in the fundamentals; the final two are devoted to the broad questions of appropriate use of statistics in many different applications.

Two very useful statistically oriented works that consider policy applications and problems are Philip M. Hauser, *Social Statistics in Use* (New York: Russell Sage Foundation, 1975); and James S. Coleman, *The Mathematics of Collective Action* (Chicago: Aldine, 1973). Hauser is especially good on demographic data, including their collection, manipulation, use and impact on social problems (e.g., the labor force, family, education, social security, welfare, housing, recreation, land use, and other topics are discussed and illustrated well). Coleman, an experienced policy analyst, skillfully advances an earlier technical contribution by focusing on the relationship and interactions of individuals in groups constituted for purposive action, i.e., for policy purposes.[8] It is a sophisticated work, and reflects in many important aspects our concerns about the extreme difficulty of doing useful estimation. A technically difficult, but rewarding, book in this vein is Albert Ando, Franklin Fisher, and Herbert A. Simon, *Essays in the Structure of Social Science Models* (Cambridge, Mass.: MIT Press, 1963).[9]

Politically oriented, but still statistically based, references are numerous; however, Hayward R. Alker, Jr., *Mathematics & Politics* (New York: Macmillan, 1965); and Edward R. Tufte, *Data Analysis for Politics and Policy* (Englewood Cliffs, N.J.: Prentice-Hall, 1974), provide breadth of coverage in measure equal to technical competence.[10] A useful, practical supplement is Kenneth Janda, *Data Processing: Applications to Political Research* (Evanston, Ill.: Northwestern University Press, 1965).

Econometrics, especially that part of the subfield of economics related to realistic applications, has many excellent sources. One that has stood the test of time and provided many clear illustrations is N. R. Draper and H. Smith, *Applied Regression Analysis* (New York: John Wiley & Sons, 1968).[11]

Mathematics has supplied many useful tools for policy analysis, and the neophyte is well advised to gain as much familiarity with several of these tools as with statistical ones. Many social problems lend themselves to representation in what is known as difference equation form (e.g., situations where time is considered directly, cycles, growth and decline, sequences); Samuel Goldberg, *Introduction to Difference Equations* (New York: John Wiley & Sons, 1961), is both readable and filled with diverse examples. A more challenging extension of these tools is Thor A. Bak and Jonas Lichtenberg, *Series, Differential Equations, and Complex Functions* (New York: W. A. Benjamin, 1967).

Mathematical programming has evolved over the years and, in its more technically sophisticated versions, has been used for purposes of system control. E. M. L. Beale, ed., *Applications of Mathematical Programming Techniques* (New York: American Elsevier, 1970), demonstrates a range of uses of these powerful tools. Norman J. Driebeck, *Applied Linear Programming* (Reading, Mass.: Addison-Wesley, 1969); and Richard Bellman and Robert Kalaba, *Dynamic Programming and Modern Control Theory* (New York: Academic Press, 1965), represent variations on the basic programming theme; both are clear statements of the techniques and suggest many potential applications.

Game theory, conceived as a branch of applied mathematics, has received attention over the years since its initial theoretical statement by John von Neumann and Oskar Morgernstern, *The Theory of Games and Economic Behavior* (Princeton, N.J.: Princeton University Press, 1953). Martin Shubik, among others, has taken responsibility for the extension of the theory into various practical social settings: Shubik, ed., *Game Theory and Related Approaches to Social Behavior* (New York: John Wiley & Sons, 1964); and, idem, *Games for Society, Business and War* (New York: Elsevier, 1975).

While admittedly overstating the case to make the point, it is useful to think of many mathematical tools in terms of their appropriateness for well-defined or well-understood problems—problems often marked by their simplicity in the sense used throughout this book. In response to limitations of application discovered for many ill-defined and poorly-understood problems, i.e., those of organized complexity, gaming and simulation approaches and tools have been created and used. Shubik's *Games for Society, Business and War* bridges the gap between tools for simple and complex problems and illustrates a central argument of Chapters 4 and 5: Problems should suggest and stimulate the development of tools, not the reverse. Many practical applications of gaming are given in Shubik, *The Uses and Methods of Gaming* (New York: Elsevier, 1975). A rich source of operational policy applications of simulation (and closely related) techniques is contained in U.S. Environmental Protection Agency, *A Guide to Models in Governmental Planning & Operations* (Washington, D.C.: Office of Research and Development, Environmental Protection Agency, 1974). A well-balanced survey of these tools in realistic decision and planning settings is offered in Martin Greenberger, Matthew A. Crenson, and Brian L. Crissey, *Models in the Policy Process* (New York: Russell Sage Foundation, 1976). Specific examples of some extraordinary weaknesses of simulation applications are also worth consulting to give one a sense of many difficulties that inhibit policy use of these tools. Brewer's *Politicians, Bureaucrats and the Consultant* (New York: Basic Books, 1973); Brewer and Shubik, *The War Game* (Cambridge, Mass.: Harvard University Press, 1979); Holcomb Research Institute, *Environmental Modeling and Decision Making* (New York: Praeger Publishers, 1976); and Karl W. Deutsch, Bruno Fritsch, Helio Jaguaribe, and Andrei S. Markovits, eds., *Problems of World Modeling: Political and Social Implications* (Cambridge, Mass.: Ballinger, 1977), adopt somewhat different points of view, and hence illuminate the situation differently; all contribute specific detail to the general arguments and themes of this part.[12]

A tool has little meaning or value until brought into use. But experience accumulated in using these tools for policy purposes (discernible by reading many of the selections just referenced) has been highly qualified—qualified enough to lend credence to Barrett's pessimism about the methodological holy grail. A few possible explanations for this have been suggested earlier and can be summarized here.

Many of the tools were created in a rational/positivistic mode, i.e., they were meant to penetrate naturalistic and mechanical puzzles; they are object and thing oriented.

A tool is a means; however, when prior specification of the end or goal sought is indeterminant, changing, or subject to dispute, the finest tool (means) may be of no assistance—and may even worsen the problem.

Many of the available tools emphasize average or aggregate system properties and tendencies that are irrelevant to specific and individual needs. Every problem context is unique, and every individual with an interest or stake in a problem is worthy of consideration.

Selection and use of a tool, respectively, project an order on problems that, in turn, bias potential outcomes that can be realized.

Tools have, in short, been used too often in the absence of sufficient understanding of the problems to which they have been applied. Appropriate and effective use requires a systematic mode of inquiry or process of thought to attain such understanding. Several general procedures to fulfill this need have been created.

Procedures to use tools: A synthesis of methods

Operations research, systems analysis, and policy sciences represent three apparently similar, but actually quite different, estimation philosophies. Each was created and has evolved in response to realistic problem settings, and all provide systematic procedures to use tools and to synthesize methods in the general interest of solving problems.

Operations research first came to prominence in World War II, as teams of scientists and engineers turned their skills and talents to solving problems of efficient allocation and management of scarce military resources. Most agree that the initial creation of OR, as the field is commonly known, occurred in Great Britain, although by around 1951 it had taken root in America as well.[13] Operations research is based on a rationalistic premise and a positivistic view of the world, or, according to two influential exponents, "The approach of operations research is that of the scientific method. In particular, the process begins by carefully observing and formulating the problem and then constructing a scientific (typically mathematical) model that attempts to abstract the essence of the real problem."[14] It emphasizes an institutional level of analysis or detail: "Operations research is the application of scientific method to the decision problems of business and other units of social organization including government and military organizations."[15] And, elsewhere, "the objectives being sought must be consistent with those of the overall organization."[16] It favors a team or multidisciplinary approach: "[For complex systems] experts in other disciplines [than mathematics and the physical sciences] become more useful as members of the operations research team. Persons with backgrounds in economics, psychology, and other social sciences have expertise which can greatly assist in the analysis."[17] To identify another important characteristic, operations research aims to find optimal solutions: "[OR] attempts to find the best or optimal solution to the problem under consideration. . . . [T]he goal is to identify the best possible course of action."[18]

With reference to an earlier discussion ("Estimation as Simplification"), it is fair to claim that operations researchers operate mainly with an estimation paradigm much like that Strauch identifies as the "Common Perception of Analysis" (Figure 5–2). Accordingly, genuine success has been achieved in understanding and solving both simple and some disorganized-and-complex problems.[19] However, despite both willingness and considerable effort, operations researchers have had far less success in cracking complex-and-organized (squishy in Strauch's terms) social problems of interest in this book.[20] By now the reader should have some appreciation for this, and reference to the underlying premises and bases of the OR philosophy helps one see possible reasons for the shortcomings.

> Many problems cannot be represented with a rational, scientific model; furthermore, what the essence of the problem might be is an open question resolved uniquely for each individual participant in the problem, based on his or her identifications, expectations, and demands.

> Institutions are but one potential focus and level of analysis. Others, such as the individual or collections of institutions in interaction, exist and need to be accounted for, too.

> A team approach is commendable for the additional perspectives and information it may yield. However, the heavy burden OR places on mathematical representation has resulted in a dominance of mathematicians and others who have invested heavily in the mastery of tools and techniques. Evidence of explicit consideration of qualitative and softer data, concepts, and methods is scarce.

> Determining an optimal solution is equivalent to establishing a single goal. Most social problems defy such determination and, hence, limit or obviate optimal analyses.

Systems analysis, as a second philosophy, is closely associated with individuals and work emanating from The Rand Corporation, particularly during the late 1950s and early to middle 1960s.[21] The idea of systems analysis has been cogently stated by two of its practitioners, E. S. Quade and W. I. Boucher, as "a systematic approach to helping a decision maker choose a course of action by investigating his full problem, searching out objectives and alternatives, and comparing them in the light of their consequences, using an appropriate framework—insofar as possible analytic—to bring expert judgment and intuition to bear on the problem."[22] A careful reading of this statement helps one understand the philosophy better.

Help a decision maker: the client-analyst relationship is central and if the analyst does the job well, both client and analyst benefit—and the converse. *Choose a course of action:* estimation needs to be oriented to decisions whose effects will occur in the future. *By investigating his full problem:* this stresses the needs of problem identification and contextual specification, both of which need to be done with respect to the needs of the decision maker; comprehensiveness is sought, too. *Search out objectives and alternatives:* the creative dimension of estimation is underscored and, by interpretation of the sense of the whole statement, one can infer that such alternatives will require assessment in light of the goals of the participants, with primacy given those of the client. *Compare them in light of their consequences:* prediction of likely costs and benefits of the alternatives needs to be carried out. *Use an appropriate framework —insofar as possible analytic:* appropriateness refers to incorporation of all the previous tasks noted, and analytic stresses the responsible use of data. *Bring expert judgment and intuition to bear:* the essential role of the analyst, as emphasized throughout this book, is recognized explicitly.

Distinctions between systems analysis and operations research can be drawn, subject to legitimate differences of interpretation; these are summarized in Table 6–1.

Many specific contributions have been made by systems analysts, and these will not be detailed here.[23] Several generic innovations do warrant mention, however, because they have not only been used to advantage but they have also passed into the analytic culture at large. Among the more prominent of these would be cost-benefit analysis,[24] planning, programming, and budgeting systems,[25] and the use of a wide variety of simulations

TABLE 6–1   Distinctions between operations research and systems analysis

	Premise or worldview	Main user of analysis	Main level of analysis	Disciplinary preference	Solution aim
Operations research	Rationalistic; positivist; reductionist.	Institutions; organizations.	Institutions; organizations.	Mathematics, engineering, natural sciences.	Optimality.
Systems analysis	Rationalistic, but with allowance for judgment and intuition. Reductionist.	"Client," variously conceived as single decision maker or institution represented by such.	"Comprehensive," mitigated by judgment of the analyst of client's needs.	Economics, management sciences, engineering, natural sciences.	Cost-benefit; efficiency.

and games for operational or policy purposes.[26] In terms of specific systems analysis studies, the *ne plus ultra* is commonly regarded as the "Rand bomber basing study" (described earlier in Chapter 3).[27]

The approach and those who rely on it to do estimation have not been without problems and critics, however.[28] Several limiting features of systems analysis can be identified.

Heavy reliance on efficiency has naturally guided systems analysts to use economics and economic tools for many of their analyses. To the extent that this discipline fails or comes up short in specific application, so, too, will systems analyses that depend on it.[29]

The scope of the potential values considered frequently is narrowed to wealth and power concerns—mirroring prevalent disciplinary preoccupations and emphasizing the privileged position of many clients for this kind of work. Questions about "whose costs?" and "whose benefits?" are often presumed to include mainly those of the commissioning client and/or institution.[30]

Unself-conscious submersion of one's own (and society's) preferences and interests in the pursuit of those favored by a client has occurred and has resulted in embarrassment[31] and even harm to one analytic institution.[32]

Data and theory problems (of the sort noted earlier in Chapter 5) have constantly inhibited systems analysts and, as a consequence, reliance on objective measurements and proxies for direct observation has frequently overtaken otherwise well-intentioned analyses.[33]

In short, systems analysis works quite well for problems having both simple and disorganized complexity aspects, particularly those in which a client's preferences can be identified and sought out through estimation; it has been less successful in coping with problems marked by their organized complexity, especially where a full range of human values, needs, and perspectives must be considered and taken directly into analytic account. Little in the philosophy, per se, would necessarily lead to these outcomes; rather, it appears as though the practical matters of working to satisfy a single client and doing so under resource constraints (time, talent, and money) both contribute to this situation. Time particularly stands out here. Deadlines must be met—and these are ordinarily prespecified in precise contractual terms—and answers must be rendered. While we have noted that some analysis is better, in principle, than none, many qualifications of time-constrained analyses tend to be lost as attention focuses on the one or a few best action alternatives.[34] Fixation on efficiency as a general objective and criterion for assessment of many systems analyses downgrades use of legitimate alternatives, such as equity, consensus, pluralism, conflict reduction, freedom, and human dignity. Such fixity of aim has led to a reduction in the nature and quality of work associated with this philosophy.

Policy sciences, the approach and philosophy recommended in this book, has already been characterized in the book's Introduction. The following summary highlights those aspects of it that serve to distinguish it from alternatives, laying particular emphasis on its potential contributions to estimation.[35] Its relation and concern for the whole of the decision process cannot, however, be overlooked.

The importance of contextuality is explicitly treated in concern for *contextual mapping:* a comprehensive framework and collection of procedures intended to improve one's understanding of relationships between parts and wholes; to provide a sense of their interaction through time, from the past, to the present, and into the future; to remind the analyst of the multiple perspectives, goals, and needs at stake in a given problem setting; and to give a basis for assessing the meaning or significance of each problem component, including the symbolic or analytic representation of each. When properly used, contextual mapping has the possibility of making the analyst a more powerful and independent thinker than one who delegates responsibility for organizing the frame of analytic attention to someone else (as occurs in both operations research and systems analysis).[36]

The *developmental construct,* another of Lasswell's contributions, is worth consideration because it is explicitly policy-oriented, combining as it does, one part expert, one part scenario (or image of the future), one part model-building (or analytic representation), and a solid proportion of normative specification. It is a method in that consistent procedures and rules underlie its execution and use. Its key objective—to allow decision makers to adapt rapidly to emerging conditions in changing contexts—is simple and worth achieving. Described and used in various policy settings,[37] a key strength of the developmental construct is its appreciation for the contingent and intentional status of the future, or as its inventor puts it, "the construct is tentative and exploratory, not dogmatic. Words that refer to future events are inferences from the existing supply of scientific and historical knowledge, and of provisional projections. They are not, however, science. They do not conjoin theory and data, since data are not available about the future." To emphasize its instrumental and intentional (in Dewey's senses) character:

> It is not put forward with the primary purpose of forecasting; rather, the construct is understood to afford a present modification of communicated events at the focus of attention. A future consequence may be the initiation of acts that prevent a forecast from coming true. This is the problem-solving demand to "create" or "invent" the future, not to remain passively content with the forecasting role.[38]

The developmental construct serves a clarifying function for specialists interested in locating particular research, personal, and professional interests in a broader social context. It does so by helping them choose and time their work with respect to the planned observation of the future, past, and present. Estimation is facilitated by orienting the analyst to the problem from a distinctly humanistic basis rather than from an institutional or client-centered one.[39]

Prototyping responds to several known features of the policy setting, including its complexity, uncertainty, and potential for conflict among affected participants. It represents a positive response to the need for innovative or creative initiatives in decision settings. It differs from experimentation (including social experimentation) in that one need not consider and measure every conceivable permutation of a proposed change or policy,[40] but only those found to be most consequential for those whose lives are likely to be affected by such changes.[41] A chief purpose of the prototype is "to see whether the innovation [policy recommendation] is capable of . . . attaining a consensus that includes a willingness among the most effective participants to give the innovation a fair test."[42] When a prototype is enacted, inevitable errors of formulation become evident, institutional and motivational difficulties emerge for attention and correction, and a more complete picture of the real costs and benefits—in more than simple economic terms—can be drawn before putting the amended innovation into full-scale use.

Scenarios, games, and computer simulations are all possible techniques available to the policy scientist. As noted previously, each has been created to a certain extent to help an analyst bridge the gap between simple and organized-and-complex problems. The scenario especially lends itself to estimation requirements in that it usually relies on a verbal (and hence accessible), tentative (and hence alterable), and future-oriented (and hence policy-relevant) depiction of past, present, and both likely and desired future possibilities.[43] Games and simulations, when skillfully and appropriately employed, are also relevant.[44]

Finally, the creation and use of *decision seminars* has been shown to achieve several desirable estimation objectives, including context-specific and disciplined integration of diverse problem perspectives and purposes.[45] Starting with simple, relatively abstract games and verbal-visual scenarios of plausible policy innovations, seminar members may move to field tests and controlled experimentation (prototypes), and finally arrive at policy recommendations. Participants represent diverse specialties, methodological skills, and viewpoints—all selected with due consideration for a tentative appreciation of the problem, which is subject to revision as is the composition of the group.[46] Emphasis is placed on the critical use of imagination, methodological flexibility, and an orientation to the future.[47]

In short, policy sciences provides a comprehensive intellectual and analytic orientation to problem solving. It is a difficult and challenging discipline, but one that has shown itself to be particularly responsive to the difficulties presented by most social decisions. Thus, it can be stressed that

TABLE 6–2   Distinguishing features of policy sciences

Premise or worldview	Instrumental; comprehensive; value-based and problem oriented.
Main user of analysis	Variable, depending on specification of the policy problem. No one excluded a priori.
Main level of analysis	Humankind, or "hominocentric" basis of analysis. The individual and relationship of all potentially affected individuals to collectivities (institutions and institutions in interaction) explicitly treated.
Disciplinary preference	None. All intellectual fields and traditions in principle relevant to the totality of problems that may, given time and circumstances, require consideration and resolution.
Solution aim	Increasing human dignity through inclusion in all the value-shaping and -sharing processes and institutions, existing and conceivable.

policy sciences are not simply a modification of operations research or systems analysis; they represent an entirely different worldview and epistemology (Table 6–2).

We conclude this section on methods by pointing out some of the more practical, even mundane, tasks that an analyst is frequently required to attend to.

Practical procedural matters

Practically, analysis may proceed in any number of ways;[48] however, many fundamental matters recur so often as to require discussion, a view seconded by Edward Quade, whose experiences as a systems analyst are exceeded by few.[49]

The first thing the analyst should do, according to Quade, is to "interrogate the decision-maker or whomever it was that commissioned [the] analysis and all other persons within the organization or associated with the problem who seem likely to be able to help."[50] The initial interrogation has many purposes, not the least of which is trying to arrive at a workable, if not clear, definition of the problem. Among other details, the analyst probes to determine the origins of the problem, who the various participants are within the context of the problem—including what seem to be their interests and objectives; whether there are existing programs and policies that bear on the situation as presented by the client; who has responsibility for decision alternatives that could in time flow from analysis; what a solution or answer might look like and, for such tentative formulations, whether or not they could be feasible, appealing, or even relevant to those commissioning the work; and, given an emerging sense of the problem, whether sufficient resources are available to undertake the project.

Arriving at some preliminary definition of "What's the problem?" helps the analyst achieve a sense of what lies ahead. One needs to understand, however, that the task of problem definition is open-ended and continually subject to revision as estimation advances. Often a client's initial conception of the problem turns out to be misguided or erroneous. Ideally, calling this to attention will result in a redefinition; practically, doing so may reveal that one is working for the wrong client or that the client's obduracy may impede full or productive exploration.

As a procedural matter, Quade suggests the generation of an "Issue Paper," intended to ensure that no key factors have been overlooked prior to launching the analysis. The key elements of the Issue Paper are reproduced (Table 6–3) to summarize the initial analytic steps.

Depending on the many factual details and uncertainties uncovered in this preliminary reckoning of the problem, the analyst could be faced with choices and may react variously to them. One responsible reaction is to decline further work, that is, deciding not to do an analysis.[51] The prospec-

---

TABLE 6–3   Items for an issue paper

Source and background of the problem
Reasons for attention
Groups of institutions toward which corrective activity is directed
Beneficiaries
Related programs
Goals and objectives
Measures of effectiveness
Framework for the analysis:
   Kinds of alternatives
   Possible methodologies
   Critical assumptions
Alternatives:
   Description
   Effectiveness
   Costs
   Spillovers
   Comments on ranking
   Other considerations
Recommendations that might follow

Source: Edward S. Quade, "Initiating the Analytic Process," in Quade, *Analysis for Public Decisions* (New York: Elsevier, 1975), pp. 69–70.

tive client may have already made plans and commitments to a specific course of action: in which case analysis is being enlisted merely to provide additional scientific support for such preferences. The client may be concerned with only an insignificant portion of the whole problem, as perceived by the analyst, the solution of which would do little or could even worsen the larger situation. There may not be sufficient resources available to conduct what, in the analyst's opinion, would be a responsible and thorough job. Or, the analyst may be repelled by the subject matter, by the implications likely to flow from the work, or by the client. Whatever the reason, and this list is only suggestive, there may be grounds for the analyst not to do the work.[52]

Particularly if resources are not lavish, the analyst may recommend addressing a portion of the initially specified job. Deciding on priorities should be a joint responsibility of the analyst and the client and one in which analytic feasibility is matched against imagined importance or need. Many projects have unfolded in this manner, with tasks being treated serially and informed by the data and information produced in earlier partial efforts. However, should this occur, the analyst needs to be aware of the dangers that such a reductionist or partist strategy impart.[53]

Presuming that initial problem specification and planned estimation efforts can be harmonized with only minor modifications and clarifications, the analyst proceeds next to research management responsibilities of finding a staff, defining tasks and objectives for the analytic group—including establishing schedules and milestones, assigning responsibilities by allocating funds according to tasks, and planning the overall research strategy to be followed. Any one of the practical matters, if left unattended or done poorly, may result in poor or deficient estimation. For instance, the apparently simple matter of staff selection may be thwarted because key individuals are already fully employed (talented people are seldom idle); or, the ideal collection of professional expertise may be simply unmanageable because of personal idiosyncracies, mutual intellectual disrespect, or for dozens of other seemingly trivial, but nevertheless consequential, reasons. As it is with many elaborate planning exercises, one of the first casualties of action may be the plan itself: data one thought would be available and suitable turn out not to be; personnel crucial to some aspect of the effort perform below expectations, or not at all; computers "crash" and take irreplaceable data or programs with them; clients change—the list is as long, diverse, and bothersome as it is challenging to the research manager.

The sum and substance of this discussion can be stated simply: Analysis is an art where the artists are overwhelmed by house painters. Resort to specific systematic procedures may be a necessary component of analysis, but it is by no means sufficient. Also required are experience, skill, judgment, taste, and plain old-fashioned luck—all in ample measure. Failing to understand this, the way things are, has doomed more than a few analyses.[54]

EXPERTS

We have alluded to estimation (and other) experts from time to time. Experts of many kinds are encountered during estimation, a stage in the overall process where specialized skills and insights are required, and a clearer understanding of who these people are, what they do, and their impact on the overall process of decision and policymaking is needed.

Estimation concerns all interested or having a stake in the policy process, but it is the special domain of the expert adviser. An expert is a person who has acquired detailed and often exotic skills in a particular subject. Such expertise may derive from formal training, experience, or a combination; a specialist is one who has concentrated on a very limited field of learning. Technique and knowledge join in terms of an "expert-specialist," a common label for many who do estimation. However, knowing more about fewer basic topics, and relying on a limited set of well-oiled tools to do so, present difficulties for those wishing to use expert advice.[55] Discrepancies are common between the narrowly defined and highly detailed information the estimation expert ordinarily deals with; the somewhat more general and comprehensive information required by a bureaucratic decision maker; the broad, general, and summary information required by an elected official, where details of one problem compete with myriad others for time and attention; and that accessible to the average citizen, whose awareness of problems may be shaky or doubtful.[56] While understandable, these discrepancies in information needs and capabilities are merely symptomatic of a deeper set of issues related to the disparate ways in which experts, decision makers, and citizens perceive, order, value, and interpret common settings.

Nevertheless, as problems demanding attention and resolution proliferate and become more noticeably complex, decision makers find themselves less able to manage or even understand them. Experts and reliance on experts increase apace.[57] Consulting services for the federal government, in 1980 for example, may have been running at as little as $2 billion or as much as $9 billion a year; no one knew for certain according to the U.S. General Accounting Office: "The use of consulting services in the Federal Government is extensive. However, there currently is no single reliable source for information as to how many consulting service contracts are being used to supply goods and services to the Federal Government or how much it is costing."[58] What is sure is that much of the consulting resources is being used for tasks related to estimation, e.g., technical knowledge, added comprehension, independent opinions, and specialized experience.[59]

Returning to the matter of differences that exist between the analyst and the decision maker helps one understand why different estimation results occur (e.g., the rational or optimal answer that conflicts with the decision maker's intuitive sense of what to do, noted earlier as adding up but not feeling right);[60] it also suggests a need for clarification and consideration of the decisions flowing from either an analytic or intuitive premise. Clarification is often not forthcoming because of the parochial requirements of those concerned, i.e., the expert's need to stay in business and the decision maker's desire to appear decisively in control.[61] Scientifically inclined experts, for instance, concentrate on rigorous measurement, theoretical development, and the refinement of tools and, hence, tend to produce results of marginal or only occasional interest to others in the decision process. Alternative consequences, according to Millikan, are that "The scientist is apt to have a strong conviction that applied research cannot be 'fundamental,' . . . [and] that the operator has asked the wrong questions, that the questions are too vaguely or too narrowly formulated, or that as formulated they are incapable of being clearly answered."[62] Those who market analyses are concerned about money to support expensive technical personnel and, in turn, the institutions and paraphernalia that support them. Selling often means that more is promised than can be delivered, and whatever the particular case, analysis ends up being less beneficial than it otherwise might have been.[63]

Many of these real features of analysis in use, with reference to military and national security experts, are captured in the following sharp comments from former Air Force General Glenn A. Kent: "I am not so sure that analysis as a credible ingredient in decision-making will necessarily have a brilliant future [because] decision-makers are becoming increasingly annoyed that different analysts get quite different answers to the same problem . . . [T]here must be something wrong when quantification of some particular problem produces such radically different results."[64] Kent's experienced assessment strengthens the previous recommendation for multiple advocacy; for complex social problems, no single analysis can carry decision making's full burden, and a variety of analyses representing the individuals and interests at stake is required.

The attraction of power has long stimulated, if not beguiled, the estimation expert, or, as George Kelly puts it: "Power attracts advice. Where a measure of centralized power exists, there, too, is the expert, sometimes in sun, sometimes in shade; in harmony with the rationale of power or working to change it."[65] For some, the analytic profession has given exposure and entree to decision-making, or power, positions; for others, confusion of role has sometimes resulted. The point is nicely made by Walker:

> On the one hand there is the analyst as scientist—pure in heart with the objective of gaining insight, discovering and revealing truth. On the other hand, there is the analyst as advocate—no longer disinterested and above the battle, but deeply involved in extolling the virtues of a particular policy or decision in seeking to persuade an executive or decision-maker or even en-

gaged in adversary proceedings where he seeks to discredit some rival analyst or to demolish some competing argument.

In actual practice, of course, the analyst is often in some intermediate situation where he is part scientist and part advocate. Not only may he have varying roles, but he may also typically have a multiplicity of relationships with a wide range of people in different organizations and at different levels in hierarchies. Some may expect the analyst to be an advocate whereas others may expect him only to reveal the absolute truth.[66]

The schizophrenic character of estimation becomes especially noticeable as analyses move ever closer to decision.[67]

Experts and expert analyses influence the decision process, and several consistent types of influence have been listed by Ascher, based on his comprehensive survey and appraisal of expert policy forecasts.[68]

Forecasts help define problems, by selecting out certain aspects while downplaying others and by fixing boundaries concerning the size and timing of potential events. Poor forecasts may easily result in poorly specified problems, with consequent misallocation of time, attention, and other resources.

Forecasts aid in problem recognition (in the senses considered here and in Part I), and, if poorly done, can result in missed opportunities or a reduction in decision-making effectiveness.

Forecasts aid in the creation of possible decision options and hence influence the kind and quality of choices and outcomes realized.

Forecasts help create a general mood or climate with respect to a given problem, e.g., optimism-pessimism, hopefulness-fearfulness.

With respect to usability, that is the chances that any one forecast will gain and hold the attention of decision makers, the following characteristics according to Ascher seem to have a positive influence: *Sponsorship*, if the work was paid for by the rich and influential, it tends to be recognized and acted on by the powerful; *impartiality*, if the experts responsible for the work are known to have no vested interest in the outcomes, then odds improve that it will have influence on decision makers; *simplicity*, plain language and few qualifications in the analysis aid comprehensibility and hence chances that the message will be heard and acted on; *diversity*, if a number of different policy options are framed, instead of a single or best recommendation, then consideration and acceptance levels rise; and *consensuality*, if an organization has consensual goals, e.g., a private corporation, then a forecast done on its behalf is more likely to accord with these goals, be accurate, and hence, be heard and used.[69]

One interpretation of these findings, attuned to the more general needs of policy estimation, is that few of these characteristics can be counted on to hold, or, if they do, to have unambiguous impacts on the whole decision process. For instance, the rich and influential are important actors, but not the only actors; representation of other legitimate interests cannot be over-looked. Impartiality is a relative concept having many subtle dimensions, and while an expert may claim no vested interest in a problem, the very qualities that constitute expertness confer an interest. A simple and unqual-ified estimate and recommendation may very well attract a decision maker's attention; it may also misstate the real complexity of the problem suf-ficiently to lead to poor choices. And consensus, particularly when vastly divergent interests and values coexist, is a sometimes thing. Of all the noted characteristics, diversity once again stands out; however, in the realistic world of choice, too much diversity has been shown to contribute to con-fusion about which option to select and to temporizing about decisions in the interest of clarifying each possible choice.

A clear statement of the role and place of the expert in the decision process—and one with which we agree—has been offered by Bernard Crick:

> Politics defines what the inhabitants of a state think should be the problems to be solved. They may not all be capable of solution. But it is a pity that so many of the experts or technologists who are called in to attempt the solution of some of these problems feel that they know best what order or priority should be attached to these attempts, and feel that politics impedes, rather than clears the way, for their use of their techniques. So many problems are only resolvable politically that the politician has special right to be defended against the pride of the engineer or the arrogance of the technologist. Let the cobbler stick to his last. We have a desperate need of good shoes—and too many bad dreams.[70]

We aim not to discourage the would-be estimator, but, rather to provide a sense, and sensitivity, for the numerous, enormous difficulties one en-counters in plying those tasks. Were it a simple calling, doubtless there would be many more successes ("good shoes") and far fewer "bad dreams."

ESTIMATION IN THE POLICY PROCESS

As customary, we now summarize and locate estimation within the whole decision process. We do so by describing common linkages between it and the other five stages.

Selection is the stage most noticeably and immediately affected. Ideally, a problem that passes from estimation to selection will have been narrowed and sharpened, and attention given to its important aspects, to the point where improved clarity about both problem and means to its resolution results. Improved clarity could mean that the attention of the mass and the elite is directed to a truer and more realistic picture of the situation (and away from erroneous and narrower ones); it could mean that many initially conceived options are set aside because of feasibility, desirability, or cost considerations; or it could mean that, because of prototyping or other analytic procedures, actual experience with decision alternatives is at hand. In similar vein, estimation may result in a better informed citizenry and more knowledgeable decision makers. If conducted openly, estimation may also allow the inevitable value differences which confound all but political resolution to crystalize and achieve articulate forms.

In contrast to this generally beneficial list of linkages and consequences, some that are less so can be imagined. Confusion of role and responsibility may result as estimators move, unasked and unwanted, into the political arena to press for options they prefer or believe to be in society's best interest. Such movement may actually impede effective selection from taking place, by bewildering the public and creating a situation where intuitive or self-serving and authoritarian decision making flourishes, e.g., If the experts cannot agree, who should one believe or trust? And, "if expert opinion is so uncertain, I'll just have to do what 'seems best' or 'what I wanted to do anyway'. " Estimates may lead decision makers to postpone or otherwise subvert selection processes. If study results are, or can be made to appear, inconclusive, this may lead to procrastination, with more studies being commissioned; or, the indiscrete use of carefully picked aspects of a study may be used to justify continuation of policies and programs, where change is in fact indicated, or the destruction of others, where continuation or expansion is actually needed.

Many other contingencies can be dreamed up or have actually occurred; however, at some point the major focus of problem interest and activity will pass from estimation to selection. It may happen quickly, as for a crisis demanding speedy or instantaneous reaction, or it may take years, as for problems which have not reached a state of political ripeness.

The connection of estimation to implementation is less definite, although certain features and characteristics can be noted. Presuming that a choice is reached equivalent to, or nearly-related to, one of the estimated options, valuable information about how to do it will have been created during estimation. Some appreciation of what doing the job should cost provides a rough sense of the resources required for implementation: Too few resources (e.g., resulting from political or economic constraints imposed during selection) may mean selective implementation or doing only the most needed or most beneficial things first. Estimation could very well have something to say about such priorities and the ordering of tasks. Talent to carry out the decision is often revealed in the person of those who earlier did the estimation. Particularly for novel options or those known to be extraordinarily complicated or technically specialized, calling on expert analysts for operational help is a well known tradition. For instance, Alice Rivlin's analytic reputation certainly counted in her favor as the first Director of the Congressional Budget Office; Robert McNamara's celebrated reliance on systems analysts during his tenure as Secretary of Defense is a related example.[71]

Administrative, legal, and procedural matters may have been anticipated during estimation, and several of these could be useful in the development of rules, regulations, and guidelines by those entrusted to carry out the job.[72] Were Quade's suggested "Issue Paper" actually used in some fashion, parallel (conflicting and complementary) policies and programs will have been identified, and this could be important information for the agency finally made responsible for an option's implementation. Besides implications of how to do it, estimation often helps determine who should do it. Indeed, many policy analyses explicitly designate either the agency most suited (legally obligated) or the need to create a new agency to accomplish certain tasks.

The primary link between estimation and evaluation is the establishment of first approximations of expected performance. That is, estimates will have been made, subject to the normal discounts one needs apply on account of their error and imprecision, about what could and should occur if an option were enacted in the ways foreseen. The idea of first approximations to performance standards is important and reflects evolving circumstances, alterations imposed by selection acts, and other aspects. Many of the same data sources used to formulate an estimate will be pertinent to those who in time do evaluation. Furthermore, many of the same analysts themselves may be used for this purpose. A more subtle contribution of estimation to evaluation concerns the prior identification of those who are meant to benefit (or pay) for the alternative; knowing who was supposed to gain or lose helps in actually determining whether they did.

Termination can be affected as a result of prior estimation acts, too. For instance, an analysis may describe the terms under which an option's cessation will result, e.g., the attainment of certain objectives or their nonattainment at specified levels of cost and effort. (When a decision to build x number of a specific airplane at y total dollars is reached, both terminal contingencies are provided for: When x is reached, the option ends; or if y dollars are exceeded before all planes are delivered, redress will be sought through renegotiations or the courts, for instance.) Provision may also have been made for the unintended consequences of an alternative, as in the case of insurance or other indemnification stipulations; e.g., "Swine Flu" vaccination insurance is illustrative here.

Finally, estimation often has backward links to the previous, or initiation, stage. New problems may have been uncovered during the course of estimation that are judged important enough to require initial specification, including all aspects discussed in Part I above. Feedback about the adequacy and efficacy of initiation actors and institutions may follow from and be conditioned by the estimation experience. A form this has taken is the bolstering of initiation capabilities so as to lengthen lead times available throughout the whole of the decision process; or it might come in terms of guidance to those responsible for initiation to be tuned or more sensitive to selected aspects of the environment, or to downplay others felt to be of less importance, e.g., shake-ups that occur in the aftermath of intelligence failures in war or improvements sought by strengthening long-range planning and forecasting operations.[73]

NOTES

1. William Barrett, *The Illusion of Technique* (Garden City, N.Y.: Doubleday/Anchor, 1978), p. 22. We are sympathetic to many of Barrett's main themes, but not the polemic nature with which these are rendered.

2. Jay W. Forrester, *Urban Dynamics* (Cambridge, Mass.: MIT Press, 1969); and idem, *World Dynamics* (Cambridge, Mass.: Wright-Allen, 1971), are the cases in point.

3. The direct follow-on to *World Dynamics* (Donella H. Meadows, Dennis L. Meadows, Jørgen Randers, and William W. Behrens III, *The Limits to Growth* [New York: Universe Books, 1972]), caused a firestorm of attention and criticism. For instance, H. S. D. Cole et al., eds., *Models of Doom* (New York: Universe Books, 1973), present a multidisciplinary dissection of the Meadows et al. work. "Overreach" figures prominently in the criticism.

4. Harold Orlans, "Neutrality and Advocacy in Policy Research," *Policy Sciences,* June 1975, pp. 107–19, touches on this. See also, Ida Hoos, *Systems Analysis in Public Policy* (Berkeley: University of California Press, 1972).

5. Harold Orlans, *Contracting for Knowledge* (San Francisco: Jossey-Bass, 1973), contains such enumeration. Herbert Goldhamer, *The Adviser* (New York: Elsevier, 1978), presents an enlightened historical perspective.

6. The relation of social and natural science measurement, from an historical perspective, is well stated in Harry Woolf, ed., *Quantification: A History of the Meaning of Measurement in the Natural and Social Sciences* (New York: Bobbs-Merrill, 1961). A close reading is amply rewarded.

7. E. L. Lehmann, *Nonparametrics* (San Francisco: Holden-Day, 1975), explores an often useful branch of statistics to good advantage.

8. James S. Coleman, *Introduction to Mathematical Sociology* (New York: Free Press, 1964).

9. John W. Tukey, *Exploratory Data Analysis* (Reading, Mass.: Addison-Wesley, 1977), is a different, but equally rewarding, approach.

10. A good general orientation can be obtained by a careful reading of Eugene J. Meehan, *The Theory and Method of Political Analysis* (Homewood, Ill.: Dorsey Press, 1965), chaps. 6 to 8 on, respectively, "Epistemology," "Method and Technique," and "Values."

11. Henri Theil, *Applied Economic Forecasting* (Amsterdam: North-Holland, 1966); and S. Weisberg, *Applied Linear Regression* (New York: John Wiley & Sons, 1980), are advanced follow-ons to this.

12. Saul I. Gass, ed., *Utility and Use of Large-Scale Mathematical Models* (Washington, D.C.: National Bureau of Standards, NBS Special Publication 534, 1979), explores the matter from the point of view of the size of the analytic undertaking vis-à-vis numerous applications. Increasing model size to "capture" more of a context's reality is not necessarily the same as increasing one's understanding. Many findings reported in Gass also lend credence to the specific, case and survey, examples cited in this passage.

13. A thorough history can be found in Philip M. Morse and G. E. Kimball, *Methods of Operations Research* (New York: John Wiley & Sons, 1951), chap. 1; for the British version, see J. R. Lawrence, ed., *Operational Research and the Social Sciences* (London: Tavistock, 1966).

14. Frederick J. Hillier and Gerald J. Lieberman, *Operations Research* (San Francisco: Holden-Day, 1974), p. 3.

15. Shiv K. Gupta and John M. Cozzolino, *Fundamentals of Operations Research for Management* (San Francisco: Holden-Day, 1975), p. 1.

16. Hillier and Lieberman, *Operations Research*, p. 3.

17. Philip M. Morse, ed., *Operations Research for Public Systems* (Cambridge, Mass.: MIT Press, 1967), p. 2.

18. Hillier and Lieberman, *Operations Research*, p. 3.

19. The list is long, but a representative sampling would include success in inventory management, production scheduling, queueing (i.e., waiting line problems), making assessments of equipment reliability, and minimizing risk in investment and other decision situations.

20. Lawrence, *Operational Research*; and Morse, *Operations Research*, state the main intention. Garry D. Brewer, *Politicians, Bureaucrats and the Consultant: A Critique of Urban Problem Solving* (New York: Basic Books, 1973), is one assessment of the dubious results attained in one social application. Richard C. Larson, *Urban Police Patrol Analysis* (Cambridge, Mass.: MIT Press, 1972), as detailed earlier, is a rare exception to the general claim.

21. Bruce L. R. Smith, *The RAND Corporation: Case Study of a Nonprofit Advisory Corporation* (Cambridge, Mass.: Harvard University Press, 1966), gives historical perspective.

22. E. S. Quade and W. I. Boucher, eds., *Systems Analysis and Policy Planning* (New York: American Elsevier, 1968), p. 2. The book is subtitled, *Applications in Defense*, the substantive field in which the philosophy has had most notable success.

23. Military and defense applications are described in Quade and Boucher, *Systems Analysis and Policy Planning;* and in Charles J. Hitch and Roland McKean, *The Economics of Defense in the Nuclear Age* (New York: Atheneum, 1965). The promise of the philosophy for other applications is presented in Roland McKean, *Efficiency in Government Through Systems Analysis* (New York: John Wiley & Sons, 1958); and Guy Black, *The Applications of Systems Analysis to Government Operations* (New York: Praeger, 1968). A more recent stock-taking, with easy to follow tips on "how-to-do-it," is E. S. Quade, *Analysis for Public Decisions* (New York: Elsevier, 1975).

24. Richard Zeckhauser et al., eds., *Benefit Cost and Policy Analysis* (Chicago: Aldine, 1975); E. J. Mishan, *Economics for Social Decisions: Elements of Cost-Benefit Analysis* (New York: Praeger Publishers, 1973); and, A. R. Prest and R. Turvey, "Cost-Benefit Analysis: A Survey," *The Economic Journal*, December 1965, pp. 638–735, cover the field.

25. David Novick, ed., *Program Budgeting* (Cambridge, Mass.: Harvard University Press, 1965); and, F. J. Lyden and E. G. Miller, eds., *Planning, Programming and Budgeting: A Systems Approach to Management* (Chicago: Markham, 1967).

26. Martin Shubik, *Games for Society, Business and War* (New York: Elsevier, 1975), part IV; and Garry D. Brewer and Martin Shubik, *The War Game: A Critique of Military Problem Solving* (Cambridge Mass.: Harvard University Press, 1979), chaps. 5–10.

27. A. J. Wohlstetter, F. S. Hoffman, J. R. Lutz; and H. S. Rowen, *Selection and Use of Strategic Air Bases* (Santa Monica, Calif.: The Rand Corporation, R–266, April 1964).

28. Ida Hoos, "Can Systems Analysis Solve Social Problems?" *Datamation*, June 1974; and, idem, *Systems Analysis in Public Policy*, represent the extreme in criticism. Richard R. Nelson, "Intellectualizing About the Moon-Ghetto Metaphor," *Policy Sciences*, December 1974, pp. 375–414, is more balanced—and constructive—in its treatment. Response and interest in his ideas in this article led Nelson to amplify and illustrate them in much greater detail. See his, *The Moon and the Ghetto* (New York: W. W. Norton, 1977).

29. Sir John Hicks, *The Crisis in Keynesian Economics* (New York: Basic Books, 1974), provides essential intellectual guidance to the limitations of one prevalent body of economic theory upon which many policy analyses have been based. See also, William Ascher, *Forecasting: An Appraisal for Policy-Makers and Planners* (Baltimore, Md.: Johns Hopkins University Press, 1978), chap. 4, for supporting evidence in the area of econometric forecasting models, which are extensively used for policy analysis.

30. Robert F. Clark, "Program Evaluation and the Commissioning Entity," *Policy Sciences,* March 1975, pp. 11–16, is instructive. Guy Beneveniste, *The Politics of Expertise* (Berkeley, Calif.: Glendessary Press, 1972), offers a fact-filled, broad exposition.

31. The celebrated disclosure of the "Pentagon Papers," in which an economist "went public" with results he believed the public had a right to know, but which were being withheld (i.e., classified) by the government for its own reasons, is notable here. *The Pentagon Papers, Senator Gravel Edition* (Boston: Beacon Press, 1971).

32. In the period of the early to middle 1970s, The Rand Corporation established a separate corporate entity in New York City to bring systems analysis to bear on the city's numerous problems. Close identification with Mayor John Lindsay, it became somewhat of a liability subsequently. A version of the story is told in Martin Greenberger, Matthew A. Crenson, and Brian L. Crissey, *Models in the Policy Process* (New York: Russell Sage Foundation, 1976), chaps. 7 and 8.

33. Richard R. Nelson emphasizes this in his *Moon and the Ghetto.*

34. Ralph Strauch, *A Critical Assessment of Quantitative Methodology as a Policy Analysis Tool* (Santa Monica, Calif.: The Rand Corporation, P–5282, August 1974), is excellent on this and closely related topics.

35. Harold D. Lasswell, *A Pre-View of Policy Sciences,* (New York.: American Elsevier, 1971); and Harold D. Lasswell and Abraham Kaplan, *Power and Society* (New Haven: Yale University Press, 1950), are the authoritative sources.

36. Lasswell, *Pre-View of Policy Sciences,* pp. 63–67.

37. Harold D. Lasswell, *World Politics and Personal Insecurity* (New York: McGraw-Hill, 1935), chap. 1, pp. 3–20, is an early statement of the idea; and idem, "The Garrison State," *American Journal of Sociology,* January 1941, pp. 455–68, is an early and vivid example of the construct in use. The basic procedure is elaborated and refined in Lasswell, "Current Studies in the Decision Process," *Western Political Quarterly,* June 1955, pp. 381–85; and startling prescient constructs of emerging problem areas of energy, armaments, production, evolution, and human rights are displayed in idem, "The Political Science of Science," *American Political Science Review,* December 1956, pp. 961–79. Lasswell's "guesses" were seldom, if ever, random or trivial, but, rather they were the product of a powerfully disciplined and marvelously creative intelligence.

38. Lasswell, *Pre-View of Policy Sciences,* p. 68.

39. Myres S. McDougal and William T. Burke, *The Public Order of the Oceans* (New Haven: Yale University Press, 1962); and Myres S. McDougal, Harold D. Lasswell, and Ivan A. Vlasic, *Law and Public Order in Space* (New Haven: Yale University Press, 1963), exemplify this.

40. A rational, consider-all-permutations, orientation is evident in Rae W. Archibald and Joseph P. Newhouse, *Social Experimentation: Some Whys and Hows* (Santa Monica, Calif.: The Rand Corporation, R–2479, May 1980); and, more explicitly in the influential, Donald T. Campbell and J. C. Stanley, *Experimental and Quasi-experimental Design for Research* (Skokie, Ill.: Rand McNally, 1966). Large social experiments take time and are usually very expensive; the longer they take, the more likely the problem setting has evolved, perhaps sufficiently so to call the original design into question. Furthermore, the simple existence of a large experiment has consequences, not the least of which are political ones. Alice M. Rivlin, "How Can Experiments Be More Useful?" *American Economic Review,* May 1974, pp. 345–54; and John O. Wilson, "Social Experi-

mentation and Public Policy Analysis," *Public Policy*, Winter 1974, pp. 15–37, touch on time and money matters. Political ones are highlighted in Margaret Boeckman, "The New Jersey Income Maintenance Experiment," *Policy Sciences*, March 1976, pp. 53–76; and Edward M. Gramlich and Patricia P. Koshel, *Educational Performance Contracting* (Washington, D.C.: The Brookings Institution, 1975).

41. The recommended use is documented in Robert Rubenstein and Harold D. Lasswell, *The Sharing of Power in a Psychiatric Hospital* (New Haven: Yale University Press, 1966), pp. 13–15, 268–92, where this key difference (and advantage) of the prototype over the social experiment stands out.

42. Lasswell, *Pre-View of Policy Sciences*, p. 71.

43. Peter deLeon, "Scenario Designs: An Overview," *Simulation & Games*, March 1975, pp. 39–60; and Harvey DeWeerd, "A Contextual Approach to Scenario Construction," *Simulation & Games*, December 1974, pp. 403–14, provide, respectively, an overview and necessary elaboration for creating and using scenarios for policy purposes.

44. These techniques are essentially neutral, until put to use. While attractive for treating organized-and-complex problems, the blame for their misapplication rests on the analyst, not the techniques. This point is stressed in Garry D. Brewer, "On Duplicity," *Simulation*, April 1980, pp. 140–43. See also, Shubik, *Games*, chaps. 1, 7, 8, 14.

45. The decision seminar is proposed in Harold D. Lasswell, "Technique of Decision Seminars," *Midwest Journal of Political Science*, August 1960, pp. 213–36. An early prototype of the decision seminar was used by and for the Committee for Economic Development, a New York-based research organization. Lasswell, in collaboration with Beardsley Ruml, William Benton, Gardner Cowles, and others, bore primary responsibility. See H. D. Lasswell, *National Security and Individual Freedom* (New York: McGraw-Hill, 1950), generally, and pp. 235–50, for details.

46. Brewer, "Dealing with Complex Social Problems: The Potential of the 'Decision Seminar'," in Garry D. Brewer and Ronald D. Brunner, eds., *Political Development and Change: A Policy Approach* (New York: Free Press, 1975), draws together both theory and practice.

47. Some of the possibilities are enumerated in Harold D. Lasswell, "Decision Seminars: The Contextual Use of Audio-Visual Means in Teaching, Research, and Consultation," in Richard L. Merritt and Stein Rokkan, eds., *Comparing Nations* (New Haven: Yale University Press, 1966), pp. 499–524.

48. Gordon Tullock, *The Organization of Inquiry* (Durham, N.C.: Duke University Press, 1966), offers several possibilities.

49. Quade served for many years as the Head of the Mathematics Department of The Rand Corporation, a role which allowed him access to hundreds of problems and problem-solving adventures. At retirement, he continued his analytic efforts for several more years at the International Institute for Applied Systems Analysis in Laxenberg, Austria, near Vienna.

50. Quade, "Initiating the Analytic Process," in his *Analysis for Public Decisions*, chap. 5. The book merits careful reading for the insights it gives on systems analysis.

51. This theme, and choice, get play in Robert G. Brown, "Ten Ways to Get Rich in Consulting by Not Taking on Clients," *Interfaces*, February 1979, pt. 1, pp. 30–36.

52. A sophisticated treatment of many of these matters is contained in Robert Behn, "Policy Analysis and Policy Politics," *Working Paper Series* (Durham, N.C.: Duke University, Institute of Policy Sciences and Public Affairs, September 1979).

53. L. Wirth, "Responsibility of Social Science," *Annals of the American Academy of Political and Social Science*, January 1947, pp. 143–51.

54. Orlans, *Contracting for Knowledge*, is replete with horror stories.

55. It has nearly always been so: Goldhamer, *The Adviser*, gives ample historical testimony; most pertinent to the current discussion are his introduction and chap. 5. Arnold J. Meltsner, *Policy Analysts in the Bureaucracy* (Berkeley: University of California Press, 1976), supplies an up-date.

56. Don K. Price, *The Scientific Estate* (Cambridge, Mass.: Harvard University Press, 1965), is a masterful statement and analysis of expert matters.

57. Michael Young, *The Rise of the Meritocracy: 1870–2033* (Baltimore, Md.: Viking Penguin, 1961), gives the longer historical view and speculates on the future. *Sputnik I*, the Soviet's (and the world's) first man-made satellite orbited in October 1957. This achievement, and all that it signified, contributed to demands for science and scientific expertise in government. James R. Killian, Jr., *Sputnik, Scientists, and Eisenhower* (Cambridge, Mass.: MIT Press, 1977), is a definitive source.

58. U.S. General Accounting Office, *Controls Over Consulting Service Contracts at Federal Agencies Need Tightening* (Washington, D.C.: Government Printing Office, PSAD–80–35, March 1980), p. 1, is the source of this quote and the $2 billion per-year figure. John Yemma, "Capitol Hill Seeks Limits on the Use of Consultants," *Christian Science Monitor*, June 30, 1980, p. 12, suggests the higher figure and characterizes Congressional reactions to the GAO's earlier report. Historical perspective, and some estimates of use, are contained in U.S. Congress, House, Committee on Government Operations, *The Use of Social Research in Federal Domestic Programs* (Washington, D.C.: Government Printing Office, April 1967).

59. Ibid. The GAO flags as deficiencies the following issues: failure to consider in-house capability; unsolicited proposals; spending in the final quarter of the fiscal year out of proportion to the previous quarters, indicative of hasty and questionable use of the resources; dubious use of results produced by consultants; and other, specific research management and use practices.

60. C. P. Snow, *Science and Government* (New York: The New American Library Inc., 1962), earlier identified this as the clash of the "Two Cultures" of science and humanism. Many present-day perspectives on science policy, with specific reference to experts and expertise, are assembled in Joseph Haberer, ed., *Science and Technology Policy* (Lexington, Mass.: D. C. Heath, 1977).

61. These, and many other worrisome topics, are treated generally in Jack D. Douglas, ed., *The Technological Threat* (Englewood Cliffs, N.J.: Prentice-Hall, 1971); and Eugene W. Schwartz, *Overskill* (Chicago: Quadrangle, 1971). Specific bureaucratic elaboration is in W. Richard Scott, "Professionalism in Bureaucracies: Areas of Conflict," in Howard M. Vollmer and Donald M. Mills, eds., *Professionalization* (Englewood Cliffs, N.J.: Prentice-Hall, 1966), pp. 265–75.

62. Max F. Millikan, "Inquiry and Policy: The Relation of Knowledge to Action,"in Daniel Lerner, ed., *The Human Meaning of the Social Sciences* (Cleveland, Ohio: Meridian, 1959), p. 161.

63. Promotional excesses certainly confounded the San Francisco and Pittsburgh community renewal analysis projects documented in Brewer, *Politicians, Bureaucrats, and Consultant*. Elsewhere, too: Orlans, *Contracting for Knowledge*.

64. Kent was responsible for most Air Force studies and analyses between 1968 and 1972 and, hence, speaks with special authority about this. Glenn A. Kent, "Decision-Making," *Air University Review*, May/June 1971, p. 62.

65. George A. Kelly, "The Expert as Historical Actor," *Daedalus*, Summer 1963, p. 533.

66. John K. Walker, Jr., "General Session V: Professional Ethics and Standards," *Proceedings of the 27th MORS* (Alexandria, Va.: Military Operations Research Society, 1971), p. 1.

67. Philip Handler, "Public Doubts About Science," *Science*, 6 June 1980, p. 1093, characterizes two consequences of expert advocacy: diminishing public confidence in science as a separate entity and a rising current of anti-intellectualism in the body politic. He firmly urges a prompt return to basics: "Scientists best serve public policy by living within the ethics of science, not those of politics. If the scientific community will not unfrock the charlatans, the public will not discern the difference—and science and the nation will suffer." An extensive treatment of the advocacy problem is found in: George W. Weber and G. J. McCall, eds., *Social Scientists as Advocates* (Beverly Hills, Calif.: Sage Publications, 1978). The overriding concern for "Professional Identity," is covered in Lasswell, *Pre-View of Policy Sciences*, pp. 112–31.

68. Ascher, *Forecasting*, chap. 2. Since estimations are aimed at the future, the link between Ascher's work and findings and this discussion is strong and close.

69. Ibid.

70. Bernard Crick, *In Defense of Politics* (New York: Penguin Books, 1964), p. 110.

71. Alain C. Enthoven and K. Wayne Smith, *How Much Is Enough? Shaping the Defense Program, 1961–1969* (New York: Harper & Row, 1965), is a first-hand account of this.

72. See *Policy Sciences*, December 1976, a special issue dedicated to these matters.

73. In concept, the Office of Technology Assessment of the U.S. Congress was created mainly for the latter reason. See, U.S. Congress, House, Committee on Science and Technology, *Long Range Planning* (Washington, D.C.: Government Printing Office, May 1976).

Discussion questions

1.   Is the systematic examination of policy alternatives useful? Desirable? Can such investigations be integrated into the policy process in advantageous ways? Why or why not? One could think about these broad questions in terms of (a) alternative ways to reach policy decisions; (b) the sophistication required of decision makers to judge the value, worth, or utility of technical information; (c) the social and commercial pressures on analysts to produce answers or to demonstrate solution competence; (d) the role of advocacy; (e) political reforms that could be imagined to improve the use of expert advice; and (f) unintended consequences and mislessons that flow from analyses.

2.   A society seems unable to cope with problems confronting it until these problems reach crisis proportions. What are some of the reasons that might account for this? What might be done to alleviate crisis decision making? What are some of the common characteristics of crisis, as compared with noncrisis, decision making? Consequences?

3.   Discuss the differences between analytic and intuitive problem-solving and decision orientations. Under what conditions does one generally appear to be more attractive than the other?

4.   Why is there such a heavy reliance on mathematical and natural science models and methods in policy analysis? How do these tools normally re-

spond to the needs of social decision makers? Please consider both intrinsic and extrinsic reasons that may limit quantitative approaches to social problem solving. What are some practical implications that lead from these limitations, and how might they be overcome?

5.   Systems analysis has evolved in the 30 or so years since its creation to the point where it is now used to solve policy problems of great diversity and complexity in numerous substantive fields. In some applications it seems to have been more successful than in others. What are the key elements and purposes of the systems analysis philosophy, and how do these contribute to its success or limitations in policy analysis?

6.   Consider and discuss the following assertion: Policy analysis is merely one specific form of what one generally recognizes and labels science. It is conducted in similar ways; it is subject to scientific constraints and guidelines; and it will stand or fall, i.e., be assessed, based on the criteria and standards of science.

7.   Are there inherent ethical or normative biases in policy estimation (considered as both process and product)? Discuss the following: Does the attempt to base analysis on hard data have harmful or beneficial consequences for the number, kind, and quality of options and alternatives being estimated? Does the rigorous definition of a problem necessarily result in a narrowed conception of the realities of the situation being analyzed? Does the fact that an analyst has been paid by an agency or organization to find an answer to some problem necessarily mean that the resulting product will be biased?

8.   Inadequate, nonexistent, and erroneous data plague many efforts to do competent estimation. What are the examples and usual courses resorted to in the data-impoverished situation often facing the analyst? What are the implications of each of these routine and/or expedient courses: for the analysis, for the chances of anyone's taking and using the analysis, for scientific concerns of theory development, and for the stature and development of the analytic profession?

9.   What kinds of technical estimation lapses seem (a) gross and preventable, (b) wrong but not preventable, and (c) honest and likely always to be present? For each contingency, what could be done (and by whom) to reduce adverse consequences?

10.   Demographic data in one way or another lie at the base of most policy analyses. However, few appear to appreciate this or the importance associated with excellent, i.e., accurate, timely, relevant, not merely good, demographic estimation. Why is this so? What might be done about it?

11.   What are the prospects for the eventual development of a system of national social indicators or a social accounting system? Consider this in

terms of theoretical, technical, and practical obstacles and opportunities that must be, respectively, overcome and seized.

12. The expert adviser has been a long-time feature of decision making and problem solving in both public and private arenas. What features of current life might account for the seeming increase in the number, diversity, and penetration of experts in a wide range of problem-identifying and problem-solving situations? What are some likely consequences of this? Is the trend toward increased expert dependence likely to change, and if so, how and why?

13. Consider and discuss the following:

> It seems to me that in economics and finance, . . . the thing we emphasize, naturally, is efficiency. That's what economists are doing. They're trying to maximize things. They're trying to get the optimal solution under all the circumstances, so that the key word in the whole endeavor is efficiency.
>
> However, anyone who has spent some time around the political world knows that things are not that simple. The key word is really equity. So I think that the question we're really dealing with is this: Can we do the things that will give us the efficiency we need in our system . . . and can we do all these things in a way that is consistent with the demand of the political process for equity? [George Schultz, Former Secretary of the Treasury and Director of the Office of Management Budget (Interview Notes)]

14. Design your ideal undergraduate educational program from the perspective of one who intends to become a policy analyst. Sketch out the kinds of courses that would be necessary and appropriate to provide the criteria; allocate the total program according to the proportion of time and effort which should be spent on general fields or areas of inquiry (e.g., quantitative, theoretical, practical—or some other categories); and speculate on what differences this ideal program would make for you in coming to terms with yourself and life in the world of the next 20 years. Think of this explicitly as a problem in policy estimation, where client and analyst are one in the same: you.

Supplementary readings

Considering the central role of estimation—at least in terms of the purposes of this book, if not with regard to the whole policy process—this part has covered a large and quite diverse body of literature. Accordingly, it has *been liberally cross-referenced and annotated so that specific topics and questions of interest to the reader could be pursued by reviewing the same materials we have relied on to develop our arguments. These materials are among the best and most appropriate available on the topics addressed. Rather than simply repeating all of the chapter references here, we have abstracted them and placed them into an organizational scheme that approximates that used in Part II. Additional citations are provided in the interest of even coverage.

A CONCEPTION OF COMPLEXITY

Ando, Albert; Franklin Fisher; and Herbert A. Simon. *Essays on the Structure of Social Science Models.* Cambridge, Mass.: MIT Press, 1963.

Brunner, Ronald D., and Garry D. Brewer. *Organized Complexity.* New York: Free Press, 1971.

Buckley, Walter. *Sociology and Modern Systems Theory.* Englewood Cliffs, N.J.: Prentice-Hall, 1967.

Hirschman, Albert O. "The Search for Paradigms as a Hindrance to Understanding." *World Politics*, March 1970, pp. 329–43.

LaPorte, Todd R., ed. *Organized Social Complexity: Challenge to Politics and Policy*. Princeton, N.J.: Princeton University Press, 1975.

Miller, George. *The Psychology of Communication: Seven Essays*. New York: Basic Books, 1967.

Simon, Herbert A. *The Sciences of the Artificial*. Cambridge, Mass.: MIT Press, 1969.

Steinbruner, John D. *The Cybernetic Theory of Decision*. Princeton, N.J.: Princeton University Press, 1974.

Weaver, Warren. "Science and Complexity." *American Scientist* 36 (1948), pp. 536–44.

COPING WITH COMPLEXITY

Rationalizing the irrational?

Axelrod, Robert. "Schema Theory." *American Political Science Review*, December 1973, pp. 1248–66.

Barrett, William. *The Illusion of Technique*. Garden City, N.Y.: Doubleday/Anchor, 1978.

————. *Irrational Man*. Garden City, N.Y.: Doubleday/Anchor, 1958.

Garthoff, Raymond L. "On Estimating and Imputing Intentions." *International Security* 2, no. 3 (1978), pp. 22–32.

Janis, Irving L., and Leon Mann. *Decision Making*. New York: Free Press, 1977.

Jervis, Robert. "Hypotheses on Misperception." *World Politics* 20, no. 4 (1968), pp. 454–79.

Nelson, Richard R. *The Moon and the Ghetto*. New York: W. W. Norton, 1977.

Rationalism versus instrumentalism

Boulding, Kenneth E. "The Ethics of Rational Choice." *Management Science*, February 1966, pp. 161–69.

"Concept of Value." *International Encyclopedia of the Social Sciences*. New York: Macmillan & Free Press, 1968.

Dewey, John. *Reconstruction in Philosophy*. Boston: Beacon Press, 1948.

Lasswell, Harold D., and Abraham Kaplan. *Power and Society*. New Haven: Yale University Press, 1950.

"Going outside the boundaries"

Brewer, Garry D., and Ronald D. Brunner, eds. *Political Development and Change: A Policy Approach*. New York: Free Press, 1975, "Introduction."

Ravetz, J. R. *Scientific Knowledge and Its Social Problems*. Oxford, England: Clarendon Press, 1971.

A survey of general procedures

Kaplan, Abraham. *The Conduct of Inquiry*. San Francisco: Chandler, 1964.

Lasswell, Harold D. *A Pre-View of Policy Sciences*. New York: American Elsevier, 1971.

THE HUMAN OUGHT AND THE RATIONAL IS

Boulding, Kenneth. *The Image*. Ann Arbor, Mich.: Ann Arbor Paperbacks, 1961.

Bronowski, Jacob. *Science and Human Values*. New York: Harper & Row, 1965.

Calabresi, Guido, and Philip Bobbit. *Tragic Choices*. New York: W. W. Norton, 1978.

Jones, W. T. *The Sciences and the Humanities: Conflict and Reconciliation*. Berkeley: University of California Press, 1967.

Kaplan, Abraham. *American Ethics and Public Policy*. New York: Oxford University Press, 1963.

Leys, Wayne A. R. *Ethics for Policy Decisions*. Englewood Cliffs, N.J.: Prentice-Hall, 1952.

Loeb, Jacques. (ed., Donald Fleming). *The Mechanistic Conception of Life*. Cambridge, Mass.: Belknap Press of the Harvard University Press, 1964.

Myrdal, Gunnar. *Objectivity in Social Research*. New York: Pantheon, 1971.

Platt, John R. *The Step to Man*. New York: John Wiley & Sons, 1966.

_____, ed. *New Views of the Nature of Man*. Chicago: University of Chicago Press, 1965.

Vickers, Geoffrey. "Commonly Ignored Elements in Policymaking." *Policy Sciences*, July 1972, pp. 265–66.

_____. *Freedom in a Rocking Boat: Changing Values in an Unstable Society*. New York: Basic Books, 1971.

_____. *Value Systems & Social Process*. New York: Basic Books, 1968.

ESTIMATION AS SIMPLIFICATION

Estimation paradigms

Brown, Steven R. *Political Subjectivity*. New Haven: Yale University Press, 1980, chaps. 1 and 2.

Strauch, Ralph. " 'Squishy Problems' and Quantitative Methods." *Policy Sciences*, June 1975, pp. 175–84.

Prevalent analytic orientations

Berlinski, David. *On Systems Analysis*. Cambridge, Mass.: MIT Press, 1976.

Boguslaw, Robert. *The New Utopians*. Englewood Cliffs, N.J.: Prentice-Hall, 1965.

Churchman, C. West. *Prediction and Optimal Control*. Englewood Cliffs, N.J.: Prentice-Hall, 1961.

_____ _Challenge to Reason._ New York: McGraw-Hill, 1968.

Florman, Samuel C. _The Existential Pleasures of Engineering._ New York: St. Martin's Press, 1976.

Illustrative applications (emphasing policy sciences contributions)

Brewer, Garry D., and Ronald D. Brunner, eds. _Political Development and Change: A Policy Approach._ New York: Free Press, 1975.

Brewer, Garry D., and James S. Kakalik. _Handicapped Children: Strategies for Improving Services._ New York: McGraw-Hill, 1979.

Dobyns, Henry F. _Peasants, Power, and Applied Social Change._ Beverly Hills, Calif.: Sage Publications, 1971.

George, Alexander L. _Propaganda Analysis: A Study of Inferences Made From Nazi Propaganda in World War II._ Evanston, Ill.: Row, Peterson, 1959.

Hobbs, Nicholas. _The Futures of Children._ San Francisco: Jossey-Bass, 1975.

Holmberg, Allan R. "The Research and Development Approach to the Study of Change." _Human Organization,_ Spring 1958, pp. 12–16.

Hyman, Sidney. _The Lives of William Benton._ Chicago: University of Chicago Press, 1969.

Johnston, Douglas M. _The International Law of Fisheries._ New Haven: Yale University Press, 1966.

Larson, Richard C. _Urban Police Patrol Analysis._ Cambridge, Mass.: MIT Press, 1972.

Lasswell, Harold D. _National Security and Individual Freedom._ New York: McGraw-Hill, 1950.

_____. "The Policy Sciences." _International Encyclopedia of the Social Sciences,_ vol. 12. New York: Macmillan and Free Press, 1968, pp. 181–89.

_____. "The Prospects of a World University." In _The Place of Value in a World of Facts: Nobel Symposium,_ vol. 14. New York: John Wiley & Sons, 1971.

Lasswell, Harold D., and Daniel Lerner, eds. _World Revolutionary Elites._ Cambridge, Mass.: MIT Press, 1965.

Lasswell, Harold D.; Daniel Lerner; and John D. Montgomery, eds. _Values and Development._ Cambridge, Mass.: MIT Press, 1976.

Lasswell, Harold D., and Lung-chu Chen. _Formosa, China, and the United Nations: Formosa's Future in the World Community._ New York: St. Martin's Press, 1967.

McDougal, Myres S., and William T. Burke. _The Public Order of the Oceans._ New Haven: Yale University Press, 1962.

Montgomery, John D.; Harold D. Lasswell; and Joel S. Migdal, eds. _Patterns of Policy: Comparative and Longitudinal Studies of Population Events._ New Brunswick, N.J.: Transaction Books, 1979.

Ophuls, William. _Ecology and the Politics of Scarcity._ San Francisco: W. H. Freeman, 1977.

Reisman, W. Michael. *Nullity and Revision: The Preview and Enforcement of International Judgments and Awards.* New Haven: Yale University Press, 1971.

Rogow, Arnold, ed. *Politics, Personality, and Social Science in the Twentieth Century: Essays in Honor of Harold D. Lasswell.* Chicago: University of Chicago Press, 1969.

Rubenstein, Robert, and Harold D. Lasswell. *The Sharing of Power in a Psychiatric Hospital.* New Haven: Yale University Press, 1966.

Wright, Quincy et al. *Preventing World War III: Some Proposals.* New York: Simon & Schuster, 1962.

DATA, THEORY, AND POLICY ANALYSIS

Alker, Hayward R., Jr., and Bruce M. Russett. *Comparing Nations: The Use of Quantative Data in Cross-National Research.* New Haven: Yale University Press, 1968.

American Statistical Association. *The American Statistician* 27, no. 2 (1973).

Bell, Daniel. "The Idea of a Social Report." *The Public Interest,* Spring 1969, pp. 72–84.

Chen, Milton M.; J. W. Bush; and Donald L. Patrick. "Social Indicators for Health Planning and Policy Analysis." *Policy Sciences,* March 1975, pp. 71–89.

Duncan, Otis Dudley. *Toward Social Reporting.* New York: Russell Sage Foundation, 1969.

Ferriss, Abbott L. *Indicators of Trends in American Education.* New York: Russell Sage Foundation, 1969.

Gitter, George A., and David I. Mostofsky. "Toward a Social Indicator of Health." *Social Science and Medicine,* April 1972, pp. 205–09.

Goldsmith, Seth B. "The Status of Health Status Indicators." *Health Services Reports,* March 1972, pp. 212–20.

Gross, Bertram M. "The State of the Nation: Social Systems Accounting." In Raymond A. Bauer, ed. *Social Indicators.* Cambridge, Mass.: MIT Press, 1966, chap. 3.

Jones, Martin V., and Michael J. Flax. *The Quality of Life in Metropolitan Washington.* Washington, D.C.: The Urban Institute, 1970.

Land, Kenneth C. "On the Definition of Social Indicators." *American Sociologist,* November 1971, pp. 322–25.

Land, Kenneth C., and Seymour Spilerman, eds. *Social Indicator Models.* New York: Russell Sage Foundation, 1975.

Sheldon, E. B., and Wilbert Moore, eds. *Indicators of Social Change: Concepts and Measurements.* New York: Russell Sage Foundation, 1968.

Stone, Richard. *Demographic Accounting and Model Building.* Paris: Organization for Economic Cooperation and Development, 1971.

Taylor, Charles Lewis, and Michael C. Hudson. *World Handbook of Political and Social Indicators.* 2d ed. New Haven: Yale University Press, 1972.

Webb, Eugene J.; Donald T. Campbell; Richard D. Schwartz; and Lee Sechrest. *Unobtrusive Measures.* Skokie, Ill.: Rand McNally, 1966.

Westin, Alan F. *Databanks in a Free Society.* New York: Quadrangle, 1972.

METHODS, TOOLS, AND PROCEDURES

Because this section was presented in annotated, bibliographic form, no additional citations will be given here.

EXPERTS

Bernstein, Ilene N., and Howard E. Freeman. *Academic and Entrepreneurial Research.* New York: Russell Sage Foundation, 1975.

Brooks, Harvey. *The Science of Government.* Cambridge, Mass.: MIT Press, 1968, especially "The Scientific Adviser."

Cronin, Thomas E., and Sanford D. Greenberg, eds. *The Presidential Advisory System.* New York: Harper & Row, 1969.

Flash, E. S. *Economic Advice and Presidential Leadership: The Council of Economic Advisors.* New York: Columbia University Press, 1965.

Gilpin, Robert, and Christopher Wright, eds. *Scientists and National Policy-Making.* New York: Columbia University Press, 1964.

Lakoff, Sanford A., ed. *Knowledge and Power.* New York: Free Press, 1966.

Morgenthau, Hans J. "Henry Kissinger, Secretary of State." *Encounter,* November 1974, pp. 57–61.

Neustadt, Richard E. *Presidential Power.* New York: John Wiley & Sons, 1980.

Price, Don K. *Government and Science: Their Dynamic Relation in American Democracy.* New York: Oxford University Press, 1962.

Primack, J. R., and Frank von Hippel. *Advice and Dissent.* New York: Basic Books, 1974.

Siu, R. G. H. *The Craft of Power.* New York: John Wiley & Sons, 1979.

Spiegel-Rösing, Ina, and Derek de Solla Price, eds. *Science, Technology and Society: A Cross-Disciplinary Perspective.* Beverly Hills, Calif.: Sage Publications, 1977.

Wiesner, Jerome B. *Where Science and Politics Meet.* New York: McGraw-Hill, 1961.

York, Herbert. *The Advisors: Oppenheimer, Teller and the Superbomb.* San Francisco: W. H. Freeman, 1976.

PART III

Selection

Most simply, selection is the choice among policy alternatives that have been generated and their likely effects on the problem estimated. It is the decision-making stage of the policy process. It is the most overtly political stage insofar as the many potential solutions to a given problem must somehow be winnowed down and but one or a select few picked and readied for use. Obviously most possible choices will not be realized and deciding not to take particular courses of action is as much a part of selection as finally settling on the best course. Many individuals and groups are certain not to get what they want or only obtain substantially modified versions of their preferences as a result of the consensus building and conflict resolution inherent in politics.

7

Estimation and selection are different

There is often tension between analysis and political acts leading to policy decisions. Such tension stems less from disagreement about whether or not analyses should be used and more from disputes over what the analyses mean in social or political terms. Not only do the analytic facts represent different things to different social groups and individuals, but decision makers themselves may make matters more difficult as they seek compromises and coalitions to secure the passage of legislation. The process often takes the form of blurred goals and objectives sought: Decision makers "often leave goals phrased in ambiguous language, hence open to misunderstanding," and as a result, "the goals enunciated by the makers of policy are inconsistent or even contradictory."[1]

Analysts obviously prefer clear statements of goals and objectives, yet the political process is often incapable of providing such clarity. Policy studies are supposed to illuminate goals and establish priorities for their attainment. However, decision makers have their own preferences. This divergence of purpose and role has been expressed as a paradox. The political process requires consensus, but the very act of exploring options and trying to attain consensus heightens awareness of the many interests and values at stake. Often, it becomes nearly impossible to produce a logically consistent set of policies and programs. Similarly, it becomes more difficult to build and hold the essential, underlying consensus that enables a democratic society to function.[2]

The difficulty of reaching policy consensus means that research on policy issues rarely enjoys the consistency of interpretation found in scientific work. The correct answer is seldom known, and often "no solution . . . can be proved to be right or even to be the best."[3] Research on the housing crisis, for example, may produce a recommendation to lower mortgage rates to make homes affordable to more families, but it may be infeasible to translate this recommendation into policy because of other pressures, such as the feared contribution to inflation reduced mortgage rates might produce. Different interest groups will interpret the same research results in different ways, according to their peculiar values and perceptions. Even the most straightforward and logical recommendation seldom emerges from the selection phase unaltered by these, and other, considerations.

With respect to the environment, fundamental questions about the legitimacy of authority, political accountability, private ownership versus public needs, and many other questions loom large. Public statements by Secretary of Interior James Watt, with regard to his intention to open up vast tracts of offshore territory to oil exploration through the sale of leases to private developers and to cut back on federal oversight of state strip-mining regulations by shutting down five regional offices of his department, quickly generated heated resistance.[4] In the first case, environmental groups raged with sufficient intensity to gain the support of California Governor Jerry Brown and to begin legal challenges, and a subcommittee of the Democratic-controlled House Appropriations Committee ordered Secretary Watt not to use any funds from the fiscal year 1982 Interior appropriations for lease sales.[5] In the second case, the Supreme Court, on June 15, 1981, ruled unanimously against challenges to the federal strip-mining authority and thus reaffirmed preservation over profit and exploitation goals.[6] Prior to the court decision, the House Appropriations Committee warned Secretary Watt not to close Interior's Denver field office, a key source of expertise and authority backing enforcement of the strip-mining legislation. Ideology, ethics, politics, economics, and other considerations are involved. Policy is determined by the complex resolution of all the relevant factors, of which rational analysis is but one.

In moving from estimation to selection, one needs to understand and appreciate the role of ideology and values in politics.[7] "Prior to politics, beneath it, enveloping it, restricting it, conditioning it, is the underlying consensus on policy . . . among the politically active members. . . . Without such a consensus no democratic system would long survive."[8] To attain that consensus and hence sustain the democratic process, full consideration of issues from the diverse points of view of all politically active participants deserves attention. In addition, ideological and technical information must be reconciled. Ideological information refers to the thoughts, feelings, attitudes, and conduct of human beings; technical information refers to the material and measurable aspects of an issue. Any policy goal, the decision or decisions reached in its pursuit, and the consensus sought to justify the choices will have ideological and technical elements intertwined. A major purpose of politics (and selection generally) is the blending of pertinent ideological and technical information in the interest of consensual decision making.

For instance, energy independence is an ideological goal based on thousands of technical facts about the current and projected patterns of energy consumption, the worldwide distribution of energy resources, the use and availability of technologies, and future scientific and engineering advances. Even stating a goal in technical terms—i.e., the production of enough synthetic fuel from nonpetroleum sources to maintain current levels of consumption without increasing U.S. dependence on foreign oil—clearly implies feelings about being dependent and being dependent on Persian Gulf oil in particular; feelings about sinking huge amounts of capital into the uncertain technology of producing synthetic fuels; and feelings about having to pay a larger share of income for something hitherto taken for granted. The decision maker must be aware of all of these as policy choices about energy independence are debated.

Politics has been described as a process by which emotional consensus is sought and sustained:

> Politics is the transition between one unchallenged consensus and the next. It begins in conflict and eventuates in a solution. But the solution is not the "rationally best" solution, but the emotionally satisfactory one. The rational and dialectical phases of politics are subsidiary to the process of redefining an emotional consensus.[9]

If correct, this description provides partial insight into what occurs during the selection phase. To remain effective, the politician must sustain an emotional consensus, especially among constituents. Other things being equal, the politician makes decisions about allocation and distribution to maintain that consensus, even when doing so seems irrational to an analyst.

Decision makers are not immune to emotional factors, which may vary considerably in degree and kind. Cool rationality, a favorite assumption of scholars of decision, is frequently tempered by—or gives way to—warmer human traits, such as blind passion, panic, hope, wariness, and fear. Emotion, in this sense, could be considered as an integrated mind set that summarizes one's experiences and expectations and serves as an instantly accessible basis for action. It is quite difficult to analyze, given its complexity and specificity for different individuals in various cases. Nonetheless, the emotional make-up or mood of key decision makers is often extremely important. Abraham Lincoln's melancholy, for instance, has been cited regularly by historians recounting his key decisions. We touch on the general issue later in discussing personalities as a factor in selection.

The climate of public opinion enters the decisional milieu, too. With respect to foreign policy, Klingberg has identified two extremes of mood (introverted and extroverted) and periodic cycles between them that appear to help account for many specific decisions.[10] In the extroverted phase, a willingness to "exert positive pressure (economic, diplomatic, or military) outside [our] borders," sets the tone of foreign policy.[11] In the introverted phase, distrust of established institutions or outright antagonism toward authority contributes to more reticent and cautious international dealings. Changes in society due in part to demographic shifts, cultural evolution, and specific historical events and experiences lead to the emergence of new value systems competing with established authority.

The environmental movement, for example, has drawn strength from young adults, but the reins of control over the economy are held by others. New problems, such as pollution and waste management, are fueling phobias about the longer-range consequences of technologies many believe to be poorly understood. New strategies to cope with these and other problems are coming into public awareness and debate. In times of introspection, the views of counterelites or utopians have often flourished.[12] That phenomenon may account in part for the current popular interest in the so-called soft path in energy that places little reliance on centralized authority.[13] In periods when the governing authority is trusted, respected, and the populace satisfied, there is apt to be greater acceptance of the policies proposed by an existing elite; the enabling consensus is left unchallenged. But, despite an apparent distrust of authority, citizens are demanding that someone take charge to clean up the mess or to make America strong. Such ambivalence in mood may have more effect on the eventual resolution of the energy, national security, and other policy problems than all the commissioned, elegant, technically based analyses.

Chance has always played an important role in political decision making. The unforeseen capture and prolonged internment of American diplomats in Iran charged the U.S. decision-making atmosphere with embarrassment and anger; the incident occupied inordinate amounts of the time and attention of top leadership which might have been better devoted to other problems and matters. With the release of the hostages, attention shifted dramatically away from Iran; political energies, and the consensus potential they represent, settled on entirely different issues.[14] Over the longer term, other chance occurrences will help shape and color the enabling consensus.

Taken individually, the events that seize public attention may be insufficient to challenge the policymaking consensus; cumulatively, however, they contribute to the popular mood, for good or ill. Events having a direct impact on energy policy include periodic gas lines, soaring prices for fuels, fears about atomic reactor accidents, and power blackouts. Distrust of government following the Vietnam War, moral outrage in the wake of Watergate and other governmental scandals, and a sense that no one is able to provide firm leadership all take their toll.

Not knowing whom to trust, the public retreats into cynicism: "What energy crisis? There are gallons of the stuff out there, but the oil companies are just trying to rip me off. Look at the prices; look at the obscene profits."

Indeed, the issues that dominate public attention and decision making, such as inflation, unemployment, taxes, and personal security, are relatively tangible ones. Energy, when considered directly, is filtered through the price one pays to heat homes and drive cars. Energy serves as a symbol of what generally ails the economy and stimulates the drive to reach a new emotional consensus and political equilibrium.[15]

To illustrate many of the general points made so far, let us look at the economic concept of price and how politicians deal with it in times of instability and turmoil.

To an economist, price is central and familiar as a signal, as a market equilibrator, and as an efficiency mechanism. An economist would not regard price as a conspiracy. Yet consider how the public reacted to the post-1973 rise in the price of gas. To the public, the pre-1973 period of no gas lines and stable prices was the familiar and fair situation. People viewed the price rise as unjust, with the spoils going to some unseen, manipulative conspiracy composed of the petroleum industry and the Arabs, with the benign acquiescence of the federal government. These attitudes are of slight concern to the economic analyst but crucial to the politician, whose business is to decide among competing groups who gets what, why, and how. The economic analyst is trained to accept the economic reality of an increased price; the politician may compromise or ignore it if doing so preserves the consensual foundation that makes politics possible.

Democratic politics is the struggle for advantage among society's competing groups. When a technical issue enters the political arena, the politician treats it more or less like any other issue, as a possible constraint or opportunity. While the technician's arguments will be heard, they will amount to just another piece of information—to be believed if convenient, rationalized and adapted if necessary, and ignored if not. Little wonder, therefore, that the language of politics has been characterized as "designed to make lies sound truthful. . . . murder respectable . . . and give an appearance of solidity to pure wind."[16]

One of the more troubling dilemmas in the democratic societies is how much decision-making power the individual should relinquish to others with presumed special competence.[17] Such relinquishment is commonplace in some aspects of life: we routinely submit ourselves to the care of airplane pilots and surgeons, for example. But in political matters, especially in a democracy, there is concern that political equality is undermined when most decisions are made by those with presumed moral, functional, technical, or other special competence.

Is the ordinary man competent? The answer to that question is decisive in determining preferences and attitudes about governance.

> If you believe . . . that on the whole the ordinary man is more competent than
> anyone else to decide when and how much he shall intervene on decisions he
> feels are important to him, then you will surely opt for political equality and
> democracy. But if you believe that he is less competent in this fundamental

way than some particular person or minority, then I imagine that like Plato your vision of the best government is an aristocracy of this qualified person or elite.[18]

Another has pointed out, "we find the requirements for democratic participation more and more in collision with requirements for internal consistency in the social management of technology."[19] It may be all to the good to begin with a wise and righteous aristocracy, but controlling it, keeping it from becoming "a cunning and voracious oligarchy" is a monumental task, one that has occupied American politics since the days of Hamilton and Jefferson.[20]

National security and defense are often represented as problems requiring superior technical competency and knowledge for sound decisions.[21] Crucial decisions must be made, and the average citizen lacks the background, time, and interest to comprehend the innumerable technical facts underlying them. Even the language used by those entrusted with responsiblity for national security is itself a formidable deterrent to informed, nonexpert participation.[22] But if the average citizen is not judged competent, will elected representatives be much more so? The question is all the more perplexing when experts themselves disagree and call one another's competency into question, as was the highly visible case of the analyses and decisions made for the antiballistic missile system some years ago and the more recent controversy over the MX missile system.[23]

The problem is not easy or simple. But its solution seems fairly clear for policy analysts. Analysis must not be allowed to substitute for a full assessment of solutions to a problem, nor must the analyst be allowed to usurp the decision-making responsibility of those entrusted with it. Rather, analysis must illuminate the nature of a problem and its ramifications, and the analyst must strive to inform political authorities of the full range of available choices. Analysis that fails in those key tasks serves neither society nor the science on which its legitimacy and success have traditionally been based. Decision makers who abdicate their rightful authority and who belie their public trust by deferring excessively to experts likewise serve neither society nor the political principles on which it is based.

> The statue of Janus, the two-faced god, is the true image of the state and expresses the most profound of political realities. The state—and in a more general way, organized power in any society—is always and at all times both the instrument by which certain groups dominate others . . . and also a means of ensuring a particular social order, or achieving some integration of the individual into the collectivity for the general good.[24]

The general good is seldom fostered by equivocation, nor is it enhanced by the hope that others will make ideal choices for their constituents.[25] At base is the issue of trust, as embodied in the idea of the enabling consensus, for "government remains government only insofar as it can extract submission from the poeple. It needs to assure itself of this power on a continuing basis."[26]

This discussion is not to be mistaken as a plea for total participation in which all issues are subjected to plebiscite; the sheer magnitude and complexity of modern life prohibit this. Still, Americans are neither persuaded by expert claims of superior competence, nor are they willing to relinquish essential elements of political equality to technocrats to decide what is best. We claim, along with Dahl, Lasswell, Dewey, and other democrats, that the ordinary man is competent to decide on matters of importance. The problem, therefore, facing democratic governments is ensuring that its citizens have sufficient information and means to assess that information in light of their own interests. Including the populace more in the policy and decision-making processes is not easy, but failing to do so is costly. Not the least of these costs is the erosion of legitimate political control and the degradation of political efficiency some fear have overtaken us in many specific problem arenas.[27] In a reflection on his tenure as Vice President, Walter Mondale captures the essence of this discussion.

> Our system is not supposed to run on time. When issues are serious, when they are controversial, they are supposed to simmer for a while. They are supposed to slow down so that the public is engaged—so that the people can take a whack at us before final decisions are made.[28]

He thus surfaces the essential matter of consensus and support: "So when you want to enter into a SALT Agreement, when you want to pass a windfall profits tax, it is supposed to take time—it should take time. And when you are done, you will have something better, and the American people will support it."[29]

Selection is the political step in the policy process.[30] It is as irrational as rational. It is more art and craft than technique or science. It involves the use of power as individuals strive to strike a balance between the invented and estimated options that analysts and others have presented for choice and the multiple, changing, and conflicting goals of those having a stake in the problem and the society at large.[31] The resolution, embodied in the choices made and the programs enacted in their behalf, is the primary business of the politician who must balance numerous factors and forces, weigh competing values while applying judgment as to the consequences of acting in certain ways or not acting at all, and then stand ready to accept eventual responsibility measured in terms of continuing public trust in what has been created.[32]

The political role and task are well captured by Auspitz and Brown:

> The politician, then, operates almost entirely in the gray area between neat categories of the moralist and technocrat. His concern is not to impose values upon objective facts but to decide what shall be taken as the relevant fact or value. Those with a specifically political sensibility (and they are by no

means confined to elected officials) acquire a habit of seeing things the other person's way, even when they reject it. . . . At his best, the politician acquires a sense of trade-offs between interests that cannot be measured on the same scale, a knack for persuading people to take other perspectives into account. . . . Also, there may be occasions when civic accommodation is impossible and force must be used. The political life amply teaches the uses of coercion.[33]

Stressed in these observations are concern for technical and ideological information, the variety and diversity of legitimate values that may come into play as decisions are sought, the need for leadership and promotional talents, and a willingness and ability to use force, if necessary, to maintain the underlying political order. Each and every one of these features will, in specific circumstances, be visible as the process of decision making unfolds during the selection process.

In the following we begin with a discussion of the nature of selection and explore several main reasons and conditions that may make its existence and consequences hard to discern and track. Our focus then shifts to notable factors that confront decision makers, and in doing so, we emphasize the "knowlege in" aspects of the policy process. "Knowledge of" the process, taken to mean perspectives and approaches one encounters in political analyses and theories about politics, is then discussed with prominence given to the leadership and promotional aspects of selection. As per practice, selection is related to each of the other phases at the conclusion of this part. First, we need to ask:

DOES SELECTION EXIST?

Are policy solutions ever clear-cut and identifiable? For a large number of decisions, the answer is no; many daily problems are solved by a variety of routine means. But in important, complex problems that do not lend themselves to solution by standard operating procedures, a decision may be equally difficult to pinpoint because of the nature of the policy process. That is, if the policy problem cannot be isolated from its environment, then one is left without a specific decision point to identify and study. Bauer states the general problem: "One of the fallacies of treating the policy process simply as 'decision making' is that it assumes that someone is aware of the problem, [and] can devote full time and attention to it, and that the issue has a clear-cut beginning and end."[34] Schoettle is more explicit: "any analysis of the decision-making process [must] recognize two factors. Decision-making is, first, an ongoing process and, second, it cannot be isolated from its contextual setting."[35] This school of thought particularly rejects the concept of the "economic man" as a decision maker in favor of the limited knowledge, bounded rationality, "incremental" concept of decision making,[36] in which actions iteratively lead to decisions and policies.[37]

Observers have noted four specific instances in which a policy decision fails to constitute a formal and identifiable event. The first is when the policymaker merely acknowledges ongoing actions and reifies them by making a decision.[38] For example, in 1970, the National Welfare Rights Organization initiated a drive to increase expenditures under Elementary and Secondary Education Act (ESEA), Title I, for clothing for the poor. The movement started in Rhode Island, where the local administrator rejected the request, but demands continued and increased. Murphy notes that to "neutralize this pressure, the Rhode Island Title I coordinator urged the USOE [U.S. Office of Education] to promulgate a strong guideline . . . setting forth numerous requirements." After similar movements arose in four other locales, the USOE, again responding to local pressure, issued another "guideline [stating] that Title I is 'an education program, not a welfare program' and that funds could be used for clothing 'only in emergency situations'."[39] Another example is the American response to the invasion of South Korea in June 1951. President Truman's decision to defend South Korea was based on a series of incremental commitments already made by armed forces stationed in the Far East.[40] In both cases, decision makers merely acted to formalize actions already taken.

The second instance is when the decision is so embedded in the estimation process that it does not constitute a formal decision. In other words, by the time the options reach the decision maker, various contending factions have already resolved their conflicts over the issue and the decision maker is in effect presented with a Hobson's choice.[41] This condition may even be preferred, since it relieves responsibility for making what could be a difficult and thankless decision. There are many examples, even in foreign policy, where the president is reputed to have a dominant voice. The Multilateral Force (MLF) became a major U.S. foreign policy initiative in the early 1960s because its State Department formulators were able to marshall it through the highest councils of government. The achievement was remarkable because its proponents had few allies—indeed, many opponents—in the government; MLF was generally rejected by its intended clients, the Europeans, and it was bitterly opposed by the Soviet Union. That it was declared U.S. policy in spite of these liabilities owed largely to the president being given no other alternative until late in 1964.[42] Similarly the CIA representation of the refugee invasion of Castro's Cuba left President Kennedy with little choice.[43] The lack of alternatives is the precise issue raised by Alexander George, who argues that by the time the decision reaches the president, the die is already cast.[44]

A third instance in which the decision event is obscured is what Bachrach and Baratz have termed the "nondecision."[45] They argue that some decisions are never considered because the prevailing political atmosphere would not permit it. In some ways, this is impossible to validate because a nondecision is analogous to a nonevent, and how does one test for a phenomenon that does not exist? However, examples can be imagined: a school principal might be hesitant to bring the subject of sex education before a rural elementary school board; President Kennedy reportedly refused to consider recognizing the People's Republic of China "until the second term."[46]

Finally, policymakers may not want a clear statement of a decision. For a variety of reasons, they may let a choice be enacted in such a way that they keep open an option to "distance" or deny association with it: the jargon term, plausible denial, was used frequently during the Watergate era in recognition of this possibility. Not making a decision may also buy time in hopes a problem will solve itself or go away. Or a decision may be postponed to gain better information. Whatever the reason, formal decisions are sometimes quite deliberately avoided.

Although these interpretations in many cases accurately characterize the selection stage—e.g., the lack of clear-cut decision or even a decision phase—we reject them for a number of reasons. First, in many cases where prior actions seem merely to have been formalized, clear-cut decisions were actually made. In the ESEA Title I example cited above, the clothing controversy went far beyond the issued USOE guidelines. The welfare supporters took their case past the USOE bureaucracy and presented their demands to Secretary of Health, Education, and Welfare Elliot Richardson, who ordered the ceiling on clothing expenditures removed.[47]

In certain decisions cited for the second instance, the estimation process did not dictate the decision; the policymaker either made a decision in the absence of intensive lobbying or made a decision against the advice of advisers. An example of the former was President Johnson's idea to provide surplus federal lands for low-cost public housing, which later became the Department of Housing and Urban Development's New Towns In-Town Program.[48] The latter is exemplified by President Kennedy's rejection of the recommended surgical air strike option during the 1962 Cuban missile crisis, and President Johnson's decision to scuttle the MLF in December 1964.[49]

Therefore, the primary reason for not accepting the incremental decision-making model is that we can often identify a clear-cut decision. The decision process is too important to be left hidden within a black box that permits observation of only inputs and outputs.[50] Likewise, it is too important to be left obscured within the overall policy process. Although agreeing that the policy process has structural integrity, we argue that the selection phase has unique dimensions and components. Because they exist and are important, we isolate and observe the selection process within the body politic, just as a physician might isolate and observe the circulatory process. Neither we nor the physician, however, claim that the object of our respective studies can or should be taken out of its real-life context.

The focus on selection is crucial because of the multiple perspectives of the policymaker and the other participants in the policy process. Human beings, especially in groups, are limited in ability to collect and process information.[51] Therefore, individuals and groups will make different, biased interpretations of a situation reflecting their differences in expectations, identifications, and demands. The individual differences may stem from personality,[52] cultural,[53] socialization,[54] ideological,[55] and institutional[56] (and other) factors.[57] Individual differences are compounded when individuals aggregate into groups[58] and groups into the coalitions necessary to ensure that action is taken.[59] In all likelihood, then, the analyst and the decision maker will have different objectives because they view the problem and solution with a different set of clients, criteria, and values in mind.[60] The analyst's client is often the policymaker, who in turn has a distinctly different client.[61] Few advisers would have based their analysis of the Cuban missile crisis on President Kennedy's assumption that his failure to remove the Russian missiles would be an impeachable offense. In this case the analyst's client was the President, while Kennedy viewed his client as Congress, and, indirectly, the American electorate.[62] Similarly, criteria and weights differ depending on how a given policymaker perceives the problem.

Only in the unusual case where the analyst can convince a policymaker to accept the analysis and also the values underlying it can agreement on criteria and values be expected. Even then, client perceptions and requirements will probably differ slightly. These differences between the policy analyst and the policymaker are too important to be subsumed under the argument that both individuals are, by and large, the same sort of creature. Whether they are or not is moot, but they do have distinct and isolatable roles in the policy process that warrant separate examination.[63] The decision maker cannot engage in lengthy estimation or evaluation of alternatives; the decision functions powerfully rule against this. It is the policymaker's or politician's role to reconcile and decide among the differing perspectives and arguments, a task more difficult than generally conceded and fraught with risk.[64] As Lasswell notes, "it is a source of perpetual concern to political thinkers that . . . uncertainty and risk are inseparable from decision."[65]

FACTORS IN SELECTION: "KNOWLEDGE IN" THE PROCESS

The policymaker probably considers, either consciously or unconsciously, at least five factors before making a choice. Although these factors are intertwined, we treat them separately and sequentially for the sake of clarity.

The first factor is the *context of the problem*. How is the problem defined and bounded in relation to its environment? What are the environmental, normative, technological, and political constraints? When or how soon must the decision be made? What are the rules of the game and the players? These can be defined personally, institutionally or culturally. What are the decision maker's relevant reference points? In short, on what precedents is the decision based, and how do they relate to present conditions?

A second important decision factor concerns *points of leverage,* that is, which variables can be manipulated by the decision maker? A major contribution of Keynesian economics was its explicit identification of economic variables that could be manipulated for policy purposes.

Consideration of the *importance of the problem,* a third factor, governs how much of the decision maker's limited time, attention, and political resources will be expended on a given policy. Will the policies be more substantive or symbolic? This represents a political cost/benefit calculation.

A fourth factor concerns the *availability of information.* What and how much information is available? Unavailable? What information can be trusted, and how much information can be processed and assimilated by the decision maker? The information factor is complicated by time constraints.[66]

As a host of case studies attest, the *personality of the participants* has an important bearing on the decision process. This factor includes the temperament of the individual, interactions with others, and small-group behavior and role patterns. It also encompasses the cultural, sociological, and ideological influences on the decision maker that condition the decision process.

Let us examine each of these factors more closely.

Context of the problem

A primary consideration for the decision maker is the overall context of the problem and the alternatives proposed to solve it. The policymaker should determine what values or ends are being pursued (e.g., power or enlightenment, wealth or affection), and what interactions with other persons and groups within the general political, social, and economic environment are necessary to attain these ends.[67] Lasswell's five intellectual tasks necessary for problem solving—goal clarification, trend description, analysis of conditions, projection of developments, and the invention, evaluation, and selection of alternatives—suggest that there is much more to the selection process than merely choosing among alternatives.[68] To understand selection, one must have an appreciation for the entire policy process as well as the institutional and personal interactions that compose the political environment. Here we will consider the broader contextual questions, especially the general political environment; personal and institutional interactions will be discussed later.

Although a decision maker must comprehend the problem as it fits within the larger political environment, at the same time one must be careful not to include this environment in the analysis. Indeed, a primary contextual task is to bound the problem, to restrict the scope of the analysis so as to address the problem substantially and realistically. Policymakers need to compare the bounding criteria used in generating and estimating the policy alternatives with their own personal perceptions. If the first contextual question is, Where does the problem fit into the decision-maker's universe? the second question must be, How can the problem be bounded? If boundaries are not set, the problem will assume unmanageable proportions, even with the aid of giant computers.[69] For example, to choose among policies designed to alleviate the causes and effects of unemployment and poverty in the United States would be an impossible undertaking; a better strategy is to attack unemployment in specified subsections of the economy.

The policymaker may find, as is common, that advisers have set too narrow boundaries to the problem, and expansion of the problem's scope may be required. For example, with the context unspecified, an analyst may design a survey of the operations of a city bureau of detectives with the aim of improving its effectiveness, when what the chief of police really wants is a lever for controlling a recalcitrant and independent group of detectives. The policymaker should share realistic perceptions of the problem with the analysts or else a great amount of work may be wasted.

Time is critically important because the passage of time can alter the entire context and necessitate a complete reformulation of the problem and alternative solutions. The mutability of the context cannot be overstated; the static world of the academic analyst simply does not exist for the policymaker. For this reason, time, as the managerial bromides "time is money" and "buying time" suggest, is not a costless good.[70] Senators will filibuster a bill, that is, buy time, until they can either accumulate enough votes to defeat the measure or convince their fellow senators that the lost time and the opportunity costs it represents are so great that the measure should be removed from consideration.

Both the importance of time and its effect on the context of an issue are illustrated by the Cuban missile crisis. In the first instance, President Kennedy deliberately provided Premier Khrushchev enough time so that he could appreciate the consequences of American actions and then mobilize his government to meet U.S. demands. According to Robert Kennedy, "Against the advice of many of his advisers and the military, [President Kennedy] decided to give Khrushchev more time. 'We don't want to push him to a precipitous action—give him time to consider'."[71] At the same time, Soviet technicians in Cuba increased the pace of their work on the missile launching pads so that as the crisis period progressed, President Kennedy found himself increasingly pressured into action by the imminent operational status of the missiles. The context of the crisis had been significantly altered with the passage of time.[72]

Another contextual issue is assuring the proper level of attention. The decision maker can choose among four primary levels of analysis to decide which one, or combination, is most relevant to the given problem. The first, the individual level, focuses on the individual and often uses formal psychological and psychiatric profiles of the key persons involved in the problem.[73] The second level is that of group or institutional interactions, with special attention to small-group behavior and role patterns.[74] The third level encompasses the general system in which the problem occurs,[75] and the final level of analysis addresses the interaction of major systems.[76] Each level has its strengths and deficiencies; e.g., the first may include too much detail for ready aggregation into a policy decision but does capture personal idiosyncrasies that often define a policy. In this regard, powerful personalities may be determining of decisions, as in the case of Lyndon Johnson in his prime as a Senator:

> Every time he bargained there was always the implicit threat—never voiced, but inherent in the very disproportion of power and rewards—. . . . He was essentially a coercive personality, working in a situation in which bargaining and persuasion were the necessary forms for the acquisition of power and the exercise of control.[77]

While a sophisticated analyst may be able to incorporate various levels of analysis into consideration of a given problem, the decision maker must eventually decide on the best or most pertinent level or combination of levels in moving toward a workable solution.

The political culture of the system should be considered. Almond and Verba have argued that distinctive political cultures are a function of education, traditions, laws, and the overall system.[78] These help to define the general rules of the game within which a policymaker operates. These rules can vary from government to government, even from one level of government to another. For example, the American political system has a much lower tolerance for governmental censorship than the Soviet or even the British system. Swift's genteel Houyhnhnms had very different standards from his rude Yahoos though they shared the same land.[79] The policymaker should recognize and act upon a change in these rules, for it could have a significant bearing on the efficacy of the considered alternatives, and thus ultimately on selection.

Mexico's emergence as a major oil producer provides a clear illustration of several of the main issues here. A prevailing American view is that Mexico's petroleum bounty should be shared with its northern neighbors. The technical information about Mexico's oil is compelling: proven reserves range from 100 to 200 billion barrels, sufficient to make Mexico the second most important oil region in the world; and Mexico needs what the United States can provide in abundance, such as food, technical know-how, and financing. However, the ideological aspects, especially as concerns the Mexican political culture, severely constrain any policy or decisions regarding these resources. Ronfeldt goes directly to the heart of the matter:

> [F]or Mexicans, petroleum and Pemex [the national oil corporation] represent "symbolic realities" of extraordinary—even mystical—significance. Were Pemex to become a high exporter of petroleum, it would imply a radical

transformation of traditional principles of Mexican nationalism. And coping with these symbolic challenges could prove more difficult than coping with the technical challenges of exploration and development.[80]

Key elements of the culture include national dignity, economic independence, and state sovereignty, which "in foreign policy issues . . . often become important forces that constrain policy choices open to Mexico's leaders."[81] Thus what Ronfeldt terms the fateful triad of dignity, independence, and sovereignty weighs heavily for any and all choices a Mexican decision maker might conceive of and take.

Violation of community ethics, as another important contextual element, may seriously restrain a decision maker's authority. Nixon's illegal use of wiretaps to monitor conversations of his National Security Council staff resulted in a lengthy court case and a judgment in favor of those whose privacy had been violated; it also did little for his rapidly waning authority when disclosed in the twilight of Watergate. There is, of course, the possibility of amending the rules or even temporarily abrogating them, either publicly or through deception, which might be viewed as an additional set of alternatives to consider. Prior to the 1973 passage of the War Powers Resolution (P.L. 93–148), a succession of presidents had invoked their authority to commit American forces to hostilities abroad. Vietnam, in the eyes of many, symbolized a height of bending the constitutional rules and served as the occasion for debate and passage of the resolution.[82] But, as the *Mayaguez* incident (in which President Ford, in May 1975, used force to recapture an American ship off Cambodia),[83] the abortive Iranian hostage rescue attempt, and several other presidential actions attest, time and circumstances may join in such a way as to favor unilateral, deceptive, and even illegal commitment of troops.[84]

In addition to the society-specific rules of the game, other priorities may follow from or depend on the situation. The timing and sequencing of events, some fraction of which may be controlled, are two critical aspects. Siu underscores this point in terms of a management principle to "Be Propitious," i.e., to develop "elegance and style in getting things done," and to allow "time to build up a psychological head of steam, . . . infractions to be forgiven, . . . and to allow people to become bored or impatient." Most people, "fail to lay the basis for the resolution of conflicts before their actual onset."[85] A sharp example of propitiousness was Congressman Wilbur Mills during his long and effective tenure as the chairman of the House Ways and Means Committee. Rather than taking the lead on an issue, i.e., presenting a solution early in the debate, Mills typically held back, listened, tested the political whims and winds, and only when the time was right did he present a version of a bill that would gain the necessary consensus and support.[86]

A prudent decision maker knows when to move and when not to. For example, in 1964–65, Congress passed a spate of civil rights and poverty legislation, largely as a result of Lyndon Johnson's overwhelming victory over Barry Goldwater (and the consequent Democratic majority in Congress) and partly as a result of the national mood after the assassination of President Kennedy. Earlier, President Roosevelt was able to enact a tremendous amount of social legislation during his first administration because of the conditions and climate created by the Depression.[87] In the early days of his Administration, President Reagan succeeded in getting large-scale budget and tax changes from a Congress still stunned by the liberal losses of 1980. In other situations, comparable legislative activity certainly would not have been possible.

More recently, the power of the public's mood has been dramatically reflected first, in the last half of the 1970s, in Congressional willingness and concern for increased defense budgets and, with the ascendancy of the Reagan Administration, in tandem with the Executive. In the aftermath of the Vietnam War, the defense budget received scant attention, save to cut it back in certain aspects or to hold others steady, to be reduced by inflation. However, beginning in 1976, an era of defense cutbacks ended, and by 1980–81, the pendulum had swung heavily in favor of increased military spending.[88] By June 1980, the Harris Survey reported that of 20 potential areas for reducing federal spending, only social security ranked lower than defense in public opinion; more than two-thirds of those asked opposed any cuts in defense.[89] Iran, Afghanistan, and many other world events[90] had worked their way into the public consciousness; the folks back home were, in increasing numbers, letting their elected officials know about their extroverted feelings. The context and, hence, the possibilities in defense and national security matters had altered fundamentally in a five-year period.

However, even where ground swells of public support appear, there are limits. Stringent federal firearms legislation did not grow from the almost back-to-back assassinations of Martin Luther King, Jr. and Robert F. Kennedy, nor did it come in the wake of prominent shootings in 1981 of a Beatle, a president, and a pope.[91] Roosevelt was unable to pack the Supreme Court even after his reelection by an overwhelming majority in 1936. Presidents Johnson and Roosevelt had overreached the political bounds of the situation and were stopped short, Johnson by the gun lobby and Roosevelt by public indignation. President Reagan's long-standing public position against gun control appears to have overpowered whatever personal pain and fears his own shooting engendered.

Finally, there are some universal political rules. For example, policymakers must rely on and operate through bureaucracies, which are not passive, selfless or unitary bodies.[92] They must also retain a consensus among their constituents if they are to keep their position of authority. Many of these conditions are just as real in totalitarian systems as in the democracies,[93] in developed as in underdeveloped nations.[94]

A final consideration is the reference points, or contextual analogs, on which a decision is based. There is no fault in preparing for the next war by studying the last one if the next and last wars' technologies, arenas, and motivations are basically the same, as they largely were during the European wars of the 16th and 17th centuries. However, this is rarely the case today, and all too often decision makers choose faulty reference points. Alexander George argues that President Johnson based his unsuccessful escalatory policy toward North Vietnam in 1964–65 on the crisis management procedures employed by President Kennedy in the Cuban missile crisis two years earlier.[95] Similar problems can be seen with the decision maker's training or disciplinary frame of reference. Physicists are trained to look at events in terms of their academic discipline; to expect a physicist to understand the flux of the urban housing market in economic, political, or social perspectives is probably asking too much.[96] The comprehension and management of the policy process cannot be confined to a single discipline or methodology.

Points of leverage

A policy decision must reflect the power or points of influence that are necessary to correct the problem or implement the proposed alternatives. Following Gergen, we refer to these as "points of leverage" so as "to avoid the surplus meanings often attached to such terms as 'power' and 'influence,' and to facilitate a more general analysis of methodology. . . ."[97] Besides avoiding the connotative difficulties of "power," the notion of leverage is more descriptive because it suggests the decision maker's view of the causal links in the policy process. Our use of the term focuses on the points of leverage that the selector can manipulate and apply to phenomena that are malleable.[98] In other words, a drought might be alleviated by a series of thunderstorms, but that knowledge does the policymaker little good; Mother Nature is quite immune to bureaucratic leverage. Rather than review the entire range of instruments that could affect the solution to a problem, the decision maker must reduce the choice to those which can be manipulated.

Manipulation, as used here, includes both the threat of force and the possibility of inducement. The prevalence of inducement suggests, however, that the matter is not as simple as it first appears, particularly when conceived as a two-party, test-of-strength proposition. Actually there are usually at least four basic parties or interests involved in decision acts: a representative (or agent) and a constitutency (or principal) on either side of a point at issue. In this simplest case, discrepancies between the interests and objectives of all parties permit possibilities for compromise and accommodation not found in the bilateral relationship. The scope or range of choice, and hence possibilities to discover and pull various levers, is thus richer and more diverse than one might expect.

Furthermore, such a set of leverage points is not constant. Two decision makers, looking at the same problem but from different agencies or vantage points, might well utilize different levers to manipulate the problem. One union leader might obtain a wage increase for his members by threatening a strike while another leader might achieve identical results by agreeing to governmental arbitration. By the same token, people can agree on ends but have completely different concepts of the proper program means; education is a particularly contentious arena.[99] The set can also vary according to time and situation. A president who has just been reelected by a large majority certainly has more leverage over Congress than does one nearing the end of a second, lame duck, term.

A decision maker can increase leverage when a problem seems to be either growing beyond or resisting conventional means. A spectacular example was the collapse of the Fourth French Republic in May 1958. Faced with civil war over the Algerian situation, French President Coty invited Charles deGaulle to become premier and to use the emergency powers the French National Assembly had just voted to Premier Pflimlin to restore order. DeGaulle, realizing that he would still lack the necessary authority, agreed to accept only if the National Assembly would dissolve itself for six months, thus giving him complete power to, among other things, write a new constitution and thereby terminate the Fourth Republic system of government.[100] A less spectacular example occurred when the Federal Communications Commission, facing a potentially rapid expansion in cable television, voted to include cable television within its regulatory purview.[101]

Another aspect of leverage is what Galbraith has called "countervailing power."[102] That is, a decision maker may have only tenuous leverage on a problem, which can be effectively neutralized by other actors or elements in the context. For example, the Nixon-Ford Administration in 1974 was faced with an economic conundrum of simultaneous recession and inflation. Use of the tools available to attack either one of the problems would only have worsened the other, unassaulted one; not surprisingly, Nixon chose to do nothing. Reagan's new federalism, especially as it concerned proposals to redirect funds targeted for cities to the states in the form of block grants, energized many concerned and powerful groups: "The block grant proposal, which Mr. Reagan intended as a sweetener to balance concern over his budget cuts, hit stiff opposition in two critically important House and Senate Committees," and the "added strong opposition of the [U.S.] Conference of Mayors could strengthen that existing roadblock and lead to the development of a detour as a compromise."[103] Another example might be where an urban redevelopment agency wants to build low-cost public housing on federal land that conservationists want to preserve as a park or a wildlife refuge.[104] In each case, those in favor and those opposed to the proposed change tend to move to block each other until one side is able to increase its leverage sufficiently to win, perhaps by developing allies to help swing the issue. We examine the issues of coalition building and compromising more thoroughly below.

Importance of the problem

The decision maker must figure out just how important the particular problem is and what the costs of various solutions are likely to be. Available resources of time, funds, attention, and so on constrain actions. Without determining the relative importance of the problem, one cannot allocate resources effectively. Writing about the American chief executive, Neustadt argues that presidential power is "the product of his vantage points in government. . . . Accordingly, his choice of what he should say and do, and how and when, are his means to conserve and tap the sources of his power."[105] Without priorities, valuable resources may be expended on a problem that is actually trivial in comparison to other pressing matters, a misallocation that could prove disastrous. In December 1939, the French and British governments were prepared to aid Finland in combating the Soviet invasion, even though both were at war with Nazi Germany. They were prevented from honoring this quixotic pledge only by the firm adherence to neutrality by Norway and Sweden, which refused to permit the transit of armed forces across their territories.[106] In times of crisis, however, priority systems are often abandoned, for multiple crises can undermine an ability to manage the situation, a phenomenon Bell refers to as a "crisis slide."[107]

After assigning priorities, the policymaker can then engage in a political cost/benefit analysis. Such a calculus might include who is benefited and who is hurt by the initial problem as well as the various alternatives.[108] Is there a question of legitimacy? Who is the client? What are the bases of support and what kind of resources or leverage can be brought to bear?[109] Can the situation be helped by symbolic treatment or will substantial changes be required? Again, answers to these questions will probably change over time. The Senate's refusal to approve President Nixon's nomination of Harold Carswell to the Supreme Court is an example of coalitions changing dramatically over time in respect to a single, fairly specific issue.[110] Obviously the coalitions will vary on different issues, even if the political environment remains relatively stable. Dahl comments: "Although the kinds and amounts of resources available to political man are always limited and at any given moment fixed, they are not . . . permanently fixed as to either kind or amount."[111]

Once tentative answers to these questions are found, the decision maker is faced with a series of tactical and strategic challenges. If the issue is important, other things being roughly equal, an alternative will be formulated that can most easily build a winning, or at least a supportive, coalition.[112]

If the issue is relatively unimportant, it might be used as a bargaining chip and, in effect, sacrificed for future consideration.[113] At the same time, expectations held by others must be fulfilled. For example, an appearance of support for one's staff is needed to reduce risk of serious morale problems.[114] Thus, the head of an agency or a congressman may end up supporting a program for which there is little personal enthusiasm. At times, these expectations can be lessened or amended, but to ignore them completely is to invite criticism from various quarters and to mortgage needlessly valuable political capital for use in future contests. One must thus decide: Can such criticism be weathered for the sake of present and future coalition building?

The various complicated judgments regarding the importance of a specific policy issue cannot be rigorously formalized into a set of concrete rules. Often the decision maker makes these judgments and estimates based on an informal, impressionistic sense of a situation that can best be described as visceral. As Crick argues so well, one should not denigrate those who use a seat-of-the-pants model, for the politician not only makes a final decision but must also stand ready to accept its consequences.[115] Or as Wilensky notes, "Top executives typically incorporate analytical judgments, value judgments, practical experience, and intuition into policy decisions."[116]

Nonetheless, one need not glorify politicians plying their arcane trade but one should understand it and them better. Practical experience, for instance, may be decidedly two-edged, or as Jervis comments, "masses of information at the decision-maker's disposal carried less weight than the scattered incidents that, although possessing no claim for special importance or representativeness, were personally witnessed."[117] Groping for consistency, in terms of past experiences, personal identifications, and expectations about the future, decision makers seek to strike a delicate balance between what they know, who they are, and what they hope will occur and the complex, highly uncertain circumstances presented with many new problems. The all-too-frequent end results, according to Jervis, are rigid adherence to old and outmoded images, inflexibility in the face of necessary adapatation and change, unwarranted belief in the correctness of decisions finally reached, an unwillingness to consider the worthiness of competing alternatives, and a tendency to accent the more superficial or sensational aspects of a problem while ignoring or denying its more consequential or significant ones.[118]

An additional outcome, termed the "51–49 principle" by Allison, is that once a choice is made, those responsible tend to argue for and defend it with more fervor and zeal than a nonpartisan assessment of the attending uncertainties would allow. It is quite understandable, for "he who is uncertain about his recommendation is overpowered by others who are sure."[119]

Availability of information

A policymaker must rely upon information or data to make decisions. At least two crucial questions exist about this evidence: What information is available (or lacking)? and What information can be trusted?

The first basically asks the question, "Do I have enough information to make a decision?" Implied are "Do I have *right* information?" and "How is it structured?" Recent attention to social indicators suggests that some decision makers have recognized the inadequacy of their data base and have sought to correct its shortcomings. However, there is no coherent theory or statement of goals underlying efforts to improve data collection or even what is to be demonstrated.[120] For example, by most objective measures (e.g., housing quality, real income, health, pollution), the Swedish society enjoys outstanding circumstances, yet other indices (e.g., rates of alcoholism, divorce, and suicide) all strongly argue to the contrary. Hence, decision makers could think that they have the necessary information. A classic example of this concerned the Japanese attack on Pearl Harbor: Roberta Wohlstetter demonstrates how American decision makers had ample evidence of Japanese intentions to attack Pearl Harbor but still were unable to identify or discern it among the masses of data gathered by American intelligence offices.[121]

This suggests another facet of information management—misinterpretation. Prior to their entry into the Korean War, the Chinese Communists tried in a number of subtle ways to signal American decision makers that they would intervene if U.S. troops advanced toward the Chinese border through North Korea. American refusal to recognize Peking's warnings resulted in the longest retreat in U.S. military history.[122] This is a complex problem, for there are times when a source of information is deliberately vague or ambiguous.[123] Even with a trusted source and reliable data, information is always open to misperception or misinterpretation. Woodrow Wilson simply refused to accept or even consider the warning of his counselors at the Versailles Peace Conference that European diplomats were taking advantage of him and that the treaty he was negotiating would almost certainly never be accepted by the Senate.[124] Richard Neustadt has shown how even the closest of allies can innocently but seriously misinterpret each other's actions, with dire consequences. [125]

The second question—What information can the decision maker trust?—has been pivotal in many situations. Barton Whaley argues that Nazi Germany provided Russian intelligence sources with so much false information (or disinformation) that Soviet intelligence neglected evidence that would have led to early discovery of Germany's planned invasion of the Soviet Union.[126] The policymaker should also realize that virtually no information is neutral; almost all information will have already been processed, interpreted, and evaluated according to sets of objectives that are not guaranteed to jibe with one's own.

For example, "according to a former Defense Intelligence Agency (DIA) analyst, DIA estimates concerning Vietnam were written so as not to undercut the action recommendations of the U.S. Military Commander in Vietnam and the Joint Chiefs of Staff."[127] Yet DIA estimates were the basis for decisions made by President Johnson and his civilian advisers. Similarly, data emphasizing successful U.S. efforts (e.g., the number of pacified villages) were highlighted by being sent via cable to Washington; discouraging information (e.g., Viet Cong recruitment data) was deemphasized by being sent via diplomatic mails, which took up to five weeks. Another example of the repercussions of not questioning one's data was George McGovern's 1972 campaign statements on taxation programs. Careful pencil work would have revealed that his figures were badly mistaken and would have spared his campaign much embarrassment.[128]

Even technical information can be suspect if it is based on a rule of thumb, as, perhaps surprisingly, it often is. For instance, the von Neumann committee projected that the first generation of U.S. ballistic missiles should carry a one-megaton warhead, have a range of 5,500 miles, and level of accuracy of landing within 5 miles of a target. These technical estimates "were based respectively on a round number, a quarter of the earth's circumference, and compromise between those who were optimistic and those who were pessimistic about accuracy."[129] Suspicion may still prevail in situations where the technical information is both necessary and reliable, as Nisbett and others have demonstrated experimentally,[130] a situation not helped by incidents such as Three Mile Island where, both at the time and in retrospect, data and interpretation were highly questionable.

Such examples lead decision makers to question the validity of the information they are given. Schlesinger writes that President Kennedy was so dissatisfied with the information he had received prior to the Bay of Pigs invasion that he was extremely skeptical of the assessments provided by the military during the Cuban missile crisis.[131] The need for validating information is one reason why a policymaker, especially the president, will attempt to establish multiple sources of information to help calibrate the reliability of the information received.

There is a secondary consideration. In some situations the decision maker may have important information but not be able to use it because preservation of the information source may outrank taking an action which reveals, and hence compromises, the source. Police informers are an example. A more spectacular one was the American decision in World War II to intercept and shoot down over Borneo the aircraft carrying Japanese Admiral Yamamoto. American intelligence had learned of his flight plan because it had broken the most secret Japanese code. The policy question concerned whether American pilots should intercept Yamamoto's flight and possibly indicate to the Japanese that the United States had broken their code or permit the top Japanese military thinker to go untouched. The American high command in the Pacific decided to intercept his flight only after devising an elaborate cover story suggesting another source of information.[132] A similar dilemma confronted Winston Churchill during World War II when British intelligence broke the most secret German code. He was thus given advance warning of a German contingency plan to launch a massive bombing attack on Coventry. Rather than order an evacuation of the city and thereby possibly reveal his intelligence source, Churchill chose to withhold the information and hence subjected Coventry to one of the most devastating raids mounted against an English city.[133]

Personality

Although difficult to address in specific terms, the personalities of those involved in the program (including one's own) are important for the decision maker to consider. Costello identifies three different personality aspects that "crucially affect the way in which a policymaker uses the policy forming process": motivational elements, risk-taking behavior, and cognitive style.[134] One person's personal characteristics, temperament or work habits might clash with those of the policymaker and thus vitiate their working relationship, such as occurred between Chester Bowles and President Kennedy.[135] Personal idiosyncracies can determine the best manner in which to couch a proposal. Colonel Edward House and Senator Henry Cabot Lodge both knew how to manipulate President Woodrow Wilson, although, of course, their ends were hardly complementary.[136]

Some study has been made of the linkage of personality with policy, often utilizing psychoanalytic techniques.[137] Although the linkage is still unclear, there is little doubt that such a phenomena as charisma can significantly affect decision makers' influence.[138]

Finally, in times of stress or crisis, it has been demonstrated that persons and groups have markedly different tendencies and reactions. If the policymaker can observe these variations and adjust for them in a crisis, it will improve the ability to discern the relevant issues and make appropriate decisions.[139] The matter can be conceived not only at the individual or group level, but at the system level of analysis, too.[140]

The foregoing discussion of factors, though scarcely exhaustive, illustrates the many and varied considerations that underlie and complicate the policymaker's choice. Obviously when a major policy decision is being made, it will be impossible to quantify or even estimate all these factors. However, they serve as a basic checklist of items to be considered before choosing. Choice is seldom simple, and the difference between what a decision maker wants and what actually happens can be large.

NOTES

1. Harold D. Lasswell, *The Analysis of Political Behaviour* (London: Routledge & Kegan Paul, 1947), p. 130.

2. Michel Crozier, Samuel P. Huntington, and Joji Watanuki, *The Crisis of Democracy* (New York: New York University Press, 1975).

3. Geoffrey Vickers, "Commonly Ignored Elements in Policymaking," *Policy Sciences*, June 1972, p. 266.

4. Under the provisions of the Surface Mining Control and Reclamation Act of 1977.

5. Ward Morehouse III, "More Coastal Areas Soon to Feel Oil Drill Bits?" *Christian Science Monitor*, June 16, 1981, p. 3.

6. Two separate cases were heard as one and involved disputes in Virginia and Indiana.

7. Roy C. Macridis, *Contemporary Political Ideology* (Cambridge, Mass.: Winthrop, 1980).

8. Robert A. Dahl, *A Preface to Democratic Theory* (Chicago: University of Chicago Press, 1956), p. 132.

9. Harold D. Lasswell, *Psychopathology and Politics* (New York: Viking Press, 1960), pp. 184–85.

10. Frank L. Klingberg, "The Historical Alternation of Mood in American Foreign Policy," *World Politics*, January 1952, pp. 239–73.

11. Ibid., p. 239.

12. H. C. Kelman, ed., *International Behavior* (New York: Holt, Rinehart & Winston, 1965), pp. 339–53.

13. Amory B. Lovins, *Soft Energy Paths* (Cambridge, Mass.: Ballinger, 1977); authorities seldom take these challenges lightly and often fight back threatened changes in the status quo. See Colin Norman, "Renewable Power Sparks Financial Interest," *Science*, 26 June 1981, pp. 1479–81, wherein the political realities contained in one section of the Public Utilities Regulatory Policies Act of 1978 stimulated a strong reaction from the utilities as they sought to quash competition from decentralized energy producers encouraged in the Act.

14. "Where Have All the Crises Gone?" *Christian Science Monitor*, June 9, 1981, p. 24. In this thoughtful editorial the ebb and flow of crises are characterized and this key conclusion is reached: "All of which is to say that the public, no less than diplomats, needs to face up to the world's disturbing pictures with fewer swings of euphoria or despair, to guard against either being lulled to sleep or getting overexcited. What is a flaming crisis today becomes just an ordinary, if not less importunate, problem tomorrow. The issues, it seems, are always complex and the solutions never facile; it takes time and patience to work through them."

15. These themes are represented in Aaron Wildavsky and Ellen Tanenbaum, *The Politics of Mistrust: Estimating American Oil and Gas Resources* (Beverly Hills, Calif.: Sage Publications, 1981).

16. George Orwell, *Collected Essays* (Garden City, N.Y.: Doubleday, 1954), p. 177.

17. Robert A. Dahl, *After the Revolution? Authority in a Good Society* (New Haven: Yale University Press, 1970), part I.

18. Ibid., p. 35.

19. Harvey Brooks, "Technology: Hope or Catastrophe?" *Technology In Society*, Spring 1979, p. 15.

20. Dahl, *After the Revolution?* p. 37.

21. A sharply contrary view is presented in Harrison E. Salisbury, "De-Professoring Foreign Policy," *New York Times*, November 17, 1980, p. A-23. "The record is clear. Presidents need academics for their expert knowledge. But that expertise does not make scholars first-rate practitioners or gifted confidential advisers to statesmen." Elsewhere in Salisbury's editorial, politics "is a pragmatic art, not an exact or scientific one. The fine-tuned scholarly approach may sound remarkably simple in the Oval Office but if it doesn't work with Leonid Brezhnev, it probably won't play in Peoria."

22. Most notable and egregious is a new dialect termed "Haiguition," in recognition of its principal creator. "General Haig has contexted the Polish watchpot somewhat nuancely. How, though, if the situation decontrols, can he stoppage its mountingly

conflagrating? . . . Experts in the Kremlim thought they could recognition the word-forms of American diplomacy. Now they have to afreshly language themselves up before they know what the Americans are subtling." "Haiguition—A Capital Offense," *Phalanx: The Newsletter of the Military Operations Research Society,* May 1981, pp. 9, 18.

23. The entire issue of the journal *Operations Research,* September 1971, treats the debate and issue from the analysts' perspective; the historical and political contexts are well described in Ernest J. Yanarella, *The Missile Defense Controversy: Strategy, Technology, and Politics, 1955–1972* (Lexington: The University Press of Kentucky, 1977).

24. Maurice Duverger, *The Idea of Politics* (Chicago: Henry Regnery, 1970), p. xiii.

25. An earlier discussion is directed to these themes: See Chap. 4, "The Human Ought and the Rational Is."

26. R. G. H. Siu, *The Craft of Power* (New York: John Wiley & Sons, 1979), p. 34.

27. Thomas Parke Hughes, *Changing Attitudes Toward American Technology* (New York: Harper & Row, 1975); and Ronald D. Brunner and Weston E. Vivian, "Citizen Viewpoints on Energy Policy," *Policy Sciences,* August 1980, pp. 147–74.

28. Godfrey Sperling, Jr., "Reflections from Fritz," *Christian Science Monitor,* December 29, 1980, p. 23.

29. Ibid.

30. Politics is, of course, everywhere present in the policy process. It is generally just more noticeable during selection.

31. Geoffrey Vickers, *Value Systems and Social Process* (New York: Basic Books, 1968); and Robert A. Dahl and Charles E. Lindblom, *Politics, Economics and Welfare* (Chicago: University of Chicago Press, 1976).

32. Bernard Crick, *In Defense of Politics* (New York: Penguin Books, 1964).

33. Josiah Lee Auspitz and Clifford W. Brown, Jr., "What's Wrong with Politics," *Harper's,* May 1974, pp. 51–61, at p. 59.

34. Raymond A. Bauer, "The Study of Policy Formation: An Introduction," in Raymond A. Bauer and Kenneth J. Gergen, eds., *The Study of Policy Formation* (New York: Free Press, 1968), p. 16.

35. Enid Curtis Bok Schoettle, "The State of the Art in Policy Studies," ibid., p. 160.

36. One of the early and most precise critics of the rational schools of decision making was Herbert A. Simon, *Administrative Behavior* (New York: Free Press, 1957). The incremental approach was first proposed by Charles E. Lindblom, "The Science of 'Muddling Through'," *Public Administration Review,* Spring 1959, pp. 79–88, and has been more thoroughly delineated in David Braybrooke and Charles E. Lindblom, *A Strategy of Decision* (New York: Free Press, 1963). Problematic search, bounded rationality and "satisficing" behavior are discussed by James G. March and Herbert A. Simon, *Organizations* (New York: John Wiley & Sons, 1958).

Up-dates are contained in James G. March and Johan P. Olsen et al., eds., *Ambiguity and Choice in Organizations* (Bergen, Norway: Universitetsforlaget, 1976); and Herbert A. Simon, "On How to Decide What to Do," *Bell Journal of Economics* 9, no. 2 (1978), pp. 494–507.

37. See Bauer, "Study of Policy Formation."

38. Although distinctions can be made between "policymaker" and "decision maker," here they will be used interchangeably. Similarly, "selection" and "decision" are treated as synonyms.

39. Jerome T. Murphy, "Title I of ESEA: The Politics of Implementing Federal Education Reform," *Harvard Educational Review,* February 1971, p. 51.

40. Truman's decision is detailed in Glenn D. Paige, *The Korean Decision* (New York: Free Press, 1968); and Alexander L. George, "American Policymaking and the North Korean Aggression," *World Politics*, January 1955, pp. 209–32.

41. This is an extension of the group theory of politics, which is represented by a sizable literature; for example, see David B. Truman, *The Governmental Process* (New York: Alfred A. Knopf, 1951).

42. The history of MLF is documented in John D. Steinbruner, *The Cybernetic Theory of Decision* (Princeton, N.J.: Princeton University Press, 1974). The European issues are carefully analyzed by Henry A. Kissinger, *The Troubled Partnership* (New York: McGraw-Hill, for the Council on Foreign Relations, 1965), chap. 5. For Soviet attitudes, see Zbigniew Brzezinski, "Moscow and the M.L.F.: Hostility and Ambivalence," *Foreign Affairs*, October 1965, pp. 126–34.

43. The President's decisions regarding the Bay of Pigs invasion are discussed in Arthur M. Schlesinger, Jr., *A Thousand Days: John F. Kennedy in the White House* (Boston: Houghton Mifflin, 1965), chaps. 9–11. Irving L. Janis, a psychologist, argues that Kennedy and his advisers all but surrendered their decision-making prerogatives by falling victim to what Janis calls "Group Think"; if such a phenomenon exists, it further obscures the decision-making process. Irving L. Janis, *Victims of Group Think: A Psychological Study of Foreign-Policy Decisions and Fiascoes* (Boston: Houghton Mifflin, 1972).

44. Alexander L. George, "The Case for Multiple Advocacy in Making Foreign Policy," *American Political Science Review*, September 1972, pp. 751–85. This and many other key themes are amplified in idem, *Presidential Decisionmaking in Foreign Policy* (Boulder, Colo.: Westview Press, 1980).

45. Peter Bachrach and Morton S. Baratz, "Decisions and Non-Decisions," *American Political Science Review*, September 1963, pp. 632–42. A critique of this concept is offered by Raymond E. Wolfinger, "Non-decisions and the Study of Local Politics," *American Political Science Review*, December 1971, pp. 1063–80. An excellent case analysis is provided by Matthew A. Crenson, *The Un-Politics of Air Pollution: A Study of Non-Decisionmaking in Cities* (Baltimore, Md.: Johns Hopkins University Press, 1971).

46. David Halberstam, *The Best and the Brightest* (New York: Random House, 1969), p. 102.

47. Murphy, "Title I of ESEA," p. 52.

48. Martha Derthick, *New Towns In-Town* (Washington, D.C.: The Urban Institute, 1972).

49. See Elie Abel, *The Missile Crisis* (Philadelphia: J. B. Lippincott, 1966). Years later, proponents of the air strike still contended that President Kennedy made the wrong decision; see Dean Acheson, "Homage to Plain Dumb Luck," *Esquire*, February 1969.

50. In the language of systemic political analysis, inputs become "demands" and "resources" and outputs are "allocations" and "distributions," and the decision process is enclosed in the black box; David Easton, *A Systems Analysis of Political Life* (New York: John Wiley & Sons, 1965). We do not accept this model of the decision process.

51. The point is related to the individual in George A. Miller, "The Magical Number Seven, Plus or Minus Two," *The Psychology of Communication: Seven Essays* (New York: Basic Books, 1967); and to the organization in March and Simon, *Organizations*.

52. See Harold D. Lasswell, *Power and Personality* (New York: W. W. Norton, 1948), especially chaps. 2–4; Lucian W. Pye, "Personality and Changing Values," in *Aspects of Political Development* (Boston: Little, Brown, 1966), chap. 5.

53. See Henry Tajfel, "Social and Cultural Factors in Perceptions," in Gardner Lindzey and Elliot Aronson, eds., *The Handbook of Social Psychology*, vol. 3 (Reading, Mass.: Addison-Wesley, 1968), pp. 315–94.

54. A standard reference is Herbert H. Hyman, *Political Socialization* (New York: Free Press, 1959); more recently, see Stanley Renshon, *Handbook of Political Socialization: Theory and Research* (New York: Free Press, 1977).

55. See Robert E. Lane, *Political Ideology: Why the American Common Man Believes What He Does* (New York: Free Press, 1962). A broader focus and scope is exemplified in Macridis, *Contemporary Political Ideology.*

56. The impact of organizations on decisions is described in Allison's Model II: Graham T. Allison, *Essence of Decision* (Boston: Little, Brown, 1971), chap. 4. For specific illustrations from business and public lobbying, see, respectively, Edwin A. Epstein, *The Corporation in American Politics* (Englewood Cliffs, N.J.: Prentice-Hall, 1969); or, for a more individualized view, Charles E. Lindblom, *Politics and Markets* (New York: Basic Books, 1977); and Jeffrey M. Berry, *Lobbying for the People: The Political Behavior of Public Interest Groups* (Princeton, N.J.: Princeton University Press, 1977).

57. A fine collection of several of these differences, taken from a foreign policy decision perspective, is Lloyd S. Etheredge, *A World of Men: The Private Sources of American Foreign Policy* (Cambridge, Mass.: MIT Press, 1978).

58. See Heinz Eulau, *Micro-Macro Political Analysis* (Chicago: Aldine, 1969).

59. James G. March, "The Business Firm as a Political Coalition," *Journal of Politics,* November 1962, pp. 662–78, is one statement of the "pulling and tugging" among factions necessary to arrive at a consensus; also see Allison, *Essence of Decision.*

60. This simple-sounding idea has many distinct implications for politics, science, and analysis—three quite different activities. See Garry D. Brewer, "Where the Twain Meet: Reconciling Science and Politics in Analysis," *Policy Sciences,* June 1981, pp. 269–79.

61. Recall, from Chap. 6, that the policy sciences approach leaves open the question of "Who is the client?"

62. See Robert Kennedy, *Thirteen Days: A Memoir of the Cuban Missile Crisis* (New York: W. W. Norton, 1969), p. 67.

63. The scant evidence regarding the similarity of the policymaker and the policy analyst is inconclusive. Thomas B. Smith, "Policy Roles: An Analysis of Policy Formulators and Policy Implementors," *Policy Sciences,* September 1973, pp. 297–308, argues that the two have very similar backgrounds and perceptions; the main differences seem to stem from their positions. Garry D. Brewer, *Politicians, Bureaucrats, and the Consultant* (New York: Basic Books, 1973), chap. 13, distinguishes between the participants of two urban housing simulation models and finds great differences in their skills, background and perceptions. Brewer was working with a more varied group, but that should not vitiate the findings.

64. This point is well made by an English political scientist, Crick, *In Defense of Politics.*

65. Harold D. Lasswell, "Some Perplexities of Policy Theory," *Social Research,* Spring 1974, p. 177.

66. Recall Chap. 5, "Data, Theory and Estimation."

67. The use of contextuality in problem solving has long been championed by Harold D. Lasswell. See his "Contextuality: Mapping the Social and Decision Processes," *A Pre-View of Policy Sciences* (New York: American Elsevier, 1971), chap. 2.

68. See Lasswell, "Problem Orientation: The Intellectual Tasks," ibid.

69. Failure to bound their system is a major deficiency of the world model defined by Donella H. Meadows, Dennis L. Meadows, Jørgen Randers, and William W. Behrens III, *The Limits of Growth* (New York: Universe Books, 1972).

70. Economists are particularly aware of the cost of time. See Charles Wolf, Jr., "Heresies

About Time: Wasted Time, Double-Duty Time, and Past Time," *Quarterly Journal of Economics*, November 1973, pp. 661–67.

71. Kennedy, *Thirteen Days*, pp. 76–77.

72. See Allison, *Essence of Decision*.

73. For example, see E. Victor Wolfenstein, *The Revolutionary Personality: Lenin, Trotsky, Gandhi* (Princeton, N.J.: Princeton University Press, 1967); or Walter C. Langer, *The Mind of Adolph Hitler* (New York: Basic Books, 1972).

74. An excellent example is Nathan Leites, *The Operational Code of the Politburo* (New York: McGraw-Hill, 1959); also see Harold D. Lasswell and Daniel Lerner, eds., *World Revolutionary Elites: Studies in Coercive Ideological Movements* (Cambridge, Mass.: MIT Press, 1965); and, regarding roles, Talcott Parsons, *The Social System* (New York: Free Press, 1951). For examples in urban-related areas, see John P. Crecine, *Governmental Problem-Solving* (Skokie, Ill.: Rand McNally, 1969); and Michael Lipsky, *Protest in City Politics: Rent Strikes, Housing, and the Power of the Poor* (Skokie, Ill.: Rand McNally, 1970).

75. Although it has serious shortcomings, Jay W. Forrester, *Urban Dynamics* (Cambridge, Mass.: MIT Press, 1969), looks at the city with a systemic perspective.

76. See T. H. von Laue, *The Global City* (Philadelphia: J. B. Lippincott, 1969). Other examples are regional government planning—in such matters as transportation and air pollution—and intergovernmental relations.

77. Doris Kearns, "Lyndon Johnson's Political Personality," *Political Science Quarterly*, Fall 1976, pp. 385–409, at p. 394.

78. Gabriel A. Almond and Sidney Verba, *The Civic Culture* (Princeton, N.J.: Princeton University Press, 1963). A cross-national comparison stressing cultural and system variations in the concept and practice of secrecy in democracies is Itzhak Galnoor, ed., *Government Secrecy in Democracies* (New York: Harper & Row, 1977).

79. Jonathan Swift, *Gulliver's Travels*, in *The Portable Swift*, Carl van Doren, ed. (New York: Viking Press, 1948), offers a remarkably relevant set of policy observations on: war (over which end of an egg is opened first), in "A Voyage to Lilliput"; government, in "A Voyage to Brobdingnag"; policy analysis (as practiced in the Grand Academy), in "A Voyage to Lagado"; and the conflicts between the Yahoos and the Houyhnhnms, in "A Voyage to the Country of the Houyhnhnms."

80. David Ronfeldt, *Mexico's Oil and U.S. Policy: Implications for the 1980s* (Santa Monica, Calif.: The Rand Corporation, R–2510/2–DOE/RC, November 1980), p. 7.

81. Ibid., p. 8.

82. Arthur M. Schlesinger, Jr., *The Imperial Presidency* (Boston: Houghton Mifflin, 1973), is one historical source.

83. Gerald Ford, "The War Powers Resolution" (Lexington: University of Kentucky, April 11, 1977). [Speech.]

84. U.S. Congress, *Congressional Record*, "President Jimmy Carter's Position on the War Powers Resolution" (Washington, D.C.: Government Printing Office, June 30, 1977), p. S. 11318.

85. R. G. H. Siu, "Management and the Art of Chinese Baseball," *Sloan Management Review* 19, no. 3 (1978), pp. 83–89, at p. 87. The entire article is a sophisticated reminder of the important place context plays in decision making and action.

86. J. F. Manley, *The Politics of Finance: The House Committee of Ways and Means* (Boston: Little, Brown, 1970). Significant differences in the particulars of the U.S. House of Representatives and in the personality of Mills' successor saw major changes in style and legislative efficiency: see R. E. Cohen, "Al Ullman—The Complex, Contradictory Chairman of Ways and Means," *National Journal*, March 4, 1978, pp. 345–50.

87. James MacGregor Burns, *Roosevelt: The Lion and the Fox* (New York: Harcourt Brace Jovanovich, 1956), focuses on the political skills of FDR.

88. Joshua Muravchik, "The Senate and National Security: A New Mood," in David M. Abshire and Ralph D. Nurnberger, eds., *The Growing Power of Congress* (Beverly Hills, Calif.: Sage Publications, 1981), pp. 197–282.

89. Ibid., pp. 261–62, citing *ABC News-Harris Survey* II no. 71 (New York: Chicago Tribune–N.Y. News Syndicate, 1980).

90. John M. Collins and Anthony H. Cordesman, *Imbalance of Power: Shifting U.S.-Soviet Military Strengths* (San Rafael, Calif.: Presidio Press, 1980), is one accounting.

91. See Robert Sherrill, *The Saturday Night Special* (New York: Charterhouse, 1973), for an account of the politics of gun control.

92. This is the thrust of the "bureaucratic politics" approach; see Allison, *Essence of Decision*.

93. This is a theme of the Social Science Research Council's series on comparative politics; for example, see Richard Rose, *Politics in England* (Boston: Little, Brown, 1966). Carl A. Linden, *Khrushchev and the Soviet Leadership 1957–1964* (Baltimore, Md.: Johns Hopkins University Press, 1966), provides an excellent illustration of how a leader must maintain a constituency even in a totalitarian government or else be deposed.

94. Harold D. Lasswell, Daniel Lerner, and John D. Montgomery, eds., *Values and Development* (Cambridge, Mass.: MIT Press, 1976), is one representative source.

95. Alexander L. George, "Comparisons and Lessons," in Alexander L. George, David K. Hall, and William R. Simons, *The Limits of Coercive Diplomacy* (Boston: Little, Brown, 1971), chap. 5.

96. Brewer notes that the San Francisco housing model, which was designed by a physicist, compared rental prices with the physics phenomenon of hysteresis and comments: "If a model builder has never been sensitized to the details of a specific empirical context, one should not find faults with his great inferential leaps . . . from expanding and collapsing magnetic fields to expanding and collapsing rentals." Brewer, *Politicians, Bureaucrats and Consultant*, p. 143.

97. Kenneth J. Gergen, "Assessing the Leverage Points in the Process of Policy Formation," in Bauer and Gergen, *The Study of Policy Formation*, p. 182.

98. Amitai Etzioni, "Policy Research," *The American Sociologist*, June 1971, Supplement, pp. 8–12, suggests that the policy analyst's concern with "movable" variables is what distinguishes policy analysis from academic work.

99. Clark Kerr et al., "A Symposium on Financing Higher Education: The Policy Dilemmas," *The Public Interest*, Winter 1968, pp. 99–136. None of the 10 contributors questioned the need for or value of higher education, but each proposed a different manner of providing the funds.

100. These events are described by Roy C. Macridis and Bernard E. Brown, *The DeGaulle Republic* (Homewood, Ill.: Dorsey Press, 1960).

101. See Walter S. Baer, *Cable Television: A Handbook for Decisionmaking* (Santa Monica, Calif.: The Rand Corporation, R–1133–NSF, February 1973).

102. John Kenneth Galbraith, *American Capitalism: The Concept of Countervailing Power* (Boston: Houghton Mifflin, 1952).

103. Lucia Mouat, "Mayors Ask Assurance that Block Grant Funds Will Filter Down to Them," *Christian Science Monitor*, June 15, 1981, p. 3.

104. These were in fact, the battle lines drawn over HUD's New Towns In-Town proposal for public housing in San Francisco; the conservationists were successful in keeping the Fort Funston area as undeveloped parkland. Derthick, *New Towns In-Town*, chap. 8.

105. Richard E. Neustadt, *Presidential Power* (New York: John Wiley & Sons, 1960), p. 179.

106. The diplomacy of this war is described in Vaino Tanner, *The Winter War: Finland Against Russia, 1939–1940* (Stanford, Calif.: Stanford University Press, 1957).

107. Coral Bell, *The Conventions of Crisis: A Study in Diplomatic Management* (New York: Oxford University Press for the Royal Institute of International Affairs, 1971). The psychological effects of an accumulation of stimuli upon individuals are discussed by Leon Festinger, ed., *Conflict, Decision, and Dissonance* (Stanford, Calif.: Stanford University Press, 1964); for a somewhat different theoretical interpretation that emphasizes "hypervigilance" (read: "panic") and "bolstering" (meaning exaggeration of wished-for favorable consequences of decision), see Irving L. Janis and Leon Mann, *Decision Making* (New York: Free Press, 1977), especially chap. 7.

108. Eugene Bardach, *The Skill Factor in Politics* (Berkeley: University of California Press, 1972), sect. I, does an exemplary job of what he calls "mapping the contours of the attentive public" (which includes existing policies, ideologies, and factions) regarding the mental commitment laws in California.

109. These issues are discussed in Martin Rein, "Social Planning: The Search for Legitimacy," *Journal of the American Institute of Planners,* September 1969, pp. 233–44.

110. The Carswell nomination and rejection reads like a mystery novel; see Richard Harris, *Decision* (New York: E. P. Dutton, 1971).

111. Robert A. Dahl, *Who Governs?* (New Haven: Yale University Press, 1961), p. 227.

112. Game theorists have debated the size of a winning coalition. William Riker, *The Theory of Political Coalitions* (New Haven: Yale University Press, 1962), argues that political coalitions tend to the minimal number that still constitutes winning.

113. This issue is discussed in a game-theoretic mode by Robert M. Axelrod, *Conflict of Interest: A Theory of Divergent Goals with Applications to Politics* (Chicago: Markham, 1970).

114. For instance, Congressional dependence on burgeoning staffs brings this possibility into sharp focus. See Abshire and Nurnberger, eds., *The Growing Power of Congress,* pp. 121–23.

115. Crick, *In Defense of Politics,* presents the positive side of the argument, while S. E. Taylor and S. T. Fiske, "Salience, Attention, and Attribution: Top of the Head Phenomena," in L. Berkowitz, ed., *Advances in Experimental Social Psychology,* vol. 11 (New York: Academic Press, 1978), explore many of the argument's scientific limitations.

116. Harold L. Wilensky, *Organizational Intelligence* (New York: Basic Books, 1967), p. 183.

117. Robert Jervis, *Perception and Misperception in International Politics* (Princeton, N.J.: Princeton University Press, 1976), p. 245.

118. Ibid., pp. 230–92, passim.

119. Allison, *Essence of Decision,* p. 171.

120. The issue of social indicators is important and was treated in the preceding chapters on estimation.

121. Roberta Wohlstetter, *Pearl Harbor: Warning and Decision* (Stanford, Calif.: Stanford University Press, 1962).

122. The episode is well documented in Allen Whiting, *China Crosses the Yalu* (New York: Macmillan, 1960).

123. The pros and cons of ambiguous signals, indices, and information are weighed by Robert Jervis, *The Logic of Images in International Politics* (Princeton, N.J.: Princeton University Press, 1970); on the overall issue, idem, *Perception and Misperception.*

124. Thomas A. Bailey, *Woodrow Wilson and the Lost Peace* (New York: Macmillan, 1944).

125. Richard E. Neustadt, *Alliance Politics* (New York: Columbia University Press, 1970).

126. Barton Whaley, *Codeword BARBAROSSA* (Cambridge, Mass.: MIT Press, 1973). German counterintelligence was so effective in concealing German intentions that Stalin

refused to believe communiques from the Russian border troops that Panzer divisions were striking across the border.

127. Patrick J. McGarvey, "DIA: Intelligence to Please," *Washington Monthly*, July 1970, cited in Graham T. Allison and Morton H. Halperin, "Bureaucratic Politics: A Paradigm and Some Policy Implications," *World Politics*, Special Supplement, Spring 1972, p. 62.

128. Theodore H. White, "The Web of Numbers: A Message from the Census to Politics," *The Making of the President, 1972* (New York: Atheneum, 1973), chap. 6. The failure to examine numerical estimates critically is common; see Max Singer, "The Vitality of Mythical Numbers," *The Public Interest*, Spring 1971, pp. 3–9; and Amos Tversky and Daniel Kahneman, "Judgment Under Uncertainty: Heuristics and Biases," *Science*, 27 September 1974, pp. 1124–31.

129. Herbert York, *Race to Oblivion* (New York: Simon & Schuster, 1970), p. 89; cited in a quotation from Allison and Halperin, "Bureaucratic Politics," p. 75.

130. R. E. Nisbett et al., "Popular Induction: Information is not Necessarily Informative," in J. S. Carroll and J. W. Payne, eds., *Cognition and Social Behavior* (Hillsdale, N.J.: Lawrence Erlbaum Associates, 1976).

131. Schlesinger, *A Thousand Days*, chap. 30. In some ways, the fiasco of the Bay of Pigs can be seen as a small price because its lessons served the Kennedy Administration well during the Cuban missile crisis.

132. David Kahn, *The Code Breakers* (New York: Macmillan, 1967), chap. 17.

133. Papers documenting British access to the top secret Nazi code only became public in the mid 1970s; see Frederick W. Winterbotham, *The Ultra Secret* (New York: Harper & Row, 1974); this interpretation is disputed by R. V. Jones, *The Wizard War* (New York: Coward, McCann & Geoghegan, 1978), chap. 18.

134. Timothy Costello, "Psychological Aspects: The Soft Side of Policy Formation," *Policy Sciences*, Summer 1970, p. 163.

135. See Roger Hilsman, *To Move A Nation* (New York: Doubleday, 1964), sec. II, "The Organizational Structure"; or Halberstam, *Best and the Brightest*, chap. 5.

136. Alexander L. George and Juliette L. George, *Woodrow Wilson and Colonel House* (New York: John Day, 1956), provide an illustration of balanced psychohistorical research and the way the personality of the policymaker can affect national policy.

137. For example, see Erik H. Erikson, *Childhood and Society* (New York: W. W. Norton, 1950).

138. One of the earliest statements about charisma was by Max Weber, "The Sociology of Charismatic Authority," in H. H. Gerth and C. Wright Mills, eds., and trans., *From Max Weber: Essays in Sociology* (New York: Oxford University Press, 1958), chap. 9.

139. See Bell, *Conventions of Crisis;* and Ole R. Holsti, *Crisis, Escalation, War* (Montreal: McGill-Queen's University Press, 1972), chap. 8, for views of this phenomenon.

140. Glenn H. Snyder and Paul Diesing, *Conflict Among Nations: Bargaining, Decision Making, and System Structure in International Crises* (Princeton, N.J.: Princeton University Press, 1977).

8

Bargaining and the essential art of compromise

One of the most notable characteristics of the American political system and process is its explicit reliance on bargaining:

> Decisions are made by endless bargaining; in perhaps no other national political system in the world is bargaining so basic a component of the political process. In an age when the efficiencies of hierarchy have been re-emphasized on every continent, no doubt the American political system is something of an anomaly, if not, indeed, at times an anachronism.[1]

While one can readily grasp the benefits of such a system, measured in terms of ready access and opportunity for numerous diverse interests to be heard as decisions are sought, its costs have become apparent to many in recent years, in terms of a perceived inability to reach any decisions. John Gardner, former president of the Common Cause citizen lobby, has dubbed the problem "The War of the Parts Against the Whole," in which each particular interest "has achieved veto power over a piece of any possible solution, and no one has the power to solve the problem. Thus, in an oddly self-destructive conflict, the parts wage war against the whole. And the conflict will destroy us unless we get hold of it."[2] We therefore need to examine the bargaining characteristics of the selection process Gardner identifies in both its more beneficial and negative aspects.[3]

The American political system owes much of its characteristic style to the considerable fear of power shared by those who created it. The dominant practical responses were a deliberate diffusion of authority among competing institutions and the alignment of a federal system of government against a diverse state-based one.[4] Not only are the institutions arranged to encourage cooperative and consensual decision making, but the individuals who perform essential governmental functions are rarely allowed tenure for periods long enough to enable any one of them to acquire disproportionately large or unchallenged power. A consequence is registered in the degree of tentativeness apparent in seasoned democratic leaders, who have more often risen and sustained through the art of persuasion than by the use of force.[5] Equally apparent in the longer view of American history is the leadership's awareness of the fluidity of opinions, from day to day and from one administration to the next. Fanatics occasionally surface and radical claims get aired, but neither has traditionally been commonplace nor long-lived. Finally, the riskiness of anyone's claiming to speak for all Americans, or even for any large number of them, has been routinely demonstrated.

Through it all, the imperative of bargaining, making deals, or compromising stands out prominently. No one or institution is immune. The president must bargain with Congress to get legislation, or as Neustadt puts it, "Their formal powers are so intertwined that neither will accomplish very much, for very long, without the acquiescence of the other . . . what one demands the other can resist."[6] Much presidential success owes to what we have called leverage, which in turn seems to depend on a variety of considerations, including one's current standing with the public and reputation for political adroitness.[7] We have already noted Roosevelt's and Johnson's historical successes during periods when their prestige and reputations were high and much admired; however, as Jimmy Carter's experience suggests, accomplishing political ends by avoiding bargains while simultaneously enduring prestige and reputational reverses is exceedingly difficult.[8]

A president must bargain with subordinates, too, a process rarely smooth or free of conflict.[9] While political appointees are liable to be dismissed for flagrant or chronic failure to do what the president wants, such sanctions do not exist with regard to careerists in the civil service, many of whom have their own patrons in Congress.[10] These and other matters have been alleged in describing the how and why of the Social Security Administration's successful expansion during the Eisenhower and Nixon administrations— both had to give a little here to get support for other programs they favored.[11]

Congress is especially built on the bargaining principle. Few pieces of legislation emerge from the two houses in identical form, and most federal law is the product of incalculable gives and takes, deals, and accommodations.[12] Because the legislative branches are decentralized and the number, scope, and diversity of interests vying for attention are huge, party discipline and cohesion are extremely difficult to maintain—tendencies many believe have been aggravated by the legislative reforms of the 1970s.[13] A Lyndon Johnson or a Sam Rayburn was often able to craft intricate trades to obtain workable coalitions; today's leaders more often despair as each member strikes minibargains with both colleagues and the Executive Branch.[14]

Even the august body of the Supreme Court "cuts deals." For justices, according to Murphy,

> bargaining is a simple fact of life. Despite the conflicting views . . . cases have to be settled and opinions written; and no opinion can carry the institutional label of the Court unless five Justices agree to sign it. In the process of judicial decision-making, much bargaining may be tacit, but the pattern is still one of negotiation and accommodation to secure consensus.[15]

One result of judicial dealing, as it is with legislative and executive bargaining, is that clear and unequivocal statements of what the decision is and means do not commonly occur. Many thought, for instance, that the landmark capital punishment decision, *Furman* v. *Georgia*, ended the fatal practice once and for all; actual experience later proved otherwise as numerous loopholes, created by internal Court bargains required to obtain an opinion, came to light and got used.[16] Generally, trying to figure out what to do and how to do it in such ambiguous circumstances is troublesome—a point considered at length in the following part on implementation.

Nor is Court bargaining limited to internal affairs; other individals and institutions must be dealt with.[17] Congress has the constitutional power to impeach, and as Representative Gerald Ford pointed out in his vendetta against Justice William O. Douglas, an impeachable offense is whatever the House chooses to call an impeachable offense. Furthermore, the Constitution provides Congress an opportunity to limit the Court's jurisdiction;[18] e.g., Senator Jesse Helms, in 1981, proposed removing the school-busing issue from the Court's agenda. As a practical matter, of course, an individual justice or the entire Court would never deal directly with a Gerald Ford or a Jesse Helms; rather, tacit bargains are entered into: "In exchange for the end of a political attack, the justices hold back or back down from policies which they have been pursuing."[19]

At the state level, the need to bargain is often even more pronounced.[20] Although it varies a great deal, many department heads are elected officials and must work out quid pro quos with their governors for anything to happen. Legislative discipline here is at least as problematic as it is at the federal level.[21] The cities are often no better.[22]

Coalition building, in which bargaining plays an essential role, is one way political leadership relates to its constituents. While the scholarship here is considerable,[23] so, too, are disputes among political scientists and others about whether individual votes are bargained for with respect to positions one takes on specific issues or whether party loyalty or many other factors dominate.[24] Recalling the earlier discussion of the underlying and enabling emotional consensus may help here. As long as the number of specific issues needing governmental treatment remains relatively small and/or the importance of the issues is perceived to be high by a relatively large number of the body politic, then a good prospect for finding and building a consensual coalition exists. But as the number of issues individuals and groups bring into the public arena multiplies and/or the importance attached to most of them is generally perceived to be slight (save for a hard-core few in each), then the prospect for effective governance fades apace with the receding consensus and splintering coalitions.[25] This argument is summarized in Table 8–1.

Several very practical implications are suggested here. The total number of issues pressing for attention must be kept small, and for those treated, their importance must be minimized (cell 1) or diligently focused (cell 3)—depending on one's control over the situation and preference for governance. This kind of advice was suggested for President Carter on numerous occasions to little avail.[26] If a coalition is to be successful, those who participate in it must be willing to moderate and compromise to gain necessary support, which may mean that aberrant ideological strains will fail if they do not evolve through bargaining or other means. For immediate, short-term, relatively well understood objectives, e.g., "cut this year's federal budget 10 percent," coalitions can be formed of individuals or groups who retain antithetical ideologies. For instance, Russian Communists united with the bourgeoisie Social Democrats against the czar, then, as the revolution progressed, with Mensheviks and Social Revolutionaries against the

TABLE 8–1   The number and importance of issues: Consensus, coalitions, and governance

		Issues	
		Few	*Many*
Perceived importance of issues	Slight/ Diffuse	1. Tacit or latent consensus. Indeterminant to few coalitions. "Invisible" to nominal governance.	2. Weak, vulnerable consensus. Numerous, fractious, unstable coalitions. Problematic, inept, visible governance.
	High/ Focused	3. Strong, dependable consensus. Easy, stable coalitions. Effective, visible governance.	4. Brittle, tense consensus. Overload coalitions. Chaotic and/or authoritarian governance.

bourgeoisie, and then with small farmers against large landowners, and at last with peasants against kulaks.[27] For a broader-based and more durable coalition in which goals are less specific, e.g., "end the federal budget deficit," ideological leveling will probably be required. However, coalitions are hard to build and at least as hard to maintain. As a coalition emerges, enlarges, and matures, so, too, do opportunities for diversity of opinion and belief—despite best efforts to discover an acceptable middle ground. As this occurs, the differences mount up and force fractures and splits, and all the more so as individuals are drawn into competing and conflicting situations. Finally, conditions that join large numbers of issues numerous citizens perceive to be important (cell 4) are to be avoided. Efforts to reduce the absolute number of issues, e.g., symbolically through propaganda, operationally by transferring or shifting responsibility elsewhere, or actually by solving some of them, will all be encountered as tension, brittleness, and overloading take their toll on governmental effectiveness.

Compromise is a very high order principle. Uncompromising pursuit of narrow and specialized interests at the expense of the enabling consensus jeopardizes the system of governance itself. The problem may be endemic, and insoluble:

> [T]here is this strong bias against majorities in the political system the framers helped to create. Because they succeeded in designing a system that makes it easier for privileged minorities to prevent changes they dislike than for majorities to bring about the changes they want, it is strongly tilted in favor of the status quo and against reform.[28]

Such anxiety appears warranted, especially as government presents itself as being increasingly incapable of working for the good of the whole, considered in terms of resolving conflicts, building coalitions, and producing results (conditions characterized in cell 2, Table 8–1). Nowhere is the problem more evident than in various complex, highly technical decisions; or as Nelkin states it, "participation as an ideology in American society is increasing in importance even as technical complexity acts to limit effective political choice."[29]

The argument is as much pragmatic as it is moralistic, as Gardner articulates precisely: "If the larger system fails, the subsystems fail. That should not be such a difficult concept for the contending groups to understand." Elsewhere, "Let us honor the reasonable striving of groups to achieve goals that they share, but let us also have regard for the health and coherence of the whole society. If we do not it will surely fail."[30]

Failure has always been an alternative; although many policies have failed over the years, the system and the society have proven remarkably durable and flexible. There is no reason to expect these qualities to disappear. The citizenry can be trusted, and it is generally competent. But, according to V. O. Key, it must be informed, for it "behaves about as rationally as we should expect, given the clarity of the alternatives presented to it and the character of the information available to it."[31] What- ever the merits or demerits of bargaining or political compromise, however, it is clear that it is a critical factor in the selection process and must be taken into account by the analyst.

POLITICAL PROMOTION: MAKING "LIES SOUND TRUTHFUL"

Propaganda or education?

Presenting the alternatives clearly and comprehensibly emphasizes an essential communication task that binds rulers and ruled. Whether one elects to accept Orwell's cynicism or to stress Key's constructive potentials is more a difference in degree than substance, because, at some time or another, the essentials of the decision must be communicated to those going to be affected by it. Components of the communication act include a source, a target, a means of transmission, and content.[32] Simply issuing a decree is not, for instance, the same as ensuring that the recipient also understands why the decree exists, what it means, and what action consequences it portends: all necessary but still insufficient conditions. Also required are a predisposition and willingness to act—or at least not to interfere. "A tacit consent from the ruled for the ruler to rule seems necessary. There is an increasing need as time goes on for a voluntary surrender of freedom on the part of the people at large or at least for a relative passivity toward en- croachments on it," ventures Siu in his realistic portrayal of elite-to-mass communication requirements.[33]

Sharp differences of opinion exist, with related differences in practical means, about how one achieves consent, willingness, and noninterference. Those cleaving to a cynical cast of mind emphasize propaganda's darker aspects. Witness this from Ellul:

> The aim of modern propaganda is no longer to modify ideas, but to provoke action. It is no longer to change adherence to a doctrine, but to make the individual cling irrationally to a process of action. It is no longer to lead to choice, but to loosen the reflexes. It is no longer to transform an opinion, but to arouse an active and mythical belief.[34]

And in explicitly rejecting the educational objectives noted earlier by Key:

> The propagandist . . . does not normally address himself to the individual's intelligence, for the process of intellectual persuasion is long and uncertain, and the road from such intellectual conviction to action even more so.

This is not to say that education does not matter for Ellul, rather he gives it a quite different purpose—that of "pre-propaganda," or a nonstop condi- tioning of minds with incoherent information, for "Only when conditioned reflexes have been created in a man and he lives in a collective myth can he be readily mobilized."[35]

While not arguing with the action emphasis in this vision of political communication, others have pointed out some important mitigating aspects of this and related societies based on the democratic ideal.[36] Even when the elite-to-mass channel is working as the rulers intend, this is no guarantee that elite-to-elite circuits necessary for decisions to be implemented are working as well.[37] Diplomacy, bargaining, compromise, and control are all, to varying degrees in different circumstances, involved. High-level political leaders are thus responsible for mobilizing community attention on behalf of and support for specific issues or problems, but they must also work to make the details of their policies, programs and projects intelligible in an authoritative way to those empowered to act.[38]

Communication is a two-way process and involves the transmission of both technical and ideological information:

> The dependence of elite members on a common stream of information goes considerably beyond the need for technical detail. They are in need of a stable map of the context; likewise, they require access to information that nourishes fundamental perspectives of faith, belief, and loyalty. [For] unless the focus of attention of elite members is reached and perspectives are patterned by media of communication, common experiences fade, common goal values are in confusion, and common identities dissolve.[39]

The results of this are not desirable, and "as the ideological structures that confer a measure of continuity on the problem-solving process lose coherence, behavioral maladaptations are more frequent and more threatening to public order."[40]

These challenging theoretical ideas have direct realistic analogs. Early in the preceding part we presented what is perhaps the most ambitious program in the history of the nation—MX, the "Missile/Experimental" intercontinental ballistic missile system—and reported the exceptional political difficulties the program encountered.[41] Good politics as well as good analysis depend on a comprehensive consideration of a variety of points of view and values at stake in addition to the more apparent technical matters of fact. For MX, presumptions of common experience, goal, and identity were seemingly misplaced. The underlying consensus was missing. Forceful attempts by decision makers to have their way may, in the final outcome, undermine public order more than the MX augments national security. This is not to say that public hearings were not held, albeit belatedly and after initial decisions about MX were reached; nor is it to say that propaganda was not used. Numerous, well-attended, and provocative hearings were held; besides extraordinary public relations activities of the Pentagon, three primary contractors for MX—GTE Systems, Boeing, and Martin Marietta—hired the advertising firm of Smith & Harnoff to establish an "MX Education Bureau."[42] What it does say is that poor communications in both directions may well add up to a political bill at least as large as the actual one expected for MX. Or it may signal and stimulate compromise and modification of the program based on a improved two-way flow of communication.

Ideology's functions

Ideology is a difficult concept; consistent definition and interpretation have not materialized.[43] For our purposes, the concept refers to thoughts, feelings, attitudes, and beliefs—taken in appropriate combinations—that prevail in political settings. The relationships of such nontechnical contextual features to political promotion are sometimes hard to discern, but they are usually important.

Among other possible functions, ideology provides the following:[44]

An illustrative framework to aid recognition and discrimination of emerging events.

A sense of history for use in grasping and understanding the past, present, and future.

Basic expectations about the future.

Explanatory categories that enrich one's understanding of events—past, present, and future.

A basis against which goals and objectives of public policy can be clarified and assessed.

For the policymaker, during all phases of the decision process, the prevalence of ideology is not to be discounted or ignored. How, for instance, does one appreciate and respond to new problems discovered during initiation? Certainly an aggregate sense of what's important, and for whom, figures here, as do the means by which these feelings are communicated to decision makers.[45] In Part II we argued that scientists and analysts are not only motivated by distinctive attitudes (about what constitutes a problem's important aspects) but that the means of sharing the same with decision makers and the society at large contribute to the conception and shape of choices posed and eventually reached. In estimation, the cognitive, discriminative, and categorical functions of ideology can all be appreciated. Likewise, the historical and expectational functions gain prominence during selection as decision makers appeal, persuade, and otherwise labor to keep in touch with and modify the consensual bases of public order. Implementation works best, as we will see, when the goals and objectives of public policy are not only clarified and assessed, but also communicated authoritatively and in accordance with the prevailing ideology. The evaluation and termination phases of the overall process are also implicated, but we defer consideration of them until later.

Opinions, attitudes, and beliefs are essential to understanding the purposes of ideology and its relationship to political communication and decision. What, for instance, do we mean by opinion? Is this the same as an attitude? How do these terms and concepts relate to beliefs and belief systems? Finally, can we understand why certain key individuals speak and act as they do, why the great mass of public opinion either supports or rejects those in power, and how or whether the complex human dimensions of a given problem and setting can be emphasized? It is usually very hard to answer any or all of these questions once and for all. Rather, one usually needs to be reminded of them periodically so that tentative answers may be framed and injected into an evolving sense of "What's the problem?" and "What are some answers?"

Opinions are the elementary statements or expressions made by an individual about the state of the world. Opinions reflecting general preferences based on particular factual interpretations are called biases; a desire for a particular end or course of action is a wish; and a preference for the best means of achieving desired ends is a policy or policy preference. Differences in opinion are caused by differences in one's view of facts, differences in the appraisal of various ends, or differences in the estimation of the best means of attaining desired ends.

Opinions are an essential element of sophisticated political communication, analysis, and acts, and they should be an integral component of theories of social decision making. For instance, opinions may be evaluated according to their diffuseness, persistence, intensity, and reasonableness where: diffuseness refers to the volume of opinion and the number of people who hold an opinion, persistence refers to the extent an opinion is perpetuated, and intensity and reasonableness refer to the earnestness and rationality with which opinions are held, especially as compared to vague preferences.[46]

With respect to any given situation or context, these four opinion concepts can in principle be separated. For instance, the categories of expert, authority, special interest, and the average citizen prove useful in sorting out characteristics of opinions surrounding issues or policy problems. Furthermore, the tasks of coping with and integrating opinions into both practical and theoretical work are made somewhat more tractable by the fact that the nearly limitless total of opinions is likely to stand for far fewer attitudes: statements summarizing numerous opinions about a given situation. Attitudes are relatively stable for individuals and groups over time and may be interpreted differently as to their meaning, features Ellul stresses in his work on propaganda, which is notably subtitled, "The Formation of Men's Attitudes."[47] Interpretations themselves are referred to as beliefs (or belief systems, when numerous people are the object of study, analysis, or manipulation).

Opinions contribute to the general climate or mood of public policy in the ways they relate to preferences about the distribution and enjoyment of all human values, e.g., respect, wealth, well-being, power, skill, and enlightenment. Past experiences influence these preferences and the symbol systems and myths to which various segments of the public respond. Taken altogether, they provide the emotional basis for politics and policy.

As practical matter, however, popular opinions and attitudes present inordinately difficult problems of interpretation; that is, determining what a given attitude or belief means and what one should do in response to it are seldom simple tasks. Not the least of the difficulty stems from the much-reported inconsistencies in such matters. For instance, over the years most Americans have been found to disapprove generally of government welfare programs while simultaneously approving specific assistance to poor families with dependent children and food stamps to the hungry. Such helps one understand, if not explain, the mixed messages embedded in popular desires to reduce the size of government but not by cutting specific governmental programs. Decision makers somehow must come to terms and deal with this.

Intentionality

A decision is a landmark signifying action or movement, and because it is, one can see that a decision is laden with intention—about objectives and goals, instrumental means, and timing and sequencing of events. Aspects of political communication are inextricably bound with each intentional element.

Following closely on the definitional efforts of Stech, intentions are found to involve four different elements: an *action*, the *object* or *target* to which the action is directed, the *context* or *situation* in which the action is to take place, and the *time* at which the action is to be performed.[48] The most detailed specification of intentions is the project or plan, in which all phases of action, object, context, and time are set out; the least detailed is exemplified in political myths and slogans as represented broadly in statements about policy and policy preferences. We have emphasized projects, plans, and programs—the easiest, most concrete forms intentions take. However, the role of political myths and slogans is at least as important in terms of their capacities for creating and maintaining the enabling emotional consensus upon which political order depends. Siu makes the point well: "No power of major proportions can effectively be exercised over a prolonged period of time without an array of myths to sustain it. Regulations and laws are largely the practical outcroppings of accepted myths," and the "foundations of power are the practical fruits of flourishing myths."[49] The main point is that the myth is a statement of expectation about behavior, the violation of which rightfully invites sanctioning. In this sense, a serious appreciation of the diverse myth structure of any given society helps illuminate essential social and cultural constraints and hence delimits the scope and range of political possibilities. For instance, a persistent myth in the American culture is one favoring the free enterprise system in commercial affairs. While, objectively, dozens, if not hundreds, of violations of the myth can be observed (e.g., government dominance of research and development, a large and expensive system of public education at all levels of instruction, private corporations wholly, or quite nearly so, dependent on the government),[50] the myth still has great force in forming and limiting political action.[51]

To bring the discussion full circle, the extent of trust, satisfaction, and general acceptance of the ruling elite's legitimacy weighs in as decisions are sought, made, and enacted. In periods when these conditions are high and stable, or can be made to appear so through judicious use of political communication, mass compliance with the wishes of that elite, including acquiescence to its intentions (projects, programs, and policies), is routine—it can be counted on for purpose of analysis and control. When disturbed in terms of the ways the ruled perceive themselves, their rulers and events (determined in assessments of opinion, attitude, and belief), the authoritative bases of governance constrict and, in limiting cases, crumble as the arguments and preferences of new elites mount and alter both political mood and the status quo; witness Iran in 1979.

This is not the appropriate time or place to delve deeply into these matters. However, their total effect is to focus attention on a generally neglected aspect of decision making—considered as both an analytic and practical matter—that is, the inherent subjectivity in all political and authoritative acts which surfaces in the operational concept of intentionality. A basic message is that the meaning of more or less objective facts cannot be presumed and this should be explored directly as an important intellectual and practical matter.[52]

Everyone plays

Elite-to-mass promotion has already been discussed primarily in terms of propaganda, which is the specialty field most directly concerned with this particular form.[53] Elite-to-elite promotion can be discovered in nearly any expert study or analysis having resource claiming implications; the rise of expert consultants and the mobilization of an impressive array of procedures to press special interests into the focus of decision both attest to this form of promotion.[54]

Mass-to-elite initiatives and procedures are manifest in polling (and its private sector analog, marketing surveys),[55] lobbying (when broad rather than narrow interests are represented),[56] and in advocacy and adversarial efforts having wide-ranging implications, e.g., class-action suits.[57]

The possibility of mass-to-mass promotion has heretofore been impeded by physical constraints; however, as systems of personal communication continue to improve and diffuse in modern society, this situation may very well change. Consider the possibility of mass meetings in which numerous individuals may elect (or not) to pursue common interests but where no one of them leaves the privacy (and safety) of the home to do so.

USING FORCE

A most profound political reality, to recall Duverger's conception of the state, is that organized power is a means by which a very few control the many in the interest of public and social order.[58] By and large social control stems from the consent of the ruled; but, as any revolutionary experience demonstrates, those in control will stop at little to extinguish dissent and ensure their continuance. Capital punishment is one extreme form of using force, and it is significant that the crime of treason to the state (at least in time of external threat or war) ranks equally with homicide in terms of expected social sanctions.

War provides a parallel, but more massive, illustration of the exercise of power on a grand scale. No one knows for sure how many Jews died in the Nazi holocaust, certainly more than enough to make the point. No one knows either how many might perish in a nuclear exchange. It is frightening just to imagine: 2 to 10 million in a "counterforce" strike at the enemy's military assets, or 80 to 100 million in an all-out "countervalue" attack against its cities and citizens?[59] While the taking of life is in some sense an ultimate sanction, the threat of doing so in the interest of the common social good is inescapable. Fortunately, killing is a last-resort means of using force.

At the other end of the spectrum of controlling means, one finds education, a topic already treated at length. Between killing them and teaching them a variety of possibilities exists:[60]

Eliminating them: exile, the prison or political prison camp, "psychiatric hospitals" (in the Soviet practice), reassignment to a bureaucratic Siberia.

Damaging them: character assassination, smear and innuendo or black propaganda, stealing and publicizing confidential or personal facts, e.g., Watergate, J. Edgar Hoover's alleged "personal files" of private pecadillos and perversions, harassment, rigorous tax audits.

Threatening them: by indicating a willingness and capacity to take actions that eliminate or damage.

Bribing them: cash payments, buying votes or horsetrading, and acceptable bribes, e.g. perquisites, junkets.

Cajoling them (emphasis on individual level): flattery and other blatant, usually unwarranted, appeals to the ego (Orwell: "give an appearance of solidity to pure wind").

Persuading them: debates, rational arguments, "come, let us reason together," oratory, propaganda, bargains, compromising; (the normal means and forms).

Seducing them: charm, charisma, guile.

Attracting them: much the same as seducing them but without as much guile.

Educating them: as previously discussed.

This list is not definitive, nor are all the categories mutually exclusive, but it does help one think about the many and varied ways force can be applied. Depending on circumstances, any or all of its distinctive forms may come into play, for no decision of importance will be taken in the absence of some authoritative resort to force.

Curiously, the standard decision-making theories, or knowledge of the policy and decision processes, give little or no prominence to the many forceful aspects of selection characterized here. By aiming at concise and coherent specifications, and inordinantly simplified perspectives of what decision making is, does, and entails, most theories omit a great deal of practical importance and tend to overstate highly selected aspects at the expense of a more complete comprehension of the whole. At best, the more prominent schools or approaches to theories of decision are simple caricatures of a rich, highly complex, and decidely human phenomenon.

THEORIES OF DECISION: KNOWLEDGE OF THE PROCESS

While a full-scale review is beyond the scope of this effort, it is probably worthwhile to mention at least several of the standard contributions to current knowledge about decision making. We touch briefly on work in psychology, economics, and political science.[61]

Psychology

Paralleling the many rational theories and methods discovered in the last part ("Coping with Complexity" and "Methods") are simple, rational psychological theories of individual and group decision making. Most share several core assumptions:

An optimal alternative is the end result sought.

Additional information is unambiguously set off against competing values.

Alternatives are appreciated and their implications can be known (measured) with confidence.

Costs and benefits can be calculated and trade-offs assessed.

Stating these assumptions so boldly does not mean that all psychological theories of decision exhibit each in equal measure, nor does it rule out the possibility of informed dissent and criticism.[62] Neither does it imply that psychological theories cannot on occasion be insightful and even helpful to one facing a tough choice. Rather, the point is one well stated by Kinder and Weiss in their review of the literature:

> [D]ecision making is not a unitary phenomenon. Although the very label creates the illusion of a single process, making a single choice involves a complex of processing tasks—defining the need for a decision, structuring the problem, finding alternatives worth considering, deciding what information is likely to be relevant, assimilating that information, assessing the probability of various consequences, living with the chosen alternative, and a variety of others. Each of these sub-tasks may be regulated by a different psychological process; each may require a somewhat different skill from the decision maker. There is no guarantee that intelligent performance of any one translates into intelligent performance of the others. *All models of decision making focus on some subset of these tasks while ignoring or making ceteris paribus assumptions about other potentially critical processes.* [Emphases added.][63]

Under these conditions it is difficult to imagine a single psychological theory of decision of sufficient scope and power to encompass the empirical facts of life—the realities of political decision making.

Economics

Which does not mean that theorists will cease their quest. In economics the rational versus irrational split is also evident. Before the 1950s, economists viewed the decision maker as a rational economic man having a full view of the appropriate arena, perfect information, and the ability to value and weigh all alternatives. The theoretical skein continues to unravel even today in the work of the so-called rational expectations school,[64] much microeconomics,[65] certain versions of game theory,[66] and in hybrid combinations of these subfields.[67]

Herbert Simon and James March, jointly and individually, challenged the rational view beginning in the late 1950s.[68] Limitations in innate cognitive capacity, explicit institutional peculiarities, expectational and volitional aspects, uncertainty, and many other important decision-making concepts which had been overlooked or assumed away in the rational paradigm were called to attention and treated directly by Simon and his various followers.[69] The perspective is broader in scope and works to include behavioral with purer economic insights; however, many important decision-making aspects are still left out (e.g., coercive or forceful events) or downplayed (e.g., actual differences in decision stemming from variations in contextual features, elements of timing, symbolic and mythical components). It is, in short, a more interesting conception but far from an inclusive one.[70]

A "pox on all your houses" critique of economics as a suitable paradigm for applied work was leveled by Shubik in 1970 and remains a benchmark—

both as a criticism and as an enumeration of the primary limitations of economic theories of choice.[71]

Political science

As a first approximation, the literature from political science dealing with decision making can be divided into incremental and piecemeal categories. The incremental approach, typified in Lindblom's works, replaces one form of rational construction with another arguing that organizational goals and sufficient information are not clear and abundant enough, respectively, to satisfy theoretical requirements for complete cognitive, volitional, and emotional specification.[72] Thus, one decides at the margin of experience. The piecemeal school of thought is more complex and is represented by numerous and different intellectual trends, such as pluralism,[73] group process/elite models,[74] bureaucratic politics,[75] and the public choice movement.[76] While differing in specifics, they all share the idea that policy-making is basically the aggregation of many disaggregated, often non-communicating, suboptimizing activities; decisions result in policies representing a distribution of goods (or values, in the terms used here) in accord with the prevailing configuration of power.

Both approaches may have merit, but the choice between the two is largely dependent upon a clear specification of the context or situation to assess the relevance of either for a particular policy setting. Such clarity is more exception than rule, however; many problems do not fit very well in either decision-making perspective.[77] For example, nonincremental, indivisible policies having enormous size or threshold effects (e.g., send a man to the moon, renew the nation's cities, create a national health insurance program, go to war then sue for peace) or those having extended time lags between the execution of a decision and any tangible outcomes (e.g., nuclear and other large-scale and time-bound endeavors) are difficult to explain with either paradigm, a point well made by Morone: "[T]here may be only one general species of complex problems and one general strategy for dealing with it, but *there seem to be many subspecies, and for these, variations of the general strategy are required.*"[78] After a thorough exploration of the decision-making literature in hopes of finding a variation that would shed light on the case of nuclear reactor development, Morone summarizes these essential points:

> There are variations among the strategies described in the literature. The variations, however, usually reflect differences in the institutional settings within which problems must be handled rather than differences in types of complex problems. Lindblom's strategy, for example, is adapted to pluralistic, fragmented policy arenas; March and Simon's to formal organizations in general; Steinbruner's also to formal organizations but to governmental organizations in particular; and Cyert and March's to business organizations. These variations are important. There is no question that decision strategies

must be adapted to their institutional settings. But this study suggests that strategies must also be, and at least in some cases are, adapted to a second variable: the nature or type of complex problem that the decision maker faces. There is more variety in such complex problems than our literature suggests, and therefore, there should be (and perhaps is) more variety in the strategies for dealing with them.[79]

In sum

The complexity of decision settings of interest to us in this book outstrips or overwhelms the individual theoretical approaches mainly relied on by scholars and analysts to specify and comprehend policy choices. Each approach may have partial merit in helping one come to terms with a specific problem or situation in context, yet no one of them has proved capable of capturing enough of the important, workaday features of organized and complex problems to be of general utility. Decisions having social and policy consequences are usually *multifaceted* and hence call for a variety of disciplinary methods and approaches to aid understanding; *value based* and *value oriented* and hence demand explicit consideration of more than just the wealth or power consequences of prospective acts; and *comprehensive* and hence require the use and integration of perspectives from many different levels of analysis. Simply focusing on one or a very few suspected determinants of decision, as psychological theorists have preferred doing, fails to illuminate many other aspects that may have as much (or more) significance in a given situation. Assuming that human beings were rational, as many economic theorists do, is not the same as confronting the observed irrationality or nonrationality that pervades individual and collective choices. Emphasizing a particular institutional or analytical milieu, the political scientist's tendency, without giving weight to or allowing for the possibility of alternative ones, can often result in a far less than comprehensive appreciation of decision's many rich manifestations. Furthermore, a failing common to all general approaches is lack of concern for the unique qualities of each and every problem requiring analysis and decision: problems should suggest theoretical approaches; theoretical approaches do not define problems.

SELECTION IN THE POLICY PROCESS

While for purposes of exposition we have isolated selection out of the total policy process, it is unquestionably highly integrated in usual experience. Let us conclude this part by elaborating these links.

Through a variety of means, selection connects to and influences initiation. A shared cultural heritage, commonality of outlook, and broad consensus about desired collective outcomes bind decision makers to those specialized in problem recognition and initial, tentative solution specification. More explicitly, those primarily responsible for choice will, over the course of time, demonstrate preferences about important problems and appropriate solutions—information about the needs, distribution, and amounts of power available for social problem solving—and thus provide guidance to those supplying initiation services. Problem recognition, in this conception, becomes partly a function of the issues and topics already demanding the decision makers' attention and partly a function of their willingness and success in dispatching these problems. For instance, the Iranian revolution was no less of a revolution in 1981 than it was in 1980; however, because attention shifted dramatically to other problems and American decision makers had slight interest in it, there is little reason to think that intelligence and information collection pertinent to Iran continued at the superheated rates of 1980.

The selection-initiation link is reciprocal. New problems occur and their nature, form, and urgency are weighed and, if sufficiently important, are communicated to those most directly implicated. The agenda of public policy shifts in response to new challenges and in accord with popular needs and strivings.

As the policy process advances to estimation, crude visions of a problem's nature and possible solution begin to give way to more refined and detailed analyses. Such analyses will be conditioned by the realities of the decision setting in numerous ways: Is the problem really important, or is it ephemeral, transient, or symbolic? How much time is there to do analyses—10 minutes, 10 months, 10 years? Who are the clients for the analysis, and what can each conceivably do to facilitate matters? What sorts of options or alternatives appear, from the record, to be feasible and which do not? For whom? Under what conditions? The list is long and in total suggests many concrete links between selection and estimation.

One needs to appreciate the fact that analysis has the effects of limiting and shaping choices, a point that emphasizes the forward connection between estimation and selection. Those relied on for analysis project order on problems as a result of their own experiences, training, and role—this even in the best of circumstances. In the worst of circumstances, analysts may be inclined to substitute their own judgment and preferences for those with constituted authority: estimation becomes selection, in effect. However, as we have emphasized at length, the decision maker not only has a different policy perspective from the analysts, but also bears responsibility for the choices finally made: This fact frequently surfaces as "finished" analyses are returned for more work, additional data, newer or more appropriate options, or is simply ignored. Even though this necessitates some repetition, it does not necessarily represent slack or fat in the system; rather, it demonstrates the realistic, iterative nature of the policy process.

The implementation of a policy is often overlooked during selection (at times deliberately), but it should not be because, without addressing implementation issues, a decision will almost certainly not be translated into the programs envisaged by the decision makers. Or, as Rein states the matter: "[T]he ruthless pursuit of a problem, without regard to the question of implementation, may lead to a solution that, while it is rational, is not politically relevant."[80]

Neglect has many sources. A decision maker may intend to leave implementation to subordinates having more detailed procedural skill and practical familiarity with the problem. This often happens in cases where the administrative details are numerous or onerous and where the decision makers have other demands on their available time; it also occurs when a decision maker seeks to avoid criticism for subsequent, faulty implementation. Even if an executive order is well designed and clearly stated, subordinates may alter it according to their own personal and institutional needs, carry out only parts of the order because of resource or jurisdictional limitations and constraints, or ignore it altogether. In any event, the transition between the policy the decision maker thought was being ordered and what actually occurs provides some of the most difficult and vexing moments in the policy process.

Implementation's link backward to selection can be illustrated with a series of operational questions: What are the stakes? How serious is the decision maker about really doing something, and what might that something be? How much time is there to implement the decision; was it expected yesterday, or is there time to do some planning and thinking about the matter? How constricting is the decision; is the intent clearly spelled out? Are there sufficient resources at hand to do the job right or to just go through the motions? Are we going to have to hire (fire) personnel to get the job done?

If program implementation is an occasional afterthought during selection, evaluation is often considered but rarely specified. Evaluation criteria are generally delegated to program managers—a poor choice since they are usually too busy managing the program to design and execute an objective monitoring procedure.[81] In addition, there are ethical questions about the advisability of program managers evaluating their own programs. Furthermore, would a program manager even want to manage a program whose evaluative system allowed others to monitor the work easily? Basically, monitoring programs is a critical component of policy. If decision makers want to ensure that a policy meets their requirements, they must decide on and specify evaluation standards during selection, a requirement that may well affect the choice taken.

A different perspective occurs when decisions are viewed from the evaluation standpoint: the evaluation-selection linkage. Who was successful in the decision-making phase? Why? If a policy turned out to accomplish all or most of what was expected of it, was it because of the wisdom, foresight, and skill of the decision makers or not? Are there consistently productive, good decision makers and the converse? Why? In general, are there some unrealized ways to tie evaluation and selection together better in the interest of improving the overall policy process?

Termination is rarely considered during the selection phase; virtually no decision maker will include contingency plans to terminate a program that proves ineffective or no longer useful. To do so would, among other things, violate Allison's 51–49 principle of oversell needed to secure consent and acceptance of specific recommendations. The possibility of termination is imagined to be so remote in time as not to warrant explicit consideration. Or contemplation of termination conjures up thoughts of political strife and personal distaste sufficient to allow the matter to pass unattended. Simple faith in the system to do a good, efficient, and useful job on the decision also exists as a plausible, though remote, reason for a decision maker to overlook terminal needs. Whatever the reason, the issue of termination is rarely addressed when decisions are made.

When terminations are encountered, do these create different problems for decision makers—or signal a need to initiate the policy process from the beginning? Since termination has been a rare matter of explicit policy in our common experience until relatively recent times, scant attention has been devoted to the termination-selection connection. As we experience more, however, opportunities will undoubtedly occur to learn more about decision making and the range of alternatives open to government in the future. One of those lessons may be that the government is being asked to do things for us which are simply infeasible, inappropriate, or better done in other ways.

The liturgy of programmatic failure, to which we next turn our attention, strongly suggests the validity of this lesson.

NOTES

1. Robert A. Dahl, *A Preface to Democratic Theory* (Chicago: University of Chicago Press, 1956), p. 150.
2. John W. Gardner, "The War of the Parts Against the Whole," *The Seventeenth Cosmos Club Award* (Washington, D.C.: Cosmos Club, April 3, 1980). [Speech.]
3. Many ideas in this section owe much to Jack Pitney of Yale's Political Science Department.
4. Bernard Bailyn, *The Ideological Origins of the American Revolution* (Cambridge, Mass.: Belknap Press, 1967), chaps. 1 and 2.
5. An interesting book on the key issue of power is Dennis H. Wrong, *Power: Its Forms, Bases, and Uses* (New York: Harper & Row, 1979), in which four fundamental types of power are categorized and carefully refined: force, manipulation, persuasion, and authority. A classic statement is Harold D. Lasswell and Abraham Kaplan, *Power and Society* (New Haven: Yale University Press, 1950).
6. Richard E. Neustadt, *Presidential Power* (New York: John Wiley & Sons, 1960), p. 105.
7. Ibid., chaps. 4 and 5.

8. Some have treated the matter in terms of variations in leadership qualities and opportunities. James MacGregor Burns, *Leadership* (New York: Harper & Row, 1978).

9. Joseph A. Califano, Jr., *Governing America* (New York: Simon & Schuster, 1981), is only one of a long list of "insider" accounts that inevitably herald an out-going administration.

10. Hugh Heclo, *A Government of Strangers: Executive Politics in Washington* (Washington, D.C.: The Brookings Institution, 1977), pp. 134–42. Longevity, familiarity, and power all matter: "A close affinity often exists between a committee chairman and the senior career staff of the departments and agencies under his jurisdiction. The chairmen and ranking committee members probably know more about the details of an agency's program and are better acquainted with the senior career staff than most agency heads who serve for relatively brief periods." Harold Seidman, *Politics, Position, and Power* (New York: Oxford University Press, 1980), p. 53.

11. Martha Derthick, *Policymaking for Social Security* (Washington, D.C.: The Brookings Institution, 1979), chap. 3.

12. Lewis A. Froman, Jr., *The Congressional Process* (Boston: Little, Brown, 1967); and Charles O. Jones, *The United States Congress* (Homewood, Ill.: Dorsey Press, 1982).

13. David M. Abshire and Ralph D. Nurnberger, eds., *The Growing Power of Congress* (Beverly Hills, Calif.: Sage Publications, 1981), part II.

14. Informal networks play an important role here. See Ross K. Baker, *Friends and Foes in the U.S. Senate* (New York: Free Press, 1980); and R. Douglas Baker, *Congress and the Bureaucracy* (New Haven: Yale University Press, 1979), pp. 210–41.

15. Walter F. Murphy, *Elements of Judicial Strategy* (Chicago: University of Chicago Press, 1964), p. 57.

16. Bob Woodward and Scott Armstrong, *The Brethren* (New York: Simon & Schuster, 1979), pp. 205–20. Lest one harbor civics-class illusions about the majesty of the court, we recommend this rather unseemly book as an antidote.

17. Louis Fisher, *The Constitution Between Friends: Congress, the President, and the Law* (New York: St. Martin's Press, 1978), develops the idea.

18. Article II, section 2.

19. Murphy, *Elements of Judicial Strategy*, p. 174.

20. Herbert Jacob and Kenneth N. Vines, eds., *Politics in the American States* (Boston: Little, Brown, 1978).

21. Alan Rosenthal, *Legislative Life* (New York: Harper & Row, 1981), chap. 8.

22. Douglas Yates, *The Ungovernable City* (Cambridge, Mass.: MIT Press, 1977), chaps. 4–6.

23. Summarized admirably throughout Seymour Martin Lipset, ed., *Emerging Coalitions in American Politics* (San Francisco: Institute for Contemporary Studies, 1978).

24. Edward G. Carmines and James A. Stimson, "The Two Faces of Issue Voting," *American Political Science Review*, March 1980, pp. 78–91, survey disputes.

25. Ralph M. Goldman, *Search for Consensus: The Story of the Democratic Party* (Philadelphia: Temple University Press, 1979), presents a particular version of this idea.

26. James MacGregor Burns, "Jimmy Carter's Strategy for 1980," *Atlantic Monthly*, March 1979, pp. 41–46.

27. R. G. H. Siu, *The Craft of Power* (New York: John Wiley & Sons, 1979), p. 110, comments on this sequence in which simple, short-term control objectives dominated longer-range and more complex goals.

28. Robert A. Dahl, "On Removing Certain Impediments in Democracy in the United States," *Political Science Quarterly*, Spring 1977, pp. 1–20, at pp. 5–6.

29. Dorothy Nelkin, ed., *Controversy: The Politics of Technical Decisions* (Beverly Hills, Calif.: Sage Publications, 1979), "Introduction," p. 14.

30. Gardner, "War of the Parts."

31. V. O. Key, Jr., *The Responsible Electorate* (Cambridge, Mass.: Harvard University Press, 1966), p. 7.

32. A thorough inquiry is Colin Cherry, *On Human Communication* (Cambridge, Mass.: MIT Press, 1966), particularly chap. 1 for the points covered here.

33. Siu, *Craft of Power*, p. 134.

34. Jacques Ellul, *Propaganda: The Formation of Men's Attitudes*, trans. Konrad Kellen and Jean Lerner (New York: Vintage Books, 1973), pp. 25–26.

35. Ibid., p. 32. He claims that the Soviet Union has tended to rely on conditioning through reflex while the United States has emphasized the myth.

36. Satish K. Arora and Harold D. Lasswell, *Political Communication: The Public Language of Political Elites in India and the United States* (New York: Holt, Rinehart & Winston, 1969).

37. Murray Edelman, *Political Language: Words that Succeed and Policies that Fail* (New York: Academic Press, 1977), expands on this and other related themes, several of which carry over from his earlier, *The Symbolic Uses of Politics* (Urbana: University of Illinois Press, 1967).

38. Part IV, "Implementation," amplifies this theme in some detail.

39. Arora and Lasswell, *Political Communication*, p. 5.

40. Ibid.

41. Eliot Marshall, "MX Faces Stiff Political Test in Nevada," *Science*, 29 February 1980, pp. 961–65. In simple physical terms, the MX promises to be the *largest construction project in history*.

42. "Washington Update," *National Journal*, June 6, 1981.

43. Much has been written about it, but David E. Apter, ed., *Ideology and Discontent* (New York: Free Press, 1964), provides an initial exposure.

44. Arora and Lasswell, *Political Communication*, chap. 1.

45. Various media exist and are relied on, e.g., surveys, public opinion polls, letters from citizens. The press, in this society, has always played a key role. See Herbert J. Gans, *Deciding What's News* (New York: Pantheon Books, 1979).

46. Steven R. Brown, *Political Subjectivity* (New Haven: Yale University Press, 1980), helps map out the requirements for including ideological information in policy analysis and political action.

47. Ellul, *Propaganda*. Also see Ronald D. Brunner, "An 'International' Alternative in Public Opinion Research,"*American Journal of Political Science* 21 (1977), pp. 435–64.

48. Frank J. Stech, *Political and Military Intention Estimation* (Bethesda, Md.: MATHTECH, November 1979), chap. 2.

49. Siu, *Craft of Power*, pp. 64, 67. A rigorous and instructive exposition of the role and function of myth throughout history is G. S. Kirk, *Myth: Its Meaning and Functions in Ancient and Other Cultures* (Berkeley: University of California Press, 1970).

50. James Fallows, *National Defense* (New York: Random House, 1981), paints an informative picture of the weapons business.

51. Imagine the consequences of deciding to nationalize the steel, automobile, or food industries.

52. A rare example of this kind of inquiry is Raymond L. Garthoff, "On Estimating and Imputing Intentions," *International Security* 2, no. 3 (1978), pp. 22–32, which concentrates on the specialized field of strategic weaponry. See also, Brunner, "An 'Intentional' Alternative."

53. Besides the works previously cited, see also: Alexander L. George, *Propaganda Analysis* (Evanston, Ill.: Row, Peterson, 1959); J. S. Bruner, "The Dimensions of Propaganda," *Journal of Abnormal and Social Psychology* 41, no. 3 (1941), pp. 311–77; Robert Merton, *Mass Persuasion* (New York: Harper & Row, 1949); and Kenneth Burke, *Language as Symbolic Action* (Berkeley: University of California Press, 1966).

Advertising and marketing, from the private sector, have a political component insofar as they create expectations about wealth and other human values. Wealth and power are directly treated in William H. Read, *America's Mass Media Merchants* (Baltimore, Md.: Johns Hopkins University Press, 1976). The joining of politics, advertising, and the communication media is one of the last decade's more significant events. See Newton N. Minow, John Bartlett Martin, and Lee M. Mitchell, *Presidential Television* (New York: Basic Books, 1973), for the harbinger of what Edwin Diamond disparagingly refers to as *The Tin Kazoo: Television, Politics, and the News* (Cambridge, Mass.: MIT Press, 1975). The presidential campaign of 1968 is treated in a similar fashion by Joe McGinniss, *The Selling of the President, 1968* (New York: Simon & Schuster, 1976).

On the issue of elite control of the mass media, see: Martin H. Seiden, *Who Controls the Mass Media? Popular Myths and Economic Realities* (New York: Basic Books, 1974); and Bernard Rubin, *Media, Politics, and Democracy* (New York: Oxford University Press, 1977).

54. Much of Part II can be considered fruitfully in these terms. For a very specific guide or "handbook" for methods by which businessmen communicate with decision makers, see Edward A. Grefe, *Fighting to Win: Business Political Power* (New York: Law & Business Inc./Harcourt Brace Jovanovich, 1981).

55. An enormous field; Angus Campbell, Philip E. Converse, Warren E. Miller, and Donald E. Stokes, *The American Voter* (New York: John Wiley & Sons, 1960); and Philip E. Converse, "Public Opinion and Voting Behavior," in Fred I. Greenstein and Nelson W. Polsby, eds., *Handbook of Political Science*, vol. 4 (Reading, Mass.: Addison-Wesley, 1975), present its contours.

56. Jeffrey M. Berry, *Lobbying for the People: The Political Behavior of Public Interest Groups* (Princeton, N.J.: Princeton University Press, 1977).

57. An easy-to-understand, how-to-do-it for neophyte advocates is Elizabeth Berger, "The Compleat Advocate," *Policy Sciences*, March 1977, pp. 69–78.

58. Maurice Duverger, *The Idea of Politics* (Chicago: Henry Regnery, 1970), p. xiii.

59. A much discussed topic by strategic analysts. Fallows, *National Defense*, refers to it and them as "Theologians," chap. 6.

60. Siu, *Craft of Power*, p. 123, is the source of this list, which he refers to as "the push-pulling of power." The examples are our own.

61. The practice of reviewing decision-making theories has become de rigueur in the social science literature; we suggest reading John D. Steinbruner, *The Cybernetic Theory of Decision* (Princeton, N.J.: Princeton University Press, 1974), part I: "Paradigms of the Decision Process," for a general orientation.

62. A curmudgeonly critique is contained in Paul Slovic, Baruch Fischoff, and Sarah Lichtenstein, "Behavioral Decision Theory," *Annual Review of Psychology* 28, no. 1 (1977), pp. 1–39. As part of the criticism, the bulk of the field is identified.

63. Reprinted from Donald R. Kinder and Janet A. Weiss, "In Lieu of Rationality: Psychological Perspectives on Foreign Policy Decision Making" *Journal of Conflict Resolution*, July 1978. © 1978 Sage Publications, Inc., with permission.

64. A seeming contradiction in terms, and a dubious attempt to subsume within a technical (rational) straitjacket ideological (not necessarily "rational") conceptions of the individual as decision maker. "All [psycho-analytic] schools view human conduct for the most part

in terms of motives, purposes, and intentions, in terms of desires, emotions, moods, thoughts, hopes and fears. Attempts at primarily physical, mathematical, biological, or other nonteleological forms of understanding are rarely made." Herbert Fingarette, *The Meaning of Criminal Insanity* (Berkeley: University of California Press, 1972), pp. 89–90.

65. William Eckhaus, *Basic Economics* (Cambridge, Mass.: MIT Press, 1972), is illustrative; and James S. Henderson and Richard E. Quant, *Micro-economic Theory: A Mathematical Approach* (New York: McGraw-Hill, 1971), offer the quantitative basics.

66. A classic is John von Neumann and Oscar Morgenstern, *The Theory of Games and Economic Behavior* (New York: John Wiley & Sons, 1954); Anthony Downs, *An Economic Theory of Democracy* (New York: Harper & Row, 1957), provides standard exemplification; and Martin Shubik, "Game Theory Models and Methods in Political Economy," in Kenneth J. Arrow and Michael C. Intrilligator, eds., *Handbook of Mathematical Economics* (Amsterdam: North-Holland, 1981), is an up-to-date review.

67. Jacob Marschak, "Decision Making: Economic Aspects," *International Encyclopedia of the Social Sciences*, vol. IV (New York: Macmillan and Free Press, 1968), pp. 42–55, provides a thorough summary.

68. The standard works: Herbert A. Simon, *Administrative Behavior* (New York: Free Press, 1957); James G. March and Herbert A. Simon, *Organizations* (New York, John Wiley & Sons, 1958); and Richard M. Cyert and James G. March, *A Behavioral Theory of the Firm* (Englewood Cliffs, N.J.: Prentice-Hall, 1963).

69. Budgetary decision making in three American cities is couched in these terms in John P. Crecine, *Governmental Problem Solving* (Skokie, Ill.: Rand McNally, 1969): decision making in the trust department of a bank serves as the substantive focus of G. P. S. Clarkson, *Portfolio Selection: A Simulation of Investment Trust* (Englewood Cliffs, N.J.: Prentice-Hall, 1962).

70. Much of the literature on economic applications to public policy decision making is reviewed in Herbert A. Simon, "Theories of Decisionmaking in Economics and Behavioral Science," *The American Economic Review*, June 1959, pp. 253–83; and in Richard Zeckhauser and Elmer Schaefer, "Public Policy and Normative Economic Theory," in Raymond A. Bauer and Kenneth J. Gergen, eds., *The Study of Policy Formation* (New York: Free Press, 1968), pp. 27–101.

71. Martin Shubik, "A Curmudgeon's Guide to Microeconomics," *Journal of Economic Literature*, June 1970, pp. 405–34.

72. Charles E. Lindblom, *The Intelligence of Democracy* (New York: Free Press, 1965), is a complete statement of the incremental view.

73. Robert A. Dahl, *Pluralist Democracy in the United States* (Chicago: Rand McNally, 1967).

74. David B. Truman, *The Governmental Process* (New York: Alfred A. Knopf, 1961); and C. Wright Mills, *The Power Elite* (New York: Oxford University Press, 1956), represent the group and elite approaches, respectively.

75. Richard E. Neustadt, *Alliance Politics* (New York: Columbia University Press, 1970); and Graham T. Allison, *Essence of Decision* (Boston: Little, Brown, 1971).

76. James M. Buchanan and Gordon Tullock, *The Calculus of Consent* (Ann Arbor: University of Michigan Press, 1962); and Robert S. Ross, ed., *Public Choice and Public Policy* (Chicago: Markham, 1971).

77. The theoretical and practical limitations are treated variously in Todd R. LaPorte, ed., *Organized Social Complexity: Challenge to Politics and Policy* (Princeton, N.J.: Princeton University Press, 1975); Ronald D. Brunner and Garry D. Brewer, *Organized Complexity* (New York: Free Press, 1971); and Herbert A. Simon, *The Sciences of the Artificial* (Cambridge, Mass.: MIT Press, 1969).

A recent addition to the literature critical of the incremental approach, which incorporates most of its antecedents, is Ian Lustick, "Explaining the Variable Utility of Disjointed Incrementalism," *American Political Science Review*, June 1980, pp. 342–53.

78. Joseph G. Morone, "Trial and Error, Time Lag, and the Potential for Catastrophe: Decision Making in Nuclear Reactor Development" (New Haven: Yale University, Department of Political Science, unpublished Ph.D. dissertation, 1981), p. 190. (Emphasis in original.)

79. Ibid., pp. 190–91.

80. Martin Rein, "Social Planning: The Search for Legitimacy," *Journal of the American Institute of Planners*, September 1969, pp. 233–44.

81. Jeffrey L. Pressman and Aaron Wildavsky, *Implementation* (Berkeley: University of California Press, 1973), point out that the federal administrators had almost no concrete idea as to what the results of their funding the Oakland project (treated in the book) would be; in such a situation, evaluation of the project is virtually impossible unless the criterion is little more than survival.

Discussion questions

1. How might it be that two individuals (or institutions) could take the same study or analysis and arrive at very different—even diametrically opposed—conclusions about what to do? Consider this occurrence in terms of the role and responsibility of the policy analyst who conducts estimates of various social problems. It may also be helpful to think about a concrete situation—e.g., energy analyses, urban analyses, military analyses—to trace the transition from estimation to selection.

2. How do the incredibly complex aspects of people's values, preferences, and volitions surface in the selection stage of the policy process? What steps could be undertaken to better prepare policymakers to recognize and consider disparate values? To accomplish the same ends for the average citizen? A consistent theme in this book stresses the importance of increasing participation—the shaping and sharing of many different human values. How, in effect, can this overriding goal be accomplished while at the same time minimizing interference with effective practices of governance?

3. Robert Penn Warren's novel, *All the King's Men*, emphasizes the role of powerful individuals in the selection process. A sense of his perspective on politics and politicians is contained in the following:

    > The Boss knew all about the so-called fallacy of the *argumentum ad hominem*. "It may be a fallacy," he said, "but it is shore-God useful. If you use the right

kind of *argumentum* you can always scare the *hominem* into a laundry bill he didn't expect." [New York: Harcourt Brace Jovanovich, 1946, p. 231.]

Consider two or more theoretical works on decision making in light of the kinds of personal interactions portrayed in these comments. Can such eccentricities be accounted for analytically or not? If they can, explain how. If they cannot, discuss what this might imply for empirical studies of decision making.

4.   In his Nobel address, author Saul Bellow made the following comments:

> What is at the center now? At the moment, neither art nor science but mankind determining, in confusion and obscurity, whether it will endure or go under. The whole species—everybody—has gotten into the act. At such a time it is essential to lighten ourselves, to dump encumbrances, including the encumbrances of education and all organized platitudes, to make judgments of our own, to perform acts of our own.

What does this mean to you personally? Do you read these comments to be either pessimistic or optimistic for the human enterprise? Develop and defend your arguments. This is not an easy question, but then, neither is the problem.

5.   The bureaucratic politics model of decision making, popularized in the works of Graham Allison and others, has gained extraordinary attention in the academic and policy communities. As is the case with any simplification of complex reality, however, the model has limitations or blind spots. Identify several of these and consider them in light of alternative decision-making models or approaches. (For instance, treat different levels of analysis, key points in the respective models, possible outcomes, issues emphasized and so forth.) Offer concrete examples. In light of these weaknesses and alternative formulations, how would you judge the contribution of the bureaucratic politics model to our understanding and practice of decision making?

6.   Watergate, corruption in America's cities, scandals in defense contracting and weapon system planning and procurement, payoffs by high officials and executives of multinational corporations, and other notable undesirable behavior appears to have become disturbingly commonplace. Discuss whether this is actually the case, a temporary phase that we are progressing through, or a more permanent feature of American political life. If it is not the case, explain what you think is in fact happening and why. If it is temporary, what could the immediate and longer-term future hold in store? If permanent, what are some of the likely consequences for this society? How does your answer relate to the selection process?

7.   In the American system, according to the distinguished democratic theorist Robert Dahl,

Decisions are made by endless bargaining; perhaps in no other national political system in the world is bargaining so basic a component of the political process. In an age when the efficiencies of hierarchy have been reemphasized on every continent, no doubt the normal American political system is something of an anomaly, if not, indeed, at times an anachronism. [R. A. Dahl, *A Preface to Democratic Theory* (Chicago: University of Chicago Press, 1956), p. 150.]

Comment and critique. For example, is the U.S. political system's reliance on bargaining really so anomalous?

8. Contained within the idea of decision making is altering the present or status quo situation in a given setting. But while a politician may intellectually appreciate the analyst's rational justification for change, that same politician may be emotionally driven to oppose it for the injustices it would create. To remain effective, the policymaker and politician must sustain an emotional consensus. Other things being equal, the politician will use the main tools at hand—decisions about allocation and distribution—more to maintain consensus than to improve government programs.

If this characterization is acceptable to you, what are some of its implications for decision making, policy coherence, implementation potentialities, and the setting of evaluative performance criteria for subsequent use to the policy analyst?

9. Consider the concrete example of site selection and construction of a nuclear power plant. For what kinds and classes of decisions related to this task could rational analysis be helpful, appropriate, or essential? For what kinds and classes of decision do rational calculations either misspecify or even worsen the decision-making activity? In framing your response, you might keep in mind what Michel Crozier has called a fundamental paradox of democratic systems: "We require consensus, but the very act of exploring options and trying to attain consensus heightens our awareness of the many interests and values at stake. As a result, it becomes nearly impossible to produce a logically consistent set of policies and programs." [Michel Crozier, Samuel P. Huntington, and Joji Watanuki, *The Crisis of Democracy* (New York: New York University Press, 1975).]

10. Selection allows the lunacy of societies to flower, or as one student of politics puts it:

Politics . . . is the sphere of conflict, and brings out all the vanity, venom, the narcissism and aggression, of the contending parties . . . politics is the process by which the irrational bases of society are brought out into the open.

The collective craziness is exposed when "the moral order [is] devalued and called into question," which prompts the political actor to find a "reflectively defensible solution of the resulting conflict." [Harold D. Lasswell, *Psychopathology and Politics* (New York: Viking Press, 1960), p. 184.]

Pick a specific situation and trace the existence and influence of such psychotic elements in terms of decisions posed and reached.

11.   High technology settings are often represented as requiring superior technical competency and knowledge for sound decisions. Crucial decisions must be made, and the average citizen lacks the background, time, and interest to comprehend the technical facts involved in making them. But if the average citizen is not judged competent, will one's elected representatives be much more so?

Discuss, taking as a departure point a common situation in which experts themselves disagree about even the basic technical facts and possibilities surrounding policy decisions.

Supplementary readings

The following list of supplementary readings is highly selective but suggestive of many of the topics and ideas treated in these chapters. It is organized in approximately the same manner as Part II but diverges on occasion to indicate avenues of possible interest stemming from the discussion. Within each subcategory in the list, an effort was made to introduce some order on the readings with the objectives of facilitating and encouraging the reader. For instance, under the category of "Using Force," readings providing general and theoretical treatments of power as a concept are mixed with illustrative methods encountered to observe and measure the phenomenon and with diverse examples of force from a practical angle. The pattern, or comparable ones, can be discerned in each of the listings. The lists themselves should be considered and treated as reader's guides to help organize supplementary reading. Furthermore, the many references used throughout the part, some of which are not repeated in this listing, can be profitably pursued—either by themselves or, better, in consultation with this collation.

ESTIMATION AND SELECTION ARE DIFFERENT

(See "Supplementary Readings," Part II: Especially, "The Human Ought and the Rational Is," and "Experts.")

FACTORS IN SELECTION

Personality/leadership

Barber, James David. *The Presidential Character*. Englewood Cliffs, N.J.: Prentice-Hall, 1972.

Burns, James MacGregor. *Leadership*. New York: Harper & Row, 1978.

Erikson, Erik H. *Young Man Luther: A Study in Psychoanalysis and History*. New York: W. W. Norton, 1958.

Geis, Florence. "Machiavellianism." In H. London and J. Exner, eds., *Dimensions of Personality*. New York: John Wiley & Sons, 1978, pp. 305–63 and passim.

Lasswell, Harold D. *Power and Personality*. New York: W. W. Norton, 1948, chap. 3, "The Political Personality."

Lipset, Seymour Martin. *Political Man*. Garden City, N.Y.: Doubleday, 1960.

Schlesinger, Joseph A. *Ambition and Politics: Political Careers in the United States*. Skokie, Ill.: Rand McNally, 1966.

Stodgill, Ralph. *Handbook of Leadership: A Survey of Theory and Research*. New York: Free Press, 1974.

Information

Argyris, Chris, and Donald Schon. *Organizational Learning: A Theory of Action Perspective*. Reading, Mass.: Addison-Wesley, 1978.

Axelrod, Robert M., ed. *Structure of Decision: The Cognitive Maps of Political Elites*. Princeton, N.J.: Princeton University Press, 1976.

Jervis, Robert. *Perception and Misperception in International Relations*. Princeton, N.J.: Princeton University Press, 1976.

Reitman, Walter R. *Cognition and Thought: An Information Processing Approach*. New York: John Wiley & Sons, 1966, chaps. 2, 5, 8, 9.

Importance (emphasizing crisis-decision behavior)

Hermann, Charles E., ed. *International Crises: Insights from Behavioral Research*. New York: Free Press, 1972.

Hermann, Margaret G. "Indicators of Stress in Policymakers During Foreign Policy Crises." *Political Psychology* 1, no. 1 (1979), pp. 27–46.

Holsti, Ole R., and Alexander L. George. "The Effects of Stress on the Performance of Foreign Policy-Makers." In Cornelius P. Cotter, ed. *Political Science Annual*, vol. 6. Indianapolis, Ind.: Bobbs-Merrill, 1975, pp. 255–319.

Janis, Irving L. *Victims of Groupthink: A Psychological Study of Foreign-Policy Decisions and Fiascoes*. Boston: Houghton Mifflin, 1972.

President's Commission on the Accident at Three Mile Island. *The Need for Change: The Legacy of TMI*. Washington, D.C.: Government Printing Office, 1979.

President's Commission on Emergency Preparedness, Staff Report. *Emergency Preparedness, Emergency Response*. Washington, D.C.: Government Printing Office, 1979.

(See "Supplementary Readings," Part I: "Recognition of the Problem.")

Context

Crenson, Matthew A. *The Un-Politics of Air Pollution: A Study of Non-Decision-making in the Cities.* Baltimore, Md.: Johns Hopkins University Press, 1971.

(See "Supplementary Readings," Part I: Identification of the Problem Context.")

BARGAINING AND THE ESSENTIAL ART OF COMPROMISE

Theoretical and research approaches

Bower, Joseph L. "The Role of Conflict in Economic Decision-Making Groups." *Quarterly Journal of Economics,* May 1965, pp. 263–77.

Brams, Steven J. *Game Theory and Politics.* New York: Free Press, 1975.

Buchanan, James M. "An Economic Theory of Clubs." *Economica* 32, no. 1 (1965), pp. 1–14.

Guetzkow, Harold, and John Gyr. "An Analysis of Conflict in Decision-Making Groups." *Human Relations* 23, no. 3 (1970), pp. 288–317.

Hare, A. Paul. *Handbook of Small Group Research.* New York: Free Press, 1976.

Ofshe, Richard J., ed. *Interpersonal Behavior in Small Groups.* Englewood Cliffs, N.J.: Prentice-Hall, 1973.

Olson, Mancur, and Richard Zeckhauser. "An Economic Theory of Alliances." *Review of Economics and Statistics* 48, no. 2 (1966), pp. 266–79.

Shubik, Martin. *Games for Society, Business and War.* New York: Elsevier, 1975, part II.

Verba, Sidney. *Small Groups and Political Behavior.* Princeton, N.J.: Princeton University Press, 1961.

Examples of group and individual bargaining

Barber, James David. *Power in Committees.* Skokie, Ill.: Rand McNally, 1966.

Berry, Jeffrey M. *Lobbying for the People: The Political Behavior of Public Interest Groups.* Princeton, N.J.: Princeton University Press, 1977.

Mackenzie, G. Calvin. *The Politics of Presidential Appointments.* New York: Free Press, 1980.

Ziegler, Harmon. *Interest Groups in American Society.* Englewood Cliffs, N.J.: Prentice-Hall, 1974.

Considerations of large-scale coalition and consensus building

Fiorina, Morris R. *Representatives, Roll Calls, and Constituencies.* Lexington, Mass.: D. C. Heath, 1974.

Goldman, Ralph M. *Search for Consensus: The Story of the Democratic Party.* Philadelphia: Temple University Press, 1979.

Holsti, Ole R., and James N. Rosenau. "Vietnam, Consensus, and the Belief Systems of American Leaders." *World Politics,* October 1979, pp. 1–53.

Lipset, Seymour Martin, ed. *Emerging Coalitions in American Politics.* San Francisco: Institute for Contemporary Studies, 1978.

Nelkin, Dorothy, ed. *Controversy: The Politics of Technical Decisions.* Beverly Hills, Calif.: Sage Publications, 1979.

Bargaining viewed from a budgeting and appropriations perspective

Arnold, H. Douglas. *Congress and the Bureaucracy: A Theory of Influence.* New Haven: Yale University Press, 1979.

Fenno, Richard F., Jr. *The Power of the Purse: Appropriations Politics in Congress.* Boston: Little, Brown, 1966.

Fesler, James W. *Public Administration.* Englewood Cliffs, N.J.: Prentice-Hall, 1980, chap. 10, "Decision Making: The Budgetary Process."

Gist, J. R. "Appropriations Politics and Expenditure Control." *Journal of Politics,* February 1978, pp. 163–78.

Havemann, Joel. *Congress and the Budget.* Bloomington: Indiana University Press, 1978.

Wildavsky, Aaron. *The Politics of the Budgetary Process.* Boston: Little, Brown, 1979.

Bargaining in the White House

Hess, Stephen. *Organizing the Presidency.* Washington, D.C.: The Brookings Institution, 1976.

Johnson, Richard T. *Managing the White House.* New York: Harper & Row, 1974.

Neustadt, Richard E. *Presidential Power.* New York: John Wiley & Sons, 1980.

Sorenson, Theodore C. *Decision-Making in the White House.* New York: Columbia University Press, 1964.

. . . in the legislative branch

Fenno, Richard F., Jr. *Home Style: House Members in Their Districts.* Boston: Little, Brown, 1978.

Fox, H. W., Jr., and S. W. Hammond. *Congressional Staffs: The Invisible Force in American Lawmaking.* New York: Free Press, 1977.

Kingdon, John W. *Congressmen's Voting Decisions.* New York: Harper & Row, 1973.

Lowi, Theodore L., and Randall B. Ripley, eds., *Legislative Politics U.S.A.* Boston: Little, Brown, 1973.

Matthews, Donald R., and James A. Stimson. *Yeas and Nays: Normal Decision-Making in the U.S. House of Representatives.* New York: John Wiley & Sons, 1975.

Mayhew, David R. *Congress: The Electoral Connection.* New Haven: Yale University Press, 1974.

. . . in the bureaucracy

Heclo, Hugh. *A Government of Strangers: Executive Politics in Washington.* Washington, D.C.: The Brookings Institution, 1977.

. . . in the judiciary

Krislov, Samuel. *The Supreme Court in the Political Process.* New York: Macmillan, 1965.

Murphy, Walter F. *Elements of Judicial Strategy.* Chicago: University of Chicago Press, 1964.

Spaeth, Harold J. *Supreme Court Policy Making: Explanation and Prediction.* San Francisco: W. H. Freeman, 1979.

. . . in other settings

Epstein, Edwin A. *The Corporation in American Politics.* Englewood Cliffs, N.J.: Prentice-Hall, 1969.

Lindblom, Charles E. *Politics and Markets.* New York: Basic Books, 1977.

Saloma, John S., III, and Frederick H. Sontag. *Parties: The Real Opportunity for Effective Citizen Politics.* New York: Alfred A. Knopf, 1972.

POLITICAL PROMOTION

Symbols and semantics

Boulding, Kenneth. "National Images and International Systems." *Journal of Conflict Resolution* 3 (1959), pp. 120–31.

Edelman, Murray. *Political Language: Words that Succeed and Policies that Fail.* New York: Academic Press, 1977.

———. *The Symbolic Uses of Politics.* Urbana: University of Illinois Press, 1967.

Lasswell, Harold D. "The Structure and Function of Communications in Society." In L. Bryson, ed., *Communication of Ideas.* New York: Harper & Row, 1978.

Meadow, Robert G. *Politics as Communication.* Norwood, N.J.: Albex Publishing, 1980.

Namenwirth, Zvi, and Harold D. Lasswell. *The Changing Language of American Values.* Beverly Hills, Calif.: Sage Publications, 1970.

Weldon, T. D. *The Vocabulary of Politics.* Baltimore, Md.: Viking Penguin, 1953.

Propaganda

Ellul, Jacques. *Propaganda.* Trans. Konrad Kellen and Jean Lerner. New York: Vintage Books, 1973.

George, Alexander L. *Propaganda Analysis.* Evanston, Ill.: Row, Peterson, 1959.

Lasswell, Harold D. *Propaganda Technique in the World War.* New York: Alfred A. Knopf, 1927.

Lasswell, Harold D., and Dorothy Blumenstock. *World Revolutionary Propaganda.* New York: Alfred A. Knopf, 1939.

Ideology

Almond, Gabriel A. *The Appeals of Communism.* Princeton, N.J.: Princeton University Press, 1954.

Clausen, John, ed. *Socialization and Society.* Boston: Little, Brown, 1968.

Key, V. O., Jr. *Public Opinion and American Democracy.* New York: Alfred A. Knopf, 1961.

————. *The Responsible Electorate.* Cambridge, Mass.: Harvard University Press, 1966.

Lane, Robert E. *Political Ideology.* New York: Free Press, 1962.

Renshon, Stanley. *Handbook of Political Socialization.* New York: Free Press, 1977.

The media—as means and ends

Gans, Herbert J. *Deciding What's News.* New York: Pantheon Books, 1979.

Rubin, Bernard. *Media, Politics, and Democracy.* New York: Oxford University Press, 1977.

Tunstall, Jeremy, and David Walker. *Media Made in California: Hollywood, Politics and the News.* New York: Oxford University Press, 1981.

USING FORCE

Theoretical contributions

Dahl, Robert A. "The Concept of Power." *Behavioral Science,* July 1957, pp. 201–15.

————. *Modern Political Analysis.* Englewood Cliffs, N.J.: Prentice-Hall, 1963, chap. 5, "Power and Influence."

Lasswell, Harold D., and Abraham Kaplan. *Power and Society.* New Haven: Yale University Press, 1950.

Moore, Barrington, Jr. *Political Power and Social Theory.* Cambridge, Mass.: Harvard University Press, 1958.

Analytical contributions

Nagel, Jack H. *The Descriptive Analysis of Power.* New Haven: Yale University Press, 1975.

Simon, Herbert A. "Notes on the Observation and Measurement of Political Power." *Journal of Politics,* November 1953, pp. 500–16.

Exemplifications

Calabresi, Guido, and Philip Bobbit. *Tragic Choices.* New York: W. W. Norton, 1978.

Milgram, Stanley. *Obedience to Authority.* New York: Harper & Row, 1974.

Roloff, Michael E., and Gerald R. Miller, eds. *Persuasion: New Directions in Theory and Research.* Beverly Hills, Calif.: Sage Publications, 1980.

Siu, R. G. H. *The Craft of Power.* New York: John Wiley & Sons, 1979.

THEORIES OF DECISION

Psychological

Abelson, Robert P.; E. Aronson, W. J. McGuire; T. M. Newcomb; M. J. Rosenburg; and P. H. Tannenbaum, eds. *Theories of Cognitive Consistency: A Sourcebook.* Skokie, Ill.: Rand McNally, 1968.

de Rivera, Joseph. *The Psychological Dimension of Foreign Policy.* Columbus, Ohio: Charles E. Merrill Publishing, 1968.

Festinger, Leon. *A Theory of Cognitive Dissonance.* Stanford, Calif.: Stanford University Press, 1957.

Janis, Irving L., and Leon Mann. *Decision Making: A Psychological Analysis of Conflict.* New York: Free Press, 1977.

Economic

Harsanyi, John C. *Rational Behavior and Bargaining Equilibrium in Games and Social Situations.* Cambridge, Eng.: Cambridge University Press, 1977.

Luce, R. Duncan, and Howard Raiffa. *Games and Decisions.* New York: John Wiley & Sons, 1957.

March, James G., and Herbert A. Simon. *Organizations.* New York: John Wiley & Sons, 1958.

Marschak, Jacob. "Decision Making: Economic Aspects." *International Encyclopedia of the Social Sciences,* vol. IV, New York: Macmillan and Free Press, 1968, pp. 42–55.

Simon, Herbert A. *Administrative Behavior.* New York: Free Press, 1957.

_____. "A Behavioral Model of Rational Choice." *Quarterly Journal of Economics* 69, no. 1 (1955), pp. 99–118.

_____. *The Sciences of the Artificial.* Cambridge, Mass.: MIT Press, 1969.

Critiques

Lustick, Ian. "Explaining the Variable Utility of Disjointed Incrementalism." *American Political Science Review,* June 1980, pp. 343–53.

Shubik, Martin. "A Curmudgeon's Guide to Microeconomics." *Journal of Economic Literature,* June 1970, pp. 405–34.

Slovic, Paul; Baruch Fischoff; and Sarah Lichtenstein. "Behavioral Decision Theory." *Annual Review of Psychology* 28, no. 1 (1977), pp. 1–39.

PART IV

Implementation

Implementation is an important but frequently overlooked step in the general policy process model. Lacking proper implementation, policy innovation and selection may end up being little more than intellectual exercises; indeed, faulty policy implementation can invalidate the earlier, carefully considered steps in the policy process and thereby intensify the original problem. The process, then, warrants our careful attention.

However critical the implementation problem might be, little concerted attention had been paid to it until the mid-1970s.[1] One report commented:

> We became increasingly bothered in the late 1960s by those aspects of the exercise of government authority bound up with implementation. Results achieved by the programs of that decade were widely recognized as inadequate. One clear source of failure emerged: political and bureaucratic aspects of the implementation process were, in great measure, left outside both the considerations of participants of government and the calculations of formal policy analysts who assisted them.[2]

The neglect was hardly restricted to policy analysts or bureaucrats-turned-author. In 1972, Pressman and Wildavsky conducted a review of the social science literature thinking that there "is (or there must be) a literature about implementation in the social sciences—or so we have been told by numerous people." Their expectations were not confirmed: with a few

249

important exceptions, they were "unable to find any significant analytic work dealing with implementation."[3]

This situation no longer exists; in fact, the literature on implementation has grown from a vacuum to an excess.[4] As Berman comments, "Everybody seems to be studying it, if not solving its problems. . . . In the rush to get on the bandwagon, studies of bureaucratic politics, organizational analyses of resistance to change, analyses of policymaking and decision making, and cases in public administration have a new focus—'implementation analysis'."[5] The reasons are not hard to fathom: too many highly visible social programs have produced too many disappointing results; in the words of one observer:

> [T]heir accomplishments are a pale reflection of their intentions. The big ideas that have shaped social policy—maximum feasible participation, equality of opportunity, self-sufficiency, compensatory treatment, to name a few—seem to have become caricatures of themselves the moment they ceased to be ideas and began to be translated into action. Concern about the implementation of social programs stems from the recognition that policies cannot be understood in isolation from the means of their execution. A large collection of carefully documented case studies . . . points consistently to the same basic pattern: grand pretensions, faulty execution, puny results.[6]

Programmatic failures have been observed in a large number and range of social programs—housing,[7] education,[8] even drug supplies[9] and city sanitation.[10] Policy analysts are now being forced to examine implementation—the apparent elusive missing link between policy selection and the delivered product.

Much early work was presented in the form of case studies in which implementation was only an analytic tangent. However, in the past few years, several authors have proposed moving beyond case descriptions toward conceptual frameworks of implementation analysis.[11] Berman details the couplings between federal policy and local-level programs;[12] Elmore considers different organizational models which affect implementation strategies;[13] and Rein and Rabinovitz discuss how "potentially conflicting imperatives" can alter and shape the actual course of events.[14] Bardach has developed a taxonomy of implementation games bureaucrats play,[15] and Yin has proposed specific research strategies for studying implementation.[16] There is, in short, a current embarrassment of riches in implementation research, but as we shall see, there is still very little on the subject of how best to implement. That is, everybody seems willing to accord implementation its distinctive position and importance in the policy process, but few have been able to offer suggestions to the policy analyst or the policymaker about conducting effective implementation.

The following chapters aim to do this by consciously alternating between the theory and practice of implementation in successive sections. We attempt to break the implementation phase down into various components so as to constitute them into an internal process within the overall framework of the policy process. After that, we consider what appear to be basic and general practical implementation problems and experiences. This results in some confidence in the utility of the process framework; it also suggests and establishes a basis for discussing various general factors that condition and affect implementation. Taken together, "Confronting Reality" and "Factors Influencing Implementation" provide a distillation and synthesis of the implementation facts of life and set the stage for a theoretical exploration of distinctive perspectives that have been underused by those grappling with implementation problems. Innovation theory, organization theory, communication theory, small group theory, and interest group theory are all characterized in terms of their possible contributions to improved understanding of implementation. These theories, the contributing factors, and our evolving sense of the internal process of implementation are then compared with several case examples having increasingly complex practical aspects. This part concludes with some thoughts about relationships that exist between system complexity and policy prescription. If the analysis is even partly correct, a quite different attitude and set of expectations about policy and program implementation than those usually entertained need to be proposed and tested.

NOTES

1. The field of public administration, one could reasonably argue, has treated implementation in great detail for years. One exceptional exposition from this tradition is James W. Fesler, *Public Administration: Theory and Practice* (Englewood Cliffs, N.J.: Prentice-Hall, 1980), chaps. 8–10.

2. The Research Seminar on Bureaucracy, Politics, and Policy, *A Report on Studies of Implementation in the Public Sector* (Cambridge, Mass.: Harvard University, John F. Kennedy School of Government, March 1973), p. 1.

3. Jeffrey L. Pressman and Aaron Wildavsky, *Implementation* (Berkeley: University of California Press, 1973), p. 166, reviewed a number of case studies in poverty and civil rights programs and the academic disciplines of psychology, political science, operations research, and public administration.

4. Much of the early literature is reviewed by Erwin C. Hargrove, *The Missing Link: The Study of Implementation of Social Policy* (Washington, D.C.: The Urban Institute, 1975).

5. Paul Berman, "The Study of Macro- and Micro-Implementation," *Public Policy,* Spring 1978, p. 158.

6. Richard F. Elmore, "Organizational Models of Social Program Implementation," *Public Policy,* Spring 1978, p. 186.

7. See Martha Derthick, *New Towns In-Town* (Washington, D.C.: The Urban Institute, 1972); and Francine Rabinovitz and Helene V. Snookler, "Rhetoric vs. Performance: The National Politics and Administration of U.S. New Communities Legislation," in Harvey S. Perloff and Neil Sandberg, eds., *New Towns, Why and For Whom?* (New York: Praeger Publishers, 1973).

8. Important work has been and continues to be done in the area of innovation in education: Neal C. Gross, Joseph B. Giaquinta, and Marilyn Bernstein, *Implementing Or-*

ganizational Innovations: A Sociological Analysis of Planned Education Change (New York: Basic Books, 1971); Jerome T. Murphy, "Title I of ESEA: The Politics of Implementing Federal Education Reform," *Harvard Education Review,* February 1971, pp. 35–63; and, most significantly, the study of the Change Agents Program by Paul Berman and Milbrey Wallin McLaughlin, *Federal Programs Supporting Educational Change: A Model of Educational Change* (Santa Monica, Calif.: The Rand Corporation, R–1589/1, September 1974); and idem, *Educational Change: Implementing and Sustaining Innovations* (Santa Monica, Calif.: The Rand Corporation, R–1589/8, 1978).

9. Mark H. Moore, "Reorganization Plan #2 Reviewed: Problems in Implementing a Strategy to Reduce the Supply of Drugs to Illicit Markets in the United States," *Public Policy,* Spring 1978, pp. 229–62.

10. Jerry Mechling, "Analysis and Implementation: Sanitation Policies in New York City," *Public Policy,* Spring 1978, pp. 263–84.

11. The transition from case studies to analytic frameworks is summarized by Robert T. Nakamura and Frank Smallwood, *The Politics of Policy Implementation* (New York: St. Martin's Press, 1980), chap. 1.

12. Berman, "Macro- and Micro-Implementation."

13. Elmore, "Organizational Models."

14. Martin Rein and Francine Rabinovitz, "Implementation: A Theoretical Perspective," in Walter D. Burnham and Martha Weinberg, eds., *American Politics and Public Policy* (Cambridge, Mass.: MIT Press, 1978), pp. 307–35.

15. Eugene Bardach, *The Implementation Game* (Cambridge, Mass.: MIT Press, 1977).

16. Robert K. Yin, *Studying the Implementation of Public Programs* (Golden, Colo.: Solar Energy Research Institute, SERI/TR–352–577, February 1980).

9

The internal process of implementation

Two rather contradictory reasons might be cited to explain implementation's long neglect. Basically, it was thought to be either too simple or too difficult to merit special study. The first reason is based on the idea that implementation is an automatic extension or spillover of the decision-making process and therefore warrants little separate attention. It was treated as a continuation of the public administration tradition of faithful transmittal and execution of policy.[1] As evidence of this evolutionary idea's prevalence, witness the vast (and still growing) literature on decision making compared with the still relatively scant literature on implementation.

To the casual observer, the very definition of implementation seems to imply its simplicity. Brewer defines implementation as "executing a selected option"; Levine defines it as "carrying out a program of actions"; and Pressman and Wildavsky merely cite and abide by *Webster's Third International Dictionary* and *Roget's Thesaurus*.[2] This view of implementation as simple or automatic could well explain the lack of rigorous analysis of the subject within the public administration literature. The spillover perception is reflected in the following comment by Graham T. Watt, former director of the Office of Revenue Sharing in the Nixon Administration: "[The implementation of revenue-sharing regulations] was an evolutionary thing in that we *merely converted the requirements of the law* into administrative regulations."[3]

As convenient as this view might be, it is spurious and misleading. Policy implementation is distinct from policy initiation and selection and has an unique set of causes and conditions. Too many projects have foundered because implementation was not distinguished from the earlier steps in the total process, thus making it almost impossible to translate a policy into its component, operational programs with any fidelity.[4] A special effort is required to identify the proper implementation strategy that will execute an intended change.[5]

The second reason why implementation has been subject to such neglect is its complexity, which makes it resistant to rigorous analysis. Implementation is extremely difficult to describe and classify analytically because so many factors influence it and thereby cloud our understanding. Some simply equate implementation with politics and leave .t at that.

A distinction is often made between the policymaker and the policy implementor, which mistakenly suggests that the two roles are different and separable.[6] In the practicing bureaucratic world in which policies take everyday form, the policy implementor is in many ways the policymaker; teachers and policemen may implement programs, but the manner and enthusiasm they employ often effectively define policy.[7] Douglas Bunker's prescription that "administrative representatives are preferably a party to the policy-making process" is correct in helping to coordinate implementation plans but overlooks the reality that the administrator often makes policy simply carrying out the tasks at hand.[8] This distinction is particularly difficult to reconcile within the "incremental" view of decision making.[9] Interview data compiled by Thomas Smith have revealed very little difference in perceptions and backgrounds between the policy formulator and the policy implementor;[10] while the roles might differ in name, in practice they are virtually indistinguishable.[11] Usually administrators are left such broad discretion in carrying out legislation or an executive order (for a variety of reasons that will be discussed below) that they can easily modify the policy to fit bureaucracy's particular interests or personal requirements. By doing so, they may undermine or alter the purpose of the original policymaker. Certainly it should have been easy to conceal a bag of "dirty tricks," but the failure of the Watergate conspiracy to implement (or at least hide) such plans tumbled an entire administration. A second example of undermining a policy through personal interpretation was the liberal use of "protective reaction" air strikes by Air Force General John Lavelle in Vietnam during the 1971 secret peace negotiations.[12]

Further obscuring the distinction between policymaker and policy implementor is the fact that policy can bubble up as well as trickle down; in the terms of our six-step model of policy process, implementation may precede and motivate selection. For instance, during the Second World War, local gasoline rationing boards began allocating, on their own initiative, extra gasoline to returning veterans out of a sense of patriotic obligation, although the action was not sanctioned by legislative or national guidelines. The national board later revised its standards to conform to local procedures, "bowing in part to the bureaucratic rationality of local sub-units, and in part to regional fear of losing control over local boards as an outgrowth of this set of *ad hoc* decisions."[13] Similarly, local education (and other) innovations are often adopted subsequently on a state-by-state or a national level.[14]

An additional example of the policy-formulating capability of policy implementors is the latter's capability to modify a program beyond the recognition of its originator's intent or even to ignore such intentions. Harold Seidman quotes Jesse Jones, director of the Reconstruction Finance Corporation under Franklin D. Roosevelt, as saying that when the President "asked me to do something which in my opinion we could not or should not do—and that happened only a few times—we just did not do it."[15]

One should never underestimate the power of even a small, apparently politically disadvantaged group to redefine the policy intentions of those with formally constituted authority. In a compelling investigation of the origins and success of a small group within the U.S. Army, Bergerson has provided ample documentation on how *The Army Gets an Air Force*, which at one point in 1970 had the "third-largest aviation fleet of any military organization in the world."[16] One needs only pause momentarily to consider the relatively high agreement on values and personal orientations, the hierarchical command structure, the communality of language, and many other characteristics of the military organization[17] and then contrast these with ordinary bureaucracies to realize the core truth—the illusion—inherent in simplistic notions of command-obey. Paranoid resort to "cabal theories" of non- or misimplementation are not needed to explain what is a far more general reality of bureaucratic existence.[18] Ellul captures the essence of the matter:

> From the very moment that a general policy decision has been made by the minister, it escapes his control; the matter takes on independent life and circulates in the various services, and all depends eventually on what the bureaus decide to do with it. Possibly, orders will eventually emerge corresponding to the original decision. More frequently nothing will emerge. The decision will evaporate in the numerous administrative channels and never really see the light of day.[19]

A prevalent view in the implementation literature describes the entire policy process as a seamless web such that differentiation between decision making (selection) and implementation equates to a destruction of one's ability to conceive of the entire process.[20] In many ways the view has merit. Thus Smith finds that policymakers and policy implementors are cut from the same cognitive cloth,[21] and many who are identified with the "incremental" school of policy formulation argue that policymaking is fundamentally the cumulative result of discrete program actions—implementation and selection are conceived as one and the same.[22] In large part, our separation of implementation reflects a disenchantment with incrementalism, discussed at some length in earlier chapters. A brief review of several of the main arguments against incrementalism establishes our case for separate treatment: incremental policies mechanistically evolve with scant concern for human intentions, as represented in planning and other analytic activities; the main criterion for a policy's success is its survival, thus undercutting the evaluation of programs; and it inhibits breaks with the established, on-going policies, that is, it denies significant innovation. For example, in retrospect, the United States would have been advised to leave Vietnam in 1963, but a true incrementalist could not have conceived of such a policy.[23] Moynihan explicitly attacks all these short-comings in recounting Nixon's welfare reform legislation.[24]

The difficulty of isolating the implementation process, then, is a major obstacle to understanding, analyzing, and managing it. However, as we have argued, implementation is too important to be considered part of initiation or selection, even if policies are selected consciously with imple-mentation strategies in mind. Even though implementation is an integral, interactive component of the policy process, it must be singled out for special attention and understanding. Failure to do so undermines the policy process and relegates our ultimate ability to manage it to chance.

Drawing upon Bardach, we therefore define implementation as "the social activity that follows upon, and is stimulated by, an authoritatively adopted policy mandate. . . ." It thus represents a transition that "takes whatever social, political, and economic arrangements [that] exist before the policy mandate is adopted and sets them in different configurations."[25] This definition stresses the process aspect and sets up a clear distinction between policy implementation and politics, for it permits us to assess implementation in terms of its inherent effectiveness.[26]

Furthermore, implementation is a first opportunity to validate various options or alternatives against reality. Prior to implementation all steps taken are synthetic and represent only the hopes, fears, and imaginings of those who have participated along the way.[27] Implementation transforms conceived policies into actual programs and hence provides an important social check. It is a time where hopes are often dashed and fears confirmed in the wake of the "often imperfect correspondence between policies adopted and services actually delivered."[28] This is the reality of public policy analysis.

CONFRONTING REALITY

Implementation is a complex process by which the broad statement of public policy, including goals, objectives, and rough means, are transferred into specific actions. In this sense, various distinctive programs (including multiple, constituent projects associated with each) can all in some degree be aimed at the same, overriding policy goals. The following example helps make these distinctions.

National industrial policy

The need to develop a national industrial policy is being expressed with increasing frequency—one which would work to stimulate business, increase productivity, make American goods and services more competitive in world markets, improve the industry-university connection, reduce the alleged burden of government interference in commerce, alter tax laws to encourage the purchase of newer, more productive equipment, increase profitability, improve long-range planning, foster quality control, add to the number of qualified scientists and engineers, reduce inflation, increase employment, and so forth; the list is expansive.[29] Reciting these commonly stated goals for a national reindustrialization policy forces one to realize that no one program could ever account for all of its diverse components. Furthermore, simply taking one goal—such as improving long-range planning—and then appreciating the large differences that exist in various sectors of the economy with respect to product types, capital/labor mixes, relevant planning horizons, regional differences in labor availability and capability, energy circumstances, and a host of other significant aspects, leads one to appreciate the quite different programs and projects that will be necessary to achieve "improved long-range planning," only one of many pieces in the national industrial policy puzzle.

Much of this general idea is illustrated in Figure 9–1, to help one understand the interrelationships between policies, programs, and projects. To illustrate implementation better, consider $goal_1$ to be something like "improve long-range planning." $Program_a$, one means of helping attain this specific goal, then could be "data acquisition and management for planning purposes"; $program_b$ could be "planning methods development"; and $program_c$ could be "training of industrial planners," or some such. The point is that all programs at this level have taken specific form and are directed toward attaining related objectives contributing to the specific long-range planning goal. For example, bolstering planning involves at least the generation of more and better data, the design and production of improved and/or more efficient means of using this increased flow, and the training and positioning of individuals capable of bringing both data and methods to bear on industry's planning problems. Further reduction and subdivision to the project level can also be envisioned. In this case, within $program_a$ (data acquisition and management), various projects might be allocated to an assortment of action agencies. One may decide that raw material assays using advanced satellite and space sensors are important but are either not presently being collected or, if collected, not well used.[30] $Project_\alpha$ might be mounted to remedy this by modifying existing reconnaissance satellite programs;[31] $project_\beta$ could involve new initiatives to identify and collect urgently needed data not available from existing

FIGURE 9–1   Policy, programs, and projects: An illustration

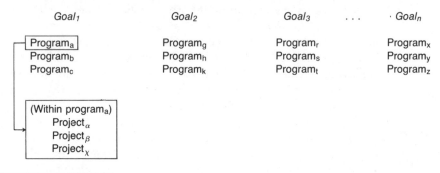

Policy: *Implement a National Industrial Policy*

(Characterized in terms of multiple goals [G_1, G_2, G_3, . . . G_n] whose collective attainment would constitute some version of a "successful" national industrial policy.)

$Goal_1$	$Goal_2$	$Goal_3$ . . .	$Goal_n$
$Program_a$	$Program_g$	$Program_r$	$Program_x$
$Program_b$	$Program_h$	$Program_s$	$Program_y$
$Program_c$	$Program_k$	$Program_t$	$Program_z$

(Within program$_a$)
Project$_\alpha$
Project$_\beta$
Project$_\chi$

sources; and project$_\chi$ undertaken to integrate the results obtained from the former two efforts into a coherent and useful data file for later industrial planning uses.

This exercise could be delineated for each of the identified, constituent goals and ordinarily injects opportunities and difficulties totally unexpected in the areas of institutional overlap, competition, and occasionally, coordination. Project$_\alpha$, in the hypothetical example, involves modification of existing practices: in this case, trying to use natural resource satellite images collected for primarily scientific purposes for somewhat different ones. NASA officials responsible for these data may be unconcerned with industrial planning, may not even know what a national industrial policy is, and may legitimately work well beyond the span of authority of those responsible for the project$_\alpha$ mission. In such realistic circumstances, faithful execution of the project's particulars may become very difficult, if not impossible.

Comparable difficulties may further impede realization of other project and programmatic ends. Policy success, in this rendition, is directly tied to the outcomes of many specific, subsidiary acts, the sum total of which may in practice be very hard to appreciate, much less analyze. The stunning potential for complication of the instrumental means, i.e., programs and projects, thus contributes much to ineffective policy implementation in a wide range of problem settings.

Failure of one or more of the enabling programs or projects may or may not, however, undermine the total policy. In some situations, remedial actions may be taken to improve individual program performance and thereby enhance policy implementation. In others, supplementary or complementary programs and projects may be indicated that, when finally enacted, contribute to overall policy success. Making such appraisals of individual program success or failure, including a determination of its contribution to overall policy goals, is naturally an ongoing process—one that stresses the relative continuity, wholeness, and dynamism of the total policy process. Because policy goals can be attained through many conceivable instruments, creating and testing a variety of enabling programs to achieve such goals is a demanding, open-ended task. To press the industrial planning illustration to the limit: Data acquisition could be achieved through covert means, such as industrial espionage, or it could be reduced in importance because of other actions taken, such as cornering the market for a raw material or inventing a superior substitute or replacement for it.

A broad view of the realities

Broad conditions can be imagined that are both necessary and sufficient for implementation to occur: General goals and objectives must be identified and specified in operational terms; enabling legislation and action programs need to be designed and responsibility for their conduct assigned; and resources must be allocated to support the programs. This is easily enough said; actually executing the necessary tasks is far more demanding.

We have previously discussed the chronic problem of specifying goals and objectives, particularly in situations involving diverse, sometimes conflicting, interests. Not only do we have the standard problem of trying to cope with the inherent complexity of most social situations, but the many individuals and institutions who have stakes in the given policy do not necessarily or readily perceive the situation, the ends sought, or the means for arriving at these ends in a consensual, consistent, or coherent way. Further complicating matters is the phenomenon of institutional inertia, an organizational concept denoting resistance to change in the absence of overriding external force. Policy implementation implies not only the expenditure of resources simply to bring something new into existence, but also forceful efforts to overcome inertia created by the status quo. Implementation to many is as much a destructive act as it is a creative one to others (a point discussed subsequently), one to be resisted or opposed.

The actual policy selected may itself present formidable problems to the would-be implementor. Vagueness and ambiguity, especially in the wake of prolonged or heated political debates attending decision making, frequently present a variety of interpretations and meanings to those tasked with implementation; public statutes are seldom models of clarity.[32] Indeed, attaining agreement is often paid for at the expense of intentional vagueness. Elliot Richardson, while Secretary of the Department of Health, Education, and Welfare, noted:

> Exaggerated promises, ill-conceived programs, over-advertised "cures" for intractable ailments, cynical exploitation of valid grievances, entrenched resistance to necessary change, the cold rigidity of centralized authority, and the inefficient use of scarce resources—all these add to frustration and foster disillusionment.[33]

Still, one can view the matter in a more useful perspective. In many areas, the goals sought through implementation means have simply become more difficult to achieve, for as many have noted, the attainment of pressing needs (e.g., shelter, sustenance, security) tends to call attention to more ambitious and diverse expectations. Practically, as Richardson describes it, "There is a fallacy abroad in the land—and rampant in the Congress—to the effect that passing legislation solves problems"; however, many problems cannot be so simply or readily dispatched, and "new legislation [often] merely publicizes a need without creating either the means or the resources for meeting it."[34] To attempt implementation of this kind of legislation means stretching limited resources more thinly, which in turn may yield failure in the eyes of those whose expectations exceed an institution's practical capabilities.

Implementation failures can come not only from reaching too high—and for too many different goals—but also from inefficient, corrupt, or deceitful practices,[35] inappropriate delegation of responsibility to agencies ill-suited or even opposed to the proposed change,[36] inadequate allocation of resources to accomplish the policy goals,[37] or from a host of other operational reasons. We touch on several of these in discussing the context of implementation, the enabling nature of legislation, and several particular features of the implementation process.

The importance of context

A sensitive appreciation of specific, realistic contexts in which decisions are made and results are sought is a necessary prerequisite to understanding and action.[38]

Who participates? Imagine a program you know and work through the following list of likely candidates: Congress (or comparable legislative authority in other settings) surely plays a role and influences implementation, not only in terms of formal statements of "what to do" embodied in law but in many other ways. Legislative committees and subcommittees exercise oversight over action agencies to ensure compliance with legislative intent, and such follow-up frequently is expressed in close scrutiny by particular senators and representatives.[39] Legislative staffs have grown greatly in total number over the last decade, and much of their activity involves daily interaction with various implementing agencies. The subordinate, specialized arms of the legislature, such as the General Accounting Office, the Congressional Budget Office, the Library of Congress, and the Office of Technology Assessment all, in different ways, have the potential for affecting implementation.[40]

The executive, of course, has the central role in policy implementation, but even in the bureaucracy diversity and individual details often count heavily in trying to determine how and why certain programs and projects occur as they do.[41] At the federal level, for example, the president's personal staff appendages have grown to unprecedented size and influence: the Office of Management and Budget, the National Security Council, the Council of Economic Advisors, and special counselors, assistants, and liaisons from the White House are all empowered to "work" various issues on behalf of the president. In addition, there are numerous rival agencies, diverse appointed and career officials,[42] and parallel authorities and institutions at the state and local levels.[43]

The judicial system, although perhaps reluctantly, also becomes involved in the implementation act.[44] In most specific policy areas, the enforced assumption of implementation by courts has been neither smooth nor efficient and free of conflict; school integration and prayer have been notable focuses of judicial involvement in implementation.[45]

Then there are the interest groups, often as numerous as they are powerful.[46] One should not underestimate the peculiar powers of strategically placed individuals in affecting implementation. The location of specific water control projects, military installations, railroad stops along the AMTRAK route, post offices, and dozens of other examples is often more easily understood in terms of who happens to be situated where in Congress or how certain special interest groups pressed their cases with crucially placed individuals than it is by calculating the efficient allocation of program expenditures—or anything else.

One should also consider the likely beneficiaries or recipients of the policy's outcomes and those who bear the costs, either directly in terms of paying a share of the resources tied up in associated programs or indirectly in the case of suffering unexpected or unwanted consequences of a program. The determination of who gets what and who pays is always an important ingredient in the implementation stew.[47]

The imperative of the contextual setting is a matter of practical consequence. For instance, bureaucratic rivalry certainly plays a role in arriving at some understanding of why economic policies seldom mesh smoothly or attain the success hoped for them; the clash of the Federal Reserve with administrations of quite different economic philosophies is one consistent illustration.[48] The Department of Defense, to note one instance, sought jurisdiction for the synthetic fuels program under the terms of the Defense Production Act; the Department of Energy was equally convinced of its rightful claims; and the Synthetic Fuels Corporation, a hybrid institutional form known in the United Kingdom as a QUANGO, or quasi-autonomous, nongovermental organization, is the compromise result. Intra-agency rivalries are not to be discounted either, as the case of the creation and subsequent conflict for the National Institute of Education within the broader education and health and human services bureaucracies demonstrates.[49]

Legislation: The selection-implementation connection

Having begun to appreciate the numerous parties to implementation, one must next understand that the initiation and execution of a policy or program do not start afresh, with a clean slate, or from virginal first premises. Indeed, the accumulated baggage may be overwhelming. Simple procedural matters, for instance, may have significant effects, as in the assignment of a bill to a particular committee where either a friendly or hostile reception is certain even before any discussion occurs,[50] or in the case of conference committee tugging and hauling to reconcile discrepant details contained in House and Senate versions of the same bill.[51] A limit of procedural silliness of sorts occurs in "Christmas tree" amendments which are often tacked onto bills in the closing moments of the legislative session.[52] Any or all of these procedural matters produce results that are neither straightforward nor simple.

Many fail to appreciate the intricacies of the budgetary process and its impacts on implementation.[53] For instance, the authorization of a piece of legislation does not necessarily result in the appropriation of requisite resources to carry out the assigned tasks; it frequently does not. One explanation of why this occurs emphasizes prevailing incentives for members of Congress. One may attain constituent gratification by laboring to put a piece of legislation on the books in the authorization stage; however, because appropriations are often handled by different committees and individuals, blame for meager funding, should that be the result, can easily be shifted elsewhere. "Elsewhere" may be onto the bureaucracy, where blame for weak execution of poorly funded but highly publicized programs is commonly placed. Maternal and Child Health Services (MCHS), within the former Department of Health, Education and Welfare, certainly illustrates this problem.

In the mid-1970s, as one of dozens of programs, MCHS provided resources throughout the country to screen about 10 million children per year for sight deficiencies.[54] Even disregarding legitimate questions about the validity of screening programs, other implementation questions loomed large: What happened to the children found to have visual problems? Were follow-up and treatment services provided to those in need? Did anyone keep track of identified children to see that they received what they required? Were efforts made to discover problems other than visual ones thought to exist at the time of screening? Most of these questions cannot be answered "because of vague objectives, inadequate resources, poor coordination, and lack of accountability data."[55] MCHS simply did not have the wherewithal to do everything expected of it, and as a result, it is not surprising that MCHS and other closely related programs came under fire. The selection-implementation connection was inadequate.

A characteristic feature of much social legislation passed in the era beginning with Franklin D. Roosevelt was the creation of new agencies to carry out mandated policies and programs. Indeed, one important element in the long-term growth of government is traceable to this particular implementation strategy.[56] Rather than trying to reeducate or redirect the energies of an existing agency, one might start afresh with new individuals, new plans, and as little old baggage as possible. In the hands of the master Roosevelt, this strategy became very sophisticated as he created alternative, competing authorities to enhance both information gathering and control purposes. In the words of Arthur Schlesinger, Jr.:

> His favorite technique was to keep grants of authority incomplete, jurisdictions uncertain, charters overlapping. The result of this competitive theory of administration was often confusion and exasperation on the operating level; but no other method could so reliably insure that in a large bureaucracy filled with ambitious men eager for power the decisions, and the power to make them, would remain with the President.[57]

We seem to be well into a period of diminishing returns for this particular administrative style; the sheer size of government now not only works against legislating new bureaucratic authority, it may well be self-destructive. In his inquiry into the red-tape phenomenon, Kaufman observes:

> The sheer mass of binding official promulgations and interventions in the marketplace begins to be oppressive. The number seems to increase steadily. . . . It is certainly undeniable that the output of the federal government is prodigious. Congress alone produces over a thousand printed pages of public laws in an average session. . . . [I]t is easy to understand why red tape has become a matter for concern. The stream appears to be at flood stage and relentlessly rising.[58]

Under such circumstances, the assignment of responsibility for new programs rests ever more with existing agencies, many of which are facing pressures to level off or contract. Not only is there the routine problem of bureaucratic inertia to contend with where old values, established procedures, an organizational history, and the like all may figure prominently, but in periods of financial stringency or cutback, the prospects for faithful or effective implementation may dim even more.[59]

Another strategic alternative is to shift programmatic responsibility away from the public or governmental sector and into the private one.[60] This may be accomplished legislatively by abolishing bureaucratic functions or by allowing them to dry up or wither away through underfunding. Deregulation is a specific form of this,[61] which might be appropriate, considering the lengths to which the regulators have gone. In one case cited by Kaufman, the "length" was a stack of regulatory documents "seventeen feet high."[62]

Legislation can produce perverse incentives for those tasked with implementation, resulting in programs that may fail to accomplish legislative intent and even make the underlying problem worse. The incentive problem has been discussed by Schultze in citing implementation difficulties structured into Medicaid and Medicare legislation, various statutes affecting the lives of those on flood plains, and several other compelling examples.[63] Besides simple lack of appreciation for the concepts embodied in legislation (the form stressed by Schultze), Ingram also stresses the politically comprehensible but practically troublesome example of legislation passed that lacks enforcement authority or instruments, e.g., the power of sanctions may be intentionally omitted, as with formula or block grant programs to the states and localities or water control programs.[64] In the formula grant example, there appears to be a fundamental tension or contradiction between intentions embodied in the legislation. On the one hand, there is evidence that the grant mechanism is chosen so as to build broad political support for a class of activities. But on the other hand, it seems to be at the expense of program effectiveness in the absence of enforcement powers.[65]

A variation on the perverse incentives theme may result from initial lack of legislative concern for measures of effectiveness—a deficiency filled in time through bureaucratic guidelines and standard operating procedures. In the human services field, for example, vocational rehabilitation services, "creaming" is a well-known phenomenon which results when performance standards are established that reward the total number of cases closed within a period of time, rather than the difficulty or appropriateness of the individual case.[66] Such an incentive rewards simple quantity—which is best boosted by skimming the cream so as to take mainly those with the slightest needs or the easiest problems. The Vocational Rehabilitation Act of 1973, as amended, finally attempts to close this bureaucratic loophole by assigning priority weights to those with the severest handicaps.[67]

The implementing agent and agency

Many agencies are seemingly incapable of controlling the numerous programs they have been called on to execute over the years. Simple matters of increasing size and decreasing ability to know and guide the complex workings of an agency figure prominently in explaining poor implementation. Efforts to delegate or decentralize[68] and to extend the reach of central authority through improved information technologies and management are two common but contradictory reactions to increased size and devolving control.[69] Neither strategy is a panacea, however; uniform and consistent performance standards may prove impossible to establish and enforce in the first case,[70] and the resort to mechanistic devices, such as management information systems, performance reporting, and the like, has in many circumstances created as many or more problems than it has solved.[71]

When variations occur in the worldview or dominant values of those at highest levels of policy formulation and those in the field entrusted with the implementation job, problems should be expected. If the 1970s illustrated nothing else, it is that variation in view and value has come to dominate collective public endeavor.[72] For even the best-intended policies, one will always encounter action agents more interested in spending the money as they see fit instead of striving to understand and faithfully execute programs as they were intended.[73] This becomes especially bothersome in cases where the action agent and the new program are mismatched, as for instance, in the case of the Energy Research and Development Administration where nuclear advocates in the bureaucracy were often given responsibility for solar and other alternative energy technologies in which they had little faith and even less interest.[74]

Finally, one should not forget that bureaucrats are human and suffer from the general failings of the species. Even the most carefully worded directive will still be open to legitimate interpretation—and misrepresentation.[75] The civil service is not noted for its risk taking, and any new venture will have by definition elements of bureaucratic risk involved,[76] particularly so in new areas of endeavor or where the proposed changes depart severely from the accustomed norm or involve large-scale activities.[77]

This hardly ends our survey of practical problems associated with implementation; we next consider a set of factors that are often and widely enough encountered as individuals try to carry out various responsibilities to merit general attention. In one sense, these factors provide a distillation and synthesis of much diverse practical experience.

FACTORS INFLUENCING IMPLEMENTATION

Many potential categories or lists could be imagined that would capture reasons for implementation success or failure. In fact, Fesler has proposed such a list: program success is related to the existence of able and committed leadership, clear objectives, and initial success; program failure has resulted from inertia, diffuseness of program clientele, inadequate scope of effort, weak congressional support, inadequate funds, and the loss of leadership.[78] We offer our own rendition as a complementary, additional perspective on the problem. Combining them may even enhance one's grasp and understanding more than having to choose between them.

A list of implementation factors might include:

Source of the policy.

Clarity of the policy.

Support for the policy.

Complexity of the administration.

Incentives for implementors.

Resource allocation.

Each factor is affected by other conditioning features of the context, such as legal restrictions and the need for bureaucratic rationality (e.g., does the administering agency have the requisite skills?).[79] While such conditions are themselves worthy of discussion, we examine only the main factors listed above.

Source of the policy

The sources of policy are numerous. First, a policy could arise from a presidential declaration, such as President Nixon's 1973 executive order to the armed forces to reduce energy consumption by 7 percent and to the states to reduce highway speed limits to 55 mph, or President Carter's ordered boycott by U.S. athletes of the 1980 Olympic Games. Second, a policy might originate in the passage of legislation—for example, the Omnibus Crime Act of 1968. Third, and probably most typically, Congress and the president might cooperate in their constitutional and functional mandates to formulate a policy; most federal policies, such as the creation in 1980 of a government-subsidized synthetic fuels industry, are the product of this partnership. It is important to note that while these products are carried out by the bureaucracy, the policies have been conceived by elected officials. Fourth, many policies originate within the upper levels of governmental bureaucracy, quite often without specific congressional or executive mandate, approval, or support; the Economic Development Administration's (EDA) decision to reduce its rural emphasis and fund the Oakland, California, development project is a prime example.[80] Finally, the courts often determine policy; we need only consider the courts' impact on civil rights, education, and conservation to appreciate their policymaking capacity.[81]

The significance of the policy source as a factor influencing implementation is that each policy originator has different roles, powers, and functions in the government which determine its capacity to define, select, and execute a particular policy. Although the legislature is not without its policy implementation powers (e.g., the budget and oversight committees can serve these purposes indirectly), the executive branch, sometimes through its personal powers but usually through the bureaucracy, has the most influence on implementation.[82] There was no implementation gap in President Ford's executive pardoning of former President Richard Nixon, as Ford held both the policy selection and implementation powers completely within his hands.

The courts are most removed. Under the constitutional separation of powers, the court must rely on the administrative branch to ensure that its rulings are enforced, a charge not always honored. President Andrew Jackson refused to enforce the 1830 Supreme Court decision in favor of the Cherokee Indians, and the 1954 Supreme Court decision abolishing racial discrimination in public schools is still not completely implemented.[83]

To complicate matters, the different policy sources do not always complement each other in carrying out a policy; indeed, in some cases, they can stand in stark opposition to each other. The battles between the Congress and president over general policy and specific legislation and how they are later enacted is the stuff of both everyday journalism and policy research. For example, the question over whether a president can legally impound funds Congress has voted for a specific purpose was raised by President Carter over the continued development of the liquid metal fast breeder nuclear reactor. The constitutional mandate of the court system can easily place it in stern opposition to both presidential and congressional preferences; the Supreme Court dismantled Roosevelt's New Deal legislation in spite of its widespread support.[84]

Clarity of the policy

A second factor is the clarity with which a policy's underlying intent is articulated, either formally or informally. In some cases, especially judicial decisions, the intent may be clear but the means of carrying it out are left completely to the administering agency, e.g., the landmark school desegregation decision in 1954, *Brown* v. *Board of Education*. The more precisely the intent is stated—be it by the legislature, the courts, or the executive— the more likely the policy will be implemented in harmony with the original intent and possibly the more likely it will be implemented at all.[85] This is what Berman refers to as "programmed implementation."[86]

This precision is generally lacking, even at the highest levels of governmental policy formulation. Imprecision can occur when there is confusion about the purpose of the legislation, as there was during the congressional Medicare debate,[87] or when the different sponsors of a bill have different reasons for their support, as in the enactment of the Elementary and Secondary Education Act (ESEA) in 1965.[88] The individual decision maker can deliberately obscure intentions. President Lyndon Johnson was careful not to reveal his long-range intentions when he opted for the limited deployment of an antiballistic missile system because he had to satisfy both Secretary of Defense Robert McNamara (who was opposed to any ABM deployment) and the Joint Chiefs of Staff (who favored a heavy, anti-Soviet ABM deployment).[89] How a policy is to be translated into actions is usually not specified until much farther down the policy implementation ladder as one engages in problems of microimplementation, that is, approaches those who actually carry out the policy, such as the street-level bureaucrats, the schoolroom teachers, and the cop on the beat.[90]

It is essential here to pause and distinguish between "intent" and "policy." Intent refers to desired outcomes of perceived problems, while policy encompasses the programs designed to effect those outcomes. High-level policymakers usually have to be rather general and abstract in their statements of intent, for it may be difficult or impossible for them to foresee all the contexts in which a policy will be carried out and to formulate specific guidelines for each one. In practice, overspecification or micromanagement can undermine program implementation. A policy can be specified so minutely as to make its execution in varying conditions virtually impossible; a required capability or resource might not be available. A similar failure can result from misspecification, which is likely to occur if a policy's operations are defined prematurely.[91] Further, overly strict guidelines can destroy local initiative and creativity, conditions which ordinarily should be encouraged.[92]

Whether through insufficient, over-, or misspecification, an administrator who does not understand the intent of a policy is likely to distort it (or feel free to distort it) by inappropriate implementation. Rather than being concerned with the minutiae of policy implementation strategies, the policymaker needs to make certain that the policy objectives are clear through careful specification of intent and a well-considered plan for feedback or evaluation.

Support for the policy

How a policy is implemented—or whether it is implemented at all—depends on the support the policy generates among those who are affected. In other words, what are the external (as opposed to the internal or bureaucratic) politics of policy implementation? The basic questions implied in this consideration include the following: Who are the potential clients? What parties—both inside and outside the government—are likely to support or oppose the policy? What resources do these parties bring to bear, and how much are they willing to expend on this issue? What are the intensity and duration of their commitment? These questions can be asked of both the policy itself and the alternative ways to implement it, although our focus here is on the latter.

To understand the implementation process and to prepare for it systematically and strategically, it is necessary to estimate the total value (i.e., positive and negative) of these factors of support. The lower the summed value of such a political calculus, the lower the chances a policy will accord with the policymaker's intent. But even a high total does not guarantee success because many other obstacles remain to be overcome. A high score on the calculus of support is thus a necessary but not sufficient condition for successful implementation.

Almost no program is enacted within the federal executive or legislative branches without "counting the ducks," that is, determining which groups will support and oppose a particular policy or set of programs; energy is currently a visible and contentious example.[93] Subtle factors can be part of that calculation. A key one is the degree of interest of the original decision maker. Degree of interest is, in turn, affected by the duration of the individual's or agency's concern, especially as their attention is diverted by competing policy or other issues. The original mover of the Department of Housing and Urban Development's "New Towns In-Town" program was President Johnson. Its early development and support benefited from his enthusiasm and prestige. However, when his attentions were increasingly consumed by the Vietnam conflict and he decided not to seek reelection, Johnson's potential usefulness in helping HUD overcome the obstacles to implementing the program was severely diminished.[94] In the Cuban missile crisis, President Kennedy's Executive Committee maintained direct and meticulous control over the naval blockade during the quarantine exercise. As Allison has commented, "For the first time in U.S. military history, local commanders received repeated orders about the details of their military operations directly from political leaders. . . ."[95] Still, even with such high-level attention, the Navy positioned the blockade farther from Cuba than Kennedy wanted and moved it closer to the island only after heated debate. This degree of control was thus maintained only with considerable friction.[96] There is also a cost to other policies that go unattended while the policymaker's attention is fixed on the details of implementation of just one.

Another component of degree of interest is the relative amount of power a policymaker can amass and especially the willingness—both real and perceived—to use this power to assist a policy's implementation. In 1961, President Kennedy was able to convince the Soviet Union of the American military commitment to Laos when he ordered American military advisers there to don their U.S. Army uniforms. Domestically, Kennedy was able to force the major steel manufacturers to roll back their announced price hikes by ordering federal departments to purchse their steel supplies from companies not participating in the price raise.[97] President Carter, however, was much less successful in having Congress approve a coherent national energy program, for he basically lacked the authority to force the necessary legislation.

There are situations where the federal government has very little leverage to ensure that a policy is implemented as intended. A good example is the relative impotence of the federal government in carrying out some educational reforms because of the extreme decentralization of American education and the autonomy of the state and local education administrations. "In practice the only real control that the Federal government has over district use of funds is the relatively unlikely option of withdrawing support."[98] This option has rarely been employed in the case of education, but it has been increasingly threatened to enforce compliance with equal employment statutes. Another example is the government's inability to fine-tune the nation's economy; President Ford's aborted WIN (Whip Inflation Now) campaign demonstrated just how little control the government had over economic forces, short of Draconian measures (such as wage and price controls), which also have severe costs attached (as Nixon's wage and price freezes showed).

Virtually every policy confronts an array of opposing agencies, interest groups, and individuals. They may oppose the policy itself—as the American Medical Association opposed Medicaid, the National Rifle Association continues to fight gun control legislation, and various groups battled the Equal Rights Amendment—or a certain means of implementing it. In the latter case, the opposing groups are likely to try to amend the implementation and interpretations to fit their interests, as oil and gas companies have been doing successfully for years.

Such alterations are also illustrated in the services and programs for the nation's handicapped youth.[99] Serious deficiences in services should not be attributed to insufficient or inadequate laws on the books, nor to any malice among individuals responsible for the delivery of services. Rather, the fault rests with implementation, which raised problems that were more complex and subtle than the initial policymakers had imagined. For example, Medicaid is relied on by a significant portion of poor and handicapped children as the main source of payment for medical treatment; however,

> the nature and quality of the various state programs is highly variable, . . . the payment schedule is often significantly lower than private rates [leading] more than a few physicians to avoid Medicaid patients. . . . Program emphasis has been concentrated on treatment, but since 1967 there have been provisions for mandatory early and periodic screening, diagnosis and treatment of Medicaid-eligible children. Compliance and full implementation of these provisions have been hard to attain from the states.[100]

State programs have subverted the importance of finding and diagnosing handicapped or potentially handicapped children by emphasizing treatment after the occurrence of a handicap. The nature and quality of coverage varies widely because the states have been allowed to design and implement their own programs, owing largely to the formula-grant character of the basic Medicaid program. Few systematic evaluations have been conducted of the total program or even the individual state programs, except in cases of suspected misfeasance.

A policy may be implemented inequitably through action by special interest groups. For example, legally blind persons in this country are entitled to an extra personal exemption on their federal income tax, but no other severely handicapped group is so entitled, a clearly discriminatory condition.[101] It appears that the blind were better organized as an interest group and were better able to alter a policy to their benefit.

Complexity of administration

Usually, several different administrative agencies must be considered, both horizontally and vertically, for a policy to work. Obviously, the greater the number of institutional entities involved—each with its own set of expectations, interests, and perceptions—the more difficult the process of implementation.[102] The difficulties in working with multiple agencies and governmental levels have been pointed out in studies of the EDA and New Towns In-Town,[103] but they are equally apparent in the Model Cities program, environmental protection acts,[104] and education programs.[105]

Generally, the farther removed the decision maker is from the implementing agent and the client—either horizontally in managerial controls and coordination within a given bureaucracy or vertically in the multiple agencies of government that separate the policymaker from the consumer—the greater the opportunities for distortion or variation of the policy from its original intent. As an example of the problem of horizontal coordination, the eight branch offices of the District Attorney for Los Angeles County were found to vary greatly in their patterns of case filing, arraignment, and disposition. Similar variations were found and statistically verified in judicial sentencing patterns in county courts. These discrepancies existed in spite of explicit policy standards set by the District Attorney (for the branch offices) and the California State Judicial Council (for the courts).[106]

When the policy must be implemented through the vertical coordination of several different agencies, each agency adds its own objectives and possibilities for policy distortion. As Levine states, a "major . . . difficulty in getting a policy executed as designed . . . is the diffusion of decision-making through large numbers of operating units."[107] The point is probabilistically underscored by Pressman and Wildavsky, who found that for the EDA to provide funds for hangar construction in the Port of Oakland, 70 separate agreements had to be reached within the participating agencies. The authors assumed that the probability of each agreement was independent of any other. If the probability of each agreement being reached were 80 percent, the overall probability of the program's implementation after 70 decision points would only be one out of a million; if the individual probabilities were raised to 99 percent, the overall probability of success after 70 clearances would still be less than half (.489).[108]

This issue resurrects the essential question of how involved the high-level decision maker should become to ensure that the project is implemented as intended, or in Berman's phrase, what is the nature of the "coupled structure."[109] Naturally the administrator cannot become involved in the day-to-day details of implementation (except in anomalous cases that tend to prove the rule). Implementation is best served by early attention to project evaluation, careful specification of intent, and thorough consideration of the motivations and incentives of the policy implementors.

Experience with various forms of revenue sharing, a policy in which the federal government turns back tax revenues to states and localities to be used for either general or specified purposes, provides fertile ground for one interested in administrative complexity and implementation.[110] As at least one careful evaluator of this experience has discovered, uniformity of program content and quality across cases is mostly absent.[111] Others have gone so far as to wonder how revenue sharing even works as an implementation process.[112]

Incentives for implementors

Whether or not a policy is successfully implemented may depend on the incentives for the administering agency built into the policy.[113] The issue has been treated generally in the context of work and motivation,[114] but others have observed that the lack of information or "market signals" for the bureaucracy makes it very difficult to understand exactly what motivates the implementing agencies and to reward (or punish) them for good (or bad) service.[115] Many public programs have been poorly implemented because they inadvertently were not congruent with the interests of those responsible for formulating and implementing them—a finding consistent with behavioral theory.[116] For example, as medical service costs have continued to rise, "the individual has had a diminishing share to pay directly out of his pocket. Private health insurance, philanthropy, and industry (through industrial in-plant services) have helped reduce the consumer's direct payments."[117] Thus, while medical and hospital costs have declined for those who hold either private or government (e.g., Medicare) health insurance, absolute health costs have soared, and especially so for the uninsured. High-quality medical care has become unaffordable to all but the very wealthy or well-insured because medical insurance has removed incentives to keep hospital costs down.

Charles Schultze points out that incentive problems can arise with budget allocations "when the major elements of cost are not charged to the decision unit responsible for making decisions which involve those costs."[118] An example is the Department of Defense's subsidy of the U.S. merchant marine; if the subsidy were charged directly to the Defense budget, one would expect it eventually to be reduced in size. The incentive problem becomes acute when an agency is ordered to carry out a program that it considers outside its primary role, its organizational "essence"[119] (such as the Internal Revenue Service's monitoring the Cost of Living Council's Economic Phase guidelines and the General Accounting Office's overseeing electoral practices) or considers it politically distasteful or bureaucratically unpopular (witness the changing role of the National Guard in the mid-1960s from an Army reserve unit to one increasingly used to quell urban riots and the resulting Kent State tragedy).

The need to provide the organizational incentives to encourage policy implementation has received increased attention recently. For example, Bardach structures the implementation game to favor a program's success.[120] A second suggestion is to restructure the organization so that it views the conduct of a specific program as being in its own best interest.[121] However, as an incentive the budget is not narrowly enough targeted; it might affect the wrong program. Even if it were specifically targeted, most bureaucracies are so well entrenched as to be relatively immune from all but the most drastic budgetary threats.[122]

Robert Levine has proposed a contingency theory of three incentive modes.[123] In the first, the economic marketplace can be replicated where the goal is efficient allocation of resources; school voucher programs are an example. Second, a political-bargaining mechanism can be used to change the structure of the government or the bargaining power of coalitions in the government; the elevation of the role of labor unions under the amended National Labor Relations Act and the political groups growing out of the Community Action Programs of the 1960s are cited as cases in point. Third, bureaucratic competition can be used to spur more responsive implementation within bureaucracies seeking greater responsibilities; an example is the competition that existed between the various manpower training programs sponsored by the Office of Economic Opportunity and the Department of Labor.[124]

Finally, McLaughlin has pointed out in her study of ESEA Title I that negative incentives should not be expected to provide sufficient motivation for adherence to the policy. She implies that successful implementation is not likely without positive incentives.[125]

Resource allocation

Resources include money and time. It is a truism that there is rarely enough of either to implement policies as fully as desired. The constraints posed by these resources thus heavily influence policy implementation. These constraints include the amount of money and time allocated for implementation and their distribution. For example, the Defense Department might be ordered to reallocate its internal priorities by spending a certain increased percent of research and development funds on a new weapons system (e.g., developing a supersonic manned bomber) while decreasing a like amount for manpower retention programs; the overall amount of money in the Defense budget would remain unchanged, but its distribution would be altered. The financial implications of the reallocation of resources are not always immediately obvious. For example, no additional government funds would apparently be required were the courts to rule that abortions are legal. However, that ruling might significantly increase the requests for abortions from those covered by Medicaid or a national health insurance, thus incurring an unexpected cost to the government. The imposition of many air pollution reduction laws in the early 1970s raised the demand for petroleum-based fuels, which heightened the energy crisis in late 1973; in the wake of the crisis, many pollution standards were relaxed. Policymakers and implementors should be careful to consider the unanticipated consequences or costs—the externalities—that can result from a resource allocation and how they affect policy implementation.[126]

Few projects are funded at the level requested by either Congress, in the appropriations cycle, or the Office of Management and Budget. The recent executive tendency to impound funds makes even congressionally approved appropriations less certain of reaching their intended programs. The courts also have their effect; school financing was fundamentally altered when the California Supreme Court ruled in 1972 that the existing method for school financing was unconstitutional (*Serrano* v. *Priest*).[127]

Time is also a vital factor. Agencies are often forced to meet a deadline that restricts their ability to implement a program efficiently. Alice Rivlin suggests that political pressures forced a premature evaluation and termination of the New Jersey Graduated Work Incentive project (the negative income tax experiment) before it had had sufficient time for a fair test.[128]

At this point we return to a more theoretical vein and consider a few potentially helpful paradigms from subspecialty fields in the social sciences. Most of these are suggested by having gained a rough familiarity with the ways in which implementation operates (or fails) in political arenas.

NOTES

1. See Robert T. Nakamura and Frank Smallwood, *The Politics of Policy Implementation* (New York: St. Martin's Press, 1980), chap. 1.

2. Respectively, Garry D. Brewer, "The Policy Sciences Emerge: To Nurture and Structure a Discipline," *Policy Sciences*, September 1974, pp. 239–44, at p. 240; Robert A. Levine, *Public Planning: Failure and Redirection* (New York: Basic Books, 1972), p. 4; and Jeffrey Pressman and Aaron Wildavsky, *Implementation* (Berkeley: University of California Press, 1973), p. xiii.

3. Juergen Haber, "Revenue Sharing Report: Ehrlichman Promises Audits and Strict Evaluation of Local Programs," *National Journal*, January 1973, p. 234; emphases added.

4. Although pointing out how education planners regularly confuse the two stages, John Pincus, "Incentives for Innovation in the Public Schools," *Review of Educational Research*, Winter 1974, pp. 113–44, fails to make the necessary distinction.

5. An illustration is Paul Berman, "Thinking About Programmed and Adaptive Implementation: Matching Strategies to Situations," in Helen M. Ingram and Dean E. Mann, eds., *Why Policies Succeed or Fail* (Beverly Hills, Calif.: Sage Publications, 1980), pp. 205–27.

6. One is reminded of the debate in public administration on the distinction between "politics" and "administration." See Dwight Waldo, *The Study of Public Administration* (New York: Random House, 1964), chap. 2.

7. Michael Lipsky, "Street-Level Bureaucracy and the Analysis of Urban Reform," *Urban Affairs Quarterly*, June 1971, pp. 391–409.

8. Douglas R. Bunker, "Policy Sciences Perspectives on Implementation Processes," *Policy Sciences*, March 1972, p. 73.

9. Incrementalism is discussed above in Part III. David Braybrooke and Charles E. Lindblom, *A Strategy of Decision* (New York: Free Press, 1963), is a standard work on the subject.

10. Thomas B. Smith, "Policy Roles: An Analysis of Policy Formulators and Policy Implementors," *Policy Sciences*, September 1973, pp. 297–308.

11. Further evidence: those who draw up program guidelines from legislative mandates also have a powerful influence on policy formulation and implementation; see the articles collected by Francine Rabinovitz, Jeffrey Pressman, and Martin Rein, eds., *Policy Sciences*, December 1976, entire issue.

12. The more general policy of coercion through bombing is well treated in Wallace J. Thies, *When Governments Collide: Coercion and Diplomacy in the Vietnam Conflict* (Berkeley: University of California Press, 1980), chap. 5. See also, Raphael Littauer and Norman Uphoff, eds., *The Air War in Indochina* (Boston: Beacon Press, 1973).

13. Described by William H. Riker, "The Veteran's Gas Ration," in Harold Stein, ed., *Public Administration and Policy Development* (New York: Harcourt Brace Jovanovich, 1952), pp. 744–59, as cited in, Martin Rein and Francine Rabinovitz, "Implementation: A Theoretical Perspective" in Walter D. Burnham and Martha Weinberg, eds., *American Politics and Public Policy* (Cambridge, Mass.: MIT Press, 1978), pp. 307–35, at p. 322.

14. Jack L. Walker, "The Diffusion of Innovations in the American States," *American Political Science Review*, September 1969, pp. 880–99.

15. Jesse H. Jones, *Fifty Billion Dollars: My Thirteen Years with the RFC* (New York: Macmillan, 1951), p. 262, as cited in Harold Seidman, *Politics, Position, and Power: The Dynamics of Federal Organization* (New York: Oxford University Press, 1970), p. 63.

16. Frederic A. Bergerson, *The Army Gets an Air Force: Tactics of Insurgent Bureaucratic Politics* (Baltimore, Md.: Johns Hopkins University Press, 1980), p. 1. The Army's air force was superseded in size only by the air forces of the United States and the Soviet Union.

17. John M. Swomley, Jr., *The Military Establishment* (Boston: Beacon Press, 1964); and Morris Janowitz, *The Professional Soldier* (New York: Free Press, 1960).

18. For treatment of the "cabal theory" of implementation, see Tom Burns, "The Reference of Conduct in Small Groups: Cliques and Cabals in Occupational Milieu," *Human Relations*, November 1955, pp. 467–85.

19. Jacques Ellul, *The Political Illusion*, trans. Konrad Kellen (New York: Alfred A. Knopf, 1967), p. 143.

20. Raymond A. Bauer, "The Study of Policy Formation: An Introduction," in Bauer and Kenneth J. Gergen, eds., *The Study of Policy Formation* (New York: Free Press, 1968), is illustrative.

21. Smith, "Policy Roles."

22. Braybrooke and Lindblom, *Strategy of Decision*.

23. Leslie H. Gelb with Richard K. Betts, *The Irony of Vietnam: The System Worked* (Washington, D.C.: The Brookings Institution, 1979), elaborate this precise theme.

24. Daniel Patrick Moynihan, *The Politics of a Guaranteed Income* (New York: Random House, 1973).

25. Eugene Bardach, "On Designing Implementable Programs," in Giandomenico Majone and E. S. Quade, eds., *Pitfalls of Analysis* (New York: John Wiley & Sons, 1980), p. 139, offers four usages of the word "implementation" as it is found in the literature.

26. For an example of appraising implementation as a process antecedent to later program evaluation, see J. David Roessner et al., *Turning Laws into Incentives: The Implementation of State Solar Energy Initiatives* (Golden, Colo.: Solar Energy Research Institute, February 1979).

27. Abraham Kaplan, *American Ethics and Public Policy* (New York: Oxford University Press, 1963), p. 103ff, is a sharp treatment of this point.

28. D. Van Meter and C. Van Horn, "The Policy Implementation Process," *Administration & Society*, February 1975, p. 446.

29. Constance Holden, "Innovation: Japan Races Ahead as U.S. Falters," *Science*, 14 November 1980, pp. 751–54, is an excellent summary.

30. Eliot Marshall, "Senate Skeptical on SALT Verification," *Science*, 27 July 1979, pp. 373–76, 378, inspired this example. Such a deficiency exists, p. 376.

31. Thomas H. Maugh II, "ERTS: Surveying Earth's Resources from Space," *Science*, 6 April 1973, pp. 49–51.

32. Rein and Rabinovitz, "Implementation," discuss this point; also see the essays collected by Daniel A. Mazmanian and Paul A. Sabatier, eds., *Effective Policy Implementation* (Lexington, Mass.: Lexington Books, 1981).

33. Elliot L. Richardson *Responsibility and Responsiveness: The HEW Potential for the Seventies* (Washington, D.C.: Government Printing Office, DHEW Publication No. OS 72–19, 1972), p. 20.

34. Ibid.

35. James Scott, *Comparative Political Corruption* (Englewood Cliffs, N.J.: Prentice-Hall, 1972), is an excellent general source; and idem, "Corruption, Machine Politics and Political Change," *American Political Science Review*, December 1969, pp. 1142–58. Deceit is treated in David Wise, *The Politics of Lying* (New York: Vintage, 1973).

36. Seidman, *Politics, Position and Power.*

37. Frederic V. Malek, *Washington's Hidden Tragedy: The Failure to Make Government Work* (New York: Free Press, 1978), is a partisan view of shortcomings of the Nixon Administration in which this rationale figures prominently.

38. An excellent book in which this point is elaborated for the implementation phase is Merilee S. Grindle, ed., *Politics and Policy Implementation in the Third World* (Princeton, N.J.: Princeton University Press, 1980).

39. Morris S. Ogul, *Congress Oversees the Bureaucracy: Studies in Legislative Supervision* (Pittsburgh: University of Pittsburgh Press, 1976); Randall B. Ripley and Grace A. Franklin, *Congress, the Bureaucracy and Public Policy* (Homewood, Ill.: Dorsey Press, 1980); and Walter J. Oleszek, *Congressional Procedures and the Policy Process* (Washington, D.C.: Congressional Quarterly Press, 1978), treat the legislative-bureaucratic connection in complementary ways.

40. Frederick C. Mosher, *The GAO: The Quest for Accountability in American Government* (Boulder, Colo.: Westview Press, 1979), introduces this important institution.

41. Dozens, if not hundreds, of books have been written on this general subject; a good starting place is Hugh Heclo, *A Government of Strangers: Executive Politics in Washington* (Washington, D.C.: The Brookings Institution, 1977).

42. The internal workings of bureaus and the influence individual bureaucrats exert over

public policies and programs are treated, respectively, in Anthony Downs, *Inside Bureaucracy* (Boston: Little, Brown, 1967); and Gordon Tullock, *The Politics of Bureaucracy* (Washington, D.C.: Public Affairs Press, 1965).

43. Again, a well-studied topic. For orientation see, James W. Fesler, ed., *The 50 States and Their Local Governments* (New York: Alfred A. Knopf, 1967); and Willis D. Hawley, ed., *Where Governments Meet: Emerging Patterns of Intergovernmental Relations* (Berkeley, Calif.: Institute of Governmental Studies, 1967).

44. Martin Shapiro, *The Supreme Court and Administrative Agencies* (New York: Free Press, 1968); and Samuel Krislov, *The Supreme Court in the Political Process* (New York: Macmillan, 1965), both describe the various ways in which this occurs; also see Lawrence Baum, "Comparing the Implementation of Legislative and Judicial Policies," in Mazmanian and Sabatier, *Effective Policy Implementation.*

45. Kenneth M. Dolbeare and Phillip E. Hammond, *The School Prayer Decision* (Chicago: University of Chicago Press, 1971); William K. Muir, Jr., *Prayer in the Public Schools: Law and Attitude Change* (Chicago: University of Chicago Press, 1967); and Gary Orfield, *The Reconstruction of Southern Education: The Schools and the 1964 Civil Rights Act* (New York: John Wiley & Sons, 1969), all play on these themes. The general case is well treated in both Theodore L. Becker, *The Impact of Supreme Court Decisions* (New York: Oxford University Press, 1968); and Richard M. Johnson, *The Dynamics of Compliance: Supreme Court Decision-Making from a New Perspective* (Evanston, Ill.: Northwestern University Press, 1967).

46. Simple reference to the Washington, D.C. telephone directory or a perusal of lists of registered lobbyists confirms the quantity point; the matter of power and influence is also probably correct, but must be assessed in each circumstance. Lynn Rosellini, "Lobbyists Row All Alert for Chance at the Budget," *New York Times*, February 26, 1981, p. B-14, indicates that something on the order of 107,000 persons are employed in Washington as lobbyists, that a payroll of some $5 billion per year is involved, and that lobby groups are forming at the rate of one per week. On one block of Washington's K Street, N. W., according to Rosellini, some 60 different groups have offices.

47. An illustrative treatment of environmental policy in these terms is Henry M. Peskin, "Environmental Policy and the Distribution of Benefits and Costs," in Paul R. Portney, ed., *U.S. Environmental Policy* (Baltimore, Md.: Johns Hopkins University Press for Resources for the Future, 1978), chap. 5.

48. Francis X. Clines, "Reagan Plan: A New Theology," *New York Times*, February 25, 1981, pp. D-1, D-14, amplifies a religious theme.

49. Lee Sproull, Stephen Weiner, and David Wolf, *Organizing an Anarchy: Belief, Bureaucracy, and Politics in the National Institute of Education* (Chicago: University of Chicago Press, 1978).

50. U.S. Congress, Senate, Committee on Finance, *Hearings on Crude Oil Tax* (Washington, D.C.: Government Printing Office, July 18, 1979).

51. U.S. Congress, Joint Committee on Taxation, *Conference Comparison on H. R. 3919, Crude Oil Windfall Profit Tax of 1979* (Washington, D.C.: Government Printing Office, December 18, 1979).

52. The label refers to Christmas tree ornaments, and the analogy aptly describes the substantive content of many of these amendments, which may have absolutely nothing to do with the main bill, or "tree" to which they have been attached.

53. Aaron Wildavsky, *The Politics of the Budgetary Process* (Boston: Little, Brown, 1979), is particularly helpful here.

54. The full story is told in Garry D. Brewer and James S. Kakalik, *Handicapped Children: Strategies for Improving Services* (New York: McGraw-Hill, 1979), chap. 9.

55. Ibid., p. 259.

56. Thomas E. Borcherding, ed., *Budgets and Bureaucrats: The Sources of Government Growth* (Durham, N.C.: Duke University Press, 1977).

57. Arthur M. Schlesinger, Jr., *The Age of Roosevelt: The Coming of the New Deal*, vol. II (Boston: Houghton Mifflin, 1959), p. 528.

58. Herbert Kaufman, *Red Tape: Its Origins, Uses and Abuses* (Washington, D.C.: The Brookings Institution, 1977), pp. 6–7.

59. Charles H. Levine, "Organizational Decline and Cutback Management," in Levine, ed., *Managing Fiscal Stress: The Crisis in the Public Sector* (Chatham, N.J.: Chatham House, 1980), pp. 13–30.

60. As Lasswell reminds us, however, government regulations exist for a reason, to bring private acts into conformance with the best interests of the community; as such, regulations represent powerful norms to secure compliance. Harold D. Lasswell, *A Pre-View of Policy Sciences* (New York: American Elsevier, 1971), p. 109.

61. Paul W. MacAvoy, *The Regulated Industries and the Economy* (New York: W. W. Norton, 1979).

62. Kaufman, *Red Tape*, p. 7. [Citing *The Federal Paperwork Burden*, U.S. Senate Report 93–125 (Washington, D.C.: Government Printing Office, 1973), p. 4.]

63. Charles L. Schultze, "The Role of Incentives, Penalties, and Rewards in Attaining Effective Policy," in Julius Margolis and Robert Haveman, eds., *Public Expenditures and Policy Analysis* (Chicago: Markham, 1970), pp. 145–71, at, respectively, p. 158 and p. 162.

64. Helen M. Ingram, "Policy Implementation Through Bargaining: The Case of Federal Grants-in-Aid," *Public Policy*, Fall 1977, pp. 499–526.

65. Ibid., p. 509.

66. U.S. General Accounting Office, *Effectiveness of Vocational Rehabilitation in Helping the Handicapped* (Washington, D.C.: Government Printing Office, No. B–164031–3, April 3, 1973).

67. Brewer and Kakalik, *Handicapped Children*, pp. 518–19.

68. Paul Goodman, *People or Personnel: Decentralizing and the Mixed System* (New York: Random House, 1965).

69. Herbert Kaufman, *Administrative Feedback* (Washington, D.C.: The Brookings Institution, 1973), takes a practical view; Richard W. Brightman, *Information Systems for Modern Management* (New York: Macmillan, 1971); and Thomas L. Whisler, *Information Technology and Organizational Change* (Belmont, Calif.: Wadsworth, 1970), emphasize the technological dimension. Both aspects are joined and treated extensively in Manfred Kochen and Karl W. Deutsch, *Decentralization* (Cambridge, Mass.: Oelgeschlager, Gunn & Hain, 1980).

70. Michael Q. Patton, *Utilization-Focused Evaluation* (Beverly Hills, Calif.: Sage Publications, 1978), argues that uniformity may not be a self-evident "good," however.

71. James L. Perry and Kenneth L. Kraemer, "Innovation Attributes, Policy Intervention, and the Diffusion of Computer Applications Among Local Governments," *Policy Sciences*, April 1978, pp. 179–205.

72. Roger Benjamin, *The Limits of Politics: Collective Goods and Political Change in Post-industrial Societies* (Chicago: University of Chicago Press, 1980), amplifies and documents this theme.

73. Neal C. Gross, Joseph B. Giaquinta, and Marilyn Bernstein, *Implementing Organizational Innovations: A Sociological Analysis of Planned Educational Change* (New York: Basic Books, 1971), discuss this in light of educational program reforms.

74. J. Robert Holloman and Michel Grenon, *Energy Research and Development* (Cam-

bridge, Mass.: Ballinger, 1975), treat this controversial topic. See especially chaps. 3 and 4.

75. C. K. Ogden and I. A. Richards, *The Meaning of Meaning* (New York: Harcourt Brace Jovanovich, 1947), is a thorough discussion of most aspects of this problem.

76. Herbert Kaufman, *The Limits of Organizational Change* (University: The University of Alabama Press, 1971).

77. Paul R. Schulman, *Large-Scale Policy Making* (New York: Elsevier, 1980), is a rare discussion of the scalar dimension of the problems of decision making.

78. James W. Fesler, *Public Administration: Theory and Practice* (Englewood Cliffs, N.J.: Prentice-Hall, 1980), pp. 275–77.

79. These conditioning factors of legality and rationality "imperatives" are defined and elaborated in Rein and Rabinovitz, "Implementation."

80. See Pressman and Wildavsky, *Implementation,* chap. 2, for a description of this decision. Eugene Bardach, *The Implementation Game* (Cambridge, Mass.: MIT Press, 1977), pays special attention to these.

81. Nakamura and Smallwood, *Politics of Policy Implementation,* devote chap. 6 to the "Special Case of Judicial Implementation."

82. While the president, as head of the administrative branch of government would appear to have a great deal of power, most presidential scholars agree with Richard E. Neustadt that the president's main source of power is his ability to persuade. The entrenched bureaucracies have a great deal of power in regards to the implementation of a particular program and, hence, the final form of the general policy. Richard E. Neustadt, *Presidental Power* (New York: John Wiley & Sons, 1980). See also, Kaufman, *Administrative Feedback,* for some thoughts on the replacement (or displacement) of elected officials by key governmental personnel.

83. Frederick Aaron Lazin, "The Failure of Federal Enforcement of Civil Rights Regulations in Public Housing, 1963–1971: The Co-optation of a Federal Agency by Its Local Constituency," *Policy Sciences,* September 1973, pp. 263–73, reports how the Department of Housing and Urban Development was unable to enforce court orders to integrate Chicago public housing.

84. Bernard Sternsher, *Rexford Tugwell and the New Deal* (New Brunswick, N.J.: Rutgers University Press, 1964), pp. 380–88.

85. Gross et al., *Implementing Organizational Innovations,* chap. 6, identify ambiguity of intent as a major cause of failure in implementing educational innovation.

86. Berman, "Programmed and Adaptive Implementation."

87. Rosemary Stevens and Robert Stevens, "Medicare: Anatomy of a Dilemma," *Law and Contemporary Problems,* Spring 1970, pp. 348–425.

88. Philip Meranto, *The Politics of Federal Aid to Education in 1965: A Study in Political Innovation* (Syracuse, N.Y.: Syracuse University Press, 1967).

89. Morton Halperin, "The Decision to Employ the ABM," *World Politics,* October 1972, pp. 62–95; and idem, *Bureaucratic Politics and Foreign Policy* (Washington, D.C.: The Brookings Institution, 1974), chap. 16.

90. Berman, "Study of Macro- and Micro-Implementation"; and Lipsky, "Street-Level Bureaucracy."

91. The problems inherent in over- and misspecification are especially evident in the development of weapon systems. For examples, see Thomas Marschak, "The Role of Project Histories in the Study of R&D," in Thomas Marschak, Thomas K. Glennan, Jr., and Robert Summers, *Strategy for R&D: Studies in the Microeconomics of Development* (New York: Springer-Verlag, 1967), chap. 3. Although the examples are not as clear, many of the failures of the War on Poverty programs and ESEA Title I grants can

likewise be attributed to misspecification of the problem, the intent, the policy, or a combination of these.

92. For an excellent example of the value of local implementation of national policy, see Ronald D. Brunner, "Decentralized Energy Policies," *Public Policy*, Winter 1968, pp. 71–92.

93. See Barry Commoner, *The Politics of Energy* (New York: Alfred A. Knopf, 1979), for one account of this debate.

94. See Martha Derthick, *New Towns In-Town* (Washington D.C.: The Urban Institute, 1972), for an elaboration.

95. Graham T. Allison, *Essence of Decision: Explaining the Cuban Missile Crisis* (Boston: Little, Brown, 1971), p. 128.

96. Secretary of Defense Robert McNamara is reported to have come to harsh words with Chief of Naval Operations Admiral George Anderson over the Navy's plans for possibly boarding Soviet ships. According to one source, "The encounter ended abruptly when Anderson said to McNamara: 'Now, Mr. Secretary, if you and your deputy will go back to your offices, the Navy will run the blockade'." Although the account has been questioned, it might be noted that Anderson was not reappointed. See Elie Abel, *The Missile Crisis* (Philadelphia: J. B. Lippincott, 1966), p. 156.

97. Kennedy's tactics in both instances are described by Arthur M. Schlesinger, Jr., *A Thousand Days: John F. Kennedy in the White House* (Boston: Houghton Mifflin, 1965), chaps. 12 (Laos) and 23 (steel).

98. Pincus, "Incentives for Innovation," p. 126. Frederick M. Wirt and Michael W. Kirst, *The Political Web of American Schools* (Boston: Little, Brown, 1972), argue that such a threat by the federal education authorities is little more than symbolic and usually fails.

99. For an evaluation of those services and programs see Brewer and Kakalik, *Handicapped Children*.

100. G. D. Brewer and J. S. Kakalik, *Improving Services to Handicapped Children: Summary and Recommendations* (Santa Monica, Calif.: The Rand Corporation, R–1420/1, May 1974), p. 28. [This earlier component of Brewer and Kakalik, *Handicapped Children*, contains somewhat more detailed administrative information than the later book version.]

101. Brewer and Kakalik, *Handicapped Children*, p. 540.

102. The administrative problems of coordination are addressed in the literature of organization theory. For example: "The more sources of uncertainty or contingency for the organization, . . . the larger the number of political positions in the organization," and "organizations group positions to minimize coordination costs." James D. Thompson, *Organizations in Action* (New York: McGraw-Hill, 1967), pp. 129 and 57, respectively.

103. Again, see Derthick, *New Towns In-Town;* and Pressman and Wildavsky, *Implementation*, for details of these two cases.

104. A. Myrick Freeman III and Robert H. Haveman, "Clean Rhetoric and Dirty Water," *The Public Interest*, Summer 1972, pp. 51–65.

105. Paul Berman and Milbrey Wallin McLaughlin, *Federal Programs Supporting Educational Change: A Model of Educational Change* (Santa Monica, Calif.: The Rand Corporation, R–1589/1, September 1974).

106. Peter W. Greenwood et al., *Prosecution of Adult Felony Defendants* (Lexington, Mass.: Lexington Books, 1976).

107. Levine, *Public Planning*, p. 138.

108. Pressman and Wildavsky, *Implementation:* Table 8: "Program Completion Doubtful Unless Level of Agreement Among Participants is Terribly High," p. 107. The authors' calculated values are impressive but methodologically suspect. They assume both

independence of agreement and a binary yes/no decision, neither of which is particularly realistic. They also operate under the weak link hypothesis, in which a policy fails if there is one nonagreement (or weak link). This serial assumption makes the probabilities multiplicative, thus producing extremely pessimistic probabilities against success. It can be argued that the individual decisions are made in parallel rather than serially. The adoption of a continuous-variable decision model with parallel, interdependent decision nodes would probably result in more realistic estimates of successful implementation.

109. Berman, "Study of Macro- and Micro-Implementation."

110. Edward C. Banfield, "Revenue Sharing in Theory and Practice," *The Public Interest*, Spring 1971, pp. 34–45.

111. Patrick D. Larkey, *Evaluating Public Programs: The Impact of General Revenue Sharing* (Princeton, N.J.: Princeton University Press, 1979).

112. Robert Cassidy, "Revenue Sharing: It's Working, But Nobody Knows How or Why," *Planning*, December 1974, pp. 8–9. See also, Haber, "Revenue Sharing Report."

113. Bruno Stein and S. M. Miller, eds., *Incentives and Planning in Social Policy* (Chicago: Aldine, 1973).

114. Victor H. Vroom, *Work and Motivation* (New York: John Wiley & Sons, 1964); and Daniel Katz, "The Motivational Basis of Organizational Behavior," *Behavioral Science* 9, no. 2 (1964), pp. 131–46.

115. Charles Wolf, Jr., "A Theory of Non-Market Failures," *The Public Interest*, Spring 1979, pp. 114–33, refers to this as a problem of "internalities." For a lengthier exposition, see idem, "A Theory of Nonmarket Failure: Framework for Implementation Analysis," *Journal of Law & Economics*, April 1979, pp. 107–39.

116. Abraham H. Maslow, "A Theory of Motivation," *Psychological Review* 50, no. 4 (1943), pp. 370–96.

117. Dorothy P. Rice and Barbara S. Cooper, "National Health Expenditures, 1929–71," *Social Security Bulletin*, January 1972, p. 10; also see Joseph Newhouse and Vincent Taylor, "How Shall We Pay for Hospital Care?" *The Public Interest*, Spring 1971, pp. 78–92.

118. Schultze, "Role of Incentives, Penalties, and Rewards," p. 154.

119. The phrase is discussed in Morton H. Halperin and Arnold Kanter, eds., *Readings in American Foreign Policy: A Bureaucratic Perspective* (Boston: Little, Brown, 1973), p. 11. Specific examples are found in Robert K. Yin, *Changing Urban Bureaucracies: How New Practices Become Routinized* (Lexington, Mass.: Lexington Books, 1979).

120. Bardach, *Implementation Game*, chap. 11.

121. One of the earliest and best books on organizational development is Warren G. Bennis, *Changing Organizations* (New York: McGraw-Hill, 1966).

122. Schultze, "Role of Incentives, Penalties, and Rewards."

123. These incentives are elaborated in Levine, *Public Planning*.

124. See, inter alia, William A. Niskanen, "Competition Among Government Bureaus," in Carol H. Weiss and Allen H. Barton, eds., *Making Bureaucracies Work* (Beverly Hills, Calif.: Sage Publications, 1980), chap. 11.

125. Milbrey Wallin McLaughlin, *Evaluation and Reform: The Elementary and Secondary Education Act of 1965, Title I* (Cambridge, Mass.: Ballinger, 1975).

126. Wolf, "Theory of Non-Market Failures."

127. See John Pincus, ed., *School Finance in Transition* (Cambridge, Mass.: Ballinger, 1973).

128. Alice Rivlin, *Systematic Thinking for Social Action* (Washington, D.C.: The Brookings Institution, 1971), chap. 5.

10

Expanding the possibilities
and practical applications

THEORETICAL PARADIGMS

Something is gained by reconsidering implementation through a variety of disciplinary perspectives, several of which at first glance might seem irrelevant. The basic purpose is to increase our understanding of implementation as both process and practice. One such possibility is suggested by Pressman and Wildavsky: "Our normal expectation should be that new programs will fail to get off the ground and that, at best, they will take considerable time to get started." This summary assessment follows a survey of various implementation failures, which according to Pressman and Wildavsky should be regarded as the norm: "The cards in this world are stacked against things happening, as so much effort is required to make them move. The remarkable thing is that new programs work at all."[1] Much the same has been said about innovations in general: most fail, successful diffusion usually takes far more time than early proponents imagined, and when anything new is put into practice, it often takes forms and shapes never conceived by its creators.[2]

These thoughts led to others and enabled us to imagine a number of subtle theoretical ideas which might have practical use in understanding given realistic circumstances.

Scientific management and the "mechanical bureaucrat"

Paralleling an earlier discussion about fundamental theoretical and practical worldviews[3] is the scientific management theory espoused by Frederick Taylor and his followers.[4] Working from an engineering premise that bureaucracies could be treated as closed mechanical systems, this style of management readily lends itself to studies of organizational and individual efficiency, time-and-motion studies of activity, and other forms of optimal-seeking behavior. The persistence of Taylorism, as the movement came to be called, gained certain normative legitimacy when alloyed with the theoretical insights of Max Weber, most particularly with respect to his general thesis concerning the superiority of the bureaucracy over other forms of social organization to conduct defined programs for the common good.[5] Not only is the bureaucracy a mechanistic device, but it ought to be as well.[6] The theory also applies to the individual: the "mechanical bureaucrat."[7]

In reaction: The innovation perspective

Human beings are not machines. As there are both central tendencies and wide variations in the species homo sapiens, one should not be surprised to discover comparable characteristics in the ways human acts begin, take hold, and operate outside of controlled laboratory environments.[8]

What Taylor and his followers failed to understand is that a proposed change impinges on existing social practice and structure. Distinct and persuasive incentives must be built into such changes, and these, together with a clear characterization of the change itself, must be spelled out in understandable, attractive, and nonthreatening ways to those entrusted with operations. Specific details and features of the contexts or sites where change is being tried also require attention and may stimulate adaptations to the general plan. Changes that attain more than superficial permanence are usually made cooperatively, not coercively; furthermore, change seldom occurs in exactly the ways or as rapidly as the external change agent originally imagines or prefers.[9]

Knowing a setting in precise detail is fundamental. There is no substitute for knowing one's business, and when the business is changing the status quo, subtle nuances and simple matters of fact count heavily. For instance, many federal programs begin with a hope that compliance and performance will be relatively uniform across all cases;[10] however, the variety of effects observed in the wake of implementation efforts often leads one to conclude that the individual cases were far more complex, and the initial concept underlying the programs far less clear, than anyone imagined.[11]

Replacing one set of practices and procedures with another is a perspective on implementation few take. One person's innovation could be another's destruction. The creation-as-destruction view presumes that innovations are not introduced *de novo* but rather disrupt or supersede existing practices and arrangements. This view allows one to appreciate the many difficulties encountered by those attempting to implement a new policy or program, particularly when the novelty has wholesale or readily apparent implications.[12]

Disturbing the status quo is seldom easily or painlessly done. Institutions, like personal habits, persist and aggrandize;[13] those heavily invested or captive can be expected to fight efforts at change.[14] Prolific bureaucracies testify to this point, as do lame attempts to contain or control them.[15] All of this needs to be taken directly into account as one prepares and then attempts implementation.

Characterizing a new policy or program is deceptively difficult. Much formal legislative debate, a prime source of social change, deals less with the comparative advantages among distinct alternatives than it does with definitions and interpretations describing only one. This problem may continue and limit effective conduct of the program or policy: the frequency with which new social programs are called into judicial question to clarify, define, or interpret operational terms is indicative.[16]

Assuming that everyone agrees about what an innovation is meant to accomplish is unwarranted. Reducing the costs of a given social program is a clear statement of purpose. Its simplicity may mislead one not to bother discussing a range of costs (frequently nonmonetary in nature) to be exacted from those already dispensing and receiving services under the program. It is a rare change that benefits everyone at no cost to anyone; and while those most directly affected by the proposed change may intellectually appreciate the need for cost-cutting measures, they may be emotionally opposed to them for the injustices they create. Short-run victories over obstructionist and unenlightened beneficiaries of change may, in the longer run, result in perversion or even defeat of the initial plan.

Psychological perspectives

The personalities, interests, and training of individuals have identifiable effects on the implementation process. Much theoretical work coming from the specialty field of organizational behavior exists and can be productively consulted in trying to design incentives into a proposed change or determining why an in-place program does not work as it should.[17] Empirical studies of implementation, taken from an individual psychological perspective, stress aspects of change although they are not nearly so numerous as theoretical ones. Downs, in a detailed survey, found that a principal explanatory factor underlying bureaucratic innovation is the influence of a key, ideologically (as determined by psychological measurements) committed director within an affected institution.[18] Psychological theories may also help one understand differences between innovators, imitators, and resistors, that is, persons who create, those who do not create but who see enough value in a change to take and use it, and those who reject change.

Differences between early and late adopters should also be measureable with psychological instruments.

Individual predispositions may be reflected at the institutional or profession-wide levels. Little is known about the effects on acceptance and use such factors as professional ethos or institutional attitudes have. For instance, a group that imagines itself to be modern and scientific will be, all else being equal, more likely to search out, try and adopt new technologies than a comparable one shaped by conservative and humanistic biases; the experiences of the New York City Rand Institute in dealing with John Lindsay's administration and then that of Abe Beame tend to lend weight to this general observation.[19] Such factors must play a role in implementation, but little systematic knowledge exists to specify what that role might be. Intensive work is needed to locate and analyze the personalities and attitudes of creative implementors (e.g., change agents and the like)[20] to help account for the considerable differences that exist in rates and styles of getting something done.[21] Detailed individual data could very well yield insights about group, institutional, and higher-level practices, too.

Small group theory

Political science has a long tradition of analysis at the group level.[22] To a certain—although debatable—extent, groups have been implicated in the outcomes of particular decisions. Dahl, for one, comments: "All other things being equal, the outcome of a policy decision will be determined by the relative intensity of preference among the members of a group."[23] A contribution to understanding implementation from this particular perspective is heightened sensitivity to the existence and interplay of many interested groups in the eventual determination and shape of policies and programs. Thus, a well-organized and venerable group, such as the American Medical Association, may play a significant role in shaping and determining a policy outcome in specific circumstances.[24] For many other groups and for many other issues, the cause and effect linkages will not be as clear nor as predictable. Nevertheless, the group approach may be useful as a descriptive aid and organizing concept for more focused policy analyses. It may be a means to characterize a specific issue or experience, but it will most likely not be the only means, nor will it be the determining one.[25]

Organization theory

Organizational studies are numerous in the literature of administrative science, psychology, public and business administration, and policy studies. Within administrative science, the subfield of organizational development has been one prolific source.[26] Much of what has been written about the administration of both public and private sectors is based on an organizational theoretical perspective.[27] Several common themes of much of this literature and scholarship can be identified and related to implementation.

No two places are precisely the same, and the peculiarities of time, circumstance, personality, and institutional form all play a part and will affect the intended action.

Change affects individuals and institutions.

Securing change is difficult, and presuming that a new program or policy is self-evidently valuable, worthwhile, and appealing helps far less than appreciating the hard work and promotion needed to make something happen in organizations.

Demonstrable near-term benefits—in reduced costs, lessened work, enhanced prestige, and so forth—nearly always smooth implementation, especially when contrasted with situations of real and immediate costs or benefits to be captured at some time in the distant future.

Communication theory and cybernetics

Studies of networks of formal and informal communication, especially those in which elites have prominence, play a central role in thinking about implementation.[28] This is especially true with respect to what Wilensky has called the "contact man," who "supplies political and ideological intelligence the leader needs in order to find his way around modern society,"[29] and to the tightly drawn communication systems between the media and officials.[30] As many have discovered, the formal organization chart is at best a crude first approximation to actual operational channels of communication; appreciating this can frequently improve the transmission and realtime monitoring of implementation procedures.[31]

Ideas from cybernetic control theory concentrate on system-level, as contrasted with individual-level, details that are often essential in comprehending how specific actions are accomplished. Thus, concepts such as lead time, loads, and lags in system responsiveness have all been employed to theoretical and practical advantage by those interested in implementation.[32] For instance, increasing lead time through initiation and estimation actions may enhance implementation by allowing those responsible to anticipate and prepare for new or additional responsibilities. A great deal of the postwar Japanese commercial success can be traced to conscious efforts to extend the lead time associated with specific policy and program decisions.[33] Systems that are overloaded, such as the drug enforcement component of New York City's Police Department, must necessarily treat criminals differently than those in which police manpower, courts, and prisons are not as constrained.[34] One should not expect instantaneous response to commands from systems, especially if they are complex, encumbered by lengthy chains of communication and dispersed authority, or hindered by insufficient resources.

PULLING THE THREADS TOGETHER

Implementation is a complex subject. No one theory of implementation exists, nor, given the difficulty and richness of the topic, is it ever likely to be created. This does not mean, however, that theories are irrelevant to implementation; the previous discussion is intended to demonstrate that they are, if at least in a preliminary manner. Indeed, for particularly troublesome or important instances of implementation, it may very well be worth the time and effort to consider the matter from several theoretical perspectives so as to obtain a better understanding of just how complicated such matters can be. Ignoring the complication has far less to commend it.

Programs and policies that accord with the needs and values of those asked to execute them stand a better chance than those in which conflicts are created. This idea is stimulated in reflecting on the often extreme differences that exist between demonstration programs and their subsequent adoption. For example, in the Vietnam War, pacified villages or strategic hamlets seemed to be a very promising way to "win the hearts and minds" of rural Vietnamese; model or demonstration projects "proved" the feasibility and desirability of the concept and resulted in massive expenditures to bring the program to all of the countryside. The expanded version was a failure, of course, and a key element certainly had to be related to the differences in need and value that existed between administrators of the demonstrations and those ordered to carry out the larger program.[35] Issues of ability—measured in talent and resources—counted, too, but not nearly so much as those engendered at a more fundamental human level.[36]

If respect, deference, or prestige attend a new program or policy—from the perspective of those being asked to carry it out—compliance and effective execution are often enhanced. Military commanders realize the value of objectively valueless little bits of ribbon and metal; according to Ralph Siu, "There has never been a person of great power who failed to recognize the indissoluble relationship between ceremonial reinforcement and social control."[37]

Organizational theorists regularly describe the relationship between the size of new undertakings, their inherent complexity, and the difficulty and time required to see something happen.[38] Small and simple are preferred to big and complex if the objective is efficient and effective implementation.[39] Likewise, if one can actually see an example of what is being asked, particularly for bureaucratic or institutional practices, compliance and easier and speedier implementation often occur.

Implementation may be considered as a social process quite akin to innovation, thus providing a temporal perspective and points of reference to enhance our working definition of the term. At the very beginning, when choices have been made about what to do, few will be able to appreciate the numerous and important difficulties that in time will be encountered. Practical matters, such as the feasibility of the policy or program, typically play second fiddle to political ones, such as the desirability of making the proposed changes. Let us call this *initial introduction,* a time of high hopes and expectations about what can and must be done. Another way of thinking about it is by relating initial introduction to the transition between selection and implementation, in the more general scheme of this book.

The second phase is *reaction.* Those with vested interests realize that they could be involved and—if threatened—mobilize accordingly.[40] The creation-as-destruction phenomenon is most pronounced at this point. Whether or not the threat is real matters less than the general heightening of structural, economic, and power insecurities associated with the proposed change. There is usually a time lag between introduction and reaction as coalitions form and responsive routines evolve for and against the proposal. Depending on the collective perceptions of the threats presented, the reaction may be even unnoticeable. A common institutional pattern is to ignore the proposal in hopes that it will simply disappear or at least become neutralized. In this case, resistance is downplayed out of concern for provoking or challenging those responsible for the decision to stiffen their resolve. At the other extreme, the reaction may be hostile and even result in open confrontation between the proponents and the targets of the new endeavor. Blends of these reactions are to be expected in different circumstances. Whatever the reaction, response of some sort is predictable; it will add time to the unfolding implementation act and can, varying from context to context, alter the initial proposal. If sufficiently hostile and powerful, the reaction may result in deadlock or serious modifications based on reconsiderations of costs, benefits, feasibility, and overall worthiness. Many case studies of implementation failures focus on this particular aspect of the process and fail to consider its totality.

The next and usually less stressful phase is *partial incorporation,* during which time the limitations and opportunities afforded by the proposal are exposed. There is real experience, not merely imaginings and fears; threats and conflict levels are appreciated, if not understood and reduced. Accommodations have had time to be worked out, and individuals have learned to cope with the new programs and their ramifications. Determining the responses of all relevant participants yields an expected course and pattern for the actual, modified proposal. Partial incorporation allows roles, practices, and procedures to be adjusted and, in due course, may lead to general acceptance and routine operations.

Acceptance and *routinization,* the final phase, are analogous to diffusion in the theoretical literature on innovation. Very few proposals ("The remarkable thing is that new programs work at all,"[41]) reach this state and, if they do, they are substantially modified from the initial concept. The proposal or decision (or new policy or program), much changed in character and perhaps altered in purpose, is now accepted and becomes part of the established routine. Or it may be adopted by others in locations removed from the site of original incursion; for instance, studies have been done on the progression of new policies and programs from state to state[42] and city to city[43] in recognition of this possibility. For each new location, however, one expects some version of the introduction/reaction/partial incorporation/acceptance sequence to occur—with less difficulty and over less time, if learning has been occurring apace.

In keeping with our plan to alternate between the theory and practice of implementation, we now review a variety of actual examples.

FROM CASE TO SYSTEM EXAMPLES

As is evident in the discussion to this point, most literature and scholarship on implementation derive from case study examples. We have sampled these experiences to relate their more prominent features to representative and emerging bodies of theoretical insight. In case after case, one discovers that the multiplication and proliferation of programs intended, in various ways and with quite different means, to accomplish policy ends have tended to get out of control. We next discuss relatively coherent and definable fields or systems, including human services, oceans, and national defense. These illustrations treat only selected aspects—those thought to be interesting from a control perspective—but they help one appreciate implementation processes from a more complex standpoint than the solitary case study.

Human services

Health, education, and welfare services have, over the last 40 years, evolved into a highly fragmented, ad hoc, and complicated patchwork of programs often found to be incapable of satisfying the diverse demands placed upon them. This view is articulated by former Health, Education, and Welfare Secretary Richardson:

> There is, in my opinion, a developing crisis—still largely hidden—facing the human service sector of our society, a crisis which may challenge the fundamental capability of our society to govern itself.
>
> *   *   *   *   *
>
> It is a crisis of control—in many fundamental respects the human service system is developing beyond the scope of Executive control . . . or of Congressional control . . . or of consumer control . . . or of public control.[44]

If this assessment is even partly correct, and events of the last decade particularly seem to sustain it, we must begin diagnosing the problem so as to resolve it. Implementation, in the sense of institutional performance that lives up to expectations, is an important element in such a diagnosis.

Complexity of administration, taken to mean numerous policies and programs with attendant action agencies and bureaus, has consequences for the development of new proposals and for effective service delivery. In the field of programs and services for exceptional children, a representative case, implementation has haphazardly occurred over the years in the absence of any comprehensive, guiding policy. It has been left to a bewildering array of offices and agencies at all levels of government, and the results have been far from satisfactory. With respect to any defined population of exceptional children (e.g., gifted and talented, learning disabled, sensorially impaired, malnourished, abused, retarded), no one really knows very well the whole collection of programs and services that exists and to which these individuals are entitled.[45] In the words of Hobbs, "In Washington, programs for exceptional children are lodged in a myriad of agencies on authorization of hundreds of separate pieces of legislation that defy complete understanding and make coordination of effort extremely difficult."[46] For example, the task of inventorying existing programs for exceptional children has not been done; it is no one institution's responsibility. But lacking such basic information, no agency or individual can know how a new policy or program proposal is likely to relate, complement, or conflict with those already in place. Simply, no one knows. No parent or family, in the present situation, can be expected to know either: to know what is available, what their child needs and could benefit from, and what they are entitled to. As it stands, the system currently providing services to the nation's exceptional children—a more than $15 billion federal outlay each year—is so complex and disorganized as to defy efficient and effective operations.[47]

Oceans

The world's oceans are rapidly becoming the focus of extraordinary opportunity and even more formidable difficulties.[48] The lack of a guiding policy in this realm has resulted in numerous implementation difficulties; the Reagan Administration's decision "not to decide" about the United States' role or participation in the complex Law of the Sea Convention and agreements only served to underscore a chronic incoherence of policy objectives.[49] While one may quibble with the details in the following assessment, its basic message and insights into implementation matters are hard to dispute:

> Despite all the efforts of the American people, the Congress, and the President to focus on a national ocean program, despite the several acts and administrative reorganizations within the federal government, and despite the extraordinary resources channeled to scientific research, surveys, vessel construction, subsidies, and other forms of aid to the marine community . . . it was doubtful whether the resources of the eleven departments and agencies closely involved with marine affairs "are being applied to best serve national purpose." What troubled many observers of the development of American policy for the oceans was the fragmentation of the decision-making process into several agencies, often competing or overlapping in their functions. Washington, beset not only by the organized interests of the shipping indus-

try, fishermen, energy producers, environmentalists, and others but also traumatized by the politics of its bureaucracies, seemed inept in setting priorities and incapable of implementing a strong purposeful ocean policy to embrace both domestic and international needs.[50]

Careful analysis of the situation reveals that serious gaps, breakdowns, and inconsistencies characterize U.S. marine and ocean policy and contribute heavily to the general unsatisfactory state of affairs.[51] Not surprisingly, implementation errors sharply contribute to the current chaos. For instance, determining what agencies have the lead responsibility for the various decisions that have been put into effect, i.e., the source of policy, has never been definitely resolved. Policy comes from multiple origins: presidential directives (various reorganization plans affecting marine affairs); the passage of legislation (e.g., Outer Continental Shelf Lands Act of 1953); simple administrative decisions (allocation of the U.S. Coast Guard's annual budget to various activities); and actions of one of several types of courts, conferences, or international bodies (Law of the Sea Conferences). Each source has performed different functions and represents different roles that often determine how a policy and related programs are defined, selected, and implemented. In the case of the Merchant Marine Act of 1953 (P.L. 91–469), the fact that federal legislation is the most obvious source of policy is essential, but it is not the only fact worth examining. A careful reading of its hearings and the subsequent law indicates that only scant consideration of its many complex provisions; likewise, a relative handful of powerful special interests participated in the enabling debate.[52] Support for the bill was not overwhelming and leads one to suspect that the resulting vague language of the statute might well have occurred in the interests of consensus building and eventual passage. This interpretation is quite plausible in light of the implementation experience. How are the actions of other policy sources, e.g., local courts, regional bodies, national agencies (such as the Defense Department), or international commissions, likely to influence or reshape the policy through time? Little is known here because necessary follow-up analysis has not taken place. In this case, it appears as though effective implementation was rendered nearly impossible, and a careful assessment of the source, including the incentives and motivations of the key participants, could have led to this judgment even as the legislation was being formulated.[53]

The complexity of administrative processes figures here, too. Generally the further removed the decision maker from the implementing agent and the client, the greater the opportunity for distortions or variations of the policy from its original intent. The Commercial Fisheries Research and Development Act of 1964, as amended, illustrates some of what is at issue here. According to Mangone, intent and reality are sharply at odds:

The overblown expectations of invigorating the American fishery industry while assisting the developing nations of the world were thwarted by the initial high costs of manufacture, wrangling within the industry and government, bureaucratic inertia, and weak responses in the undernourished countries. Least hopeful was the conservative attitude of the U.S. Food and Drug Administration, which first regarded the crushed fishmeat and bones as "filthy" and then as possibly dangerous with their residues of lead and fluoride.[54]

This again calls attention to the essential question of how involved high-level decision makers should become to ensure that a program is implemented as intended. Out of necessity, one cannot expect them to be involved in the day-to-day details. A more parsimonious strategy is to stress evaluation, careful specification of intent, and a thorough consideration of the motivation and incentives of those detailed to carry out the program. In this case, such an appreciation and style were absent, leading to the conclusion that, "whether the total investment of public revenues into fisheries had justified the return to the economy of the nation was debatable."[55]

More than economic costs are involved, and the persistent, nettlesome relations the United States sustains with both Canada and Mexico are only one indication. Failure to ratify a bilateral fishery treaty with the Canadians, after many years of difficult negotiations, has transformed fishing disputes into heated exchanges which may "affect the planned construction of a U.S. natural gas pipeline across Canada and joint measures under discussion to combat acid-rain pollution."[56] In the Mexican case, a failure of policy and inconsistent treatment of American tuna boats encroaching on Mexican territorial waters led the Lopez Portillo government in 1981 to terminate a variety of fishing accords with the United States and has resulted in a "mushrooming into a major issue and concern growing in the U.S. over the illegal or undocumented worker situation."[57] In the latter case, it appears as though existing policy has been largely determined by and in favor of a small, highly influential special interest group of tuna-boat owners.

Defense

Grave questions must be raised regarding the nation's abilities to control its weapons of war—an implementation problem of extraordinary magnitude and devastating potential consequence. For instance, in a 1977 assessment, the Office of Management and Budget framed the problem as follows: "Serious questions persist about the effectiveness of the command structure for the conduct of war, for peacetime activities, and for crisis management."[58] Others have raised the alarm over the years,[59] but planning for strategic operations and the development of operational forces and doctrine both continue as if flexible, reliable, and positive control over the forces were a reality.[60] It is not.

There is a consistent tendency among strategic analysts and decision makers to shortchange the institutional matters related to control—

implementation.[61] For instance, former Secretary of Defense James Schlesinger postulated some preconditions for success to implement a strategy of flexible response, the prevailing mode: "Maintain continued communications with the Soviet leaders during the war [and] indoctrinate and plan in anticipation of the difficulties involved."[62] But as many point out, the institutional supports for those conditions are sketchy, superficially analyzed, and usually treated as givens, implying that large and complex organizations could be managed effectively during nuclear war. A more realistic conclusion has been stated by Steinbruner:

> There are strong reasons to believe, or to fear . . . that realistic flexibility—the availability under combat conditions of more than a single plan—is sharply limited by the vulnerability of command channels, and that the dangers of losing central command over strategic operations shortly after the initiation of even very moderate levels of warfare are very great indeed.[63]

The underlying problem, in somewhat oversimplified terms, appears to be related to "the principle preoccupation of the U.S. military" with the "acquisition of more and especially more expensive hardware, such as computers, satellites, secure transmission lines, and the like. All this miraculous gadgetry and the formidable acronyms that go with it have consistently come up short on performance."[64] One's ability to generate and process ever-increasing amounts of data is not the same as being able to interpret the meanings contained in them, nor is it the same as guaranteeing control over the individuals and institutions the data might portray. The sheer complexity of the military systems edges them toward chaos. Implementation has been ignored and disconnected from sources of authority and control.[65]

Ironically, even technical issues seem to have been shortchanged. A stunning series of articles in *Science* has publicized the existence and likely consequences of a physical phenomenon known as electromagnetic pulse or EMP.[66] "Defense strategists today assume that a single Soviet warhead detonated 200 miles above Nebraska would knock out unprotected communications equipment all across the United States. The reason is electromagnetic pulse, a byproduct of high-altitude nuclear explosions that blankets huge tracts of the earth with peak fields of 50,000 volts per meter."[67] The implications of EMP are spelled out: "A single nuclear blast high above the United States could shut down the power grid and knock out communications from coast to coast."[68] One possibility of this is that, "the President might not be able to issue the last call to arms due to the chaos-producing effects of electromagnetic pulse."[69]

Such a terrifying and exotic event may not even be necessary to paralyze the strategic command structure. According to the U.S. General Accounting Office, reported in *Science*, the World Wide Military Command and Control System "is unreliable and inadequate because of poor design and management," a condition known to exist "all the way back to 1970," when officials "complained about the . . . equipment," but to no avail as "the Joint Chiefs . . . ignored their pleas."[70]

One would hope that something could be done about these problems, although the capacity for learning in such matters appears slight. This from a sensitive observer of World War I:

> Men are reluctant to believe that great events have small causes. There-fore, once the Great War started, they were convinced that it must be the outcome of profound forces. It is hard to discover these when we examine the details. Nowhere was there conscious determination to provoke a war. States-men miscalculated. . . . This time things went wrong. The deterrent on which they relied failed to deter; the statesmen became the prisoners of their own weapons. The great armies, accumulated to provide security and preserve the peace, carried the nations to war by their own weight.[71]

And from Vietnam: "[E]very generation is doomed to fight its war, to endure the same old experiences, suffer the loss of the same old illusions, and learn the same old lessons on its own."[72] The nuclear environment leaves little time to learn but would exact a terrible tuition.

The foregoing discussions are far from complete in their coverage of implementation experiences. They do, however, help to emphasize several consistent points and themes. Implementation is a significant problem; an appreciation of the enormity of the implementation task helps one under-stand why analysts and practitioners alike have been loathe to address the topic with enthusiasm.

IMPLICATIONS: WHAT MIGHT ALL OF THIS MEAN?

It is a wonder that anything ever gets done, much less according to anyone's rational plan for action. Faced with tremendous complexity suf-ficient to make the understanding of all but commonplace problems ques-tionable, and beset with multiple and conflicting renditions of what is desired and how best to attain it, those responsible for policy and program implementation should not be faulted when even the best laid plans run amok.[73]

Successful implementation can be conceived of in terms of command-obey only in situations where relatively certain knowledge about a prob-lem's causal structure is joined with a clear and widely shared commitment to outcomes. In such rare instances, implementation can and should be swift, sure, and efficient. Should goals be uncertain or in fundamental conflict or should knowledge about a problem in which answers are sought be dubious, different styles of implementation and different criteria of acceptability hold (Table 10–1).

Experience strongly suggests that conditions marked by certainty of knowledge and certainty about desired outcomes (cell 1) are exceptional in most public policy arenas. Were this not the case, rational calculation and

TABLE 10-1   Certainty, knowledge, and goals: Implementation styles and criteria

		Knowledge about problem	
		Certain	Uncertain
Goals *(outcomes desired)*	Certain	1. Implementation by calculation; efficiency.	2. Implementation by judgment; goal attainment— "Yes" or "No"?
	Uncertain	3. Implementation by adjustment; institutional learning.	4. Implementation by inspiration; maximal participation . . . social learning.

Source: John Gerard Ruggie, "Complexity, Planning, and Public Order," in Todd R. La Porte, ed., *Organized Social Complexity: Challenge to Politics and Policy.* Copyright © 1975 by Princeton University Press. Adaptation of Table 4–1, p. 149, by permission of Princeton University Press. Reprinted by permission of Princeton University Press.

efficiency maximization—behavior exemplified by many estimation specialists and their methodologies—would have solved far more social problems than has been the case.[74] Rather, as we have argued, the reliance on rational analysis, computers, and other scientific tools consistently has been misplaced and has often contributed to the difficulties of implementation.[75]

In those few circumstances where a consistent set of goals can be determined, but where realistic knowledge of the problem is uncertain (cell 2), implementation can be left to the judgment of those to whom the task has been entrusted or delegated; appraisal of their efforts, in time, becomes a relatively straightforward matter of deciding whether or not the goal or goals have been achieved.

In situations of military conflict, winning may appear to be a consistent and clear goal whose attainment should be left to military specialists. Even here, however, one can be misled by the apparent simplicity of the concept of winning, which may mean very different things to those involved. The Vietnam War offers multiple divisive experiences. In his memoirs, Maxwell Taylor, who was deeply involved in Vietnam decision making during the Kennedy Administration, asserts that U.S. expectations of probable North Vietnamese objectives and negotiation behavior were based on a simple assumption about winning: "We were inclined to assume . . . they would seek an accommodation with us when the cost of pursuing a losing course became excessive. Instead, the North Vietnamese proved to be incredibly tough in accepting losses which, by Western calculation, greatly exceeded the value of the stakes involved."[76] Clearly this implementation problem existed in neither a cell 1 or a cell 2 environment, as Taylor and others mistakenly presumed.

When one presumes that knowledge about a problem is certain (or can be readily obtained) but clarity about goals or outcomes is not, implementation may proceed by adjustments or steps that allow various individuals or institutions to try out or learn from different experiential possibilities (cell 3). For many but no means all social problems, this style of implementation and associated criterion of appraisal may suffice.[77] However, convinced of the uncertainty of knowledge associated with problems of organized social complexity and further saddled with multiple, uncertain, and often conflicting renditions of what a policy or program should accomplish—again, the prevalent case—a very different style of implementation and criterion of appraisal are indicated (cell 4). Bluntly, implementation in these circumstances is best considered as error making in the face of complexity, the practical implications of which have scarcely been considered.

One general implication for the policy analyst is to design implementation strategies and means as simply as possible.[78] Given the usual complexity of problems and settings, great ingenuity and no small amount of inspiration will be required. Both are necessary to stem the tide of implementation failures caused in part by excessively complicated administrative machinery. As the military command-and-control example points out, the machinery has been allowed to grow so cumbersome and complicated that serious doubts exist about its ability to function at all. The resort to novel approaches and out-of-the ordinary talent, described by Broad, to grapple with this problem may be interpreted as an attempt to regain control through simplification, or it may be seen as an act of desperation.[79]

Inspiration, taken to mean flexibility and adaptability, also suggests a fundamental change in bureaucratic thinking about the appropriateness of single solutions to difficult problems. Prior to implementation, the weight of knowledge about a problem is largely imaginary or synthetic; only during implementation is there a reconciliation of preconceptions and hopes with realistic experience. Hence, there is no logical basis to fix on single answers to poorly understood problems having numerous potential solutions and outcomes. Recognition of this point could be reflected in a restructuring of bureaucratic incentives and rewards, much as Campbell has suggested in distinguishing between "trapped" administrators (the prevalent case) and "experimental" ones.[80] One result of this is the social experiment,[81] although the large-scale and complication of many of these have created implementation problems of exactly the sort we seek to avoid.[82] Rather, what is envisioned is a reward system that encourages administrators to search for solutions to local problems where it is expected that specific circumstances—and specific solutions—will differ from place to place. Moderation and commonsense will be essential, as will periodic assessments of the kind and quality of adaptations actually encountered. Implementation success is thus not preordained but derives from realistic situations.[83]

A specific implication worth analytic attention is the need to weigh changes in the patterns of resource availability and distribution likely to result from proposed policies or programs. More than just a reminder to attend to contextual matters, this point stresses that little opposition will come from those who stand to gain, but resistance from those who bear the costs nearly always occurs. Appreciation of this can, to a certain extent, be translated into implementation acts having compensatory provisions, or at least one will have a better idea of where the opposition resides. The ocean policy example illustrates that concern narrowly favoring only the beneficiaries of many specific marine programs resulted in unexpected and negative reactions from those disadvantaged by them; at least this is a plausible explanation for the intensely negative responses stimulated in the Mexicans and Canadians.

A general implication for the policymaker is to consider the possibility that a given requirement could be accomplished through non- or quasi-governmental means.[84] There is no hard and fast rule stating that problems being resolved publicly must be administered entirely by public officials and institutions. This is not a plea for marketplace solutions to every problem, nor is it an excuse for public officials to shirk their responsibilities. It is a recognition that governments are often not very adept at delivering the goods. A certain degree of inspiration and a willingness to take additional risks appears warranted here. Chase makes the general point vividly for the health field, where "most services in the United States are delivered by the private voluntary sector. It makes sense, at least conceptually, to tap these resources when appropriate."[85]

Broadening and enriching the base of participation in decision making and implementation are warranted on several grounds, not the least of which is an overriding goal of enhancing democratic values. The matter is more than symbolic, however. In situations where uncertainty predominates about what is to be accomplished and for whose account, it is important to secure a solid understanding of the variety of goals and values implicated in policy actions. This can hardly be done if significant points of view are excluded intentionally or overlooked inadvertently. This does not mean that everyone must get directly into the act; it does mean that representative viewpoints need to be considered in light of proposed and eventual action.[86] As shown in the previous human services example, citizens are often able to perceive their own needs and the circumstances surrounding those needs with sensitivity and realism. The citizen viewpoint of the handicapped children's system was essential in calling expert and authoritative attention to many fixable implementation problems and in helping set priorities for future action.

Social learning is also strongly implied in this prescription and stresses the essential connection between implementation and evaluation phases of the overall policy process. If mistakes are the rule in implementation, and they seem to be, then one needs to consider action strategies having reversible consequences. For example, scientists know that a nuclear power plant will not last forever; at some point these facilities begin to wear out or to be superceded by more efficient, technologically advanced ones. However, this practical matter has not been incorporated directly in the planning and execution of nuclear power plants, with the result that adequate provision for plant decommissioning has not been made. In part provision has not been made because no one required the utilities to factor in these considerable costs—in their planning, rate structure, or set-asides to pay for decommissioning. One must consider more than just the costs of doing something; the costs of undoing something, should it not work out or when time comes to stop, are also relevant and may be large.

CONCLUSIONS

The foregoing discussions suggest some of the difficulties in understanding and analyzing implementation and getting it to work. These difficulties are inherent in the governmental system; we should not seek to find scapegoats in venal or incompetent bureaucrats. Martha Derthick comments:

> If the federal government is unable to do in domestic affairs what its leaders say it will, this is not necessarily because the men who run it, either as elected officials, presidential appointees, or high-ranking civil servants, are lazy, incompetent, or deceitful. If they delude the public as to what to expect of government, it is because they delude themselves as well. They too are puzzled and disillusioned when things go wrong and government programs do not fulfill their promise.[87]

This is not say that bureaucratic incompetence and fraud do not exist. Both exist and take their toll.[88] However, the impact of corruption or incompetence is probably minimal next to the effect of the tremendous problems endemic in implementation.

More serious than simple incompetence is the enormous stress that implementation puts on program managers, especially those responsible for large, innovative programs. Writing about the Elementary and Secondary Education Act, Bailey and Mosher express the doubt and uncertainty that attend implementation.

> When, as in the case of ESEA, a law unprecedented in scope has to be administered through state and local instrumentalities, on an impossible time schedule, by an understaffed agency in structural turmoil, beset by a deluge of complaints and demands for clarification of the legislation at hand, as well as cognate legislation already on the books, the wonder is not that mistakes are made—the wonder is that the law is implemented at all.[89]

The sentiment is echoed by Levine drawing on his experiences in the Office of Economic Opportunity to observe that projects have

> to be implemented by program operators who may or may not have been in sympathy with the plans, may or may not have even understood them, but in any case will certainly be governed by their own motives and imperatives,

both personal and programmatic. . . . It is a wonder that anyone ever thought it would work.[90]

When we consider the resources necessary to put a given program into effect, the number of people involved, the amount of coordination required within and among agencies, the visibility of activity (as contrasted with other phases of the policy process), and other numerous factors, we begin to appreciate the magnitude of the task of effective implementation. It is understandable that analysts have been largely unable to treat the subject with any appreciable analytic rigor, let alone prescriptive insight.[91] Policymakers appear equally reluctant to tackle the substantive issues of implementation. Relating anecdotes and pleading *nolo contendere* to Murphy's Law, they promise better implementation the next time and to that end issue a new set of rules or initiate new planning procedures. But rules themselves are subject to varying interpretations by the actors throughout the system; conditions change and plans generally fail to account for the unexpected organizational or personal obstacles that arise. Such realities must somehow be grasped and made more operational and appropriate implementation strategies devised and matched to prevailing conditions.

To borrow Bardach's metaphor, the rules and players of the implementation game are still obscure, let alone one's even being able to imagine what winning means.[92] To gain these important insights, we must systematically investigate the dynamics of implementation and understand how it functions in the entire policy process before we can expect to understand and improve the execution of policy. The task is hardly easy, but we have already seen the cost of ignoring implementation in the wages of policy failure.

IMPLEMENTATION IN THE POLICY PROCESS

The many important relationships between implementation and selection phases of the process have been covered extensively in this and the preceding chapters. One needs only be reminded that explicit separation of the two phases only occurred within recent memory in the scholarly consciousness and literature, and then only when repeated discrepancies between intended decisions and actual results brought the distinctiveness out in the open.

Even before policy and program results begin to amass, there is both need and opportunity to consider evaluation. Beginning with formal statements decreeing or authorizing action and careful analysis of key contributing features, one is often able to discern performance criteria or expectations about "What is supposed to happen, when, at what cost?" and the like. As a program unfolds, especially in its earliest stages, evaluation can be expected to signal difficulties and alert those responsible to needed corrections. The path between implementation and evaluation can be clear and frequently traveled, and it usually is in more successful programs.

Later in a program's life or in the event that early returns are far afield from what was expected, major changes may be called for, including fundamental reestimates of the problem or amendments or alterations to its enabling decisions. Another possible connection between implementation and evaluation occurs when the lessons learned by doing something in one locale are codified and readied for use in another. Expanding from a narrow experience base of demonstration or pilot programs to full-scale operations nearly always demands some sort of evaluation.

Implementation's linkage to estimation could be less tenuous than it usually is. Were this so, the information generated during implementation could improve analyses of subsequent problem-solving activities. To what extent were prior estimation efforts accurate in prejudging and anticipating actual problems encountered in implementation? Where inaccurate, can the causes be discovered and improvements made?

Additionally, implementation may cause new or unexpected problems of sufficient importance or scope to require separate treatment, again, from the very beginning, or initiation. Experience may indicate that the problem was simply misunderstood, in which case a recycling through the policy process from the very beginning may be called for.

As stressed previously, one person's implementation is quite often someone else's termination—as concerns the disruption or destabilization of the status quo.

NOTES

1. Jeffrey Pressman and Aaron Wildavsky, *Implementation* (Berkeley: University of California Press, 1973), p. 109.

2. Garry D. Brewer, "On Innovation, Social Change, and Reality," *Technological Forecasting and Social Change* 5, no. 1 (1973), pp. 19–24.

3. Chap. 5, "Estimation as Simplification."

4. Frederick W. Taylor, *The Principles of Scientific Management* (New York: Harper & Row, 1911), especially pp. 9–29, where the underlying assumptions are noted.

5. H. H. Gerth and C. Wright Mills, eds., trans. *From Max Weber: Essays in Sociology* (New York: Oxford University Press, 1946), pp. 210–14.

6. Luther Gulick and Lyndall Urwick, eds., *Papers on the Science of Administration* (New York: Institute of Public Administration, Columbia University, 1937).

7. Chester Barnard, *The Functions of the Executive* (Cambridge, Mass.: Harvard University Press, 1938), is a pronounced example of this.

8. The following summary discussion is freely drawn from a much larger status report: Garry D. Brewer, "On the Theory and Practice of Innovation," *Technology In Society,* Fall 1980, pp. 337–63.

9. The issue of implementation incentives is the theme binding the articles collected by John Brigham and Don W. Brown, eds., *Policy Implementation: Penalties or Incentives?* (Beverly Hills, Calif.: Sage Publications, 1980).

10. Milbrey Wallin McLaughlin, *Evaluation and Reform: The Elementary and Secondary Education Act of 1965, Title I* (Cambridge, Mass.: Ballinger, 1975), is a specific illustra-

tion in which contextual matters overpowered the best, albeit simplistic, federal intentions in the education field.

11. Erwin C. Hargrove, *The Missing Link: The Study of Implementation of Social Policy* (Washington, D.C.: The Urban Institute, 1975), details the necessary intellectual connection.

12. Recall our earlier discussion of Franklin Roosevelt's administrative style. See also, P. G. Zimbardo and E. E. Ebbesen, *Influencing Attitudes and Changing Behavior* (Reading, Mass.: Addison-Wesley, 1969), for a theoretical treatment of many of the same issues.

13. Thomas E. Borcherding, ed., *Budgets and Bureaucrats: The Sources of Government Growth* (Durham, N.C.: Duke University Press, 1977).

14. Warren G. Bennis, *Changing Organizations* (New York: McGraw-Hill, 1966); and Daniel Katz and Robert L. Kahn, *The Social Psychology of Organizations* (New York: John Wiley & Sons, 1966).

15. Herbert Kaufman, *Are Government Organizations Immortal?* (Washington, D.C.: The Brookings Institution, 1976). With few exceptions, the answer seems to be "Yes."

16. Richard M. Johnson, *The Dynamics of Compliance: Supreme Court Decision-Making from a New Perspective* (Evanston, Ill.: Northwestern University Press, 1967).

17. Chris Argyris, *Personality and Organization* (New York: Harper & Row, 1970); Robert H. Guest, *Organizational Change: The Effect of Successful Leadership* (Homewood, Ill.: Dorsey Press, 1962); and Zimbardo and Ebbesen, *Influencing Attitudes and Changing Behavior*, all represent approaches from this perspective.

18. George W. Downs, Jr., *Bureaucracy, Innovation and Public Policy* (Lexington, Mass.: D. C. Heath, 1976).

19. Martin Greenberger, Matthew A. Crenson, and Brian L. Crissey, *Models in the Policy Process: Public Decision Making in the Computer Era* (New York: Russell Sage Foundation, 1976), contains a thorough and nonpartisan reconstruction of the events.

20. Paul Berman and Milbrey Wallin McLaughlin, *Federal Programs Supporting Educational Change: A Model of Educational Change* (Santa Monica, Calif.: The Rand Corporation, R–1589/1, September 1974), is an excellent exploration of this possibility.

21. An example of what we have in mind here is Steven R. Brown, "Consistency and Persistency of Ideology: Some Experimental Results," *Public Opinion Quarterly*, Spring 1970, pp. 60–68.

22. David B. Truman, *The Governmental Process: Political Interests and Public Opinion* (New York: Alfred A. Knopf, 1951).

23. Robert A. Dahl, *A Preface to Democratic Theory* (Chicago: University of Chicago Press, 1956), p. 147.

24. Lester W. Milbrath, *The Washington Lobbyists* (Skokie, Ill.: Rand McNally, 1963).

25. M. Margaret Conway and Frank B. Feigert, *Political Analysis* (Boston: Allyn and Bacon, 1976), chap. 8.

26. Charles Perrow, *Organizational Analysis* (Belmont, Calif.: Wadsworth, 1970); Paul S. Goodman and Johannes M. Pennings, *New Perspectives on Organizational Effectiveness* (San Francisco: Jossey-Bass, 1977); and Peter M. Blau and W. Richard Scott, *Formal Organizations* (San Francisco: Chandler, 1962), represent different versions of the field.

27. James W. Fesler, *Public Administration: Theory and Practice* (Englewood Cliffs, N.J.: Prentice-Hall, 1980), is a starting point for exploration of the public dimension; he provides thorough coverage and an excellent bibliography of the field. A recent collection with a private sector slant is P. C. Nystrom and W. H. Starbuck, eds., *Handbook of Organizational Design* (New York: Oxford University Press, 1980).

28. Eugene Bardach, "Subformal Warning Systems in the Species *Homo Politicus,*" *Policy Sciences*, December 1974, pp. 415–31.

29. Harold Wilensky, *Organizational Intelligence* (New York: Basic Books, 1967), p. 10.

30. Leon V. Sigal, *Reporters and Officials* (Lexington, Mass.: D. C. Heath, 1973).

31. Harold Guetzkow, "Communications in Organizations," in James G. March, ed., *Handbook of Organizations* (Skokie, Ill.: Rand McNally, 1965), pp. 534–73.

32. Karl W. Deutsch, *The Nerves of Government* (New York: Free Press, 1966); and John D. Steinbruner, *The Cybernetic Theory of Decision* (Princeton, N.J.: Princeton University Press, 1974), both can be viewed in this manner, although neither was written from a specific implementation perspective. General systems theory, particularly its sociological interpretations, can be similarly reinterpreted: See Ludwig von Bertalanffy, *General Systems Theory* (New York: Brasiller, 1968); and Walter Buckley, *Sociology and Modern Systems Theory* (Englewood Cliffs, N.J.: Prentice-Hall, 1967), respectively.

33. Chitoshi Yanaga, *Big Business in Japanese Politics* (New Haven: Yale University Press, 1968), chaps. 3 and 4, is illustrative.

34. Gilbert Levin, Edward B. Roberts, and Gary B. Hirsch, *The Persistent Poppy* (Cambridge, Mass.: Ballinger, 1975), develop a computer model having precisely this operational feature.

35. Douglas Pike, *Viet Cong* (Cambridge, Mass.: MIT Press, 1966), pp. 61–73, is one source on strategic hamlets.

36. This opinion is based on Brewer's experience with 20 or more of the strategic hamlets in the middle 1960s. They "worked" if the desire to make them work existed. A question remains, however, whether success of a full-scale program might have ever been attained, given the extreme cultural difference between the Vietnamese and the Americans and the limited number of committed administrators.

37. R. G. H. Siu, *The Craft of Power* (New York: John Wiley & Sons, 1979), "Orchestrating Ceremonies," pp. 143–59, at p. 143.

38. Gerald Zaltman, Robert Duncan, and Jonny Holbek, *Innovations in Organizations* (New York: John Wiley & Sons, 1973).

39. Paul R. Schulman, *Large-Scale Policy Making* (New York: Elsevier, 1980).

40. Eugene Bardach, *The Implementation Game*, (Cambridge, Mass.: MIT Press, 1977), addresses many of these conditions from the bureaucratic perspective.

41. Pressman and Wildavsky, *Implementation*, p. 109.

42. Jack L. Walker, "The Diffusion of Innovations in the American States," *American Political Science Review*, September 1969, pp. 880–99; and Paul Berman and Milbrey Wallin McLaughlin, *Federal Programs Supporting Educational Change* (Santa Monica, Calif.: The Rand Corporation, R–1589/8, 1978).

43. Robert K. Yin, *Changing Urban Bureaucracies: How New Practices Become Routinized* (Lexington, Mass.: Lexington Books, 1979).

44. Elliot L. Richardson, *Responsibility and Responsiveness*, vol. II (Washington, D.C.: Department of Health, Education and Welfare, January 18, 1973), pp. 1–2. [Note: This is a different document than the one of the same title cited earlier in Chapter 9; this is volume II.]

45. These general themes are taken and developed throughout Edward Zigler, Sharon L. Kagan, and Edgar Klugman, eds., *Children, Families, and Government* (New York: Cambridge University Press, 1983). A detailed examination of special education, the most costly of all exceptional-children's services, is contained in Erwin C. Hargrove et al., *Regulations and Schools: The Implementation of Equal Education for Handicapped Children* (Nashville, Tenn.: Institute for Public Policy Studies, Vanderbilt University, March 1981).

46. Nicholas Hobbs, *The Futures of Children* (San Francisco: Jossey-Bass, 1975), p. 185.

47. Garry D. Brewer and James S. Kakalik, *Handicapped Children: Strategies for Improving Services* (New York: McGraw-Hill, 1979). The consumer's perspective is considered at length in chap. 8 and calls attention to the particularly demanding implementation problem of coordinating a mix of often very expensive services on behalf of the individual child, every one of whom presents a unique problem.

48. The opportunity and difficulty themes are highlighted in United Nations Food and Agriculture Organization, *FAO Fisheries Report No. 236* (Rome: FAO, FIRM/R236– En, 1980). Among other conclusions, the FAO report stresses the harm done to the world's stock of fish resources as a result of an unsystematic, piecemeal approach to its management.

49. "U.S. Says It Won't Review Sea-Law Proposal 'Till Fall," *Christian Science Monitor*, April 16, 1981, reports on the last-minute Reagan administration pull-back from the seven-year-old negotiations. U.S. General Accounting Office, *The Need for a National Ocean Program and Plan* (Washington, D.C.: Government Printing Office, Report B– 145099, October 1975), supplies the broader context of "nonpolicy" in the area.

50. Gerard J. Mangone, *Marine Policy for America* (Lexington, Mass.: D. C. Heath, 1977), pp. 39–40. Internal cite refers to U.S. General Accounting Office, *Need for a National Ocean Program.*

51. Francis Hoole, Robert Friedheim, and Tim Hennessey, eds., *Marine Policy Papers* (Boulder, Colo.: Westview Press, 1981), is one attempt at comprehensive diagnosis and remedy.

52. U.S. Congress, House, Committee on Merchant Marine and Fisheries, *Hearings on President's Maritime Program* (Washington, D.C.: Government Printing Office, No. 91– 17, 1970).

53. Charles L. Schultze, "The Role of Incentives, Penalities, and Rewards in Attaining Effective Policy," in Julius Margolis and Robert Haveman, eds., *Public Expenditures and Policy Analysis* (Chicago: Markham, 1970), pp. 145– 71; and Bardach, *Implementation Game*, provide, respectively, the practical and theoretical grounding that would aid one in reaching such a conclusion.

54. Mangone, *Marine Policy for America*, p. 137.

55. Ibid.

56. "Mending the US– Canada Fishing Net in Georges Bank," *Christian Science Monitor*, July 17, 1980.

57. James Nelson Goodsell, "Why Mexico Threw Its US Fishing Accords Overboard," *Christian Science Monitor*, December 30, 1980.

58. Office of Management and Budget, "Memorandum for the Secretary of Defense: Defense Reorganization" (Washington, D.C.: OMB, WH54276, September 20, 1977), p. 8.

59. Blue Ribbon Defense Panel, *Report to the President and the Secretary of Defense on the Department of Defense* (Washington, D.C.: Government Printing Office, July 1970). "[The existing command structure] provides little flexibility and a considerable potential for confusion in crisis situations." Pp. 53; and William J. Broad, "Philosophers at the Pentagon," *Science*, 24 October 1980, pp. 409– 12: "[Recent investigations by outsiders are meant] to find the means of orchestrating the cacophony now rampant in the U.S. command-control domain. . . . Our capability to deter world war is increasingly inhibited by our inability to cope with the problem [of command and control]."

60. This point is thoroughly documented in Kevin N. Lewis, "Planning Nuclear Defense: Force Structures, Employment Plans, and War Objectives" (Cambridge, Mass.: MIT, Department of Political Science, unpublished Ph.D. dissertation, October 1980).

61. Such a view is the central theme of Paul Bracken, *The Command of Nuclear Forces* (New Haven: Yale University Press, 1983).

62. U.S. Congress, Senate, *U.S.—U.S.S.R. Strategic Policies* (Washington, D.C.: Government Printing Office, 1974), pp. 9–13.

63. John Steinbruner, "National Security and the Concept of Strategic Stability," *Journal of Conflict Resolution*, September 1978, pp. 411–28.

64. Broad, "Philosophers at the Pentagon," p. 409.

65. Michael Getler, "U.S. Ability to Retaliate after Nuclear Blast Attack Concerns Officials," *Washington Post*, January 26, 1981, presents an up-to-date appraisal.

66. William J. Broad, "Nuclear Pulse (I): Awakening to the Chaos Factor," *Science*, 29 May 1981, pp. 1009–12; and idem, "Nuclear Pulse (II): Ensuring Delivery of the Doomsday Signal," *Science*, 5 June 1981, pp. 1116–20.

67. "Nuclear Pulse (II)," p. 1116.

68. "Nuclear Pulse (I)," p. 1009.

69. "Nuclear Pulse (II)," p. 1116.

70. William J. Broad, "False Alerts and Faulty Computers," *Science*, 5 June 1981, p. 1123. See also, idem, "Computers and the U.S. Military Don't Mix," *Science*, 14 March 1981, pp. 1183–84, 1186–87, where this summary assessment is made of the U.S. computer-based command-and-control system: "It seems, in short, that the sprawling military bureaucracy cannot cope with the rapid evolution of computer technology." P. 1187.

71. A. J. P. Taylor, *The First World War* (New York: Capricorn, 1972), p. 16.

72. Philip J. Caputo, *A Rumor of War* (New York: Holt, Rinehart & Winston, 1977), p. 81.

73. Many of these comments have been suggested in Todd R. La Porte, ed., *Organized Social Complexity: Challenge to Politics and Policy* (Princeton, N.J.: Princeton University Press, 1975); see especially the essays by John Gerard Ruggie, "Complexity, Planning, and Public Order," pp. 119–50; and the concluding comments of La Porte, "Complexity and Uncertainty: Challenge to Action," chap. 10.

74. Recall Chap. 4, "A Conception of Complexity" for the parallel discussion.

75. Richard R. Nelson, "Intellectualizing about the Moon-Ghetto Metaphor: A Study of the Current Malaise of Rational Analysis of Social Problems," *Policy Sciences*, December 1974, pp. 375–414, is conceptually on target; Alan Altschuler, *The City Planning Process* (Ithaca, N.Y.: Cornell University Press, 1965), is one notable practical illustration.

76. Maxwell Taylor, *Swords and Plowshares* (New York: W. W. Norton, 1972), pp. 400–401. Again, an opportunity to learn something from previous experience was missed, or as a different Taylor puts it with respect to World War I: "To a detached view, the military deadlock ought to have produced a willingness to compromise. It did the opposite. Both sides asked: 'Why should we compromise when we cannot be defeated?' Only victory seemed to promise security; and men went on fighting the war in order to make certain that there would never be another." A. J. P. Taylor, *First World War*, p. 163.

77. See Chap. 4, "A Conception of Complexity," and especially Fig. 4–1, for a recapitulation of the basic ideas. Wildavsky, *The Politics of the Budgetary Process*, exemplifies the incremental perspective characterized in cell 3.

78. Eugene Bardach, "On Designing Implementable Programs," in Giandomenico Majone and E. S. Quade, eds., *Pitfalls of Analysis* (New York: John Wiley & Sons, 1980).

79. Broad, "Philosophers at the Pentagon," provides several instances of efforts to reconceive and simplify the system.

80. Donald T. Campbell, "Reforms as Experiments," in Francis Caro, ed., *Readings in Evaluation Research* (New York: Russell Sage Foundation, 1971), pp. 233–61.

81. Garry D. Brewer, "Experimentation and the Policy Process," in *Twenty-Fifth Annual Report of The Rand Corporation* (Santa Monica, Calif.: The Rand Corporation, 1973), pp. 151–65; social experiments are treated in more detail in Part V ("Evaluation"). See also,

Alice Rivlin, *Systematic Thinking for Social Action* (Washington, D.C.: The Brookings Institution, 1971), chap. 5, "Can We Find Out What Works?"

82. Margaret Boeckmann, "Policy Impacts of the New Jersey Income Maintenance Experiment," *Policy Sciences*, March 1976, pp. 53–76, documents this claim.

83. This idea has taken concrete form in Japan and has been implicated in improved productivity, high quality, and job satisfaction; its more general appropriateness merits consideration. Rodney Clark, *The Japanese Company* (New Haven: Yale University Press, 1979), chaps. 6 and 7; Constance Holden, "Innovation: Japan Races Ahead as U.S. Falters," *Science*, 14 November 1980, pp. 751–54, p. 753; and Christopher Byron, "An Attractive Japanese Export," *Time*, March 2, 1981, p. 74.

84. Gordon Chase, "Implementing a Human Services Program: How Hard Will It Be?" *Public Policy*, Fall 1979, pp. 385–435, considers this possibility with regard to an array of human services in New York City.

85. Ibid., p. 428.

86. Geoffrey Vickers goes directly to the heart of the matter and traces out the implications of continuing to ignore citizen views in *Freedom in a Rocking Boat: Changing Values in an Unstable Society* (New York: Basic Books, 1971). Steven R. Brown, *Political Subjectivity* (New Haven: Yale University Press, 1980), provides both technical procedures and practical justifications to this end.

87. Martha Derthick, *New Towns In-Town* (Washington, D.C.: The Urban Institute, 1972), p. xiii.

88. James Scott, *Comparative Political Corruption* (Englewood Cliffs, N.J.: Prentice-Hall, 1972), is a thorough, cross-national source.

89. Stephen K. Bailey and Edith K. Mosher, *ESEA: The Office of Education Administers a Law* (Syracuse, N.Y.: Syracuse University Press, 1968), p. 69.

90. Robert A. Levine, *Public Planning: Failure and Redirection* (New York: Basic Books, 1972), p. 9.

91. Erwin C. Hargrove, "The Search for Implementation Theory" (Nashville, Tenn.: Institute for Public Policy Studies, Vanderbilt University, May 1981), emphasizes this.

92. Bardach, *Implementation Game*.

Discussion questions

1.   One reason that the implementation process is little understood is its complexity, which renders it resistant to rigorous analysis. There are so many factors that influence and obscure the implementation process, and therefore impede our understanding, that we can neither comprehend nor manage implementation with a fraction of the requisite sophistication. Discuss various general implementation problems with specific reference to promising analytic improvements that one could imagine.

2.   Policymaking is a disjointed and not easily modeled process, a condition that appears to hold especially true during implementation. Many believe that the disjointness of the process is merely a reflection of an underlying irrationality created by the play of political factors and events. How might the policy analyst examine the diverse interests, values, and perspectives that operate, modify, or thwart the faithful execution of new policies and programs? What are some of the expected costs involved in rendering such an accounting, or not bothering to do so?

3.   There are 50 state governments, thousands of county systems, tens of thousands of cities and towns, and millions of people in the United States. What different techniques could be employed by the national leadership to secure even the most minimal compliance and conformity on behalf of these diverse entities with the centralized goals of those in Washington? What

key aspects of implementation and what crucial dimensions require close attention? What can be ignored or given less attention?

4. Consider and then explain why heaven and earth are so disparate:

> Administrative feedback is a vital element in organizations because subordinate compliance does not automatically follow upon the issuance of orders and instructions by leaders. When managers die and go to heaven, they may find themselves in charge of organizations in which subordinates invariably, cheerfully, and fully do as they are bid. Not here on earth. [Herbert Kaufman *Administrative Feedback* (Washington, D.C.: The Brookings Institution, 1973), p. 2.]

5. Motivation and incentives as topics have served to focus attention on the weak connections that exist between selection and implementation phases of the overall policy process. What is meant by motivation and incentives? What are some plausible reasons that may exist to account for the wrong or unintended incentives that can be observed operating in many policy and program areas?

6. Nuclear energy authorities caution that there are a large number of nuclear reactors which are either obsolete or no longer needed. The facilities are candidates for decommissioning. However, no one knows how much it will cost, and great conflict among the experts marks discussion about how to do it. Whatever the cost, who pays? No private utility is setting aside a fund for ultimate decommissioning of the existing commercial nuclear facilities. Current rates to consumers do not reflect decommissioning costs. The Nuclear Regulatory Commission does not require owners of the nuclear facilities to develop specific plans or to make financial provision for decommissioning. How could this have happened? Who is responsible? Who will have to pay the price of decommissioning? What policies need to be considered to (a) correct the present situation and (b) lessen its impact in the future?

7. A chronic problem with the federal administrative system is the recruitment and selection of appropriate and competent individuals to fill high-level positions of public trust and responsibility. The problem is complicated by the distinctive roles performed by career civil servants, political specialists and generalists; it is made all the more thorny by the conflicting objectives of administrative continuity and responsiveness to the administration in power. Discuss this issue in terms of its causes, effects, and possible resolution as it relates to policy implementation.

8. While everyone seems to get into the act in the formulation of new policies and programs (e.g., political parties, legislators, the mass media, special interest groups, experts), most of what is implemented—for better or worse—can be traced to the specific actions taken by bureaucratic offi-

cials. Comment, taking special care to support your arguments in response to this assertion.

9.   Controlling the bureaucracy is a major issue and problem in current American life. What are the main available strategies for gaining such control? What new strategies can you imagine to accomplish the same objective? In considering this, be sure to assess the relative strengths and weaknesses of each strategy identified.

Supplementary readings

Implementation is such a difficult concept and collection of activities that one is hard pressed to pick out a single, appropriate list of readings capable of representing both concept and actions. However, the following selections aim to be both diverse and inclusive. As is our convention, they have been organized according to the topical breakdown of the two chapters. Finally, we urge the seriously interested reader and student to take the time to pursue the numerous endnote references made throughout the chapters. It helps to think about the part itself as a map or reader's handbook to implementation.

THE INTERNAL PROCESS OF IMPLEMENTATION

Bardach, Eugene. *The Implementation Game*. Cambridge, Mass.: MIT Press, 1977.

Bunker, Douglas R. "Policy Sciences Perspectives on Implementation Processes." *Policy Sciences*, March 1972, pp. 71–80.

Fesler, James W. *Public Administration*. Englewood Cliffs, N.J.: Prentice-Hall, 1980, chaps. 8–10.

Hargrove, Erwin C. *The Missing Link: The Study of Implementation of Social Policy*. Washington, D.C.: The Urban Institute, 1975.

Nakamura, Robert T., and Frank Smallwood. *The Politics of Policy Implementation*. New York: St. Martin's Press, 1980.

Pressman, Jeffrey, and Aaron Wildavsky. *Implementation*. Berkeley: University of California Press, 1979.

Van Meter, Donald S., and Carl E. Van Horn. "The Policy Implementation Process." *Administration & Society,* February 1975, pp. 445–88.

Waldo, Dwight. *The Study of Public Administration*. New York: Random House, 1964, chap. 2.

Williams, Walter, and Richard Elmore, eds. *Social Program Implementation.* New York: Academic Press, 1976.

CONFRONTING REALITY

A broad view of the realities

Jones, Charles O., and R. Thomas, eds. *Public Policy Making in a Federal System.* Beverly Hills, Calif.: Sage Publications, 1976.

Seidman, Harold. *Politics, Position, and Power: The Dynamics of Federal Organization*. New York: Oxford University Press, 1975.

Legislation: The selection-implementation connection

Dodd, Lawrence C., and Richard C. Schott. *Congress and the Administrative State.* New York: John Wiley & Sons, 1979.

Ogul, Morris S. *Congress Oversees the Bureaucracy: Studies in Legislative Supervision*. Pittsburgh: University of Pittsburgh Press, 1976.

Oleszek, Walter J. *Congressional Procedures and the Policy Process*. Washington, D.C.: Congressional Quarterly Press, 1978.

Ripley, Randall B., and Grace A. Franklin. *Congress, the Bureaucracy, and Public Policy*. Homewood, Ill.: Dorsey Press, 1980.

The implementing agent and the agency

Gawthorp, Louis C. *Bureaucratic Behavior in the Executive Branch: An Analysis of Organizational Change*. New York: Free Press, 1969.

Heclo, Hugh. *A Government of Strangers: Executive Politics in Washington*. Washington, D.C.: The Brookings Institution, 1977.

Kaufman, Herbert. *Administrative Feedback*. Washington, D.C.: The Brookings Institution, 1973.

Malek, Frederic V. *Washington's Hidden Tragedy: The Failure to Make Government Work*. New York: Free Press, 1978.

Ripley, Randall B., and Grace A. Franklin. *Bureaucracy and Policy Implementation*. Homewood, Ill.: Dorsey Press, 1982.

FACTORS INFLUENCING IMPLEMENTATION

Source of the policy

(All citations noted under "Legislation: The selection-implementation connection," above).

Congressional Quarterly. *Congresssional Quarterly's Guide to the U.S. Supreme Court*. Washington, D.C.: Congressional Quarterly, 1979.

Handler, Joel F. *Social Movements and the Legal System: A Theory of Reform and Change*. New York: Academic Press, 1978.

Hardin, Charles. *Presidential Power and Accountability*. Chicago: University of Chicago Press, 1974.

Krislov, Samuel. *The Supreme Court in the Political Process*. New York: Macmillan, 1965.

Neustadt, Richard E. *Presidential Power*. New York: John Wiley & Sons, 1980.

Rose, Richard. *Managing Presidential Objectives*. New York: Free Press, 1976.

Shapiro, Martin. *The Supreme Court and Administrative Agencies*. New York: Free Press, 1968.

Wasby, Steven L. *The Impact of the United States Supreme Court*. Homewood, Ill.: Dorsey Press, 1970.

Clarity of the policy

Gross, Neal C.; Joseph B. Giaquinta; and Marilyn Bernstein. *Implementing Organizational Innovations*. New York: Basic Books, 1971, chap. 6.

Le Breton, Preston P. *Administrative Intelligence-Information Systems*. Boston: Houghton Mifflin, 1969.

Morris, C. K. *Signification and Significance*. Cambridge, Mass.: MIT Press, 1965.

Ogden, C. K., and I. A. Richards. *The Meaning of Meaning*. New York: Harcourt Brace Jovanovich, 1947.

Smith, A. G., ed. *Communication and Culture*. New York: Holt, Rinehart & Winston, 1966.

Complexity of administration

Kaufman, Herbert. *Red Tape*. Washington, D.C.: The Brookings Institution, 1977.

Levine, Robert A. *Public Planning: Failure and Redirection*. New York: Basic Books, 1972.

Thompson, James D. *Organizations in Action*. New York: McGraw-Hill, 1967.

Incentives for implementors

Bennis, Warren G. *Changing Organizations*. New York: McGraw-Hill, 1966.

Katz, Daniel. "The Motivational Basis of Organizational Behavior." *Behavioral Science* 9, no. 2 (1964), pp. 131–46.

Rodgers, Harrell R., Jr., and Charles S. Bullock III. *Coercion to Compliance*. Lexington, Mass.: Lexington Books, 1976.

Schultze, Charles L. "The Role of Incentives, Penalties and Rewards in Attaining Effective Policy." In Julius Margolis and Robert Haveman, eds. *Public Expenditures and Policy Analysis*. Chicago: Markham, 1968, pp. 145–71.

Stein, Bruno, and S. M. Miller, eds. *Incentives and Planning in Social Policy.* Chicago: Aldine, 1973.

Vroom, Victor H. *Work and Motivation.* New York: John Wiley & Sons, 1964.

Resource allocation

Caiden, Naomi, and Aaron Wildavsky. *Planning and Budgeting in Poor Countries.* New York: John Wiley & Sons, 1974.

Hirschman, Albert O. *Exit, Voice and Loyalty.* Cambridge, Mass.: Harvard University Press, 1970.

Kaufman, Herbert. *The Limits of Organizational Change.* University: The University of Alabama Press, 1971.

Miles, Rufus E., Jr. *Awakening from the American Dream: The Social and Political Limits to Growth.* New York: Universal Books, 1976.

Okun, Arthur. *Equity and Efficiency: The Big Tradeoff.* Washington, D.C.: The Brookings Institution, 1975.

Shefter, Martin. "New York's Fiscal Crisis: The Politics of Inflation and Retrenchment." *The Public Interest,* Summer 1977, pp. 98–127.

THEORETICAL PARADIGMS

In reaction: The innovative perspective

Downs, George W., Jr. *Bureaucracy, Innovation and Public Policy.* Lexington, Mass.: D. C. Heath, 1976.

Schultz, Randall L., and Dennis P. Slevin. "Implementation and Management Innovation." In Schultz and Slevin, eds., *Implementing Operations Research/ Management Science.* New York: American Elsevier, 1975, pp. 3–20.

Zaltman, Gerald; Robert Duncan; and Jonny Holbek. *Innovations and Organizations.* New York: John Wiley & Sons, 1973.

Psychological perspectives

Argyris, Chris. *Personality and Organization.* New York: Harper & Row, 1970.

Weick, Karl. *The Social Psychology of Organizing.* Reading, Mass.: Addison-Wesley, 1969.

Zimbardo, P. G., and E. E. Ebbesen. *Influencing Attitudes and Changing Behavior.* Reading, Mass.: Addison-Wesley, 1969.

Small group theory

Hayes, Michael T. "The Semi-Sovereign Pressure Groups." *Journal of Politics,* February 1978, pp. 134–61.

Stockman, David A. "The Social Pork Barrel." *The Public Interest,* Spring 1975, pp. 3–30.

Truman, David B. *The Governmental Process.* New York: Alfred A. Knopf, 1951.

Organization theory

Blau, Peter M., and W. R. Scott. *Formal Organizations*. San Francisco: Chandler, 1962.

Buckley, Walter, ed. *Modern Systems Research for the Behavioral Scientist*. Chicago: Aldine, 1968.

Downs, Anthony. *Inside Bureaucracy*. Boston: Little, Brown, 1967.

Etzioni, Amitai. *A Comparative Analysis of Complex Organizations*. New York: Free Press, 1961.

Fesler. *Public Administration*.

Goodman, Paul S., and Johannes M. Pennings. *New Perspectives on Organizational Effectiveness*. San Francisco: Jossey-Bass, 1977.

March, James G., and Johan P. Olsen et al., eds. *Ambiguity and Choice in Organizations*. Bergen, Norway: Universitetsforlaget, 1976.

March, James G., and Herbert A. Simon. *Organizations*. New York: John Wiley & Sons, 1958.

Perrow, Charles. *Organizational Analysis*. Belmont, Calif.: Wadsworth, 1970.

Communication theory and cybernetics

Deutsch, Karl W. *The Nerves of Government*. New York: Free Press, 1966.

Steinbruner, John D. *The Cybernetic Theory of Decision*. Princeton, N.J.: Princeton University Press, 1974.

FROM CASE TO SYSTEM EXAMPLES

Intergovernmental relations

Derthick, Martha. *The Influence of Federal Grants*. Cambridge, Mass.: Harvard University Press, 1970.

Dolbeare, Kenneth M., and Phillip E. Hammond. *The School Prayer Decision*. Chicago: University of Chicago Press, 1971.

Pressman, Jeffrey L. *Federal Programs and City Politics*. Berkeley: University of California Press, 1975.

Reagan, Michael D. *The New Federalism*. New York: Oxford University Press, 1972.

Williams, Walter. "Implementation Problems in Federally Funded Programs." In Williams and Elmore. *Social Program Implementation*, pp. 15–42.

Yates, Douglas. *The Ungovernable City*. Cambridge, Mass.: MIT Press, 1977.

Foreign policy/defense

Halperin, Morton H. *Bureaucratic Politics and Foreign Policy*. Washington, D.C.: The Brookings Institution, 1974.

Kanter, Arnold. *Defense Politics: Bureaucratic and Programmatic Success in Government*. Cambridge, Mass.: Harvard University Press, 1972.

Environment

Andrews, Richard N. L. *Environmental Policy and Administrative Change.* Lexington, Mass.: Lexington Books, 1976.

Crenson, Matthew A. *The Un-Politics of Air Pollution.* Baltimore, Md.: Johns Hopkins University Press, 1971.

Jones, Charles O. *Clean Air: The Politics and Policies of Pollution Control.* Pittsburgh: University of Pittsburgh Press, 1975.

Liroff, Richard A. *A National Policy for the Environment: NEPA and Its Aftermath.* Bloomington: Indiana University Press, 1976.

Education

Bailey, Stephen K., and Edith Mosher. *ESEA: The Office of Education Administers a Law.* Syracuse, N.Y.: Syracuse University Press, 1968.

Berke, Joel S., and Michael W. Kirst. *Federal Aid to Education.* Lexington, Mass.: D. C. Heath, 1972.

McLaughlin, Milbrey W. *Evaluation and Reform: The Elementary and Secondary Education Act of 1965/Title I.* Cambridge, Mass.: Ballinger, 1975.

Orfield, Gary. *The Reconstruction of Southern Education.* New York: John Wiley & Sons, 1969.

Health

Feder, Judith M. *Medicare.* Lexington, Mass.: D. C. Heath, 1977.

Marmor, Theodore R. *The Politics of Medicare.* Chicago: Aldine, 1973.

Development administration

Benveniste, Guy. *Bureaucracy and National Planning.* New York: Praeger Publishers, 1970.

Grindle, Merilee S., ed. *Politics and Policy Implementation in the Third World.* Princeton, N.J.: Princeton University Press, 1980.

Hirschman, Albert O. *Journeys Toward Progress.* New York: Twentieth Century Fund, 1963.

La Palombara, Joseph, ed. *Bureaucracy and Political Development.* Princeton, N.J.: Princeton University Press, 1967.

Montgomery, John D. *Technology and Civic Life: Making and Implementing Development Decisions.* Cambridge, Mass.: MIT Press, 1974.

Scott, James. *Comparative Political Corruption.* Englewood Cliffs, N.J.: Prentice-Hall, 1972.

IMPLICATIONS

Hackman, J. Richard, and Greg R. Oldham. *Work Redesign.* Reading, Mass.: Addison-Wesley, 1980.

Jackson, J. A., ed. *Professions and Professionalization.* Cambridge, Eng.: Cambridge University Press, 1970.

Kneese, Allen V., and Charles L. Schultze. *Pollution, Prices and Public Policy.* Washington, D.C.: The Brookings Institution, 1975.

Landau, Martin. "Redundancy, Rationality, and the Problem of Duplication and Overlap." *Public Administration Review,* July/August 1969, pp. 346–58.

McFarland, Andrew S. *Power and Leadership in Pluralistic Systems.* Stanford, Calif.: Stanford University Press, 1969.

March, James G. "The Uncertainty of the Past: Organizational Learning Under Ambiguity." *European Journal of Political Research* 3, no. 2 (1975), pp. 147–71.

Schulman, Paul R. "Non-Incremental Policymaking: Notes Toward an Alternative Paradigm." *American Political Science Review,* December 1975, pp. 1354–70.

Schultze, Charles L. *The Public Use of the Private Interest.* Washington, D.C.: The Brookings Institution, 1977.

Wescott, J. H., ed. *An Exposition of Adaptive Control.* New York: Pergamon Press, 1962.

PART V

Evaluation

As soon as experience begins to collect and tangible results from decisions and implementation efforts exist, one needs to find out how matters are progressing. Or in the jaunty slogan of New York City's Mayor Ed Koch, "How am I doin', folks?" Evaluation is concerned with individual responsibility, as in Koch's case, and with the performance of policies, programs, and projects, including parts and whole systems of each. Typical topics and questions reflected in the idea of evaluation include the following: What policies and programs were successful or unsuccessful? How can that performance be measured and assessed? What criteria were used to make those measurements? Who did the assessment, and what were they trying to accomplish? Who sought the evaluation, what were they after, and how did they use the results? To what ends and for whose account was the evaluation directed, and were the ends attained and the accounts adjusted accordingly?

Evaluation is a necessary phase in the policy process, but the incidence of comprehensive and competent efforts in a wide variety of decision settings is not great.[1] Evaluation can be either internal to an organization (in-house) or external (such as an auditing firm, a consultant, or a troubleshooter). Evaluation can be considered as a separate phase of the policy process, although realistically it is usually quite integrated with all other phases. For instance, one real dilemma confronting a budget cutter is

319

determining what programmatic elements can sustain a reduction and which are truly essential. Seasoned bureaucrats are aware of this problem and the linkage between termination and evaluation it represents. And, in the absence of appropriate evaluations, many have been able to take serious advantage of the situation, as evidenced in the "Washington Monument Syndrome": e.g., when those responsible for a specific policy area are told to cut back their total budget some amount, they have occasionally responded by "sacrificing" specific programs they know to be absolutely essential or beyond serious consideration. In this example, the need to cut the Park Service budget results in a proposal to shut down the Washington Monument rather than an offer, based on responsible evaluation, to trim more selectively. The game is more general, and its persistence reflects in part a lack of useful evaluation and a disjunction between this phase and the others. Linkages exist with all phases of the process. For instance, evaluation may serve as an attention-directing device in which new problems are signaled, the initiation phase begun, and the total policy sequence mobilized. McLaughlin's evaluation of the Elementary and Secondary Education Act, for instance, not only called attention to many serious problems with the implementation of a specific piece of legislation, but also raised key questions about the general federal involvement in educational and related policy matters.[2]

Much as was the case with implementation, there is no commonly accepted definition of the terms *evaluation research* or *evaluation analysis*. Nor are efforts to do evaluation the special province of any particular discipline or professional specialty. This may present particular problems; for instance, an education specialist might be conducting a "summative evaluation" and be unaware that these efforts mean more or less the same as an "impact evaluation" or a "program evaluation" to someone else trained in any of the several disciplines that also do evaluations.[3] Likewise, no one method prevails; the gamut ranges from what accountants do in institutions small and large[4] to full-blown, highly complex, experimentally grounded studies of complicated policy proposals—as in the case of the social experiment.[5] Both are, in varying ways, evaluations, despite the considerable differences in the approaches taken, the observational tools used, the clients served, and the standards of execution and reporting that pertain.[6]

Institutional responsibility for evaluation is also widespread. It can be discovered in all branches and levels of government, as well as in most other formal and informal organizations.[7] For instance, the legislative branch is constitutionally mandated to exercise oversight (a distinctive call for evaluation) and discharges its responsibility through standing and select committees as well as through the efforts of subsidiary agencies such as the U.S. General Accounting Office.[8] Comparable patterns exist in other political jurisdictions. Executive branch evaluations are important and ubiquitous, as reflected in the usual institutional entities, such as assistant secretary level divisions for planning and evaluation, regulatory bodies, inspectors general, boards of inquiry, high-level advisory boards, commissions, panels, and many other instrumental means. While each may exist and operate for somewhat different reasons and with variable powers and constraints, each shares elements of a common evaluation purpose. Courts perform an essential evaluation function, especially in situations where decisions rendered result in reinterpretations of social standards and practices.[9]

Citizens perform an evaluation by casting ballots. While perhaps lacking the clarity and trappings of science one has come to expect from evaluation research, the results are no less telling. At a narrower and more precisely targeted level, individual citizens may band together in pursuit of particular interests, especially so in cases in which sufficient numbers of them share a sense of having been deprived or wronged in some way or another (an implicit evaluation stimulating pressure for change).[10] A variant on the individual theme is the whistle-blower, a usual reference to disgruntled or disaffected bureaucrats who elect to go public with specific details of misfeasance, incompetence, inefficiency, and corruption.[11]

The press and other communication media play a role, too, as spectacularly demonstrated by Woodward and Bernstein in their reporting of the Watergate Affair during the Nixon Administration.[12] Equally compelling and tightly focused are the televised investigative reports in which specific deficiencies are alleged at the same time as they are transmitted into thousands if not millions of living rooms.[13] Books, including fictional ones, have often performed even more diffuse evaluation tasks, e.g., informing the public, creating expectations about individual and collective behavior, and creating or reaffirming ethical and normative standards for later adoption in the social process.[14] Political cartoons have likewise been powerful critical devices, clearly providing another medium for assessment and dissent. Indeed, art as a general cultural activity has always contributed essential ingredients to the social and political processes,[15] a point concisely stated, it is alleged, by playwright Berthold Brecht: "All art is political. Whoever believes not merely reaffirms the status quo."[16]

By now it should be apparent that the scope of potentially relevant evaluation activities is vast. Doing justice to them all, furthermore, is too demanding a chore, especially considering the more diverse purposes of this book. Certain simplifications are required. But how to do this?

Taking a budgeteer's approach and trying to identify everything in, for instance, the federal budget that pertains to evaluation is one way. For one year, at least, estimates of about $300 million for federally sponsored evaluation studies have been derived.[17] A large figure, it still must understate by a considerable margin the actual level of resources spent to evaluate federal policies and programs. For instance, a great deal of administrative data collection is not counted here, although its basic purpose is obviously related to performance monitoring and assessment. Similarly, there is no accounting for the thousands (or more) hours that are spent in supervisory and controlling functions throughout the government, time which if not spent would certainly result in degraded levels of performance. For a variety of understandable reasons,[18] the budgeting approach at best yields a partial insight into the matter.[19]

Another approach would be to consider evaluation as a profession and then attempt to identify its specific characteristics, e.g., societies having memberships, journals and books related to evaluation, training programs, and certifying and sanctioning bodies. This helps in understanding something about evaluation's research aspects. Within the last decade at least two societies have been created and operate to advance evaluation research's cause: Evaluation Research Society and Evaluation Network (the latter for education specialists). Several specialized journals exist: *Evaluation, Journal of Evaluation and Program Planning*, and *GAO Review*, to name but three of the more prominent ones; and many more general publications have devoted significant space to articles about evaluation, e.g., most of the policy journals, such as *Public Interest* and *Policy Sciences*, and several of the functional journals, such as *Public Administration Review*. Training programs exist in a wide variety of academic disciplines and departments, but these are marked more by their diversity than singleness of orientation, emphasis, and purpose (picking up on an earlier observation that everyone is getting into the act). At least one attempt has been made to create and exercise professional standards,[20] but actual and continuing practice seems to indicate that these are not uniformly observed.[21]

On balance, it seems that evaluation exists well enough, but most attempts to bound or delimit the activity and field are deficient in various ways. It is clear, nonetheless, that our consistently sought objectives of comprehensiveness, multiple methods, and problem-centeredness are being approximated in various ways by existing examples of work in the field, albeit rarely all for any one given instance. Evaluation research, as one noticeable component of the field, has in the 1970s, in the words of two main exponents, "emerged a still somewhat gawky and floundering adult . . . destined to have a long, successful, and influential life."[22] Perhaps evaluation is entering a reformation period during which the proliferation of terms and approaches, literature, and disparate practices will in time be winnowed down and rendered into a more coherent and comprehensible whole, as Cronbach and his associates urge throughout their work, which begins forcefully: "This book calls for a reformation in evaluation, a thoroughgoing transformation. Its priests and its patrons, as well as those who desire its benefits, have sought from evaluation what it cannot, probably should not, give."[23]

Whatever the actual state of evaluation as an analytic (research) enterprise concerns us only insofar as its limitations interfere with the operations of the policy process. Reflecting momentarily back on the incredible difficulties one encounters in policy and program implementation, these limitations must be substantial. For now let us conjecture that the enormous complexities of the policy process are no less evident and no less perplexing during evaluation than they have been in all antecedent phases. Doing so lets us concentrate less on specific technical or theoretical disputes (which are legion) and allows us to think a bit more clearly about evaluation's practical realities and requirements.

The following discussion begins with a consideration of a broad concept of system performance: a choice predicated on the belief that evaluation should inform and improve the operations of the social system by contributing constructively to the entire policy process. We next think about criteria—standards on which judgments or decisions may be based—for, among other reasons, no one can effectively answer the "How am I doin' folks?" question unless the question "As compared to what?" has been raised and answered beforehand. Various tools, techniques, and approaches are surveyed to give a flavor of representative knowledge of the evaluation component of the policy process, but far more attention is devoted to evaluation practicalities—or knowledge in the policy process.

NOTES

1. The desired features are central in Harold D. Lasswell, "Towards a Continuing Appraisal of the Impact of Law on Society," *Rutgers Law Review,* Summer 1967, pp. 645–77. In normal practice, however, the grand view of comprehensive evaluation is seldom encountered.

2. Milbrey Wallin McLaughlin, *Evaluation and Reform* (Cambridge, Mass.: Ballinger, 1975). Not the least of her conclusions reflects back on the appropriate role and function of evaluation: "An important lesson . . . is that the logic of inquiry should be perceived as relative, not absolute, and that a realistic and useful evaluation policy should acknowledge the constraints of the policy system and the behavior of bureaucracies." P. 120.

3. These terminological differences and the confusion they cause are discussed in Lee J. Cronbach and Associates, *Toward Reform of Program Evaluation* (San Francisco: Jossey-Bass, 1980), chap. 1.

4. An interesting inquiry into the broader social functions of accounting is Lawrence A. Gordon, ed., *Accounting and Corporate Social Responsibility* (Lawrence: The University of Kansas Press, 1978).

5. A general orientation in the policy-process terms used in this book is Garry D. Brewer, "Experimentation and the Policy Process," in *Twenty-Fifth Annual Report of The Rand Corporation* (Santa Monica, Calif.: The Rand Corporation, 1973), pp. 151–65. Specific, psychologically based, elaboration is Donald T. Campbell, "Reforms as Experiments," *American Psychologist* 24, no. 4 (1969), pp. 409–29, a standard source of inspiration for much subsequent social experimentation.

6. All of these distinctions are treated in Robert F. Rich, ed., *Translating Evaluation into Policy* (Beverly Hills, Calif.: Sage Publications, 1979).

7. One attempt to summarize evaluation efforts throughout the federal government is E. A. Chelimsky, ed., *A Symposium on the Uses of Evaluations by Federal Agencies,* vols. 1 and 2 (McLean, Va.: MITRE Corporation, 1977).

8. Both possibilities are demonstrated in U.S. Comptroller General, *Finding Out How Programs Are Working: Suggestions for Congressional Oversight* (Washington, D.C.: Government Printing Office, 1977). A thorough investigation of the General Accounting Office (GAO) is Frederick C. Mosher, *The GAO: The Quest for Accountability in Amer-*

ican Government (Boulder, Colo.: Westview Press, 1979). A more general survey of legislative evaluation is Franklin M. Zweig, ed., *Evaluation in Legislation* (Beverly Hills, Calif.: Sage Publications, 1979).

9. Historical perspective is provided in Jerome Frank, *Law and the Modern Mind* (New York: Doubleday, 1930); and explicit treatment of the political component of judicial evaluation anchors the discussion of Jesse H. Choper, *Judicial Review and the National Political Process* (Chicago: University of Chicago Press, 1980).

10. Norman J. Ornstein and Shirley Elder, *Interest Groups Lobbying and Policymaking* (Washington, D.C.: Congressional Quarterly Press, 1978), especially "Interest Group Resources and Strategies," pp. 69–94.

11. Charles Peters and Taylor Branch, *Blowing the Whistle: Dissent in the Public Interest* (New York: Praeger Publishers, 1972). The lot of the whistle-blower is unenviable, as attested in a series of case studies presented in Taylor Branch, "Courage Without Esteem: Profiles in Whistle-Blowing," *Washington Monthly*, May 1971, pp. 23–41.

12. Bob Woodward and Carl Bernstein, *The Final Days* (New York: Simon & Schuster, 1976).

13. General points are made in David Anderson and Peter Benjaminson, *Investigative Reporting* (Bloomington: Indiana University Press, 1976). A specific example, which began as a television documentary and ended with the publication of a book about the experience, is Geraldo Rivera, *Willowbrook* (New York: Vintage Books, 1972)—an exposé of then prevalent conditions in a Staten Island, New York mental institution.

14. Far too numerous to relate here, one has only to reflect momentarily on the effect of Rachel Carson's *The Silent Spring* (Boston: Houghton Mifflin, 1962), on the environmental movement and subsequent policy initiatives to appreciate the general point.

15. An interesting extension and exploration of this and other diverse ways of thinking about evaluation is Nick L. Smith, ed., *Metaphors for Evaluation: Sources for New Methods* (Beverly Hills, Calif.: Sage Publications, 1981).

16. We have also heard this comment expressed as follows: "All art is political. The artist who claims to be apolitical has merely chosen the side of the ruling class." We are unable to find specific attribution here, although the point itself retains validity. On the general question of culture as the matrix constraining individual activity, see Musafer Sherif, *Social Interaction: Process and Products* (Chicago: Aldine, 1967), especially, "Conformity-Deviation, Norms and Group Relations," pp. 168–89.

17. W. H. Shapley and D. I. Phillips, *Research and Development in the Federal Budget: FY 1979, R & D, Industry and the Economy* (Washington, D.C.: American Academy for the Advancement of Science, 1978).

18. Many of which are cogently stated in Martin Rein, "Comprehensive Program Evaluation," in Robert A. Levine, Marian A. Solomon, Gerd-Michael Hellstern, and Hellmut Wollman, eds., *Evaluation Research and Practice* (Beverly Hills, Calif.: Sage Publications, 1981), pp. 132–48.

19. A general conclusion implied, but not clearly stated, in U.S. Congress, Senate, Committee on Human Resources, *Cost, Management, and Utilization of Human Resources Program Evaluation* (Washington, D.C.: Government Printing Office, 1977), is that program evaluation is a large and rapidly growing field and that human services is a key stimulant to that growth.

20. Hale Champion, *FY 1980 Guidelines for Evaluations, Research, and Statistical Activities* (Washington, D.C.: Government Printing Office, 1980). (For the Department of Health and Human Services.)

21. "Evaluating the evaluations" has occurred, but seldom in more than a case-by-case or anecdotal fashion. See A. Bernstein, "Evaluating the Evaluators," *Change* 6, no. 9

(1977), pp. 8 and passim. A specific technical complaint is noted in Donald T. Campbell and A. E. Erlebacher, "How Regression Artifacts in Quasi-Experimental Evaluations Can Mistakenly Make Compensatory Education Look Harmful," in J. Hellmuth, ed., *The Disadvantaged Child*, vol. 3 (New York: Brunner/Mazel, 1970), pp. 185–210.

22. Howard E. Freeman and Marian A. Solomon, "The Next Decade in Evaluation Research," in Levine et al., *Evaluation Research and Practice*, chap. 1, at p. 13.

23. Cronbach et al., *Toward Reform of Program Evaluation*, p. 1.

11

System purposes and performance

To understand a system's purposes, one needs to understand its operating goals. Where is the system heading? To measure its performance, one needs criteria. Has the system arrived where it was meant to go, and if not, how far off the mark is it?[1]

GOALS

Goals are categories of preferred events, whether events desired in themselves or events desired because they are instrumental, e.g., health is desired in itself and is preferred to illness, and productive employment is desired as an instrumental event and is preferred to mass unemployment.[2]

Criteria and value are different. Value refers to the worth or utility of an event, not the measures or criteria on whose scale such valuation is made. For example, efficiency is a standard measurement criterion for evaluating programs; however, assessing wastefulness is not the same as deciding whether waste matters as much as many other aspects might and thus whether other criterion measures are more appropriate—literally, more valuable. Furthermore, values and criteria can be distinguished from norms, which are rules governing behavior. Once criteria are established, the valuation of events on those criteria provides the grounds for rejecting or accepting particular norms as undesirable or desirable.[3]

In practice the major point is that values influence choices about possible goal events to be considered (creation of the social agenda and the later development of a menu of a program's potential goals), the preference ordering of these goals, the selection of one set (including a particular weighting among the set's elements), and their eventual assessment.[4] It is important to determine whose values regarding what events are at stake in any given setting throughout the entire policy process. For those participating in a social system in which economic and social development are sought, for example, change itself is often valued as an outcome, but done so without due regard to the full range of other outcomes and effects it generates. The anthropologist's distinction between "cool" and "hot" cultures illustrates the problem. Valuing stability, those in a cool culture act to reduce or dissipate forces that would lead to disruptive social changes. Such acts often take the form of creative rituals and complex myths intended to ensure the place of the individual in a stable, dependable world. Valuing change, those in a hot culture act to increase and stimulate dynamic forces that intentionally disrupt the existing social fabric. Acting thus, however, often overlooks the extraordinary strains placed on individuals in the society. Industrial societies have been more dynamic and flexible than nonindustrial ones, but in the process, such societies have taken more daring and costly risks with the psychic well-being of their people.[5]

In other terms, the narrow pursuit of increases in wealth and power frequently results in significant costs in terms of other values foregone or sacrificed in the process. The point holds for individuals (obsessive business executives who literally work themselves to death) and higher levels of analysis (the plight of Iran is a most stunning example). What are the realized and likely outcomes of policies and programs, that is the more immediate and observable results of policy and program intervention; and what are the longer-term, second-, third-, and higher-order effects, measured in individual and collective respect, rectitude, affection, well-being, and other value terms (in addition to wealth and power)? The cumulative "benefits" of vastly increased wealth and military power during a relatively brief period in Iran's historical experience were acquired at "costs" in respect, well-being, rectitude and other values at levels high enough to erode the underlying basis of popular consent any political leadership requires to sustain. A continuing revolution, in which the areas of greatest previous value deprivation figure prominently, was the result.

Goals are a multifaceted problem whose understanding and accommodation are necessary if an evaluation is to proceed. For instance, take a general hypothetical case of the poor in a society, as a class. If one were to analyze what individuals in this class sought, goals of the "greatest good for the greatest number" variety might well dominate. For instance, the group would want assurances that their needs for programs and services, such as housing, medical care, food, education and the like, are adequately met. Or this might be represented in terms of assurances that each poor person has the opportunity to develop his or her capabilities to a maximum potential consistent with one's innate physical and mental gifts.[6] In actual practice, these goals will not be consistent for each member of the class, e.g., government need not meet every need, but somehow these needs must be met and the potentials realized. This can occur because many of the poor want to be as self-sufficient and self-reliant as possible. Attaining the greatest good for the greatest number and fostering social and economic independence are in this case complementary and mutually supportive goals.

Realistically, these goals have only partly been met because society has not been willing to make the necessary financial commitment. Evaluation, in this instance, centers on determinations of the distance existing between goal and experience, the speed with which this distance is either being closed or is opening, and the breadth and fairness of coverage those in need and holding these goals have realized.

The goals of officials responsible for contemplating and executing specific policies and programs are reflected in the form and substance of these interventions, as revealed during implementation. At one level the goals will be broad and somewhat ambiguous as, for instance, in statements of intention found in most legislation or general statements of policy and in more detailed interpretations contained in program rules, regulations, and guidelines.[7] Generally, program goals conform to goals sought by individuals for whom the program is intended; however, they typically cannot fit the wishes and expectations of all such individuals. A role for evaluation is thus suggested: monitoring the fit between official and individual statements of goals, with particular consideration given to large discrepancies discovered for segments of the targeted group. These discrepancies nearly always exist. Individuals and groups have different needs and expectations, not all of which can be accommodated with a general prescription. Furthermore, the phrase "subject to budget constraints" is the key implicit or explicit qualification of nearly every program objective.

Society's goals, taken in total, are fundamentally a collective ethical problem and hence not easily determined.[8] At a very rough level of approximation, social goals can be appreciated by considering the sum total of all governmental actions over a whole range of programs for a specified group. In the case of the poor, this would mean paying attention to everything done on their behalf—targeted programs as well as those having incidental impacts—at all levels of government and then doing the monumental job of aggregating them all to contrast their consequences with individual and collective needs and expectations. Having made this global observation, the analyst is provided cold comfort and very little guidance as to how such an assessment could possibly be made. Furthermore, unique and conflicting aspects of the actual goals tend to predominate and make the determination of society's valuation of goal events nearly impossible. The armed forces, for instance, contribute to improved national educational levels through programs of remedial and vocational education—programs that benefit poorer segments of the society disproportionately, given the proportion of these classes serving in the armed forces. However, the goal of reducing poverty or increasing education is not the main reason for the existence of such educational programs—improving war-fighting and military competence are. The problem of disentangling immediate outcomes realized for the military goal and the longer-range effects stemming from the incidental, social welfare benefit goal is practically insurmountable.

Other more common trade-offs in goals sought exist, and many of these take extreme forms: (Continue using the poor as a reference group.)

> Restrict current public expenditures—which implies low emphasis on expensive services, such as public education.
>
> Minimize total expected public expenditures over the lifetime of a group in need, such as the poor—which implies high emphasis on job training and considerably less emphasis on welfare.
>
> Emphasize expenditures to those most in need—which implies a conscious discrimination against those with less substantial, albeit still notable, needs.
>
> Emphasize programs that yield greater effectiveness per dollar expended—which implies concentration on those with borderline needs who can be readily satisfied and discrimination against those with severest need.
>
> Increase the distribution of expenditures to the maximum number of those in need (to increase equity)—which implies that those with greatest need will either not be served or served at ineffective levels of quality.

These stark illustrations are seldom encountered in policy or program goal statements; one usually infers them from specific, concrete details. Nor are they the only dilemmas one discovers. The relevant time frames and perspectives of different participants also enter. For instance, "The person or group with a time orientation toward the present [e.g., politicians] will have difficulty in seeing the value of innoculations against disease, a future occurrence."[9] This insight helps one partly understand why preventive social programs—not just those centered on health issues—are quite hard to promote politically and why resources typically are spent in treating problems already at hand.[10] (The insight obviously fails in the case of national defense.) As compared with the politician, a poor person's time frame contains both an appreciation of how long it might take to become economically secure and an expectation of continuing difficulty for one's children.[11] For many, poverty has been the total life experience, and quick fixes are not likely to be taken very seriously.

Another realistic difficulty for the would-be evaluator is the usual condition, according to Geoffrey Vickers, that "When we open our eyes to the scene around us, we find goals already set. Policies are being implemented, institutions are in action with all the historical momentum of buildings and establishments. . . . Budgets, even budget headings, have acquired prescriptive rights."[12] In other words, the context influences evaluation by providing cues and constraints which cannot be ignored; new policies and programs do not exist in a vacuum but are being shaped in their goal potentials (and in many other ways). Nonetheless, certain general social goals can often be discovered in specific program statements: e.g., increase participation, improve accountability, become aware of unintended consequences of individual policies and programs, improve the structure and function of service-providing institutions, and increase human dignity. It is the operational specification, in given circumstances, of any or all of these general prescriptions which causes difficulty. Not the least of the problem is trying to measure the status and progress in achievement of such goals— the matter of criteria.

CRITERIA

Many different measures are required to assess system performance and to evaluate policy impacts. Considering the number and diversity of possible outcomes and effects for even the simplest program, one nearly always must use multiple criteria to evaluate. The sheer complexity of most interventions means that a single measure of effectiveness probably will not suffice;[13] it also demands considerably more basic data than is usually available to conduct a responsible evaluation.[14]

A criterion, in the sense used here, is a standard on which a judgment or decision may be reached. Basic subjectivity, "Whose judgment?" and a requirement to be rooted firmly in specific circumstances, "Decisions about what?" are essential ingredients in creating and then using such criteria. Reliance on absolute standards provides few practical guidelines or little help. Or as Kaplan states the matter:

> The maxim of the greatest good for the greatest number . . . is useless as a basis of choice when, as is almost always the case, one alternative [e.g., actual program] provides a greater good for some while the other benefits more people though to a lesser extent; what, on this basis, is an equitable distribution of the tax burden?[15]

We agree with Kaplan's view that evaluation can only be undertaken in concrete settings: "The lessons of operationism are as important for policy as for science. To be able to guide practice, [ethical] theory must be formulated in terms that connect it with determinate behavior."[16] Moreover, every concrete setting requires evaluation because of the possibility for both gains and losses that exist for affected individuals and because of the inherent uncertainties that always follow intervention. There are no pat answers; programs can seldom be enacted with perfect foreknowledge of their eventual outcomes and effects. Indeed, adherence to the idea of neatly prespecified criteria has been implicated as a deterrent to learning and good policy:

> The prior specification of criteria and the prior specification of evaluational procedures that depend on such criteria are common presumptions in contemporary social policy making. They are presumptions that inhibit the serendipitous discovery of new criteria. Experience should be used explicitly as an occasion for evaluating our values as well as our actions.[17]

Discovering criteria

Besides being contextual, criteria depend on, among other things, who one is, where one sits, and what one intends—or intended and expected when decisions underlying policies and programs were reached. Criteria are suggested in statements of legislative intent often found in the opening paragraphs of a public law. More importantly, criteria can be inferred from careful readings of hearings preceeding passage of legislation, in rules and regulations governing implementation, in antecedent legal rulings and complementary programs having the force of precedent, and in statements (both formal and informal) of those wielding influence or controlling the "levers" that allow or constrain actions. More unsettling to the evaluation task are those criteria defined well after the fact (i.e., after the program has been operating). These can often be seen as post hoc rationalizations in defense of the program and are, on occasion, proposed by people who had little involvement in the program's formulation. These criteria can especially complicate the evaluator's work.

The Education for All Handicapped Children Act, P.L. 94–142, passed in 1975, states that the intention of Congress is "to assure that all handicapped children have available to them, within the time periods specified . . ., a free appropriate public education."[18] Implied in this statement is a need to remove deficiencies in equality of educational opportunity for handicapped children. But this does not mean equal resources or equal objectives for both handicapped and nonhandicapped children. Generally, the educational resources and goals established for each handicapped child will be different and based on the child's needs and potential.[19] At this stage at least, the prospective evaluation chore is so immense as to be impracticable. The law describes a condition in which some 8 million children across the nation are believed to be handicapped, but 4 million of these "do not receive appropriate educational services which would enable them to have full equality of opportunity."[20] Besides having to identify and locate a very large number of individuals, the would-be evaluator must also contend with the problem of discriminating between a case of opportunity versus a case of nonopportunity: What would each look like; do standards vary across the country; is equality of opportunity the same for a young handicapped child as it is for an older one? These and dozens of other operational questions come immediately to the fore. Most are not easily resolved.

Consultation of the hearings discloses the civil rights protection intention implied in equal opportunity, but it also reveals much more of possible interest to an evaluator. Securing long-term economic advantages as a result of educating the handicapped was sometimes cited as a justification for the law and might have provided one useful criterion for evaluation.[21] However, the hearings weighed civil rights and humanitarian factors at least as heavily: In the words of Congressman Robert Cornell, "I think that we also ought to stress the fact that this education is necessary just to give them a greater enjoyment, and appreciation of living." Elsewhere, Cornell clarifies, "Some of these people are never going to be able to be self-supporting, or to obtain gainful employment."[22] Perfectly understandable, but these statements do not help very much in identifying potential criteria or standards by which the law might be assessed.[23]

Historical or preceding factors, "historical momentum" in Vicker's phrase, add another important dimension and suggest standards of expected performance for possible use in measuring the Education for All Handicapped Children Act. In one important way, the collective inadequacies of many programs already in force to aid handicapped children served as a main stimulus for yet another piece of legislation—to remedy the shortcomings. Knowledge of these programs, e.g., their limitations, is thus an essential precursor to the creation of criteria for determining improvements realized with the new one. Gaining this knowledge, however, is in itself a demanding task. More than 20 different federal educational programs existed to assist handicapped children in November 1975 when the new legislation was passed, and these were complemented by hundreds, if not thousands, of separate initiatives already in progress at the state and local levels.[24] The level-of-analysis problem, that is, trying to bound the evaluation task so as to keep it manageable, is unavoidable given the distinctive roles of states and localities in education and the certain impact less-than-federal efforts were having on education for the handicapped. In short, criteria were already in place, being used, and affecting existing practice. Given the diversity of programs around the country, uniformity was not to be expected in their operating criteria.

Federal regulations develop and stress all three classes of concern or social goals for this legislation (humanitarian, civil rights, and economic) and begin to specify terms somewhat. In this case, six separate objectives guided implementation of the law.[25]

Assurance that every handicapped child is receiving an appropriately designed education.

Assistance to states to provide appropriate educational services to the handicapped.

Assurance that handicapped school-leavers have had career educational training relevant to the job market, meaningful to career aspirations, and realistic to one's fullest potential.

    Assurance that handicapped children served in schools have competent instructors to assist each in reaching a full potential.

    Enrollment of preschool handicapped children in federal, state, local educational and day care programs.

    Provision of special attention to severely handicapped children to reduce need for institutional care and to ensure development of their full potential.

While some of the vagueness and contradiction evident in previous statements of intention is removed, these regulations introduce a different class of problem. What do the key words mean, particularly with respect to their operational specification for implementation and later evaluation purposes? Words such as "appropriate," "realistic," "relevant to the job market," "competent," and "full potential" all possess complex and highly varied possibilities of interpretation and meaning. These differences matter. For instance, appropriateness of educational opportunity is quite likely to be construed in different ways by the family of an eligible child than it is by a local school principal whose already thin resources are further diluted by the addition of children presenting special needs and problems—children heretofore taken care of somewhere else. For a state official concerned about the possibility of civil rights litigation, appropriateness may mean working diligently to see that as many handicapped children as possible are included in the program, even though some (or many) of them will not get nearly as much service as they actually need. For the federal official, the term may mean making some progress in reducing the total numbers of those believed to be unserved while at the same time concentrating on a few promising locations so that anecdotal, but truthful, testimonials of success may be offered in the next round of the budget.[26] The exercise is easily strung out with respect to other participants and for each of the key, operational terms contained in the regulations.[27] It would be difficult to overemphasize that the identification of criteria is far more challenging than simply answering questions such as, "How efficient is such-and-such a program? How effective? How many? How equitable? How adequate?" And because it is, evaluation is one of the most difficult phases in the entire policy process.

    This observation also reminds us that criteria may have evolved in advance of selection and implementation. During estimation, for instance, rough performance measures and standards, especially for relatively new or ambitious programs, are established. When creating and then estimating various candidate program alternatives, expectations about eventual costs and consequences are a normal part of the exercise (e.g., program X is preferred to other plausible options because one expects it to be more beneficial, less costly, more effective). However, these expectations may not be realistic because of analytic shortcomings (errors of specification and technique), significant uncertainties about the problem (random effects as well as unknown-unknowns), and modifications the program X option sustains during the give-and-take of selection and implementation. Still and all, some basis of judgment exists during estimation to help guide the analysis and to order its findings. Differences in predicted performance and those later observed may themselves shed light on and improve estimation in future iterations of the policy process (e.g., gaps in the data base are filled, better observational techniques are created, improvements in the underlying theories are made). As a practical matter, such differences often stem from the quite different criteria used by various participants in the respective phases of the policy process (e.g., an analyst's standards for weighing options are not the same as a politician's, and neither necessarily conform to an administrator conducting the program). One should not be surprised by this, for criteria are linked to an evolving context much as the specific steps undertaken to solve society's problems. What may have started out as a concern for efficient resource allocation could in time evolve and become more matter of equity or adequacy. It commonly happens this way.

Efficiency

A technical definition of efficiency is easy: the ratio between inputs (I) and outputs (O).[28] Inputs are resources transformed through activities to produce outputs. For two programs (production units in usual usage), X and Y, using comparable inputs and outputs, program X is more efficient than Y if,

$$\frac{O_x}{I_x} > \frac{O_y}{I_y} \quad \text{or} \quad \frac{I_x}{O_x} < \frac{I_y}{O_y}$$

Inputs and outputs may be measured in different terms *within* a program (e.g., enumerated according to money, manpower, time), but they must be equivalent *between* programs if a comparison is to be valid.

Examples of efficiency-based evaluation approaches are also easy to identify.[29] However, because of some considerable differences that exist between the private sector, manufacturing setting from which many efficiency studies derive and the public sector settings in which most social problems are treated, direct and constructive application of efficiency as a criterion has been rare.

When producers compete for a consumer's dollars, the most efficient in time survive and/or increase their share of the market by driving out inefficient competitors. Noticeable inefficiencies in a market may also attract the attention of new producers and encourage them to enter and compete. Producers are gauged according to the profits they can capture, and efficiency of operations is a key means to improve profitability. A social condition of strong property rights coupled with a right to retain a portion of the aftertax money residual links performance and efficiency directly.[30] Efficiency is not the only criterion under these conditions, but it is a very strong one.[31]

This condition is not much the case in the public sector. Because the public sector manager is not allowed to maximize profits or to capture the residuals, profit maximization is converted to budget maximization.[32] Efficiency in this situation becomes a negative incentive, for any effort to economize may lead to reduced budgets, which in turn could mean a reduced capacity. The manager, however, will still be asked to produce—to carry out the assigned responsibilities. So where is the incentive to be efficient?

Furthermore, there is no clear-cut production process for public goods as there is for private ones. This is not to say that in certain, very limited service activities something akin to the industrial production function cannot be imagined: picking up the trash is one case where buyers and sellers are reasonably clear about what they want and the efficient means of providing for it. Comparisons with private trash collectors or comparable operations in other cities can be made and some determination of relative efficiency of operations reached, with consequent improvements in service if inefficiencies are discovered.[33] For most public services and programs, however, the variety of goals associated with any given activity makes efficiency much more problematic. For instance, what is the goal of public education? There is no single answer here for public education has been tasked to provide many different products, e.g., suitably prepared students for higher education, vocational training, rehabilitative training, a holding pattern for hard-to-employ adolescents, a baby-sitting function, a health mission (disease identification and nutritional programs), an employment opportunity for educational specialists, socialization and citizenship building, and many other possibilities. Not only is there nothing remotely like agreement about the total list of what public education is to accomplish, different participants in the production process of public education will view various outcomes and effects differently and will apply different weights to the importance of any or all of them.

For these and many other reasons, efficiency in public programs is often not a realistic criterion. Because production functions are not well defined, and because many masters are realistically being served, sharp focus and agreement about goals or operational objectives are rare. One common consequence is that separate line items in a bureaucrat's budget are subjected to scrutiny based on the particular views and weights constituents place on them. This in turn leads to an incentive to produce justification for what is being done, in defense of one's budget, regardless of standard evaluation criteria such as efficiency (such also makes the objectivity of program data for evaluation suspect). Furthermore, where efficient provision of services does occur, it can often be traced to a bureaucratic desire to please specific political patrons or to placate particular interest groups.[34]

Equity

Equity as a criterion implies that similarly situated people be treated equally. Equity claims in simple, two-party contracts, for instance, are complicated enough to fill volumes of legal casebooks. This complication is heightened several orders of magnitude when considering issues of social contract where nothing is explicit and the consensus on interpretation of the contract shifts on a daily basis. Income maintenance for the poor, for example, has been a major focus for battles over equity—a problem made all the more difficult because of the genuine confusion that exists between the criterion of equity and the norm of equality. The former provides an opportunity for operational assessment, the latter, absolute standard is less amenable.[35] Income maintenance represents a claim by the poor against the rest of society—it is a claim without specific instrumental means, however. Some recognize it in the form of private charity, others a guaranteed income; the claim may be interpreted as an opportunity, a guarantee, or an insurance policy (safety net) against failure. Usually, all these and more complications will surface and impede an evaluator's efforts to determine a program's equity element.

Additionally, conflicts can be discerned in separate equity claims. For example, efforts have been periodically made to reduce the level of expenditures under the Aid to Families with Dependent Children (AFDC) program, a considerable federal initiative to provide assistance to families with children based on individual need. It is basically an income maintenance program.[36] Cut-backs threaten violation of equity of the people denied access to be treated similarly to equally situated people; they also portend increasing inequities for those already receiving services based on the observed differences that exist from state to state in coverage and extent of assistance already being provided.[37] In the case of social security, proposals to limit eligibility based on a rationale of preserving the insurance base needed to meet future equity claims present the simultaneous dilemma of creating inequities for those who will be denied now or in the immediate term. The point is not to dishearten, but rather to present some of the concrete realities confronting and inhibiting evaluation.

Equity, as is the case with other general criteria, can still be a useful guideline. To measure how fairly a service is distributed among various target groups and to measure unmet needs, one must consider whether and how much of a needed service the individuals in each recipient group get. Because the individual's needs and abilities to benefit from services will differ, equity does not mean that equivalent amounts of each service are necessarily provided to each individual. Rather, equity involves two types of measurable criteria: the percentage of a group needing service that actually receives it and the variance among groups in the quantity of services received.

Adequacy

Equity and adequacy are not the same. Equity generally refers to social choices that distribute services fairly across the population. Increasing equity with fixed levels of resources implies providing lower levels of service to greater numbers of people. Adequacy refers to the availability of enough service to meet the need and can be illuminated by raising and then answering the following question: "What portion of those in need receive quality services?"

Adequacy is very hard to pin down. Standards created to evaluate adequacy are bound up intimately with perceptions outside the program or policy setting in which evaluations are undertaken; these perceptions are not static nor are they invariant from place to place. For instance, many have noted that perceived poverty seems to be increasing at the same time that American society is prospering. What might have been considered adequate to alleviate poverty in the Depression (a chicken in every pot, a car in every garage, to paraphrase one political slogan of the times) would be considered far from adequate in the 1980s, where the perception of need and a habit of entitlement, an equity consideration, both change the common perception. Competing and inconsistent conceptions of a policy's main purpose also enter in: Is adequacy of income maintenance considered a matter of equal opportunity, a promise to bring the poor into the economic mainstream, or is it mainly a promise to provide a safety net to those "truly in need," however one cares to define that category? Depending on the dominant concept, very different standards of adequacy will follow.

Effectiveness

Effectiveness, as was the case with efficiency, may be defined technically with relative ease: it is a ratio measure relating observed output to the planned output over some time period. Because both outputs are measured in the same units, the ratio expresses the percentage of effectiveness for the assessment period. It is important to note that unless two programs are nearly identical in the missions or goals set for them, and the resources allocated to accomplish these goals, comparisons of effectiveness between programs will not make much sense. Furthermore, the nature of the measure introduces a perverse incentive: an ambitious program that is also efficient in its production can look bad in effectiveness terms when compared with a conservative program that is inefficient.[38]

An earlier distinction between outcome and effect in program evaluation needs to be made especially clear in determining effectiveness. For the income maintenance illustration, the two may actually trade-off against each other. Were eligibility standards for the AFDC program to be eased, a proximate outcome could well be an increase in per-capita income among a select number of families below the poverty level. A longer-run effect, however, may be a reduction in labor force participation of the new beneficiaries, consequent increases in overall dependency, and longer average durations on aid. In the more general case, welfare payments (such as AFDC) may actually result in a drop in long-term earnings and an increasing proportion of the incomes of the poor. In such a situation, can one realistically call the program effective or a success?[39]

What's left?

Pick any substantial policy arena and the criteria problem will be discovered. Indexing benefits was mandated because of equity considerations to maintain real standards of living in the face of inflation, but indexing has been implicated as a primary cause of inflation and faulted for actually increasing benefit levels beyond what was intended. Political wars then degenerate into squabbles about the levels of adequacy realized and actually needed. Or efficiency questions pop up in related discussions about in-kind and complementary programs, such as food stamps or public housing.

What's an evaluator to do? Trade-offs and conflicts are inescapable. Ignoring them has far less to recommend it than trying to reckon with them. As a practical matter, all of the general criteria we have identified should be considered and blended in an evaluation. But one must guard against overemphasis on any one of them: none will be best in actual circumstances, and all may be helpful in gaining an appreciation of a program's many possible outcomes and effects.[40] Extreme care needs be given the matter of the many different and valid perspectives that will pertain in a given program setting; these require explicit elaboration and illumination. A success for one participant could very well be a failure for another depending on the standpoint. One should resist a temptation, as an analyst, to show consistent preference for any single criterion over others. The matter of weighting or valuing is a highly subjective issue not made any easier by misguided efforts to stress precision in measurement; e.g., "the benefit/cost ratio for Program X is +2.3." Depending on the goals, purposes, and objectives of the consumer of one's evaluation, strikingly different overall assessments will be encountered. In any event, great precision should not be expected based simply on the sketchy data one usually has.[41] Often about the only thing one can say with any confidence is that such-and-such a policy or program has had some positive relationship to intended goals, or the reverse, some negative relationship. This may be enough. Sound choices can often be made if such general statements are known to be valid in the large, even though specific cause-effect sequences are not well understood and precise data describing the context are not available.

This is a very different attitude than that found in many evaluation research studies, as we shall see in the following chapter. It is what we chose to call a pragmatic-constructive approach to evaluation—one that stresses the contextual features of particular policies and programs nearly as much as it does their enormous complexities, generally reflected in problems of locating criteria.

NOTES

1. Much of the material covered in this section continues an earlier discussion found in Chap. 4: "The Human Ought and the Rational Is."

2. Daniel Lerner and Harold D. Lasswell, eds., *The Policy Sciences* (Stanford, Calif.: Stanford University Press, 1951), pp. 9–10; and Harold D. Lasswell and Abraham Kaplan, *Power and Society* (New Haven: Yale University Press, 1950), p. 16.

3. Cultural and community norms provide the general structural framework in which behavior and individual activity are confined. Because norms are generally internalized (in the individual case) over a prolonged period of socialization and enculturation, they are nearly as unchangeable as they are taken more or less for granted. Violation of them tends to be readily apparent; one does not have to look hard ("do evaluations") to find them. Excessive violation of this kind of norm (great deviation by one individual or cumulative minor infractions by numerous individuals) is usually cause for reaction, for not to do so threatens the underlying social order. Sanctions are expected and encourage conformance. One only has to think about the extreme repressions of authoritarian regimes to grasp the significance of this point.

4. See concept of "Value," *International Encyclopedia of the Social Sciences* (New York: Macmillan/Free Press, 1968); and Kenneth E. Boulding, "The Ethics of Rational Decision," *Management Science*, February 1966, pp. B–161–69.

5. William Barrett, *Time of Need* (New York: Harper & Row, 1972), pp. 271ff, has generalized these points and related them to what he perceives to be several strong philosophical currents flowing in contemporary Western intellectual life. The "cool" and "hot" illustration is derived from Garry D. Brewer and Ronald D. Brunner, eds., *Political Development and Change: A Policy Approach* (New York: Free Press, 1975), "Introduction," p. 11.

6. This interpretation appears to conform reasonably well with the various programs undertaken in the "War and Poverty," for instance. See Robert H. Havemann, ed., *A Decade of Federal Anti-Poverty Programs: Achievements, Failures, and Lessons* (New York: Academic Press, 1977), in which the complications and confusions attending goals figure prominently.

7. See Chap. 9, "Confronting Reality," for a recollection of problems created by a need to translate broad pronouncements of goal into specific programmatic terms.

8. Besides their complexity and resistance to specification, society's goals are dynamic (by the time an ambitious analyst believes they have been measured, they may well have changed—and substantially). As John Dewey characterized it: "[T]he foundation for value and the striving to realize it is found in nature, because when nature is viewed as consisting of events rather than substances, it is characterized by *histories*, that is, by continuity of change proceeding from beginnings to endings." As cited in James Gouinlock, *John Dewey's Philosophy of Value* (New York: Humanities Press, 1972), p. 134.

9. S. H. King, *Perceptions of Illness and Medical Practice* (New York: Russell Sage Foundation, 1962), p. 53.

10. A "lesson" from one unfortunate preventive health effort, the swine flu vaccination program, may even reinforce this general tendency. As Califano reports, the political costs for attempting swine flu immunization are quite real whereas the benefits redound

to no one's account. Joseph A. Califano, Jr., *Governing America* (New York: Simon & Schuster, 1981), chap. V.

11. Alternatively, a hope that poverty will not be the lot for one's children, as considered within policies and programs undertaken in the present.

12. Geoffrey Vickers, "Who Sets the Goals of Public Health?" *The Lancet*, March 1958, p. 599.

13. Recall the lengthy discussion in Chap. 5, "Data, Theory, and Estimation." Points made there in consideration of estimation requirements apply for evaluation with equal force.

14. A fundamental constraint limiting advances in the social indicator movement (also discussed in Chap. 5) has been stated thusly by Bell: "The nation must decide which objectives [*goals,* as used here] should have the higher priorities, and choose the most efficient programs for attaining these objectives. Social reporting cannot make the hard choices the nation must make any easier, but ultimately it can help to ensure that they are not made in ignorance of the nation's needs." Daniel Bell, "A Social Report in Practice," *The Public Interest,* Spring 1969, pp. 98–105, at p. 105.

15. Abraham Kaplan, *American Ethics and Public Policy* (New York: Oxford University Press, 1963), p. 98.

16. Ibid., p. 91.

17. James G. March, "Model Bias in Social Action," *Review of Educational Research,* February 1972, pp. 413–29.

18. 20 U. S. C. 1402 as amended; P. L. 94–142.

19. In the terms of two leading advocates of the legislation: Equal opportunity means "equal access to differing resources for differing objectives." Frederick C. Weintraub and A. Abeson, "Appropriate Education for All Handicapped Children: A Growing Issue," *Syracuse Law Review* 23 (1973), p. 1056.

20. P. L. 94–142, Section 3(b).

21. U.S. Congress, House, Subcommittee on Select Education of the Committee on Education and Labor, *Extension of the Education of the Handicapped Act* (Washington, D.C.: Government Printing Office, 1975), pp. 35–46.

22. Ibid., pp. 49–50.

23. Erwin C. Hargrove and his colleagues have done a commendable job in carrying this exercise through. Hargrove et al., *Regulations and Schools* (Nashville, Tenn.: Institute for Public Policy Studies, Vanderbilt University, March 1981).

24. Garry D. Brewer and James S. Kakalik, *Handicapped Children* (New York: McGraw-Hill, 1979), chap. 10. Knowledge of the 20 educational programs is itself insufficient to grasp the significance of total federal involvement affecting this group of children. Medical, vocational, rehabilitation, welfare, and other programs would, in varying degrees and in varying ways, have potential consequences for the children and for the shape and implementation of the new piece of legislation. Such consequences, judged according to appropriate criteria, need to be considered.

25. *Code of Federal Regulations,* Title 45, Public Welfare, Part 121; General Provisions, Section 121.3. (Note: Precise terms have been paraphrased somewhat for brevity.)

26. During the late 1970s, the Department of Health, Education, and Welfare emphasized a "best practices" campaign that gave recognition to exemplary, site-specific programs.

27. For some the simple existence of the legislation is a sufficient criterion, that is, success is gauged according to the placing of the law on the books: "Money is not the primary issue. . . . The first thing is to get commitment to assure that our children get the education they need." U.S. Congress, *Extension of the Education of the Handicapped Act,* p. 35. Statement by Mr. Fred C. Weintraub, Council for Exceptional Children. Success, initially at least for Weintraub, was more symbolic than substantive.

28. The following discussion borrows heavily and with permission from Otto A. Davis and P. D. Larkey, "Improving the Financial Discipline of States and Cities," in David Solomons, ed., *Proceedings of the Arthur Young Professors' Roundtable 1979* (Reston, Va.: Council of Arthur Young Professors, 1980), pp. 43–81. We have also benefited from Larkey's, *Evaluating Public Programs* (Princeton, N.J.: Princeton University Press, 1979).

29. A sample would be Robert N. Anthony and Regina Herzlinger, *Management Control in Nonprofit Organizations* (Homewood, Ill.: Richard D. Irwin, 1975); and Fremont J. Lyden and Ernest G. Miller, eds., *Planning Programming Budgeting* (Chicago: Markham, 1967).

30. Eric A. Furubotun and Svetozar Pojovich, "Property Rights in Economic Theory: A Survey of Recent Literature," *Journal of Economic Literature*, December 1972, pp. 1137–62.

31. Humane working conditions, social responsibility, and a variety of other constraints exist and must be taken into account by even the most single-minded profit maximizer. See Thomas Donaldson and Patricia H. Werhane, eds., *Ethical Issues in Business* (Englewood Cliffs, N.J.: Prentice-Hall, 1979), for a thorough treatment of the issue.

32. William A. Niskanen, Jr., *Bureaucracy and Representative Government* (Chicago: Aldine, 1971), presents the starkest version of this theme.

33. We are grateful to J. A. Stockfisch for illumination of these points and the examples.

34. Harvey Leibenstein, "Allocative Efficiency vs. 'X-Efficiency'," *American Economic Review*, June 1966, pp. 392–415.

35. "Equality as a value does not depend upon a belief that men were created equal by their Maker or that men are by nature equal . . . such appeals are normatively ambiguous: they mainly serve to conceal personal preferences and to rationalize these preferences as the logical outcomes of shared principles. . . . Values can remain ideals and absolutes only to the extent that they are divorced from real choices." Brewer and Brunner, *Political Development and Change*, p. 9. We acknowledge the assistance of James B. Query in the development of the illustrations here.

36. U.S. Department of Health, Education, and Welfare, *Findings of the 1967 AFDC Study* (Washington, D.C.: National Center for Social Statistics, NCSS Report AFDC–3, 1970).

37. Significant inequities in payment levels and eligibility requirements for AFDC have been reported across the 50 states; the federal involvement is intended to reduce these discrepancies through an income redistribution mechanism from the richer to the poorer areas of the country. A reduction in direct federal involvement will necessarily have the likely consequence of widening the discrepancies by returning the situation to something approximating the previous, "nonleveling" condition.

38. Davis and Larkey, "Improving the Financial Discipline."

39. This claim is made by Lester C. Thurow, *The Zero Sum Society* (New York: Basic Books, 1980), especially chap. 7.

40. We agree with the spirit of Robert Dorfman, ed., *Measuring the Benefits of Government Investments* (Washington, D.C.: The Brookings Institution, 1967), in this difficult matter.

41. A reminder: There are very few incentives to produce "objective" data from a program manager's standpoint, and most evaluations depend extensively on exactly this source for much of the data they use.

12

Evaluation: Science, analysis,
and control

A great deal has been written, reflecting a large body of social scientific effort, on the general subject of policy and program evaluation. It is extremely difficult to make sense of this whole activity. It is equally challenging to determine instances of successful and unsuccessful evaluation applications. Part of the problem no doubt stems from the very high standards that many have set for evaluation, and part of the problem results from a demonstrated inability to approximate those standards in practice. We have accordingly elected to summarize many of these standards into a description of an idealized view of evaluation; we next consider several typologies, including one of our own, to aid and orient one to the general field of evaluation research. Various methods and purposes for evaluation are then considered to acquaint the reader with the wide variety of tools and techniques that have been used and may in the future be encountered. The discussion concludes with some reasons that may account for the disparity between ideal and reality.

AN IDEALIZATION

A point of departure for the following discussion is contained in John Dewey's characterization of the social process:

Every situation or field of consciousness is marked by initiation, direction or intent, and consequences or import. What is unique is not these traits, but the property of awareness or perception. Because of this property, the initial stage is capable of being judged in the light of its probable course and consequence. There is anticipation. Each successive event being a stage in a serial process is both expectant and commemorative. . . . [And] the terminal outcome when anticipated . . . becomes an end-in-view, an aim, purpose, a prediction usable as a plan in shaping the course of events.[1]

Several key ideas are thus suggested for evaluation research. We are able to imagine, plan, and implement according to different perceptions of need and results desired. Furthermore, experience in dealing with common problems can be subjected to scrutiny and appraisal with respect to our initial conceptions of aim or purpose: that is, what did we wish to accomplish and how successful were we? What are needed in this scheme are indicators capable of expressing (a) the nature and magnitude of the needs, considered from the perspectives of all relevant stakeholders; (b) the means selected to satisfy those needs, represented as policies, programs, and projects; (c) the magnitude and direction of various activities undertaken and realized to satisfy those needs, best thought of as the history of implementation; and (d) the desirability or value of those activities.[2] Many factors conceivably enter into the construction, application, and interpretation of performance measures, as most of what we have said about the policy process to this point suggests. Some, but by no means all, of these factors can be observed and measured—necessary components of any scientific research endeavor.[3]

The selection of indicators for use in evaluation has been termed a *measurement strategy*, whose general purposes include assistance to an analyst in observing institutional and program activities and in assessing various consequences.[4] Performance measures are typically classified as being either absolute or relative, absolute when performance is assessed with respect to some previously defined or ideal feature and relative when compared to a standard performance or to a comparable aspect of another institution's performance.[5] Measures are either direct or indirect. The former evaluate performance as expressly as possible, while the latter key on related behaviors, often through the use of surrogate or indirect measures.[6] Ideally, such measures should be as objective as possible when concerned with quantitative and quantifiable aspects of performance;[7] however, qualitative matters should not be overlooked and would include efforts, for instance, to define excellence, satisfaction, sufficient, and similar hard-to-define and harder to measure attributes.[8]

Because multiple objectives characterize the usual institutional agenda and these objectives are pursued in the form of various definable, programmatic activities, there is a clear requirement to use multiple measures.[9] There is an even more essential requirement to identify and understand the objectives themselves; many will, upon examination, be ill-considered or inappropriate.[10] Stated and unstated goals for the assessment are themselves worthy of detailed analysis.[11]

Data must be accurate, and they must be collected systematically. The one-shot approach has traditionally been misleading, and data definition, gathering, and analysis activities require continuing appraisal.[12]

Finally, performance measurement must be set off against a variety of plausible and potential purposes to be served by measurement.[13] For instance, if the assessment is to be made for the internal purposes of an agency, then agency staff members will be most likely to be responsible for the effort. If the evaluation is part of a general assessment of the sponsoring agency, done on behalf of the public interest, outside and less directly involved specialists are required. In either case, the personal and professional identifications of the evaluator are important and have consequences for the type, comprehensiveness, and severity of the evaluation.[14]

These are well-intentioned but idealized characteristics of evaluation taken from a research perspective that seeks to measure and assess program and institutional performance. They are seldom observed altogether in actual experience. Indeed, as is suggested and indicated in many critiques of evaluation research, there is mounting disillusionment.[15] Such a situation stems in no small part from the setting of impossibly high ambitions, from a failure to specify the type and purpose of evaluation, and from a noticeable lack of concern and attention to situational or contextual matters.

TYPES OF EVALUATIONS

Far and away the most prevalent evaluation type is informal. As suggested in our earlier survey of many different forms evaluation may take (e.g., investigative reporting, special interest group activities, art), scientific evaluation as a product of formal research is only one way social policies and programs may be assessed. It may not even be the most relevant or telling approach, at least as concerns a capacity for affecting decision making and institutional behavior. For instance, if evaluation is thought of very generally as mere information about ongoing activities to responsible officials, then the innumerable informal evaluations of this type plainly dominate: they are the most common, the least expensive, the least disruptive (under normal circumstances), and in toto probably the most effective type. Informal evaluations are important for other reasons, too. Besides being timely and more or less continuous, they may signal a need for more formal and detailed assessment, especially in situations where simple correctives do not yield improved performance or where the complexity and stakes involved in a given program are, respectively, beyond easy comprehension and large. Additionally, informal evaluations may serve the useful purpose of cross-checking or calibrating formal analyses, particularly those emphasizing more qualitative biases; they have proved very useful in capturing political and popular attention necessary to gain support for needed changes.

Many formal evaluation typologies exist and have been used in specific applications.[16] However, the unsettled state of evaluation research theory (suggested in the foregoing discussion) appears to have contributed to a great deal of confusion, not the least of which derives from labeling more or less equivalent processes and practices very differently. For example, educational evaluations are often termed either *formative* or *summative*.[17] The former refers to tactical observations and recommendations made to decision makers to guide midcourse corrections and to improve on-going program performance. The latter are more encompassing evaluations intended to inform high-level policymakers (and indirectly, the public) about overall consequences of both large-scale programs and significant policies. Alternatively, and in terms previously defined, formative evaluations are more nearly concerned with program outcomes, while summative ones emphasize program and policy effects. Because of this distinction, formative evaluations are best seen as being tightly linked to the previous implementation stage, but summative inquiries connect more often to the termination, selection, estimation, and initiation stages.

The public health tradition has contributed much to evaluation research, including another typology which underlies many evaluations outside the public health area. A foremost exponent of the tradition, Edward Suchman, concentrates on the process of evaluation and identifies increasingly difficult and expensive levels of evaluation inquiry: effort, performance, adequacy of performance, efficiency, and process.[18] Effort evaluation measures the quantity and quality of program inputs; performance evaluation compares outputs (as measured) to program objectives; adequacy evaluation connects performance to measures of how much a given program is needed; and efficiency evaluation relates program outputs to effectiveness indicators and total program costs (dollars are the usual metric here). Process evaluations attempt to determine causal and structural aspects of a program. As the labels indicate, there is very little overlap with the formative-summative typology, and there is some considerable confusion internal to the Suchman scheme. For example, how can one realistically compare outputs and objectives (performance evaluation) without having a reasonably clear understanding of the internal causal structure of the black box responsible for the conversion of one into the other? This is particularly true for anyone interested in improving performance—a basic rationale for conducting evaluation. Much of the difficulty with this particular typology centers on a need to specify criteria, a variety of which will, in given circumstances, be needed to guide one's evaluation efforts. Such criteria are, as discussed earlier, highly sensitive to the requirements and perspectives of those doing the evaluation, those being evaluated, and those whose lives are touched by the program-object of study. This typology is rather silent on this matter. Its relative strengths, on a more positive note, are its emphasis on program efficiency—which in many public health instances is perfectly appropriate—and its tight focus on internal (process) details of program operations.[19]

Which leads us to a somewhat different view of evaluation and a typology to understand, structure, and conduct many specific evaluations. Performance may be assessed in terms of *process, response,* or *impact*. The first concentrates on the internal workings of an institution or program; the second attends to an institution's or program's responses to the surrounding environment; and the last attempts to assess the environment's response to an institution's or program's activities.[20] Elemental distinctions are portrayed in the following figure.

For most institutions and programs, resources are seldom extravagant or, in any event, one works to ensure their efficient use—a process consideration in the main. However, for even this simplest type of evaluation, serious conceptual and practical problems intrude. Simple economic efficiency, for instance, can be defined in terms of a single economic entity pursuing its goals in such a way that "no alternative [operation] would yield it a higher payoff when all costs and outputs are taken into account."[21] However, at this apparently simple level of conceptualization and activity, the multiplicity of meanings and interpretations individuals bring to bear is notable. Such a definition of efficiency (quite analogous and in keeping with the technical definition provided in the previous discussion of criteria) fails to account for the likely influence exerted on the surrounding environment by the operation, for the realistic determination of capital and labor mixes to yield measures of technological efficiency pertinent to the specific setting, for the social consequences of failing to achieve collective or multiperson and multiunit efficiency, for risk and uncertainty, and for the different perceptions and values individuals have about the single economic entity and their relationship to and responsibility for it.[22] Despite these

FIGURE 12–1

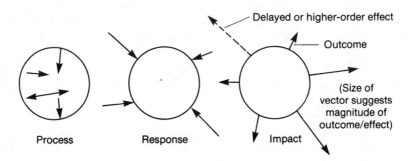

Process   Response   Impact

Delayed or higher-order effect

Outcome

(Size of vector suggests magnitude of outcome/effect)

problems, internal auditing, accountability, managerial and fiscal analyses, and other tools and techniques are available and used to enhance administrative practice and control. In common parlance, these are referred to as process or internal assessments.

In contrast, one may also wish to know and assess the consequences for a program or institution of external demands, threats, and opportunities. Such inquiries would seek to determine the responses observed in light of constantly changing external events. Response recognizes the reciprocity of defined interventions, e.g., programs, and the settings in which these are located. For instance, in international affairs, a major crisis, such as the Cuban missile crisis or the Iranian hostage crisis, has consequences for the normal workings of many other organizations and institutions (specifically the programs for which these are responsible). These consequences even bear on programs not immediately involved with dealing with the crisis, as in the case of top leadership's attention being riveted on the details of the crisis and thus not being available to deal with what in other circumstances would occupy it. To the extent that such attention is diverted (and the length of time of the diversion), this may have unwanted or harmful consequences in other areas. Executive branch efficiency generally declines and many opportunities are foregone. In short, external events have internal consequences, and these are often significant.

In the realm of special education, for example, the status and rate of change of demands for service are both important variables having a large external component (that is, external to the scope of responsibilty defined in the Education for All Handicapped Children Act itself). If preventive actions not connected directly to the act and the various programs undertaken in its behalf were to increase, improve, or otherwise realize better success, in time fewer children would be presenting themselves for service within the program domain defining the act. Better service could thus be provided those remaining in need (which assumes a constant level of resources expended but reduced total number served), or the total magnitude of the program could be scaled back in proportion to dwindling demand while holding the amount and quality of care provided constant on average. Likewise, better identification of potentially handicapping conditions through high-risk registries of women presumed likely to bear handicapped children, prenatal identification and remediation, improved pediatric practice, better screening programs for handicapping conditions, and the like could well result in faster and more appropriate medical interventions, at an earlier age, with the further reduction in number and degree of severity of those eventually needing service under the provisions of the act. A response evaluation would be sensitive to and take such contingencies into account.

Determining the consequences of program and management actions (including inaction) on the encompassing environment is a third type generally known as impact evaluation. What are the proximate outcomes and longer-range effects of a program? Who or what is responsible for successful or unsuccessful results? Can they be recognized and rewarded to enhance and encourage performance, in the first case, or to correct and ameliorate, in the latter? Determining impacts is often very hard to do or to do well. The explicit use of outside and consultative assistance is often indicated to improve the scope and objectivity of this kind of evaluation. Furthermore, the concept of impact assessment is explicitly comprehensive. One works to determine the impact on the relevant whole of the setting not simply a few of its routine and commonplace parts. The matter is complicated even more by making appropriate distinctions between spatially and temporally proximate outcomes and longer-term, spatially removed effects.

Consider a manufacturing or assembly operation making jet aircraft, for example. Absolute performance measures can be devised to aid assessment of efficiency and productivity. Were the target goals achieved? In a timely fashion? At least per-unit cost? And so forth. Relative measures, such as did the plant measure up to others in the corporation's scope of business or to those of competitors, may also be applied. The more successful and prevalent of these evaluation efforts will be of the process type and hence will stress relatively simple auditing and control tools and techniques. Typically, they will also emphasize direct measurement, save for instances where lagging productivity or inefficient performance fails to yield to it, in which case indirect observations and measurements may be utilized. In either case, however, the thing being observed and measured will be outcomes, where causal linkages are short and predominantly transparent. Far less time or energy will be expended in pursuit of individual reactions and concerns about being a part of or responsible for the process, and even less will focus on matters concerning short- and long-term efficiencies.

The evaluation problem is considerably harder when taken from a response perspective. How, for instance, does one recognize and then calculate the consequences of something as prevalent and chronic as worker absenteeism? Workers exhibit a variety of motivations when they elect to stay away. Sickness may be a legitimate reason, but its legitimacy blurs when occurrences are repeated, habitual, or prolonged. It is far less acceptable when used as a cover for other, actual reasons one might use for not coming to work. But how does one determine such deceptions and, once determined, devise ways to cope with them? Besides trying to understand, come to terms with, or minimize sickness in the normal interests of efficiency and productivity, management is also confronted with demands to comply with contractual constraints (e.g., healthy and safe working conditions) and with other external demands on its time and attention (e.g., regulations). That these and numerable other factors have consequences for the operation of the plant is indisputable. What both cause and consequence might be is far more problematic. What are the costs that result from management's preoccupation with absenteeism and the resultant lack of attention and concern for other less pressing, perhaps more significant, matters?[23] Especially when the neglect only becomes recognized as full-blown crises of one sort or another?

Assessing impacts is perhaps the most difficult matter of the three. For the aircraft manufacturer, it is a simple matter to determine how many individuals it employs, their gross contribution to the local economy, the number of aircraft they produce within a given period of time, and other such outcomes. But where does one bound assessment? Who bears responsibility for the heavy economic dependence placed on the plant by local authorities, e.g., municipalities or states, especially in times of market downturn? At what point and under what conditions is the manufacturer absolved for deaths that occur as a result of aircraft malfunction and crashes? What are the costs associated with aircraft manufacture (notably military aircraft) as compared with alternative uses of the same resources?[24] What is involved, to carry the point farther, in determining responsibility for environmental degradation that many believe occurs as a consequence of jet aircraft and their use?[25] Or to put it somewhat differently, what is the trade-off between a dollar of profit, one additional job, or one extra jet and one additional death, one more unit of pollution, or one more surplus military aircraft for transfer to an underdeveloped country somewhere in the world? All such questions could be relevant in impact assessment.

A main implication of this discussion is that one needs to be very specific about the type or form of evaluation at hand. As suggested in our hypothetical aircraft example, certain types of assessment can be conducted; others are far more difficult; and many may be simply impossible. Even the most cursory experience in dealing with those who commission and use evaluations leads one to conclude that expectations often outstrip possibilities.[26]

Other points are also worth noting. Evaluation is fundamentally historical in orientation and concentrates on what has happened or is happening in specific settings. This is not to say that evaluation does not have future consequences; the idea of policy-as-process strongly suggests that it does.[27] Qualitative and quantitative features of a context are equally important in conducting an evaluation, and precision may give way to gross characterizations (e.g., more or less, improving-deteriorating, better-worse) and admittedly subjective judgments. Furthermore, balanced consideration needs to be given to matters of outcome, which are generally more amenable to observation and measurement, and effect, which are far more problematic. Evaluation normally strives to compare results with specified objectives, expectations, standards, or conditions; in this matter, the problem of criteria stands out most prominently. Such criteria, however, are not to be limited simply to formal statements of intention or single-purpose standards, such as efficiency. Nor should they emphasize only the perspective or standpoint of a client or any other single participant. In principle, all stakeholders merit consideration, and one comes to expect many different criteria to be useful and used in making program assessments. Finally, no one method, theory, typology, or analysis will be sufficient to accomplish the full evaluation task. Each may have worth, but all will in various ways have limitations that matter.

Evaluation research, as a field and collection of methods, has tended to emphasize specific methodologies while giving less attention to many of these other considerations.

METHODS

Understandably, many of the main analytic tools and methods encountered during the estimation activities of the policy process are also used to conduct evaluations.[28] It is understandable when one sees that estimation is firmly rooted in past experience—data are a form of history—and concentrated on making judgments about likely and desired future courses of action. Tools and theories that aid the policy estimator will often be as useful to the policy evaluator. And where differences occur, these can usually be linked to unavoidable consequences flowing from the observed complexity of realistic circumstances an evaluator must confront—as opposed to the synthetic, prior-to-experience situations with which estimators deal. For example, value preferences or conflicts and confusion about what a program's real purposes are nearly always confound the evaluator and must be treated. While these are usually just as important and pronounced during estimation, the analyst may occasionally ignore or finesse them by carefully selecting the data, formulating assumptions, or otherwise failing to deal with messy aspects of the analysis. The messy aspects nearly always surface during evaluation.

For instance, it is often very difficult to relate observed outcomes and effects directly to program interventions. Programs exist in the operational world, not in sterile laboratory conditions where randomness, coincidence, and plain old luck can be controlled. As a result, numerous plausible explanations accounting for actual observed performance will be needed. Additionally, evaluation results do not generalize very well in practice. The specific conditions and circumstances attending an exemplary, successful program will not necessarily exist in other settings. Thus, a promising demonstration program, done under close scrutiny with highly motivated administrative talent and ample resources, may very well fail when transplanted elsewhere and operated by indifferent administrators with fewer resources to dispense. In such circumstances, does one assess the total program as a failure?[29] The main point is that evaluation seeks to answer specific, contextually constrained questions; it is far less valuable as a basis for broad generalization.

As with all policy analysis, evaluation is extremely sensitive to the time selected, both with respect to the choice of elapsed time of a program's life (e.g., brand new programs are usually less efficient than tried-and-true, time-tested ones) and the amount of time available for the evaluator-analyst to do the work.[30] The time span of an evaluation will be determined in part by the importance a research sponsor ascribes to the program (and hence the amount of resources made available to do the analysis) and in part by the tools and techniques relied on by the analyst to do the work. This helps one appreciate the high incidence of informal evaluations, the reliance on cross-sectional (as opposed to prolonged, time-series) analyses, and the large number of case study assessments that together make up the bulk of the evaluation research field. Formal evaluations are usually more expensive and time-consuming than informal ones; time-series data collection and analysis are more challenging and error prone than cross-sectional ones; and case studies, given the problems of generalizability and comparative analysis, are usually more satisfying to both researchers and study users. But there is no inherent reason why a program's value should be arbitrarily confined to some preset period of time. It is alleged that premature evaluation of the New Jersey Income Maintenance experiment resulted in unfavorable reactions to what some thought was a very promising program.[31] It also led to its termination. In other words, evaluation needs to be regarded as a continuous, on-going activity in recognition of the dynamic nature of the policy process and of the possibility that longer-term costs and benefits may accrue that were not evident in the first blush of success or failure.

The evaluation of research and development (R&D), particularly in high-risk or high-technology settings, is illustrative of many more general methodological considerations.[32] By nature and definition, many R&D programs seek to make breakthroughs, discoveries of new ways to do things or new products. Evaluation in advance of such discovery will, strictly speaking, turn up negative results; and the creative process itself defies rigid scheduling and prespecification. Not only will results not come in on time, but they may occur in very different guises than those expected when the program began. Cost overruns,[33] scheduling problems, and not getting precisely what one wanted in the first place are common enough conditions in the R&D realm, and evaluations that pinpoint any or all of these deficiencies may very well end up squelching longer-term benefits of the creative process. Care must also be taken not to make unwarranted comparisons between competitive technologies at different stages of development or realization. Hence, it makes very little sense to compare an emerging technology, such as solar energy, to an established one, such as nuclear power, especially because the former will have many more observable, near-term costs than benefits. Also, a comparison between a conventional power source and an evolving, alternative one will tend to overstate the near-term benefits of the existing technologies and understate or neglect longer-term effects, such as pollution or resource depletion—both of which can only be estimated (guessed at) for the alternative source.

This brief treatment of common evaluation dilemmas is a necessary precursor to the following discussion of evaluation designs that, in varying degrees, one encounters in the field. While a diversity of specific methods may help one in carrying out any of these designs, the approaches and attitudes about evaluation research each represent are fairly standard.

The *pre-experimental* design matches program results with program actions in the absence of any control groups or settings against which judgments of what kind of and how much impact an intervention has had. The one-group, pre-test, post-test design is a common example here: measurements are made of variables that one wishes to influence with a new program to establish baseline data and a point of reference; the program is implemented (the matter of how much time to allow for implementation figures here); and then an equivalent set of measures to the initial set of variables is made to determine what happened. Changes in the before and after states are then related to specific aspects of the program. An alternative version of this design compares treatment and nontreatment groups or variables according to prespecified (expected) criteria. Again, differences are imputed to the treatment or program influence. The case study evaluation is the most common form of pre-experimental design. Here evaluation criteria are usually determined after the fact of implementation (although consideration of intent or expectation of eventual performance occurs). Despite their prevalence, pre-experimental designs are methodologically the least rigorous and satisfying. They are also the least costly and the easiest to perform.

Quasi-experimental designs are more scientific (e.g., more rigorous, more quantitative) and more costly. Two general forms occur: the time series and comparison group.[34] The time-series design relies on successive measurements of the prior, during, and post-treatment condition of criteria variables; a more complex variant involves simultaneous time-series measurement and comparison between treatment and nontreatment groups or settings. A main point of the time-series design is to detect and measure trends—rates of change—in the variables of interest. So a program meant to reduce drug abuse might be measured according to decreases in numbers of drug overdose admissions to hospitals within the treatment area, of arrests for drug-related offenses, and of individuals coming forward for rehabilitation or medical treatment, depending on the kind of program put into effect. For the period of analysis a usual assumption is that everything but the program will remain relatively stable or constant, an assumption that loses credibility the longer the analysis. The comparison group variant is employed to help the analyst make judgments about the true influences of the program intervention by reducing uncertainty about happenstance or coincidental events in the treatment setting. Thus, reduction of drug abuse may very well occur in the treatment area simply because of external factors (e.g., disruptions in heroin or cocaine production) and not because of the specific program under review. With two groups (treated and untreated, program and nonprogram), the opportunity for additional information to be brought to bear over time is often attractive. However, the selection of comparison groups is usually not easy and seldom results in a perfect match;

this is particularly so when large, complex units of analysis, such as a city, are the object of study.

The *true experimental* design is the holy grail of evaluation research. Not surprisingly, it tends to be extremely hard to do and usually quite expensive.[35] The social experiment is perhaps the most notable representation of this design strategy or approach.[36] The scientific model from which the experimental design takes most cues is a common one in experimental psychology,[37] although attention to it can be more generally discerned throughout the various social science disciplines.[38] In this approach, great care is given to the matter of selection of control and treatment groups (e.g., random, statistically valid selection), to the prespecification and measurement of criterion variables (e.g., definitions must be unambiguous and measurement must be capable of high precision, reliability, and validity), and to the control of factors external to the field of observation and study (e.g., sharp bounding of the problem in spatial and temporal terms). It follows, therefore, that many programs will not be amenable to the true experimental approach, especially those of large scale, great complexity, variable contexts, or an evolutionary sort (e.g., as the program gets started its rules change in light of fluctuating resources or other realistic and unforeseen events).

As was the case with many estimation approaches and tools, there seems to be a trade-off between analytic rigor and policy utility—a matter recognized in many calls to be mindful of and incorporate qualitative and subjective factors into one's analyses. At base, one comes back to a policy reality: The quality of one's evaluation will ultimately depend as much on the skill and judgment of the responsible analyst as it does on the selection and use of any one or collection of tools and techniques. As we discovered in estimation, the stated and unstated purposes underlying an analysis, such as evaluation, will have a significant bearing on its eventual form, operation, and results.

PURPOSES: KNOWLEDGE VERSUS CONTROL

A great deal of what passes for evaluation research is inspired by a desire to create and contribute to knowledge, a perfectly reasonable goal as seen from the perspective of social science researchers. Questions of the following sort suggest main lines of inquiry and kinds of information a knowledge-oriented evaluation pursues: How much does an observed phenomenon deviate from a norm or expectation for it? Why? Are the divergences related to intentional manipulations or are they related to other things? Which ones? And how strong are the relationships? However, those who commission and attempt to use evaluation research are often searching for something quite different. From the user's perspective, concern for control dominates creation of knowledge as an end in itself. Control in this sense is found in efforts to improve accountability of programs, to enhance managerial flexibility and potency, and to maintain or improve one's position of authority or dominance: that is, to succeed politically. Knowledge is, of course, needed for one to control, but it is a rather different sort of knowledge than that sought by the typical evaluation researcher.[39] Knowledge is, in this case, instrumental and serves the interest of better control.

In situations of continuing conflict, where program operations contribute to tension and stress among members of a responsible organization or between insiders and outsiders, evaluation may serve the very useful controlling purposes of cushioning or damage limiting: cushioning in the sense that precise terms or inflated expectations may be changed or aligned with reality and limiting in the sense that stressful or onerous aspects of a program may be appreciated and contained at something less than open hostility. Building ships for the U.S. Navy is an illustrative program, "which has been plagued by delays, high costs, and acrimonious disputes."[40] While a variety of problems have surfaced in a succession of evaluations—by the Senate Armed Services Committee, the House Appropriations Committee, and the U.S. General Accounting Office, all functioning in their oversight role—a root cause of chronic poor performance is a lack of agreement about what shipbuilders are expected to accomplish:

> the Navy is addicted to buying the most technologically advanced ships, even if this means that initial plans are vague, even if constant changes must be made during construction, and even if costs escalate and production is delayed.[41]

In other words, program expectations are not only hard to discern, they are constantly changing and creating conflicts and poor performance. The problem has become so serious as "to threaten the Navy's ability to fulfill its strategic role at a time when that very role is the subject of widespread debate."[42] The need to regain control, by limiting conflict among other things, underlines virtually all evaluations concerning Navy shipbuilding; elegance of research design, reliability and validity of measurements of performance, and other scientific niceties simply do not compare in importance.

Single evaluations have occasionally resulted in significant social changes, but change has been served at least as well by the cumulative impact over time of hundreds of routine appraisal activities. Improvements in civil liberties, for example, are commonly tied to the results of one or a few landmark judicial assessments, such as *Brown* v. *Board of Education* in 1954. But the aggregate social impact of numerous other small assessments, meant to advance civil rights more than to measure details of compliance (or its lack), clearly accounts for more in deciding where change originated and why it sustained. In other words, evaluations can be used to foster social change and to enhance the authority backing the means to accomplish it.

Social experiments contain a large element of social change, and their conduct may be based as much on this purpose as the more scientific ones discussed in the relevant literature. An experiment, taken from a social change perspective, means that a limited variety of programs will be tried out and their various results assessed. Decisions and commitments, plans and experiences all get made and worked out. The key point is that conducting an experiment has consequences, not the least of which are a partial vindication for those favoring the changes tried out in the experiment and the creation of experiences and dependencies that may persist and flourish.[43] The social experiment, thought of as evaluation to foster change and enhance control, presents a very different slant on the kinds and quality of data and information a user will require than simply thinking about it as a scientific, measurement enterprise. Many do not consider this possibility.[44]

To one interested in control, evaluation offers a chance to explore both assumptions and behavior in given program settings. As one engages in evaluation, a very common reaction is to make conscious implicit or vaguely understood presumptions and preferences. Such introspection extends to cover both evaluators and those being observed and appraised. Evaluation often allows program personnel to step back momentarily from their day-to-day responsibilities to think about what they are doing and trying to accomplish. Experienced evaluators, in various ways, are aware of the controlling influences their presence and probing have. Experienced evaluation sponsors and users are at least as aware of this valid and beneficial reason for assessing performance. Self-examination occurs among evaluators, too. Heightened self-righteousness and an assumption that everything being assessed is corrupt or misguided may moderate as familiarity with the operational realities accumulates in the course of doing the evaluation. Alternatively, one's predispositions may intensify in light of the experience. In either case, evaluation offers a chance to examine pertinent assumptions and to modify behavior accordingly.

Burnishing one's image is a political fact of life, and evaluation has been implicated more than once here. Such a purpose need not be inappropriate, particularly if the sponsor is sincere and wants to know what is happening to make improvements. Plus, perceived respect for the integrity and effectiveness of a program or organization cannot hurt in other competitive arenas—in cases where responsible officials know a program is accomplishing what it was meant to. For instance, if legislators believe that some agency is behaving responsibly, because of its vigorous evaluation efforts (among other reasons), it stands to reason that the organization will be viewed more favorably than others not having this image. In recent memory, comparisons between operations of the supersecret National Security Agency and the parallel Central Intelligence Agency suggest the worth of this point. The former has a general reputation for competency and efficiency of operations, including tight internal controls over its personnel and operations; the latter's reputation is quite different, as any number of official and renegade evaluations attest.[45]

Sincere assessment and whitewash or eyewash efforts done for deceptive or self-promotion reasons are different. Nagging questions about evaluations done of the controversial and trouble-plagued, U.S. Army M-1 tank help make the distinctions. In the words of an unnamed Defense Department armor analyst, "American soldiers will get killed in this tank—I mean unnecessarily killed," as a result of numerous unreported defects and alleged contrived assessments.[46] Evaluation as whitewash is charged by this individual as follows: "What they mean by assessing is throwing out the stuff they don't like. By the magic of this they reduce 1,007 maintenance actions [a key performance criterion] to 171 . . . which just happens to be a hair above the requirement. . . ."[47] The disclosure continues and identifies many other possible defects, all of which Army officials denied. A different version of self-promotion comes through in the case of Senator William Proxmire's celebrated Golden Fleece Awards for supposedly flagrant misuses of the taxpayer's dollars.[48]

The Golden Fleece is not only self-promotional, but it shares in common with many other evaluations a desire to assign responsibility. Boards of inquiry, trouble-shooters, and hatchet men are other common indicators that those in charge are trying to fix blame or to spread its ill effects around. Certainly when a political judgment lets the hatchet men loose, the nature, form, and substance of the assessments concocted will differ greatly from those expected of a more scientific evaluation. Responsibility is a complex idea, and an appraisal can acknowledge excellence as well as incompetence; personnel evaluations (a process type) have this characteristic. But some have come to question personnel evaluation systems, specifically those relied on by the armed forces to recognize excellence in the officer corps, as having become severely distorted as an objective indicator while at the same time increasing in importance as a means to force conformance of those whose lives it controls.[49]

In its purest state, evaluation works to generate objective measures of observed experiences in the interests of improved decision making and operations. Such are the often stated purposes or objectives encountered in the literature of evaluation research. However, equally evident in the literature is a finding that evaluation has either failed to have much impact on decisions and operations or that much more fundamental social science remains to be done before improvements will occur. Accordingly, a great deal of evaluation research has emphasized methodological, measurement, and theoretical ends—not practical ones. Improvements in decisions and operations are tendered far less weight. Other routine purposes, characterized generally as matters of control, are hardly treated at all. But any analyst or scholar who wants to conduct evaluations needs to be aware of possibly significant purposes other than the limited academic ones that prevail. Our discussion has been designed to heighten this awareness.

CRITIQUE

The slight influence evaluation research has had on decision making and program operations is well known.[50] But the common requirements postulated that would be necessary to improve matters are neither as well known nor are they especially realistic. For instance, the following three "conditions" have been listed as necessary precursors if "evaluation research is likely to lead to better program performance."[51]

Condition 1: Program objectives are well defined.

Condition 2: Program objectives are plausible/realistic.

Condition 3: Intended uses of information are well defined.

It is obvious that attainment of any or all of these conditions would make the experimental design approaches of evaluation research work better. It is equally obvious that most real programs are not likely to satisfy the conditions. A sketchy recollection of the salient features of conventional evaluation research approaches helps explain why.

Researchers trying to assess a program's effectiveness must measure the relevant attributes of the target population before and after the program. Differences between the measures indicate the extent and direction of the program's influence. An effective program produces improvements in the relevant attributes, an ineffective program no change, and a detrimental program a decline. The challenge is to ensure that the results (or lack of them) are due to the program rather than to extraneous, contaminating, or unforeseen factors. This basic model is limited. Policymakers care about a program's influences but they care about lots of other things, too. Prime on this list would be the value of a program's outcomes and effects, and evaluation research is mute on this. The experimental design demands clarity of objectives, but the decision maker typically has broad and diffuse objectives. Decision makers allow their objectives to evolve as a program unfolds and unexpected limitations and possibilities present themselves; the evaluator demands constant objectives so that valid measures can be made before and after the program. Program officials seek to tailor-make or individualize their operations to meet the special needs of clients and to adapt to peculiarities in the context; the evaluator demands standard treatments, invariant from place to place, so that responsibility for outcomes and effects can be assigned accurately. An administrator seeks out clients in a variety of ways (sometimes working not to attract them at all); the evaluator requires clients to be selected randomly from among those eligible so as to determine differences between treatment and nontreatment control groups unaffected by the program. Everyone is disappointed in the process. Program people get upset when evaluations fail to address their concerns, even in cases where they make efforts to bend their responsibilities to fit the experimental mold. Researchers are frustrated as they discover the facts of program life will not fit the constraints of the experimental method and thus resort to bending programs into familiar (and illegitimate) forms or to falling back on case study descriptions of dubious scientific merit. Obviously, a different approach is called for.

EVALUATION AS CONTROL

Evaluation occurs in real circumstances. It involves human beings with various motivations, talents, and inclinations. Evaluation exposes these conditions, and as it does, mundane and irrational aspects of the policy process emerge into full view. Not the least of these realistic—and important—aspects depicts evaluation as a key means to control. This useful perspective helps one appreciate many practical difficulties encountered during evaluation.

A concept of control

A key source of disappointment for many evaluation researchers is that while their products are good, decision makers simply do not use the knowledge provided to achieve better, more rational, outcomes. But as stressed throughout this book, more than rational considerations inhabit the policy process. Policymakers not only seek enlightenment, they also wish to control their environments.

> And, because knowledge-seeking has costs (in time, energy, and scarce staff resources), policymakers may be more likely to invest in acquiring knowledge that serves pressing needs for control than in acquiring knowledge that serves the desirable but abstract goal of enlightenment.[52]

Control, in this perspective, involves the many uses of force treated earlier in Chapter 8 and can be generally summarized as the means by which some individuals get others to do their bidding to secure some policy or program goal. So, for instance, when the federal government passed the Education for All Handicapped Children Act, it was seeking fundamental control over states and localities, e.g., to comply with provisions of the statute, to change their behavior for various reasons, and to accede to some version of the collective, federal will. The federal initiative was predicated on the sense that previous experience has been deficient; the overriding intent of the legislation was to force changes to reduce these deficiencies. To the degree that changes occurred and deficiencies receded in the wake of the new law, one may say a certain amount of control was exerted.

Evaluation plays a central role in all of these steps. The perception of deficiency is determined through cumulative evaluations, large and small, formal and informal. The prescription for change is based on an explicit statement of preferences about the future. Finally, determining the kinds of changes that eventually occur is a way to discover how much control one has over the situation. Policymaking, from this perspective, resolves to the matter of persuading, coercing, or seducing by some groups to get others to go along with decisions which they otherwise might not.[53]

Many different ways, besides doing evaluation, exist to enhance control of this sort. Hiring people with built-in controls is a common one.[54] Political loyalty and professionalism are representative. Decision makers of all kinds seek subordinates who share their beliefs, and to the degree the quest yields compliant and obedient executors, the need for evaluation per se may be reduced. But as a practical matter in most large organizations, the number of political or personal loyalists will never be large enough to guarantee completely faithful performance. This becomes all the more so as the norm of loyalty conflicts with that of merit or competence.[55] Furthermore, completely faithful performance may not result in completely desirable outcomes when taken from perspectives other than those who control, as the Nixon era amply demonstrates. "In the case of Watergate, like-minded associates . . . developed a warped and unbalanced perspective where excesses reinforced and fed upon one another," with the devastating consequences all know too well.[56]

Professionalism is another means by which demands for evaluation might be lessened. The general argument in its favor proceeds as follows: If there are well-understood and generally accepted norms for behavior, transmitted through reputable training and other socialization means, then those aspiring to a specific trade or calling can be counted on to perform predictably.[57] For those who transgress or violate the norms, sanctions must exist and be used to punish aberrant behavior. In selected circumstances, professionalism has reached a level where top leadership scarcely needs to worry about subordinate behavior, but in other times and places, the norm has failed to live up to its textbook billing.[58] In commenting on municipal authorities' inability to deliver the goods, Yates concludes: "Professionalism in service bureaucracies has not produced the rational, well-ordered system of service delivery that the advocates of professionalism envisioned."[59] Because of such breakdowns, evaluation, as an alternative way to control, gains prominence.

Reliance on professionalism often runs afoul of the realistic conditions and ambiguous decisions that defy even earnest professional efforts at unraveling and implementation.[60] Furthermore, the explicit or formal norms thought to be governing professional conduct may be at odds with implicit and informal ones; large enough differences here produce corruption and scandals.[61] Whether well-meant or corrupt, the resulting problems usually demand many kinds of evaluation to set matters straight.

Strong reasons not to evaluate

Despite many reasons for doing evaluation, it is still often not done or done according to the specifications of evaluation researchers. It is important to understand why.

Good evaluation has its costs. It takes highly trained talent, money, and time. Not all policies or programs will be considered important enough to warrant detailed and expensive probing. More to the point, from the control perspective, evaluations disrupt, reveal institutional weaknesses and limitations, and threaten individual policies and their sponsors. Most of these real aspects of evaluation are emphasized by Szanton:

> Using discontent is productive; attempting to create it is not. Since nothing works as well as it might, and since evaluators demonstrate their acuteness most readily by finding fault, program evaluations are almost always critical. Even when they propose correctives, evaluations focus mainly on fault: questionable policies, probable inefficiencies, inadequate foresight, perhaps a taint of fraud. That may be tolerable for a new administrator but not for a veteran. And in either event it makes enemies of his career subordinates. . . . More important, it serves little purpose. Proposals for change can document clearly enough, though implicitly, what is wrong. And their emphasis is far more welcome and more useful: not what is wrong and who should take the blame, but how service or policy or operations can be improved.[62]

Several lessons are suggested by these comments. Evaluation will probably occur in a hostile setting; inadequate, poor, or fraudulent performance is, to a large degree, a matter of judgment and relative perspective; and as is the general case with policy analysis, evaluation will be sought and its results used more to enhance control than to improve understanding. An evaluator's arguments may be heard, but they will be treated as just another piece of information—to be believed if convenient and ignored if not.

Because evaluation is commonly perceived to be a destructive process, its conduct stimulates hostility in those being appraised. Staff resistance is bolstered by a general abhorrence of failure found in the society at large. Furthermore, evaluation threatens the status quo. A presumption of misfeasance prompts many assessments and this, in turn, readily leads to fears that familiar ways of doing business will be faulted and changed. Individuals[63] and institutions[64] usually resist both changes and threats to stability posed by evaluations. Restating these points (developed elsewhere in the book) reminds one that human, motivational issues will have real consequences for evaluation.

Judgment and perspective also matter. In a sobering disclosure of reviewing practices at the National Science Foundation, the following conclusion stands out: "An experiment in which 150 proposals submitted to the National Science Foundation were evaluated independently by a new set of reviewers indicates that getting a research grant *depends* to a significant extent *on chance.*"[65] Even in this relatively specialized case of judging the merits of scientific (as contrasted with policy) work, serious differences of opinion exist that make evaluation suspect. The problem is widespread,[66] and helps to remind us once again of the many valid perspectives and value biases that reside in real settings where policy is created and carried out.[67] Because even qualified experts may disagree and different participants will see and value identical circumstances differently, consistent and binding evaluation results are rare.

This is not to say decision makers should cease doing evaluations, nor is it justification for the many, diverse, and variable-equality evaluations that already exist. Rather, it says that evaluations will continue to be used selectively by those in control to advance their own purposes, many of which are not readily apparent to the unwary analyst.[68] An illustration from the general field of management information systems clarifies many of these points.

Management information systems (MIS) have been proposed as a way of improving top leadership's effectiveness, efficiency, and the like.[69] An evaluative purpose, stressing the process form of internal assessment, dominates. However, a common reaction to many MIS efforts is that they are mostly symbolic and do not provide much substantial assistance: they contain a great deal of data, most of which is not particularly decision relevant. The reaction varies from place to place but is common enough to mention. A usual response or explanation takes a rational tack: decision makers really do not know what they need to know, they are not sophisticated enough to make the best use of the data at their disposal, or the system requires more development and expansion. A contrary and unconventional interpretation helps put the MIS tool into a different light.

Some proportion of the data collected is probably not very useful to anyone; it is collected because it is easy to do so and the computer's appetite must be sated. Another proportion is probably relevant to some levels of the organization but not to all nor to top management except in unusual circumstances. Nonetheless, it clutters up the common information system files. Some smaller segment is important to top management, is monitored regularly and carefully, and provides sufficient worth to cover its associated costs. This core of essential data is not static; needs change, as one would expect, in an evolving setting. Furthermore, and this is the key point, it may be in the leadership's interest to keep this core data hidden amidst the clutter of the rest of system in which it is embedded. Were this high-interest, critical data separated out—by being identified as such—a grave risk presents itself of compromising the operation by identifying for one's competitors, including those within the organization, realistic elements most critical for planning, evaluation, and control.

Is it irrational to have large, unused management information systems? Of course not. So it is with evaluation. Much, if not most, evaluation is informal, routine, and hidden from easy view. Data that count most are precisely those the leadership protects and covets for its own uses. Many evaluations will be conducted to create noise and clutter in the environment. Finally, the symbolic ends of evaluation—whitewash, eyewash—serve leadership as well as most substantial ones of improving an organization's efficiency or a policy's effectiveness.

Evaluation results: Substantial or symbolic?

Whether or not evaluation leads to substantial results is never a foregone conclusion. It all depends on many other aspects of the operational environment in which the evaluation occurs.

Hard and unyielding recommendations may be politically infeasible. Evaluations of the social security system in America in the 1970s and during the Reagan Administration converged on policy options that, if not infeasible, were certainly very unattractive to the political leadership.[70] In similar circumstances, in other policy areas, even were evaluation to work well, this may still be insufficient to stimulate the required political actions.

Good evaluation findings may be distorted as they pass upward through chains of command until most or all substantive content is drained away. Besides not wanting to take responsibility for deficient performance, many subordinates fear the boss's wrath when bad news is announced. Besides not wanting to be the target in the classic "shoot the messenger who bears bad tidings" situation, cover-ups and other obstructions may impede faithful transmission of bad news to those who ought to be hearing it.

Problems can be misspecified, and evaluation results that follow may be misguided or harmful. In the 1960s, numerous assessments urged urban renewal as a policy to restore America's cities.[71] The bulldozers roared and thousands of blocks were demolished. Whether or not the outcomes were justified should be considered in each case; but the longer-term effects have been questioned by many:

> This kind of program is not logical, it is not practical, and it is not moral. For no government program should exist that threatens the life, the liberty or the property of *any* person. No person, no matter who he is, should be sacrificed for the esthetic pleasure or personal gain of anyone, no matter how educated, how rich or how powerful.[72]

In all instances political and symbolic requirements can be discovered undermining evaluation's most defensible and substantial findings. The problem is deep-seated and irresolvable. As long as bargaining and compromise underlie political consensus, actual programs will reflect diverse interests. Policy goals and program objectives will be inconsistent and sometimes contradictory, and so will the policies and programs that flow from them. Much of what transpires has heavy symbolic and rhetorical overtones because politics depends on both symbol and rhetoric at least as much as it does on hard facts.

Why bother?

If evaluation is so hard to do, why bother? It is essential that the reasons for carrying out evaluation are as well understood as are the many and varied problems one encounters doing it. Evaluation is a critical phase in the overall policy process, just as it is significant in the life of particular policies and programs.

At the most general level, evaluation offers realistic experience and adds to our knowledge of social and political behavior. Evaluation is the point during the policy process when problem, solution, and experience converge and provide opportunities to gauge and calibrate our collected knowledge about specific problems. Slowly and erratically, to be sure, we learn. Evaluation is one means by which we do.[73]

But we learn not for its own sake nor to rationalize particular institutional arrangements. Rather, evaluation is best conceived as a way to advance human fulfillment which means seeing "the person as a whole, in all his aspects, not as the embodiment of this or that limited set of needs or interests." And its accounting through evaluation, "prizes not the glory of a depersonalized state of the efficiency of a social mechanism [e.g., a nation, an organization, a program, a policy], but human dignity and the realization of human capacities."[74] Human dignity includes freedom, the sharing of power among the many rather than the few, as well as widespread participation in all value processes. The most general task for policy scientists is the specification of ways human dignity can be achieved in concrete circumstances, so that whatever potential for progress exists can be realized. Evaluation—the assessment of outcomes and effects—is an essential means to this end.[75]

Paying specific attention to the differences between program and policy outcomes and effects enables responsible authorities to adjust management and implementation approaches to attain a variety of human objectives. Merely determining that program X has consumed a certain number of resources to yield outcomes Y and Z is a necessary, but insufficient, condition for evaluation. One also needs to find out about effects—the influence of program X on the lives of all touched or implicated by it. So what if 10,000 people are served at a cost of $1 million over a period of time? Were they the right people? Did the service make any difference in their lives? Would some other intervention have done better in advancing basic social welfare and personal fulfillment?

By some reckonings, the policies and programs pursued in Germany between 1936 and 1945 were extraordinarily efficient and effective. Certainly the industrial miracles performed by Albert Speer in harnessing a relatively limited resource base for the national purpose represent outcomes far in excess of anyone's initial expectations. But the total tragic costs incurred in terms of human dignity and fulfillment sharply underscore the key point in our argument: Social mechanisms are good only to the extent they advance fundamental human needs.

EVALUATION IN THE POLICY PROCESS

As it must be tied directly to human needs, so too must evaluation link-up with the other phases of the policy process.

Evaluation often uncovers problems unforeseen and unimagined and thus stimulates initiation to begin anew. Economists sometimes speak of externalities—outcomes and effects outside of the specific field of vision and concern. Such may, in time, become important enough to warrant explicit treatment through the policy process but only if their nature, magnitude, and consequences are adequately assessed through evaluation. For instance, in the Aid to Families with Dependent Children (AFDC) example used earlier, one unexpected program result for many appears to be increased dependence and continuing poverty. Some remark that this follows from a general tendency to blame the victims for their plight.[76] While others see the problem as rooted in a lack of attention to the goal of human dignity: "Human-development goals can never be effectively achieved with the victim-blaming, short-term relief arrangements which derive from current ideas about poverty."[77] Whatever the validity of the diagnosis, AFDC is at best a partial answer, which itself creates new demands on society.

Initiation and evaluation are closely linked. Trying to define and come to terms with new problems discovered during evaluation may reveal or suggest different—and more appropriate—characterizations of the problem during initiation. If blaming the victims produces consistently unsatisfactory outcomes and effects, in many different programs for the poor, perhaps other definitions of the problem are required.

Estimation is implicated, too. As evaluation results mount, an opportunity is created to refer back to previous analyses on which program decisions were based. Were estimated outcomes—costs and benefits— achieved? If not, were the analyses at fault? What needs to be done to improve future estimation activities? Furthermore, evaluation generates new data which, in time, may inform existing theories or improve methods for the same or related problem areas. Were the criteria and goals used during estimation realistic, reasonable, valuable? Whose preferences were emphasized, after all, during the earlier analyses?

Blame for poor or substandard performance will be lodged somewhere. Politicians and others concerned with selection are understandably loath to bear the brunt here, especially for the harm it may cause in constituent esteem. Nonetheless, evaluation may discover decision errors needing correction. Many pieces of legislation are thus amended, clarified, or otherwise adapted in light of experience. Evaluation may even provoke more sweeping adjustments: Demands for constitutional change, "sweeping the rascals away" through the ballot box, and extra-legal responses such as civil disobedience and revolution should not be rejected in extreme cases.

Taken from the selection-evaluation vantage point, other changes may occur. Better informed and more realistic expectations about performance could be created to improve implementation and to provide better guidance for evaluation. As a general matter, the growth and diversification of the U.S. General Accounting Office are concrete examples of the selection-evaluation connection.[78]

If one recalls that most evaluations are informal and occurring nearly all the time, the intimate relationship between them and implementation comes clear. Indeed, numerous simple feedback mechanisms between evaluation and program operations—exemplified in the process form of assessment—yield one of the strongest connections in the policy process.

As small errors are sensed, midcourse corrections are effected. As corrections are experienced, evaluations determine whether previous errors are reduced or new problems are created. Larger and more noticeable mistakes may not be as easily dispensed with. Evaluation that uncovers gross malfunction or misfeasance could foreshadow wholesale changes in implementation procedures and personnel.

Considerably less well developed, in either practice or theory, is the link between evaluation and termination.[79] While it is reasonable to expect that many problems will be resolved to some satisfactory degree (if not solved outright), there is very little evidence that evaluation findings smoothly or routinely result in program or policy termination. There are many reasons for this, which we discuss in the next part. However logical the connection between evaluation and termination seems, it does not occur often. Programs grow old and become dysfunctional. Priorities and resources to meet problems are not static. Deciding about all of this involves evaluation, and carrying through may mean termination.

Once termination happens, questions could occur about the accuracy, fairness, or propriety of the evaluations that preceded it. Were the evaluations accurate, e.g., was the program in fact no longer needed, were its costs truly in excess of its benefits? Did the assessments meanly disadvantage some for the unfair benefit of others? Were they carried out according to acceptable and defensible practices and standards, or were the evaluations contrived—science and analysis be damned?

One suspects that this final list of questions is as important as it is unasked. Our experience with termination suggests as much.

NOTES

1. John Dewey, *Experience and Nature* (New York: Dover Publications, 1958), p. 101.

2. Harold D. Lasswell, *Politics: Who Gets What, When, How* (Cleveland: Meridian, 1958), part III, "Results." Measurement demands are treated in R. A. Berk, "Performance Measures: Half Full or Half Empty?" *Social Science Quarterly*, March 1974, pp. 762–64.

3. The measurement and quantification emphasis is most pronounced in selections collected in Francis G. Caro, ed., *Readings in Evaluation Research* (New York: Russell Sage Foundation, 1971); Edward A. Suchman, *Evaluative Research* (New York: Russell Sage Foundation, 1967); and Leonard Rutman, ed., *Evaluation Research Methods: A Basic Guide* (Beverly Hills, Calif.: Sage Publications, 1977). The nonquantitative elements are discussed in different ways in Robert K. Merton, "The Role of Applied Social Science in the Formation of Policy," *Philosophy of Science* 14, no. 2 (1949), pp. 161–81; Laurence E. Lynn, Jr., ed., *Knowledge and Policy: The Uncertain Connection* (Washington, D.C.: National Academy of Sciences, 1978); and Charles Fried, *An Anatomy of Values: Problems of Personal and Social Choice* (Cambridge, Mass.: Harvard University Press, 1970).

4. James S. Coleman et al., *Policy Issues and Research Design* (Chicago: National Opinion Research Center, 1979).

5. J. Child, "What Determines Organizational Performance? Universals vs. It All Depends," *Organizational Dynamics*, March 1974, pp. 2–14.

6. Elinor Ostrom, "Exclusion, Choice, and Divisability," *Social Science Quarterly*, March 1974, pp. 691–99; Bertram M. Gross, ed., *Social Intelligence for America's Future: Explorations in Societal Problems* (Boston: Allyn and Bacon, 1969), generally, but especially chap. 2, Amitai Etzioni and E. W. Lehman, "Some Dangers in 'Valid' Social Measurement," pp. 45–62; and Eugene J. Webb, Donald T. Campbell, Richard D. Schwartz, and Lee Sechrest, *Unobtrusive Measures* (Skokie, Ill.: Rand McNally, 1966).

7. R. L. Kenney and Howard Raiffa, *Decisions with Multiple Objectives: Preferences and Value Trade-Offs* (New York: John Wiley & Sons, 1976).

8. Judith Innes deNeufville, *Social Indicators and Public Policy* (New York: Elsevier, 1975), chaps. I, XII. A collection emphasizing the quality and quantity interrelationships is Thomas D. Cook and Charles S. Reichardt, eds., *Qualitative and Quantitative Methods in Evaluation Research* (Beverly Hills, Calif.: Sage Publications, 1979).

9. M. M. Provus, *Discrepancy Evaluation* (Berkeley, Calif.: McCutchan, 1971); problems in not conforming to this ideal are the centerpiece of Frederick Mosteller and Daniel P. Moynihan, eds., *On Equality of Educational Opportunity* (New York: Random House, 1972).

10. E. S. Quade, *Analysis for Public Decisions* (New York: American Elsevier, 1975), chap. 5.

11. Martin Rein, *Social Science and Public Policy* (New York: Penguin, 1976), chap. 4.

12. M. Carley, *Social Measurement and Social Indicators* (London: George Allen & Unwin, 1981), chap. 5; and Carol H. Weiss, *Evaluation Research: Methods of Assessing Program Effectiveness* (Englewood Cliffs, N.J.: Prentice-Hall, 1972).

13. Geoffrey Vickers, "Who Sets the Goals of Public Health?" *The Lancet*, March 1958, p. 599; Donald T. Campbell and A. E. Erlebacher, "How Regression Artifacts Can Mistakenly Make Compensatory Education Look Harmful," in J. Hellmuth, ed., *The Disadvantaged Child*, vol. 3 (New York: Brunner/Mazel, 1970), pp. 185–210; and U.S. General Accounting Office, *Follow Through: Lessons Learned from Its Evaluation and Need to Improve Its Administration* (Washington, D.C.: Government Printing Offfice, 1975).

14. Walter Williams and J. Evans, "The Politics of Evaluation," *Annals of the American Academy of Political and Social Science*, no. 385 (1969), pp. 118–132; Robert F. Clark, "Program Evaluation and the Commissioning Entity," *Policy Sciences*, March 1975, pp. 11–16; Harold Orlans, "The Political Uses of Social Research," *Annals of the American Academy of Political and Social Science*, no. 394 (1971), pp. 28–35; and idem, "Neutrality and Advocacy in Policy Research," *Policy Sciences*, June 1975, pp. 107–19.

15. Lee J. Cronbach and Associates, *Toward Reform of Program Evaluation* (San Francisco: Jossey-Bass, 1980); W. G. Smith, "The Ideal and the Real: Practical Approaches and Techniques in Evaluation," in J. Zusman and C. R. Wurster, eds., *Program Evaluation* (Lexington, Mass.: Lexington Books, 1975); and U.S. General Accounting Office, *Assessing Social Program Impact Evaluations: A Check-List Approach* (Washington, D.C.: Government Printing Office, 1978).

16. A more thorough than usual accounting of types is contained in W. James Popham, *Educational Evaluation* (Englewood Cliffs, N.J.: Prentice-Hall, 1975).

17. Michael Scriven, "The Methodology of Evaluation," in R. E. Stake, ed., *Perspectives on Curriculum Evaluation* (Skokie, Ill.: Rand McNally, AERA Monograph Series on Curriculum Evaluation, no. 1, 1967); and idem, "Two Main Approaches to Evaluation," in R. M. Bossone, ed., *Proceedings, Second National Conference on Testing* (New York: Center for Advanced Study in Education, City University of New York, 1978), is generally regarded as the author of these distinctions.

18. Suchman, *Evaluative Research*.

19. Consider efforts to prevent disease through a widespread vaccination program: One

certainly needs to know the prevalence and seriousness of the disease before the program is undertaken, how much effort will be expended in its control, how well these efforts succeed in reducing disease according to some previous specification, and for how many dollars. The causal linkages are mostly well-known or can be adequately interpreted from observation. We maintain that most, or all, of these conditions are exceptional in other social problem settings and hence reduce considerably the overall utility of the public health typology and model for evaluation research. Compare, for example, the public health model in application with respect to the swine flu vaccination program, in which external events figured prominently. Joseph A. Califano, Jr., *Governing America* (New York: Simon & Schuster, 1981), chap. 5. A definitive account is Richard E. Neustadt and Harvey V. Fineberg, *The Swine Flu Affair: Decision-Making on a Slippery Disease* (Washington: Government Printing Office, 1978).

20. We claim no particular pride of authorship here. Comparable distinctions can be found elsewhere. Harry P. Hatry, "Measuring the Effectiveness of Nondefense Public Expenditures," *Operations Research*, September 1970, pp. 772–84.

21. Martin Shubik, "On Concepts of Efficiency," *Policy Sciences*, April 1978, pp. 121–26, at p. 123.

22. Ibid.

23. The point is fairly general. Consider the "costs" associated with a school principal's being entangled in trying to fire a recalcitrant teacher while at the same time not being able to spend time on other matters, such as integration, busing, and student performance.

24. A provocative line of thought is provided in D. Allan Bromley, "The Fate of Seed Corn," *Science*, 10 July 1981, p. 159. Industry is demanding, in the near term, far more scientists and engineers than society is capable of producing under current budget and institutional circumstances. The result has been a rapid, perhaps accelerating, depletion of the ranks of those capable of training the next generation and providing the innovations (research based) industry will need in a wide variety of fields in the long range.

25. Some concern has been expressed about upper atmospheric effects of supersonic aircraft, although the evaluation is at this time both inconclusive and highly controversial.

26. U.S. General Accounting Office, *Assessing Social Program Impact Evaluations*.

27. Our conviction here is supported elsewhere. See Harry P. Hatry et al., *Practical Program Evaluation for State and Local Government* (Washington, D.C.: The Urban Institute, 1973), as one example.

28. See Chap. 6, "Methods and Estimation in the Policy Process."

29. The matter of generalizability is overlooked, for example, in Robert E. Klitgaard, "Identifying Exceptional Performers," *Policy Analysis*, Fall 1978, pp. 529–48.

30. The time issue is explicitly treated in Lester M. Salamon, "The Time Dimension in Policy Evaluation: The Case of the New Deal Land Reform Experiments" (Durham, N.C.: Institute of Policy Sciences and Public Affairs, Duke University, August 1974).

31. Margaret Boeckmann, "Policy Impacts of the New Jersey Income Maintenance Experiment," *Policy Sciences*, March 1976, pp. 53–76.

32. Peter deLeon, *The Evaluation of Technology R&D: A Continuing Dilemma* (Santa Monica, Calif.: The Rand Corporation, P–6655, August 1981).

33. Military R&D programs stand out here, although reasons for cost overruns, centering on the highly uncertain and ambitious objectives set out initially, have been appreciated. See Edmund Dews et al., *Acquisition Policy Effectiveness: Department of Defense Experience in the 1970s* (Santa Monica, Calif.: The Rand Corporation, R–2516, October 1979), for a summary exploration of this matter.

34. The literature is growing here, but a representative sample would include: Donald T. Campbell and Julian C. Stanley, *Experimental and Quasi-Experimental Designs for Re-*

search (Skokie, Ill.: Rand McNally, 1969); and James A. Caporaso and Leslie L. Roos, Jr., eds., *Quasi-Experimental Approaches: Testing Theory and Evaluating Policy* (Evanston, Ill.: Northwestern University Press, 1973).

35. Henry Acland, "Are Randomized Experiments the Cadillacs of Design?" *Policy Analysis*, Spring 1979, pp. 223–42.

36. Alice M. Rivlin, *Systematic Thinking for Social Action* (Washington, D.C.: The Brookings Institution, 1971), is a standard source here.

37. Donald T. Campbell, "Reforms as Experiments," *American Psychologist* 24, no. 4 (1969), pp. 409–29; and Julian C. Stanley, ed., *Improving Experimental Design and Statistical Analysis* (Skokie, Ill.: Rand McNally, 1967). A collection with a variety of case examples is Paul McReynolds, ed., *Advances in Psychological Assessment V* (San Francisco: Jossey-Bass, 1981).

38. F. S. Chapin, *Experimental Design in Sociological Research* (New York: Harper & Row, 1947), sets the common tone. The philosophical grounding is provided in Karl R. Popper, *Conjectures and Refutations* (New York: Basic Books, 1963).

39. A complicated matter, the difference in purposes has caught the attention of many interested in the uses of knowledge. See, Robert F. Rich, "Uses of Social Science Information by Federal Bureaucrats: Knowledge for Action versus Knowledge for Understanding," in Carol H. Weiss, ed., *Using Social Research for Public Policy Making* (Lexington, Mass.: D. C. Heath, 1977), pp. 199–211. Charles E. Lindblom and David K. Cohen, *Usable Knowledge* (New Haven: Yale University Press, 1979), is more comprehensive.

40. Deborah Shapley, "Addiction to Technology is One Cause of Navy's Shipbuilding Crisis," *Science*, 19 May 1978, pp. 741–44.

41. Ibid., p. 741. In his indictment of defense research and development, James Fallows considers many other causes of conflict and failure. *National Defense* (New York: Random House, 1981), especially chaps. 1–3.

42. Shapley, "Addiction to Technology."

43. Garry D. Brewer, "Experimentation and the Policy Process," in *Twenty-Fifth Annual Report of The Rand Corporation* (Santa Monica, Calif.: The Rand Corporation, 1973), pp. 151–65, considers this and other possible outcomes and effects of social experiments.

44. R. W. Archibald and J. P. Newhouse, *Social Experimentation: Some Whys and Hows* (Santa Monica, Calif.: The Rand Corporation, R–2479–HEW, 1979), is representative in its overwhelming focus on technical details.

45. Tyrus G. Fain, comp., *The Intelligence Community: History, Organization, and Issues* (New York: R. R. Bowker, 1977), especially the striking differences between chap. 5, "Central Intelligence Agency," and chap. 7, "National Security Agency." One of the first of many exposé accounts—the beginning of a parade—is Victor Marchetti and John D. Marks, *The CIA and the Cult of Intelligence* (New York: Alfred A. Knopf, 1974).

46. Stephen Webbe, "M–1 Tank Already in War—Of Words," *Christian Science Monitor*, April 22, 1981, p. 6.

47. Ibid. Prevalence of this reason for doing evaluation is not limited to tanks. Fallows, *National Defense*, reports the practice in numerous weapon procurement cases.

48. An engaging examination of the award and the Senator is provided by Vic Gold, "Calling to the Yahoo," *Harper's*, October 1976, pp. 32, 34–35.

49. William J. Gregor, "The Leader as Subordinate: The Politics and Performance of Unit Commanders in the United States Army" (New Haven: Yale University, Department of Political Science, unpublished Ph.D. dissertation, 1980), chap. II, especially pp. 44–54. The Officer Evaluation Report has a maximum numerical value of 200; in 1976 for the rank of captain, the Army-wide *average* stood at a remarkable 196! And, "the key to

career success is not the receipt of high evaluation report scores; it is rather avoiding low ones." P. 46. One presumes avoidance is in large measure achieved by doing what the Army superiors expect—a control matter.

50. Joseph S. Wholey, *Evaluation: Promise and Performance* (Washington, D.C.: The Urban Institute, 1979), is honest and authoritative on this score.

51. Joseph S. Wholey, "Using Evaluation to Improve Program Performance," in Robert A. Levine, Marian A. Solomon, Gerd-Michael Hellstern, and Hellmut Wollman, eds., *Evaluation Research and Practice* (Beverly Hills, Calif.: Sage Publications, 1981), pp. 92–106, at p. 95.

52. Janet A. Weiss, "Knowledge as Control in A Federal System" (New Haven: Institution for Social and Policy Studies, Yale University, April 1981). (Unpublished manuscript.) James W. Fesler, *Public Administration: Theory and Practice* (Englewood Cliffs, N.J.: Prentice-Hall, 1980), chaps. 10 and 11, develops the general idea for the Congress and the courts, respectively.

53. Weiss, ibid., has a parallel, but different, slant on the matter in her discussion of federal educational policymaking. We have also profited from several insightful comments about these matters from Jack Pitney of Yale's Political Science Department.

54. Charles Perrow, *Complex Organizations* (Glenview, Ill.: Scott-Foresman, 1979), p. 26.

55. Herbert Kaufman, "Emerging Conflicts in the Doctrines of Public Administration," *American Political Science Review*, December 1956, pp. 1057–73, at p. 1070.

56. Richard P. Nathan, "The Administrative Presidency," in Frederick S. Lane, ed., *Current Issues in Public Administration* (New York: St. Martin's Press, 1978), pp. 68–78, at p. 75.

57. Garry D. Brewer, "Professionalism: The Need for Standards," *Interfaces*, November 1973, pp. 20–27; and idem, "What Ever Happened to Professionalism?" *Interfaces*, August 1978, pp. 63–72.

58. Herbert Kaufman, *The Forest Ranger* (Baltimore, Md.: Johns Hopkins University Press, 1960), is a well-known illustration of nearly ideal professionalism.

59. Douglas Yates, *The Ungovernable City* (Cambridge, Mass.: MIT Press, 1977), p. 171.

60. Chap. 9, "Factors Influencing Implementation."

61. James Q. Wilson, "Corruption: The Shame of the States," *The Public Interest*, no. 2 (1966), pp. 28–38.

62. Peter Szanton, *Not Well Advised* (New York: Russell Sage and Ford Foundations, 1981), p. 138. The book itself is an evaluation of sorts—of many less-than-completely successful policy analyses done on behalf of municipal authorities.

63. Much of the issue has been captured in the rubric, "cognitive dissonance": individuals ignore or fight information from their immediate environment that does not conform to their psychological needs and expectations. Leon Festinger, *A Theory of Cognitive Dissonance* (Stanford, Calif.: Stanford University Press, 1957).

64. Garry D. Brewer, "On the Theory and Practice of Innovation," *Technology In Society*, Fall 1980, pp. 337–63.

65. Stephen Cole, Jonathan R. Cole, and Gary A. Simon, "Chance and Consensus in Peer Review," *Science*, 20 November 1981, pp. 881–86, at p. 881. (Emphases added).

66. Sheila Jasanoff and Dorothy Nelkin, "Science, Technology, and the Limits of Judicial Competence," *Science*, 11 December 1981, pp. 1211–15; and Philip M. Boffey, "Science Court: High Officials Back Test of Controversial Concept," *Science*, 8 October 1976, pp. 167–69.

67. Kenneth R. Hammond and Leonard Adelman, "Science, Values, and Human Judgment," *Science*, 22 October 1976, pp. 389–96.

68. Recall the previous discussion in this chapter, "Purposes: Knowledge versus Control."

69. Richard W. Brightman, *Information Systems for Modern Management* (New York: Macmillan, 1971), is representative.

70. Califano, *Governing America,* chap. IX. Carter, according to Califano, tried to tackle the beast: "This is not a politically popular proposal . . . but in the long run, we have got to make sure that . . . the allocation of funds goes to those who need it most, who don't have any other way to derive benefits. And with a limited amount of money, it is imperative that the system be efficient and that benefits go where they are most needed." Be that as it may, the proposal to reign in social security was termed by then Vice President Mondale, "the worst political mistake in the 1980 budget and legislative program." All at p. 397.

71. An extensive literature exists here, but Scott Greer, *Urban Renewal and American Cities* (Indianapolis, Ind.: Bobbs-Merrill, 1965), provides a concise overview.

72. Martin Anderson, *The Federal Bulldozer* (New York: McGraw-Hill, 1967), p. xix.

73. This argument is exemplified well in Lloyd S. Etheredge, "Government Learning: An Overview," in Samuel L. Long, ed., *The Handbook of Political Behavior*, vol. 2 (New York: Plenum, 1981), pp. 73–161.

74. Harold D. Lasswell and Abraham Kaplan, *Power and Society* (New Haven: Yale University Press, 1950), p. xxiv.

75. A more complete discussion of the general issue is contained in Garry D. Brewer and Ronald D. Brunner, "Harold D. Lasswell and Political Science," *In Commemoration and Continuing Commitment: Essays in Honor of Harold Dwight Lasswell* (New Haven: Yale School of Law, 1980), pp. 22–32.

76. William Ryan, *Blaming the Victim* (New York: Random House, 1971). Increased illegitimacy, husbandless families, and other ill effects of AFDC are also alleged or suspected.

77. Nicholas Hobbs, *The Futures of Children* (San Francisco, Jossey-Bass, 1975), p. 63.

78. Frederick C. Mosher, *The GAO: The Quest for Accountability in American Government* (Boulder, Colo.: Westview Press, 1979), chaps. 9 and 10.

79. Peter deLeon, *Policy Evaluation and Program Termination* (Santa Monica, Calif.: The Rand Corporation, P–6807, October 1982).

Discussion questions

1.   The variety and incidence of evaluation studies are noticeably increasing and broadening in recent years. Why do you think that this is happening? How does the information contained in such evaluations relate to the other five phases of the overall policy process? Could these links and relationships be strengthened, and if so, how? Would one want to strengthen them: why or why not? What outcomes and effects would you forecast for doing so?

2.   Three evaluations of three programs lead to three separate conclusions. Program A is faulted for not implementing accepted practices expected of any sophisticated endeavor. Program B, while doing what it did very nicely, did the wrong thing. Program C is chastised for doing something that resulted in entirely unintended consequences, most of which were undesirable. Discuss and describe the possible types of evaluations that might have resulted in these findings. What difference does it make if the sponsor or the evaluator is inside or outside the program or organization? Why do many evaluations focus on the technical and efficiency aspects of programs?

3.   "In principle" arguments advancing the need for evaluation of programs and policies have been developed by scholars; many of these either imply or require changes in the normal business as usual of program operations to work with best effect. Identify two or three of these arguments and contrast

them with "in practice" reasons that mitigate and otherwise thwart evaluation efforts.

4.   The sense that there is a deficiency of ethical preparation in the professions (e.g., law, medicine, research, analysis, politics) has gained prominence in the light of Watergate, periodic scandals in the practice and administration of medicine, faking important research results, atrocities— like the New Mexico and Attica prison riots and the My Lai massacre— corruption in the courts and Congress, bribery in large corporations, and so forth through a long and tiresome list. What might be done with the current generation of aspiring professionals to counter this apparent trend toward amoral behavior? Define and discuss what you mean by amoral. Why should the deficiency exist at all? Is it a problem with existing institutions? With incentives? The character of individuals attracted to various professions? Weaknesses in the systems of sanctions that currently exist to protect society from such acts? Weaknesses in the underlying moral fiber of the society? You might consider treating this question by concentrating on one profession, e.g., doctors, lawyers, businessmen; or you might want to focus on a specific institution, e.g., the U.S. Congress, General Motors.

5.   In recent years there has been a series of attempted administrative improvements, going by the names of Planning, Programming, Budgeting Systems (PPBS), Management by Objectives (MBO), and performance contracting. Based on your appreciation of the complexities of implementation and the difficulties of evaluation, what prospects do these, and similar, techniques hold? Why is it that administrative reforms, such as these, often stimulate countermeasures that tend to reduce the intended, beneficial effects? (Thinking about this question from the perspective of evaluation-as-control might be useful.)

6.   The simple threat of an impending evaluation may have consequences for the operations of a program or organization. Think about what some of these might be and develop conditions under which the threat may be lessened while at the same time allowing the evaluation to proceed.

7.   Some (unnamed) statesman has remarked: "If it ain't broke, don't fix it." Argue both the pro and con sides of this imperative.

8.   From the *New York Times*, April 14, 1981, p. A–11:

> The General Services Administration is resisting reforms that could save taxpayers millions of dollars and safeguard against fraud and organized crime infiltration, a Government auditor told a Congressional subcommittee today.
> "Very frankly, we're considerably frustrated," said Howard David, an Assistant Inspector General. "We don't feel we're getting cooperation. We're more and more alarmed at the potential for fraud, waste and abuse."
> Mr. David said agency officials might be reluctant to accept reform because it would be a tacit admission of past failures.

Why do you think that admission of past failures should figure so prominently here—to the extent that demonstrated misfeasance would be allowed to continue? What steps could one consider to confront the issue, either generally or with specific respect to reforms of the General Services Administration?

9.   Select a specific program with which you have had some direct, personal experience (e.g., student loans, unemployment or workman's compensation, local criminal justice). Define operationally, for this program, the following terms: equity, efficiency, adequacy, effectiveness. Again, with specific reference to this program, identify the various goals and objectives, trade-offs, contradictions, and other difficulties one might encounter in trying to decide how good or bad the program might be.

Supplementary readings

Because evaluation is perhaps one of the most studied and written-about phases of the policy process, it would be impossible to represent all perspectives and points of view. We did attempt, in the body of the chapters, to sample widely while at the same time working to bring together this large body of literature into a coherent and constructive picture of the theory and practice of evaluation. Hence, the chapters' documentation provides one rendition of the field and could be consulted for either specific points or questions or to develop one's general sense of the whole. The following supplementary readings provide another avenue to the topic and field. It is highly selective, but we have also tried to provide diversity—of disciplinary perspective, types and forms of evaluation, and subject matters considered. The organizing principle used for these readings differs somewhat from that in the chapters, although the general orientation and intent are similar.

GENERAL SOURCES (INCLUDING COLLECTIONS WITH NUMEROUS ADDITIONAL REFERENCES)

Cook, Thomas D., et al., eds. *Evaluation Studies Review Annual*, vol 3. Beverly Hills, Calif.: Sage Publications, 1978.

Guttentag, Marcia, ed. *Evaluation Studies Review Annual*, vol. 2. Beverly Hills, Calif.: Sage Publications, 1977.

377

Lasswell, Harold D. *Politics: Who Gets What, When, How.* Cleveland: Meridian, 1958, part III, "Results."

————. *A Pre-View of Policy Sciences.* New York: Elsevier, 1971, chaps. 5–8.

Nachmias, David, ed. *The Practice of Policy Evaluation.* New York: St. Martin's Press, 1980.

Rein, Martin. *Social Science and Public Policy.* New York: Penguin, 1976.

Rossi, Peter H., and Walter Williams. *Evaluating Social Programs.* New York: Seminar Press, 1972.

Stromsdorfer, Ernst W., and George Farkas, eds. *Evaluation Studies Review Annual,* vol. 5. Beverly Hills, Calif.: Sage Publications, 1980.

Weiss, Carol H., ed. *Evaluating Action Programs.* Boston: Allyn and Bacon, 1972.

GOALS AND VALUES: INDIVIDUAL AND SYSTEM RESPONSIBILITY

Fried, Charles. *An Anatomy of Values: Problems and Personal and Social Choice.* Cambridge, Mass.: Harvard University Press, 1970.

Jonas, Hans. *Philosophical Essays: From Ancient Creed to Technological Man.* Englewood Cliffs, N.J.: Prentice-Hall, 1974.

Kaplan, Abraham. *American Ethics and Public Policy,* New York: Oxford University Press, 1963.

Keeney, R. L., and Howard Raiffa. *Decisions with Multiple Objectives: Preferences and Value Trade-Offs.* New York: John Wiley & Sons, 1976.

Means, R. L. *The Ethical Imperative.* New York: Doubleday, 1969.

Winter, Gibson. *Elements for a Social Ethic.* New York: Macmillan, 1966.

The ultimate trade-off—life or death?

Anderson, Odin W. *Health Care —Can There Be Equity? The United States, Sweden, and England.* New York: John Wiley & Sons, 1972.

Ramsey, Paul. *Ethics at the Edges of Life: Medical and Legal Intersections.* New Haven: Yale University Press, 1978.

Wertz, Richard W., ed. *Readings on Ethical and Social Issues in Biomedicine.* Englewood Cliffs, N.J.: Prentice-Hall, 1973.

Williams, Preston, ed. *Ethical Issues in Biology and Medicine.* Cambridge, Mass.: Schenkman, 1973.

Ethics in the professions

Donaldson, Thomas, and Patricia H. Werhane, eds. *Ethical Issues in Business.* Englewood Cliffs, N.J.: Prentice-Hall, 1979.

Hazard, Geoffrey C., Jr. *Ethics in the Practice of Law.* New Haven: Yale University Press, 1978.

Kugel, Yerachmiel, and Gladys W. Gruenberg, eds. *Ethical Perspectives on Business and Society.* Lexington, Mass.: Lexington Books, 1977.

CRITERIA: SELECTED VIEWS

Chapple, Eliot D., and Leonard R. Sayles. *The Measure of Management*. New York: Macmillan, 1961.

Coleman, James S., et al. *Equality of Educational Opportunity*. Washington, D.C.: Government Printing Office, 1966.

Feldstein, Martin S. *Economic Analysis of Health Service Efficiency*. Chicago: Markham, 1968.

Mosteller, Frederick, and Daniel P. Moynihan, eds. *On Equality of Educational Opportunity*. New York: Random House, 1972.

U.S. Congress, Joint Economic Committee. *Economic Analysis and the Efficiency of Government*. Washington, D.C.: Government Printing Office, 1970.

RESEARCH METHODS, APPROACHES, AND PROBLEMS

Caro, Francis G., ed. *Readings in Evaluation Research*. New York: Russell Sage Foundation, 1971.

Coleman, James S. *Policy Research in the Social Sciences*. Morristown, N.J.: General Learning Press, 1972.

_____ et al. *Policy Issues and Research Design*. Chicago: National Opinion Research Center, 1979.

Rutman, Leonard, ed. *Evaluation Research Methods: A Basic Guide*. Beverly Hills, Calif.: Sage Publications, 1977.

Simon, Julian L. *Basic Research Methods in Social Science*. New York: Random House, 1978.

Struening, E. L., and Marcia Guttentag, eds. *Handbook of Evaluation Research*, vol. I. Beverly Hills, Calif.: Sage Publications, 1975.

Suchman, Edward A. *Evaluative Research*. New York: Russell Sage Foundation, 1967.

Weiss, Carol H. *Evaluation Research: Methods of Assessing Program Effectiveness*. Englewood Cliffs, N.J.: Prentice-Hall, 1972.

Measurement issues

Bauer, Raymond A., ed. *Social Indicators*. Cambridge, Mass.: MIT Press, 1968.

Carey, M. *Social Measurement and Social Indicators*. London: George Allen & Unwin, 1980.

de Neufville, Judith Innes. *Social Indicators and Public Policy*. New York: Elsevier, 1975.

Webb, Eugene J.; Donald T. Campbell; Richard D. Schwartz; and Lee Sechrest. *Unobtrusive Measures*. Skokie, Ill.: Rand McNally, 1966.

Design issues

Campbell, Donald T., and J. C. Stanley. *Experimental and Quasi-Experimental Designs for Research*. Skokie, Ill.: Rand McNally, 1963.

Caporaso, James A., and Leslie L. Roos, Jr., eds. *Quasi-Experimental Approaches: Testing Theory and Evaluating Policy.* Evanston, Ill.: Northwestern University Press, 1973.

Fairbrother, George. *Methods for Experimental Social Innovation.* New York: John Wiley & Sons, 1967.

Patton, Michael Quinn. *Qualitative Evaluation Methods.* Beverly Hills, Calif.: Sage Publications, 1980.

_____. *Utilization-Focused Evaluation.* Beverly Hills, Calif.: Sage Publications, 1978.

Provus, M. M. *Discrepancy Evaluation.* Berkeley, Calif.: McCutchan, 1971.

Reicken, H. W., and R. F. Boruch, eds. *Social Experimentation.* New York: Academic Press, 1974.

Saxe, Leonard, and Michelle Fine. *Social Experiments: Methods for Design and Evaluation.* Beverly Hills, Calif.: Sage Publications, 1981.

Smith, Nick L. *New Techniques for Evaluation.* Beverly Hills, Calif.: Sage Publications, 1981.

Experiences from government

Bureau of the Budget. *Measuring Productivity of Federal Government Organizations.* Washington, D.C.: Government Printing Office, 1964.

Dorfman, Robert, ed. *Measuring Benefits of Government Investments.* Washington, D.C.: The Brookings Institution, 1965.

Goldman, T. A. *Cost-Effectiveness Analysis.* New York: Praeger Publishers, 1967.

Hinrichs, Harley H., et al. *Program Budgeting and Benefit-Cost Analysis.* Pacific Palisades, Calif.: Goodyear Publishing, 1969.

Kloman, Erasmus H., ed. *Cases in Accountability: The Work of the GAO.* Boulder, Colo.: Westview Press, 1979.

Nay, Joseph, and P. Kay. *Government Operations and Evaluability Assessment.* Washington, D.C.: The Urban Institute, 1978.

Novick, David. *Current Practices in Program Budgeting (PPBS).* New York: Crane, Russak, 1972.

U.S. Congress, Joint Economic Committee. *The Analysis and Evaluation of Public Expenditures: The PPB System.* Washington, D.C.: Government Printing Office, 1969.

U.S. General Accounting Office. *Civil Agencies Make Limited Use of Cost-Benefit Analysis in Support of Budget Requests.* Washington, D.C.: Government Printing Office, January 14, 1975.

EVALUATION AS CONTROL: USES

Abramson, Mark A. *The Funding of Social Knowledge and Application: A Survey of Federal Agencies.* Washington, D.C.: National Academy of Sciences, National Research Council, 1978.

Chelimsky, E. *An Analysis of the Proceedings of a Symposium on the Use of Evaluation by Federal Agencies*. McLean, Va.: MITRE/METREK, M–77–39, vol. II, July 1977.

Hatry, Harry P., et al. *Practical Program Evaluation for State and Local Government Officials*. Washington, D.C.: The Urban Institute, 1973.

U.S. Congress, House, Committee on Government Operations. *The Uses of Social Research in Federal Domestic Programs*. Washington, D.C.: Government Printing Office, 1967.

U.S. Congress, Senate, Committee on Human Resources. *Hearings on the Cost, Management, and Utilization of Human Resource Program Evaluation*. Washington, D.C.: Government Printing Office, 1977.

U.S. Congress, Senate, Committee on Rules and Administration. *The Program Reauthorization and Evaluation Act of 1978*. Washington, D.C.: Government Printing Office, July 1978.

U.S. General Accounting Office. *Assessing Social Program Impact Evaluations*. Washington, D.C.: Government Printing Office, 1978.

Van Mannen, John. *Program Evaluation: A Guide for Managers*. Washington, D.C.: National Training and Development Service Press, 1973.

Weiss, Carol H., ed. *Using Social Research in Public Policy Making*. Lexington, Mass.: Lexington Books, 1977.

Wholey, Joseph S.; John W. Scanlon; Hugh G. Duffy; James S. Fukumoto; and Leona M. Vogt. *Federal Evaluation Policy*. Washington, D.C.: The Urban Institute, 1978.

EXAMPLES, APPROACHES AND STYLES OF EVALUATION

Acton, Jan Paul. *Evaluating Public Programs to Save Lives: The Case of Heart Attacks*. Santa Monica, Calif.: The Rand Corporation, R–950–RC, 1973.

Brewer, Garry D., and Martin Shubik. *The War Game: A Critique of Military Problem Solving*. Cambridge, Mass.: Harvard University Press, 1979.

Chayes, Abram, et al. *ABM: An Evaluation of the Decision to Deploy an Anti-Ballistic Missile System*. New York: New American Library, 1969.

Glennan, Thomas K., Jr. *Evaluating Federal Manpower Programs*. Santa Monica, Calif.: The Rand Corporation, RM–5743, September 1969.

Greenbaum, W.; M. S. Garet; and E. R. Solomon. *Measuring Educational Achievement*. New York: McGraw-Hill, 1977.

Greer, Scott; Ronald D. Hedlund; and James L. Gibson, eds. *Accountability in Urban Society: Public Agencies Under Fire*. Beverly Hills, Calif.: Sage Publications, 1978.

Hudson Institute. *The Future of American Poverty: Some Basic Issues in Evaluating Alternative Anti-Poverty Measures*. Croton-on-Hudson, N.Y.: Hudson Institute, 1968.

Levin, Henry M. *Cost-Effectiveness Analysis and Educational Policy: Profusion, Confusion, Promise*. Stanford, Calif.: Center for Research and Development in Teaching, December 1968.

Limaye, Delip R., ed. *Energy Policy Evaluation*. Lexington, Mass.: D. C. Heath, 1974.

Moynihan, Daniel P. *The Politics of a Guaranteed Income*. New York: Random House, 1973.

Pauly, Mark V. *Medical Care at Public Expense*. New York: Praeger Publishers, 1972.

Ribich, Thomas. *Education and Poverty*. Washington, D.C.: The Brookings Institution, 1968.

Ridker, Ronald G., ed. *Economic Costs of Air Pollution*. New York: Praeger Publishers, 1966.

Rivlin, Alice M., and P. Michael Timpane, eds. *Planned Variation in Education: Should We Give Up or Try Harder?* Washington, D.C.: The Brookings Institution, 1975.

Stufflebeam, D. L.; W. J. Foley; W. J. Gephart; E. G. Guba; R. L. Hammond; H. O. Merriman; and M. M. Provus, eds. *Educational Evaluation and Decision Making*. Itasca, Ill.: F. E. Peacock, 1971.

Titmus, Richard M. *The Gift Relationship: From Human Blood to Social Policy*. New York: Pantheon, 1971.

Weisbrod, Burton A. *Benefits of Manpower Programs: Theoretical and Methodological Issues*. Madison: University of Wisconsin, May 1969.

PART VI

Termination

On June 30, 1977 President Jimmy Carter cancelled the Air Force's B–1 strategic bomber.[1] The decision was a controversial one, and its death did not come summarily. On September 28 of that same year, the House Appropriations Committee voted to continue the project by authorizing an extra $426 million for the construction of two more B–1s to go along with the four already built (which Carter had decided were enough to ensure a "continuing research effort").[2] The program did not end with six however. By October 1981, the B–1 was reincarnated as an important component of President Reagan's comprehensive strategic arms program, and in November of the same year, the full 100, B–1 fleet easily survived a congressional vote and thus moved one step closer to realization.[3] What happened in the intervening period to so change political minds? Among other things, times and circumstances had changed; so, too, did the ideology of the commander-in-chief: "If a President of either party says he wants a weapons system, he's going to get it," according to one opposition congressman. In the words of another, "There is sort of a general consensus among the public at large that we have allowed the Russians to gain an advantage in strategic weaponry. . . . Building the B–1 is one way [to regain the advantage]."[4]

There are many reasons why the termination of the B–1 bomber program did not occur automatically in the wake of the Carter decision. We have mentioned two, but undoubtedly many more, once pointed out,

383

would seem plausible—perhaps even obvious and compelling. The more important question is why President Carter or anyone else connected with the B–1 death sentence expected it to be executed in the first place. In other words, why did they think that termination would be swift, sure, and final? Part of the answer probably relates to the underdeveloped, incomplete state of knowledge of termination as an integral component of the policy process and another part from our simple lack of experience in ending policies and programs.

It seems, therefore, appropriate to begin by offering some working definitions of termination as a distinct phase in the policy process; by framing questions usually encountered during the termination phase (almost irrespective of the specific content of the entity being ended); and finally by moving quickly through some of the existing research on the subject to provide a feeling for many of the difficult analytic problems and practical issues that possibly explain the thin scholarship and meager experience.

Many candidate topics are suggested for treatment in the following material, more than we could be expected to deal with completely. Certainly, the many obstacles that impede the understanding and practice of termination stand out as general issues of importance, and we try to characterize the more prevalent of them. As we have suggested, termination does happen, and sometimes the experiences suggest lessons that may be applicable in other settings and situations; we take up several of these successes and then attempt to build on them in a following section devoted to design considerations, both tactical and strategic, that may serve to improve termination. We next examine termination as experienced during periods of severe budget constraints, the situation under the Reagan Administration; in other words, how do different political and economic contexts influence or affect termination analysis and policies? Lastly, we address future policy and research objectives for termination activities and conclude by placing termination in the overall context of the policy process.

NOTES

1. Nicholas Wade, "Death of the B–1: The Events Behind Carter's Decision," *Science*, 5 August 1977, pp. 536–39.

2. Nicholas Wade, "B–1 Raises Head from Grave," *Science*, 14 October 1977, p. 177; a similar lugubrious metaphor was employed by Bruce Ingersoll four years later when the program was resurrected, "B–1 Back from Dead Stronger than Ever," *Chicago Sun-Times*, September 30, 1981.

3. Steven V. Roberts, "House Voted Funds on the B–1 and MX, Backing President," *New York Times*, November 19, 1981, p. A–1.

4. Ibid., p. A–21.

13

Of beginnings . . . and endings

WHAT IS TERMINATION? (AND OTHER BASIC QUESTIONS)

Termination generally refers to the adjustment of policies and programs that have become dysfunctional, redundant, outmoded, unnecessary, or even counterproductive. As termination is the finish of one set of expectations, rules and practices, a sense of finality is easily seen in the concept; however, less evident but perhaps more important is the idea that termination is frequently only the replacement of one set of practices with another: Termination signals a beginning of the policy process as much as it does its end.[1]

The dictionary defines termination as "The spatial or temporal end of something; . . . conclusion or cessation. A result or outcome of something."[2] Such a definition allows for many personal and institutional examples of termination, which can sometimes be quite instructive. Death, divorce, retirement, bankruptcy, revolution, and surrender can all be viewed in this perspective. However, public policy termination is usually more complex than the personal types and at least as hard to understand or forecast as some of the institutional ones. It is certainly much less studied than either. Let us therefore initially define public policy termination as *the deliberate conclusion or cessation of specific public sector functions, programs, policies, or organizations.*

Even as a starting point, this definition is as restrictive as the *American Heritage* was expansive. For instance, it excludes significant changes in policy emphasis, direction, or jurisdiction. The March of Dimes did not conclude its operations with the discovery of the Salk polio vaccine, nor did the U.S. Army's horse cavalry tamely canter off into the sunset with the advent of the mechanized army.[3] The definition also fails to account for contextual or circumstantial changes, as we discovered in the case of the phoenix-like B–1 bomber. To include such phenomena, we need to appreciate the idea of partial termination, in which specific government functions, programs, policies, or organizations significantly redirect their activities and thus remain viable.[4] We also need to consider the multitude of fine-tunings that occur as policies and programs are adjusted in response to experience coping with problems or are adapted to changes in the evolving context. Hence, the probability that partial termination activities routinely occur is almost certain.

The idea of termination-as-beginning as much as termination-as-end also must be recognized. When the state of California decided to end its primary reliance on state mental institutions for the care of the mentally handicapped, a strong presumption was that those released would somehow be cared for, probably in community-based facilities. It was an erroneous presumption, particularly for the most seriously disabled.[5] While the closure of the state facilities struck a certain note of finality in one sector, it merely initiated a whole series of new problems for several others—cities, counties, the community mental health systems, the criminal justice system, the welfare system, and various private mental health providers. The problem did not go away, it got shifted elsewhere. Another recognition dilemma: at times policies might work so well that the problem seemingly disappears. The incidents of skyjacking have rapidly dwindled—which implies the success of airport metal detectors—but few would argue for the termination of airport security programs.

These examples and numerous others suggest certain questions about termination that merit thought and attention. This seems especially so now that agency and program terminations have become a central feature of President Reagan's reduction of the size and scope of the American federal government, and local governments and the private sector are expected to assume program responsibilities.[6]

The fundamental issue concerning termination is how can a policy or program be rationally and humanely adjusted or ended without having had a thorough evaluation of the program and the effects of its demise? This raises a number of practical questions. Who will suffer from the termination and in what ways? What obligations do authorities have to those disadvantaged, such as due process, severance and other compensation, or ethical and moral responsibilities? What costs—not limited to simple monetary ones—accrue to individuals affected by termination? Can these be accounted and compensated for? One must consider the context in which termination takes place and what objectives are sought to tailor the most appropriate strategies. For instance, are terminations being proposed to promote governmental efficiencies (e.g., better health care delivery programs) or to reduce governmental spending (e.g., decrease government health care expenditures)? Should the targeted agency participate in the termination planning, or should a detached agency have the primary responsibility?[7] What might be learned from specific terminal acts that will inform new policies and improve programs in the same or related fields? How can that knowledge be preserved and transmitted to others?

More basic questions surface as well. Why is it so hard to terminate public policies and programs? Can, or even should, new programs with uncertain effectiveness or a high risk of failure be constructed so that they can be terminated easily if they later prove deficient? What is the salvage value of an ended program, and how are its recoverable resources (e.g., personnel, assets) reclaimed and recycled to productive use? What incentives can be created to encourage needed terminations? How might the overwhelming expectation of permanence found in the bulk of public policies and programs be shifted in favor of flexibility, adaptability, and appropriate transcience and the uncertainties these engender?[8] What possible political, economic, and social dangers attend wholesale demolition of large, well-established organizations? How might citizens as well as policymakers be educated and involved in needed termination decisions?

There are no simple answers to these and similar questions. Policy analysts are only recently beginning to pose and grapple with them. Lacking the necessary intellectual command of such questions, decision makers (even the most well-intentioned) appear either to avoid termination choices as much as possible or to assume that they can be implemented easily and effectively. Neither attitude is correct for a large number of termination cases, which is not the same as saying that termination should be continually avoided or naively undertaken. It is as essential as any of the other phases of the policy process, despite its lack of intellectual development and actual practice.

There are convincing political and economic reasons to include termination as part of the policy process.[9] Policies get old, they wear out, or they keep solving problems that have long since been resolved or replaced by more pressing social priorities. Political power is just too valuable to be wasted on obsolete policies and programs. Economic resources are similarly scarce. Releasing dollars and other resources invested in outdated programs makes them available for deployment against new problems. Indeed, a great challenge confronting modern societies is learning how to adapt attitudes and habits formed during times of sustained economic growth—where some of the newly created wealth is available for solving social problems—to conform better to a condition of economic stagnation or decline—where a surplus is not so dependable or has become a deficit.[10]

Reform, even in the absence of Draconian budgetary stimuli, may not be possible, or as readily achieved, in the absence of prior termination experiences. For instance, the reforms sought in the Education for All Handicapped Children Act (discussed at length in Chapters 11 and 12) could very well be undermined by the continuing existence of numerous competing programs for handicapped children. At the very least, the sheer complexity that all such programs represent has not been lessened by the passage of yet another piece of legislation, and in this case, complexity had already proven to be a major obstacle to providing improved service.[11]

Experimentation and learning-by-doing are impeded in cases where acceptable end conditions are not built into risky ventures. Many pilot or demonstration programs, for example, are initially justified as experimental; their persistence long after a reasonable trial period, however, suggests that other implicit motives are at work and that inadequate concluding conditions were established before the demonstrations began. Indeed, one argument against trial or experimental programs is that, once operational, it may be impossible to evaluate them or to end them even after their experimental purposes have been served. "Temporary" commissions, like quonset huts, have remarkable staying power, as one might observe in reading the *Sixteenth Annual Report of the Temporary Commission of the State of New York.*[12]

Finally, when the threat of termination lacks credibility—because it is infrequent or no one knows how to do it—perverse incentives are created by default that encourage persistent performance even in situations where policies and programs have obviously lingered far too long. A strong demand exists to make termination real, expected, and acceptable if government performance is to improve. Under present circumstances, it is usually none of these things, and the policy process and performance suffer accordingly.

THE STUDY OF POLICY TERMINATION

Most scholarly work to date has focused on case studies and the tactics used by key individuals to secure terminations of specific programs or organizations. The result has been a disjoint and noncumulative body of literature. Major government research programs have been abruptly stopped—such as the supersonic transport and the nuclear airplane[13]—but very little thought is evident in the case histories relating the general questions and problems of termination.[14] Closing mental institutions has received scholarly attention, and one discovers in this literature an occasional insight about general termination strategies;[15] however, caution needs to be exercised to avoid mistakenly applying the lessons from this one issue area to different and possibly inappropriate ones. Other case examples are slowly coming into the literature, but their total impact on scholarship or practice has not been great.[16]

A handful of studies exists which emphasize such procedures as zero-base budgeting[17] and sunset legislation[18] as means to stimulate termination.

The procedures themselves have had limited success, and thorough inquiries to determine why have not been forthcoming. We suggest that a major part of the difficulty with these two governmental innovations is a lack of understanding of the intellectual and contextual factors (e.g., bureaucratic, political, and personal motivations) that impede termination—a lack of knowledge both in and of this phase of the policy process.

"Cut-back management" has been coined as a slogan representing various means to cope with budgetary decline, primarily in the governmental sector (an occasional case example from private or nonprofit experiences crops up).[19] Here, too, lack of knowledge and experience looms large; the analytic community interested in cutbacks is seldom able to provide decision makers with much more than descriptions rather than feasible suggestions for dealing with the problem.

Ethical, moral, and legal dimensions of termination have not been well considered, a serious shortcoming. One needs to ask what legal and moral obligations inhere in a policy or program slated for termination. As opposed to the usual case of policy creation, policy termination involves real beneficiaries whose lives have already been affected, often substantially. The courts are increasingly being petitioned to adjudicate termination actions as vested interests seek legal redress. Consider the following:

> The California Supreme Court Monday ordered the Los Angeles County Department of Health Services not to fire or demote 610 of its employees. The court order suspended notices of 345 layoffs and 265 demotions in rank and pay that the county had served earlier in the day. At the request of the Legal Aid Foundation of Los Angeles, the high court . . . ordered the county not to proceed with the layoffs.[20]

How and to whom is the terminating authority obligated by what Behn refers to as the "entitlement ethic"?[21] At the moment, these kinds of questions are considered on a case-by-case basis, a practice resulting in lengthy and expensive judicial and administrative proceedings of sufficient difficulty to discourage many other would-be terminators.[22]

It is instructive to ask what are some approximate reasons for termination's neglect, particularly by policy analysts and scholars? Four principal reasons come to mind. First, strong negative connotations are generally ascribed to most termination acts, especially the more common personal ones we all experience, such as death, which many Westerners find almost impossible to confront with any detachment.[23] Bankruptcy and surrender also have been accorded pejorative overtones—failure of the individual or institution in the first and of the state and society in the latter. Strong, sometimes primitive, emotions are conjured up in these experiences, and we find a similar occurrence in other realms where termination is sought or required. Emotions run high, and dispassionate analyses wane or pale by comparison. The political debate over abortion laws and funds is one of many such examples. No matter the specific reason, it is clear that people do not like to think about the unpleasant and, for most, termination is an unpleasant experience.

As true as it seems to be, this aversion has notable adverse and unnecessary consequences for the policy process. In primitive cultures, death has been structured into one's life expectations; thus, its reality and consequences are more easily accepted than in Western cultures.[24] As Herman Kahn has vividly demonstrated, thinking about the unthinkable does not mean that one has to invite or condone it.[25] To master the policy process, the analyst needs to accept it in its entirety, and this means coming to terms with all the contextual facts of life, not continuing to be made insecure by them. Divorce, bankruptcy, and retirement once were considered admissions of failure; more recently, they are being viewed as opportunities for new and creative beginnings.[26] Adjusting perceptions and changing attitudes about policy and program termination could, with concerted effort, be accomplished, too, for, as Biller states, "One's ability to take advantage of discovery is directly proportional to one's ability to terminate prior policy and organizational commitments."[27]

A second possible reason for termination's neglect is that there are still not enough examples from which one might generalize.[28] Kaufman writes that one of the reasons he posed the question *Are Government Organizations Immortal*? "is to call attention to this gap."[29] His answer to the question was a qualified yes. He found only 27 federal government agencies out of a sample of 421 that had gone out of business since 1923.[30] Further, as Bardach observes, "one always suspects that each instance of the phenomenon is bound to be so idiosyncratic that no interesting generalizations will be possible."[31] But if the previous explanation rests with psychological reluctance, then this one is comparable to analytic oversight or indulgence. There is an impressive number of reported experiences with termination, although these are often not labeled as such.[32] For instance, the Supreme Court's 1954 decision to ban public school segregation by race was a profound act of termination, culminating some 60 years of judicial activity beginning with *Plessy* v. *Ferguson* in 1896.[33] Court rulings and subsequent legislation in the environmental field have had similar pervasive effects.[34] Organizations do die, as in the cases of President Nixon's abolition of the Office of Economic Opportunity, the linchpin of Lyndon Johnson's War on Poverty,[35] and Reagan's closing of the Community Services Administration.[36] Many experiences have been recorded, although these rarely have been cast from a termination or policy process perspective. Kaufman, for instance, notes that the number of terminated agencies he found "though small, was not trivial. And if someday more frequent readings on the organizational population of the government are taken, there is reason to believe the death rate will turn out to be even higher."[37]

There appears, then, to be ample evidence to begin describing termination conditions, strategies, and tactics and projecting the likely outcomes and effects of each. The need for both is certainly great and growing. As Foster and Brewer caution, the exigencies of nuclear war do not permit the luxury of pursuing previous war termination strategies.[38] When government funds are increasingly restricted, with all that implies for cutting back and redirecting resources and attentions, different termination strategies may be necessary than when termination's objectives are increased government efficiencies.[39]

A third reason termination has been overlooked is intellectual. Termination is very hard to think about and at least as hard to master conceptually. For instance, at what point does the fine-tuning inherent in policy implementation become partial termination? At what point does institutional reorganization become termination? How does one account for the terminal outcomes (or, more challenging, the longer-term and more-removed effects) of decisions made for other reasons and on other grounds? When Franklin D. Roosevelt decided to create numerous new organizations to deal with the Great Depression, he did so to circumvent the bureaucracy he thought would be incapable of or unresponsive to the new challenges. Would this be an example of termination? Or when reelection-seeking politicians withhold planned expenditures to yield budget surpluses or reduced deficits, the termination consequences are usually not considered—as the wholesale erosion of municipal infrastructure caused by under- or deferred maintenance attests.[40] If studying termination is difficult, it is so in no small measure because the politics of termination are rife with byzantine coalitions and hidden agenda.[41] Policy analysts have avoided the subject nearly as much as policymakers, and both must bear the responsibility.

A final reason why termination studies have been largely underattended is that, until recently, there have been few incentives to examine such cases. Not only were they relatively rare, difficult to fathom, and perhaps even unpleasant, but there were few rewards inherent in such research beyond one's immediate intellectual colleagues. During a period of relative governmental largess, there was little public policy reason to understand why and how programs should be curtailed. It was easier to create new programs overlaid on the old and questionable than to curtail existing programs; witness the multiple uncoordinated programs that exist in the education policy area. Termination discussions were not seen as ways to ingratiate program managers with their bureaucratic peers; nor were policy analysts quick to propose termination options to their superiors who, more often than not, were trying to expand rather than contract their bureaucratic realms. There was in short, scant call for termination activities.[42] While this is perhaps not a compelling reason, in a research discipline characterized by its responsiveness to perceived needs, the low demand for termination studies cannot be ignored. In retrospect, however, we can see this as being extremely shortsighted, especially as the industrialized nations are being forced to adopt extreme budget constraints which require as much intelligence as possible if they are to be accomplished with any significant degree of equity and efficiency.

THINKING ABOUT THE CONCEPT

Termination provides a different perspective on many social problems, but few have thought about specific situations by using it. For example, the need to reduce the number of weapons (especially nuclear ones) worldwide is a reduction many believe to be as necessary as it is long overdue.[43] However, usually absent in such proposals are considerations about what to do about the severe economic dislocations arms reduction or limitations would create. Arms production and acquisition are gigantic businesses in the United States, the Soviet Union, and elsewhere.[44] As one well-placed observer has noted, "Arms sales have become, more than ever before, a crucial dimension of world politics. They are now major strands in the warp and woof of international affairs."[45] Size itself may provide both its own justification and momentum for continuing along a course of business as usual. Or, to take another example, arguing for tax reductions reveals few opponents—who looks forward to paying a tax bill? But as long as the argument is disconnected from its consequences, e.g., deciding on what government services will be curtailed or terminated, it maintains little but rhetorical value. Politicians are, of course, aware of this and have benefited. They do so mainly because others have not habitually linked such provisional and symbolic statements with their concrete and substantial implications—something that would naturally happen if termination were given its full weight as a distinctive element in the total policy process.

Social theorists, scholars, and analysts have likewise failed to appreciate some of termination's important realities. During the estimation phase, it is often easy and technically convenient to neglect distributional, humanitarian, and other subjective matters. But during termination, their reality—with attendant contradictions, uncertainties, and conflicts—is so evident and pressing that it cannot be readily ignored or denied. To do so misses an opportunity to assess the theories and methods used previously to determine which of them worked (i.e., were reasonably accurate), and which did not, or even contributed to the conditions calling forth the termination option. Failing to close the theoretical and analytic loops may, in its own way, be as difficult for scholars as not thinking through termination's possible consequences is for policymakers.

Both examples stress an understandable human reluctance to admit past mistakes or to disrupt comfortable procedures and certain practices. Both aversions are common in understanding why specific and necessary terminations do not occur routinely.

Concentrating the mind

"The prospect of death," observed Dr. Samuel Johnson, "wonderfully concentrates the mind." It also evokes a fairly general set of emotional reactions, including initial shock, denial that anything so terrible could be happening, irritation with one's self for not having lived differently or taken better precautions, anger with others who survive, and, lastly, final acceptance of the inevitable.[46]

In varying degrees and ways, something akin to these emotional stages can be discerned in the behavior of individuals in institutions slated for termination. In bureaucracies, for example, it is common to find false and inflated optimism following news of reductions in force (RIF) or wholesale cutbacks. A form of denial, the unexpectedly strong personnel evaluation of a RIF-ed subordinate, may help assuage the guilt and hopelessness of the superior by placing the blame elsewhere and broadcasting a message that this office has good people doing useful work. Highly positive evaluations of the institution itself also count as denial and contribute to the release of anger next encountered when political allies in "just wars" are sought to prevent the reductions. In 1973, Caspar Weinberger, then Nixon's Secretary of Health, Education, and Welfare, took the lead in trying to secure cut backs in a variety of health programs. In the Senate hearings that occurred soon after one proposal was announced, a common aspect of denial came to light:

> During the hearing, [Senator] Kennedy [of Massachusetts] repeatedly quoted studies, either done by or commissioned by the department, testifying to the value of the programs under discussion. Mr. Weinberger countered that too much emphasis had been placed on such studies, adding that they often tend to reflect the vested interests of those involved in the program. "The poverty, education, health complex is getting very large," he said.[47]

Providing that the fight against termination fails,[48] grudging acceptance must in time replace anger and hostility.[49]

A similar pattern is often seen among beneficiaries of programs threatened with termination. These antitermination campaigns can be expected to be particularly intense, for the program clientele are already the recipients of a program's benefits, goods to which they have become accustomed or even entitled. Nor are the program sponsors in the bureaucracy indifferent. For instance, because of sharp reductions in the number of school-aged children across the country, hundreds of local school officials are being forced to "concentrate the mind" on shutting down or trying to find other uses for the emptying facilities. The biological metaphor came readily to the mind of one hard-pressed school administrator: " 'Closing a school is a major political problem,' says San Francisco school board member John Mayer. 'Each school is a living organism, and no organism dies quickly and politely'. "[50] The emotional aspects were as easily described: "There is a kind of territorial imperative involved, a very strong emotional tie."[51] Confounding termination and the search for alternative uses for the threatened schools are the facts that individual schools are usually embedded within larger systems having relatively high fixed costs; union contracts often prevent teacher layoffs; and the school facilities themselves are not easily recycled because of their distinctive purpose and character.[52] Each factor becomes a weapon in the war to keep a school open or a bureaucracy functioning.

The school-closing example points out a more general flaw in conceptualizing termination, one especially prevalent in the pluralist or incremental approach. If one assumes that the political system is a self-correcting mechanism, then its internal processes must yield politically acceptable results, roughly analogous to the competitive marketplace in the economist's supply and demand model. Policies and programs that no longer have political support will be terminated, and those sustaining constituency support will continue. The logic is clear enough, but empirical evidence is lacking, thus rendering the conclusion suspect, especially in light of the extraordinary problems encountered in trying to get governments at all levels to adapt and adjust to changing circumstances and opportunities.

Pluralist and incremental theories emphasize the selection phase of the policy process, as we have noted. But doing so deemphasizes the institutional transformations that occur in implementation (e.g., designing for institutional permanence), and naively concentrates on aggregate and expected outcomes of economic and political choices (e.g., specific contexts, beneficiaries, and providers that are unimaginable at the point of decision). The U.S. government's role in developing and fostering the American nuclear reactor industry is illustrative. One can argue that the U.S. Atomic Energy Commission's atomic power reactor development programs would have been substantially different if anybody had predicted the subsequent environmental and legal difficulties, made accurate cost estimates, used a low energy demand forecast, recognized the waste disposal/reprocessing problems,[53] or envisioned the difficulties in closing down a radioactive reactor after its 30 years of operation.[54] It cannot be conclusively demonstrated, of course, but had these matters been taken into account during the early 1950s, the government and industry might well have terminated the nuclear reactor R&D program before it ever reached the construction of the Shippingport demonstration reactor. Certainly the R&D strategies and products would have been altered. Whatever the outcome, it illustrates the several limitations of the pluralist approach to termination matters and how an integrated, policy-process approach with an explicit termination-contingency strategy might have been more appropriate.

Levels of termination

We have generally been using *policy* termination as an umbrella term to include the cessation of government institutions, functions, and programs as well as specific policies. It is, however, important to recognize that each of these levels must be treated differentially when considering termination, for each represents a different level or set of termination requirements. Admittedly, in practice, the distinctions might be impossible to honor; one can hardly distinguish the curtailment of the Environmental Protection Agency's pollution regulation and monitoring activities without understanding the agency's political vulnerabilities.[55]

We can examine the termination of programs, policies, organizations, and functions.[56] *Programs* are, relatively speaking, the easiest of the four to terminate; they have the fewest political resources to protect them and represent the smallest investment on the part of the sponsoring organization. *Policies* are program aggregates, usually characterized by guiding themes and objectives. As such, a change in governmental policy can be manifested in a policy termination exercise; the change in strategic arms limitation policy between the Carter and Reagan administrations represented an end to the policy of strategic detente between the United States and the Soviet Union. More often than not, since policies reflect greater amounts of political resources and commitment than other component programs, they are more resistant to termination activities and, perhaps, more susceptible to partial termination.

Organizations are deliberately designed for long-term operations; indeed, they "have as one of their principal strengths the ability to resist change and termination—that is, persist in the face of information that may warrant discontinuity."[57] Thus, it is not surprising that there are few examples of organizations—especially large, public sector agencies—being terminated. Finally, *functions* (which we define as services provided by the government for its citizens) transcend organizations and policies; many agencies and policies can attend the same function. Since functions are service demands upon the government by its constitutents, it is not surprising that Kaufman found "the functions performed by the agencies were even more enduring than the organizations themselves. In most of the twenty-seven [agency] deaths, the activities were not terminated; they were reassigned or taken up by other units, for the most part."[58] President Reagan has, in functional terms, stated that "The government will no longer try to manage every aspect of energy supply and consumption." Still, the administration's proposed reorganization did not surrender the responsibilities of ill-starred Department of Energy, but parceled out these responsibilities or functions to other cabinet level departments. Thus, it acted to abolish the organization but to retain control over energy-related functions (e.g., protect against energy supply disruptions, sponsor high-risk, long-term energy R&D, and perform certain regulatory duties).[59] Relatively straightforward program termination strategies, such as offered by Behn, are much less effective when dealing with organizations and functions.[60]

The points to be stressed here are twofold. First, termination activities are not uniform. They affect different levels of activities (programs, policies) and different levels of government. Reagan's New Federalism directly translates into terminations at the federal level of government; some predict that two to three thousand government employees could have their jobs abolished in the Department of Energy alone.[61] The Reagan New Federalism will also have profound ripple effects down to the state and local levels; Georgia Governor George Busbee has stated that "the wave of federal budget-cutting has created 'disarray and chaos' in state and local governments and is paralyzing their ability to plan their own budgets."[62] To the international observer, such activities may be even more confusing and disheartening.[63] Second, and more important from the policy standpoint, is that the multiple levels of termination targets mean that no single termination strategy (or perhaps even set of strategies) will suffice, that specific termination tactics must be tailored for the particular context. Again, as demonstrated throughout our discussions of the policy process, complexity precludes the simple.

All-or-nothing versus partial termination

While not prepared to cite specific figures, it appears that the wholesale and complete termination of functions, programs, policies, and organizations is far less frequent than less-drastic partial terminations. One might even think about total termination as a relatively uninteresting and limited case. However, the emotional and political intensity attending usual proposals for cutbacks and reductions suggests that most people fix on the limit too readily. Thinking about and clarifying the intermediate states of partial termination might temper out-of-proportion fears and stimulate more positive thoughts about the creative potentials of termination-as-beginning as much as end.

Five general categories of partial termination can be identified:

Replacing—where something old is replaced with something new to satisfy more or less the same need.

Consolidating—where existing arrangements are reorganized and outmoded aspects eliminated.

Splitting—where a constituent element is restructured as a separate entity.

Decrementing—the most common category, where the evolving and dynamic properties of human systems and arrangements are recognized by program adjustments.

Discontinuing—where the old is replaced with something new, and the needs and objectives are altered.

Replacement is easily seen as a consequence of innovation: better methods or procedures are devised and, in time, drive out the less efficient or effective ones. The process is far more involved than this, but this characterization is adequate for present purposes.[64] Consolidations occur routinely in business as firms merge or operations are centralized to improve control or to obtain economies of scale. Mergers usually involve casualties, and a whole industry has emerged to service RIF-ed employees.[65] Larger-scale displacements, especially of blue-collar workers as opposed to executives, usually exceed private means and necessitate unemployment compensation from public sources. Policies and programs are sometimes consolidated, too, but personnel reductions (especially in the public sector) are less common.[66]

As the antitrust settlement between the U.S. Department of Justice and the American Telephone and Telegraph Company is carried out, its local operating companies will be separated from the parent corporation. Most attention has concentrated on the possible increases in charges for local customers the split may create; however, many other results may have as much importance as the old arrangements give way to the new. Most of these can only vaguely be imagined at the moment.[67]

The concept of decrementing has been defined by Tarschys as "an expenditure policy for an era of retarded growth or economic stagnation,"[68] and a necessary conceptual and practical supplement to conventional incremental—and upward or growth-oriented—ones. The prevalence of marginal institutional changes suggests we carefully consider Tarschys' ideas.

Five key features distinguish the decremental approach:

It is marginalist, with an emphasis on the negative margin. Efforts to examine the budget in its entirety to secure terminal benefits, e.g., zero-base budgets and sunset, are "in grave error."

Analyses preceding the decrement must be selective and able to discrimate "to make wise decisions about cuts."

A medium-to-long range perspective or time horizon is required: "quick and short-term operations have little chance of succeeding."

Maximum support for the proposed measures must be sought from the agencies and interest groups affected.[69]

Termination or contraction of organizations, policies and programs "must be built into [them] from the very outset." Expenditure escalators must give way to phasing-down and reduction; control stations, with the power to respond to changing or declining demand need to be constituted; and planning itself must consider rolling policies and programs backward as often as they now consider rolling them forward.

These suggestions are not the idlings of an ivory tower academic but a former member of the Swedish Parliament and chairman of the Swedish Commission on Public Policy. They are practical, sensible, and warranted as Sweden and other industrial nations learn to cope with stagnation or decline.[70]

Discontinuity is more straightforward; the helicopter airborne assault division's replacement of the traditional horse cavalry in the U.S. Army is a clear example.[71] The new needs extended well beyond a capability for rapid assault to include close-air support with helicopter gunships, logistics support and troop transport, and sustained operations wherein the landed troops performed more in an infantry than a cavalry role.

The common feature of all these forms of partial termination is that some thing or some process has been supplanted because of changes in the context or improvements in the underlying and enabling technologies. In each case, the continuity of the policy process occurs as specific problems are confronted and treated in different ways.

OBSTACLES TO TERMINATION

In many different guises, an inability to cope with failure is a root cause inhibiting termination efforts. A success-orientation dominates modern, Western culture. Failure is rarely tolerated, and in extreme cases, even warrants punishment, e.g., blaming victims for their poverty or other deficiencies.

The problem stems in part from inattention to different kinds of failure. In social and policy terms, failure is condemned with heavy connotations of guilt and inadequacy. A sense that failure can be constructive and necessary for progress to occur is almost always lacking. But such an operating premise occurs in technical programs where the discovery of errors in previously held theories or procedures often indicates new thinking and product improvement. In this sense, failure is prerequisite to learning; it is expected and accepted. Analogously, "failure" must be regarded and accepted in its general social and policy senses if an integrated idea of the policy process is to prevail.

More specifically, one needs to be aware of different obstacles to termination—most of which, in some form or other, emanate from the failure-as-bad premise. Thus, we can segregate institutional/structural, political, economic, psychological, ethical/moral, ideological, and legal categories for special attention.

Institutional/structural issues

One necessary element for organizational success is its survival, for nothing else an organization might try to accomplish matters without it. To survive, organizations adapt to stresses and opportunities in their environments.[72] When this survival instinct is linked to the success premise, exceptionally durable institutions are the result. Thus, few opportunities are created which allow organizations to pass away easily when no longer needed. If one knows what's right and will work best to solve problems, why build institutions that allow for doubt and consequent failure to realize ambitions? Institutions, therefore, come to embody certainty about successful solutions to problems or at least our attempts to minimize uncertainty.[73]

This is a complicated matter. It is often important to ensure that policies and organizations are sufficiently resilient to combat challenges to their existence and to persist despite the vicissitudes of political and bureaucratic sponsors. This requirement is easily appreciated for chronic problems (imagine the consequences of dismantling the armed forces with every change of national leadership), although it also holds for other problem types to varying degrees.

We are less concerned here, however, with the utility or value of organizational life and death than with the reality of bureaucratic and policy longevity and its consequences. In this, Biller offers several insights:

> [I]t is not surprising to find system designers choosing, in the name of making operation "easy," to focus on amortizing a long operational run by setting up standard operating procedures and templates that are as difficult as possible to change. . . . Coupled with our primary dependence in the public sector on administered bureaucratic operations . . . it really is unremarkable that we have come to assume basic persistence and perpetuity rather than termination to be the appropriate assumption to be used in dealing with most public policies and organizations.[74]

Organizations do change, as do the environments in which they are embedded and the policy goals they seek. The interesting aspect of this is that organizations also notably influence both environments and goals.[75] Simply attaining a policy objective is usually not reason enough to disband an organization; new objectives can and usually will be defined to allow continuation. Initially, United Nations' involvement in the Korean War was to repulse North Korean forces from the south. Hostilities did not cease following North Korea's retreat from the south, however. U.N. commander General Douglas MacArthur then defined new objectives that led to an invasion of North Korea, Communist China's entry into the war, and a very different conflict than had been originally imagined.[76] The March of Dimes charity continued to function after the discovery of a polio vaccine and the effective eradication of the disease. Rather than disband, the organization redirected its medical research attentions to other unconquered diseases. Nor did the Woman's Christian Temperance Union abandon its efforts after Prohibition became law. These examples all suggest that attaining a policy goal is not a sufficient reason for organizational termination.

We also find that lack of success in achieving goals may not be reason enough to cease pursuit of a policy or to terminate an organization. The Vietnam War, for much of its duration, illustrates this point—although a reasonable question about the goals various South Vietnamese and American authorities sought clouds the example.[77] Initial lack of success may also cause policy supporters to seek other organizational means, as was the case

400 / Chapter 13

when proponents of performance contracting in education were unable to convince Department of Health, Education, and Welfare (HEW) officials of the value of this approach, but were able to find a more receptive audience in the Office of Economic Opportunity. Threatened policy termination by one organization was fended off by taking the program to another.[78] Poor performance by itself need not lead to termination; it may increase its odds but not guarantee it. Organizations can and will alter their sponsors, clientele, policies, and objectives if necessary and hence make termination more difficult.[79]

Political aspects

Much as Jimmy Carter discovered how difficult killing the B–1 bomber turned out to be, so will practically any chief executive, especially in a pluralistic system where compromise and consensus are constant ingredients. Clear understanding and unambiguous interpretation of decisions are sometimes neglected or poorly attended during selection; they almost never are considered during termination where a clear and immediate appreciation of likely gains and losses stimulates quick and determined political responses.

Candidate Reagan promised that he would abolish the Department of Energy if elected. It was a useful campaign ploy, but it also alerted opponents of markedly different views to prepare for a "guerrilla warfare directed at preventing the dismantling of the four-year-old agency."[80] Politically disparate groups combined to fight the decision. Initial supporters of the department's creation coalesced to protect their previous political investments; other argued that abolition "would send a message overseas that the nation was weakening its commitment to energy independence";[81] environmentalists joined forces, fearing the department's demise would retard the search for alternative energy sources; and pronuclear advocates aligned with these other groups to protect DOE's nearly $5 billion nuclear weapons production program. Nor was Congress dormant as key legislators moved to block the Administration's reorganization plan.[82] Even James B. Edwards, Reagan's Secretary of Energy, appeared to change his mind between his confirmation hearings early in 1981, when he made no bones about wanting to scrap the department as quickly as possible, and December 1981, when "White House aides . . . report[ed] that privately, Mr. Edwards resisted the dismantling of his agency."[83]

Effective blocking coalitions characterize most terminations. Internally, those in threatened organizations will move to demonstrate their value and to publicize the dire consequences of shut down. At the same time, they can be remarkably creative at developing new objectives and rationales for continued existence. Procrastination and compromise can be used to buy time, placate foes, and gain new supporters. Simply refusing to obey orders also occurs. In November 1969, President Nixon "announced that the United States had decided to renounce the uses of biological weapons" and ordered all supplies of them destroyed. Dr. Nathan Gordon, director of the CIA's biological branch, ignored the order despite his department's research in shellfish toxins. When later quizzed by a Senate committee, he reportedly explained that these toxins were excluded from the presidential order because they were chemical, not biological, agents. In February 1970, Nixon clarified his initial order to include all chemical and biological toxins. Gordon again ignored the order because, in his words, "the second order was directed to the Defense Department, and the CIA is not part of the Defense Department."[84]

Political strategies opposing termination are different than ones found in policy and program startups. A main reason is that an entrenched bureaucracy has "easy and regular access to powerful governmental and other allies."[85] Once an organization has time to cultivate clients and supporters, who can be mobilized in its defense, termination becomes a very difficult political act. Some outsiders have their own bases of political support which, when called on, effectively multiply the political assets within the threatened agency. Thus, when the Defense Department wants to close a military base, an imposing coalition typically arises from local labor and commercial interests, affected congressmen, regional and national suppliers of military goods and services, and dozens of other groups and interests. Bases do close but not without strife nor according to any simple, rational calculus.

As the time to effect termination stretches out because of inevitable resistance and consequent delay, symbolic political costs usually mount. Apparent decisiveness at first succumbs to a perception of impotence, the more so the longer the delay. Because it is so prevalent, this political reality helps explain why successful terminations often are undertaken with stealth and dispatch. In many aspects, termination and crisis decisions are alike. Few options or details are considered to prevent compromise or leaks of the plan; very few affected by the decision are consulted for the same reasons; and the final decision consequently has large uncertainties about its eventual outcomes and effects. Concern for due process, widespread participation, careful analysis, and fair operations may all be overwhelmed by necessity in the process of ending something.

This is not to say that all terminating decisions must be covert. American automobile management and labor efforts to negotiate roll backs in contracts to improve their joint prospects[86] and the sale of troubled factories to workers (e.g., Rath's Iowa meat packing plants) are all counterexamples. It does suggest that as long as institutional permanence, a growth ethic, and an operational premise of success (versus failure-as-learning) hold when termination is called for, then brutal choices may necessarily prevail.

Economic concerns

Timing is often crucial in decision making. Large-scale terminations probably take time, invariably more than their adherents expected or can afford. Unfortunately, termination involves multiple short-run costs and few immediate benefits. Many of these costs are political, but some are economic, and their combined effect is daunting. Distinctions between business and government exist and help distinguish several important points: timing, incentives, and the number of relevant participants in respective cases of termination all differ to a considerable extent.

In early 1977, Donald H. Rumsfeld left the federal government, in which he had served as both congressman and cabinet officer, and became the chief executive officer of ailing G. D. Searle Company, primarily a drug manufacturer.[87] In short order, he began making critical decisions that included divesting "the company of 30 businesses worth $400 million," and cutting "its corporate staff from 800 to 350."[88] Some four years later, the effects could be seen. The value of Searle stock increased nearly threefold, and corporate profits increased an impressive 38 percent between 1980 and 1981, a period of general economic malaise. Rumsfeld had considerable incentive to make the needed terminations work. When hired, he was reportedly "offered 70,000 shares of the company's stock at 33 cents each and given options to buy another 150,000 at $12.28 each." This incentive was in addition to his $500,000 annual salary. Central to his success, according to Rumsfeld, is the fact that, "There is also more public scrutiny and therefore more pressure in government. In the boardroom you don't have to contend with such outside pressure."[89]

Besides lacking Rumsfeld's economic incentives, the public manager must contend with outside pressure, which is usually formidable and quick to mount. Rumsfeld did not have to bargain with congressmen in pruning Searle of its deadwood in terms of personnel and operations, nor were civil service procedures an obstacle; indeed, his appointment was contingent upon drastic action to make the ill corporation well again. He faced few bargaining and compromising demands, and his constituency was limited. Perhaps most important, he had time to make progress, and the measures of progress and success were unambiguous—increases in profits and the price of Searle stock.

The corporate model of successful termination is inappropriate and too limited for direct application to the public sector. A major source of difference is how performance is rewarded, which, in turn, relates to basic differences between service and production activities. Business executives, such as Rumsfeld, are paid if they satisfy their consumers and produce a profit in the process. Service institutions, such as most government services and the advertising, research, and legal divisions of corporations, are rewarded according to their success in budgetary terms. Service institutions exist, according to Peter Drucker, and depend on "a general revenue stream which is not tied to what they are doing but obtained by tax, levy, or tribute."[90] Performance in the corporate world is equilibrated to the numbers at the bottom line of the balance sheet, but there is no bottom line for government or most public sector services, where the proxy measure of success has become the size and growth of the budget.[91] Even though Searle was fairing poorly by business' simple performance measure and terminations were invoked, it was still no mean accomplishment to improve its condition. The alternative was eventual failure and total corporate liquidation. But for services, where goals are not so clearly defined (e.g., public education's multiple goals), many "customers" are often served in variable and counterproductive ways. The basic idea of successful performance is enigmatic; finding a simple economic justification for termination is often elusive, irrelevant, or even impossible. A Department of Energy undersecretary explaining the department's pending phase out stated that "This isn't being done for savings. There will be savings, I am sure, but it is not being done because there is a cost savings of this much or that much."[92] Other goals count and must not be ignored. Various "customers" have legitimate claims to be recognized and satisfied. Other concepts of success matter and invite pursuit.

When Rumsfeld cut back on his corporate losers, he also created resources for promising profitable reinvestment. When someone in a service industry retrenches, the resources can disappear, in effect, to be used elsewhere, by other people and for other purposes, or not to be used at all. It is commonly held that a bureaucrat's most fatal sin is to return money to the general account at the end of the fiscal year. From the administrator's perspective, returned money is lost forever and amounts to personal and institutional failure, for the size of the budget is the accepted measure of success.

Other economic insights help one grasp the problem's extent. Economists hold that sunk costs are gone forever and should not influence future investment decisions. Business people know the axiom as well. One may rue past decisions and the errors of judgment sunk costs represent, still nothing can be done about them. While many politicians may comprehend the argument, few are able to abide by it; for them, sunk costs must be justified. In many ways sunk costs stand for earlier promises, and to conclude that past promises, and the policies and programs enacted in their behalf, are ineffective or failures is much the same as indicting those responsible for them. Sunk costs, as the drawn-out Vietnam War suggests, are as much a political as an economic concern.[93]

By thinking simultaneously about termination as both beginning and end, startup and closing costs can be envisioned as two sides of the same coin. Thought of as closing costs, one must assess the expenses involved in shutting down a plant or killing a program and salvaging reusable resources, including personnel. For those fired outright, there will be severance and unemployment pay and perhaps expenses for retraining and relocation. If termination is partial, closing costs may be more subtle and involved. Union contracts, for instance, could prevent laying off workers with seniority. But because these individuals normally earn higher wages than the average, the total wage bill will not decrease in proportion to the number of workers laid off. Furthermore, in enterprises based on rapidly evolving technologies, the last hired often have superior or more up-to-date training and skills. But when last hired means first fired, the closing costs of retrenchment may involve larger than expected reductions in productivity and competitiveness. The more capable workers, to extend the thought, usually have more marketable talents and skills; and in a time of high uncertainty about an enterprise's prospects, many of the best employees may simply move elsewhere to escape the stress and turbulence of the threatened venture.[94]

The question of who pays the closing (or not-closing) costs is even more complex. When the steel industry, for example, succeeds in obtaining protective trade barriers or quotas established to keep threatened jobs, one outcome is that derivative industries, such as machine tool and automobile manufacturers, must pay more for steel and charge more for their products. A longer-term, ripple effect could thus be a reduction in the derivative industries' competitiveness and an increase in risk of their eventual failure. In this example, the short-term benefits sought by not paying the total bill tendered for closing, e.g., maintaining inefficient and expensive steel production to save some jobs, results in a serious cost to others, elsewhere, later.

When thought about as startup costs, the would-be terminator must demonstrate not only why something needs shutting down (evaluation can be very expensive) but must also pay for the estimation and analysis of the replacement alternative being proposed. The proposal will surely be scrutinized painstakingly by those who stand to lose. As a consequence, the analytic burdens may become impossibly severe; they will unquestionably add to the total time required to effect a decision and hence allow the opposition more time to organize and block the action.[95]

Psychological impediments

Termination is stressful. It also brings out emotional responses and considerations to a different, and often greater, extent than many of the other phases of the policy process.

Psychiatrists realize the emotional traumas attending termination of psychoanalytic treatment; part of many psychiatric training programs is in fact devoted to coping with them. Redlich and Freedman, two respected therapists, discuss these matters:

> The best criterion of termination is the patient's and therapist's agreement that the patient can, from a certain point on, proceed on his own power. Many

therapists set a date for termination at some juncture in the therapy; this is often arrived at through mutual agreement. The therapist may frequently encounter intensified symptoms and various attempts to continue the treatment, to reassert childish needs to cling and be dependent and these attitudes can be interpreted. Nor is it true that the patient who leaves with anger or reluctance has not been helped. Similarly, it is not necessary to prolong termination with ritualistic preparations.[96]

While we are not claiming that psychiatric experience is directly applicable to the kinds of termination problems presented so far, it seems useful to point out some standard emotional and practical consequences from this specialty. For instance, termination is enhanced through a contractual and negotiated decision sometime during the therapeutic process. The act of termination is invoked "when returns are markedly diminishing for patient and therapist," an evaluative assessment.[97] As the terminal moment approaches, childish or irrational symptoms are to be expected, and dependency usually characterizes the general situation. Anger, reluctance, and enmity are common emotions during and immediately following termination. Nor is the authority responsible—the therapist—immune from emotional reactions. A major lesson here is that training and preparation may increase awareness of the emotional obstacles and an expectation of coming to a conclusion. Terminations in therapy do occur. Perhaps similar training and awareness might become as common in social settings, thus facilitating terminations to happen there, too.

Several other ideas are suggested by the psychiatric example. It is claimed that unemployment can result in psychological stress and increased incidences of ill health and abnormal behavior, e.g., alcoholism, family abuse, drug use, and depression.[98] An ideal accounting and reconciling of termination costs would include these nonmonetary factors and assess their outcomes and effects to those responsible for them.[99] But we are far from any ideal; just beginning to make both factors and costs as explicit as possible would be an improvement. Of course, specifically affected individuals and society at large eventually assume the cost by absorbing termination's total consequences. When finished, Rumsfeld relieved 450 Searle executives, many with families, mortgages, bills, and all with individual life stories. Searle undoubtedly paid part of the bill through severance pay, health premiums, pensions, and other means, but it is safe to say that the corporation did not foot the entire bill. In part, it was unable to because of our lack of awareness of total effects, which is related, in turn, to our lack of experience with and general aversion to termination.

The expectational issue Redlich and Freedman stress stimulates other ideas. Some employment and activities are structured with a cyclic expectation of lay-offs: e.g., aerospace and other contract-based enterprises subject to boom-and-bust cycles; time-constrained or soft-money positions in government, universities, and business (political appointments or contracted services, untenured professorships or fellowships, and consulting arrangements, respectively); and industries with discontinuous, highly uneven demand (the performing arts and home construction). Participants in each of these examples expect to be laid off from time to time, and when that moment arrives, the emotional and other costs are more easily faced and paid. Among other things, the termination-as-failure stigma is not as pronounced—because it happens to everyone, one seldom takes it personally—and preparations have usually been made for the inevitable bad times that one expects to follow the good.[100] People in white-collar, managerial jobs have been relatively immune from such experiences and hence have not developed an expectational set to enable them to survive termination's distresses. However, as service industries account for an increasing share of the work force, an expectation of immunity becomes increasingly less likely, all the more so in a declining or stagnant economy.

Parallel to the psychiatrist's expected emotional travails are survivors' reactions in other settings. It is extremely difficult for a survivor not to sympathize with those being terminated, although when sympathy translates into prolonging the inevitable, no one's best interests are served: not the survivor's, where transitory emotional distresses are drawn out unnecessarily, and not the recipient's, where acceptance, readjustment, and pursuit of new possibilities are unreasonably delayed.

Survivors often harbor feelings of guilt. Friendships and other social arrangements built up over the years are stretched to the breaking point. Emotional burdens will insinuate themselves in numerous, vexing ways, not the least of which will be a notable reticence among survivors to take unnecessary risks which might fail and hence mark them for the hatchetman in the next round of pink slips. Rumors run rampant during termination (abetted by the above noted secrecy-enshrouded decision making), and productivity could well be impaired. Institutional loyalty cannot be expected to remain at previous high levels either. If it is hard to understand what marks the difference between victims and survivors, as it often is, those who remain may find it difficult to embrace the institution.[101]

Another psychological obstacle is a reluctance by individuals to plan for termination because doing so represents a form of betrayal, e.g., an extreme version is treason in war,[102] or in the corporate world, accusation of not being a team player. Lack of preparation could also stem from continued denial and an obsessive pursuit of one's work that often accompanies it.[103]

This brief discussion of the psychological and emotional obstacles to termination hardly exhausts their possibilities. Ethical and psychological considerations can be especially interactive, as is suggested by questions such as: To whom is a decision maker responsible, and from where are these attachments derived?

Ethical and moral issues

Substantial moral difficulties confront those trying to disrupt the status quo by stopping something. Rarely viewed as a reasonable and responsible managerial activity, termination is perceived as an unjust attack and irresponsible assault against systems of support and moral arrangements upon which many rely. Termination has, for many, a moral repugnance great enough to stir them in opposition to it.

When policymakers contemplate termination, the question of responsibility looms large: "To whom am I responsible for this choice?" But answers to this question differ depending on one's role and perspective, specific details of the situation, what one values, and many other factors.

Consider one's professional perspective. If primary allegiance is to a professional class, then that group's guiding norms and rules can be relied on to formulate and assist termination. For those in charge of the guillotine during the French Revolution, there was probably very little soul searching, moralizing, analysis, or hesitation about doing the job. Most professions are less bloody-minded or are, at least, not as well stocked with ready rules for termination. Some, such as the medical profession, are distinctly opposed to it.[104]

When professional norms fail to provide clear guidance or operate in opposition to needed terminations, external perspectives and details of the specific setting may weigh more heavily in the decision. Does one give preferential treatment to long-term and loyal employees? Fire troublemakers and the disloyal as a way of getting even or settling scores? How responsible is one for fired employees who have few marketable skills, e.g., those trained only to perform obsolete tasks or those too old to have continuing employment prospects? If the specific situation approximates full-scale liquidation in contrast to retrenchment, answers to each of these questions could be very different. A primary consideration in retrenchment is to minimize the declining morale of surviving employees and to restore a productive routine as soon as possible. Fair and just treatment of those relieved, including genuine efforts to help them begin again, will be far more important in attaining this goal than in the case of total liquidation.

Consider values and strategies. Decision makers facing cutbacks could choose a strategy that emphasizes consumer satisfaction above others: steps to deliver the best product or service at the lowest price would dominate as means to improve one's market share. Still, maximizing consumer service may mean slighting other values and related strategies for dealing with impending reductions. In early 1982, the Scandinavian Air System (SAS) attempted to stem declines in its profitability by luring more of the business-traveler market away from its European competitors and providing special services. The French government, on behalf of state-owned Air France, countered by increasing charges to SAS for office and ticket counters, reducing support services in French airports, and threatening to remove landing rights. Ministry-level negotiations were required to reduce the conflict, and SAS was forced to trim back its consumer strategy.

When an organization is the primary economic source for a city or region, there may be good cause to think seriously about termination's local impact. For example, officers of Cummins Engine Corporation (a manufacturer of diesel engines and other heavy equipment) have expressed concern about the possible consequences of cutbacks were they to continue their heavy investment in Columbus, Indiana, a town already highly dependent on Cummins. This worry led Cummins to locate several new plants elsewhere.

Personal relations and termination have emotional aspects, but they have ethical ones as well. Who assumes primary responsibility for the termination decision and who executes it? For many authorities, the whole business is so distasteful that no one wants to be responsible: a faceless "they," an impersonal committee, or the personnel department might be obliged to take the onus. Blame sharing is all the more likely as guilt (poor executive performance and failure to protect the organization) and fear (uncertainty about the future, including one's own prospects) mount.

What about severance for those being laid off? Economic theory would argue against it, but contractual, legal, and moral aspects make the theoretical dictum moot. But then one still might want to depersonalize the cutback as much as possible: offer everyone the option of a "golden hand-shake" (a euphemism for voluntary separation in exchange for a lump-sum payment) until enough employees are dismissed to satisfy immediate needs. However equitable or humane this approach appears, it could wreak considerable havoc on the institution, especially if desirable and valuable employees take the offer more than less desirable ones. But personalizing and making the golden handshake inequitable by singling out specific victims have their own costs and drawbacks, not the least of which might be irreparable harm done to the bonds of loyalty that sustain organizations.

Ideological/mythical issues

As discussed in the selection chapters, ideology is an important component of decision making. This holds true for termination as well. In deciding to close down several mental institutions in California, for example, ideology came into play in several telling ways.[105] Technological changes in treatment methods for many kinds of mental illness (improvements in drug therapies primarily) meant that many formerly confined patients could be released with relatively little risk to themselves or others. Besides improved technology, there was an evolving sense that mental institutions were uncivilized and inhumane places, not fit for modern society. Individual awareness of mental illness also seemed to be increasing at about the same time. "Normal" people were becoming more willing to acknowledge mental illness in associates, families, and even themselves.[106] Independent of general changes in technical means and broad shifts in humanitarian attitudes was a complementary shift in economic philosophy in the California State House. Ronald Reagan had become governor and set about cutting the budget and returning services and programs "to the people." Mental health professionals introduced a final ideological component of the decision. A nationwide movement promoting community-based care began sometime in the late 1950s and early 1960s and reached prominence in several state and federal statutes at about the same time.[107] Ideological bases for termination are not restricted to mental health programs. Similar ideological underpinning can be identified in the Reagan Administration decisions to abolish the Departments of Energy and Education, curtail support to public broadcasting, and generally reduce the federal government's social welfare programs.

Ideology is by no means the complete story, but it is important to emphasize its importance in many termination decisions. Were any one of the key ideological aspects markedly altered (in the mental health illustration, had there been an expansion-minded governor, a professional ethic of centralized institutional treatment, or a prevalent attitude of neglect toward the mentally ill), then the chance of termination actions would have been different and probably less. A decision maker needs to be sensitive to ideological matters, but mindful of the limited control any individual has over them, so as to be able to move opportunistically or not to move at all, depending on ideology's presence and implications.

Ideological conflicts can occur within individuals, too. More than one economy-minded California state legislator had to deal with the problem of reductions in the mental health budgets and their various consequences for his constituents. Many mental institutions were the main source of employment in remote regions where they were located. Such locations frequently abound in a conservative political and economic ethic; hence conflicts arose between economizing and wanting to reduce state government's control versus the fiscal reality of local unemployment and economic decline.

Organizational myths may also affect specific termination decisions. For a corporation such as General Electric, whose external image is embodied in its advertising slogan, "Progress is our most important product," it may be especially difficult to face plant closures, economic declines, obsolescence, and other "nonprogressive" facts of life. Success becomes aligned with or equated to growth and progress, and termination means failure. An internal image or myth of caring for one's employees by providing them with secure and fulfilling jobs in exchange for their dedicated productive service may also impair thinking, planning, and acting on necessary reductions.

Legal aspects

Myths and ideology take concrete form in the legal arrangements binding employer and employee, manager to consumer, and decision maker to society at large. Individually and collectively, the legal obstacles to termination can be formidable, if not completely overwhelming.

The federal government operates under the constraints of civil service regulations and due process, which may in specific cases be invoked by those "wronged" or "abused" by prospective terminations. Legislation may also exist to impede a decision maker's cutback plans. As Bardach points out, "the Administrative Procedures Act forbids the government to be 'arbitrary and capricious'," words inviting legal interpretation and contest.[108] In 1974, Washington, D.C., Police Chief Jerry Wilson decided to abolish his department's motorcycle squad. However, a suit was brought by a motorcycle officer to contest whether Wilson could reclassify his employees' position, the form the decision took. A restraining order followed to delay the chief's decision, but in time, he was successful.[109] Following President Nixon's order to abolish the Office of Economic Opportunity, threatened employees won a federal court restraining order forbidding him to impound the agency's funding and disband the agency.[110] Questions consistently occur about a president's legal right to impound congressionally appropriated funds, or to cancel programs in which contracts have been signed, or to prevent an agency from fulfilling its legal obligations in some other way. Jimmy Carter discovered such problems when he attempted to cancel the Clinch River breeder reactor program and to reduce the number of federal advisory panels and committees. For the National Science Foundation (NSF), a heavy user of outside advisors to fulfill its legislative mandate to provide "oversight and evaluation of the conduct of its programs,"[111] this meant *increasing* its use of advisors and thereby gaining Carter's ire. Still, a spokesman for the NSF claimed, "There was never any attempt to circumvent the President."[112]

We are not trained to discuss in detail the possible relationships between contract law and policy or program terminations; nevertheless, many central concepts of contract law seem applicable. Ideas such as damages, restitution, satisfaction of the parties, change in circumstances affecting one's duty to perform a promise, relief from frustrating, coerced, or unfair bargains, and many other contractual matters seem relevant to termination.[113] Certainly, were a contractual approach to programs and policies more commonplace, the connection of existing law and termination could become stronger.

As a general matter, though, the anger and frustration of termination's targets all too commonly lead to legal redress, which imposes yet another layer of obstacles to the simple desire to get rid of something.

Despite the many formidable obstacles, terminations do occur, and it is worthwhile to explore a few instances to see if they hold lessons for potential use elsewhere. We turn to this task in the concluding chapter.

NOTES

1. This termination exercise is posed in Garry D. Brewer, "Termination: Hard Choices—Harder Questions," *Public Administration Review*, July/August 1978, pp. 338–44.

2. *The American Heritage Dictionary of the English Language* (Boston: Houghton Mifflin, 1969), p. 1328. © 1981 Houghton Mifflin Company. Reprinted by permission from *The American Heritage Dictionary of the English Language*.

3. The latter episode, a classic study in termination, is described by Edward L. Katzenbach, "The Horse Cavalry in the Twentieth Century: A Study in Policy Response," *Public Policy* 8 (1958), pp. 120–49.

4. This theme is developed in Peter deLeon, "Public Policy Termination: An End and a Beginning," *Policy Analysis*, Summer 1978, pp. 369–92.

5. James M. Cameron, "Ideology and Policy Termination: Restructuring California's Mental Health System," *Public Policy*, Fall 1978, pp. 533–70; and Julian Wolpert and Eileen R. Wolpert, "The Relocation of Released Mental Hospital Patients into Residential Communities," *Policy Sciences*, March 1976, pp. 31–51.

6. For two examples, see Linda E. Demkovich, "Political Budget Pressures Sidetrack Plan for Turning AFDC Over to States," *National Journal*, September 19, 1981, pp. 1671–73; and Thomas L. Friedman, "Revolutionary Changes for Solar Field: Private Sector Must Fill Gap in Funds Cuts," *New York Times*, August 18, 1981, pp. D–1, D–6; or, more metaphorically, Burt Solomon, "Adam Smith Swoops Down on Solar Budget," *Energy Daily*, February 18, 1982, pp. 2–4.

7. These concepts are explored by Peter deLeon, "New Perspectives on Program Termination," *Journal of Policy Analysis and Management*, Fall 1982, pp. 108–11.

8. Robert Biller comments that we spend enormous resources in making a policy or organization as "continuous and persistent as possible," and that we "work extraordinarily hard to produce continuity, stability, and persistence—all features that can be understood as ways of avoiding termination." Biller, "On Tolerating Policy and Organizational Termination: Some Design Considerations," *Policy Sciences*, June 1976, p. 135.

9. Many ideas in this section were contributed by Robert D. Behn, although we have adapted them to fit our purposes. Behn, "Private Communication," October 5, 1978.

10. Robert Benjamin, *The Limits of Politics: Collective Goods and Political Change in Postindustrial Societies* (Chicago: University of Chicago Press, 1980), especially chaps. 3, 5, and 6. The thesis is a compelling and controversial one.

11. Garry D. Brewer, "Direction: The Coordination of Social Services," in Jay Chambers and William Hartman, eds., *Special Education Policies: Their History, Implementation, and Finance* (Philadelphia: Temple University Press, 1982).

12. As wrily noted in *The Washington Monthly*, June 1977, p. 31.

13. The decision to cancel the American SST is described in Mel Horwitch, *Clipped Wings: The American SST Conflict* (Cambridge, Mass.: MIT Press, 1982); the latter case is treated in W. Henry Lambright, *Shooting Down the Nuclear Plane* (Indianapolis, Ind.: Inter-University Case Program, Bobbs-Merrill, 1967).

14. W. Henry Lambright and Harvey Sapolsky creditably work to this end in "Terminating Federal Research and Development Programs," *Policy Sciences*, June 1976, pp. 199–213. Their effort is uncommon.

15. One of the first thorough studies of the "deinstitutionalization" of mental patients is Eugene C. Bardach, *The Skill Factor in Politics: Repealing the Mental Commitment Laws in California* (Berkeley: University of California Press, 1972); Cameron, "Ideology and Policy Termination," supplies follow-up data complementing the Bardach case study; and Valerie J. Bradley, "Policy Termination in Mental Health: The Hidden Agenda," *Policy Sciences*, June 1976, pp. 215–24, explores many of the political and bureaucratic incentives underlying the movement.

16. We cite many of these throughout the chapter as illustrations of specific points.

17. Zero-base budgeting tries to examine existing programs and activities by exploring what would happen if the total resources they contain were reduced or reallocated to other purposes rather than merely being taken for granted. One is supposed to consider the entire budget "from scratch" or first premises rather than concentrating on mar-

ginal adjustments. See Peter A. Pyhrr, *Zero-Base Budgeting: A Practical Management Tool for Evaluating Expenses* (New York: John Wiley & Sons, 1973); a partisan view is Joseph S. Wholey, *Zero-Base Budgeting and Program Evaluation* (Lexington, Mass.: D. C. Heath, 1978); and a valuable collection of materials and experiences (mainly from states trying to use the procedure) is U.S. Congress, Senate, Committee on Government Operations, *Compendium of Materials on Zero-Base Budgeting in the States* (Washington, D.C.: Government Printing Office, January 1977).

18. Sunset legislation calls for the automatic termination of programs and organizations unless they are affirmatively recreated by new law. One compilation of the procedure and some early results sustained with it is Common Cause, *Making Government Work: A Common Cause Report on State Sunset Activity* (Washington, D.C.: Common Cause, 1978); at the federal level, during 1977, the U.S. Senate's Committee on Governmental Affairs, *Hearings on the Sunset Act of 1977* (Washington, D.C.: Government Printing Office, 1977), is illuminating. Among the many problems revealed was the realization that a general federal sunset statute would necessitate huge additions to the evaluation staffs of both the Congress and the Executive.

19. A large segment of *Public Administration Review*, July/August 1978, pp. 325–57, presented a "Symposium on Organizational Decline and Cutback Management." The general theme is developed in Charles H. Levine, ed, *Managing Fiscal Stress: The Crisis in the Public Sector* (Chatham, N.J.: Chatham House, 1980). Also see the papers in Robert D. Behn, ed., "Leadership in an Era of Retrenchment: A Symposium," *Public Administration Review*, November/December 1980, pp. 603–26.

20. Sid Bernstein, "High Court Bars Health Staff Cuts," *Los Angeles Times*, November 3, 1981, p. II–1.

21. The entitlement ethic is best described in Robert D. Behn and Kim Sperduto, "Medical Schools and the Entitlement Ethic," *The Public Interest*, Fall 1979, pp. 48–68.

22. The legal concepts of government largess, entitlement, due process, and fair administrative procedure often conspire to make termination exceedingly difficult. The literature and experience are considerable. Charles Reich, "The New Property," *Yale Law Journal* 73 (1964), pp. 733–58, lays out some of the groundwork; Jerry Mashaw, "Management Side of Due Process," *Cornell Law Review* 59 (1954), pp. 772ff., engages several administrative and procedural details. Both contain supporting documentation and references.

23. Ernst Becker, *The Denial of Death* (New York: Free Press, 1973), offers philosophical and psychological insights into the problem; G. Zilboorg, "Fear of Death," *Psychoanalytic Quarterly* 12 (1943), pp. 465–75, works through several of the psychological themes; and Jacques Choron, *Death and Western Thought* (New York: Collier Books, 1963), explores the cultural dimension.

24. Choron, *Death and Western Thought*.

25. Herman Kahn, *On Thermonuclear War* (Princeton, N.J.: Princeton University Press, 1960), demonstrates how one can think through the strong emotions stimulated by that cataclysmic subject—and the necessity for doing so. Jonathan Schell, *The Fate of the Earth* (New York: Alfred A. Knopf, 1982), pp. 7–8, discusses the intellectual reluctance to conceptualize nuclear warfare and its resulting horrors: "And accompanying the revulsion there may be a sense of helplessness and defeat, brought about by an awareness of the incapacity of the human soul to take in so much horror. A nuclear holocaust, widely regarded as 'unthinkable' but never as undoable, appears to confront us with an action that we can perform but cannot quite conceive. Following upon these first responses, there may come a recoil, and a decision, whether conscious or unconscious, not to think any longer about the possibility of a nuclear holocaust. . . . A society that systematically shuts its eyes to an urgent peril to its physical survival and fails to take any steps to save itself cannot be called psychologically well."

26. The literature on divorce is perhaps the most pronounced here. See Esther Oshiver Fisher, *Divorce: The New Freedom* (New York: Harper & Row, 1974); Norman Sheresky and Marya Mannes, *Uncouplings* (New York: Viking Press, 1972); and William J. Goode, *After Divorce* (New York: Free Press, 1956). Written for the mass audience, these books (and most others in this burgeoning field) are not very applicable to problems of policy or program termination.

27. Biller, "Policy and Organizational Termination," p. 137.

28. Eugene C. Bardach, "Policy Termination as a Political Process," *Policy Sciences*, June 1976, p. 123, said as much six years ago; it still holds true.

29. Herbert Kaufman, *Are Government Organizations Immortal?* (Washington, D.C.: The Brookings Institution, 1976), p. 77.

30. Ibid., p. 35.

31. Bardach, "Policy Termination," p. 123.

32. Michael Handel, "The Study of War Termination," *Journal of Strategic Studies*, May 1970, pp. 51–75, claims "the amount of literature on the subject of war termination is immense, . . ." and draws upon such disciplines as international law and diplomatic history for reference.

33. Richard Kluger, *Simple Justice: The History of Brown* v. *the Board of Education* (New York: Alfred A. Knopf, 1975), documents the history of school segregation and court actions taken to end it.

34. Bruce A. Ackerman, and Susan Rose-Ackerman, James W. Sawyer, Jr., and Dale W. Henderson, *The Uncertain Search for Environmental Quality* (New York: Free Press, 1974), is an excellent illustration of this sort of scholarship—where the termination standpoint is not explicitly adopted but where the materials presented nonetheless are rich in its exposition.

35. See Robert A. Levine, *The Poor Ye Need Not Have: Lessons from the War on Poverty* (Cambridge, Mass.: MIT Press, 1970), for the rise and fall of OEO from the perspective of an administrator and an analyst.

36. The "first wholesale elimination of a major independent agency since the end of World War II" is described by David Shribman, "Death Comes to a Federal Agency," *New York Times*, September 19, 1981, p. 7. The Community Services Administration is eulogized by Hugh Price, "Minimum Feasible Participation," *New York Times*, September 21, 1981, p. 24.

37. Kaufman, *Are Government Organizations Immortal?* p. 65.

38. James L. Foster and Garry D. Brewer, "And the Clocks Were Striking Thirteen: The Termination of War," *Policy Sciences*, June 1976, pp. 225–43; the theme is integrated into a discussion of arms limitation by Garry D. Brewer and Bruce G. Blair, "War Games and National Security: With a Grain of SALT," *Bulletin of the Atomic Scientists*, June 1979, pp. 157–69.

39. Levine, *Managing Fiscal Stress.*

40. Two pertinent studies are Nan Humphrey, George Peterson, and Peter Wilson, *The Future of Cleveland's Capital Plant* (Washington, D.C.: The Urban Institute, 1979); and David A. Grossman, *The Future of New York City's Capital Plant* (Washington, D.C.: The Urban Institute, 1979).

41. The Departments of Energy and Education are illustrative: Judith Miller, "Energy Dept.'s Backers Cross Ideological Lines," *New York Times*, December 29, 1981, p. 12, explains how the Reagan plan to dismember that Department has aligned environmentalists and solar energy advocates with nuclear weapons developers. Hidden agenda are the themes of Rochelle L. Stanfield, "Breaking Up the Education Department—School Aid May Be the Real Target," *National Journal*, October 24, 1981, pp. 1907–10.

42. Although hardly a perfect indicator, the sparse literature on policy termination offers some evidence to this proposition.

43. The assessment of Herbert F. York, ed., *Arms Control* (San Francisco: W. H. Freeman, 1973), almost 10 years ago still rings true: "Thus, in the almost three decades since the atomic bomb was first used, there has been progress in both arms developments and arms control. But, compared to the great crescendo of the arms race itself, the arms control successes can scarcely be detected." And, in describing the possible consequences: "If used in the worst possible way, [the forces the United States and the Soviet Union possess] could kill many hundreds of millions of people within a half hour after a launch signal was given." From the Preface.

44. Jacques S. Gansler, *The Defense Industry* (Cambridge, Mass.: MIT Press, 1980), is one reckoning.

45. Andrew J. Pierre, "Arms Sales: The New Diplomacy," *Foreign Affairs*, Winter 1981/82, p. 266. For a more extensive account of arms transfers on a nation-by-nation basis, see idem, *The Global Politics of Arms Sales* (Princeton, N.J.: Princeton University Press, 1982).

46. Becker, *Denial of Death*, p. ix, reproduces Dr. Johnson's famous dictum and suggests the emotional distinctions noted here. Denial is given particular emphasis throughout. Inevitably, denial and the role of religion are noted in the following from Seymour B. Sarason: "That death is our destination we will of course not say or recognize, and as a society we strenuously avoid reminding our young about this—a function that religion once discharged so well." In his, "Growing Up Old," *Yale Alumni Magazine*, December 1976, p. 23.

47. Harold M. Schmeck, Jr., "Senators Resisting Nixon on Health Bill," *New York Times*, March 23, 1973, p. 22. A version of the evidence in dispute is contained in Alice M. Rivlin, "A Counter-Budget for Social Progress," *New York Times Magazine*, April 8, 1973, pp. 33, 84, 86, 91, 93, 95, and 97. A follow-up on Weinberger's response is Richard T. Cooper, "HEW Prodded to Do Research on Its Own: Weinberger Seeking to Reduce Flow of Funds to Outside Consulting Groups," *Los Angeles Times*, April 23, 1973, pp. 1, 14.

48. In the case of the Weinberger/Nixon cuts, most did not occur because of the Watergate spectacle and the diversion of attentions and political resources it represented. Timothy B. Clark, "New Federalism Report," *National Journal*, April 21, 1973, pp. 580–81, details the administrative complications inherent in the proposal and stresses the need for dutiful and persistent political effort. For an early termination assessment of Reagan's New Federalism, see Rochelle L. Stanfield, "New Federalism," *National Journal*, February 27, 1982, pp. 356–62.

49. In the "successful" terminations of previous mental health legislation and practice in California, reported in Bardach, *Skill Factor*, chaps. 3 and 4, all of these general reactions are distinguishable; also see Constance Holden, "Massachusetts Juvenile Justice: De-institutionalization on Trial," *Science*, 30 April 1976, pp. 447–51.

50. Jean Seligmann et al., "Empty Desk Blues," *Newsweek*, April 24, 1978, p. 94.

51. Ibid.

52. Some colleagues or universities threatened with closure present another argument— the dependence of the local economy on the institution. Judith Cummings, "Supporters of York College Cite Tie to Area's Economy," *New York Times*, April 28, 1978, p. B–8.

53. A description of the magnitude and potential cost of the radioactive waste disposal problem created by the civilian power reactor is provided by Fred C. Shapiro, *Radwaste* (New York: Random House, 1982); it is especially valuable in making the issues intelligible to the layperson. Also, E. William Colglazier, Jr., ed., *The Politics of Nuclear Waste* (Elmsford, N.Y.: Pergamon for the Aspen Institute, 1982).

54. The decommissioning of atomic reactors that have reached the end of their operating lifespans will soon become matters of immediate policy concern as the first generation of nuclear power reactors approaches its 30 year operating limit. See Colin Norman, "A Long-Term Problem for the Nuclear Industry," *Science*, 22 January 1982, pp. 376–79.

55. The organizational troubles of the EPA are described by Constance Holden, "EPA Hard Hit by Budget Cuts," *Science*, 16 October 1981, pp. 306–7.

56. This theme is elaborated in Peter deLeon, "A Theory of Policy Termination," in Judith V. May and Aaron B. Wildavsky, eds., *The Policy Process* (Beverly Hills, Calif.: Sage Publications, 1978), pp. 283–86.

57. Biller, "Policy and Organizational Termination," p. 137.

58. Kaufman, *Are Government Organizations Immortal?* p. 64.

59. Burt Solomon, "Commerce Department Is the Big Winner in DOE Demolition Derby," *Energy Daily*, December 18, 1981, pp. 1–2, describes the result of the interagency competition over DOE's responsibilities as "the vector-sum of everybody's desires." The extent of the "Finlandization" of the DOE empire is displayed by the 1983 energy budget in Kennedy Maize, "DOE Budget's Bottom Line Favors the Atom," *Energy Daily*, February 9, 1982, pp. 1, 3. On the side of agency continuance, see Robert D. Hershey, Jr., "Department of Energy Stays Alive," *New York Times*, February 15, 1982, pp. 21–22.

60. Robert D. Behn, "How to Terminate a Public Policy: A Dozen Hints for the Would-Be Terminator," *Policy Analysis*, Summer 1978, pp. 393–413.

61. Robert A. Rosenblatt, "Reagan to Ask Congress to Abolish Energy Department," *Los Angeles Times*, December 18, 1981, p. I–10.

62. Quoted in Gaylord Shaw, "U.S. Cutbacks Create Chaos in States, 3 Governors Say," *Los Angeles Times*, November 6, 1981, p. I–16.

63. Continual American revisions in NATO contingency plans are a constant source of bewilderment to its European allies; for a less volatile but equally irritating example, see Robert Reinhold, "U.S. Dismays Allies by Slashing Funds for Joint Science Projects," *New York Times*, May 10, 1981, pp. A–1, 6.

64. Garry D. Brewer, "On the Theory and Practice of Innovation," *Technology In Society*, Fall 1980, pp. 337–63.

65. Paul Van Slambrouck, "Consultants to the Displaced Employee," *Christian Science Monitor*, May 5, 1978. In this 1978 account, it was estimated that yearly annual revenues from "outplacement," as the service is called, exceeded $30 million.

66. A counter example: In the aftermath of wars, huge consolidations in the military always occur after demobilization.

67. See Mary Bralove, "AT&T Employees See Threat, Opportunity for Them in a Breakup," *Wall Street Journal*, January 26, 1982; and Michael Wines, "Divorce, American Style—Breaking Up AT&T Could Trigger a Battle Royal," *National Journal*, January 1, 1982, pp. 189–93; both speculate on these possibilities.

68. Daniel Tarschys, "Rational Decremental Budgeting: Elements of an Expenditure Policy for the 1980s," *Policy Sciences*, December 1981, pp. 49–58.

69. DeLeon, "New Perspectives on Program Termination," reports on the success of the Swedish National Agency for Agriculture in a collaborative venture to determine how best to secure a needed 2 percent budget reduction. A high-level committee, representing all key interests, deliberated and reported back a plan that everyone endorsed which also resulted in a 4 percent reduction.

70. See Daniel Tarschys, "Public Policy Innovation in a Zero-Growth Economy: A Scandinavian Perspective," in Peter R. Baehr and Bjorn Wittrock, eds., *Policy Analysis and Policy Innovation* (Beverly Hills, Calif.: Sage Publications, 1981), pp. 9–25.

71. Which is not to say that the transition was timely or smooth: Katzenbach, "The Horse Cavalry"; and Frederic A. Bergerson, *The Army Gets an Air Force* (Baltimore, Md.: Johns Hopkins University Press, 1980), present the respective details.

72. This is a seminal theme of Richard M. Cyert and James C. March, *A Behavioral Theory of the Firm* (Englewood Cliffs, N.J.: Prentice-Hall, 1963).

73. Herbert Kaufman, "The Natural History of Human Organizations," *Administration & Society*, August 1975, pp. 131–49.

74. Biller, "Policy and Organizational Termination," p. 136.

75. Donald Schon, *Beyond the Stable State* (New York: Random House, 1971), refers to this as "dynamic conservatism."

76. David Rees, *The Limited War* (New York: St. Martin's Press, 1964).

77. Wallace J. Thies, "Searching for Peace: Vietnam and the Question of How Wars End," *Polity*, Spring 1975, pp. 305–33.

78. Levine, *The Poor*, tells the story.

79. Albert O. Hirschman, *Exit, Voice and Loyalty* (Cambridge, Mass.: Harvard University Press, 1970), expands on this idea.

80. Miller, "Energy Dept.'s Backers," p. 12. A report in *Energy Daily*, February 9, 1962, p. 1, relates how DOE Deputy Secretary Davis ordered 7500 copies of the Department's FY83 *Budget Highlights* recalled and destroyed (at a cost of $3500) because it used the word "dismantle" three times in referring to the Department's future; reprinted editions substituted the word "reorganize."

81. Miller, ibid.

82. Congressman Jack Brooks (Dem.-Texas) threatened as much in his interview with Kennedy Maize, "Rep. Brooks Promises Slow Going on DOE Dissolution," *Energy Daily*, February 12, 1982, pp. 2, 3.

83. Miller, "Energy Dept.'s Backers."

84. The example and testimony are reported in *The Washington Monthly*, November 1975, p. 39.

85. Bardach, "Policy Termination," p. 128.

86. Donald Woutat, "Widespread Gains Seen from Ford-UAW Pact," *Los Angeles Times*, February 21, 1982, pp. V–1, 15.

87. Thomas M. Chesser, "After Rumsfeld's Pruning, Searle Blossoms," *International Herald Tribune*, February 1, 1982.

88. Ibid.

89. Ibid.

90. Peter F. Drucker, *Management: Tasks, Responsibilities, Practices* (New York: Harper & Row, 1974), p. 141.

91. Curious, but a comparable "measure of success" seems to hold for individual business executives. That is, the size and growth of their individual compensation packages determine for many how successful an individual is.

92. Quoted in Anonymous, "Delay in DOE Demise," *Energy Daily*, February 12, 1982, p. 2.

93. Theis, "Searching for Peace," covers the specific case; Fred Iklé, *Every War Must End* (New York: Columbia University Press, 1971), offers a general survey of the theme.

94. An off-setting benefit of retaining those with most seniority is the contribution it makes to the organizational myth of caring for loyal employees, even in times of crisis. This, in turn, could boost the survivors' morale.

95. Robert D. Behn, "How the Differences between Private and Public Organizations Affect Their Abilities to Terminate Their Activities" (Phoenix, Ariz.: 39th Annual

Conference of the American Society for Public Administration, April 19, 1978), addresses several of the ideas summarized here.

96. Frederick C. Redlich and Daniel X. Freedman, *The Theory and Practice of Psychiatry* (New York: Basic Books, 1966), pp. 285–86.

97. Ibid., p. 285.

98. Maya Pines, "Recession Is Linked to Far-Reaching Psychological Harm," *New York Times*, April 6, 1982, pp. 21, 23.

99. A rare case study that does so is Alfred Slote, *Termination: The Closing at Baker Plant* (New York: Bobbs-Merrill, 1969).

100. Preparations include setting money aside, acquiring alternative professional skills and potentials, looking forward to vacations, or seeking retraining or educational assistance to improve future employability.

101. Marlene Cimons, "Civil Servants See Cutbacks as Demoralizing, Punitive," *Los Angeles Times*, April 4, 1982, pp. I–1, 28.

102. Paul Kecskemeti, *Strategic Surrender: The Politics and Victory of Defeat* (Stanford, Calif.: Stanford University Press, 1958), uses this as a major thesis.

103. Recall the earlier discussion of institutional obstacles where threatened individuals tried to justify and rationalize themselves and their organizations. A former White House staff member in the Carter Administration explains: "We were so busy right up until the end that no one had any time to plan or prepare for what we were going to do next." "Private Communication," December 5, 1981.

104. Joseph Fletcher, *Morals and Medicine* (Boston: Beacon Press, 1954), gives a good historical description of the bases and evolution of these norms. A collection of essays addressed to the problem of "death with dignity" or a "right to die" is Daniel H. Labby, ed., *Life or Death: Ethics and Options* (Seattle: University of Washington Press, 1968).

105. Cameron, "Ideology and Policy Termination," takes this as a departure point in explaining the California experience of the 1960s and 1970s.

106. A prevalent attitude from about the late 1800s through the early 1960s was that the mentally ill were in various ways themselves to blame, or, at least, they should be removed from society so as not to taint it. In some measure this helps explain why so many mental institutions are in remote areas around the country.

107. Bardach, *Skill Factor*, chaps. 1 and 2, provides the general legislative and ideological context; and Valerie J. Bradley, "Policy Termination in Mental Health," *Policy Sciences*, June 1976, pp. 215–24, gives a good summary of the main state statutes.

108. Bardach, "Policy Termination," p. 129.

109. Abram N. Shulsky, "Abolishing the District of Columbia Motorcycle Squad," *Policy Sciences*, June 1976, pp. 183–97, describes the legal and other obstacles in this incident.

110. Levine, *The Poor*. Eventually, OEO also succumbed.

111. Jeffrey Smith, "Carter Versus Advisory Panels," *Science*, 12 May 1978, p. 630.

112. Ibid. The matter boiled down to which of two conflicting authorities to obey, and the NSF picked its legislative obligation.

113. A legal scholar, Thomas M. Carhart III, supplied these and other intriguing ideas in a "Private Communication," May 9, 1975.

14

It does happen: Some experiences
and challenges

As a general proposition, there appear to be certain conditions that lend themselves to termination. For instance, when a private organization's top leadership changes or when a new administration comes to power in the public sector, a distinct break with past commitments and experiences occurs that may facilitate new policies, including whole or partial terminations. When a Donald Rumsfeld assumes control of a corporation, in the example used in the previous chapter, previous arrangements and obligations are clearly subject to review and change. Similarly, when a new administration assumes office, there is a honeymoon period during which new initiatives have a better than normal chance of success. Among other things, prior political programs are suspended, and the sunk costs of the previous administration can be ignored and may no longer need to be justified. President Reagan was able to ignore the political obligations President Carter had incurred in such disparate areas as strategic arms talks, Law of the Sea negotiations, and cabinet-level departments (the very existence of the Departments of Education and Energy). The fact that a board of directors or an electorate decides to switch leadership could act as mandate for basic changes, including terminal ones.

A change in the ideological climate often facilitates termination. Some of the impetus for federal deregulation in the 1980s is understandable in these terms. Climatic cycles and ideological shifts can be used to motivate termination, if the leadership is willing to take advantage of them (e.g., deinstitutionalization in mental health). Indeed, such changes will often motivate termination activities. An earlier climate or sense that government should protect the general citizenry through regulatory means began to yield to a competing sense that government involvement was exacting too high a price.[1] Although clearly an extreme and vested perspective, the Department of Energy, in reviewing its operations, proclaimed itself

> a wholesale failure. Ill-conceived regulation impeded new development, discouraged conservation, and distorted distribution. Subsidy programs created artificial demand for energy technologies that could not stand the market test. And the drain on federal resources grew almost beyond control.[2]

Turbulent, sharp, or unexpected changes in political contexts have been seized to alter course, often radically (e.g., Franklin Roosevelt facing the Depression years). Something like an energy crisis or a recession can become a rationale to terminate ineffective individuals or marginal programs. These external events provide the excuse and motivation and hence remove the onus from those involved in termination. Fired employees or hapless executives can rationalize their plight as being the fault of the recession, the energy crisis, the Japanese, excessive regulation or government interference, and thereby avoid bearing full personal responsibility and loss of self-respect.[3]

A combination of new leadership and large contextual changes may be especially effective in achieving terminations. The Reagan Administration's first year in office is representative, at least in its general intention and direction. Newcomers can be tarred with the symbolic blame for needed cutbacks that were previously politically infeasible. Hence, American liberals in the early 1980s have an opportunity to save selected aspects of programs they know need pruning or to accede reluctantly to overwhelming conservative power to get full termination of otherwise worn-out or ineffective programs. In either case, blame rests with the conservatives, as do the political liabilities the eliminations will generate.

If support systems are already in place (for whatever reason), then getting reductions or reallocating resources is sometimes easier. The natural attrition of employees through retirement, including early retirement incentive plans, is one example, although it takes time which might not be available. Task forces set up to accomplish specific objectives are a somewhat different version of the basic idea. When a military task force is created to obtain a certain objective, it is disbanded and its resources are returned to their original units once the goal is attained. Presidential commissions and special legislative committees work in much the same fashion, as do some "matrix organizations." At the individual level, mandatory retirement has a similar character. An airline pilot knows that failure to pass required, periodic physical examinations will end a flying career.[4] Physicians and lawyers, in contrast, do not have similar built-in professional expectations, nor do they have ready support systems to help them through disbarment or decertification. In part, this helps explain why termination for cause occurs so infrequently in both of these occupations.[5]

Other enabling circumstances and conditions exist and are described in the following case examples. As often happens, however, individual cases are characterized by highly specific factors that both impede and ease termination, and caution against generalization. Many of the general conditions outlined cannot be created willfully, but some may be seized or stimulated and then used. However, the current immaturity of termination knowledge as part of the policy process diminishes those prospects.

SOME EXPERIENCES

Successful partial termination: The Village Nursing Home

The Village Nursing Home, located in the Greenwich Village section of New York City, had since 1958 provided the only skilled nursing facility for the elderly in Manhattan's lower west side.[6] But on August 5, 1975, New York State's Health Department ordered the operators to bring the facility into compliance with current regulations (far in excess of those existing when the home opened) or else cease operations. According to the state's demands, the home would have to reduce its patient population by a third and undertake extensive structural renovations. The home was severely overcrowded and had been operating below standards under a series of special waivers for a number of years, but because of heightened awareness of nursing home abuses (including media coverage and new legislation), the comply-or-desist order was issued. Pleading financial hardship, the operators responded by telling the Health Department they would close down within 30 days.

Resistance formed quickly. Physicians providing care to the residents cited studies emphasizing the life-threatening aspects of "transfer trauma" for the elderly; a precipitous change of living circumstances could literally be fatal. Village relatives and friends of the home's patients also reacted quickly as they realized that shutdown and transfers to out-of-town nursing homes would mean losing contact. Others within the neighborhood rose up in opposition to the possible loss of "their" nursing home.[7] Community meetings, petitions, letters, press and television coverage, and a steady stream of meetings with city, state and federal officials followed. A first tangible result, on September 11, was a court restraining order on behalf of several home residents that allowed the opposition to organize and react while transition plans were made.

In the following four or five weeks confusion reigned; the crisis atmosphere only intensified when newspapers reported that the facility was going to close down right after Thanksgiving ("stranding 267 patients") and the staff threatened to resign enmass unless somebody did something to resolve the problem.[8] But no one was willing to fill the breech because no one knew what to do—a usual problem when termination has not been thought through. A provision of the state's newly adopted nursing home law allowed the court to appoint a receiver to take charge of threatened or deficient facilities for as long as an 18-month transitional period. Despite never doing it before, receivership became the means to secure partial termination, satisfactory consolidation, and retrenchment of the facility.

The Village Nursing Home represented a very complex story involving dozens of participants. It was a frustrating, time-consuming, and confusing process for everyone involved. Progress would stall until deadlines or external pressures rekindled the crisis (e.g., HEW moved to decertify the home and cut off Medicare payments). A clear strategy never evolved as a basis for action; rather, ad hoc tugging and hauling by dozens of well-meaning people and organizations defined the erratic play of events. Nevertheless, through what eventually turned out to be a two-year process, progress was made. After initial lack of success, a receiver was appointed. The Jewish Home and Hospital for the Aged (a successful nonprofit operator of a number of nursing homes) agreed to accept the responsibility but *only* for the 18-month statutory period. Caring Community Inc., a nonprofit corporation already serving the Village's elderly and representing a concilium of local churches and synagogues, eventually assumed responsibility for running the home but only with considerable reservations on the part of its leaders. Village residents organized and succeeded in raising enough money to purchase the facility for Caring Community and to allow work on the necessary renovations to begin. Natural attrition of the resident population during the period reduced the total number of patients to an acceptable level.

For our purposes, the receivership provision is perhaps the case's most interesting aspect because it suggests a termination strategy with more general possibilities. Lacking legal and procedural means, such as the receivership, the nursing home operators had only two options: continued operations at a substandard, money-losing level or closure. The first was not an option after the state intervened, and the second threatened to deprive the community of an essential service while endangering the lives of 267 elderly patients. As Johnson observes:

> If community action was the foundation for the success in redeeming the Village Nursing Home, the statutory receivership was clearly the keystone in that it provided time within which the community was able to develop and execute a plan for the facility's future.[9]

Under normal circumstances, a receiver ensures the orderly closure of an organization, company, or facility. Assets and resources are accounted for and outstanding debts are met according to various legal guidelines. A receiver is usually accorded extraordinary powers, with the sanctioning of a court, to execute these duties. Receiverships may be voluntary or involuntary, depending on specific circumstances, state statutes, and court decisions in particular cases. A feature distinguishing the nursing home case was that patient services had to continue during the period of the receivership. As a more general matter, finding empty beds to relocate the patients was impractical if not impossible, since, in New York City, demand for this kind of service far exceeded the supply. In other words, closing the facility not only endangered lives, but it would also have added to an already serious social problem.

Of the many lessons learned in the Village Nursing Home case, the following stand out.

A public sector or nonprofit retrenchment will probably be more complex than its private sector analog, other factors being roughly comparable, because more people are legitimately involved.

An external authority—in this case, the courts—was needed to invest the receiver with extraordinary powers to make difficult salvaging decisions.

The period of the receivership was fixed and thus provided steady pressure on all involved to work out the many hard problems retrenchment posed.

Compromises and bargains had to be reached, and these took patience, skill and inordinate amounts of time. Among other general matters, the realization that someone would have to be responsible for the operation of the facility was particularly difficult.

The receiver was skilled at operating nursing homes and was able to put the administrative, financial, and management problems of the operation into proper order during the receivership period.

The state did *not* serve as receiver and thus avoided unnecessary and possibly harmful politicization of the strong measures required for consolidation.

Each observation merits additional comment.

The public scrutiny and outside pressure Rumsfeld found so cumbersome while serving as a public servant were unavoidable, central features of the nursing home and apply to other possible public or nonprofit cutback cases. Many different values and points of view will exist, must be heard, and addressed as the termination drama plays out. All of this usually means that more time will be needed than anyone will have allocated. It probably means frustrating delays, missed opportunities, and circuitous resolution of the problem when taken from any one point of view or set of preferences. Thus it helps if a receiver has finely honed political sensitivities and a record of political achievement to allow the process to function at all. Extraordinary, but carefully defined authority will be necessary to break logjams and force the contending parties to acceptable compromises.

Action-forcing events and deadlines serve to keep groups focused on the difficult choices at hand. Had the receivership period been too short, for example, there would not have been enough time to organize, raise money, find new management, or to get the facility into proper working order. On the other hand, lacking a definite time by which the problem had to be resolved would have led to procrastination and reluctance to make needed accommodations.

Not just any group can be a receiver. Besides political skill, a receiver must have a substantial understanding of the operation in question so as to carry out the necessary pruning while maintaining the respect of others who are involved. A court can invest a receiver with authority, but it cannot guarantee that the receiver will use it wisely or well. Additionally, it may be ill-advised to make the state the receiver. There are obvious extraneous political facts of life that may enter and interfere, but there is also a problem of scale and detail. Successful retrenchment of the Village Nursing Home hinged on locals paying close attention to many contextual details that could very well have been ignored or overlooked by state officials, who are justifiably more concerned with hundreds of nursing homes at a much more aggregate level.

Several legal lessons were also learned; Johnson summarizes them while urging their consideration and incorporation by future users of the receivership model.

> Depending on the provisions of the particular statute and the financial status of the facility, counsel for a private receiver should consider securing the following provisions in a court order as conditions of appointment as receiver: (1) the owner or operator shall post a bond to cover potential deficits; (2) any reasonable deficit not reimbursed by the operator shall be reimbursed by the state, because in most states the receiver acts as the state's designee; and (3) the facility shall be assisted in making expedited application for Medicare and Medicaid reimbursement if this will supplement the income of the home.[10]

Some may be unconvinced by this success story, believing that its peculiar details are not reproducible or the receivership model is too complicated to work elsewhere. We agree that contextual matters count heavily in the policy process and that the process is often very complex. This is not, however, tantamount to submission. Rather, this case provides rare encouragement for anyone interested in developing termination as both an intellectual and practical matter. Lessons on a larger scale are provided in the next example, the protracted but ultimate termination of Lyndon Johnson's War on Poverty.

Termination on a grand scale: The War on Poverty

The Economic Opportunity Act, enacted on August 20, 1964, amid much fanfare and exuberance, promised an end to poverty in America. Ten years later, in the fall of 1974, the Office of Economic Opportunity (OEO), command center for the war, fell victim to a congressional vote of no confidence; its programs were phased out, consolidated, or shifted to other authorities; and a new era of federal involvement in poverty policy began. In October 1981, OEO's successor agency, the Community Services Administration (CSA), closed up shop for good.[11] We are not prepared to supply the historical record of the War on Poverty; there is simply too much to tell. In the following short discussion, we call attention to several key factors that contributed to the termination of the war, omitting most details but trusting that the broader sweep and interplay of events are recognized.

A major constellation of difficulties revolved around the enthusiastic but unrealistic promises made at the onset: "What the nation got in the war on poverty was an act whose swelling rhetoric bore little resemblance to the tools it made available to carry it out."[12] As often happens with ambitious legislation, what was to be accomplished was sufficiently grandiose and ambiguous that practically any interest could be enticed to support the call to arms. "Total victory in a decade" made for a good political rallying cry, but it provided little clarity about what was to be accomplished, by whom, when, and at whose expense.[13] For Lyndon Johnson, the consummate legislator, getting laws on the books was the accepted standard of success; worrying about implementing the administrative details of the laws was basically beyond his ken, someone else's problem. The legislation piled up in the early going: civil rights, voting rights, aid to public schools, health insurance for the elderly, and more. Within the purview of OEO, community action programs, the Job Corps training program for high school dropouts and unemployed teenagers, legal services for the poor, Head Start, and VISTA all came to pass with blinding speed . . . and replete with unexpected and indigestible problems.[14]

The 1964 ideological climate of sharing America's expanding wealth markedly changed by 1974 as more citizens realized that singling out one class of Americans—the poor—for special consideration could not be done without extracting sacrifices from other groups. Similarly, presuming that a moral justification would continue to sway public opinion enough to guarantee an ever-increasing share of the federal budget for poverty programs turned out to be mistaken. And finally, expecting that massive changes in American society would not provoke reaction and resistance contributed to the general erosion of support and grossly understated the vulnerability of many specific programs to counterattack and defeat.

A recession was underway in 1974, Watergate was running at fever pitch, and the Vietnam War was coming to its ignominious conclusion. The previously expansive and generous public mood was now marked with insecurity, self-doubt, suspicion, and a dawning sense that there might not be enough money to fight a real war and American poverty simultaneously. More concretely, the poverty programs had produced a mixed record. Horror stories of ill-conceived and poorly implemented programs fueled and dominated disillusionment. An underlying, but driving economic premise that expansionist government fiscal and monetary policies would spur economic growth, create jobs, add to tax revenues, and thus make the poverty war practically self-supporting fell victim to economic contraction, a stunning energy crisis, and inflation.

Politics reflected these dynamics. Many early supporters of the War on Poverty became opponents as they experienced "combat" first-hand. Widely publicized strikes against city hall, demands for more minority jobs, civil and voting rights activities, legal skirmishes to open up welfare and other programs, and dozens of other battles on behalf of the poor all began to erode the large base of support upon which the war had been predicated and begun. Changes, compromises, and cutbacks occurred almost from the start. By 1967, Congress had moved to limit OEO's operations: Wages for poverty workers were constrained, costs for certain programs were limited, stricter evaluation standards and requirements were levied, and steps were taken to transfer some federal programs to local control. OEO itself read the legislative omens and cut back several of its more politically controversial programs, primarily in the civil rights area. Successful and popular initiatives, such as Head Start, were emphasized and enlarged, while more troublesome or sensitive ones were curtailed: "In retrospect, it can be argued that if OEO had not pulled in its horns, it would not have survived as long as it has and many of its programs would not have survived at all."[15]

One program that did not get trimmed in the mid-1960s shakedown was California Rural Legal Assistance (CRLA), a model for dozens of other legal aid programs around the country. Besides providing routine legal aid to poor Californians, CRLA challenged that state's farm industry and the public bureaucracy which had evolved over the years to support it. In a succession of successful lawsuits, CRLA advanced the cause of migratory and other farm workers at considerable expense to wealthy and powerful agricultural interests. Sufficient pressure mounted against CRLA to cause California Governor Ronald Reagan to publish a long list of charges of misfeasance and abuse and to demand that all federal funds for CRLA be cut off. A panel of judges, years later in 1971, dismissed the charges as false but not before a political message was driven home: Legal services were removed from direct OEO control and, in 1974, placed under a nonprofit, government-sponsored corporation, the Legal Services Corporation, which later was itself targeted for termination by the Reagan Administration.[16]

With a change in national leadership in 1968, many feared for OEO and the continuing War on Poverty. Interestingly enough, President Nixon worked to streamline and strengthen, rather than decommission, OEO and other elements of the poverty army. Programs developed by OEO were assigned to regular line bureaucracies: Head Start went to HEW, and the Job Corps, instead of being scrapped as Nixon had promised in his campaign, went to Labor. A research and development emphasis in OEO was strengthened as Nixon named Donald Rumsfeld its new director. That Nixon did not stop the war during his first term probably owes as much to the narrowness of his 1968 victory over Hubert Humphrey as anything else. In keeping with the "game-within-the-game" tactic previously described, Daniel Patrick Moynihan, then head of the White House's Domestic Council and serving as a liberal counterweight to Nixon's other senior staff, proposed a family assistance plan to give every American a minimum income.[17] Had it been enacted, continuation of the comparatively piecemeal aspects of the War on Poverty would not have been as necessary.

The election of 1972 augured a different story as the Nixon landslide become his license to attack the federal bureaucracy. Rumsfeld, who had labored to make OEO more efficient, was replaced by Howard Phillips, a staunch conservative ideologically opposed to using tax dollars for social change. Mass resignations of senior political appointees were sought and accepted. Perhaps the most notable form termination took was withholding appropriated funds (impoundment) to force unwanted programs to cease operation. Four months into the Nixon attack on OEO, in April 1973, a federal judge issued a restraining order forbidding Phillips—and Nixon, indirectly—from subverting the intent of Congress to continue OEO's work, at least through the end of 1974.[18] The court-created delay allowed OEO supporters, primarily in cities and states, to organize and rally. It also allowed the Nixon forces to regroup and continue chipping away at OEO by transferring a number of its programs to other government agencies, a tactic that survived another court challenge and was executed in late 1973.

By the middle of 1974, state and local officials were well enough organized to convince Congress to continue the community action and services part of the War on Poverty; Nixon had earlier announced he would request no funds in his fiscal year 1975 budget and hence kill the program. Congressional resistance meant passage of the Community Services Act of 1974 which brought the *coup de grâce* to OEO but maintained the poverty programs already spun off to other federal agencies (e.g., Head Start and VISTA). One participant's interpretation of the situation is instructive: "It was a perfect way to resolve the issue. The people who hate OEO could say, 'Look, we're getting rid of it.' The people who like the individual programs could say, 'Look, we're keeping them.' Very often, they were the same people."[19]

Seven years and many changes later, OEO's successor and the last symbolic vestige of Lyndon Johnson's poverty army died when the Community Services Administration folded its tents and laid off its more than 1,000 employees. Congress now backed CSA's termination, as contrasted to 1974. The final fate of the War on Poverty, its army scattered throughout other agencies of the federal government, then turned on the eventual outcome of President Reagan's proposal to give block grants to state and local governments. The end-as-beginning aspect of termination is specifically echoed by Dwight Ink, CSA's last administrator, the person appointed to turn off its lights:

> I don't look upon this as bringing a program to an end. I look upon it as a transition, a returning of local decisions to local governments. The elimination of a Federal agency is incidental to this process. It's a very important incidental to the men and women who work here, of course, but the main thrust of the President's program is the devolution of programs back to state and local governments.[20]

A common emotional reaction is summed up by Ink, "It's a very traumatic situation."[21]

The lessons learned throughout the 17-year history of the War on Poverty will probably never be completely understood, but they certainly will be the subject of voluminous inquiry and partisan debate. Nevertheless, several general features of the war's termination are already beginning to emerge:

Absent clearly defined goals and related guidelines for attaining them, profound questions will arise about success, or its lack, when the possibility of termination occurs. At the most elementary level, resolving the definitional question of "What is poverty?" really never happened, and perhaps it never could given its subjective and contextual determinants.

Wholesale termination of large programs or policies is far less likely than selective, partial terminations of their more vulnerable and less successful parts.

Many changes in a problem's context occur slowly, even so slowly as to be imperceptible to those most directly involved. Shifts in popular mood and attitude are among the slowest and least predictable or controllable of these, although they may be among the most important in the long run.

Termination is a fact of life in most social arrangements. The question is not so much whether to end something as it is how, when, and how well to do so. This, of course, reemphasizes termination as an integral part of the whole policy process.

Termination seldom occurs painlessly and it usually takes much more time than anyone imagines or plans for.

DESIGN ISSUES IN TERMINATION POLICY

Design begins with understanding and proceeds by keeping fundamental principles well in hand. Understanding in this sense refers to the design principles required to make termination credible, acceptable, and expected. The following section proposes basic principles and general strategic considerations, then considers finer-grained, tactical changes and approaches, and concludes with a summary of suggestions for improved policy and program design.

Basic principles

It is important to learn how to design expectations for ending social arrangements. At present, too much energy and emphasis are placed on creating simple, durable solutions to problems far more complex than analysts and decision makers have a justification to presume. Throughout this book we have illustrated forces that compel a search for best or optimal solutions, but in nearly every case, various contingencies intervene to thwart the once-and-for-all approach. Simply, our analyses and decisions are imperfect while the problems are intricate and changeable. Analysts always have the opportunity to err and usually in significant ways. Decisions are seldom perfect either because of their inherent shortcomings and because of the limitations of the analyses on which they are based. Finally, neither problem nor context stands still; they evolve both naturally and in reaction to our efforts to understand and master them.

When we treat termination as if it were unexpected, it is incredible until and when it occurs. Individuals experience shock and anger. Organizations resist and fight back. Confusion, indignation, and pathos reign; a sense of betrayal pervades. The design problem revolves about creating expectations that will enable people to understand that little is forever and that termination can be constructive and beneficial. Still, people or organizations presently expect termination could not happen to them, so it is not accepted when it does. How, then, can this rather understandable set of expectations be changed?

Suppose, for the sake of illustration, that public agencies were allowed to deposit some portion of their yearly budgets into a central credit institution for use in future program investments: a savings bank for public agencies. Rather than losing part of an operating budget because of mandated reductions, the bank innovation might encourage agencies to trim inefficient programs by guaranteeing them access to their savings for use in later, more productive programs. The savings bank would encourage those who best know about policies and programs to evaluate them continually rather than shielding "losers" from outside scrutiny and attack. It would also introduce partial termination as a smooth, routine process in the workaday world. In short, a constructive termination element would be incorporated into an agency's standard (i.e., nonthreatening) operating procedures.

A contractual approach to services, suggested earlier, may be another way of integrating organizational expectations of termination. While a large number of things that organizations do might not fit the contract model well enough, some program-level and certainly many project-level activities could be constructed this way to build in termination from the very beginning.

In several ways, the matrix organization operates as a contract model. A matrix organization is designed with relatively stable and transitory elements interlaced. A research corporation, a consulting firm, a law partnership, or many other service organizations lend themselves to this institutional design. Members of a research firm in the business of analyzing housing problems, for example, generally know that its permanent staff should contain a number of economists, sociologists, statisticians, legal and administrative experts, and probably one or two other disciplinary specialties (probably situated in departments). For most problems the firm expects to explore, these skills and people are combined in varying proportions. But because the firm does not know exactly the details of specific problems it will be working on, it cannot allocate its permanent staff to preset working groups nor can it hire fully in anticipation of the specific, but unknown, tasks ahead. Hence, the relatively permanent part of the matrix organization is responsible for hiring and maintaining a quality staff in the basic disciplines while the projects draw from the departmental pools to staff individual programs, which vary in duration and scale (Table 14–1). Adjustment occurs through an internal market mechanism; if certain staff members are consistently not employed on projects, this may signify that their specific talents are no longer needed by the firm or that as individuals their performance is unacceptable, i.e., project leaders do not want them. Or the internal market may consistently demand talents not usually provided by the departments, which might signal changes in the permanent staff, including cutbacks for those in low demand and additions of new talent. If the market is far enough out of equilibrium, major structural alterations in the departments themselves may be required.

TABLE 14–1   An illustrative matrix organization doing housing research and studies

| | Projects | | | |
Department	A-housing demand in city X	B-housing stock assessment study	C-building codes and violations study	D . . . E, etc.
Economics	150 (days)	226	0	1
Sociology	27	1	0	5
Statistics	13	6	1	1
Legal	6	51	195	2
Administrative	1	175	68	6
Other	1	30	50	3
Consultants	5	6	10	6

The contract idea is relevant in other ways, too. Permanent staff members are essentially working on contract to project leaders. They are "hired" for specific tasks and allocated fixed amounts of resources (expressed as "days" in the cells of the matrix, Table 14–1) to do specific jobs. The initial contract may not work as expected. More days might have to be added to complete the job, staff members could be relieved for not meeting their commitments, or other changes can be made as the project unfolds. On the other side of the contractual coin, individuals have some latitude in designing their own assignments under this arrangement. Some may work on only a single project for long periods of time, which allows them to get deeply involved. It also makes them vulnerable should their project not be renewed or reconstituted in some form at its conclusion. Others may work on a variety of projects simultaneously without committing themselves excessively to any one, thus ensuring diversity in their intellectual diet and hedging against the decline of one or more of them. Different ways of allocating one's time exist between these extremes, but the matrix market mechanism essentially resolves the actual mix in a continuing, dynamic manner.

The matrix organization is scarcely a cure-all for government's or business' problems. It can help improve the internal operations of an organization by enhancing evolution and fine-tuning. It does not guarantee that the organization will stay competitive in the larger, external market, nor does it exert much control over cycles and sharp changes in the outside world. In the housing research example, the best research group in the world may face unemployment if the sponsors of its work decide to be interested in quite different aspects of the problem or if the market "crashes," e.g., a new sponsor evinces different priorities than housing and cancels funds for this sort of work.

So far we have suggested two designs to make termination more expected, credible, and accepted. They are not the only ones that can be imagined, nor are they necessarily the best ones. Specific needs and circumstances must be taken into account as one works to build termination into organizations, policies, and programs. Other design ideas—roughly divided into strategic and tactical categories—also warrant consideration and possible use.

Strategic design

A common element in new strategic approaches to termination is attitudinal. Termination is not the end of the world; rather, it should be seen as an opportunity to improve a deficient condition or to reuse resources in more productive ways. It can be as creative an act as it is destructive. This attitude suggests that the possibilities of success and failure should be realized at the origin of and throughout the policy process. We have suggested that a complete policy analysis include explicit considerations of termination options as these might relate to the ordinary cost and benefit calculations dominating an analyst's attention. For example, what would a successful option look like? And, if on attaining success, what needs to be done to reduce or shut off the resources being used to solve the problem? Or what would failure look like? What steps are needed to stop spending resources on its behalf? The idea of designing fall-back positions as hedges is possible, although rarely practiced. It would be surprising if this kind of analytic thinking did not result in rather different kinds of alternatives for decision makers to consider. Just imagine the consequences of grappling with the following design question: Of all possible options considered, which would be most easily terminated, and should it prove necessary, how would it be accomplished?

Developing these sorts of termination contingency plans also depends on how an analyst treats evaluation. Knowing what success or failure might resemble alerts the analyst and policymaker to observe and measure events following selection and implementation and provides guidance for possible terminations. This does not make evaluation any easier, however. Donald Rumsfeld the businessman knew that Searle was failing—the balance sheet and his directors told him so; Donald Rumsfeld the civil servant did not have as simple a metric or as clear a mandate, primarily because public organizations pursue disparate goals for a variety of constituents and a simple yes or no to the success-fail question is seldom found. Nonetheless, room for improvement of evaluation exists and could lead to more common and acceptable terminations.

The political and ideological climate is an important strategic factor that could be better advantaged. Until recently, many policy decisions have been based on a presumption that economic growth was normal and would continue. The War on Poverty was founded on this idea, as we pointed out. Life is simpler and gentler if its various problems can be resolved from an ever-expanding economic base. But the reality of recession is less lenient. Suppose instead that all new proposals were based on a presumption of zero or even negative growth in keeping with the decremental model suggested by Tarschys. If an organization wants a new policy or program, then its analysis and decision must consider what could be cut back or terminated and how the reduction would be accomplished.

Political and ideological considerations also indicate better termination strategies. The political context of policies and programs is not immutable. Any policy has groups in favor and opposition, and the balance between them changes through time. Determining that balance is one element in forming a successful termination strategy. Natural points in a policy's existence—times and places where a policy is susceptible to change—exist and could be exploited.[22] Most obvious of these is a change in administration, e.g., Reagan replaces Carter as president or Abe Beame replaces John Lindsay as New York's mayor.[23] Less visible but sometimes more important are changes in congressional committee assignments that temporarily weaken an agency's ties to sources of political support and power and thus make it and its policies more susceptible to termination. Another point occurs when key and powerful personnel within an agency are shifted, retire, or die: J. Edgar Hoover dies and the Federal Bureau of Investigation is restructured; Admiral Hyman Rickover is retired from the Navy's nuclear power program and reorganization finally becomes possible. The lesson here is simple. Termination is difficult enough, but its chances of success can be improved if analysts and decision makers learn to take advantage of specific opportunities, even though they may have little control over them. Still, to be opportunistic, one must be prepared with a concrete plan and know when the time is right to execute it.

Time is always important, especially when planning and carrying out termination. Is the termination performed with a bang or with a whimper?[24] One usually does not have the luxury—as an analyst at least—of deciding whether to get the job over with as quickly as possible or letting it drag out. Timing's consequences can be very important, however, as the Village Nursing Home case suggests. A bang might have literally cost lives and left the community without a nursing home; buying time through the receivership purchased an entirely different outcome. The gradual approach usually means a program's clientele will be able to plan what to do next and accommodate the idea of significant changes. But it also means they will have time to organize and resist. Natural attrition of service recipients and providers is less wrenching and may be more humane if done over a long time. Or it may only prolong the agony of readjustment and coming to terms with the inevitable. Phasing down eventually means spending less, but it also means paying more in the near term (closing costs, salvage costs, receiver costs) to attain these savings. Whether a bang, a whimper, or something in between, the timing of termination will make a large difference in the strategies one selects.[25]

As a general strategic matter, it would be illuminating to amass as much formal and informal evaluation as time allows. Because most evaluations are routine—even pedestrian—affairs and because they are conducted piecemeal, one rarely assembles them into a composite portrait of events over time.[26] Systematic deficiencies, chronic gaps and redundancies, and grossly deviant individual cases will often stand out when the overall and over-time picture is used as a background and benchmark.[27] For particular weaknesses, a next logical step is to seek corroboration from other credible sources; e.g., when Chief of Police Wilson targeted the District of Columbia's motorcycle squad, he drew on several previous studies to support his attack.[28] Or if there is time or the circumstances are not quite right, the initial composite may highlight problems that a respected outside panel could concentrate on to prepare for a later termination, e.g., blue ribbon commissions are sometimes used this way, especially in the defense establishment.[29] The inevitable deviant cases that stand out from the norm—

either because they are exceptionally successful or woefully inadequate—identify strategic ammunition that can be stockpiled.

One might argue for termination because of a program's success; or one might argue for termination because of conspicuous failures; the most egregious and sensational flops can be played up to focus attention, gain support, and embarrass the policy's supporters. Either way, this strategy may be distastefully manipulative; nonetheless, effective politics often boils down to successful overselling. Just as gross oversell may be needed to start something, it may also be needed to stop something. Likewise, when a policy was initiated, not everyone supported it. There were controversial aspects, elements that certain persons and groups simply did not like or want, and so on. These are, after all, political processes. A thorough termination strategy should encompass the details and dynamics of the possible opposition so that a policy's natural opponents can be mobilized when the end is near.

Survival of the fittest, a policy analog of social Darwinism, suggests another strategic possibility. Because terminations are not common, the threat often lacks credibility. As a broad strategic matter, singling out one or two especially vulnerable policies for an early and well-publicized execution could deliver a message to a number of other agencies that a new administration is serious about project pruning and will continue to effect important reductions. At the very least, the first sacrificial program sets a tone or climate that revives the complacent agency and cautions advocates of new policies that the future may not be benign.

A more subtle strategic design problem centers on a contradiction. On the one hand, terminations may be easier during periods of economic and budgetary growth because of a relative abundance of employment options for those whose programs are cut. Relocation, transfers, and other cushions exist to ease the terminator's burden. But on the other hand, the demand for termination is highest during periods of stringency, when alternative employment and other options are relatively scarce. Organizations might therefore resist termination even more strenuously during times of fiscal contraction. Resolution of the matter depends on recognizing termination as a continuous, ongoing process through good times and bad so that when it is necessary, there will be less to do.

A common and unsatisfactory strategy during austere times is to apportion the pain of termination evenly, e.g., the 10 percent across the board approach. It is a weak strategy, even though it may be politically appealing, because it is indiscriminant. Once again, a need for continuous and meaningful evaluations stands out, as do their termination consequences, even though this does not guarantee that the evaluation will be followed.

Strategies to create specialized agencies and agents to carry out termination are in short supply. The receivership example is indicative here. Experts are needed in policy and institutional restructuring, debt management, operational "fixes," and other relevant skills.[30] Some of these exist, especially in the private sector, but not nearly enough, nor is their applicability to public sector terminations well understood. No one literally knew how to restructure the Village Nursing Home; the basic procedures of receivership were invented at the same time as they were being implemented. Felix Rohatyn had some experience in rescuing distressed corporations, but he was hardly prepared to save an entire city and had to learn the ropes at the same time as New York City was being salvaged financially by his Municipal Assistance Corporation. In both examples, extraordinary authority was required to carry out the restructuring. It was practically impossible and politically infeasible (respectively) for ordinary management processes and governance to operate. Closing something down is not the same as starting it up or running it, and experience strongly suggests that specialized talent, working with different rules, may be required to do the job. Charles deGaulle in 1958 insisted on creating the Fifth Republic (i.e., establishing a new governmental structure) rather than rescuing the Fourth.

The receivership and savings bank ideas lead to other analogies from the private sector having general strategic implications. For example, "as in bankruptcy experienced by private sector firms, there is a need for the appointment of referees able to protect legally the rights of multiple claimants (both funding sources and clients) when a public agency flounders."[31] Such an agency would make certain that a program's assets (money and personnel) were equitably redistributed. It would also provide an incentive for operating agencies to curtail their own programs when necessary rather than risking loss of control over their assets to an appointed referee. Thus, this approach offers tangible incentives for continuous policy adjustment or partial termination rather than postponing the more traumatic inevitable.

What should be done with the remnants? A demand exists for salvage specialists trained in reallocating resources freed by termination. Having knowledgeable individuals in the salvage business could alleviate staff reluctance and uncertainties and help overcome some internal resistance. The public sector is especially vulnerable in this regard. When Dwight Ink turned off CSA's lights for the last time, ". . . 1,050 employees, none of whom are being tranferred to other government agencies"[32] were left in the dark to fend for themselves, hardly a situation which encourages termination.

Biller also suggests using brokers and fiduciaries—third parties—to help with termination. For instance, an escrow system might reduce some of termination's stress and uncertainty by guaranteeing that nothing would happen unless all the precise details of the reduction—such as severance, retraining, maintenance of pensions, and other closing matters—were satisfactorily discharged. Just as the third party holding an escrow for the sale of a house delays its final transfer until all the particulars are in order (e.g., the title is clear, deposits are valid, the mortgage is issued, and all inspections are completed), so, too, might a third party insure compliance with all the complex details of a cutback or reduction.

These are by no means the only strategies worth considering, nor do they represent a how-to-do-it manual. But they do suggest that many constructive possibilities exist to alter current incentives and make termination more credible and applicable. At the moment, most incentives favor perpetuation. Shifting this bias should be the goal for strategic throughts on termination.

Tactical designs

Few termination cases in the literature go beyond a tactical emphasis. That is, the relatively fine-grained and specific details of particular termination examples catch case writers' attention, but few authors have managed to summarize or suggest which details are common or generally matter. But at least a few details occur often enough to merit attention.[33]

First of all, there must be a terminator. Some one authority has to take the unusually difficult and complex steps necessary to curtail a program. Although apparently straightforward, in case after case, the position or responsibility has been next to impossible to fill. The Phillips and Inks of the world are scarce commodities. This will probably continue as long as termination's putatively darker aspects—destructiveness, immorality, distastefulness—dominate and until two basic changes occur: a change in attitude and an appreciation for the skill required to carry out termination.

One way to cultivate such changes would be to create educational or training curricula for termination specialties, e.g., receivers, fiduciaries, salvage specialists, outplacement and midcareer counselors. Once these professional specialties existed, rules, procedures, and norms would emerge to assist individuals and guide institutions through termination's turbulences. Training programs in public and business administration, law, policy analysis, and other professional fields can contribute to filling the void. Even if students in these programs are not planning on careers in cutback management or institutional restructuring, they still could benefit from knowing something about such matters.[34]

The survival tactics threatened organizations might use are worth knowing, so as to be prepared for and to counteract them when reductions are needed. Simon, Smithburg, and Thompson identify five common tactical ploys used by public agencies:

Appealing to important extra-governmental groups.

Seeking legislative support.

Currying support of superiors and prestigious persons.

Enlisting public favor and support.

Making compromises and deals to survive.[35]

Skilled bureaucrats are adept at obstructing or even preventing program reductions by directing budget cuts where they will most directly affect powerful interest groups, who will often appeal to their congressional delegations to rescind the threatened cuts. The U.S. Weather Service, ordered to close down 75 weather stations by Reagan's OMB, was able to have most of its funds restored through congressional intervention; the *New York Times* reported that "There was speculation on Capitol Hill that Richard E. Hallgren, the weather service director, tailored the closing list to provide as much outcry as possible."[36] A second, often-employed tactic is for the threatened agency to appeal its case on relatively emotional grounds which are usually outside the considered criteria. Public safety is a common refuge. In a statement of rare candor to nominal and real objectives, weather service director Hallgren avowed that "The weather service takes its responsibility to protect the safety and property [of the public] very seriously, and I know our people are not very happy."[37]

Both the general and specific strategems against policy termination need to be considered in devising appropriate measures to counter them. A frontal assault on an entire organization is less politic than selecting more vulnerable, discrete targets of opportunity (within an organization's policy and program array) and concentrating extraordinary attention and resources on them. Termination demands spending precious political resources and, as in war, concentrating forces nearly always succeeds better than assaulting along a broad front.

Similarly, target selection is important. For example, there may be chances to "leverage" initial successes or breakthroughs. If public education is oversupplied with teachers, reductions in force might be more easily attained by curtailing teacher training programs, loan and fellowship support, construction grants and guarantees, and/or benefit packages than firing an entrenched, highly visible, and vocal cadre of teachers. It will take some time, but the odds of success are probably better. Particularly weak and susceptible programs should be identified and exploited; such a tactic could yield both immediate and symbolic victories by demonstrating how termination can work and a ripple effect would cast doubt on other programs the agency sponsors. The National Science Foundation is a favorite — some say easy—target of Senator William Proxmire's notorious Golden Fleece Award for wastes of the taxpayers' money. While the Senator scores occasionally by stopping NSF projects, his actual target is very possibly the NSF itself. Every time NSF administrators must defend a project ridiculed by a Golden Fleece, they give up credibility elsewhere.[38]

Concentrating forces occurs in other ways. One reason President Nixon's impoundment of OEO funds did not completely succeed was that its opponents finessed it by adroitly shifting the focal point of the contest from the poverty program to Nixon's legally questionable impoundment tactics. When the House of Representatives debated OEO's fate in May 1974, the issue was not OEO or the poverty war, rather, "The most hotly debated item during the four hours of floor action on the bill was an amendment, passed 290 to 91, that would prohibit the use of Federal funds for abortions."[39] In other words, the poverty coalition undercut Nixon's attacks by creating a smoke screen and a diversion.

Good tacticians do not telegraph or give away the plan. This principle also suggests the possibility of deception and feints to throw the opposition off balance. Assaulting the core of a popular program or an entrenched policy is not good tactics. What if Jimmy Carter had first feigned an attack on the U.S. Army Corps of Engineers or the Bureau of Reclamation— strong organizations responsible for water resources programs—rather than going directly after 20 or 30 dam projects he wished to cancel?[40] What might have been is, of course, uncertain, but Carter's forthwith approach foreclosed compromises to protect the organizations that could have meant their sacrifice of a couple of dams or other projects.

Tactics involve acute appreciation of details. If one expects certain legislators to block a cutback, their opposition can possibly be alleviated ahead of time by making deals or promises on other items that are most important to them. A legislator represents a district with a military base, which, for any of a variety of reasons, could be closed. But representatives have other interests which may count more. A prior appeal to these interests may create an advantage when the base closure is proposed. The legislator may publicly protest as constituents will expect, but symbolic resistance and determined opposition are not equivalent. Buying opponents off need not be malicious or deceitful; again, it is the political stuff of effective termination tactics.

A well-designed plan of operations is essential. When the California Department of Commerce was marked for extinction during Governor Reagan's administration, a carefully scripted, step-by-step plan for its dismantling was first drawn up. The plan's details not only paved the way, they focused bureaucratic attention away from the decision itself and onto routinized administrative procedures, of which the following are illustrative:[41]

Compute seniority points and related rights of civil service employees.

Inventory all furniture, accessories, office machines, supplies and equipment.

Inventory all records, files, and related and pertinent valuables for possible retention by state archives.

Send form letters to various departmental clientele announcing termination of departmental services.

Terminate lease agreements with Xerox and IBM and arrange pickup of equipment by leasors.

Disconnect telephones.

Inventory and relinquish custody of plants to Department of General Services, Buildings, and Grounds.

The administrative machinery was tasked, in effect, to ensure its own elimination.

Along this same line, private sector firms sometimes use a consulting arrangement with former employees to cushion the blow of outplacement, separation, or early retirement. The consultantship buffers both the employee and the organization. Not wishing to endanger the loss of consulting income from the organization, ex-employees are less likely to embarrass the organization or divulge proprietary information. (Inside information may be very critical in the period immediately after separation, precisely the time when emotional stresses are at their highest.) Knowing when to reduce this transitional arrangement itself presents an interesting tactical calculation: How well has the individual adjusted to changed circumstances; how much residual anger is there toward the organization; and how much does he or she know that still might cause harm?[42] Public sector organizations, particularly those dealing with sensitive or classified information, often go beyond the consultantship tactic and rely on oaths, written declarations, financial threats, and legal prosecution to inhibit and control ex-employees.[43]

Legislative and budget cycles present timing opportunities which enhance one's termination options. It may, for example, be prudent to withhold termination plans until the final hours of a budget debate and vote so that legislative opponents are forced to accept cuts to get a total budget package or to compromise to protect higher-priority budget items. To single out a program early in the legislative session may make it harder to relate it to the wave of budgetary red ink that crests at session's end. The delayed-action tactic may work even better if a strategic climate of austerity has been established beforehand so that everyone has to bite the bullet together, that is, there is some semblance of equity.[44]

Calculations of timing can be even more precise. The "Saturday Night Massacre," when Nixon fired the Watergate Special Prosecutor Archibald Cox and forced the resignation of Attorney General Richardson and Deputy Attorney General Ruckelshaus, did not happen on a Monday or a Tuesday, largely because government and the media scale down their operations on weekends, and Nixon sought minimal coverage of his decision. Likewise, moving against a program when its staunchest supporters are out of town or are otherwise occupied is better tactics than assaulting them in place; the pocket veto is one example of this tactic.[45] Or it may help to use retiring, lame duck, or hugely popular legislators to carry the battle of termination; they either do not have to stand for reelection or can afford the political consequences.

Outcomes and effects

No matter the strategy or tactics used, terminations have consequences, and these require analytic/design attention. When social systems are working smoothly, their complexity tends to be overlooked. Months or years may have passed to get something enacted and working but once it is, a deceptive orderliness sets in. Termination causes disruptions that reveal complex social connections and frailties. The analyst must anticipate termination's various outcomes and effects as well as possible. For instance, a cutback in medical research programs on a particular disease will affect researchers almost immediately. But others are just as surely affected: those afflicted by the malady, who had been praying for a timely cure; program administrators, who must now redirect their efforts; universities and research firms, which must figure out what to do with the surplus equipment and staff; and so forth. There is, however, more to explore on the termination trail than just these obvious outcomes. One must calculate future effects upon those who will suffer from the disease, for medical researchers already in training whose job prospects are diminished, and for a medical service system which must continue to treat patients for a disease that might have been cured.

The idea of tracking termination outcomes and effects is relatively unknown, but the reality of coupled systems and sequences of events is becoming more evident. The charge that "Reagan Program Edges California to Fiscal Brink" is only one representative example of the effects of federal termination decisions on other authorities.[46] California, not alone among states, is in a fiscal bind which will result in service reductions and institutional closures.[47] Governor Jerry Brown told "municipal officials in his speech [of October 21, 1981], 'The cupboard is bare'."[48] Cities, counties, and the state are being forced to retrench, although none of them decided on its own to do so, a necessity which means more than the loss of certain federal programs or a few civil service jobs. "The San Francisco health department said that cuts in medical aid programs would fall mostly on preventive services." Furthermore, "the loss of $600,000 in Federal aid for a drug- and alcohol-abuse program in San Francisco, which already had the highest alcoholism and suicide rate in the country," means, according to a health department official, "those figures will go through the roof."[49] Through the roof or not, there will undoubtedly be more reports of this sort as New Federalism forces other systems to change.[50] As intractable as it may seem, tracing important linkages within and between systems and assessing the consequences of large disruptions for them are some of this decade's most important analytic problems. They are patently termination problems, yet most have not even been recognized as such, much less dealt with.

BUREAUCRACIES AND WARS

Most of termination is unfinished. It has been so long neglected that serious challenges are found practically anywhere one turns. Difficult problems seldom yield to quick fixes or simple remedies for their solution. This point is quite apparent in the following brief discussions of two pressing termination targets which are only now being faced: runaway bureaucracy and nuclear war.

Runaway bureaucracy

Government, according to popular perception, is not doing its job very well, despite increases in its size, expense, and prominence. Several underlying causes of its growth are partly understood, and so are some reasons for failures. Larkey and his colleagues argue that despite,

> how much has been written and how little is known what differences the magnitude and composition of the public sector makes in terms of equity, efficiency, individual freedom, economic development, or anything that anyone might care about. . . . The theories and empirical work . . . are rudimentary. None of the theoretical work is sufficiently developed and tested to be persuasive as a positive theory or useful as a prescriptive theory. Few empirical regularities have been discovered and the conditions under which some of the seeming regularities might hold have not been explored.[51]

Clearly work on the problem is needed even while scholars and analysts are sorting out its precise details.

Growth of the federal bureaucracy has various roots. Since Franklin Roosevelt's presidency, the executive has increasingly called on the bureaucracy to serve the citizenry. But because termination was not considered as important as organization and policy creation, growth from this source only begat more growth. Constraints seemed unimportant as long as the economy grew and continued to satisfy the population's rising expectations and demands. The legislative branch contributed as well. During the 1960s and 1970s, public demand for more and different services increased. The turmoil of the 1960s, abetted by the Vietnam War, diversified the range of subjects attended by the federal government: health, occupational safety, crime, pollution and the environment, energy, and many other areas where the federal government had little or no previous involvement. Congressional distrust of the executive added to the problem, as it created agencies designed to resist the imperial presidency.[52] Again, bureaucratic growth led to more bureaucracy and its ever more solid entrenchment. But size alone did not guarantee solutions to the problems the bureaucracy was being dealt. Quite the contrary, many problems only intensified, thus stimulating calls for more bureaucracy, and "layered bureaucracy" became a new Washington phenomenon; the Energy Research and Development Administration was transformed into a cabinet-level department and an independent regulatory commission.

This gross oversimplification does injustices, but it at least sets the stage for the popular and negative reactions that began in the late 1970s. Taxpayer revolts to "cap" property taxes and other public spending[53]—

characterized by political rhetoric damning unfettered and arrogant bureaucracies[54] and appealingly simple proposals to slow bureaucratic growth or to stop it altogether—came to the political foreground. Plans to zero-base the federal budget and to legislate a sunset for existing laws and programs are notable. Both proposals merit brief discussion from a termination-design perspective to demonstrate that these simple solutions to complex problems, such as reining in a runaway bureaucracy, are not adequate and may even make matters worse.

Zero-base budgeting (ZBB) examines existing programs and policies from scratch, usually on an annual basis, and asks what would happen if the committed resources were reduced or completely reallocated.[55] The procedure is simple . . . and flawed. It presumes that someone will do systematic and rational evaluations of all the extant programs. It expects, based on such analyses, that rational and easy choices about termination will follow. But evaluation is inherently problem-ridden and hardly simple. Hence the zero-base idea failed to live up to its advance billing or to its advocates' hopes, not the least of whom was President Jimmy Carter, who loudly heralded ZBB early in his administration.[56]

Besides the enormous complexity of the federal budget, even more fundamental realities interfere. Ignore for a minute the political ramifications of ZBB and consider just the problem of data—the elemental component of evaluation and the linchpin of zero-basing. The bureaucracy itself supplies most of the data. Under the best of circumstances, these data are hard to use for evaluation. But the problem becomes much worse when officials know, in the zero-base world, that their data could be used against their programs. If at all sophisticated, they will be reluctant to collect or share critical data which could reflect poorly on their programs, their agencies, and ultimately them. Rather than having valid, representative indicators, an analyst will probably be faced with manipulated data to support program continuation or no data at all. This is an inherent failure in ZBB procedures; only determined, costly, independent data collection and evaluation efforts can overcome the problem.

Terminations have consequences. Merely marking a program for reduction does not relieve the analyst of the obligation to assess its various implications, nor does it suggest how the termination should be implemented. So besides a huge evaluation component to identify appropriate programs, ZBB also portends extensive analyses to plan termination strategies and tactics and to forecast its outcomes and effects. But no one ever addressed the very practical and necessary aspects of cutting back. Ameliorative practices are not well known or used, nor are they likely to be made-up ad hoc after ZBB is in place and forcing terminations.[57]

Zero-based budget endeavors initially sound good, but their design and execution both mark them as basically inadequate. Lacking the time, resources, and analytic talent for the required tasks, one is left with agencies justifying their own existences and using carefully cultivated political support to ensure survival through the next budget cycle. At best, a few egregious or trivial programs could fall to ZBB, but why expend such significant resources for this menial chore? For substantial programs protected by a politically determined opposition, ZBB is simply ineffective.[58]

Sunset legislation confronts a sprawling government bureaucracy by an action-forcing mechanism that requires legislators to attend to oversight for individual programs and policies and to allow them to continue only if a majority regularly reaffirms them.[59] Two procedures are relied upon: A formal evaluation of every program is required, and a program will be discontinued unless it is specifically reauthorized.

From the present perspective, most sunset proposals suffer from two basic design problems. First, the task has not been treated as a matter of termination and second, the sunset mechanism narrowly concentrates on oversight, only one aspect of evaluation, and not on other equally important evaluation requirements nor on the more difficult issues of termination strategies and tactics.[60]

Sunset has an intuitive appeal to those initially favoring and voting for it. Whatever political benefits accrue to sunset are collected in the short run, but the considerable costs it engenders (e.g., implementing an unworkable procedure and then having to be responsible for its failures) devolve to subsequent legislatures or to subordinate agencies. But at some point, sunset's evaluation requirements must be confronted and so must its termination consequences. Sunset laws demand thorough, ongoing evaluations to be effective and meaningful control measures. Relying on an occasional study by the General Accounting Office, on the information supplied by the bureaucracy itself, or patently self-serving political documents is not likely to provide the quantity or quality of information needed to reach termination decisions that sunset induces. Sunset requires spending a great deal of money for continuous and independent evaluations, a figure few care to estimate. Whatever it means, if the price is not paid, one should not be surprised to discover the following:

Severe overloads of legislative calendars after passage of sunset, with consequent pro forma treatment of its provisions, as evidenced in Alabama where hundreds of state programs were cursorily accorded their sunset reviews during the final session of the legislature.

Reliance on agency-generated information of dubious credibility to make evaluative assessments.

Cancellation of insignificant programs and closing small offices.

Political rather than meritorious decisions in the absence of systematic, independent, and rigorous evaluations.

Political pressure from vested interests to forgo or ignore sunset assessments of important agencies and programs for a variety of particular reasons.[61]

All of these will contribute to a general—and perhaps deserved—skepticism of the worth of sunset procedures, thereby undercutting whatever value they initially offered.

Whether knowingly or not, standards of success will be set by the passage of sunset laws. If these standards are being met as the mandated sunset date approaches, good and effective administrators will know it and not be as prone to give up or bail out—common responses to threatened termination. But when the fate of an agency is perceived to hinge on political criteria—not on the merits of performance—it is easy to forecast sunset's own demise because of the uncertainties surrounding evaluation and the considerable stress these in turn promote about continuation. DOE's 1982 mandated sunset review is an example of such politically motivated evaluation casting serious doubt on the analytical benefits of the entire concept.[62] Quality and quantity of service will probably decline as the prospect of termination because of capricious evaluation takes hold. Most or all of the dysfunctional aspects of threatened termination will be felt by every program and policy subjected to sunset, while very few of its benefits will be realized.

The integration of the policy process proposed here suggests a possible resolution to rescue sunset's better features. Assume that success thresholds were established in the enabling legislation for an agency's policies and programs. Such thresholds would set minimal acceptable standards for performance to implement the program, to guide its operations over time, and to assist in its evaluation. If an agency meets these standards by performing at or beyond the thresholds, then its sunset requirements would pose no threat. However, if the thresholds are not being matched, this would signal a more concerted review as the target date nears, with a presumption that terminations might follow. It would also alert those responsible to begin devising termination plans for the specific case at hand.

Zero-base budgeting and sunset are symptomatic. Neither approach takes account of termination's political complexities, not the least of which is the overall integrity of the policy process itself. But on the other side of the argument, any efforts to create logical conclusions in the lives of policies and programs are to be seized, for they represent at least a beginning step toward understanding and mastery of the policy process. Runaway bureaucracy is certainly one worthy focus on these probings.

Termination of nuclear wars

War is one of humanity's few dependable and consistent events. While the causes and conduct of war have always fascinated scholars, surprisingly little is known about how wars end.[63] Historians, military analysts, and defense policy specialists have concentrated almost exclusively on war initiation, war conduct, and deterrence while ignoring questions about how wars end and how prewar policies affect one's ability to terminate war on acceptable terms and costs—or to terminate it at all. While this condition was understandable when war's objectives were constrained and its destructive capabilities limited, the horrors of nuclear warfare and destruction render this neglect inadmissible.[64]

The scant literature about ending wars tends to be based on assumptions from past contests that do not pertain to a nuclear setting. Current theories of deterrence and limited war (and the expenditures and forces they represent) all posit three basic and coolly rational conditions for war's termination: (1) attrition of the adversary's warfighting capabilities or will; (2) protracted stalemate after an exchange of a limited number of nuclear weapons; and/or (3) unacceptable damage, threatened or imposed, on an adversary that changes perceptions of the costs and benefits of conflict.

None of these conditions considers the possibility that a nuclear war might run out of control, even though each presumes that complex engines of strategic warfare and nuclear exchange can be kept under tight rein and their power meted out in appropriate measures. Doubts are being expressed[65] centering on differences between war initiation, conduct, and termination:

> The capabilities for command and control, and the conditions which enable control to be exercised throughout a strategic nuclear exchange are critical to the viability of the current U.S. strategic doctrine. Without survivable command, control, and communications, (C^3) systems, for example, any limited nuclear operations involving control, selectivity, discrimination, and precision would rapidly become infeasible.[66]

Just as many new policies proceed best in optimistic and ambiguous settings—where clear goals and objectives are often not established and where real costs and benefits are not fully appreciated—so most wars begin in euphoric haze. But once begun, and lacking specific objectives, control disintegrates quickly through delegation, destruction, and default to separate, specialized individuals and organizations which conduct the war almost independently, all dealing with their own aspects of the problem.[67] The relationship of political objectives or conditions needed to terminate hostilities and combat's realities, such as the command and control problems Ball details, is everything in a nuclear setting.

Terminating nuclear war certainly depends on many factors, but most revolve around maintaining communication between adversaries while maintaining control over one's own forces. The following minimum communication elements are required: channels that remain operating to connect decision makers able to stop violent action on all sides; communicators trusted by the relevant parties; and messages that identify sources uniquely and maintain interchanges dependably. Each element has to be established before going to war, but to the best of our knowledge, none presently exists. Existence could be demonstrated by neutral and hardened communication centers having specially protected equipment, personnel in these centers who keep termination contingency plans in hand and are able to carry them out if called upon, and explicit procedures mutually agreed on before a conflict that would guarantee reliable communication between political authorities from the initiation of hostilities.

These requirements and conditions are imperative because conventional and nuclear wars are very different, even those intended to be limited in scope or demonstrative in intent. Two of these differences relate to time and political control. Nuclear war will not be measured in days, months, or weeks, but in minutes and seconds. The flight time of a nuclear-tipped submarine-launched ballistic missile aimed at Washington, D.C., is about 15 minutes, scarcely time to think about anything, let alone design, plan, order, and execute a termination strategy. Contingency plans must be written ahead of time, and the participants must know their roles. Yet most established contingency plans deal with how to conduct nuclear exchanges (e.g., what weapons to direct at which targets) rather than how to terminate an ongoing nuclear war. Maintaining political control over the military forces has been given only a fraction of the attention it warrants. In fact, much time has been spent devising strategies for the destruction of the very communication networks (e.g., satellites and C^3 centers) termination depends upon. The first strike of a nuclear war will likely be against the adversary's communication systems: antisatellite missiles will destroy an opponent's ability to detect incoming missiles and bombers while ICBMs will decapitate primary command centers to block an expected counter strike.

Threats to political control posed by an intentional attack may happen unintentionally. Loss of C^3 could follow a high-altitude nuclear detonation, for no one really knows how much communication and command capability would fail because of it. But we do know, because war-fighting has been so structured, that loss of central political control shifts authority to dispersed and decentralized military command posts. We also know that the primary training and incentives guiding those commanders are not war termination but war conduct: executing large-scale, preplanned, strategic retaliatory attacks to achieve maximum destruction. Defining limited political objectives, deciding what is meant by unacceptable damage, constraining operations to conform precisely to these objectives, and negotiating war termination are not part of their experience or assigned responsibilities. Nor is there comfort to be gained that coordination and control of operations, even by decentralized military command centers, will be restrained or possible:

> [T]he dynamics of nuclear exchange are likely to generate military and political pressures for the relaxation of restraints, even when both adversaries agree at the outset that it was in their mutual interest to avoid unwanted escalation. There are compelling military arguments both against the highly graduated application of force and for attacking the command-and-control infrastructure of the adversary's strategic nuclear forces. Differences in interests and perspectives among the various groups and individuals that compro-

mise the respective national leaderships (as well as between the leaderships) would make intra-war bargaining and conciliation extremely difficult exercises.[68]

Calling attention to this horrific problem starkly demonstrates some consequences of not giving termination its due. Rather than spending resources on the analysis of possible operations of nuclear communication, command, and control during termination, nearly all energies have focused on ensuring a response to an attack, i.e., war initiation and conduct. Years of neglect and a conceptual failure to think about termination are to blame. However, the stakes are high, and the consequences of breakdown are terrifying. Now, perhaps, this bit of unfinished business can be addressed.

This chapter has presented two basic themes. Termination is a grievously and "wrongly underattended"[69] issue in policy analysis. And even though there are formidable obstacles (both conceptual and practical), the payoffs from learning how to cope with and carry out terminations are substantial. The general outlines of future work are visible. More reports of termination experiences and cases should be compiled. Based on these, analysts must acquire understandings of the intellectual and everyday requirements for terminations under varying conditions in hopes that understanding will lead to respectable theories about termination. Finally, based on experiences and evolving theory, more and better strategies and specific tactics to promote termination need to be created, tried out, and assessed.

NEW CHALLENGES IN TERMINATION POLICY

We have described how termination, like other stages of the policy process, rarely admits to easy solutions. We have also seen how it has its own peculiar characteristics which make it especially difficult to conceptualize and implement, aspects that have resulted in the lack of research on the topic. Yet this state of naivete or ignorance cannot be permitted to continue. As Tarschys has cautioned, in a period of fiscal reductions, terminations will per force occur.[70] To permit fiscally motivated reductions in programs and policies to take place without the vaguest idea as to their implementation or consequences is to guarantee their brutality, perhaps even their counterproductiveness. The fact that these programs are operating—that is, have a real rather than an expectant clientele—means that individuals will be directly affected, possibly hurt by the termination or demise of such programs unless careful planning is part and parcel of their execution.[71]

This is not to suggest that programs should not be subject to partial or total termination. Surely we have argued that as programs, policies, and agencies are demonstrated to be lacking, they should be adjusted, curtailed, replaced, or completely eliminated. Further, we have argued that there should be no illusions about the ease or results of termination struggles. As Downs and Larkey demonstrate, the simple reduction of government expenditures does not translate into more efficient programs or expenditures of funds;[72] the Washington Monument ploy is still alive and well.[73] Perhaps because termination is yet an uncharted activity, perceived to be institutionally and personally threatening, it still remains outside the practiced purview of the policy analyst. However, the prevailing political and economic climates in the Western industrialized nations strongly argue that such luxuries will be increasingly dear.

If conditions have changed, then perspectives on termination analysis must similarly adapt. Much of the early work on policy termination was based on the assumption that termination was one way to rid the public sector of inefficient programs. Termination authors—especially Behn and Biller—proposed specific termination strategies and how to make termination more palatable by creating internal institutional incentives.[74] Funds released by curtailing faulty program A could be channeled into a new and better program B. If the Comprehensive Employment and Training Act (CETA) were (by some criteria) not producing, then it should be eliminated and another job training program created. The litmus test or underlying assumption was the effective delivery of government services.

Under more recent conditions, these assumptions are less pertinent. Termination activities are more driven by financial necessities than programmatic efficiencies. The Swedish budget paper for 1980–81 states this clearly:

> In time, the growth of public expenditure must be adjusted to the development of the economy as a whole. This requires stringent budgetary assessments over the future that is now foreseeable with any certainty. The expansion of local government expenditures must be limited in the future to the room that the economy as a whole provides. . . . These resources must be obtained in part by reassessing other efforts that are well founded as such but even less urgent.[75]

This altered motivation for policy termination means that money saved from cancelling program A will not be automatically permitted to be reallocated to new program B; it goes back to the Treasury or maybe all the way to the taxpayer (the Proposition 13 phenomenon). This creates, of course, a host of new policy termination dilemmas (in addition to most of the previous ones), such as how does one now convince bureaucrats that program reductions serve any of their purposes?[76] These changes also imply that the earlier how-to policy suggestions at least require thoughtful reexamination.

In times when there is little financial or organizational slack, policy termination might conceivably be permitted to occur without special attention paid to its economic and political consequences. Much of the earlier termination work examined how one opted for termination and possibly how it was attempted; i.e., these were case studies of a specific type of decision making and implementation. That assumption and approach are no longer sufficient if, indeed, they ever were. The Reagan Administration may cut back on job training programs to save millions of dollars, but what if, consequently, a very large number of then-out-work CETA recipients began to draw unemployment, applied for food stamps and otherwise absorbed significant amounts of welfare payments? The end result of savings in the CETA budget could be greater demands upon the social welfare systems than before and could conceivably cost more than the savings realized through CETA reductions. This does not begin to plumb the near-term psychological ramifications (on a personal, individual basis) or the possible later political effects.

In short, policy termination has become more important and relevant but no less easy. Indeed, in a period of severe financial constraints, it might be more difficult as organizations realize that they stand to lose much more than a small budget increase adjusted for inflation. As institutional survival becomes an issue, one might easily see the termination encounters become more pitched.

This part began with the example of how a change in administrations resurrected the B–1 strategic bomber; the Reagan Administration has also chosen to reinstitute U.S. chemical warfare R&D programs after a 13-year hiatus, despite international conventions which outlaw such weapons.[77] Perhaps, then, the thematic metaphor should be that termination is more Dracular than Draconian. That is, programs and policies rarely die, regardless of their contemporary irrelevance or inefficiency. In pluralist governments, changing conditions and perceptions will almost certainly create opportunities for long-dead programs to be reborn. This assessment, however, should not dissuade either the policy analyst from exploring or the policymaker from exercising the termination option, for—as we have repeatedly stressed—the key to responsive and responsible policymaking is the appropriate alternative in the correct time and setting.

TERMINATION IN THE POLICY PROCESS

To conclude, it is useful to place termination in the context of the other stages of the policy process. As problems are encountered during initiation, then is the time to think about what solutions would look like and mean, e.g., for the redeployment of resources in their solution. Martin Shubik has captured the essence of this idea when he asks: "What's the question? And, what would an answer look like if you 'bumped' into it?" The "baby bust," as the declining number of school-aged children in America has been called, is not some unexpected phenomenon but was forecast with reasonable accuracy a decade or more ago. When the educational investment problems encompassed by the preceeding baby boom were being sensed and defined, their underlying causal factors were also fairly well appreciated.[78] But their transient nature (i.e., the boom was an anomaly not expected to persist or repeat) was not well understood or communicated to those responsible for educational decisions. The result was overbuilding of permanent school facilities, excessive investment in teacher training and other professional educational programs, and a false expectation that the extraordinary one-time demand for educational services would become the norm.

This style of thinking and concern should also extend to estimation activities. In the simple calculation of costs and benefits for candidate programs, for example, greater attention to the discount rates used could reflect different perspectives on eventual termination. If one wishes to emphasize the short term by heavily discounting future cost and benefit streams, then the consequences of early termination (or an expectation that the problem can be solved quickly) could be estimated. Conversely, if one expected the problem to be difficult, persistent, or unlikely to produce benefits until sometime long after costs are incurred, a much lower discount rate would be called for. The usual case, however, does not reveal this kind of sensitivity.[79]

Other legitimate changes in estimation approaches to accommodate possible policy termination can be imagined. Were questions about the ease of terminating each proposed option raised, it is quite likely that their preference orderings would be different. At the least, promising options might be modified to make future termination less frightening. For example, should program control be highly centralized to keep the administrative apparatus as small as possible and thus more amenable or vulnerable to termination? This possibility makes sense from the termination perspective, although it runs directly counter to a preference for decentralization of control found in proposals such as the New Federalism.[80]

Might it be possible to estimate the differences that would occur between candidate programs designed to serve carefully defined or bounded target populations and those more generously intended? While having less political appeal, because of the limitations imposed on the potential number of constituents, spending more time defining and targeting programs would limit the total number of beneficiaries whose claims would have to be considered in the event of termination.[81] One of the reasons social security may be beyond the pale is precisely because it affects the lives of so many. Had it been more carefully designed to serve a more circumscribed population, securing changes in the program later on might have been less troublesome.[82]

Perhaps the easiest shift in estimation procedures would be to ensure that termination provisions were established from the start. Sunset legislation dictates a review of an agency's activities within a certain time; e.g., the Department of Energy had a sunset provision written into its charter, as did its predecessor, the Federal Energy Administration.[83] A contractual approach to public policies and programs may have some potential.

> The system of law that we have in this country . . . has compromised between enforcing all promises and enforcing no promises, and the result is that we have special classes of promises which are enforced by social control and which are known as contracts.[84]

Contract law comprises an enormous body of the legal literature and scholarship and we are uninformed of its detail and nuance. However, the general case of government's promising to do certain things for specified individuals, where needs and rights under the contract are carefully spelled out before implementation, has appeal as a general principle. Enlisted service in the military is one illustration of the possibilities; here, as in the general case, the prior elaboration of conditions of completion allows termination to occur in the individual case with greater certainty and dispatch.

Obviously, many problems will not conform to this format, and differentiating problem types could become an accepted component of policy estimation. For instance, problems may be categorized as being either chronic, recurring, or resolvable. If resolvable, a contractual approach may pertain, considering that both needs and their satisfaction might be defined beforehand. If the problem is perceived to be chronic, the contractual approach has less appeal. National security concerns in the large represent a continuing problem by this definition, although the degree is surely susceptible to peaks and valleys.[85] Recurring problems, such as disaster relief or severe or one-time unemployment, could have termination provisions addressed during their estimation stage. The Red Cross, to cite one case, does not maintain a large, standing army of disaster and relief workers; it is structured so that a relatively small number of individuals are retained permanently, with a large number of contingency personnel to be called to aid only when needed. What they possess collectively are procedural rules and guidelines for temporary mobilization of essential resources to contend with disasters when they occur. But once the problem subsides, the resources are relinquished.

We do not offer these estimation ideas for possible program drawdowns as panaceas but as suggestions for the kind of thinking needed to bring termination into better focus earlier in the policy process. We are also aware of several analytic issues such questioning surfaces. For instance, in the case of resolvable problems, there may well be an inherent dynamic that prevents them from being readily resolved and hence terminated. By turn-of-the-century standards, much illness and disease in this country have been eliminated, but we continue to be concerned about health.[86] Obviously the general perception and operational definition of good health is not immutable, nor is the problem, consequently, resolvable. Can the problem be bounded or not? The provision of unemployment benefits is a good case of a bounded problem, while worker's compensation may be open-ended with respect to the length of time involved. In the bounded case, there are definite expectations about the end point; they are shared by both provider and beneficiary. However, what happens when unemployment persists but the benefit period does not or a deepening recession or budget reductions create even greater unemployment?[87] Does one extend the benefits indefinitely, create another program to fill the need, bend the rules of a different program to grant eligibility, make do, or what?

Selection presents a different set of termination problems, but some selective means are important for conceptually linking the decision-making phase and termination. At the most general level, the decision maker needs to be more conscious of ways to change expectations about continuance or permanence as policies are considered and programs chosen. As much as anything, this will be a diffuse but consuming political activity meant to turn the climate or mood of the populace away from unrealistic demands and toward a sense of limitations or restraints.[88] If an austerity climate can be created and sustained, individuals and interest groups usually work to retain past achievements and to spend proportionately less time in seeking new areas for bureaucratic growth; this could result in serendipitious consequences.[89] For example, within the academic community of scholars when the usual sources of research support are hard pressed, many become less inclined to invest the time and effort in formulating new research proposals as the odds of success are perceived not to warrant the effort. One would expect the total number of new legislative proposals to decline during times of real or perceived austerity but hope that the quality might improve.[90] Similar claims have been expressed for military R&D policies and programs.[91]

Altered expectations could also be explicitly contained within them. So, for example, when a regulatory commission is established to modify practice and behavior in some field, it might be useful to either limit its life to a fixed number of years or to set up conditions of success that would signal its end.[92] That regulatory commissions and most other organizations will seldom contribute to their own self-destruction is a foregone conclusion.[93] Trying to impose fixed time limits after the fact on organizations, policies, and programs, e.g., sunset legislation, has also not produced many unqualified successes.[94]

In this same vein, the prior provision of grievance and redress procedures as a contingency against possible reductions may make it somewhat easier to terminate when it becomes necessary. The points here are to forewarn those concerned with a proposed decision and to ensure that fair and just practices exist to smooth subsequent events. When these standards have not been contemplated early and earnestly, those burdened with responsibility to carry out the death sentence or to wield the budget ax are often forced to dissemble (e.g., by claiming their acts produce superior collective social benefits even though disadvantaging a select few) or to move with unseemly stealth and speed. In the case of juvenile corrections in Massachusetts, the resistance its director met in trying to get changes and reductions "led him to conclude that the only way to change the system was to obliterate it entirely—and fast, before the forces of resistance had a chance to mobilize."[95] A final reluctant alternative is to lie and—if called to account—stand ready to accept the consequences.[96]

As one next considers implementation, the importance and consequences of action-forcing events and deadlines gain prominence. Major changes in the federal budget process enacted in 1974 have helped legislators curtail their enthusiasms (or at least to be aware of their sum total) in amending parts of the annual budget. While far from perfect, the effort to set limits and deadlines is a step in the right direction.[97] More to the point, however, would be concerted efforts to anticipate bureaucratic maneuvers by crafting rules, regulations, and guidelines with possibility of program termination in mind. As with most political contests, countermeasures are to be expected no matter how well drawn the rules; the battle is ongoing.

Because of its proximity, evaluation's relationship to termination is perhaps better explored than for the other phases of the policy process. Any evaluation implies that termination could be a consequence. The suggestion here is to think more clearly during the framing and execution of evaluations about explicitly considering termination's implications, should assessment require such. Whether or not a negative evaluation leads to termination remains an open question whose answer depends on many factors outside the evaluator's control, e.g., the political climate, shifts over long periods of time in the prevailing ideological temperament, and general fiscal conditions. However, the need to inform possible termination decisions with respectable, prior evaluations is not as well appreciated as it should be. A 10 percent across the board political decision to cut back affects everything indiscriminately (even the sources of the necessary evaluation data)[98] and might be less defensible were previous evaluations in place to help distinguish the good from the bad, the fat from the muscle and bone.

A twist in the rules of the game having evaluating consequences is worth considering. In an era of deregulation and relaxation of government enforcement of existing rules and regulations, a near-term outcome is a reduction in the total number of guidelines one might observe (or violate). Greater programmatic or even institutional latitude is thus created; what was previously illegal could become accepted if not acceptable. The need for and possibility of rigorous, systematic evaluation wane as a result. A longer-term effect might be more efficient markets and heightened productivity in the industrial sector, as deregulation proponents argue,[99] but it might just as well lead to greater risk taking with the public trust or to morally questionable (if not strictly illegal) behavior.

Termination requirements also increase the evaluator's need to identify a program's objectives and goals, especially their underlying political and ideological bases. Reagan appointees to the Department of Labor, when examining the CETA programs, complained that "they couldn't even measure what was right and what was wrong . . . because nobody was really looking at performance. . . . There is no standard measure out there that everybody will accept as the basis of success or failure of the program."[100] Thus, they were able to phase out CETA on political grounds even though recent CETA evaluations proved positive. Similarly, compensatory aid to education has been reduced despite strong evidence that it is instrumental in raising basic reading and mathematical skills among disadvantaged children. Nominally a victim of economic hardtimes, the unspoken justification is more ideological: "that it's simply something the federal government shouldn't be doing. Education is the province of the states and localities . . . and no matter how effective a federal program may be, it still intrudes on the state and local domains."[101] Public programs and policies rarely fall prey to simple quantitative measures or mere economics. Therefore, the requirements of termination place even greater emphasis on accurate and comprehensive program evaluation than might have previously been the case.

NOTES

1. Paul W. MacAvoy, ed., *The Crisis of the Regulatory Commissions* (New York: W. W. Norton, 1970), presents most of the deregulation arguments. It is important to remember that, despite the rigor or elegance of the analyses presented either for or against regulation, the general arguments and underlying premises are as much ideological as they are analytical.

2. Quoted from a DOE paper, *Why Reorganization is Necessary,* in Anonymous, "DOE Explains Why It's Not Entitled to Live," *Energy Daily,* January 28, 1982, p. 3.

3. All of these reasons are cited in the Chrysler Corporation's official request for financial assistance from the U.S. Government: Chrysler Corporation, *Analysis of Chrysler Corporation's Situation and Proposal for Government Assistance* (Washington, D.C., and Detroit, Mich.: Chrysler, September 15, 1979), especially pp. 1–9. A critique of the *Analysis* that squarely blames Chrysler's management is Peter Bohr, "Chrysler's Pie-in-the-Sky Plan for Survival," *Fortune,* October 23, 1979, pp. 16, 47–48, 50, 52.

4. Insurance pools exist to cover just such a contingency; pilots have often prepared themselves emotionally and substantively by acquiring other marketable skills and interests, by setting up annuities or other financial cushions, or by arranging to move laterally into administrative duties.

5. One gets a sense of this in Geoffrey C. Hazard, Jr., *Ethics in the Practice of Law* (New Haven: Yale University Press, 1978).

6. Details of the case are provided in Sandra H. Johnson, "Nursing Home Receiverships: Design and Implementation," *Saint Louis University Law Journal* 24, no. 4 (1981), pp. 681–712.

7. The Village is a well-defined entity within Manhattan; it has its own character and style as well as its own newspapers—*The Villager* and the *Village Voice*—which provided continuing information about the nursing home's plight.

8. "Village Nursing Home to Close," *New York Times,* November 29, 1975, p. 46.

9. Johnson, "Nursing Home Receiverships," p. 711.

10. Ibid., p. 712.

11. Robert A. Levine, *The Poor Ye Need Not Have: Lessons from the War on Poverty* (Cambridge, Mass.: MIT Press, 1970), describes the 1964 to 1969 period from an insider's perspective; Mark R. Arnold, "The Good War that Might Have Been," *New York Times Magazine*, September 29, 1974, pp. 56–57, 59, 61, 64, 66, 71, 83, is a succinct recounting of events up to and including the congressional action; and David Shribman, "Death Comes to a Federal Agency," *New York Times*, September 19, 1981, p. 7, describes the end of the Community Services Administration.

12. Arnold, "The Good War," p. 56.

13. Lyndon Johnson used this sort of language, as did R. Sargent Shriver, Jr., the first director of OEO.

14. An American political cliché holds that, "You want it bad, you get it bad"; for many of the war's programs, that is exactly the way things developed.

15. Arnold, "The Good War," p. 66.

16. The history and termination travails of the Legal Services Corporation are detailed by Elizabeth Drew, "A Reporter at Large: Legal Services," *The New Yorker*, March 1, 1982, pp. 97–113. Drew provides a valuable lesson in termination politics, including her observation that Governor Reagan's CRLA battles fueled President Reagan's LSC antipathies.

17. As ably described by Daniel Patrick Moynihan, *The Politics of a Guaranteed Income* (New York: Random House, 1973).

18. A further consequence of what many believed to be an inappropriate use of executive power through impoundment was eventual passage of the Congressional Budget and Impoundment Act of 1974, which clarified the possible uses of the practice at the same time as it tried to organize Congress' chaotic budgeting processes. The Congressional Budget Office is the main institutional product of the act.

19. Attributed to Representative Albert Quie of Minnesota, in Arnold, "The Good War," p. 71. Other reactions are contained in Richard D. Lyons, "House Votes to End Poverty Agency," *New York Times*, May 30, 1974, pp. 1, 9.

20. Shribman, "Death," p. 7.

21. Ibid.

22. The label is Robert K. Yin's. Yin, *R&D Utilization for Local Services* (Santa Monica, Calif.: The Rand Corporation, R–2020–DOJ, 1976).

23. But as we saw for the poverty war, a change does not guarantee termination. Nixon in 1968 was a different president than Nixon in 1972, probably due to the size of his election victory.

24. The distinction comes from T. S. Eliot's poem "The Hollow Men." It is a reasonably accurate characterization for much experience.

25. W. Henry Lambright and Harvey Sapolsky, "Terminating Federal Research and Development Programs," *Policy Sciences*, June 1976, 202–04, contrast the two timing approaches and strategies.

26. These points relate to our previous discussion of "internal evaluations," Chap. 12.

27. In The Rand Corporation's evaluation of programs and services for handicapped children (Part V), the first year of the nearly three-year project was devoted to a drawing of the composite picture, as suggested here. The results helped establish priorities for all subsequent work, some of which led to recommendations for program terminations. See James S. Kakalik, Garry D. Brewer, Laurence A. Dougharty, Patricia D. Fleischauer, and Samuel A. Genesky, *Services for Handicapped Youth: A Program Overview* (Santa Monica, Calif.: The Rand Corporation, R–1220, 1973), for the full picture; and James S. Kakalik and Garry D. Brewer, "Services for Handicapped Youth," in B. Famighetti et al., eds., *Education Yearbook 1974–1975* (New York: Macmillan Educational Corporation, 1975), pp. 174–88, for a summary.

28. Abram N. Shulsky, "Abolishing the District of Columbia Motorcycle Squad," *Policy Sciences,* June 1976, p. 190. Among other prior evaluations was a 1966 study by the International Association of Chiefs of Police.

29. The Congressional Budget Office attempts to produce balanced analyses, some of which have been used to argue for "restructuring" or "modernization," code words for partial termination that emphasize its constructive aspects. See, for example, Congressional Budget Office, *Strategic Command, Control, and Communications: Alternative Approaches for Modernization* (Washington, D.C.: U.S. Government Printing Office, October 1981), in which the word "termination" does not occur, although "modernization" could mean little else.

30. Robert Biller, "On Tolerating Policy and Organizational Termination: Some Design Considerations," *Policy Sciences,* June 1976, pp. 133–49, is a fertile resource for such ideas.

31. Ibid., p. 146.

32. Shribman, "Death," p. 7. The role the Civil Service Commission played is unclear, although employees holding tenured positions could have had a prior claim on job openings in other agencies, if they existed.

33. An exception is Robert D. Behn, "How to Terminate a Public Policy: A Dozen Hints for the Would-Be Terminator," *Policy Analysis,* Summer 1978, pp. 393–413. The present discussion overlaps Behn's but there are several differences, primarily emanating from our separation of strategies and tactics.

34. Recall the previous discussion of problems to train psychoanalysts, Chap. 13.

35. Herbert A. Simon, Donald W. Smithburg, and Victor A. Thompson, *Public Adminstration* (New York: Alfred A. Knopf, 1950), chap. 19.

36. Ben A. Franklin, "45 Weather Posts Given a Reprieve," *New York Times,* March 8, 1982, pp. 1, 11.

37. Ibid., p. 11.

38. Citing this example does not condone it.

39. Lyons, "House Votes," p. 9.

40. Adam Clymer, "President in Shift, Favors Some Funds for Water Projects," *New York Times,* April 16, 1977, pp. 1, 11.

41. "Private Communication" from John McCaffrey, a principal agent in the Department's termination, September 1977. McCaffrey lists 20 steps in all.

42. The idea of hiring people and keeping them on retainers to do nothing may strike many as strange. It actually is not when the possible harm and expenses are calculated against the modest consulting fees required to maintain some degree of institutional loyalty. Lawyers, especially in certain specialty fields such as tax and antitrust law, are sometimes retained under this arrangement; they are, in effect, paid not to work for the opposition.

43. There have been several visible failures of the tactic, most notably former CIA officers who have written "insider" accounts and violated prior agreements not to divulge such information without obtaining formal government review. To date, the courts have upheld the CIA's right of prior review and, in one case, ordered an author to return his royalties to the government.

44. See Robert J. Hershey, Jr., "Several Interest Groups Prepared to Accept Curbs on U.S. Budget," *New York Times,* March 10, 1982, pp. 1, 11, for an example of this condition.

45. It might be interesting to count how many successful terminations occur when the legislature is out of session or when key supporters are traveling or are indisposed with other business; political coups offer a number of vivid testimonies to the recognition and efficacy of this tactic.

46. Wallace Turner, "Reagan Program Edges California to Fiscal Brink," *New York Times,* October 27, 1981, p. A–27.

47. For a cogent analysis of the California condition, see John J. Kirlin, *The Political Economy of Fiscal Limits* (Lexington, Mass.: D. C. Heath, 1982).

48. Turner, "Reagan Program." A similar message was reported by Neil R. Peirce, "Reagan to Nation's Governor's—The Federal Aid Cupboard Is Bare," *National Journal,* November 28, 1981, pp. 2109–13.

49. Turner, ibid.

50. This is hardly unique. Mental patients released from California's state facilities in the 1960s did not cease needing care; rather, responsibility for them was transferred to lesser authorities who were ill-prepared to accept the burden. James M. Cameron, "Ideology and Policy Termination: Restructuring California's Mental Health System," *Public Policy*, Fall 1978, pp. 533–70.

51. A clear and thorough inventory of the theoretical speculation and empirical findings on government growth is Patrick D. Larkey, Chandler Stolp, and Mark Winer, "Theorizing about the Growth of Government: A Research Assessment," *Journal of Public Policy,* May 1981, pp. 157–220.

52. This is a main theme of Paul W. MacAvoy, *The Regulated Industries* (New York: W. W. Norton, 1979).

53. California's "Proposition 13" is notable here. A popular referendum, passed in the summer of 1978, it cut real property taxes about 60 percent and removed more than $7 billion from local tax revenues. State revenue surpluses filled the gap in 1979 and 1980. By 1981, the "cupboard was bare," and stark fiscal realities finally had to be faced; see Kirlin, *Political Economy of Fiscal Limits.*

54. A perceptive analysis is Anthony Lewis, "The War of the Bureaucrats," *New York Times,* April 10, 1978, p. A–46.

55. Peter A. Pyhrr, *Zero-Base Budgeting: A Practical Management Tool for Evaluating Expenses* (New York: John Wiley & Sons, 1973); and Joseph S. Wholey, *Zero-Base Budgeting and Program Evaluation* (Lexington, Mass.: D. C. Heath, 1978), are general sources.

56. ZBB's failure is analyzed by Aaron B. Wildavsky, *The Politics of the Budgetary Process* (Boston: Little, Brown, 1979); similar lessons can be observed in his description of the shortcomings of ZBB's analytic predecessor, PPBS.

57. Recall the previous discussion of salvage institutions, third parties, cushioning provisions, and a host of other potential matters.

58. Shades of the French Maginot Line and the British defense of Singapore in World War II, where faulty thinking led to erroneous presumptions about the opponents' behavior and to stunning defeats. Strategy is never completely fixed and tactics are always circumstantial.

59. Common Cause, *Making Government Work: A Common Cause Report on State Sunset Activity* (Washington, D.C.: Common Cause, 1978); U.S. Senate, Committee on Governmental Affairs, *Hearings on the Sunset Act of 1977* (Washington, D.C.: Government Printing Office, 1977); and U.S. Senate, Committee on Governmental Operations, *Hearings on S. 2925, The Government Economy and Spending Reform Act of 1976* (Washington, D.C.: Government Printing Office, 1976), contain most of the history and arguments for and against sunset. Samples of parallel activity at the state level are reported in George B. Merry, "Mass. Backs 'Sunset Law' to Phase Out Old Agencies," *Christian Science Monitor,* December 15, 1976; and, Robert B. Simison, "Cleaning House: New 'Sunset Laws' Seek to Curb Growth of Big Government," *Wall Street Journal,* June 25, 1976, concentrates on Colorado, which was in the vanguard of sunset legislation. For some recent Colorado sunset reports, see fn. 94 below.

60. This argument is reiterated throughout hearings on a 1977 sunset proposal in U.S. Congress, *Congressional Record*, 95th, 2nd Sess., vol. 123, no. 3, January 10, 1977.

61. Many of the conditions have occurred; see Eugene Carlson, "Success of Sunset Laws Varies and Fights Turn to Big Targets," *Wall Street Journal*, May 4, 1982.

62. The three-volume 733-page document is reported on by Burt Solomon, "DOE Memoirs to Congress," *Energy Daily*, February 11, 1982, pp. 1, 4, who observes, "The suicidal impulse is plain." P. 1.

63. Fred Iklé, *Every War Must End* (New York: Columbia University Press, 1971); and Michael Handel, "The Study of War Termination," *Journal of Strategic Studies*, May 1970, pp. 51–75, are exceptions that prove the rule.

64. See Jonathan Schell, *The Fate of the Earth* (New York: Alfred A. Knopf, 1982). Schell's alarms should not be viewed as idosyncratic; see Judith Miller, "Efforts to 'Freeze' Nuclear Arsenals Spreads in U.S.," *New York Times*, March 15, 1982, p. B–12; and Robert Scheer, "Majority in U.S. Back Nuclear Arms Freeze," *Los Angeles Times*, March 21, 1982.

65. James L. Foster and Garry D. Brewer, "And the Clocks Were Striking Thirteen: The Termination of War," *Policy Sciences*, June 1976, pp. 225–43, identified the problem.

66. Desmond Ball, *Can Nuclear War Be Controlled?* (London: International Institute of Strategic Studies, Adelphi Paper, no. 169, Autumn 1981), p. 1. Also see John D. Steinbruner, "Nuclear Decapitation," *Foreign Policy*, Winter 1982, pp. 16–28.

67. This is made even more difficult when the two major strategic actors—the United States and the Soviet Union—do not accept the other's nuclear doctrine as credible; i.e., neither contestant accepts the other's rules of the game. See Fritz W. Ermarth, "Contrasts in American and Soviet Strategic Thought," *International Security*, Fall 1978, pp. 131–55; and Leon Gouré, "The U.S. 'Countervailing Strategy' in Soviet Perceptions," *Strategic Review*, Winter 1982, pp. 51–64.

68. Ball, *Can Nuclear War Be Controlled?* p. 2.

69. Biller, "Policy and Organization Termination," p. 133, is responsible for the elegant descriptor: "wrongly underattended."

70. Daniel Tarschys, "Public Policy Innovation in a Zero-Growth Economy: A Scandinavian Perspective," in Peter R. Baehr and Bjorn Wittrock, eds., *Policy Analysis and Policy Innovation* (Beverly Hills, Calif.: Sage Publications, 1981), pp. 9–25.

71. Two recent victims: Richard Corrigan, "The Administration May Try Again to Kill Energy Aid for the Poor," *National Journal*, January 23, 1982, pp. 150–52; and Scot J. Paltrow, "Cutbacks Force Legal Aid to Reject Cases, Often Leaving Poor Helpless," *Wall Street Journal*, January 28, 1982, p. 25.

72. George W. Downs, Jr. and Patrick D. Larkey, "Fiscal Reform and Governmental Efficiency: Hanging Tough," *Policy Sciences*, September 1981, pp. 381–96.

73. See Robert D. Hershey, Jr., "The Name of the Game is Ducking the Budget Ax," *New York Times* November 6, 1981, for some current examples.

74. Biller, "Policy and Organizational Termination," and Behn, "How to Terminate."

75. Cited in Peter deLeon, "New Perspectives on Program Termination," *Journal of Policy Analysis and Management*, Fall 1982, p. 108. For a more complete statement of Swedish efforts along these lines, see the Swedish Commission on Public Policy Planning, *Policy Innovation Through Policy Reappraisal* (Stockholm: Departmentens Offsetcentral, 1980).

76. Anthony Downs, *Inside Bureaucracy* (Boston: Little, Brown, 1967).

77. David Wood, "Reagan to Seek New Chemical War Capability," *Los Angeles Times*, January 30, 1981; Richard Halloran, "Reagan Approves Airlift and Chemical Arms Plan," *New York Times*, January 27, 1982; and Anonymous, "U.S. to Resume Chemical-

Weapons Output After 13-Year Halt; $30 Million Is Sought," *Wall Street Journal,* February 9, 1982.

78. William Ascher, *Forecasting* (Baltimore, Md.: Johns Hopkins University Press, 1978), chap. 3.

79. U.S. General Accounting Office, *Civil Agencies Make Limited Use of Cost-Benefit Analysis in Support of Budget Requests* (Washington, D.C.: Government Printing Office, January 1975), lists general limitations; and David Novick, *Current Practices in Program Budgeting (PPBS)* (New York: Crane Russak, 1972), contains interesting technical issues. The usual case applies a fixed discount rate to all options.

80. Timothy B. Clark, "New Federalism Report," *National Journal,* April 21, 1973, pp. 580–81. The thrust of such proposals is relative; the policies and programs marked for termination or cutback were not designed with termination in mind, the point made in our discussion. The main consequence of such proposals is to shift the problems to the ill-prepared states and localities. Turner, "Reagan Program"; and Gaylord Shaw, "U.S. Cutbacks Create Chaos in States, 3 Governors Say," *Los Angeles Times,* November 6, 1981.

81. After the fact, these and related recommendations are being made. U.S. General Accounting Office, *What Can Be Done to Check the Growth of Federal Entitlement and Indexed Spending?* (Washington, D.C.: Government Printing Office for the GAO, March 1981).

82. The size issue—especially as it translates into political power—figures prominently in Robert J. Samuelson, "Benefit Programs for the Elderly: Off Limits to Federal Budget Cutters?" *National Journal,* October 3, 1981, pp. 1757–62. Samuelson answers his own question: "They have been so far, and because programs account for more than a fourth of federal spending, the consequence is enormous pressure on the rest of the budget." P. 1757.

83. The DOE, of course, was ticketed for dissolution for reasons entirely independent of its sunset clause, which mandated a review, in 1982. DOE's self-authored sunset review is largely negative and, not surprisingly supports the Reagan Administration's decision to abolish the Department. To wit: "Many of the Department's programs are no longer valid within the context of the federal role in the energy sector of the economy. . . . The Department was established to address a set of problems that were peculiar to their time and that were largely the result of a philosophy that stressed excessive government intervention in energy markets in the first place." Quoted by Burt Solomon, "DOE Memoirs to Congress," *Energy Daily,* February 11, 1982, p. 1. Regarding the FEA, see Karen Elliott House, "Getting Entrenched: Energy Agency Spends Much to Ensure a Long Life, Foes Say," *Wall Street Journal,* March 9, 1976.

84. Thomas M. Carhart III, "The Relationship between Termination of Policies and Contract Law" (Unpublished private communication to G. D. Brewer, 1977), p. 2.

85. Component aspects contributing to national security, however, could still be a resolvable sort, e.g., building a tank, and here ideas about contracts pertain.

86. Aaron Wildavsky, *Speaking Truth to Power: The Art and Craft of Policy Analysis* (Boston: Little, Brown, 1979), chap. 12, addresses the problems involving changing standards of medical care and their effect on public health policy.

87. Bill Curry, "Jobless Find Doors Closed at Job Services," *Los Angeles Times,* January 30, 1982, details how Reagan economy measures forced the closure of state employment offices in the face of rising unemployment, thus making it more difficult for the out of work to find new jobs and exacerbating the unemployment problem.

88. Recall in the selection chapters our discussion of political mood and climate. In this context, see Warren E. Walker and Jan M. Chaiken, *The Effects of Fiscal Contraction on Innovation in the Public Sector* (Santa Monica, Calif.: The Rand Corporation, P–6610, April 1981).

89. Hershey, "Ducking the Budget Ax," provides an account of bureaucratic strategems in a constrained fiscal environment.

90. An empirical proposition, one could assess it historically or by tabulating the number of proposals forthcoming in a given legislative setting.

91. An optimistic straw in the winds? Michael R. Gordon, "Budget Crunch Gives Shot in the Arm to Growing Military Reform Movement," *National Journal*, September 5, 1981, pp. 1572–76.

92. This and many other interesting ideas about regulation are presented in Barry M. Mitnick, *The Political Economy of Regulation: Creating, Designing, and Removing Regulatory Reforms* (New York: Columbia University Press, 1980). Strong claims to limit all regulations are contained in MacAvoy, *The Regulatory Commissions*.

93. With respect to regulatory agency behavior, see Milton Russell and Robert B. Shelton, "A Model of Regulatory Agency Behavior," *Public Choice*, Winter 1974, pp. 47–62. Public organizations are viewed thusly in Herbert Kaufman, *Are Government Organizations Immortal?* (Washington, D.C.: The Brookings Institution, 1976); private ones are discussed in Peter Drucker, *The Age of Discontinuity* (New York: Harper & Row, 1968), pp. 222ff.

94. Sunset deficiencies are stressed in Robert D. Behn, "The False Dawn of the Sunset Laws," *Public Interest*, Fall 1977, pp. 103–18. More recent pessimistic assessments are reported by Sue Lindsay, "Ex-Proponent Will Submit Bill to Repeal 'Sunset'," and "Lawmakers Move to Abolish 'Sunset'," *Rocky Mountain News*, January 29, 1981 and February 14, 1982, respectively.

95. Constance Holden, "Massachusetts Juvenile Justice: De-institutionalization on Trial," *Science*, 30 April 1976, pp. 447–51, at p. 447. The resulting sense of injustice led to numerous court and administrative actions.

96. It is hard not to avoid this opinion in the case of Reagan's Director of the Office of Management and Budget, David Stockman's treatment of the facts. William Grieder, "The Education of David Stockman," *The Atlantic Monthly*, December 1981, pp. 27–54 ff.

97. Wildavsky, *The Politics of the Budgetary Process*. A special issue of *PS* [American Political Science Association], Fall 1981, pp. 731–66, details aspects of the "Reagan Budget: Redistribution of Power and Responsibilities," in the general spirit suggested here.

98. See John Hebers, "Census Bureau Plans More Cuts; Threats to Basic Research Feared," *New York Times*, January 31, 1981, pp. 1, 16; and Rochelle L. Stanfield, "Numbers Crunch—Data Funds Cut Just When More Statistics are Needed," *National Journal*, November 28, 1981, pp. 2118–21.

99. The literature is burgeoning on this topic, but Alfred E. Kahn, *The Economics of Regulation*, vols. I and II (New York: John Wiley & Sons, 1970 and 1971), provides both scope and detail.

100. Quoted in William J. Lanouette, "Life After Death—CETA's Demise Won't Mean the End of Manpower Training," *National Journal*, February 6, 1982, p. 241.

101. Secretary of Education Terrel Bell has testified to the efficacy of the Department's compensatory education programs, while slashing the programs by approximately one-third. Rochelle L. Stanfield, " 'If It Ain't Broke, Don't Fix It,' Say Defenders of Compensatory Aid," *National Journal*, January 30, 1982, pp. 201–04, at p. 201. For a more general statement, see the interview with Secretary Bell by Marjorie Hunter, "How to Dismantle Your Own Agency," *New York Times*, February 6, 1982, p. 8, in which the secretary explains how he has come to recommend the dissolution of a department he argued a scant few years ago should be created.

Discussion questions

1.   The prospect of death, according to Dr. Johnson, "wonderfully concentrates the mind." It has many other consequences, at least as regards established institutions, relationships, and programs. Consider these in drawing distinctions between policy creation and adoption and policy termination. What are the essential differences between the two?

2.   In his classic monograph, *Are Government Organizations Immortal?*, Herbert Kaufman makes several trenchant observations about long-lived public institutions, including the following:

   a. Agencies are often accorded statutory permanence, regardless of their need or mission.

   b. Agencies' sponsors never die, they just fade into new programs.

   c. Agencies are not idle observers of their own death sentences; they are combative participants, either in the reactive or proactive modes, willing to use both internal and external resources.

   d. Agencies are protected by the incremental budgetary process, rather than threatened by it or any of its variations.

   e. Agencies are often sheltered from outside control or danger.

   What is it about this aura of permanence that has such tremendous implications for policy and agency termination? What are some different variants of termination as they apply in specific cases? How might they be generalized? Under what circumstances can you see termination not as an end but as a beginning? Aside from the above reasons, why does one see so few examples of institutional terminations? Or are there, in fact, more than we realize?

3.   In 1967, then-Senator J. William Fulbright stated:

> Priorities are reflected in the things we spend money on. Far from being a dry accounting of bookkeepers, a nation's budget is full of moral implications; it tells what a society cares about and what it does not care about; it tells what its values are.

In March 1981, the Congressional Budget office commented on President Reagan's budget revisions for fiscal year 1982:

> The Administration also proposes to increase the share of defense in the budget from 23.4 percent in 1980 to 33.2 percent in 1984. . . . In real terms, adjusting for inflation, defense spending would grow by an average of over 8 percent per year between 1980 and 1984, but nondefense spending would fall to a level 15 percent lower in 1984 than in 1980.

Comment on these two observations in terms of their implications for policy termination. More specifically, what is the relation between ideological and financial motives for program reductions?

4.   A business school has been defined as a place where a bunch of 55-year olds are striving mightily to convince a bunch of 25-year olds of the wisdom and righteousness of the status quo . . . and providing them the tools to sustain it. Discuss this point.

5.   The following conclusion appeared in the financial section of the *New York Times*, April 22, 1981, p. D–8: "Wall Street is hoping—and more than one analyst is betting—that the Lockheed Corporation will jettison its Tristar jumbo jet business soon and become significantly more profitable in the years ahead." In the balance of the article, various corporate analysts present the evidence that supported dropping the Tristar from the corporation's business, e.g., increased profitability, tax writeoffs, improved earnings, early retirement of the loans made by the U.S. government to bail the corporation out in the early 1970s. However, the article concludes: "Harold Hurlocker, publicity representative for Lockheed, said that the company had no intention of closing down Tristar." What might account for Lockheed's devotion to a 10-year, controversy-plagued, money-losing aircraft, especially since it operates in the for-profit sector? (Note: Lockheed discontinued Tristar production in early 1982.)

6.   The ascent of industrial technology led to a general strengthening of the state and a greater regulation of the urban-centered society. It also led to increased demands on the state to distribute more equitably the fruits of the new technology. It has, as well, created a totally new style of thought— technology as doctrine or even religion. Everything in society is considered

subject to rational, mechanistic manipulation, if only the techniques of power and production are understood. At the limit, power and production become one. The polity, therefore, maintains its power only so long as production (i.e., resources) expands. But then, what happens when production declines? What are the effects on the society and its members (both as individuals and organizations)?

7. As appears to be a general trend worldwide, substantial numbers of people are becoming increasingly worse off in terms of real income and quality of life. An eventual consequence of ecological scarcity and mismanagement is a lower standard of living for almost all save a privileged few. If you agree with this assessment, discuss its implications in political, economic, and social terms. Can you pose some concrete examples in terms of public sector actions?

8. In assessing the future of the Department of Education, an analyst for the National Educational Association—which favors the continuation of the department—predicted, "I think we'll win. I think we'll keep the department. If fair-minded people really listen, they'll do what's right." Comment on this observation from the perspective of policy termination; for instance, what criteria are being used that would persuade "fair-minded" people? Indeed, what (or who) are these "fair-minded" people?

9. Under the Reagan Administration's budget reductions, the National Weather Service was ordered to close down 75 local weather bureau stations. The director of the service, in seeking to restore the cuts, commented that "The weather service takes its responsibilities to protect the [public] safety and property very seriously and I know our people are not very happy." Discuss his observation, especially in light of the fact that Congress restored funds for at least 45 of the threatened stations.

10. Pascal wrote that "it is easier to endure death without thinking about it than to endure the thought of death without dying." Freud observed that "It is indeed impossible to imagine our own death: and whenever we attempt to do so, we can perceive that we are in fact still [only] present as spectators." Do either of these philosophers provide any insight to organizational termination?

11. Public sector bureaucracies have grown greatly, largely because of pork barrel politics; numerous programs and agencies have proliferated as political favors with little understanding of their cumulative effects. The result has been what some have termed "runaway bureaucracy" and a general public reaction against public sector involvements. In a period of economic retrenchment, one can imagine pork barrel terminations, i.e., reductions in government services made entirely for political reasons with, again, little appreciation for costs, efficiencies, and the cumulative effects of the reductions. Is this a valid distinction? Does it help us understand the policy termination processes?

Supplementary readings

The literature dealing with termination is not coherent, nor is the scholarship. This part itself presents one initial synthesis of both, although numerous alternative renditions most certainly exist and could be formulated to accomplish a comparable end. The challenge and need are both great. For the purpose of guiding one's own exploration of this neglected aspect of the decision process, we have compiled the following list of supplementary readings in which the emphasis is on case and historical materials. We believe that understanding of the part's organization and content will enable one to view the various illustrative materials with more sophistication and discernment than trying to comprehend and master them by themselves. Finally, the list is quite a bit shorter than for the book's other parts; this is truly reflective of the inattention to termination noted throughout.

THE BACKGROUND AND SETTING OF TERMINATION

Bardach, Eugene C. "Policy Termination as a Political Process." *Policy Sciences,* June 1976, pp. 123–31.

Hirschman, Albert O. *Exit, Voice and Loyalty: Responses to Decline in Firms, Organizations and States.* Cambridge, Mass.: Harvard University Press, 1970.

465

Kaufman, Herbert. *Are Government Organizations Immortal?* Washington, D.C.: The Brookings Institution, 1976.

———. "The Natural History of Human Organizations." *Administration & Society*, August 1975, pp. 131–49.

Starbuck, William H. "Organizational Growth and Development." In *Handbook of Organizations*, James G. March, ed. Skokie, Ill.: Rand McNally, 1965, pp. 451–533.

LIBERALISM, FEDERALISM, AND THE ROLE OF GOVERNMENT

Feldman, Paul. "Efficiency, Distribution, and the Role of Government in a Market Economy." *Journal of Political Economy,* May/June 1971, pp. 508–26.

Holden, Matthew, Jr. " 'Imperialism' in Bureaucracy." *American Political Science Review*, December 1960, pp. 943–51.

Lowi, Theodore. *The End of Liberalism.* New York: W. W. Norton, 1969.

MacAvoy, Paul W., ed. *The Crisis of the Regulatory Commissions.* New York: W. W. Norton, 1970.

Rose, Richard, and B. Guy Peters. *Can Government Go Bankrupt?* New York: Basic Books, 1978.

Wilson, James Q. "The Politics of Regulation." In *Social Responsibility and the Business Predicament,* James W. McKie, ed. Washington, D.C.: The Brookings Institution, 1974, pp. 135–68.

RETRENCHMENT AND CUTBACKS

Behn, Robert D., ed. "Leadership in an Era of Retrenchment." *Public Administration Review,* November/December 1980, pp. 603–626.

Kaufman, Herbert. *Administrative Feedback: Monitoring Subordinates' Behavior.* Washington, D.C.: Brookings Institution, 1973.

Kirlin, John J. *The Political Economy of Fiscal Limits.* Lexington, Mass.: D. C. Heath, 1982.

Levine, Charles H., ed. *Managing Fiscal Stress: The Crisis in the Public Sector.* Chatham, N.J.: Chatham House, 1980.

Levine, Charles H.; Irene S. Rubin; and George G. Wolohojian. *The Politics of Retrenchment.* Beverly Hills, Calif.: Sage Publications, 1982.

Natchez, Peter C., and Irvin C. Bupp. "Policy and Priority in the Budgetary Process." *American Political Science Review,* September 1973, pp. 951–63.

Rubin, Irene S. "Decision Making Under Conditions of Reduced Resources." *Social Science Quarterly,* Fall 1977, pp. 242–54.

Stanfield, Rochelle L. "New Federalism." *National Journal,* February 27, 1982, pp. 356–62.

Tarschys, Daniel. "Rational Decremental Budgeting: Elements of an Expenditure Policy for the 1980s." *Policy Sciences,* December 1981, pp. 49–58.

A SAMPLER OF EXPERIENCES

The individual view: Death

Becker, Ernest. *The Denial of Death.* New York: Free Press, 1973.

Crane, Diana. *The Sanctity of Social Life: Physicians' Treatment of Critically Ill Patients.* New York: Russell Sage Foundation, 1975.

Fuchs, Victor R. *Who Shall Live? Health, Economics and Social Choice.* New York: Basic Books, 1974.

Labby, Daniel H., ed. *Life or Death: Ethics and Options.* Seattle: University of Washington Press, 1968.

Deinstitutionalization

Bakal, Yitzhak, ed. *Closing Correctional Institutions: New Strategies for Youth Services.* Lexington, Mass.: D. C. Heath, 1973.

Bardach, Eugene. *The Skill Factor in Politics: The Repeal of Mental Commitment Laws in California.* Berkeley: University of California Press, 1972.

Behn, Robert D. "Closing the Massachusetts Public Training Schools." *Policy Sciences,* June 1976, pp. 151–71.

Lamb, H. R., and V. Goertzel. "High Expectations of Long-Term Ex-State Hospital Patients." *American Journal of Psychiatry* 129 (1972), pp. 471–75.

Ohlin, Lloyd E., et al. "Radical Correctional Reform." *Harvard Education Review,* February 1974, pp. 74–111.

Rothman, David J. "Prisons, Asylums, and Other Decaying Institutions." *The Public Interest,* Winter 1972, pp. 3–17.

Wolpert, Julian, and Eileen Wolpert. "The Relocation of Mental Hospital Patients into Residential Communities." *Policy Sciences,* March 1976, pp. 31–51.

War

Iklé, Fred. *Every War Must End.* New York: Columbia University Press, 1971.

Kecskemeti, Paul. *Strategic Surrender: The Politics of Victory and Defeat.* Stanford, Calif.: Stanford University Press, 1958.

Theis, Wallace J. "Searching for Peace: Vietnam and the Question of How Wars End." *Polity,* Spring 1975, pp. 305–33.

Other examples and illustrations

Behn, Robert D. "Closing a Government Facility." *Public Administration Review,* May/June 1978.

Costello, John, and Terry Hughes. *The Concorde Conspiracy.* New York: Charles Scribner's Sons, 1976.

David, Arie E. *The Strategy of Treaty Termination.* New Haven: Yale University Press, 1974.

Horwitch, Mel. *Clipped Wings: The American SST Conflict.* Cambridge, Mass.: MIT Press, 1982.

Lambright, W. Henry. *Shooting Down the Nuclear Plane.* Indianapolis, Ind.: Inter-University Case Program, Bobbs-Merrill, 1967.

Shulsky, Abram N. "Abolishing the District of Columbia Motorcycle Squad." *Policy Sciences,* June 1976, pp. 183–97.

Wallerstein, Mitchel. "Terminating Entitlements: Veterans Disability Benefits in the Depression." *Policy Sciences,* June 1976, pp. 173–82.

ZERO-BASE BUDGETING, SUNSET LAWS, AND THE OFFICIAL RESPONSES

Adams, Bruce. "Sunset: A Proposal for Accountable Government." *Administrative Law Review,* Summer 1976, pp. 511–42.

Adams, Bruce, and Betsy Sherman. "Sunset Implementation: A Positive Partnership to Make Government Work." *Public Administration Review,* January/ February 1978, pp. 78–81.

Behn, Robert D. "The False Dawn of the Sunset Laws." *The Public Interest,* Fall 1977, pp. 103–18.

Common Cause. *Making Government Work: A Common Cause Report on State Sunset Activity.* Washington, D.C.: Common Cause, 1978.

Executive Office of the President, Office of Management and Budget. *Zero-Base Budgeting.* Washington, D.C.: OMB Bulletin No. 77-9, April 19, 1977.

Pyhrr, Peter A. *Zero-Base Budgeting.* New York: John Wiley & Sons, 1973.

U.S. Congress, House. *The Legislative Oversight Act of 1978.* Washington, D.C.: Government Printing Office, January 19, 1978.

U.S. Congress, Senate. *The Program Evaluation Act of 1977.* Washington, D.C.: Government Printing Office, July 1, 1977.

U.S. Congress, Senate Committee on Government Operations. *Compendium of Materials on Zero-Base Budgeting in the States.* Washington, D.C.: Government Printing Office, 1977.

U.S. Congress, Senate Committee on Governmental Affairs. *Hearings on the Sunset Act of 1977.* Washington, D.C.: Government Printing Office, 1977.

U.S. Congress, Senate Committee on Rules and Administration. *Government Economy and Spending Reform Act of 1976.* Washington, D.C.: Government Printing Office, 1976.

DESIGN ISSUES

Behn, Robert D. "How to Terminate a Public Policy: A Dozen Hints for the Would-Be Terminator." *Policy Analysis,* Summer 1978, pp. 393–413.

Biller, Robert. "On Tolerating Policy and Organizational Termination: Some Design Considerations." *Policy Sciences,* June 1976, pp. 133–49.

Index

This book has been set VIP photocomposition in 10 and 9 point Caledonia, leaded 2 points. Part numbers are 16 point Caledonia Bold and part titles are 20 point Caledonia Bold. Chapter numbers are 24 point Caledonia Arabic and chapter titles are 18 point Caledonia Bold. The size of the type page is 30 by 47 picas.